ARGENTINA
BUSINESS

**World Trade Press
Country Business Guides**

ARGENTINA Business
AUSTRALIA Business
CHINA Business
HONG KONG Business
JAPAN Business
KOREA Business
MEXICO Business
PHILIPPINES Business
SINGAPORE Business
TAIWAN Business
USA Business

ARGENTINA
BUSINESS

The Portable Encyclopedia For Doing Business With Argentina

James L. Nolan, Ph.D.   Alexandra Woznick
Edward G. Hinkelman   Karla C. Shippey, J.D.

Molly E. Thurmond, J.D.   John DeCaire, J.D.   David L. Gold
Fred Gebhart   Maxine Cass   Robin E. Kobayashi, J.D.
Stan Draenos   Patrick Sullivan   Christopher Mahon
Patrick J. Burnson   Zenophon A. Abraham   Cynthia G. Sewell
        Mark Williams   Marcelo Sierra

Marcelo Aftalión • Luis Aguirre • María Laura Alzúa
Teodosio Brea • Alicia Caballero • Jaime Campos • Dolores Diez de Tejada
Adrián Makuc • Cecilia Nazer • Luis María Riccheri
Gabriela Ruggeri • Eduardo Zalduendo • Susana C. de Zalduendo
Fundación Invertir Argentina

Baker & McKenzie • Ernst & Young
International Chamber of Commerce • International Monetary Fund
CIGNA Property and Casualty • The East West Group Inc. • Horizons Travel
Reed Publishing (USA) Inc. • Magellan^sm Geographix

Series Editor: Edward G. Hinkelman

WORLD TRADE PRESS®
Resources for International Trade

1505 Fifth Avenue
San Rafael, California 94901
USA

Published by World Trade Press
1505 Fifth Avenue
San Rafael, CA 94901, USA
Tel: (415) 454-9934
Fax: (415) 453-7980
USA Orderline: (800) 833-8586
E-mail: WorldPress@aol.com

Cover and book design: Brad Greene
Illustrations: Eli Africa
Maps: Magellan^{sm} Geographix
Desktop design and publishing: Peter G. Jones
Charts and graphs: David Baker
Copy Editor: Michael Levy

Library of Congress Cataloging-in-Publication Data

Argentina business: the portable encyclopedia for doing busines with
    Argentina / James L. Nolan . . . [et al.].
        p.   cm. – (World Trade Press county business guides)
    Includes bibliographical references and index.
    ISBN 1-885073-04-6
        1. Argentina–Economic conditions–1983- 2. Argentina–Commerce.
    3. Argentina—Commercial policy. 4. Investments, Foreign-
    -Government policy–Argentina.   I. Nolan, James L., 1951-
    II. Series.
    HC175.A844   1996   95-18706
    658.8 '48 ' 0982–dc20   CIP

Printed in the United States of America

ACKNOWLEDGEMENTS

We owe many leaders in the international business community a debt of gratitude. Hundreds of trade and reference experts have brought this book to life. We are indebted to numerous business consultants; reference librarians; travel advisors; consulate, embassy, and trade mission officers; bank officers; attorneys; global shippers and insurers; and multinational investment brokers who answered our incessant inquiries and volunteered facts, figures, and expert opinions. To all these many individuals, named and unnamed, we extend our thanks.

Argentina Business began with a telephone call from Jaime Campos, Executive Director of Fundación Invertir Argentina. His faith and interest spurred us forward; his quest for quality shines from every page; and his network of experts have added a layer of excellence we could not have otherwise achieved.

The professional talents of many researchers, authors, and editors have been combined in this single volume. At the top of the list are the many experts in Argentina whose belief in our cause translated into hours of insightful editing, resulting in text that contains the most up-to-date information to be found in any one source. In addition to Jaime Campos, these include Marcelo Aftalión, Luis Aguirre, María Laura Alzúa, Teodosio Brea, Alicia Caballero, Dolores Diez de Tejada, Adrián Makuc, Cecilia Nazer, Luis María Riccheri, Gabriela Ruggeri, Marcelo Sierra, Eduardo Zalduendo, and Susana C. de Zalduendo. Their assistance in this endeavor was invaluable.

The kindly officials at the Argentine Consulate, San Francisco, were most obliging. An informative session with Deputy Consul Luis del Solar yielded much raw data plus many helpful resource contacts. We sincerely thank the Deputy Consul for his continued interest in this project and we wish him *buena suerte* in his travels.

Attorney John DeCaire toiled over the practical aspects of Argentina's business law and entities, interviewing Argentine practitioners to learn the current status of legislation. For taking time from their busy days to brief us on the Argentine legal system, we are most obliged to Dr. Osvaldo R. Agatiello (Latin American Regional Coordinator, Baker & McKenzie, Miami), Pablo Rueda (Resident Counsel, Marval, O'Farrell & Mairal, New York), and Alberto Gonzalez (White & Case, Miami).

The talents of attorney-author Molly Thurmond can be seen in trade agreements and culture. International trade specialist and corporate writer Stan Draenos searched source after source for hard-to-find data on Argentine labor issues and requirements. Managing editor Patrick Burnson of the trade journal *Pacific Shipper* lent his expertise to the transportation materials. News and travel writer Mark Williams gave a special spin to current issues. A hundred statistics had to be sorted and reconciled by business reporter Zennie Abraham in working out the Argentine foreign trade situation. The special research and analytical skills of Patrick Sullivan were essential to compiling accurate demographic and trade fair materials.

For unique insights into the fascinating culture of Argentina, we have to thank consultant Viviana Gaeta (owner of Horizons Travel of Marin County, California). Her respect and love for her own Argentine heritage and her focus on travel in South America today has given her an intimate knowledge of the Argentine people, which she willingly shared with us. She added unique insights into this fascinating society. We also benefited from the vast cultural experience of human resources consultant Dean Engel, senior partner in The East West Group Inc., a consulting firm that develops cross-cultural strategies for clients operating worldwide.

Renowned travel writers Fred Gebhart and Maxine Cass (Gebhart & Cass, Ltd., of San Francisco, California) take us on an Argentine business tour. International marketing analyst Cynthia Sewell sifted through the intracacies of developed and undeveloped Argentine markets. Legal author Robin Kobayashi analyzed Argentine import and export policies and sorted through often conflicting procedural data to get to the hard facts. Author Christopher Mahon delved into Argentine industries and opportunities, while investment manager David Gold (Transamerica Investment Services, Los Angeles, California) analyzed rivers of data on Argentina's foreign investment requirements and financial institutions to come up with the practical basics.

For reprint permissions, we found helpful allies in Dr. Osvaldo R. Agatiello (Baker & McKenzie, Miami, Florida); Cassie Arnold (Ernst & Young, San Francisco office); Kenneth Young (Publications Services, International Monetary Fund); Steve Fahrbach, Doug Crawford, and Rick Wood (Magellan[sm] Geographix); and Barry Tarneff (CIGNA Property and Casualty Co.). Thank you also to Denise Getty of Colliers International for coordinating the real estate market survey and to the researchers in Colliers Interamerica, Miami, and Badino Colliers, Buenos Aires, who compiled the information. We also acknowledge the valuable contributions of Philip B. Auerbach and Naomi Baer (Auerbach International, San Francisco) for translations.

We relied heavily on the reference librarians and resources available at the libraries of the University of California at Berkeley, San Francisco Public Library, San Rafael Public Library, Marin County Civic Center Library, and Marin County Law Library. Of particular note, reference librarian Gail Lockman at the San Rafael Public Library has always been a most willing accomplice in research.

DISCLAIMER

We have diligently tried to ensure the accuracy of all of the information in this publication and to present as comprehensive a reference work as space would permit. In determining the contents, we were guided by many experts in the field, extensive hours of research, and our own experience. We did have to make choices in coverage, however, because the inclusion of everything one could ever want to know about international trade would be impossible. The fluidity and fast pace of today's business world makes the task of keeping data current and accurate an extremely difficult one. This publication is intended to give you the information that you need in order to discover the information that is most useful for your particular business. As you contact the resources within this book, you will no doubt learn of new and exciting business opportunities and of additional international trading requirements that have arisen even within the short time since we published this edition. If errors are found, we will strive to correct them in preparing future editions. The publishers take no responsibility for inaccurate or incomplete information that may have been submitted to them in the course of research for this publication. The facts published are the result of those inquiries, and no warranty as to their accuracy is given.

Contents

Introduction

Argentina, the most promising nation in Latin America at the turn of the 20th century and one of the less promising ones only a decade ago, has been recovering rapidly during the early 1990s. Although its economy was pressured in early 1995 by the sudden loss of favor for emerging markets among international investors, Argentina's situation is far less structurally problematic than that of several other nations. Blessed with a large variety of rich natural and human resources, Argentina has the potential to become a major force once again in the global economy.

Long noted for commodity agricultural products and exports, Argentina's reawakening industrial sector is beginning to produce and export a broader range of more competitive, higher-value-added industrial products. Although labor costs are generally more expensive in Argentina than they are in many competing countries, these costs are still lower than in fully developed economies, and Argentina's workers are also generally better trained than those of many of its competitors. After a half-century of populist policy designed to insulate the nation from the outside, Argentina has decided that in the context of a globalized economy, integration with other nations is the path that it should follow. Accordingly, it has been dismantling many of its trade barriers, has opened the economy to foreign participation and investment, and—through its Convertibility Law, which removed foreign exchange controls and set the peso at par with the US dollar—has revised its financial structure to put its domestic and international dealings on a stronger footing. The nation is completing the privatization of its far-reaching state sector industries, opening them to outside interests, and returning them to profitability. Argentina is also looking outward, as evidenced by its adoption of the General Agreement on Tariffs and Trade (GATT) and its participation in Mercosur, the Southern Cone common market arrangement with Brazil, Paraguay, and Uruguay.

Argentina is an intriguing market and one well worth investigating from a number of perspectives. For buyers, Argentina remains one of the strongest markets worldwide for a wide variety of traditional raw materials and commodity resource products, as well as for nontraditional intermediate processed products. Its industrial sector is growing; Argentina is fast becoming a competitive producer in both world and regional markets. As part of its drive to upgrade its industry and increase its nontraditional production and exports, Argentina is actively importing a variety of goods. In 1993, 40 percent of the increase in its imports represented purchases of capital goods destined to improve its industry. Argentina needs a wide range of materials, intermediate goods, capital goods, and service inputs to support its industrialization drive and its ambitious infrastructure investments.

For manufacturers, Argentina offers the prospect of an eager labor force capable of producing a wide range of items. It is not only a potential source for those seeking suppliers worldwide, but also a prime location from which to serve Latin American markets. For investors, Argentina has opened the floodgates, allowing foreigners virtually free access to its financial and industrial markets. Almost all sectors are open to foreigners with few restrictions, and earnings and capital can be freely converted and repatriated. Even former state firms have been sold to foreign investors, and Argentina's financial markets, although they remain volatile, have posted remarkable performances in recent years.

Argentina is currently in the process of recovering the luster it had earlier in this century as it builds for the next century. The country is caught between the old, set, and protected way of doing things and the new, dynamic, open way espoused by its more forward-looking leaders. Although Argentina still has a long way to go, there is reason to be optimistic that it will continue to progress toward its goals. It remains a complex, challenging, and compelling place to do business.

ARGENTINA Business was designed by businesspeople experienced in international markets to give you an overview of how things actually work and what the current conditions are in Argentina. It will give you the head start you need to be able to evaluate and operate in Argentine markets. It also tells you where to get more information in greater depth.

The next chapter discusses the main elements of the **Economy**, including its development, present situation, and the forces determining its future prospects. **Current Issues** explains the top concerns affecting the country and its next stage of development. The **Opportunities** chapter presents discussions of major areas of interest to importers and exporters, plus additional hot prospects. The chapter also discusses the nature of government procurement processes. **Foreign Investment** details attitudes, policies, incentives, regulations, procedures, and restrictions, with particular attention to Argentina's new foreign investment law. **Foreign Trade** presents information on what and with whom Argentina trades. **Trade Agreements** presents the latest information on Argentina's trading arrangements, with special reference to Mercosur.

The **Import Policy & Procedures** and **Export Policy & Procedures** chapters delineate the nature of Argentina's shifting trade: trade policy and practical information—including nuts-and-bolts procedural requirements—necessary to trade with the nation. The **Industry Reviews** chapter outlines Argentina's nine most prominent industries and their competitive positions from the standpoint of a businessperson interested in taking advantage of these industries' strengths or exploiting their competitive weaknesses. **Trade Fairs** provides a comprehensive listing of trade fairs in Argentina, complete with contact information, and spells out the best ways to maximize the benefits offered by these events.

Business Travel offers practical information on travel requirements, resources, internal travel, local customs, and ambiance, as well as comparative information on accommodations and dining in Buenos Aires, Córdoba, Mendoza, and Rosario—the main business markets in Argentina. **Business Culture** provides a user-friendly primer on local business style, mindset, negotiating practices, and numerous other tips designed to improve your effectiveness, avoid inadvertent gaffes, and generally smooth the way in doing business with Argentines. **Demographics** presents basic statistical data needed to assess the Argentine market, while **Marketing** outlines resources, approaches, and specific markets.

Business Entities & Formation discusses recognized business entities and registration procedures for operating in Argentina. **Labor** assembles information on the availability, capabilities, and cost of labor in Argentina, as well as terms of employment and labor-management relations. Prepared with the help of international authority Martindale-Hubbell, **Business Law** interprets the Argentine legal system, providing a digest of substantive points of commercial law. **Financial Institutions** outlines the workings of the financial system, including banking and financial markets, and the availability of financing and services that foreign businesses need. Prepared with the help of the International Monetary Fund, the **Currency & Foreign Exchange** chapter explains Argentina's foreign exchange system. **International Payments** is an illustrated, step-by-step guide to using documentary collections and letters of credit in trade with Argentina. Prepared with the help of Ernst & Young, the **Taxation** chapter explains the corporate and individual tax rates and the tax status of foreign operations and individuals, information that businesspeople need to evaluate fully the financial aspects of a venture in the country. **Transportation & Communications** gives current information on how to gain access to destinations within the country.

The **Business Dictionary** is a unique resource that provides the businessperson with the basic means for conducting business in Argentina. It consists of 450 entries, focusing specifically on Argentine business and idiomatic usage. More than 750 **Important Addresses** include contact information for Argentine official agencies; business associations; trade and industry associations; financial, professional, and service firms; transportation and shipping agencies; media outlets; and sources of additional information to enable businesspeople to locate the offices and help they need to operate in Argentina. Full-color, up-to-date **Maps** aid the business traveler in exploring the major business venues in Argentina. The volume is cross-referenced and indexed to provide ease of access to the specific information that a businessperson must find quickly to succeed in a particular situation.

ARGENTINA Business gives you the information you need, both to evaluate the prospect of doing business in Argentina and to begin actually doing it. It is your invitation to this fascinating society and market. *¡Bienvenidos!*—Welcome!

Economy

INTRODUCTION

La República Argentina is perhaps the most cosmopolitan nation in South America. Located on the southeastern extreme of the South American continent, it has traditionally been closely linked with Europe, often to a greater extent than with the rest of the New World. Although Argentina has played a noteworthy role in the continent's history, its development has been unique within the larger Hispanic tradition. At the turn of the current century the envious saying "rich as an Argentine" was in common usage when discussing the country's booming economy. However, Argentina's potential began to tarnish during the 1930s, and during the 1950s the country dropped off the roster of the most prosperous nations in the world to be listed among the developing countries of the world. Those intent on looking backward continue to argue over the reasons for Argentina's failure to develop its potential. However, during the past decade, other analysts have become more interested in assessing its renewed rise. An intensely proud people, the Argentines are turning away from a period of looking inward and are accepting a greater international role in the developing new world order. Some observers would argue that rather than a different Argentina, what the world is seeing is a return of an older, more optimistic Argentina.

The Land of Argentina

Argentina claims a total surface area of 3,761,274 sq km (1,452,228 sq mi), of which about three-fourths—just under 2.8 million sq km (1.1 million sq mi)—is located on the South American continent (the rest consists of a sector of Antarctica and three groups of islands in the South Atlantic). Based on area, continental Argentina is the eighth largest country in the world, the second largest in Latin America. With an estimated population of 33.9 million in mid-1994, it ranks 31st in the world in population, with an overall population density of 12.2 per sq km (31.6 per sq mi) for the continental portion. Some 87 percent of Argentines live in urban areas; more than 12 million—36 percent of the nation's people—live in the Buenos Aires metropolitan area, which has a density of 14,827 persons per sq km (38,400 per sq mi) in the Federal Capital.

Argentina claims international frontiers that stretch across 25,728 km (16,080 mi). Most are on the Atlantic Ocean, but on the west Argentina is bounded by Chile and the Andes Mountains; to the northwest lies Bolivia; Paraguay is nearly due north; and Brazil and Uruguay are found to the northeast. The Argentine Andes rise to a height of 6,959 m (22,834 ft) at Aconcagua, the highest elevation in the Americas, but much of Argentina is low-lying and flat: some 45 percent lies below 200 m (656 ft) in altitude, while only 10 percent lies above 2,000 m (6,562 ft). Argentina's climate ranges from subtropical in the northeast, to temperate in the central region, to arid and semiarid and cold in the south and along the mountains; each of these main three climatic zones covers approximately one-third of the country's area.

Just over half of continental Argentina consists of grasslands. About a quarter is classified as forested.

Nearly 9 percent is considered arable, but less than half of that is under permanent cultivation. The rest represents urban development, undeveloped land, bare rock, and inland waters. Central Argentina holds the country's main agricultural resources: its fertile pampas, noted for production of grain, cattle, and oilseeds. Argentina ranks 11th in the world in wheat production and is a major producer of corn (maize) and meat. Argentina also produces substantial quantities of wine grapes, linseed, sugar, tobacco, rice, soybeans, and citrus fruit. Its mineral resources include oil and natural gas, manganese, lead, zinc, iron, copper, tin, and uranium.

The People of Argentina

Unlike the people in other areas of Hispanic America, Argentines are mostly of European origin. At least 85 percent of the population is White, with the remainder classified as Mestizo, Indian, or other non-White (relatively few Indians remain as genetically or culturally separate groups). Between the 1850s and 1940, more than 3.5 million immigrants arrived in Argentina, about 45 percent of them from Italy and 32 percent from Spain. Prior to the 1960s, substantial numbers also came from Britain, Germany, France, Switzerland, Denmark, Poland, Russia, the Middle East, and Japan. Other groups, such as Blacks and Asians, make up a negligible portion of Argentina's current population. Spanish is the official language and is spoken universally, but a number of Argentines also speak English, Italian, German, or French.

Despite the mix of ancestries and languages, Argentines are fiercely nationalistic, although many are sometimes unsure regarding their cultural allegiance. This ambivalence about whether they are more Latin or European is most common in Buenos Aires, which many other Argentines view as constituting a separate world. One common saying holds that "Argentina is the most European of the Latin nations because its people are from the most Latin of the European nations."

Approximately 90 percent of the population is nominally Roman Catholic. However, some studies indicate that fewer than 20 percent of Argentines are actively practicing Catholics. Protestants and Jews each account for about 2 percent of the population, with the remaining 6 percent representing adherents of various other religions.

HISTORY OF THE ECONOMY

Argentine Life and Times

The Early Period Most pre-Hispanic settlement in the land later to be called Argentina was by small-scale indigenous groups practicing village agriculture or following nomadic lifestyles. One major reason cited for Argentina's relatively slow development as a colony was its lack of the precious metals sought by the Spanish—including the silver (*argentum* in Latin) for which the country was named. An even more significant reason was the difficulty in harnessing native labor—which was scattered and mobile—into the colonial system on which Spain depended. Although the Río de la Plata (or River Plate) was discovered in 1516, hostile Indian activity kept Europeans out until Buenos Aires was finally established in 1580. (Indian warfare continued to affect development in some areas until the late 1800s.)

By Spanish law, the colony was barred from trading legally with all but a few officially licensed traders until 1776, when the country was formally separated from the Viceroyalty of Peru. At that time, it became the Viceroyalty of Río de la Plata, a region that today includes Argentina, Paraguay, Uruguay, and parts of Peru and Bolivia. Although Buenos Aires rebelled against Spain in 1810, the move was largely opposed by the *estancieros* (landed gentry) and merchants who held official trading licenses. Afterwards cleavages developed between the *unitarios*, who wanted a strong, liberal central government run from Buenos Aires, and the *federales*, conservatives who supported decentralized provincial authority.

The independent United Provinces of the Río de la Plata began to fragment almost before it came into existence. Local *caudillos* (warlords) resisted the imposition of outside authority, and different regions within the rather arbitrarily constituted entity began to break away. After decades of civil war, around 1860 the nation began to reach its modern extent; it installed basic institutions and infrastructure, and—with the declaration of Buenos Aires as a federal district (in 1880)—arrived at a working arrangement by which the traditional rivalry between that city and the rest of the country were reconciled. Massive European immigration swelled the population, commercial activity expanded, and Argentina entered a period of great prosperity and progress.

Perón and the Era of Nationalism Argentina continued to grow and generally prosper in the early 1900s. Encouraged by legal reforms, the traditional, more conservative leadership was supplanted by a Radical Civic Union reformist president in 1916. The Radicals held the presidency until 1930, when President Yrigoyen was ousted by a military coup, inaugurating an era of military intervention. In 1946, following 15 years of military influenced or direct military government, free elections were held, resulting in the election of Juan Domingo Perón as president.

Under Perón, labor took on a significant role in society, many industries were nationalized, and foreign investment and participation in the economy was restricted in an effort to allow Argentina to develop as a self-sufficient entity. However, development was inefficient and incomplete, and the country incurred massive debts to support its various projects.

By 1955 deteriorating economic conditions led to a backlash among the middle class, students, and elements of the clergy, business, and military. Perón fled the country following a military coup. If Perón had erred by catering too much to the demands of labor, the military pushed the pendulum too far in the opposite direction, offending not only leftists but also students, business interests, and Argentina's large middle class. Greater military repression triggered more intense public discontent and gave rise to armed guerrilla opposition movements during the late 1960s.

Perón returned from exile in the midst of growing anarchy, assumed the presidency in 1973, but died suddenly in 1974. The military took over again in 1976 amid worsening economic and social conditions. In contrast with most previous military interventions, the 1976 coup was designed to allow consultation and power sharing among all service branches. The junta ruled from 1977 to 1983 during a period known as the *Proceso*, during which it instituted a campaign known as "the dirty war." Rightist official and unofficial organizations sought to wipe out existing and potential subversive opposition, which was defined extremely broadly. This resulted in the death or disappearance of thousands of Argentines (the *desaparecidos*). This domestic trauma was compounded by a worsening economy. Production foundered and the country racked up foreign debts of US$36 billion at the end of 1981 as unemployment and inflation soared.

In 1982 the junta occupied the Islas Malvinas—which were taken over by Britain in 1833 and occupied under the name Falkland Islands—off the southeast coast of Argentina. This sovereignty issue was popular at home, but the junta badly miscalculated international response, particularly that of Britain, which sent elite troops to retake the islands. After a short, sharp conflict—known as the South Atlantic War—the British ejected Argentine forces. Public outrage put the military on notice that its rule was ending.

Return to Civilian Rule Despite the general expectation that the Peronists would take power, the more moderate Radicals won both the presidency and a majority in the legislature in the 1983 general elections. President Raul Alfonsín put former junta members on trial, and several high-ranking officials were convicted and jailed. Military protests came when lower-ranking individuals were charged; the government backed down and peace was restored. Meanwhile, despite a general resurgence of public confidence and the reopening of Argentine society, hard economic issues remained. The Alfonsín administration began the reconstruction of Argentine social and democratic political life, but it was able to make relatively little progress against the country's economic problems.

The resurgent *Justicialista* (Peronist) party handily won the 1989 election, putting Carlos Menem, a former provincial governor into the presidency. Although many observers expected a return to old-style Peronist populism, Menem instituted austerity measures and began privatizing state enterprises. He quickly pardoned both convicted and untried military personnel in an attempt to settle that issue, reversed isolationist policies, and opened the heavily protected Argentine economy to trade and investment. Since 1989—when inflation reached nearly 5,000 percent—the once stagnant Argentine economy has turned around and is not only showing remarkable growth, but also a very low rate of inflation.

The Paradox of the Argentine Economy

Argentina developed an economy based on the exchange of agricultural commodities for foreign capital and manufactures. It was run primarily by and for the landed aristocracy and *porteño* (Buenos Aires) business interests. However, this commodity-based economy was at the mercy of volatile international market prices and dependent on the nations which bought Argentina's low-value produce and in return sold the Argentines expensive, value-added manufactures.

The political power based on the support of labor in the mid-20th century resulted in the provision of expensive employment benefits. This policy raised production costs, without a corresponding plan to increase productivity. To sustain this built-in elevated cost structure, the government cordoned off the economy with protectionist rules, keeping out competitors during that period. The authorities also nationalized many crucial enterprises and imposed export levies in order to generate revenues. Many Argentine goods became uncompetitive in world markets.

In the last decade, Argentina's administrations have broken with the past. Restrictive trade and investment barriers have fallen and nonproductive and non-self-sustaining state companies have been privatized. Financial accounts have been placed on a current basis by means linking the Argentine peso to the US dollar under the Convertibility Law. The intransigent Argentine system of 10 years ago has been replaced by a largely open regime—a change that many find astonishing, but few will deny because it is supported by virtually all economic indicators.

Nevertheless, some substantial problems must still be conquered. Government operations and procedures need to be standardized, revenues need to be increased, expenditures need to be reduced, and all of these issues need to be approached with greater transparency and addressed more forthrightly. The country faces deteriorating social services, such as its health and education systems, and will have to begin restructuring and modernizing them. This in turn will require stricter attention to the generation and collection of revenue to fund public programs. Finally, the competing interests and conflicts between the provinces and the central government must be resolved.

In early 1995 Argentina weathered the fallout from the collapse of the Mexican peso. Although the economic situations of these two countries are substantially different, investors also noted some similarities: Argentina's foreign debt and foreign reserves situations have made it difficult for the nation to maintain currency convertibility, economic growth, and stability—keystones to its economic recovery.

Given Argentina's recent history of hyperinflation, even a small event can cause panic, and it will require some time for Argentines and outsiders alike to regain full trust. It is also necessary to recognize that to date the new economic plan has had a high social cost.

And even as the administration worked to calm market fears in early 1995, the spectre of the dirty war of the 1970s and early 1980s resurfaced with new revelations of official misconduct. Despite the efforts of two administrations to lay it to rest and a formal apology from the military in 1995, this issue continues to trouble Argentines. Although it now lies firmly in the past, the lack of resolution has left scars in the Argentine psyche.

SIZE OF THE ECONOMY

Numbers for 1994 place Argentina's gross domestic product (GDP) at US$279.4 billion, up 9.3 percent in nominal terms from the prior year's US$255.7 billion. As of the end of 1994, officials were predicting growth in 1995 of between 4.5 and 6.5 percent (to roughly US$290 to US$300 billion). However, in March 1995 the government reduced its projections to 3 percent (about US$288 billion).

Economic and many other statistics are a difficult issue in Argentina, where special conditions, hyperinflation, and general confusion formerly hampered the preparation of reliable numbers in some past years. The *Statistical Yearbook of the Republic of Argentina,* published by the Instituto Nacional de Estadística y Censos (INDEC, the National Institute of Statistics and Census), notes that Argentina changed its currency five times since 1969 and had six different foreign exchange regimes between 1980 and 1990, making currency translation difficult. INDEC is the official authoritative source for Argentine economic statistics and is accepted by the International Monetary Fund (IMF) for its authoritative *International Financial Statistics Yearbook.* Although INDEC is definitive for the economy in peso terms, it becomes difficult to

Argentina's Gross Domestic Product (GDP)

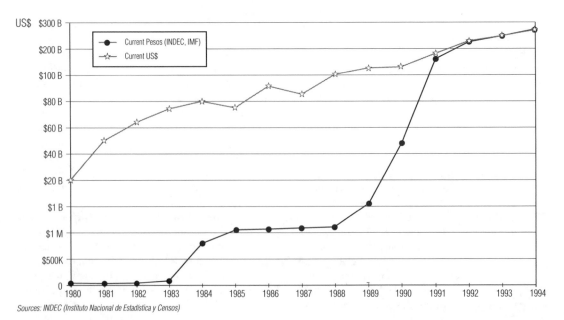

Sources: INDEC (Instituto Nacional de Estadística y Censos)

reconcile with comparative measures (such as translation into US dollars), and different sources often give widely varying figures for Argentine activity, even for such basic data as GDP. In general, more recent figures are more reliable, not only because of improved data collection based on Argentina's more open economic regime, but also because the linkage of the Argentine peso with the US dollar on a one-to-one basis allows easier translation by presuming rough equivalence.

From 1991 through 1994 Argentina's economy grew by almost 55 percent in current dollar terms, second only to China's growth during the same period. However, during the period from 1980 to 1993, INDEC's GDP figures calculated using real (constant 1986) pesos show a largely stagnant economy with total growth of less than 15 percent and a compound annual growth rate (CAGR) of about 1 percent (from 10.3 billion constant pesos in 1980 to 11.8 billion pesos in 1993). In 5 of those 14 years, Argentina's GDP fell, the largest drop being 6.6 percent in 1985. Nevertheless, the GDP grew by an of average 4.5 percent in positive years, climbing by as much as 8.9 percent in 1991. In current US dollar terms, Argentina's economy has grown, albeit erratically, by a CAGR of 19 percent since 1980 (from roughly US$20.1 billion to US$276.6 billion in 1994).

Another measure of the size of Argentina's economy is found in per capita GDP, which in 1994 was calculated as US$8,159, up 6.9 percent from 1993's US$7,632. Per capita GDP has grown at a CAGR of 17.6 percent since 1980, when the figure was US$712. In 1993 Argentina's per capita GDP—calculated in scaled terms of purchasing power parity—was about US$9,500, behind South Korea (with about US$10,000) and Portugal (at about US$10,500), but ahead of Malaysia (at about US$9,000) and Chile and Greece (at about US$8,500 each). According to another indicator, the number of persons living below the poverty line in the greater Buenos Aires area (defined as an income equivalent to less than roughly twice the cost of the family food basket) was 17.8 percent in 1993, down from a high of 47.4 percent in 1989.

CONTEXT OF THE ECONOMY

Since the government's stabilization program began to take hold in the 1990s after implementation of the Convertibility Law, Argentina has exhibited major improvement in its operations and prospects. Among the main results of the new economic plan are a greater certainty and trust in governmental policies along with social and political stabilization. With this stability, interference and turnover in the government have fallen drastically and investment and demand have grown. The privatization of state enterprises has attracted outside investment while resulting in more efficient operations, although it has also contributed to disruptions and unemployment. The availability of credit and the development of capital markets—severely restricted during the 1980s—have opened the floodgates of pent-up domestic demand. Construction and industrial production are among the strongest sectors, and a new focus on lagging high-value-added products for export markets is a particularly welcome trend.

Another indication of change in the economy is the return of flight capital. According to wildly varying estimates, between US$25 and US$50 billion in capital is thought to have fled Argentina during the 1980s. From 1991 through 1994 an estimated US$25 billion of this capital was returned to Argentina. Capitalization of the Argentine stock market—which had fallen as low as US$1 billion in 1987—rose to US$58 billion in 1993, with virtually all of this rise occurring in the years since currency convertibility took effect.

The State Sector

The Argentine economy has traditionally included a few prominent firms, which have exercised substantial control over specific production sectors and have been protected by barriers against outside investment or competition. This situation worsened with the creation of state-run firms in key sectors. Many of these firms were overstaffed, inefficient, and heavily subsidized. During the early 1980s, 14 of Argentina's top 50 firms were state-run. Even though these state firms accounted for 50 percent of total sales of the top 50 enterprises, all but four of them posted operating losses. In 1991, 77 state enterprises were in business in such sectors as telecommunications (ENTEL); energy and petroleum resources—Yacimientos Petroliferos Fiscales (YPF) and Gas del Estado; utilities including power generation, water, and sanitation systems; air (Aerolineas Argentinas) and rail transportation; ports; chemical and petrochemical production; steel; and certain defense-related industries.

This state of affairs has changed dramatically since 1990 with the privatization of most state-run firms, and few firms remain in state hands. Disinvestment has occurred through direct sales, sales of securities for cash or cancellation of debt, or grants of long-term operating concessions. As of mid-1994 a total of US$10.4 billion had been received in cash, plus an additional US$13.4 billion in face value of public debt canceled (these figures omit additional benefits from the assumption of private debt or projected future investments called for in specific contracts). After peaking at 874,000 in

1989, public employment shrank by three-quarters to 201,000 in 1993. Additional privatizations, delivery of concessions, or subcontracting of state-provided goods or services are anticipated in energy, transportation, the post office, social security, mint operations, and various defense industries, among others.

THE UNDERGROUND ECONOMY

During the late 1980s some observers estimated that the Argentine underground economy was as large as 40 percent of the formal (aboveground) economy. At that time, the sector of the population generally classified as poor—that is, persons who operated on the fringes of the formal economy—was increasing as more and more of the lower-middle class blue-collar industrial and white-collar office workers were displaced by cutbacks in inefficient operations (mainly in state-owned, but also in some private businesses). The high interest and inflation rates during the 1970s and 1980s, the inability of public and private enterprises to self-fund from their operations, and the lack of available capital and credit that stifled the economy also led to inventive and quasi-legal (or illegal) financing schemes, many of which were designed simply to pursue short-term paper gains by operating in the money markets.

Argentines have long suspected—with good reason—that many firms and individuals pay little or no tax. At least part of the government's prescription for returning to solvency has revolved around closing loopholes in the tax code and making collection procedures more efficient. Nevertheless, some estimates argue that one-third of these taxes continue to be evaded even after implementation of a fairly rigorous campaign to enforce payment. One recent tax change—dropping the rate on the tax on personal nonproductive assets from 1 percent to 0.5 percent, but extending it to cover previously exempt securities holdings—is designed to apply to worldwide holdings, thus capturing some of the billions that some Argentines hold abroad in shell companies or other accounts. Some companies have been accused of using falsified invoices to reduce the income and value-added taxes owed.

Tax evasion has been considered the rule among large numbers of new single proprietorships created by laid-off workers who are paying little or no income or value-added tax on their operations. In early 1995, tax receipts—especially from the smallest but also from larger companies—plummeted, not so much because of evasion as insolvency as the financial crisis dried up working capital. Furthermore, it has been estimated that

perhaps as much as one-quarter of the Argentine workforce consists of so-called "black labor": illegal, often immigrant or underage workers who are paid off the books, who themselves pay little or no tax, and for whom employers make no payments for social security, benefits, or taxes.

Although Argentina lacks the cultural basis that has supported widespread corruption in some other societies, the phenomenon became common in the 1970s and early 1980s. This was complicated by the extent of the bureaucracy and the monopoly and near-monopoly situation found in many industries. However, Argentina has made great strides in eliminating abuses and making its official and business dealings operate both more transparently and at arm's length. Examples of corrupt behavior may remain, but they are much reduced from even a few years ago. Part of this success has been due to the simple provision of a more stable system with more formal opportunities available to a wider range of businesses, as well as improved basic enforcement. Also, the introduction of automated systems in customs and other government agencies is beginning to ease the burden of recordkeeping and collecting.

Argentina has a relatively low crime rate. Overall reported crime has risen since 1980—partially due to the end of military rule that suppressed crime—but the numbers of actual incidents have fallen in many places, despite difficult economic times that usually promote such activity. Organized crime is a minor factor in Argentina, and overall crime is lower in the cities than in many rural areas.

Intellectual Property Rights Argentine intellectual and industrial property right protections and enforcement are relatively strong. As a signatory to the latest round of the General Agreement on Tariffs and Trade (GATT), the country is in the process of revising a few weaker areas—in particular, patent protections on pharmaceuticals. Licensing and technology transfer is protected and is eligible for certain tax benefits. Trade secrets are not specifically covered, but receive indirect protection through enforceable provisions of contract, labor, and property laws.

INFLATION

Few countries have had a worse experience with inflation than Argentina, and because of this, few countries are more sensitive to the issue. Between 1980 and 1988 consumer price rises were in the triple digit range every year except 1986, when they fell to 86 percent. Argentine inflation reached a high of 4,924 percent in 1989, dropped to 1,344 percent in 1990, and then fell precipitously to 3.9 percent in

1994. At the beginning of 1995, Argentine authorities were forecasting an increase of 3 percent in consumer prices for the year. Despite all the financial turmoil in early 1995, Argentina showed no change in inflation (which was rising at an annual rate of 5 percent) in February 1995, and is expected to remain at about that level for all of 1995.

LABOR

Labor has been one of the most important elements in Argentina's economy in recent decades, and it is arguably the element that has paid the highest cost in the restructuring of the economy. In 1991 Argentina had a potential workforce of 23,288,000. Of these, 13.2 million (57 percent) were considered to be economically active—either employed or seeking employment. Some two-thirds of the active workforce consists of men, although women's participation in the workforce is increasing, as is the incidence of those holding multiple jobs and moonlighting. Other than in allowed family enterprises, labor by children younger than 14 is forbidden; although many parents have been seeking such employment for their children in order to make ends meet, child labor is not the endemic problem in Argentina that it is in some other countries.

In 1991—before the most radical round of public sector cutbacks through privatization—8.1 million (61 percent) were employed in the private sector and 5.1 million (39 percent) in the public sector. Within the public sector, roughly one-third of workers were employed at the national level and about half at the provincial level, with the remainder employed at the municipal level. Within the private sector, 29 percent of people were employed in operations with five or fewer employees, while 56 percent worked in operations employing more than five (size information was unknown for the remainder). About 11 percent of all workers were involved in domestic service, and roughly one-fifth described themselves as self-employed.

Argentina, which boasts a literacy rate of 96 percent, has long prided itself on its educational system. Schooling is mandatory for nine years; however, in recent years there have been growing complaints that schooling has been unsatisfactory in many areas. Although many receive additional schooling beyond the basic required level, overall attendance falls to roughly half after the seventh grade. Argentina places a higher premium on education than do many other countries in Latin America, and many Argentines express concern over the perceived deterioration in the educational system.

Argentine workers have traditionally been able to achieve a higher standard of living—and have been accorded a somewhat higher status—than those in many other countries. But while the average Argentine worker may be a cut above the average worker in some other countries, there is a shortage of skilled labor in many specialized functional areas, especially outside Buenos Aires and a few other larger centers. However, pockets of extremely sophisticated production operated by well trained personnel have also been developed in specific areas.

Unemployment

Argentina keeps comprehensive statistics on employment, unemployment, and underemployment only for urban areas. Between 1989 and 1994, unemployment averaged 6.9 percent. The rate was reported to be 18.6 percent in May 1995, and

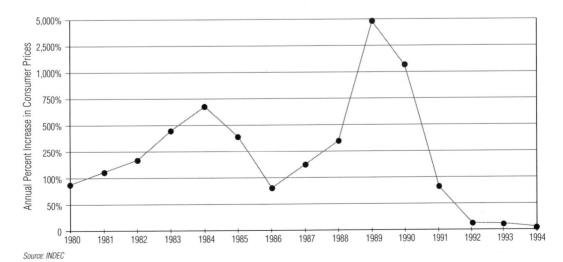

Argentina Inflation: 1980–1994

Source: INDEC

analysts predict that the rate will remain higher than 10 percent throughout 1995. Unemployment is even higher in some provinces. Argentina's urban underemployment averaged 9.1 percent from 1989 through 1994, ranging from a high of 10.4 percent in 1990 to a low of 7.5 percent in 1994.

Since 1989 urban employment—the number of jobs—has grown by 13.4 percent, while the economically active population has grown 11.7 percent and the total population has risen by 6.2 percent. Argentina appears to be keeping ahead of the demand for jobs, although the substantial numbers of underemployed suggest that even more jobs need to be created.

All countries generally undercount their unemployed workers, and it is likely that a significant percentage of those classified as economically inactive are not only eligible for, but would actually prefer to, work.

The Role of Unions

The Argentine constitution guarantees the right of workers to organize, bargain collectively, and strike, and labor unions have been a long-standing and influential phenomenon in Argentina. Various trade unions flourished around the turn of the century and were consolidated into the Confederación General de Trabajo (the General Labor Confederation or CGT), which has continued through several reorganizations as the main representative of organized labor. Argentine unions came into their own in the mid-1940s under Perón. The newly empowered unions used their increasing influence to staunchly defend the gains they had made under the new system. Some analysts argue that despite their expansion, Argentine unions served in

many cases to restrict the entry of new workers so as to defend the positions of existing members, especially during periods when the economy was trending downward. In 1945 about 529,000 workers were union members; in 1954 this number had surged to 2.2 million, about 50 percent of the workforce. By 1992 participation had fallen to about 28 percent of the labor force.

As Secretary of Labor, Perón united union and nonunion labor into a large related bloc by instituting pension and health benefits administered through his offices. Even 10 years after Perón's ouster in 1955, Peronists led about 70 percent of the unions. During the *Proceso*, the military purged many militant union leaders and co-opted others, while placing strict limits on the ability of unions to operate. Nevertheless, unions remained strong enough to thwart Alfonsín's attempts to reorganize labor after he assumed office in 1983. In that year, trade unions still represented about one-third of Argentina's workforce.

Although still powerful, unions are more fragmented. Generally considered less obstructive during the Menem administration, they have nevertheless opposed the president on numerous occasions. Unions have been most outspoken on the issue of privatization, which they contend has been extremely harmful to labor. Organized labor is particularly strong in urban industrial centers.

Wages and Benefits

Argentina has had a relatively high cost of labor during much of the 20th century, and inflation has caused nominal Argentine wages to jump at the same time that they have lost a great deal of purchasing power. Between 1985 and 1993 real

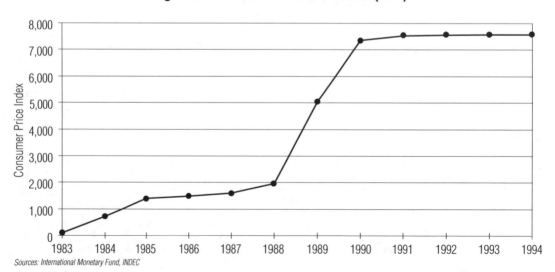

Argentina Consumer Price Index (CPI)

Sources: International Monetary Fund, INDEC

wages declined by one-third from the 1985 level (although the purchasing power of wages actually fell less—by only one-quarter from the 1985 level). Between 1985 and 1993, the real overall cost of labor rose by 50 percent, while average monthly wages rose from roughly US$382 to US$884 in current US dollars. Despite resistance, the government has been able to push through reforms making wage increases dependent on productivity, breaking the linkage with inflation.

In 1993 average monthly manufacturing wages were US$606.50; projections for 1994 show a monthly average rate of US$636.75, with a year-end monthly rate of US$652.50. Wages vary widely within specific industries, with leatherworkers earning roughly 45 percent of the average wage, while those producing high-demand electrical machinery earn roughly 30 percent more than the average. In 1994 workers in the commercial sector had monthly earnings of roughly US$700, those in specialized industry US$955, and those in finance US$1,210. The national minimum wage was doubled in 1993 to US$200 per month, but relatively little labor is actually available at this rate.

All regular workers are eligible to receive annual bonus payments equal to one month's wages, half of which is payable in June and the other half in December. Employers contribute 16 percent of the worker's annual salary toward pension benefits, 9 percent toward a family allowance fund, 6 percent toward health care, and 2 percent toward social services, totaling 33 percent to mandatory benefit programs (employees contribute 11 percent toward their pension, 3 percent toward social services, and 3 percent plus 1.5 percent for each dependent covered for health care). Employers must also provide workers' compensation, disability, and life insurance benefits for regular employees. Benefits are delivered through the *obras sociales* (social works) programs of unions or through government-approved insurance firms. Dismissed workers are usually entitled to severance benefits based on length of service.

Argentine employers customarily offer few additional benefits, although larger firms may provide subsidized meals, transportation, or housing for operations located in areas where alternative services are not available. Executive compensation and benefits packages are comparable to those in developed countries.

Workweek

Argentina's standard workweek has been 48 hours, usually spread over six days (including a half-day on Saturday). Some firms can demand overtime work, but strict rest time requirements are enforced (Saturday afternoon and all day Sunday), and unionized operations usually negotiate shorter hours. Employees are entitled to 11 national holidays annually and receive a number of paid vacation days depending on length of service.

ELEMENTS OF THE ECONOMY

In 1992, 6 percent of Argentina's GDP came from the agricultural sector, 29 percent from the industrial sector, and 65 percent from the services sector. While the contribution of agriculture has remained relatively stable—it was 6.5 percent of GDP in 1980—industry has faded from 39.3 percent of GDP as services, which accounted for 54.4 percent of GDP in 1980, gained. In 1990, 12 percent of the workforce was employed in the agricultural sector, 30.4 percent in industry, and 57.6 percent in services.

Agriculture

Farming and Ranching Argentina's wealth has traditionally come from ranching and grain growing, and agricultural commodities continue to be a mainstay of Argentine exports. Although agriculture's direct share of GDP has fallen to a relatively low level, when ancillary activities such as food processing, transport, and related services are counted, perhaps 30 percent of the economy is still dependent on agriculture. Many Argentine industries are based on the manufacture of products from primary agricultural products. As recently as the early 1980s, the export of agricultural products accounted for about three-quarters of all foreign exchange earnings from exports. In 1990 Argentine farms employed roughly 12 percent of the workforce. Many of Argentina's more than 420,000 farming establishments are small family operations, but the large estates—averaging 10,000 hectares (25,000 acres) in size—account for an overwhelming share of the production.

As has been the case worldwide, Argentine agricultural producers have seen commodity prices fall while the costs of inputs have risen. They have also suffered from inflation and exchange and interest rate rises. Credit has been scarce, while government policy has in the past acted as a negative subsidy by imposing hefty export taxes on critical agricultural products, making Argentine products less competitive in international markets.

Fisheries and Forestry The agricultural sector includes forestry, fishing, and hunting for economic purposes. Production by Argentine fisheries has continued to expand, rising by nearly 145 percent from 1980 to 1993 to 919,500 metric tons. Similarly, the number of raw logs harvested nearly doubled within these years, although production of other forestry products has dropped sharply. Among secondary products—most of which are classified as manufactured products—a few have shown significant growth (laminates, lumber, paper paste, and finished paper and cardboard).

Future Directions Increased investment incentives are being offered to modernize Argentina's fishing fleet and processing facilities, with a view toward increasing its exports. The Argentine government is targeting the development of new crops and nontraditional products, particularly processed grain, grain subproducts, prepared foods, fruit, flowers, and organically grown products. To address trade restrictions of other countries against Argentine livestock because of health concerns, the government is pressing the implementation of vaccination programs and is reaching out to improve the confidence of its trading partners in the improved sanitary conditions. Greater exploitation of agricultural potential—both for improved domestic use and greater export value—will require major investments in infrastructure (including refrigeration, processing, and transportation facilities); fertilizer and pesticide use; and marketing, promotion, and information systems. Improved credit will also be necessary to develop Argentina's agricultural potential.

Industry

The industrial sector includes manufacturing, mining, and construction. Overall, this sector employed more than 3 million workers in 1990, approximately 30 percent of the workforce. Development of this sector began during the World War II era, and has accelerated during the past 10 years. With Argentina's push during the 1990s to diversify its economy, growth has surged. Industrial development is heavily concentrated in the Province of Buenos Aires—location of 40 percent of Argentina's manufacturing operations—as well as in centers in Santa Fe and Córdoba. Pockets of specialized industrial development have developed in other areas to take advantage of local natural and labor resources. Most Argentine operations are small; firms with fewer than 30 persons employ the vast majority of Argentine industrial workers, and few operations employ more than 500 workers.

The focus of Argentine industry has changed from decade to decade. Before the 1930s, most industrial products were imported. The age of import substitution swept the nation during the 1940s, but most industrial products were not yet competitive by world standards and therefore contributed only about one-quarter of export revenues despite representing a share of GDP roughly five times greater than that of agriculture. In the late 1950s and 1960s, production expanded from its base of consumer goods to include industrial products—primarily steel, petrochemicals, and automobiles. Diversification into capital and intermediate

goods came during the 1960s and early 1970s, while markets were heavily protected from import competition. Despite a certain degree of stagnation due to restrictions and overcapacity, Argentine industry continued to expand in the 1970s, diversifying and increasing capacity in such areas as basic metals, machinery and equipment, and chemical and petrochemical production. The industrial sector has continued to grow, and pockets of extremely sophisticated state-of-the-art production now exist. The prospect of being able to reach larger markets on more favorable terms through the Mercado Común del Sur (Mercosur) is spurring interest in industrial investment and production.

Mining This sector has shown limited growth since 1980—rising from 1.3 percent in 1980 to 1.8 percent in 1992—in terms of its participation in the GDP. Foreign investment in this sector in recent years is expected to result in renewed activity. Quarry and building materials account for roughly two-thirds of the value of sector output. In 1990 this sector employed only 47,000 workers barely 0.5 percent of the workforce. To improve output value and increase this sector's export share, the government has removed controls on foreign investment and as added favorable tax treatment as further incentive to attract new capital.

Petroleum Exploration and development permits were offered to outside firms following the deregulation and privatization of the state-run petroleum monopoly (YPF) in 1991. In 1993 production rose 18 percent (topping 34 million cubic meters). Through privatization of this industry and deregulation of foreign investment, Argentina hopes to attract nearly US$9 billion in new investment to this sector by 1997.

Manufacturing In the modern era, Argentina's manufacturers have struggled against great odds. Between 1974 and 1985 the number of manufacturing establishments declined by 13 percent to reach a low of 109,000. In 1980 manufacturing accounted for 29.5 percent of GDP, a share that dropped to 22 percent by 1992. Faced with competition from imports, many sectors—such as textiles and apparel, nonmetallic mineral products, wood products, and miscellaneous manufactures—were seriously affected. Other sectors—such as food and beverage, paper, chemical products, and machinery producers—sustained level production or saw modest gains. Manufacturing employment dropped by 9 percent during this period.

However, the situation appears to be turning around in the 1990s, seen first by a slight rise in employment to encompass nearly 20 percent of the workforce. As of 1993, the production of paints and soap was showing noticeable increase, the production of new higher-value intermediate and end product petrochemicals was strong and growing,

Structure of the Argentine Economy—1992

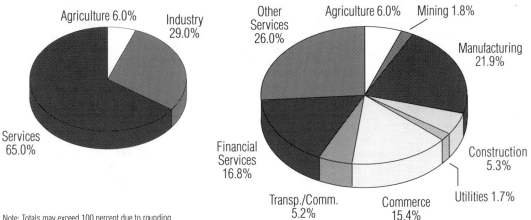

Note: Totals may exceed 100 percent due to rounding.
Source: INDEC

and production of aluminum and specialized intermediate steel products was up. Activity in the automotive industry is showing renewed strength, particularly in production of passenger automobiles, buses, and motorcycles.

Construction Construction accounted for a little more than 5 percent of GDP in 1992, down from an 8.6 percent share in 1980, although much of the difference actually represents greater growth in other areas of the economy. In 1990 construction employed 1 million workers (10 percent of the workforce), and was among the least productive sectors in terms of output per worker. The construction sector is cyclical in nature. It also has struggled because of outside forces: a lack of financing, plus former instability in the economy, have led to a drop in new construction projects. The number of building permits issued fell by half during the 1970s and 1980s.

In the early 1990s pent-up housing demand, coupled with newly available credit, led to a surge in building activity. By 1993 the number of building permits issued had risen by 44 percent, representing a cumulative addition of 31 million sq m (333.7 million sq ft) of space. Some 30 percent of this construction represented new single family housing, followed by retail space (17 percent), multifamily dwellings (16 percent), and industrial facilities (8 percent). In 1993 permits issued for extensions of existing structures added 3 million sq m (33.6 million sq ft) of space, mostly for single family homes, and retail and industrial space.

Future Directions Argentine industrial policy now operates within the context of an open economy. The country's participation in Mercosur is also expected to have a major effect on future

market-based development as industry begins to grow to complement that in the economies of member countries. Industry is generally expected to expand its scope and increasingly to target foreign markets to a much greater degree on a competitive basis.

Services

Despite rapid growth in importance, the Argentine services sector has received relatively little attention. In 1992 this sector's share of GDP was 65 percent, and in 1993 the sector grew by 7.5 percent in real terms. As of 1990, it employed nearly 60 percent of the workforce (15.741 million workers). The services sector includes utilities, transportation and communication, commerce (which includes retail and wholesale trade, lodging, restaurants, and entertainment), financial services, and miscellaneous services (including professional, personal, and government ones). The difficulty in assessing this sector's economic contribution arises from the inherent problem of measuring services output; statistics are less reliable for this sector than for other areas of the economy.

Utilities The output of Argentine utilities represented 1.7 percent of GDP in 1992, nearly the same as its GDP share in 1980. As of 1990, 103,000 workers (1 percent of the workforce) were employed in utility services. Power generation currently satisfies domestic demand, but expansion is needed to support Argentina's future growth and to reach many remote underserved areas. More than half of the electricity is supplied by thermal generation—steam, gas, and diesel-fired turbines—and another 40 percent comes from hydropower. Argentina has the most advanced nuclear energy program in Latin

America, deriving 7 percent of its total power in 1993 from nuclear plants. The development of additional hydroelectric projects is underway, and companies are undertaking the expansion and modernization of wastewater treatment systems. Argentina's water supply system is well developed in the more temperate and productive regions.

Transportation and Communications These sectors combined accounted for 5.2 percent of GDP in 1992, up from 4.5 percent in 1980. In 1993 the transportation sector grew by 5.5 percent, while communications rose by 9.8 percent. In 1990 these sectors together employed 460,000 workers, 4.6 percent of the workforce; however, since then the share of employment has fallen sharply because of privatization. Prior to 1990, Argentina's communications and transportation systems were largely inadequate and service was generally considered to be poor. Privatization has done much to change this historical situation.

Between 1990 and 1993 the number of installed lines rose by 43 percent and the number of lines in service by one-third; the number of digitized lines rose fivefold, with 45 percent of the system being digitized. Argentina leads all Latin American countries in per capita telephones and cellular telephones. Mail service is considered adequate, but slow, and foreign and domestic courier services are making inroads into the business market despite some remaining restrictions.

Most of the nation's rail systems are also being privatized on condition that the investors improve and maintain them. Privatization of part of the air transport infrastructure—navigation systems, ground structures, and the largest airports—is responsible for improving operations and injecting new capital. Similarly, privatization of the ports—an essential channel for Argentine foreign trade—is expected to increase capacity and efficiency, resulting in additional ship traffic.

Commerce The commercial sector represented 15.4 percent of Argentina's GDP in 1992, down from 16.5 percent in 1980. It grew by roughly 3.7 percent in 1993. In 1990 commerce employed 1.7 million workers, 17 percent of the workforce. A wide range of service outlets exist in Argentina. Although there are a number of national chain operations, the vast majority of retail businesses are small, and many are operated by individuals—largely as a result of the contraction in other employment sectors in recent years. However, the entry of large international retail operations into Argentina is expected to change the retail situation dramatically.

Financial Services Financial services represented 16.8 percent of GDP in 1994, up from 13.9 percent in 1980. In 1990 the financial sector employed 396,000 workers (4 percent of the workforce) placing it among the most productive in terms of output per worker. This sector grew by as much as 18 percent in 1993. The number of financial institutions in Argentina has fallen since 1990, primarily as smaller firms are forced to merge. The remaining operations are generally stronger and better capitalized than their forerunners, although most observers expect a further shakeout of smaller, weaker firms. In 1993 volume on the Buenos Aires Stock Exchange was US$58.6 billion, while volume on Argentina's over-the-counter market was US$234.6 billion. However, the Buenos Aires Stock Exchange's Merval Index fell by nearly two-thirds—from its high in February 1994 to 262 in early March 1995—before recovering somewhat, serving notice that Argentine markets are still volatile. Financial services are becoming more sophisticated and more available to both foreign and domestic users, largely as a result of the more open foreign investment regime and peso convertibility.

Other Services This catchall segment of the service economy accounted for 26 percent of Argentine GDP in 1992, up from 17.8 percent in 1980. In 1990 other services employed 3.1 million workers, 30.6 percent—the largest single sector—of the workforce. Some areas—such as education and health care—barely grew in 1993, while others—such as business services—grew by from 9 to 12 percent. Despite a sharp retrenchment in the public sector as a result of privatization, public sector service employment nevertheless grew slightly in 1993—largely as a result of increased overall employment by provincial and municipal governments. Many areas of personal, professional, and business services in Argentina are considered to be highly developed, with many operating according to the highest international standards.

TRADE

During much of its modern history, Argentina has exported low-value-added commodity products and then imported high-value-added manufactured goods. During the 1940s and 1950s Argentina imposed tariff and nontariff barriers to protect the development of domestic import substitution industries, while from the 1960s through the 1980s, policy fluctuated between more open and less open trade. After running large trade surpluses for most of the 1980s—largely because of official limits—policymakers shifted to an open-market approach, allowing the economy to run up substantial trade deficits as the country imported capital goods and other inputs to strengthen production.

In 1988 import tariff levels were a maximum of 50 percent plus a 15 percent surcharge, with a minimum charge of 15 percent, and an average rate of 39 percent. As of January 1994, tariffs were lowered to between 0 and 20 percent, with an average of 9.1 percent (these levels have since fallen further, and as a signatory to GATT, Argentina is pledged to reduce them even more). Discretionary import licensing was also dropped. Most export tariffs have also been eliminated. Total foreign trade doubled between 1980 and 1994.

Mercosur A customs union including Argentina, Brazil, Paraguay, and Uruguay, Mercosur is expected to alter the trade picture in Argentina substantially. The country's trade with neighboring Brazil represented roughly a modest 11 percent of total Argentine foreign trade from 1975 through 1989. By 1994 this figure had nearly doubled to 21 percent. Although Argentina currently maintains a trade deficit with Mercosur countries, its exports to them—especially of nontraditional, higher-value-added products—are growing rapidly, moreso than with non-Mercosur nations.

Trade Deficits During the past 30 years, Argentina has maintained a balance of merchandise trade surplus in all but 1981, 1992, 1993, and 1994. During much of this period, Argentina managed its trade to exclude imports. Based on improved export performance in early 1995, officials were projecting breakeven performance or even a slight surplus in 1995. The development of exports, especially of nontraditional, higher-value-added merchandise exports, is taking on greater urgency. In 1994, 40 percent of the growth in exports was accounted for by such nontraditional industrial products, while 40 percent of the increase in imports consisted of capital goods to boost productivity.

Exports Argentina continues to be known primarily for its agricultural exports (grain, oilseeds, and meat products), although exports of manufactured goods have seen a boom in recent years. From 1980 through 1989 Argentina's exports averaged 38 percent primary products, 37 percent agricultural manufactures (processed products), 21 percent industrial manufactures, and 4 percent fuels. However, by 1994 these positions had nearly reversed themselves, with primary products accounting for 24 percent of exports, agricultural manufactures for 29, higher earning industrial products for 37 percent, and fuels for 10 percent.

In 1994 Argentina's top single export was fuels, accounting for more than 10 percent of total merchandise exports. This was followed fats and oils, food by-products, cereals, oilseeds, and meat. Together these top six categories accounted for nearly half of all exports. Of the top 10 export categories—accounting for 64 percent of export value—only vehicles and machinery represented nonextractive products. However, these two categories showed high growth (26 and 13 percent, on top of 86 and 30 percent growth, respectively, in the previous year), allowing for a more optimistic view of Argentina's developing industrial economy.

Imports Argentina has allowed imports to grow rapidly in recent years after an extended period during which it erected barriers to outside products. Much of this increased influx has represented capital goods and intermediate inputs, which are accorded low- to no-tariff treatment, but open markets entail the import of consumer and nonessential goods, which have also grown. In 1994 intermediate goods accounted for 29 percent of

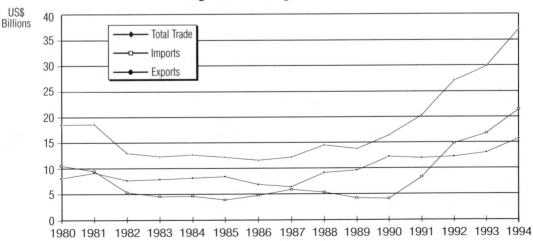

Argentina Foreign Trade

Note: Merchandise trade; exports reported on an FOB basis, imports reported on a CIF basis.
Source: INDEC

Leading Argentine Exports by Commodity—1994

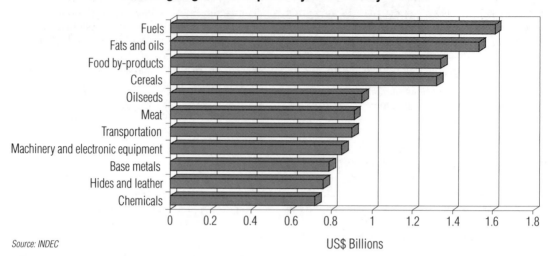

Source: INDEC

US$ Billions

imports and capital goods represented 28 percent of imports. When parts and accessories for capital equipment are included, these inputs include 73 percent of all imports. Consumer goods represented 18 percent of imports and vehicles 6 percent. Fuels and miscellaneous imports rounded out the import picture.

Machinery and mechanical equipment represented the largest single category—34 percent—of imports in 1994. Transportation equipment was second (18 percent), with chemicals in third place (12 percent). Together these three categories accounted for 64 percent of 1994 imports. The top ten import categories accounted for nearly 90 percent of all imports.

Trading Partners Argentina's dominant trade partner is its largest neighbor, Brazil: in 1994 Brazil accounted for US$7.9 billion, or 21 percent of Argentina's total trade. The second largest partner was the US, with US$6.6 billion (18 percent of total trade). Aside from these two large partners, Argentina's trade partners individually account for a much smaller proportion of its foreign activity. In 1994 Italy, Germany, Chile, the Netherlands, Spain, Uruguay, France, and Japan followed in rank order. These top ten trade partners included all the countries with which Argentina had trade valued at more than US$1 billion; together, they accounted for almost three-quarters of the country's total trade. Trade with Mercosur partners—particularly Brazil and Uruguay—is expected to continue to grow and become more important in future years.

Argentina's trade is fairly well diversified, although this is liable to change as it alters the mix of its exports to include more value-added items. In 1994 the major purchaser of Argentina's products was Brazil (23 percent), followed by the US (11 percent), the Netherlands (8 percent), and Chile (6

percent). Together these three countries took nearly half of all Argentine exports. The top 10 countries took about 70 percent of Argentina's exports.

With the exception of its top two suppliers, Argentina gets its imports from a wide range of sources, none of which accounts for a very large percentage of its generally well diversified trade. In 1994 the major sources of Argentine imports were the US (US$5 billion, 23 percent) and Brazil (US$4 billion, 20 percent). The next seven largest suppliers accounted for an additional 33 percent of the total.

FOREIGN PARTICIPATION IN THE ECONOMY

Argentina has a long history of foreign investment. Its present approach—one that is expected to continue indefinitely, given the growing climate of internationalism—is designed to attract foreign investment through the openness of its economy and the removal of disincentives to outside capital. Indeed, Argentina's official and unofficial policy is geared toward encouraging both insiders and outsiders to bring investment funds into the country to support growth and development. This extends to the privatization of Argentina's huge and crucial state-run industries and the opening of its financial markets, which for many years were closed to many Argentines and foreigners alike. After years of outright bans and de facto regulatory and procedural roadblocks that protected national and nationalized industries from outside participation and competition, foreigners are now eligible to invest to almost any degree in virtually any economic sector in Argentina. They can generally do so without obtaining prior approval, without fear of discrimina-

Leading Argentine Imports by Commodity—1994

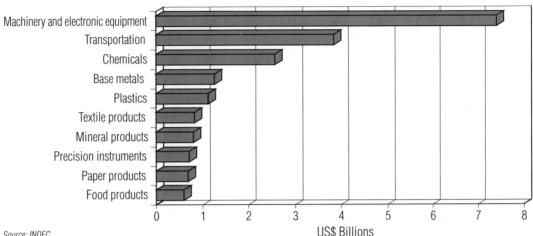

Source: INDEC

tory treatment, and without worry over the sanctity and availability of their earnings or assets.

Some usually relatively minor restrictions persist in specific areas. However, most restrictions have been removed, and many of the remaining ones are expected to fall as well in the next and final round of privatization. Even in areas where limits continue to exist, regulators may pragmatically allow foreign takeover of existing firms that need help, even when they will not authorize the creation of new competing firms by foreign interests.

Portfolio investment in securities is welcomed and generally unrestricted. And perhaps one-third of all foreign investment—especially that in privatized state industries—has come from debt-equity conversions, in which outside interests buy sovereign debt at a market discount and cancel it for a greater amount of equity value in a state industry. Such swaps are not officially available for private debt-equity conversions; however, depending on the specific circumstances, the authorities may authorize particular transactions in order to further policy goals.

The 1993 decree on foreign investment resulted in transparency and the repeal of procedural requirements that had served to limit foreign participation under preexisting law. Registration of investment is not compulsory, although Argentina asks investors to register for statistical purposes (some intracompany transfers of technology do require registration for tax purposes). Repatriation of all funds is now immediate and unconditional, whereas previously investors could not repatriate invested capital for a period of 3 years (10 years if made through a debt-equity conversion). Funds are available in any currency purchased at free market exchange rates.

Because they are granted national treatment,

foreigners are generally eligible for any incentives; however, the scarcity of funds is causing the government to phase out most incentives. Nevertheless, some incentives designed to direct new investment into undeveloped industrial and geographical areas—particularly mining, petroleum exploration, utility concessions, and tourism development—still exist.

Size of Foreign Participation

Argentina does not compile statistics on foreign investment, and information is sketchy. Such investment has been substantial and significant from the 19th century until the present, but its actual value is largely conjectural. Between 1989 and 1991, about US$30 billion in portfolio and direct foreign investment came into the country. More than 50 state enterprises were sold—largely to foreign investors—bringing in more than US$10 billion in cash (and more in the face value of canceled debt and contracted or implied additional post-acquisition capital investment). Between 1990 and 1993, foreign investment was estimated at US$28 billion, one-third of it from privatizations, placing Argentina behind only Mexico and China in terms of foreign investment channeled into emerging economies worldwide. In 1994 an estimated US$3 billion to US$5 billion flowed into Argentina. Some observers are predicting that from 1995 through the end of the decade, Argentina can expect an average annual net inflow of about US$2 billion in foreign investment funds.

Origin of Foreign Investment

Argentina has historically been closely involved with British investors, and that country provided the vast majority of investment capital during the last century. In the early 1990s, the US has become the dominant outside investor in the country, followed by investors from Europe—with which Argentina has maintained a long-term relationship—and increasing investment from neighboring Chile and Brazil. In terms of estimated total investment during the period 1990–1994, the US ranks first—accounting for perhaps 40 percent of all foreign investment made during the period— followed by Italy, Spain, Brazil, Chile, Germany, Switzerland, the Netherlands, and Canada.

Areas of Foreign Investment

Since the late 1980s the bulk of foreign investment in Argentina has been in the large privatized, formerly state-run, industries. Although these include such industrial production as steel, the main privatized industries participated in by outsiders have been the former monopolies operating the extractive sectors, utilities, and services: oil and gas, mining, telecommunications, water and sewers, transportation, and ports and port services. Following investment in these privatized companies, the next largest area has been portfolio investment in securities.

Remaining direct foreign investment has been made largely in manufacturing, with the automotive industry as the primary target sector. Based on investment plans announced by international automotive firms, this industry—arguably Argentina's most advanced—is expected to realize substantial additional investments during coming years. Many of these investments represent sums greater than US$100 million dedicated to specific projects over a relatively short period of time. Additional foreign investment has been channeled into the production of consumer durables and nondurables, particularly in the food processing industry.

GOVERNMENT ECONOMIC DEVELOPMENT STRATEGY

For too long Argentina effectively lacked a development policy. Despite the attempts of the Alfonsín administration to deal with the economic issues plaguing the country, its primary impact was in repairing the political rather than the economic sphere. Beginning in 1989 the Menem administration has worked to rationalize its policy, using an overall framework based on deregulation, decentralization, open markets, and policies designed to achieve stability in the economic sphere.

The Convertibility Law, which went into effect in April 1991, formed the core feature of Argentina's new policy. Its provisions were designed to stabilize Argentine finances and make them more transparent, providing greater confidence to both national and international investors. The success of most of its other policies now depends on the extent to which

the government continues to adhere to the convertibility plan and the degree to which it is seen to be achieving its goals.

Other aspects of the overall thrust of government policy include the maintenance of a budgetary surplus (achieved in 1992 and 1993, with an estimated 0.3 percent of GDP deficit in 1994, and an optimistic prediction of a surplus of about 1 percent for 1995) and the consolidation and control of public debt, with the issuance of new debt being contingent on the cancellation of old debt via repayment, rescheduling, or debt-equity swaps. At year-end 1994, total public debt was US$74.2 billion or 25.4 percent of GDP. Debt remains a concern, but it now accounts for a much smaller share of GDP and is scheduled in a far more manageable way.

Another goal is to promote savings and investment—in 1994 there was an estimated gap equal to 3 percent of GDP between investment and national savings, which was supplied by foreign capital and which the government hopes to close by the year 2000—while also funding current expenditures from current revenues. The government wants to reduce federal expenditures by delegating more responsibilities to provincial and local governments (particularly for education, health, and general welfare programs, funded by revenue sharing) and to the private sector (largely through privatizing most remaining state-run operations). It also wants to increase revenues reform of the tax code and better enforcement. Tax revenues grew by three-quarters from 1989 to 1992, with receipts from income taxes growing by almost 70 percent and those from value-added taxes by nearly 450 percent.

Social security reform is also a critical issue. Policies are designed to increase funding and benefits to adequate levels, while reducing evasion of contributions through standardization of collection procedures. The system is to be put on a pay-as-you-go footing and strengthened through the privatization of a portion of required contributions (which should add to national savings and available investment capital).

In contrast to past policy, in which different industries and producers were subject to varying rules, the new regime has established standard national treatment for virtually all domestic sectors as well as for foreign investors. Production; marketing; capital, financial, and foreign exchange markets access; and foreign trade have all been deregulated under the open-market policies. At the beginning of 1995, the administration's agenda included reform of the social security system and of bankruptcy law, employment law, workers' compensation, and small business regulation. As of the first quarter of 1995, the government seemed to be adhering to its stated policies—especially those regarding the defense of the convertibility regime—in an effort to weather the storm and convince domestic and foreign observers of its commitment.

POLITICAL OUTLOOK FOR THE ECONOMY

The return of government to civil authority based on popular elections led Raúl Alfonsín and the Radical Civic Union party to power in 1983. The Alfonsín administration withstood repeated threats of military coups and pressure from authoritarian elements in the country to strengthen the Argentine government, but also presided over a worsening of the economic situation. Alfonsín was succeeded by rival Justicialist party candidate Carlos Menem in 1989. Stepping down early, Alfonsín turned over a shaky Argentina to his successor.

Menem dealt forcefully with a variety of thorny issues. He pardoned convicted military personnel and halted further prosecutions, placating the armed forces. However, the president also quietly reduced the military budget by half, while privatizing defense industries and abolishing universal conscription, moves that served to put the armed forces largely under effective civilian control.

The Economic Outlook The new administration did not begin to gain control of the economy until the appointment of its third Minister of Economy, Domingo Cavallo, in February 1991. Cavallo instituted a sweeping open-market policy—based on the Convertibility Law—which resulted in a cumulative growth of 33 percent in GDP, 120 percent in real growth, and 37 percent in increased consumption from 1991 through 1994.

However, following the collapse of the Mexican peso at the end of 1994, international investors began withdrawing funds from other emerging markets, including Argentina. Nevertheless, as 1995 progressed, Argentina demonstrated both a commitment to adhere to its stated policies—primarily convertibility—and generally sound fundamentals. Between mid-1994 and mid-1995, Argentina's inflation rate—at 4.6 percent—fell below that of many countries in the world, including both developing and established industrialized nations. Free convertibility was maintained at par with the US dollar, and the money supply was kept in balance with foreign reserve positions, while the government pared expenses and worked to increase revenues, largely through improved tax collection. Meanwhile, the economy as measured by GDP continued to grow, and the business opportunities provided by Mercosur continued to increase.

Argentina's currently dormant, but still huge, foreign debt—the country owes roughly US$4 billion in interest and US$5 billion in principal in 1995 alone—would also become a live issue if there is any weakening in its currency. And having been burned before, Argentines are hypersensitive to any renewed bout of inflation. Although the government argues—fairly convincingly—that Argentina is not at risk, panic caused by a short-term liquidity shortfall could quickly accelerate into a full-blown crisis.

Between mid-December 1994 and mid-April 1995, Argentine banks lost deposits estimated as high as US$7.5 billion, while the central bank's reserves fell by at least US$2 billion as it rushed to shore up the system with the limited tools at its disposal. Several smaller, second tier banks become insolvent due to a lack of liquidity; some 30 others merged with stronger partners; and yet others pulled back and began looking for help. Skittish Argentines appeared to be moving their funds to the sidelines, hoarding them in foreign currencies in case the financial system were to collapse (some estimates suggest that about half of the funds withdrawn were sent abroad as flight capital, while the rest were converted—primarily to US dollars—and tucked under the mattress). Some short-term interest rates skyrocketed as high as 70 percent—although these fell back to 12 percent later in the month—and Argentina's Alto Paraná S.A., a major paper company, went into technical default when it had to stretch out payment on US$63.6 million of debt, causing even greater worry as it struggled to restructure. Nevertheless, the main danger has been that the situation could become a self-fulfilling prophecy, feeding on itself until the system would collapse.

The Argentine government rapidly went through a US$420 million reserve advanced by the IMF to stabilize the financial situation. The government then set about arranging a financing package of US$6.7 billion—including US$2.4 billion from the IMF, US$1.3 billion from the World Bank, US$1 billion from regional development banks, and US$2 billion in bonds, half to domestic and half to foreign investors. Plans were also set in motion to reduce government spending by US$1 billion and raise additional revenues of US$2.5 billion from increased tariffs, caps on pension benefits, higher value-added taxes (raised to 21 percent from 18 percent), and elimination of tax loopholes and stepped-up enforcement on tax collections—plus an additional US$2.4 billion from accelerated sales of state properties, including hydroelectric and nuclear power plants. However, facing an election in May 1995, the government asserted that it would not raise levies on fuel, cigarettes, or alcohol. Nevertheless, some 85 percent of Argentines polled stated that they were against devaluation and generally supported the government in its tightening of the economy to prevent such devaluation.

The immediate concern was that international investors would fail to recognize that the Argentine situation was substantially different from that of other emerging market economies. The situation had cooled by April, due partially to the government's forthright facing of the crisis, and partially to concern over the fall of the US dollar, which deflected attention away from the emerging markets' financial situation. Despite having avoided the immediate threat, Argentina continues to face not only the potential recurrence of similar problems, but also a longer range concern that its underlying revenue stream will not develop rapidly enough to cover future needs adequately. Argentina is going to need substantial inflows of foreign investment capital for an extended period, making the success of its near-term responses to the current crisis even more critical in attracting longer-term investment.

The Political Outlook Under the 1853 Argentine constitution, presidents were allowed to serve only a single six-year term. However, in November 1993 Menem and Alfonsín—as head of the next largest political party—reached what has been described by some as a power sharing agreement. They agreed to support Menem's bid to change the constitution so as to allow a second term of office. As a result, the new 1994 constitution changed the term of office to four years and allowed for self-succession; other provisions included run-off elections for president; direct election of senators; creation of the office of Prime Minister; and a clearer allocation of responsibilities between provincial and national government entities.

Congressional elections in 1994 saw a rearrangement of the prevailing political factions, with the Radicals losing ground and the rise of a new party, the Broad Front, made up primarily of dissenters opposed to Menem. Although Broad Front candidates seemed to be gaining strength in the final weeks of the 1995 campaign, Menem and the Justicialists scored an impressive victory in the May elections. Most observers felt the election served as a referendum on the government's policies and interpreted the results as support for the administration's program, the major points of which even the opposition had grudgingly endorsed.

Others have noted that winning the election was the easy part. Although the initial fears of investors have been allayed by Argentina's steadfast refusal to be stampeded into devaluation or other traditional—and largely counterproductive—reactions, as of mid-1995 many foreigners had shifted from a panic-induced pullback to more of a "wait-and-see" posture. The confirmation that the general public supported the new program was certainly welcome. Some investors have begun to venture back in, and these are likely to have a head start when the country resumes its climb.

There is still concern regarding unemployment and the fact that the radical restructuring of the economy has yet to sort itself out and stabilize to a degree that allows those displaced in it to find new roles. The issue of extending reform and economic recovery to the provinces also remains critical. Although it has come a long way, Argentina still must deal with numerous aspects of its economic; financial; labor; health, education, and welfare; judicial; and administrative systems. Nevertheless, Argentina has made a huge start in addressing these matters, has a viable model in place, and has shown the requisite political will to confront the hard choices needed to confirm and extend progress.

ARGENTINA'S INTERNATIONAL ROLE

Argentina has long been a member of a variety of international associations. Recently it has taken a greater role in regional and international activities as its new open economy pushes it into greater interaction with its international neighbors. Argentina is a charter member of the United Nations (the UN, or the Organización de Naciones Unidas—ONU—in Spanish), and of most of its affiliated bodies. It is a member of the International Monetary Fund (IMF), the International Bank for Reconstruction and Development (IBRD, or World Bank), the Inter-American Development Bank (IDB), the Organization of American States (OAS, or Organización de los Estados Americanos—OEA—in Spanish), and the Latin American Integration Association (LAIA, or Asociación Latinoamericana de Integración—ALADI—in Spanish).

Argentina subscribes to the General Agreement on Tariffs and Trade (GATT), its successor, the World Trade Organization (WTO), and to Mercosur (the Southern Common Market, or Mercado Común del Sur), while maintaining a variety of bilateral treaties with various nations. Argentina adheres to most international conventions, including the Berne and Paris Conventions regarding intellectual property, the International Chamber of Commerce (ICC), and the Customs Cooperation Council (CCC), among others.

Current Issues

ECONOMIC RESTRUCTURING: MAINTAINING THE MIRACLE

Changing Times

For the past 50 years and up until the early 1990s, Argentina's economy was essentially closed, operating within the protections provided by high trade barriers. Not only was its industrial sector protected from international participation and competition, but it was also subject to extensive and active government intervention. Political instability—caused by a series of military coups d'état together with economic instability characterized by high inflation and slow economic growth—has now given way to a sharply different scenario characterized by an outward-looking, free market economy and rapidly improving political stability.

The Turning Point

However, it took a crisis of staggering proportions—including an inflation rate that reached nearly 5,000 percent in 1989—to compel Argentina's traditionally strong and control oriented central government to take the leap of faith and try a free market economic solution and a monetary policy based on free convertibility. Although the country had suffered from greater or lesser economic and social turmoil for years, it took this sobering low point in 1989 to prod officials into taking radical action.

In 1989 Carlos Menem won the presidency and, together with his minister of economy, Domingo Cavallo, privatized and deregulated practically the

CONTENTS

entire Argentine economic system. The Convertibility Law of 1991—which established a currency board to control the Argentine money supply—fixed the value of the newly established Argentine peso equal to one US dollar and backed every peso with hard currency from the nation's central bank reserves. Given these new, more favorable conditions, foreign funds and foreign businesspeople slowly began to return and invest in Argentina. Economic growth has been stimulated by high pent-up consumer demand, fueled by improved availability of and access to credit—yet another critical plus for the economy and for Argentines at large, who had effectively been shut off from credit for many years.

President Carlos Menem won reelection to a second term in May 1995, receiving nearly 50 percent of the vote in a multi-candidate election, substantially more than the 45 percent minimum needed for a first-round victory. This victory was considered a popular endorsement of the economic policies that had defeated inflation during the six years of his first term and at least a partial seal of approval for the overall thrust of his broad program of economic reforms.

In the context of the so-called "tequila effect," in which international investors, stunned by the sharp drop of the Mexican peso in late 1994, fled emerging market economies worldwide on a massive scale. In early 1995, the uncertainty created by presidential elections led domestic small investors and savers to withdraw their funds from Argentine banks. The electoral result that consolidated the power of the Menem administration—signaling continued economic direction by Minister Domingo Cavallo—did much to calm the fears of both international and domestic investors' expectations, although they continue to remain cautious. During the first four weeks after the May 1995 elections, the Argentine banking system recovered US$2.4 billion of the estimated US$7 billion that had been withdrawn during the preceding five months; a good part of this was deposited during the three days following the elections.

Despite these intense pressures exerted by the tequila effect, Argentina maintained exchange rate parity (in which the peso remained at US$1), full convertibility of its currency, and complete international freedom of movement for capital, as well as state solvency and a very low inflation rate throughout the first half of 1995. The ability of the authorities to hold the line in this fashion led to a recovery of the deposit base of the Argentine financial system as depositors returned funds to the banks. Although significant, this return of confidence and funds to the banking system has been too slow to induce the banks to expand credit. As the beleaguered banks seek to consolidate and improve their liquidity ratios, many firms and individuals have been left without access to much-needed funds and liquidity. By August 1995, a total of US$4 billion had been recovered by the banking system, indicating that domestic and international confidence was returning.

All this demonstrates that the country has taken some crucial first steps toward its goals of sustainable economic growth and democratically led political stability. Argentina's challenge for the immediate future and beyond will be to consolidate the gains of recent years and build on this foundation over the longer term.

Structural Reforms

In the context of a country in which many businesses either underpaid their taxes—or avoided paying any tax at all—the proceeds derived from the privatization of state sector operations during the early 1990s provided the government with the funds necessary to underwrite and jump-start the new economy.

Between 1989 and 1994, fully one-third of the Argentine economy was transferred from the public to the private sector, and this transfer resulted in a massive infusion of new money from both overseas investors and from Argentines, who in many cases retrieved funds they had sent abroad as flight capital during the previous decade. Overall, the Argentine government raised substantially more than US$17 billion—US$9.3 billion in cash, US$6 billion in the cancellation of public debt and US$2.6 billion in liabilities transferred to new owners or concession-holders—by selling controlling interest in about 150 companies, roads, port facilities, and other federal assets. This figure does not include the additional funds that will be invested by the acquiring entities to upgrade the operations purchased. Nor does it directly account for the reduced the burden on the federal government in servicing retired or assumed debt or the relief from

the need to supply operating subsidies for many of these entities. During 1995 the government expects to obtain an additional US$2.4 billion from the privatization of hydroelectric and nuclear power plants, airports, the postal service, and the national mint.

These reforms have produced phenomenal results for the economy as a whole: the Argentine economy grew by more than 30 percent between 1991 and 1994, a rate surpassed only by rapidly growing China. Industrial productivity has risen by at least 40 percent. Preliminary returns for 1994 have calculated the overall consumer rate inflation at 4.2 percent, lower than that found in some developed European economies. Meanwhile, gross foreign investment doubled during the first half of the 1990s. Exports were up, and imports also doubled during this period. Despite the implications of a negative balance of trade, by and large the import situation is positive: unlike previous periods during Argentine history when imports were primarily for consumption, much of the current surge in imports represents investment in productive activities—capital goods and intermediate components for import substitution or export production. Argentina went from a trade deficit in 1994 to a surplus for the year through June 1995. Such a positive result has not been seen in Argentina since October 1992, and it has been achieved without the need for a nominal devaluation in the exchange rate.

Argentine exports are clearly on the increase. During the first four months of 1995, they increased by 47 percent, and the trend is toward additional increases in future months. During the remaining months of 1995, seasonal factors are expected to benefit exports; at the very least, it is expected that exports will remain stable. Broken out data for the first two months of 1995 show primary exports increasing 60 percent, while those of industrial goods and fuels each grew by 44 percent. At the same time, exports of agro-industrial goods rose by at least 24 percent. The performance of foreign trade serves to consolidate the growth of the production of intermediate goods (such as steel, petrochemicals, and paper) to the detriment of those linked to domestic consumption (cars and electric household appliances); this phenomenon is already being noticed in manufacturing production statistics.

In general, while the rate of growth is expected to slow, it should remain solid through the end of the century as recently privatized and new firms modernize, become competitive, and expand capacity.

Turning the Tide: Investment Flows

Since 1989 foreign investors have been subject to national treatment of their investments in Argentina; that is, they are entitled to the same rights and subject to the same obligation as domestic investors. Foreigners may invest in Argentina without being subject to prior approval and in any area of economic activity. The 1991 Convertibility Law further provided the regulatory foundation to establish the stability required to sustain foreign investment in the country.

During the last five years, Argentina has received US$13 billion in direct foreign investment. Although a large portion of this amount went into the privatization of state assets, foreign investors have been interested not only in the large-scale, high-profile privatizations, but also—increasingly—in private industry in Argentina. Growing numbers of investments represent "greenfield" (newly established) operations, and joint venture projects with and mergers and acquisitions of existing private Argentine firms are growing, both in number and importance.

Two of the most dynamic sectors attracting foreign investors have been the food processing and automotive industries. Such well-known multinational firms as France's Danone, the US firm RJR Nabisco, Italy's Parmalat, and the British firm Cadbury Schweppes have invested in Argentine food processing ventures. In the automotive sector, many of the best-known car makers in the world have decided to settle or to increase their presence in Argentina, including General Motors, Chrysler, Hyundai, Toyota, Ford, Volkswagen, Renault, Peugeot, and Fiat. All propose to use Argentine operations not only to serve the domestic market, but also as a base from which to export to the Mercado Común del Sur—the Common Market of the South, or Mercosur—currently composed of Argentina, Brazil, Paraguay, and Uruguay and anticipated to encompass other growing economies in South America in the near future.

Investment projects valued at US$7.5 billion—US$3 billion in the automobile sector, US$3 billion for activities related to oil and gas production, US$500 million in the electric energy sector, and US$1 billion in the food industry—have already been planned for implementation between 1995 and 2000. With the inclusion of additional planned investments in other sectors, the total figure for foreign investment projects announced for the next five years in Argentina doubles, to US$15 billion.

Some of the most significant investors include General Motors, Chrysler, Nabisco, Wal Mart, Procter & Gamble, and Kimberly-Clark from the US; Sadia and Brahma from Brazil; Grundig, BASF, and Warsteiner of Germany; Masisa, Luksic, and Unimarc from Chile; British Gas and Cadbury-Schweppes of the UK and the Anglo-Dutch Unilever; Danone, Air Liquide, and France Telecom from France; and Benetton, Parmalat, Ferrero, and Fiat from Italy.

WEATHERING THE FINANCIAL CRISIS

The Immediate Background

In December 1994, while immersed in serious balance of payments difficulties, the Mexican Central Bank abruptly abandoned its "dirty float" exchange rate system, allowing its currency to devalue sharply. The Mexican peso rapidly lost nearly half its value within a matter of days. Following this, US and European institutional investors drastically reduced their positions across the board in virtually all countries which were classified along with Mexico as "emerging markets."

This massive and abrupt drain of capital from emerging markets affected Argentina. The decrease in international reserves during the first quarter of 1995 was on the order of US$5 billion. During this same period, the Argentine stock exchange's Merval Index fell about 30 percent. The resulting "crisis in confidence" severely battered the Argentine financial system. Subsequently, the continued withdrawal of bank deposits reached an estimated US$7 billion before the situation began to reverse itself. As a result, credit availability shrank and interest rate rose sharply.

Argentina reacted strongly, enacting a series of fiscal, monetary, and regulatory measures. These assured the state's continued solvency and the availability of reserves in order to defend the currency's value. The private sector supported these initiatives by subscribing a total of US$2 billion in below-market interest rate bonds.

During the crisis, Argentina managed not only to maintain full convertibility of its currency at its stated fixed exchange rate and freedom of capital movement internationally, but also federal government solvency and a very low inflation rate.

Among the principal fiscal measures adopted by the government worth mentioning include the reduction of public spending by US$2 billion; a significant increase in tax revenues to be raised by upping the national value-added tax (VAT) from 18 percent to 21 percent; a new privatization plan designed to raise an additional US$1 billion; and the decision to sell government-held shares of recently privatized state sector companies for an additional US$1.4 billion. To support the financial sector, the government created a private deposit guarantee system; a US$2.6 billion fiduciary fund for the restructuring of the financial system (primarily to assist larger banks in acquiring troubled smaller institutions), and a separate US$2.55 billion fiduciary fund to support the privatization of troubled provincial banks.

Argentina's efforts to overcome this threat were reinforced by an external financing package consisting of loans worth US$7 billion from the International Monetary Fund, World Bank, Inter-American Development Bank, Bank for International Development, and Eximbank of Japan. Moreover, foreign reserves have risen substantially, export revenues are up, significant foreign and locally funded investment projects are being carried out as planned, and bank deposits are increasing steadily.

Strengthening the Banking System

Meanwhile, the Banco Central de la República Argentina (BCRA)—the central bank—still has plenty of hard work on its hands. It must supervise the concentration and strengthening of the financial system. Although the return of deposits to institutions benefits everyone, most of such deposits have gone to the official banks (especially the Banco de la Nación and the Banco de la Provincia de Buenos Aires) and secondarily to about 10 of the top private banks, while largely bypassing the even more needy small institutions.

The BCRA's idea is to convince the more solid banks to acquire these weaker organizations, bringing about a consolidation without the pain of actual bank failures. A more concentrated banking system with fewer entities having more branches, a greater diversity of services, and greater efficiency based on economies of scale, plus a greater rationalization of provincial government banks—coinciding with their privatization—are the changes to be accomplished through the use of the two parallel fiduciary funds. It is expected that following this process there will be between 80 and 100 banks remaining in Argentina (there were about 160 banks at the beginning of 1995, and about 120 at mid-year because of mergers and acquisitions during the first half of the year).

The fiduciary funds had begun to disburse funds by mid-year, although in limited amounts, making payments of about US$40 million to the Caseros Bank, an important cooperative bank which used the funds to convert to a corporate structure; the funds were made available in the form of convertible bonds at a low interest rate. As bankers negotiate to shore up their institutions, reassured by the mere availability of these funds, the less frantic pace of such negotiations has already resulted in an easing of tensions and greater confidence in the future of the system.

Dealing with Debt

During the past, foreign capital made up for lack of domestic savings, much as it does today. The difference is that in the past, too much of this borrowing went toward underwriting current consumption; at present, much more of it is being channeled into productive investment. And, also in contrast, a major theme of the current government program is to increase domestic savings.

By the late 1980s Argentina's foreign debt was the fifth largest in the world, and the debt service on these massive external obligations left few funds for investment in domestic industry and other sectors. However, since the late 1980s, Argentina's total foreign debt load has been restructured, stretched out, and effectively reduced. Also, a significant portion of the privatization of certain state assets was accomplished through debt cancellation. Although debt service payments continue to absorb a great deal of much-needed funds, the situation has been reduced enough so that it is no longer critical.

CLOUDS ON THE HORIZON: SOCIAL COSTS

Unemployment

Argentina's economic restructuring has meant a heavy dose of harsh reality for its people and some domestic industries. Privatization and systemwide restructuring have inflicted casualties: about 400,000 employees in what had been thought to be safe, private, and previously sacrosanct government operations have lost their jobs, and the stark reality is that there are as yet simply no jobs for many of these people in the new Argentine economy. Unemployment has continued to rise steadily, reaching an official rate of 18.6 percent in May 1995. In some provinces the local unemployment situation is even worse, because a much larger percentage of jobs in the provinces previously were government-related.

In shifting industries from public to private ownership, the Argentine government has made many of the concessions granted to new investors conditional, requiring that the new operators retain and reeducate their existing workers. However, a major goal of these restructuring programs is to make management and operations more efficient, in part by introducing new technology, most of it designed to improve productivity by reducing labor inputs. A number of the new, private concession grantees are balking at the substantial investment in time, training, and funds that they are being asked to invest in order to have so many workers qualify for positions in the new economy. Privatization of the relatively few remaining state-owned companies is becoming more difficult to negotiate as labor issues come to the forefront, specially at the provincial level.

But economic restructuring and growth are not producing new jobs rapidly enough to counteract the dislocations they are creating. Surveys show that more privatized businesses are cutting labor rather than increasing it. Modernization of the economy will eventually create more jobs, but for Argentine workers, the question is when. Coping with this issue will require significant retraining of the workforce in order to fill the more highly skilled jobs being created.

Defenders of restructuring claim that the poorest fifth of Argentina's workers have actually gained the most since 1989, with the number of families living below the poverty line dropping from 20 percent to about 12 percent by 1994. But for many workers, it seems the benefits of the new policies are trickling down far too slowly, and political demonstrations against the "social insensitivity" of the reform and the lack of social planning or services to help cushion the blows are becoming larger, more frequent, and more insistent. However, the turnout has been low by standards of past labor-inspired demonstrations—evidence of the fragmentation in the interests of and weakening in the strength of organized labor as a defining force in Argentine politics.

Middle Class Erosion

The middle class, much larger in Argentina—by some accounts as much as 70 percent of the population; other observers argue that in the past it comprised substantially more than half—than elsewhere in South America, has been especially hard hit by economic restructuring. Many laid-off government workers simply cannot find jobs. Previously secure managers and professionals have joined the ranks of the unemployed, and many small to medium-sized businesses, often inefficient and uncompetitive, have closed their doors. Many previously stay-at-home women are entering the workforce, and more and more Argentines are working two or more jobs to make ends meets. There has been a rise in the number of persons describing themselves as "self-employed" (often a euphemism for "unemployed"). A certain middle class solidarity, long the bedrock support of the Radical Civic Union party in particular, has been eroding since the l989 crisis. Many consider this erosion and disaffection of the middle class to be among the more unsettling aspects of the new order, because a strong and united middle class has been essential to Argentina's self-image as well as to its political and economic success in the past.

For the new economy to succeed, the middle class must once again become the leading element the nation's producing and consuming economy. The free market reforms will ultimately succeed only if the middle class is able not merely to come back from the brink, but also to resume its advance.

Defusing the Military

During the past five years, President Menem has walked a tightrope between restoring public confidence in the military and controlling it. The army is currently being "restructured" by reducing its size and slashing its budget. Successive armed services chiefs have been less and less rigid, more democratic, and more accepting of civilian control. Today Argentina's once feared military is among the more tractable on the continent and seems an unlikely threat to democracy and stability, as was the case in the past. This de-emphasis of the armed forces was made somewhat easier by the fact that the military itself gave up the reins of government, acknowledging tacitly that even it could no longer manage the old Argentina.

The Provinces

To weather the country's growing pains successfully, the Argentine government will also have to focus on another weak link in the country's economic growth: the stagnation or decline of its less developed provinces, the economies of some of which have contracted by as much as 30 percent between 1990 and 1994. One part of the problem is the nearly complete centralization of economic and power in the national government and Buenos Aires. Another is the tradition of localism and the fact that federal policies, economic, and social programs have in the past often ended up diverted by and to the benefit of local power elites. This is a problem that has existed since the colonial era and has been largely intractable throughout Argentina's history. It is now even more important than ever to solve it. The new hope is that the expansion and incipient diversification of the country's economy will allow more widespread development and opportunity, mitigating the either-or nature of the competition for scarce resources between Buenos Aires and the rest of the country. Already, there are signs of new economic life in the industrializing area around Córdoba, and the northeast corridor linking Argentina with Brazil is also beginning to develop and should prosper further as Mercosur trade builds. The problem areas are still the remote Andean and Patagonian regions.

Politics

Despite the margin of victory won by President Menem in the May 1995 elections, there remain concerns that the very strength of that victory could result in problems. Some observers argue that the total loss could make the opposition more intractable, while others worry that internal factionalism could see demands by less progressive elements for concessions. That those who benefited under the old system are unlikely to willingly give up power to the new order is a truism. However, there is a good chance that Argentina's reforms will continue because the old solutions have been shown to be unworkable and there are enough politicians committed to the new ideas, enough personnel capable of administering them, and—perhaps most compelling of all—fresh memories of a far worse past that should help both the public and the government to keep each other on a steady course.

THE SILVER LINING

Positive Trends

The basic idea that Argentina must become better integrated into the world system seems to have taken hold, however grudgingly, even among traditional isolationists. To this end, Argentina has signed a series of treaties for the promotion of trade with nations worldwide, and it has confirmed its commitment to Mercosur, the important new regional trade pact. Optimists believe that Mercosur is only the first step toward achieving the complete economic integration of the continent and unity within the hemisphere within the next generation.

In this context, Argentina is undergoing major changes in its external trade. Since 1989 the maximum import tariff fell from an average of 35 percent to 12 percent in 1994; most export taxes were also eliminated. This phenomenon, together with economic stability and growth, caused imports to grow during the first three years of the Convertibility Plan, resulting in a trade deficit. Although an important portion of these imports has consisted of capital goods necessary to modernize Argentine industry and make it more competitive, some groups have been worried about the trade deficit, insisting on the need for at least a nominal devaluation to help reverse this deficit. This trend has been reversed since the beginning of 1995, achieving a trade surplus in the first half of the year, without any modification to the exchange rate. The major growth in exports has been registered in primary products and intermediate goods, such as steel, petrochemicals, and paper.

Argentina's trade liberalization policies have been carried even further in the case of Mercosur. Trade among member countries has increased sharply and continues to do so. A large number of cross-border acquisitions, production sharing agreements, and joint ventures have already taken place among both domestic and multinational firms located in the member countries. This offers a new framework for investment and developing competitiveness.

Beyond trade, the current era marks the first time in more than three decades that foreign investors have entered Argentina in such numbers, with such a volume investment, and in such a variety of sectors. They are bringing with them modern technology to increase productivity and create new high-skill jobs.

Another important aspect is the noticeable improvement in port facilities, roads, highways, and infrastructure, and the reduction in the cost of electricity. During the next four years, hydroelectric production capacity will increase by 30 percent with the installation of new generating capacity at the Yaciretá, Piedra del Aguila, Pichi Pichu Leufú, and Casa de Piedra power plants. The mining sector has been deregulated and opened to private companies, with a large number of projects getting underway, most of them involving foreign firms. Estimated investment in this field over the next five years is on the order of US$1 billion.

The Argentine government has also initiated a project to make employment regulations more flexible. A law was signed in 1994 allows small and medium-sized firms—those with fewer than 40 employees—to set more flexible working hours and holiday schedules while allowing temporary employment and internships. Congress is considering even broader relaxations of such rules that would include all industries.

In spite of the ups and downs of the Argentine situation caused by both internal and external factors, Argentina has turned in a solid performance based on its adherence to a well conceived economic plan. The increasing investment flow across a range of sectors suggests that Argentina can be seen as a promising location for those interested in the development of Mercosur, the Southern Cone, and all of South America.

Opportunities

CONTENTS

INTRODUCTION

Argentina ranks high to many businesspeople looking for new international opportunities. It is the wealthiest nation in all of Latin America on a per capita basis. The economic stability built on the policies of the administration of President Carlos Menem, the liberalization of trade laws, the reduction of tariffs, the drastically reduced inflation rate—which has recently fallen to its lowest point in 30 years—and the country's growing economy are all features attractive to the international trader. As an exporter, Argentina is looking for ways to diversify production and increase exports, especially nontraditional, higher-value-added exports, as it revitalizes its economy. As an importer, it demands a wide range of goods to meet business expansion and upgrades in diverse sectors as well as the wants and needs of its consumers, particularly those of its battered but recovering middle class, still the largest in Latin America. Practically all areas of the economy could benefit from foreign investment. Although the government itself is scaling back through privatization, public procurement projects continue to be available as the country modernizes, rebuilds its social and transportation infrastructure, water, and sewerage systems, and cooperates with formerly state-owned corporations in the fields of electricity, oil and gas, and telecommunications.

In addition to understanding the topics covered in this chapter, the international trader and businessperson should also be aware of two recent developments:

Mercosur (the Mercado Común del Sur or Common Market of the South) On January 1, 1995 Argentina, Brazil, Paraguay, and Uruguay united to form Mercosur, a common market bringing together 200 million people with a combined annual gross domestic product (GDP) of US$900 billion. The agreement offers reduced tariffs and other trade benefits to the participating countries and sets a higher common external tariff, thus channeling more and more trade among the members, while opening the possibility of other countries—Chile and Bolivia have been mentioned as candidates in the near term—joining the arrangement at a later date. (Refer to the "Trade Agreements" chapter, beginning on page 65, for a full discussion of Mercosur).

Foreign Trade Zones Argentina has an established foreign trade zone in its southernmost province, Tierra del Fuego. It allows the duty-free import of foreign goods destined for specified high-priority industries and it also gives other tax breaks to users of the zones. Plans have been approved for the creation of foreign trade zones in each of the country's 23 provinces as well as in four other areas of the country. Although of little import at present, such zones could play a significant role in international operations in the future.

IMPORT OPPORTUNITIES

Argentina offers a wide variety of products that can be purchased at competitive prices to satisfy international requirements. These include commodity products ranging from cereals and beef to petrochemicals and basic steel to such specialized composite products as the engineering and installation of hydroelectric turbines and offshore platforms. Although it cannot match the sophistication of some European, North American, and developed Asian industries, Argentina's technological capabilities are more developed that those found in most other Latin American countries. With the establishment of free market policies, Argentine businesses operate in an open, competitive environment comparable to that found in other market economies, and survival under these conditions serves to ensure that the goods produced meet international standards and cost considerations.

The Argentine government has been waging a campaign to encourage more exports from its country. It has opened up its markets to international competition and has decreased the export barriers that had affected its domestic companies. Two important specific measures have been taken. First, the government allows total reimbursement of the value-added tax (VAT), as well as drawback refunds for duties, paid on imported inputs destined for export products. Second, the government has greatly reduced export tariffs and port costs for exporters. Port costs have been reduced on exports in the following terms: 11 percent for general cargo, 70 percent for fishing cargo, 11 percent for bulk cargo, and 8 percent for containers.

The Ministry of Foreign Affairs has been working to make sure Argentine exports are open to the world's principal markets, and has sponsored the creation of the Fundación Exportar to work toward this end. The Dirección General Impositiva (tax authority) has issued resolutions facilitating exports through trading companies.

In fact, exports have been increasing significantly: exports of manufactured goods rose 30 percent in 1993, while fuel and energy exports increased by 13 percent. Merchandise exports were US$15.7 billion in 1994, a growth rate of almost 20 percent, nearly three times the rate in 1993. Weakness in the textile, electrical equipment, and metallurgical export sectors have been offset by strength in the grain, automotive vehicle and parts, and fuel export sectors.

Argentina's primary customers are Brazil, the US, and the Netherlands. It has maintained historical trading ties with many countries of the European Union (EU) and it is beginning to establish stronger trade relationships with the other countries in Latin America as well as those in Asia. (Refer to the "Export Policy & Procedures" chapter, beginning on page 91, for a full discussion of exporting to Argentina.)

AGRIBUSINESS

More than 100 years ago Argentina was, in many ways, the breadbasket of the world, and today it still has an enormous capacity to produce grain and oilseed crops, meat products, fruit, and vegetables. Recently, agricultural products have accounted for about half of the country's exports by value. In 1993 Argentine meat exports amounted to US$750 million. The 1993 figures for exports of nonmeat agricultural products (including cereals, grain crops, oilseeds, fruit, vegetables, dairy products, and processed foodstuffs) reached about US$5 billion. Exports of organically grown crops—a growing niche market—were valued at US$5 million in 1993, an increase from US$1.6 million worth of such exports in 1991.

Despite its abundant natural resources and its historic ability to produce goods and meet domestic and international market demands, there is still room for Argentina to improve production so that it can fully meet its potential. Agribusiness in Argentina is less productive and efficient than that of a number of the world's leading industrial countries. At present the government and industry are working together to increase productivity, improve quality, and diversify production to become top competitors in the world market.

In 1991 the government reduced or eliminated

the export duties on most grains, edible oils, and subproducts (actually providing some negative export duties, or subsidies for some agricultural exports), while, at the same time increasing available financing for exportable goods. The Agriculture, Livestock and Fisheries Secretariat and the National Animal Health Office have worked recently to improve health and safety controls in all facets of the meat industry—from the raising and feeding of cattle, to the packing of meat, to the actual export of goods. In 1992 programs were introduced to improve the means by which meat is produced and traded in the Pampas region. Quality and sanitary conditions have improved markedly, and new processes have been introduced to give customers more opportunity to inspect the products and processes.

Similar attention has been given to growers of quality fruit for export markets. In the past, the major limits to export markets for fruit have centered on nominal concerns by importing countries over the introduction of pests and diseases, which concerns are being addressed by Argentine authorities.

Recent deregulation of port operations in the country has significantly decreased costs for the Argentine exporter of agricultural goods. The agricultural export industry has benefited from a 70 percent reduction in loading rates, as well as substantial cuts in pilotage, tug, and crew hiring expenses.

The combined efforts of government and industry have resulted in a more competitive agricultural industry in all of its key components: grains, meat, fruits, and vegetables. The government is particularly eager to promote investment in and the development of processed food products as nontraditional exports.

Processed Meat and Poultry Since the end of the 19th century, Argentine beef has set the standard for quality beef exports worldwide. Argentine processors generally operate state-of-the-art facilities and are in touch with international standards and demand. Greater attention is also being paid to producing well-fed poultry for international markets.

Dairy Products Milk quality is a key factor in this sector, and Argentine milk ranks extremely high because of production conditions and quality control. The industry produces a wide range of products, with an increasing concentration on higher-value-added offerings, including cheeses, yoghurt, ice cream, and other dessert products.

Edible Oils Because of its climate, experience, and modern processing plant and equipment, Argentina offers edible oils of particularly high quality and cost competitiveness. A leader in exports, it handles annual sales of around US$3 billion.

Confectionery and Cookies Argentine exporters are vertically integrated, with many producing everything from glucose to packaging, allowing them a great deal of control over production in order to maintain competitiveness. Argentine firms export a wide variety of vegetable preserves, jams, and candies, as well as inputs, such as glucose. Chocolate products are exported mainly to Mercosur countries, while cookie and biscuits are exported to the North American and European markets.

Wine Argentina produces both low priced (about US$1.50 per liter) common table and higher priced (about US$5 or more per liter) premium wines. Argentine wines are comparable to those of Europe—from which the rootstock and methods of vinification were imported more than a century ago—however, because the variation in climate is less in Argentina, the variation in quality of product from year to year is usually far less. Although the domestic market absorbs most premium production, exports of bulk wines and unfermented grape juice are growing.

Juices and Fruit Concentrates Excellent growing conditions for citrus and other fruit provide high quality materials at competitive prices. Most firms produce from their own orchards and are able to exercise careful quality control. Exports of lemon juice are particularly significant.

Some Hot Items:

- apples
- apple juice
- apricots
- asparagus
- barley
- berries
- beef
- biscuits
- butter
- candies
- canned fruit and vegetables
- cereals and subproducts
- cheese
- cherries
- chicken
- chocolates
- common bulk wines
- cookies
- corn (maize)
- corn oil (maize oil)
- corned beef
- cotton
- cottonseed oil
- crackers
- cucumbers
- dairy desserts
- *dulce de leche* jam
- eggs
- fine wines
- fruit juices

- garlic
- glucose
- grapefruit
- grapefruit juice concentrate
- grapes
- grape juice (unfermented, for wine)
- grapeseed oil
- hams
- hamburger and ground meat
- heat-processed meats
- ice cream
- jams
- jellies
- lemons
- lemon juice
- liquid eggs
- mandarins
- marmalade
- *mate*
- melons
- milk
- nuts
- oats
- oilseeds
- olive oil
- olives
- onions
- oranges
- orange juice and concentrate
- organic meats and other foods
- organic milk
- packaged beef
- peanut oil
- pears
- peppers
- plums
- pork
- potatoes
- poultry products
- powdered eggs
- powdered milk
- preserved meats
- pumpkins
- rice
- sausages
- sorghum
- soybeans
- soybean oil
- sugar
- sunflower seeds and oil
- tobacco
- tomatoes
- vegetable oils
- vegetable preserves
- vegetable protein cake
- wheat
- wines
- yoghurt

AUTOMOTIVE INDUSTRY

The Car Industry Regime currently in force encourages export production by establishing incentives for specific firms to concentrate on the production of few models designed to fill a specific market niche. This is designed to promote production at economies of scale that allow competitive costs and pricing. In exchange for giving up production of other models, the firms are to be licensed to import models of the type that they no longer produce. The regime is implemented through export and import targets established through negotiation between the individual producer firms and the government. Offsetting exports and imports thus form the basis for international trade in finished automobiles.

The Argentine auto parts industry—which deals in both original equipment and replacement parts— provides about 60 percent of the components for domestic production. It exports a significant proportion of its output, primarily to Mercosur countries. Some Argentine auto parts firms specialize in niche products expressly for the export market; such specialists include those producing replacement parts for vintage US automobiles.

Some Hot Items

- auto parts
- cars
- pick up trucks
- trucks

CHEMICALS

During 1994 Argentina exported about US$700 million petrochemical products. Argentina produces about 290,000 tons of ethylene, 270,000 tons of polyethylene, and 90,000 tons of polyvinyl chloride (PVC), among many other products. Argentine firms are heavily oriented toward exports. Because of this orientation and the abundance and low cost of natural gas, pricing and quality are generally quite competitive. Other products include agricultural chemicals—primarily nitrogen-based fertilizers—and resins for paints. Specialty chemical products, such as colorants and additives, are being developed and improved by local firms.

Some Hot Items

- additives
- agricultural chemicals
- benzene
- colorants
- ethylene
- fertilizers
- fine chemicals
- high density polyethylene

- low density polyethylene
- nytrile rubber
- polypropylene
- polystyrene
- polyvinyl chloride (PVC)
- resins
- SBR synthetic rubber
- turnkey chemical plants

FISHING

The Argentine fishing industry is oriented primarily to exports. Each year the fishing industry lands a catch marked by enormous volume and great variety, only 25 percent of which is consumed domestically. The government has taken an active interest in expanding the productivity of its fishermen by (1) deregulating the industry, (2) reducing port costs for the exporter, and (3) initiating studies to evaluate and approve new fishing exploitation programs. The new policies have brought results. In just four years, total fish caught almost doubled—from 476,000 metric tons in 1989 to 919,000 metric tons in 1993. The value of exports has shown an even greater increase, from US$285 million in 1989 to US$649 million in 1993.

Most of the fishing industry's export business is conducted with the EU, which takes nearly 60 percent of all Argentine seafood exports. In 1993 Argentina set up a special five-year trade accord with the EU designed to increase its exports to the EU, lower EU tariffs, and encourage more European investment in the Argentine fishing fleet and onshore facilities. The EU will also gain greater access to Argentine territorial waters.

The long coastline and the extended shallow continental shelf off the coast of the country offer great opportunities for the Argentine fishing industry. Argentina is now a major producer and exporter of seafood, and there is plenty of room for the industry to expand. Abundant natural resources and current policies designed to encourage investment in and deregulation of the industry offer promise for the industry's expansion.

Some Hot Items:

- anchovies
- codfish
- crabs
- dogfish
- hake
- mollusks
- oysters
- *pejerrey* (mackerel)
- shrimp
- squid

FORESTRY, WOOD, AND PAPER PRODUCTS

Argentina is naturally suited to meet part of the world's growing demand for forestry products. Demand is growing for lumber and for processed products such as containers, cardboard and paper packaging, biodegradable replacements for plastic containers, and air freight packaging. Planting and replanting of forests in industrial countries has not kept pace with the growing demand. In Argentina, forestry land is less expensive than in many industrial countries, and soil and weather conditions allow forest plantations to grow at a faster rate than in countries that are better known for their forests than Argentina. For example, in the province of Córdoba in 1992, forestry land could be bought for between US$60 and US$80 per hectare (2.47 acres). In the province of Corrientes, the price at the same time was between US$150 and US$200 per hectare. The government estimates that even with recent development, only 5 percent of the land suitable for forestry production has been brought into production.

Local forests provide the materials for a furniture industry, centered on the production of local folk furniture (*quebracho*), which is being exported to Europe and North America—as are wooden toys. Argentina also produces 750,000 tons of cellulose paste and 140,000 tons of newsprint annually. The Argentine paper industry exports mainly short fiber cellulose pulp and paper products.

The Secretary of Agriculture, Livestock, and Fishing has designated a fund of US$20 million per year to assist forestry producers in planting new trees. Currently about 777,800 hectares throughout the country are planted with eucalyptus, evergreens, poplar, salicaceous shrubs, and other trees. In 1990 the sum total of forestry products exported from Argentina was valued at US$337.4 million.

Some Hot Items:

- cellulose pulp
- chipboard
- folk wood furniture
- hardwood
- newsprint
- paper for printing
- paper and carton
- paste for paper
- plywood
- round logs
- sheeted planks
- stationery and supplies
- tannin
- wooden toys

HOUSEHOLD APPLIANCES AND ELECTRONICS

Argentine companies involved in the appliance and electronics industries export primarily to Mercosur countries. Products include refrigerators, washing machines, dishwashers, air conditioners, television sets, radios, and video cassette recorders (VCRs). Little Argentine production is exported outside Mercosur, although certain niche markets are served by high quality Argentine manufacturers. These include specialty high-fidelity equipment designed for audiophiles willing to pay in the range of US$10,000 for equipment and for concert halls, theaters, and other buildings in need of high quality audio equipment. The target market of these firms is international.

Some Hot Items

- air conditioning units
- audio equipment
- dishwashers
- radios
- refrigerators
- television sets
- washing machines
- video cassette recorders (VCRs)

INDUSTRIAL PRODUCTS AND SERVICES

The Argentine machinery and equipment industry is generally small and only moderately developed, and most traditional industrial machinery is exported to Mercosur countries.

However, Argentina has developed considerable expertise in engineering, design, and implementation, selling a wide range of often complex turnkey and specialty installation projects. These include such major installations as hydroelectric turbines, nuclear power plants, offshore platforms, and oil pipelines. Medium-range projects include industrial automation, bottling operations, and other specialized equipment that can be tailored to client needs.

Because of the surge in commercial construction in Argentina in recent years, many local firms have become skilled in state-of-the-art construction technologies and needs for the construction of intelligent office buildings, hotel and convention centers, shopping centers, and other public constructions. Privatization has provided the opportunity for many firms to update their expertise in many large scale projects, including telecommunications, highways, and hydroelectric power generating plants. This expertise, coupled with an abundance of well-trained and experienced engineers, provides the basis for the export of such services.

Steel and Aluminum Argentina has an annual production of nearly 3.3 million tons of crude steel, 1.6 million tons of hot rolled flat laminates, 1.2 million tons of hot rolled non-flat laminates, 1 million tons of cold laminates, and 600,000 tons of seamless steel tubes (most of the tube production is for export). Argentina also produces 173,000 tons of primary aluminum, of which it exports about 60 percent.

Some Hot Items

- agricultural machinery
- aluminum alloys
- aluminum shapes
- cold laminates
- crude steel
- electric power turbines
- highway construction and engineering
- hot laminates
- hotels and convention centers
- hydroelectric power plants
- industrial automation
- industrial machinery
- intelligent office buildings
- metalworking machinery and equipment
- nuclear power plants
- offshore platforms
- oil pipelines
- pipes
- primary aluminum
- seamless steel tubes
- shopping centers
- specialty steel alloys
- steel construction products
- tailor-made industrial machinery
- turnkey industrial plants

LEATHER, FUR, AND TEXTILES

Argentina is among the top five world exporters of leather and leather goods, as well as furskins. This industry is a natural outgrowth of Argentina's large cattle-raising industry. Sheep and goat hides are also produced, although in far smaller quantities. About two-thirds of the annual sales from the Argentine leather processing industry—about US$450 million out of US$700 million—come from exports. Since 1965, the export of salted hides has been banned, and Argentine tanneries now process all skins for export. The industry currently produces around 12 million hides annually, the actual number fluctuating with the availability of the cattle stock and the demand for beef.

About 80 percent of production is exported, of which nearly 60 percent of the hides and skins are unfinished. The US has been the top export market for many years, buying up more than 25 percent of Argentine skins and hides. Substantial volumes are also shipped to Hong Kong, Brazil, and Italy.

Export opportunities in the Argentine leather and

fur industries exist for both raw and processed products. Faced with increasing domestic and international competition as both its own markets and those of other countries become more open to foreign trade, the Argentine leather and fur industry is seeking to enter new overseas markets and to increase its production levels in terms of quality, quantity, and diversity of products. Because of the emphasis on exports, the industry has a good understanding of international requirements, and the large number of medium-sized companies in Argentina that competition keeps prices down. Leather and fur are supplied to a great variety of other industries, and the export potential to industrialized and developing nations is tremendous. From 1989 to 1993, exports of hides and skins rose by over 65 percent. The number of finished leather goods—still relatively small compared to exported unfinished hides—is slowly growing with the introduction of modern finishing machinery. Larger firms with access to high quality, low priced raw materials and skilled labor are able to supply footwear to the international export market, and leather apparel of recognized quality is also a standard export.

Textile Products Argentina annually produces substantial quantities of high-quality, cost-competitive cotton, which forms the basis for its cotton spinning industry. Large, vertically-integrated firms use their output to weave finished fabrics, such as denim, canvas, and duck, much of it for export. Medium-sized firms concentrate on production of commodity goods, such as sheeting, toweling, and fabrics for work clothes, usually for export.

Some Hot Items:

- cattle hides
- canvas
- cotton fiber
- cotton wool
- cotton yarns
- cut leather, particularly soles
- denim
- finished leather
- fisher pelts
- furs
- goatskins
- leather apparel
- leather footwear
- sheepskins
- sheeting
- toweling
- work clothes

OIL, MINERALS, AND NATURAL GAS

Production and exports of oil have increased dramatically since the oil industry was privatized and deregulated in 1992. Before that time, an inefficient national oil industry was mainly concerned with supplying domestic needs in a noncompetitive environment. The government controlled the industry by setting prices and volume limits for production. But deregulation and privatization has led to increased competition in the international market and expanding efforts in the exploration and exploitation of oil fields. Production of crude oil has risen from 26.7 million cubic meters in 1989 to 33.8 million cubic meters in 1993—an increase of 27 percent. Exports in 1993 increased a total of 285 percent from 1989, amounting to 2.7 million cubic meters. Production reached 38.6 million cubic meters and exports US$1.6 billion in 1994. Part of this rise is due to changes which now allow foreign producers to export Argentine crude oil—before such producers were required to refine crude in Argentine plants before it was eligible for export.

Production of natural gas reached its highest levels ever in 1993. Total production was measured at 26.6 million cubic meters. Government policies toward the natural gas industry are similar to those in the oil industry: encourage investments and create competitive markets. The transportation network for the natural gas industry has been privatized. The country is hoping to entice US$1.24 billion in investments into the natural gas industry between 1993 and 1997; some US$611 million of that amount has already been raised.

In 1994 a major natural gas and oil field was discovered off the coast of Tierra del Fuego. Initial estimates predict that the ocean field will generate 20 million cubic meters of natural gas per day, nearly a third of Argentina's current production. Two trial wells now produce one million cubic meters of natural gas per day. A natural gas pipeline under construction between Chile and Argentina is also expected to boost both production and export sales.

Argentina also has a large capacity for mining metals and nonmetallic minerals. It is aiming to increase its mineral exports fivefold during the 1993–1995 period. Current exports are valued at about US$35 million, and the country hopes to increase the exports to about US$175 million. The government is facilitating exploration and exploitation of mining fields and is setting up programs to reimburse mining companies for internal taxes on exportable minerals. Zinc, silver, and uranium are among the most common metals found in Argentina. Salt, argil, gypsum, bentonite, and borate are the most common nonmetal minerals mined. The terms of the new Mining Investment Law 24,196, passed in 1993 were designed to attract foreign investment to the mining sector though tax and other financial benefits, making mining operations more attractive and promising increased output in the future.

Some Hot Items:

- aluminum sulphate
- argil
- barite
- bentonite
- borate
- cement
- common salt
- crude oil
- feldspar
- fuel oil
- gas oil

- gasoline
- gold
- gypsum
- iron
- lead
- lubricants
- natural gas
- quartz
- silver
- uranium
- zinc

EXPORT OPPORTUNITIES

Imports into Argentina increased dramatically—from US$4.1 billion to US$21.4 billion, almost 425 percent—between 1990 and 1994, following the liberalization of import regulations in 1989. The economic reorganization plan decreed by the Menem administration called for a general modernization of domestic industry, led by the need to upgrade the newly privatized firms operating in core sectors of the economy. The elimination of most restrictions on imports was not only a key provision of the overall plan to open up the economy, but also a necessary precondition to acquiring the capital goods required to implement the revitalization of industry. During that time, all important import categories grew significantly. For example, motor vehicle imports increased by about 290 percent (in large part because of a growing integration with the Brazilian automotive industry), imports of capital and intermediate goods rose 110 percent, and imports of the still somewhat controlled consumer goods rose 60 percent. (In general, consumer items represent discretionary purchases, and despite overall improvement in the statistics, due to unemployment, the discretionary income of many consumers has fallen to nil, serving as a brake on the import of such goods.)

Since 1993 the demand for imported goods has slowed somewhat following this initial boom period, but a moderate to strong demand continues to exist virtually across the board for capital, intermediate, and consumer goods. In addition, even when domestic industries are filling most of the current demand in their particular markets, they are increasingly relying on imported materials and components, as well as on capital goods, creating additional markets for foreign suppliers. And the overall demand for goods is expected to continue to be greater than the country's ability to produce them for some time into the future. Refer to the "Import Policies & Procedures" chapter, beginning on page 77, for a full discussion of importing to Argentina.

AGRICULTURAL PRODUCTS

Agriculture and Food Products Although Argentina is one of the world's top food exporters, there are a number of items the country is importing to an ever greater extent. These include prepackaged convenience foods—especially snack foods—and processed fruit and vegetable products. In 1995 the market for processed fruit and vegetables was expected to reach US$2.2 billion, with imports accounting for US$167 million, about 7.5 percent of the total.

The country also depends on the import of a wide variety of seeds to sustain its agricultural production. Although the primary agricultural sector represents a relatively small portion of Argentina's GDP, processing and other downstream services connected with agriculture make up a much larger portion of GDP, and agricultural sector exports contribute a large percentage of Argentina's foreign exchange earnings. The total 1995 market for planting seeds was estimated at US$445 million, with imports representing about US$35 million.

Agricultural Chemicals Argentine demand for agricultural chemicals will continue to grow because of the importance of the agricultural sector to the country's economy and the shortfall in domestic productive capacity, which is unlikely to be reversed in the near term. In particular, the need to improve yields through use of fertilizers, pesticides, and herbicides—which have traditionally been used sparingly in Argentina—is expected to drive this market. The 1993 total market for these products was about US$160 million, with an annual growth rate of 12 percent, and with imports representing US$50 million, or nearly one-third. Competition from local suppliers is only moderate, and trade barriers are few. To date few international suppliers have developed a strong presence, so there is ample room for new suppliers to establish relationships.

Agricultural Equipment Argentina's government realizes that it must make additional investments in more and more sophisticated farm machinery to increase efficiency in its agriculture sector, having invested little in this area in recent years. The government is offering special lines of credit for agricultural producers and the level of investment is expected to grow, especially for tractors and tillage equipment, and particularly for used farm machinery that allows operation upgrades at a reduced cost. Modern agricultural technology is also needed because some farmers are switching to less familiar nontraditional crops—such as specialty fruit and vegetables—creating a new demand for specialized equipment. Competition from local and international suppliers is becoming more intense, particularly with the lifting of most trade barriers. The 1993 total market for agricultural equipment was US$550 million, with imports representing US$35 million.

Food Processing and Packaging Equipment The opening of the Argentine economy to competition from overseas suppliers has created an opportunity for those who wish to export state-of-the-art processing equipment and other labor-saving devices to the Argentine agricultural sector. The 1993 total market for such equipment stood at US$235 million and was growing at a 10 percent annual rate. Imports supplied about half of this market. The competition from local suppliers and other countries has been no more than moderate and the trade barriers few, offering an opportunity for suppliers of processing equipment for both traditional and nontraditional products and processes.

Some Hot Items:

- bailers, new and used
- cold storage facilities
- cookies
- cotton harvesters, gins, and modules
- dairy products machinery
- fertilizers
- fish processing machinery
- fruit and vegetable harvesting and processing equipment
- fungicides
- grass forage
- herbicides
- insecticides
- meat processing machinery
- mitecides
- planting seeds for fruit, vegetables, and grain crops
- popcorn
- potato chips
- processed fruit and vegetables
- snack foods
- urea
- used tractors

AEROSPACE

The market for commercial aircraft in Argentina has begun to rebound after a decade of stagnation. Aerolíneas Argentinas and Austral—the newly privatized national carriers—are updating their domestic fleets and are expected to begin investing in transcontinental aircraft to upgrade their international service in the near future. As a result, this US$310 million annual market is expected to expand considerably over the next several years. As the Argentine economy recovers, the market will also improve for executive jets, turboprops, and helicopters.

As Argentina moves to upgrade and modernize its air fleets to become internationally competitive, the need to improve airport conditions is growing. Argentina is seeking to upgrade its air transport infrastructure and modernize its navigation systems to support the growth in air traffic. International competition to service and supply the Argentine market is relatively heavy, and trade barriers are few. Aggressive marketing and attractive financing are the inroads into the Argentine air transport equipment markets.

Some Hot Items:

- air traffic control radars
- approach and landing aids
- avionics
- executive jets
- ground support equipment
- helicopters
- passenger aircraft

COMPUTERS AND SOFTWARE

In 1993 the total Argentine market for computers, peripherals, and software stood at about US$500 million, and was growing at an annual rate of about 10 percent for software and 15 percent for hardware. Imports account for nearly 75 percent of the software and almost all—90 percent—of hardware sales. Banks, other financial institutions—insurance companies in particular—and commercial firms have been the largest users of computer products, but demand from utilities and heavy industry is growing as these sectors are privatized and their operations are modernized and streamlined. Some government agencies—for example, tax collecting agencies—have also begun to invest in computer systems. Companies that offer a full service package, including hardware, software, installation, training, and follow-up technical assistance, are likely to be most successful. There is little competition from local suppliers, trade barriers are few, and intellectual property protection and enforcement is improving.

Some Hot Items:

- hardware for local area networks (LAN servers)
- integrated applications software
- laptop notebook computers
- minicomputers
- operating systems software
- personal computers
- printers
- software for general business applications
- word processing software

CONSTRUCTION MATERIALS

The far-reaching overhaul of Argentina's retirement system and the resurgent development of the mortgage lending sector is generating capital for new housing and commercial developments. Environmental legislation is also playing a role in this market, as industries revamp their facilities to comply with more stringent controls. In 1993 the total market for such infrastructure improvements was about US$700 million, with imports representing only about US$85 million. The annual growth rate is projected to average 16 percent for the next several years. This market has been largely supplied by domestic producers, but competition from them—especially regarding modern high-tech materials—is low, and trade barriers are few.

Some Hot Items:

- chemical additives
- concrete molds
- fastening and power tools
- prefabricated housing

ELECTRICITY

The electric energy sector in Argentina has been privatized. Many of the power distribution facilities are outdated and in need of repair. Foreign corporations can take a role in generating, distributing, and managing power operations and in providing equipment to upgrade facilities. In 1993 imports represented US$304 million of the estimated US$437 million market. Although international competition is relatively stiff, there is only moderate competition from local suppliers and few trade barriers. The market in the electric power sector is projected to grow at an annual rate of 25 percent from 1995, opening new opportunities through rapid expansion.

Some Hot Items:

- dry cells
- electrical wires for low voltage distribution
- fuses for low and medium voltage distribution

- monitoring devices for electrical generation, transmission, and distribution
- switch boxes for electrical consumption data control
- transformers

HOUSEWARES

As Argentina's middle class recovers and its buying power increases, so will the opportunity to export many household items into the country. However, this is a highly competitive market. Due to the general need for housewares of virtually all categories and all quality and price levels, and the recent reduction of import barriers, the housewares sector has attracted numerous suppliers. However, opportunities remain for new suppliers prepared to identify and serve specific market niches.

Some Hot Items:

- cleaning supplies
- coffeemakers
- dishes
- glassware
- household tools
- microwave ovens
- plastic containers
- pots and pans
- silverware
- table cloths
- toasters
- tea kettles
- vacuum cleaners

INDUSTRIAL EQUIPMENT

Plastics Processing Machine and Equipment Local industry must now upgrade its equipment to compete with finished imported goods. Sectors generating the highest demand include packaging, beverage bottling, and construction. In 1993 the market was US$80 million, with imports representing US$55 million. Competition is moderate from local suppliers, but intense from international providers. Trade barriers are few.

Pollution Control Equipment The need for pollution control equipment is growing as industry and government become increasingly aware of environmental concerns and incorporate them into the national policy agenda. Although the private sector has not yet made investment in this area a high priority, it is expected to receive wider corporate attention soon. International investors and the Argentine legislature and judiciary are beginning to demand greater environmental protection. Chemical refineries and leather and food processing industries are the likeliest immediate customers for pollution control equipment. Water quality control is also a growing concern and needs environmental consulting and modern treatment systems—especially in highly populated areas where population growth is expected to continue and where infrastructure improvements are in process.

Both private companies and the national government are looking outside the country for guidance in pollution control and solutions for contamination problems. France has been the principal supplier for environmental equipment. The 1993 market size for pollution equipment was US$12 million, with imports representing about US$3 million. Competition from local suppliers is moderate and trade barriers are few.

Some Hot Items:
- bottling equipment
- liquid industrial effluent treatment plants for medium-sized industries
- packaging equipment
- smokestack monitoring and filtering equipment
- water and sewage treatment equipment

MEDICAL AND SCIENTIFIC EQUIPMENT

Medical Equipment Although the national government has reduced its health care budget, hospitals now under municipal and provincial control continue to replace old equipment. The 1993 market for medical equipment was US$360 million, with imports representing about US$196 million. The estimated average annual growth rate in the market for the period 1993–1995 is 11 percent. Competition from local suppliers is small—especially in high-technology equipment—and trade barriers are few.

Scientific Instruments Argentina's market for scientific instruments has been damaged recently because so many high-tech, finished products are being imported into the country. Recognizing that they do not yet have the capability to compete with the quality and quantity of imports, many Argentine corporations have reduced their research and development budgets and are changing their product mix to concentrate on the lower-end equipment that they are better suited to producing. This is leaving a gap in supply for the dominant Argentine industries—agricultural and natural resources (especially oil)—which need advanced scientific instruments to remain competitive in world markets. The government is encouraging ties between national and international research scientists and industry. The 1993 market for scientific instruments was US$8.5 million, with imports representing US$6 million. The 1993–1995 estimated average annual growth rate is 15 percent. Competition is moderate from local suppliers and heavy from other countries, and there are few trade barriers.

Some Hot Items:
- amalgams
- bandages
- blood pressure measuring devices
- catheters
- cements
- clamps
- dental chairs
- dental hand instruments
- drains
- drills
- hypodermic needles
- implantable and laparascopic devices
- lasers
- magnetic resonance imaging (MRI) equipment
- ophthalmic goods
- optical microscopes
- pacemakers
- patient monitoring systems
- plaster
- portable analytic instruments
- prosthetics
- quality control instruments
- scanning microscopes
- sterilizers
- stethoscopes
- suture needles
- syringes
- ultrasonic scanning devices
- wheelchairs
- X-ray apparatus and tubes

MOTOR VEHICLES AND VEHICLE PARTS

Strengthening the important automotive industry is still a high priority for the Argentine government. Recent relaxation of import restrictions have opened up the market for automotive products from other countries, including replacement parts for these imported vehicles. Although there is a large domestic auto parts industry, it is primarily designed to serve the rather narrow range of domestically built models, leaving open the provision of parts for imports. Not all imported parts are model-specific: spark plugs, gaskets, and diagnostic equipment for computer-controlled fuel injection engines are popular generic imports.

The 1993 market for motor vehicles was US$2.8 billion, with imports representing US$740 million—roughly one-quarter of the total. The estimated annual growth rate for 1993–1995 is 5 percent. Competition from the local industry is moderate, and although the trade barriers are fairly substantial, they are falling. The market for parts during the same time period was US$1.2 billion, with imports representing about US$215 million, and a 1993–1995 estimated growth rate of 5 percent. Competition for importing parts among other countries and local suppliers is heavy, and the trade barriers are severe.

Some Hot Items:

- convertibles
- diagnostic equipment for computer-operated engines
- exhaust fume monitoring equipment
- four-wheel drive vehicles
- front-end and suspension parts
- gaskets
- recreational vehicles
- spark plugs

OIL AND GAS FIELD MACHINERY

The privatization of the oil and gas industry has created opportunities for foreign suppliers of field machinery. Private operators are now concerned with increasing both productivity and corporate profits. Equipment will need to be upgraded to expand and increase the efficiency of operations and to meet the new standards imposed by international competition. The 1993 market size for the industry was US$1.1 billion, with imports representing US$98 million. The estimated average annual growth rate of the market for 1993–1995 is 10 percent. Competition from local suppliers is only moderate because local industry lacks the capability to produce the more sophisticated equipment required; however, trade barriers designed to protect the domestic industry remain in place, making access somewhat difficult.

Some Hot Items:

- cementing equipment
- compressors
- control devices
- injection equipment
- meters
- pipeline equipment
- valves

SPORTING GOODS

The 1993 market for sporting goods in Argentina was about US$776 million, of which imports represented about US$328 million. Local competition and trade barriers are both moderate. The 1993–1995 estimated average annual growth rate in the market is about 17 percent. The high growth rate reflects returning affluence and leisure activities among the sectors of the population likely to become significant consumers of these products (and consumption is possible for many basic products at a low income level). The US dominates the import market, with about a 30 percent share, but there is a high demand for Brazilian products because of their low prices, a demand that is likely to increase with the develop-

ment of Mercosur.

Some Hot Items:

- camping and outdoor items
- fishing equipment
- gymnasium equipment
- motor homes
- soccer footballs
- tennis rackets
- outboard engines

TELECOMMUNICATIONS

ENTEL, the government-owned telephone company, was privatized and divided into two separate groups: Telecom and Telefónica de Argentina. The license to operate was granted on an exclusive basis for seven years (that is, until 1997) and may be extended for three more years to the year 2000 (a move that is considered likely). Currently, hundreds of thousands of telephone lines throughout the country are being modernized and rehabilitated to provide an underlying infrastructure to support private investment in equipment. Once the work on the lines is complete, there will be a demand for high-tech equipment and services as Argentine firms begin to upgrade their often woefully inadequate equipment with state-of-the-art telecommunications systems. The 1993 market for telecommunications products was US$1.32 billion, with imports representing US$392 million. The 1993-1995 estimated average annual growth rate in the market is 12 percent. There is little competition from domestic suppliers, but competition from foreign suppliers is substantial. Trade barriers are few.

The television and cable television market also represent significant export opportunities. The existing network of 1,000 cable operators who have a subscription base of 4 million customers—serving roughly half of the country's population, but located primarily in Buenos Aires and other large cities—is expected to grow as new areas are served.

Some Hot Items:

- cable television equipment
- cellular telephones
- facsimile machines
- fiber optics equipment
- fixed and mobile radio systems
- high capacity switching systems
- radio transmitters, transceivers, and receivers
- signal switches
- telephones
- television sets
- transmission equipment

TOYS AND GAMES

The reduction—if not the removal—of nontariff restrictions on the import of consumer goods (including toys and games) has opened up the market to imports and increased the sales of electromechanical toys and computerized games. Improved economic conditions are increasing consumer's discretionary income. Local competition is limited to manual and medium-quality toys. Toys manufactured in Brazil provide the most competition to other potential foreign suppliers. The 1993 market for toys and games was US$1.32 billion, with imports representing US$392 million. The 1993–1995 estimated average annual growth rate in the market is 15 percent. There is little competition from local suppliers, but heavier competition from foreign suppliers. Trade barriers are few, although discriminatory tariffs remain on nonessential consumer items.

Some Hot Items:

- Barbie-type dolls and other collectible dolls
- educational games for ages one to five
- electronic games

OPPORTUNITIES FOR GROWTH

Billions of dollars are being invested in a number of Argentine enterprises that the state formerly owned and operated. In the oil, gas, and electricity sector alone, about US$20 billion is expected to be spent in the next few years to upgrade and expand privatized operations. About US$1 billion will be invested in water and sewage programs. Several billion dollars will be spent to improve transportation networks, ports, and telecommunication services. And about US$6 billion will be spent in 1995 to complete and expand privatizations in the energy and petrochemical sectors. The privatization process continues. Airports, seaports, three nuclear power plants, the national post office, the federal mint, and the country's largest petrochemical plant are all scheduled to be privatized by the end of 1995. All of these privatizations will create opportunities for foreign investors who wish to participate in auctions for the facilities and in the rebuilding and expansion of these operations.

Foreign investment laws have recently been reformed and liberalized to favor the investor. Basically, the government grants the same rights to foreign investors as it does to domestic investors. According to the Foreign Investment Act of September 1993, no prior approval is necessary for a foreign investor to participate in the Argentine economy. Investors require licenses to operate in the banking, insurance, and mining industries. However, once licensed, foreign investors can operate on the same terms as domestic investors. Currently only two industries—broadcasting and atomic energy—are off limits for foreign investors. For the most part, there are few official hurdles for the foreign investor to overcome, and there are no discriminatory taxes.

AGRICULTURE

Although Argentina has long been a major producer of agricultural products—grains, meats, fruit, vegetables, and dairy products—this sector has had relatively little foreign investment. This is changing. Argentina's new stability and interest in increasing its traditional and nontraditional value-added products, both for export and internal consumption, is attracting foreign investors. Nabisco Brands recently spent US$200 million for a majority interest in one of Argentina's largest food companies, Terrabusi SAIC, and other foreign corporations have been investing millions of dollars in Argentine seed-processing plants and in its tobacco industry. Manufacturing facilities for new consumer products—processed foods and convenience foods—are to be built in the future, offering foreign investment opportunities. Some specialty foods, like ice cream—sales of which rose to more than US$500 million in 1993—also offer opportunities.

AUTOMOTIVE

The automotive industry is one of the few industries in Argentina for which the government still grants substantial protection from foreign competition, and the fact that it is betting on the development of this sector for high value-added growth provides opportunity for foreign investors. Argentine automakers have strong historical ties with Brazilian and European manufacturers, and the industry is beginning to welcome joint operations with car manufacturers from the US and Japan. As consumer demand, production, and exports increase, there will be opportunities not only in the manufacture of automobiles themselves, but also in the industries that support the manufacturers: steel, rubber, glass, plastics, and auto parts. Those interested in this sector should note that Argentina does have a balanced trade relationship with firms in the Brazilian auto industry that results in reciprocal trade benefits, meaning that newcomers will have to offer value to gain a foothold.

ELECTRICITY

The privatization of the electric industry has created opportunities for foreign investment. Demand for electricity continues to increase, and there is a concurrent need to upgrade electrical generation, transmission, and distribution facilities. Major equipment is needed to monitor electricity use, efficiently transmit electricity across a large system, and distribute it to the individual consumer. Some major hydroelectric projects have recently been completed, and others are being planned for the future, offering opportunities for foreign investors. One such project is the joint Paraguay-Argentina hydroelectric complex on the Paraná River at Corpus. Budgeted at US$3.5 billion, environmental and engineering studies are expected to take three years, and the construction to take an additional seven. The project is to be completed entirely with private funds.

FRANCHISING

Many of the industries in the Argentine economy have undergone great transformations since reforms began in the early 1990s. However, franchising is an example of an industry that hardly existed before the reforms were initiated. Now opportunities for franchising are booming in a number of product areas.

Before the 1990s the Argentine economy was primarily a mix of a relative few large state-owned corporations plus a few large privately held firms and a great number of privately owned small businesses. There are still a great many small privately owned businesses. The large public operations were, in many ways, the backbone of the Argentine economy. But with the advent of privatization, many state employees lost their jobs and were given severance pay that they needed to invest in creating new positions for themselves. Given the entrepreneurial nature of Argentine small business and the lack of alternative formal positions available, investing in a franchise has been a natural move for many. But entrepreneurial spirit and necessity are not the only forces driving the expansion. So is consumer demand. By the end of 1992, 50 local and foreign franchisors had teamed up with 500 national franchisees. Annual sales have been estimated at US$300 million, and employment at about 5,000. Estimates are calling for franchising activities to double over the previous year's level.

Franchising presents obvious advantages to the potential franchisee: with limited capital he or she can open a business that already has a level of established name recognition and a management support system behind it. Buenos Aires has been the most popular area for franchises. Its shopping malls rival those in major metropolitan areas of the US and Europe. Familiar companies like McDonald's, Burger King, Pizza Hut, Domino's, and Fuddrucker's have already established sites in Buenos Aires. And any number of other companies may follow. There is considered to be substantial potential for franchises that offer more than fast food. The list includes automotive oil changers, clothing outlets, copy centers, fitness gyms, mailing services, pharmacies, shoe stores, and specialty food shops.

Both foreign and domestic operations have opened franchises. The greatest obstacle for the potential franchisee is establishing credit. No major Argentine bank has yet offered a line of credit geared especially to financing franchise operations (what is usually available is combined commercial credit), but they are beginning to look into the possibility for the future.

LEGAL SERVICES

As Argentina creates an economy that more closely resembles the economy of other free-market industrialized nations, the need for legal services to integrate its operations with those in other countries will increase rapidly. A number of legal and consulting services were required during the time that many state-owned companies were privatized, and there will still be a need for legal services dealing with corporate mergers, international trade, capital markets, tax law, environmental regulations, and international litigation. Clients exist in both the private and public sector. In Latin America, Argentina and Brazil are the two countries with the most established domestic legal services, but the movement towards opening the Argentine economy to the international market will create opportunities for outside legal services. Although foreign attorneys are not allowed to practice in Argentina, there is a substantial and growing demand for legal consulting.

MINING

In the past, foreign companies have been hesitant to invest in Argentina's mining industry because high inflation rates, volatile interest rates, and general economic instability worked against the long-term commitment necessary for mining investments to pay off. But with Argentina's newfound economic stability, opportunities are being created for foreign investment in this sector. The government has enacted a new mining law and regulatory structure that provides the following benefits: tax regimes are guaranteed to remain stable for 30 years; costs for exploratory surveys are 100 percent deductible from income taxes; investment in mining infrastructure or expansion of existing operation are tax deductible at the rate of 60 percent for the first year of operations and 40 percent for the following two years; and investment in machinery and other equipment may be completely amortized on a straight-line basis over three years, beginning with a 33 percent write-off in the first year the equipment is placed in operation.

Argentina has all the characteristics of a mineral-rich country, but currently only 20 percent of its territory has been surveyed for possible exploitation, and mining activities now account for less than 2 percent of GDP. Thus potential is great within the mining sector, offering substantial opportunity for foreign investment. Observers are forecasting strong growth in this sector of the economy, and by 1997 it is estimated that mining production will double to account for 4 percent of GDP. Those interested should note that, according to the Argentine Mining Code, mining rights are severable and the owner of the surface land does not automatically own the underlying mineral deposits.

OIL AND GAS

Plans are being made to explore and develop oil holdings throughout the country and to pump gas across wide areas to supply domestic needs and the needs of bordering countries—in particular, Chile. Argentina's recently privatized oil company, YPF, intends to spend US$14 billion over the next 10 years to explore and exploit new wells and to upgrade pipelines and distribution equipment.

Gas pipeline projects are underway in Tierra del Fuego and across the Andes to Chile. However, the corresponding Chilean projects have been put on hold due to restrictions by both the Argentine and Chilean governments. In the Buenos Aires area, gas distributors Metrogas and Gas Natural Buenos Aires Norte, intend to invest a combined US$114 million to improve services and construct a new industrial plant.

TELECOMMUNICATIONS

There is opportunity for investors in underwriting the installation of large-scale telecommunication networks and the sale of smaller scale goods and services to private consumers. The Chilean company Entel recently announced plans to invest US$10 million in setting up a digital transmission network. Similar opportunities will be available as Argentina continues to link networks within the country and outside of its borders to foreign networks. There will also be increasing consumer demand in the cellular telephone, television, and cable television markets. Argentine cable television revenue now stands at US$1.4 billion, which represents 70 percent of total Latin American cable television revenue. Of all Latin American countries, Argentina is the most active in the telecommunications arena. By 1997 it will have the highest rate of telephone and cellular telephone use on the continent.

TOURISM

Argentina offers investors great opportunities in the tourist industry. It is a country with a great metropolitan center and great natural beauty that remains largely undiscovered by travelers outside of South America. The government would like to see the development of tourist infrastructure and wants word of the country's offerings to spread.

As the country opens its economic market to international competition, it has also opened its doors to tourists. Between 1983 and 1993 the number of tourists in Argentina grew from 1.3 million to 3.53 million. Opportunities for the foreign investor include a wide range of areas: airport services, camping sites, car rental agencies, catering services, credit lines for modernizing hotels, and for extending the business of tour operators, convention centers, cultural centers, domestic and international airlines, fast-food outlets, hotels and motels, hotel equipment, mountain and ski resorts, railroads, recreational vehicles, shopping centers, spas and health treatment installations, theme parks, tourism complexes, training for hotel personnel, vacation centers, yacht charters, and marinas. Recent plans have been announced to develop a five-star hotel in the Iguazú National Park near Iguazú Falls and a four-star hotel located on Lago Argentino, near the Glaciar Perito Moreno.

WATER AND SEWERAGE SERVICES

A total of US$450 million will be invested to improve water and sewage services in the greater Buenos Aires area. About US$200 million will be invested to bring potable and irrigation water to dry areas in five additional provinces. Much of Argentina is arid, much more is rural and sparsely settled, and even in urban zones with historically well developed water and sanitation facilities, growth and the lack of recent maintenance has led to increased needs for infrastructure development in these areas. Argentina's future economic growth depends to a substantial extent on the country's ability to provide water and sanitation services to the substantial segment of its population that can not now access them.

Opportunities exist for providing equipment to create and renovate infrastructure and for the engineering and design services needed to plan the work. Federally subsidized programs aim to bring drinking water and sanitation services to areas that have both more and less than a population of 15,000. A total of 98 drinking water projects, servicing a total population of more than 500,000, have been developed. A national credit program has been established to lend to organizations bringing drinking water and sewer networks to urban populations greater than 15,000.

OPPORTUNITIES IN PRIVATIZATION

POWER GENERATION

Federal level projects slated for privatization include the massive Yaciretá hydroelectric project on the Río Paraná. The dam—which is approximately 90 percent complete—will support a power station with 20 turbines and a capacity to generate 3,200 megawatts. Total cost of the project is estimated at US$8 billion. A binational commission involving Argentina and Paraguay is to decide whether the project will be offered as a concession or for sale.

Other power projects scheduled for privatization include Hidroeléctrica Tucumán (24 megawatts), Pueblo Viejo (15.36 megawatts), El Cadillal (13 megawatts), Hidrotérmica San Juan (43.6 megawatts), Sarmiento (33.75 megawatts), Río Grande (750 megawatts), and Pichi Picun Leufú (252 megawatts).

The federal government has also announced the planned privatization of Argentina's nuclear power system. The government has created a new quasi-public entity called Nucleoeléctrica Argentina, which will hold the existing Atucha I and Embalse nuclear plants and complete Atucha II. The Secretariat of Energy is preparing bidding documents for this proposed privatization.

Among provincial energy offerings are Empresa de Servicios Eléctricos de Buenos Aires (ESEBA), which is to be privatized through a public stock offering, with the operating company to receive 10 percent of the shares created; the Dirección de Energía of Catamarca (DECA), with bidding projected for late 1995; the Empresa Provincial de Energía of Juyjuy, with sale by bid anticipated; Electricidad de Misiones S.A. (EMSA), through contract with the reorganized state entity; and the Empresa Provincial de Energía of Neuquén (EPEN), which will administer a central system supplied by local cooperatives.

GAS AND ENERGY DISTRIBUTION SERVICES

The Empresa Provincial de Gas of San Luis Province, which primarily serves the area around the city of San Luis, is slated to be offered by bid in late 1995.

The Province of Santa Cruz is expected to privatize up to 50 percent of Empresa Provincial de Servicios Públicos (Distrigas), a quasi-public entity that administers the provision of electricity, water, and gas services. A similar offering is expected to be made for the related portion of Empresa Provincial de Servicios Públicos of Santa Cruz that specifically provides electricity.

WATER AND SEWERAGE SYSTEMS

The Dirección de Obras Sanitarias de Catamarca (OSCA) is to be privatized, although specifics of the transaction are not finalized; the Servicios de Agua Potable y Cloacas of Formosa Province is expected to be offered by tender in mid-1995; the Empresa Provincial de Obras Sanitarias de La Rioja is to be offered as a concession; the Administración Provincial de Obras Sanitarias of Misiones Province is expected to be tendered in late 1995; the Ente Provincial de Aguas y Saneamiento (EPAS) of Neuquén Province is expected to be offered on a concession basis, although final authorization has yet to be completed and the offer is expected to be delayed for some time; and the Dirección Provincial de Obras Sanitarias of Santiago del Estero Province is to be offered by concession following acceptance of a consultant's final report.

TRANSPORTATION

The federal government has announced its intention to privatize nontechnical services at national airports. Federal control is to be maintained for radar, meteorology, and air traffic control functions, but such services as ramp and repair operations are expected to be made available on a concession basis.

Officials expect submission in mid-1995 of engineering feasibility studies for a proposed bridge to be constructed between Buenos Aires and Colonia, Uruguay. Some 127 foreign and domestic firms have submitted prebid applications for various aspects of this estimated US$1 billion project. The project is not slated to receive any government support or guarantees.

The Empresa Provincial de Transporte of Mendoza Province is expected to be offered on a 20-year concession basis, pending final submission of supporting documents.

The government has also announced plans to privatize its General Belgrano freight rail line operations, although no details or schedules have been released.

FINANCIAL SECTOR

A number of Argentine provincial and municipal banks are to be offered for privatization. Although foreigners have been denied new licenses to operate financial institutions, they are being encouraged to invest in existing entities, such as the public ones being offered.

Privatization offers are expected for the Banco de Catamarca; the Banco de Mendoza, S.A.; the Banco de Previsión Social, S.A. (also of Mendoza); the Banco Provincial de Salta; the Banco de San Juan; the Banco de la Provincia de San Luis, S.A.; the Banco Provincial de la Provincia de Santiago del Estero; and the Banco de la Provincia de Tucumán. Most of these offerings are expected to be made by the end of 1995, with various levels of stock being offered to outside investors. The Salta bank is expected to offer 50 percent of its shares to outside investors; the San Juan bank 95 percent of the province's 50 percent holding; the San Luis and Santiago del Estero banks 95 percent of their holdings; and the Tucumán bank 60 percent, with an additional 35

percent to be sold within one year after completion of the initial sale.

OTHER PRIVATIZATIONS

Petrochemicals The federal government has indicated that it will offer the Bahía Blanca and Indupa petrochemical firms to the public in late 1995. The main products of these plants include ethylene, butane, propylene, and propane, among other products.

Mining Industrial y Minera S.A. of Misiones Province is to be offered in late 1995. The operation processes and markets aluminum sulphate.

Forestry The Establecimiento Forestal Sagastizabal of Misiones Province is scheduled to be offered in late 1995. The operation, located in Guaraní Department, manages 2,589 hectares (about 6,500 acres), planted primarily in *paraná* and *resinoso* varieties of pine.

Salta Forestal S.A. of Salta Province is to be offered to bidders by a private consortium organized to handle the privatization of the 400,000 hectare (1 million acre) resource.

The federal government has also announced that it intends to privatize a variety of additional government-owned and -operated firms, including grain elevators, several plants manufacturing items for national defense, the postal service, and the mint. Most of these privatizations are expected to be offered by the end of 1995, although specifics remain unclear as of mid-1995.

PUBLIC PROCUREMENT OPPORTUNITIES

The volume of public procurement has decreased in a number of areas since the privatization of many of the country's state-owned companies took effect; in particular, those that relate to oil, gas, certain transportation services, ports, and telecommunications are now in private hands and are developing their own means of bidding and financing. However, the government is still very much involved in the transition process and although many purchases are not strictly "public procurement," they will certainly be transacted, in some form or another, under the government's sponsorship or aid. In many cases, the government's role has changed from owner of public services to regulator of them, continuing to retain a certain degree of control over standards and procedures.

Some of the billions of dollars raised by the government during the privatization process, much of which was spent to reduce the federal deficit, will

also be spent on future projects. The government has established priority sectors for the investment of such public funds. These include: (1) social sectors of education, health care (especially for mothers and infants), and water and sanitation services; (2) economic sectors that integrate education with industrial production, advance scientific and technological research, rebuild transportation infrastructure, increase environmental protection, and improve health and safety systems in the production of goods and services; (3) law enforcement and public safety; and (4) governmental reform at the federal, provincial, and municipal levels.

A number of loans the country may receive from such organizations as the World Bank will also be used for public procurement. The economic emergency law of September 1989 suspended the government's "buy Argentine" requirements. Although official government policy continues to favor domestic industry, bidding is now to be conducted on a more neutral basis.

A number of government-sponsored projects have recently been initiated. A representative sample of them follows:

Computer Systems The Argentine government has recently purchased a computer system to monitor over US$30 billion of exports from and imports to the country. Upgrading of all government computer systems—involving finance, transportation, and international trade—can be predicted for the future.

Decentralization and Improvement of Secondary Education Project In 1994 Argentina received a US$190 million loan from the World Bank to improve all aspects of its secondary school system. This included rebuilding existing school infrastructure, reviewing and improving school curriculum, purchasing textbooks and teaching materials, and training instructors. Consultants are needed for teacher training, efficiency studies, and program development. Total funding for the project will be US$268.7 million, and the projected completion date is 1999.

Environmental Protection Projects Water supply treatment, the cleaning up of major rivers, the limitation of industrial and petrochemical pollution—these are all projects that the government of Argentina has become increasingly concerned with. In 1991 an office for Natural Resources and Human Environment was established to confront some of the country's most critical environmental problems. Representatives from other countries have met with Argentine officials to determine how outside consultants may be of help. There will be opportunities to work with the government on a long-term basis to solve problems involving air quality, water quality, and toxic waste.

Oil Pipelines In February of 1994, an oil pipeline between Neuquén Province in Argentina and the Chilean Pacific Ocean port of San Vicente was completed and began its operation. It will provide Chile with a substantial amount of its oil imports and increase the amount of Argentine oil exports by about US$500 million per year. And this may be just the start of a wider pipeline network across the Southern Cone. The pipeline was completed in a cooperative effort by the Chilean state-owned oil company, Enap, and Argentina's newly privatized YPF, with financial backing from Banco Río de la Plata. Future projects may involve Argentina and other Southern Cone neighbors.

Roads, Bridges, Railways, and Waterways Studies for a proposed bridge between Buenos Aires and Colonia, Uruguay are now underway. The studies were estimated to be completed in mid-1995, and construction on the project is tentatively scheduled to begin in 1996. The US$800 million project is scheduled to be completed by the year 2000. Continual projects and plans will go forward to connect Argentina with its neighbors: a railway line from the Neuquén Province to the Chilean border is scheduled for extension; a project on the Paraguay-Paraná river, which connects Argentina, Brazil, Paraguay, and Uruguay, is near completion; and Argentina and Uruguay will work together to improve navigation on the Uruguay river. Improvements will consist of a US$24 million dredging project and renovation of ports upstream.

Social Infrastructure Development In 1994 the Inter-American Development Bank proposed a US$240 million loan for the redevelopment of the Argentine social infrastructure. Funding will be used to finance works and equipment, although specific projects have yet to be determined. They will be determined with participating municipalities. The project is currently in the analysis stage, consultants will be needed, and estimated total funding is US$300 million.

PUBLIC PROCUREMENT PROCEDURES

The reorganization of the Argentine public sector and the privatization of many state-owned corporations is a process that is still in transition. Procedures for bidding on government contracts or for acquiring contracts through private corporations working in cooperation with the government are varied and in flux. Specific state agencies and private corporations should be contacted to ascertain specific project requirements.

Foreign Investment

INVESTMENT CLIMATE AND TRENDS

Historical Perspective At the beginning of the 20th century, Argentina was a liberal democracy with the tenth largest economy and the sixth highest per capita income in the world. Its abundant natural resources, coupled with some of the best agricultural land in the world, attracted immigrants and development capital from around the globe. Indeed, these factors—together with a largely middle class population of European ancestry—made for a welcome and attractive environment for direct foreign investment. In the late 19th and early 20th centuries foreign investors, primarily from the US and the UK, rushed in to develop first infrastructure—ports, railways, and electric power and natural gas production and distribution facilities—and later manufacturing operations.

For 1880 to 1930 the nation flourished with a stable currency tied to a gold standard and an annual average inflation rate of only 1.5 percent; between 1900 and 1920 gross domestic product (GDP) doubled. Moderate protectionism began to develop during the period of World War I; however, this focus on import substitution actually opened additional opportunities to establish manufacturing plants in Argentina. During these years, major foreign corporations from the US, the UK, and Germany opened plants to manufacture electrical products, chemicals, and pharmaceuticals and cosmetics. Unfortunately, the prosperous times wound down, and the Argentine economy was seriously damaged by the economic dislocations of the Great Depression.

Both demand and prices for Argentine exports fell dramatically, and the international climate of protectionism led to a domestically oriented economy and—during the 1940s—to the nationalization of some public services, such as railroads and power generation and distribution. Nevertheless, even during this period, foreign firms continued to establish Argentine plants to manufacture consumer durables for the domestic market, although they were hampered by a lack of locally available subcontractors, materials, and components. This situation led many operations to integrate vertically to produce the needed inputs. This expensive strategy was sustained by the monopoly and near-monopoly status the producers enjoyed in serving the isolated Argentine domestic market, but led to industries with a cost structure that was largely uncompetitive in international markets.

Economic recovery and pent-up demand allowed markets to develop, and—in the late 1950s—led to the enactment of a pro-foreign investment regime. This policy shift attracted investment, primarily in the automotive, petroleum refining, chemical and petrochemical, and machinery and equipment industries. The resulting surge in foreign investment led in turn to overexpansion in some areas and a subsequent halt in new investment. Until the turnaround in policy that decreed an open economic system under the Menem administration in the late 1980s that made Argentina far more attractive to international investment, most foreign investment consisted of the incremental

KEY CONTACTS AND REGULATORS

Subsecretaría de Inversiones The Undersecretariat of Investments answers inquiries about foreign investment in Argentina.

Fundación Invertir Argentina A private entity established to promote domestic and foreign investment in Argentina. It operates in conjunction with the Undersecretariat of Investments and the Undersecretariat for International Trade.

Inspección General de Justicia (IGJ) To operate in Argentina, a business must register with the provincial level entities that supervise corporations and commercial societies. In Buenos Aires, such registration is accomplished through the IGJ.

Comisión Nacional de Valores (CNV) The National Securities Commission approves listings on and regulates the operations of Argentine securities markets.

Instituto Nacional de Tecnología Industrial (INTI) The National Institute of Industrial Technology governs the transfer of technology and the registration contracts governing it.

Mercado de Valores de Buenos Aires S.A. Entities wishing to perform broker/dealer activities on local securities markets operate through this institution.

Secretaría de Energía The Secretariat of Energy oversees business activity in oil and gas exploration and production, and electric power generation and distribution.

Secretaría de Industria The Ministry of Economy's Secretariat of Industry monitors manufacturers, whether nationally or foreign owned.

Dirección Nacional de la Propiedad Industrial The registration of patents, trademarks, and industrial designs is handled by this office of the Secretariat of Industry.

Dirección Nacional del Derecho del Autor Registration of copyrighted material is accomplished through this office.

Addresses for these organizations can be found on page 56, under "Useful Addresses."

expansion and upgrading of existing operations.

Fortunately, the reforms of the Menem administration seem to be working in many critical policy areas. Argentina's economic problems are now little worse than those of many European countries. The days of high volatility in macroeconomic variables and in government policymaking seem to have come to an end. The growing maturity of the system has begun to promise the stability that enables the longer range business planning critical to attracting foreign capital, and—perhaps even more important—has begun to restore the public's confidence in the political and financial system.

Development of Liberal Investment Policies The unprecedented economic boom led by free-market reform has likely changed forever the pace of and attitude toward direct foreign investment in Argentina. Out of the depths of decades of managed economics and economic nationalism has emerged a more democratic, global market-oriented economy that is virtually wide open to foreign investors. Since 1989 Argentina has largely welcomed—and even actively encouraged—foreign investment, facilitating it to a greater extent than ever before. Argentina has, in a few short years, developed what is arguably the most liberal foreign investment regime in Latin America.

The Menem administration's free market policies have swept away a great deal of excessive regulation, reduced tariff and nontariff trade barriers, abolished the foreign exchange controls that had hamstrung its international economic posture, placed foreign and local investors on equal footing, and greatly reduced currency risk. In sum, the regime has created an entirely new playing field for foreign investors. Not surprisingly, some of the same investors who drained an estimated US$50 billion in capital out of the country during the 1980s are now leading the charge to put their funds back into the economy under more favorable terms. Since the reforms of 1989–1991, more than US$30 billion in portfolio and direct foreign investment has made its way to Argentina. The privatization of state-owned businesses—such as oil giant Yacimientos Petrolíferos Fiscales (YPF) and the national telephone company—was a leading element in attracting foreign investment. The stabilization of the Argentine peso under the Convertibility Law (which pegged the peso to the US dollar on a one-to-one exchange rate), the opening of local financial and capital markets to restriction-free foreign participation, and the reemergence of local credit have provided the market liquidity critical to direct investment.

Elimination of Investment Barriers Crippling barriers to foreign investment—such as outright bans on participation in some sectors and discriminatory operating approval procedures—have been removed. A 1989 amendment to the 1976 Foreign Investment Law provided for "national treatment," giving foreign investors the same rights and obligations as local investors. In 1993 measures contained in the 1989 Economic Emergency Law, the 1989 State Reform Law, and the 1993 Foreign Investment Law were combined in a single act known as Decree 1853, which has removed nearly all restraints on foreign investment. Now, with certain government-mandated exceptions, foreign entities may own 100 percent of Argentine companies and may repatriate capital and remit profits back to the home country without limit. In general—in contrast to recent years—Argentine laws, regulations, and policies do not interfere with foreign investment.

In addition, the 1992 Bilateral Investment Treaty with the US, Argentina's largest foreign investor, guarantees US companies the right to invest in the private sector on a most favored nation basis, that is, at terms that are at least as favorable as those accorded to domestic or third-party investors. Other bilateral investment agreements are in force with Austria, Belgium-Luxembourg, Canada, Egypt, France, Germany, Hungary, Italy, Poland, Spain, Sweden, Switzerland, and the UK. In addition, treaties with Chile and Turkey had received congressional approval and awaited final ratification, while treaties awaiting congressional approval were signed with Armenia, Bolivia, Bulgaria, Denmark, Ecuador Finland, Jamaica, the Netherlands, Rumania, Senegal, Tunisia, and Venezuela. Further treaties or additional treaty provisions were under negotiation with Ecuador, Finland, Iceland, Indonesia, Malaysia, Morocco, Norway, Russia, South Korea, and the United Arab Emirates.

Favorable results of this long-standing international interaction between Argentina and other nations include standards of business that are more or less in line with practices in industrialized countries and a net positive relationship between Argentines and foreign business interests, making Argentina an attractive place for foreign entities seeking business relationships. And Argentina is perhaps the Latin American nation that is best disposed toward European and US business culture. Argentines are familiar with and continue to demand foreign products and services, which have long set the standard in the country. At present, this is particularly true for US goods such as consumer products and entertainment items. With local firms actively seeking foreign participation to raise capital and benefit from managerial and technological transfers, and the removal of all restrictions on capital movements, there seems to be few—if any—better locations in Latin America for growth-oriented direct foreign investment.

Argentina's cumulative growth rate in its GDP of approximately 30 percent between 1991 and 1994 places it among the fastest growing in the world. However, growth has been largely concentrated in certain manufacturing industries and not all sectors have benefited. In fact, some provincial economies have actually contracted during this period. Industrial production has risen almost 60 percent since the implementation of the Convertibility Law.

LEADING FOREIGN INVESTORS

Size of Foreign Investment

Cumulative, recorded, direct, nonfinancial foreign investment (investment other than portfolio investment placed in securities that can be liquidated rapidly—the so-called "hot money") in Argentina as of year end 1993 amounted to approximately US$28 billion for the period 1990-1993, the third largest inflow among emerging markets worldwide (only Mexico and China received more foreign investment during the period). Significantly, nearly one-third of that total was in the form of investment in assets privatized by the Argentine government. Estimates for private capital inflow in 1994 vary, but should result in the addition of another US$3 to US$5 billion to the cumulative total. This is a dramatic turnaround for an economy that saw net private capital outflows of an estimated US$50 billion during the 1980s; more than US$5 billion fled abroad during Argentina's economic and financial turmoil in 1989-1990 alone.

In 1990 and 1991, more than US$15 billion in net private capital made its way back into Argentina. Foreign investment reform, currency stabilization, the beginning of effective privatization efforts, and a drastic reduction in perceived country risk—which fell to less than 3 percent from almost 32 percent by one measure between early 1990 and year end 1993—were major contributors to this reversal. In addition, macroeconomic and global financial market trends during this time, such as the beginning of a recovery from recession among the OECD nations, and a low interest rate environment that pushed global investors towards opportunities in higher-yielding emerging economies, added to favorable domestic conditions.

Foreign investment continued its heated pace during 1992, remaining strong in 1993 and 1994. The Deregulation Decree and the Bilateral Investment Treaty with the US, eliminating most restrictions on internal commerce and foreign trade, set the tone for investor optimism in 1992. Mass privatization continued unabated with foreign investors eventually becoming the beneficiary owners of more than one-third of all privatized assets. By the end of

RELAXATION OF FOREIGN INVESTMENT REGULATIONS

Foreign Investment Law

On 8 September 1993 Decree No. 1853 (the "Decree" was published in the Official Gazette. The Decree updated the wording of the Foreign Investment Law No. 21,382 ("FIL") and amended the Technology Transfer Law ("TTL"). Salient aspects of the decree include the following:

The FIL applies to any foreign-domiciled individual or legal entity investing capital in local economic activities ("foreign investors"). Under the Decree, investments by foreign investors are no longer subject to prior government approval even when they are made in an area where special prior approval was required in the past, such as banking and insurance.

The FIL declares that foreign investors will be given the same treatment as local investors, provided the investments are destined to productive activities. Those activities have been defined to be industrial, mining, agricultural, commercial, service or financial activities, or any other related to the production or exchange of goods or services.

Prior to the promulgation of the Decree foreign investors had the option of registering their investments with the foreign investment authorities. The advantage of registration was it "protected" the investor against most (though not all) of the restrictions that the government was entitled to impose on the availability of foreign exchange for the remittance of profits and/or the repatriation of capital. Currently there are no such restrictions. The Decree eliminates the "Registry of Foreign Capital Investments."

Technology Transfer

Scope of the Technology Transfer Law The TTL has been clarified by the Decree. The TTL law governs agreements which provide for the transfer, assignment or license of technology or trademarks by foreign-domiciled persons to Argentine-domiciled persons ("License Agreements"). The regulations of the TTL define "technology" as patents, industrial models and designs, and any technical knowledge applicable to the manufacture of a product, or the rendering of a service.

Prior to the issuance of the Decree the TTL provided that, where the licenser directly or indirectly controls the licensee, or was an affiliate of that controlling entity, the License Agreement had to be approved in advance by, and registered with, the National Institute of Industrial Technology ("INTI"). Failure to obtain INTI approval and registration of the agreement resulted in adverse tax treatment of the payment of royalties, both for the licensor and the licensee. INTI scrutinized License Agreements at the approval stage. Once approval was granted, registration was obtained automatically. With the enactment of the Decree, INTI approval is no longer required. Failure to obtain INTI registration of the agreement however continues to result in adverse tax treatment.

Though INTI approval is no longer necessary, the requirement that terms and conditions should comply with "normal practices between independent parties" remains in effect.

A License Agreement between related parties used to be approved and registered only if INTI determined that its terms and conditions were in accord with "normal practices between independent parties." The TTL provides that the agreed consideration must "bear a relationship" to the transferred technology. Under the regulations, it is presumed that the consideration agreed upon "bears a relationship" to the licensed technology when it does not exceed 5 percent of the net sales value of the products manufactured or the services rendered using the technology. The regulations define "net sales value" as ex-factory invoice value, less discounts, allowances, returns and excise and value added taxes.

In order to evaluate the royalty rate included in the License Agreements between related parties, INTI used to calculate the percentage of the licenser's gross income that was spent on research and development. INTI generally objected to a royalty rate that exceeded that percentage. Since 1977, the average royalty rate approved by INTI in agreements between related parties has been 3

This sidebar is reproduced from Baker & McKenzie's Latin American Legal Developments Bulletin, vol. 2, no. 1 (January 1994); authors Martin Barreiro and Marcelo Slonimsky of the Buenos Aires office. Copyright © 1994 Baker & McKenzie. Reprinted with permission of the law firm.

percent of the licensee's net sales. This, however, was merely an average, and should not be interpreted as implying an INTI policy to reject higher royalty rates or accept royalty rates that did not exceed 3 percent.

INTI will not register trademark licenses between related parties unless they are granted on a royalty-free basis and are part of another registrable agreement.

Neither the TTL nor its regulations contain provisions concerning the treatment of other terms and conditions under the "normal practices between independent parties" test.

The majority of License Agreements between related parties that have been rejected by INTI involve technology that INTI considers to be available in Argentina. Another large percentage of rejections are based on INTI's determination that the consideration for the technology is too high. A small percentage of the rejections is based on the inclusion of restrictive clauses, such as restrictions on the licensee's exports, disclaimers of liability of the licensor, requirements that the licensee acquire raw materials from a specified source and provisions fixing the price of the products to be manufactured or the services to be rendered using the technology.

Agreements Between Unrelated Parties A License Agreement executed between unrelated parties should be registered with the INTI (a routine procedure) for statistical and tax purposes.

The TTL and its regulations do not establish any specific requirements regarding the content of License Agreements executed between unrelated parties. Nonetheless, INTI from time to time has refused to register such agreements based on its determination that the actual purpose of the agreement was not the transfer of technology.

Since 1977, the average royalty contemplated by INTI-registered agreements between unrelated parties has been 4 percent of the net sales of the licensee.

Tax Consequences of Registration Royalty payments made under a License Agreement are considered Argentine-source income of the licenser and are subject to withholding. The tax rates vary depending on whether the License Agreement is registered with INTI and, if it is registered, on the type of technology to be transferred.

The failure to register a License Agreement, whether between related or unrelated parties, does not affect the validity of the agreement between the parties. Payments made to the licensor, however, may not be deducted by the licensee for income tax purposes (they are deductible if the agreement is registered), and such payments are subject to an effective income tax withholding of 27 percent, rather than the otherwise applicable 18 percent or 24 percent rates, as explained below.

Royalty payments made under a registered License Agreement are subject to an effective income tax withholding rate of 18 percent if (i) the technology is transferred in the form of technical assistance, engineering or consultancy services, (ii) the payments are made on a nonrecurring basis, and (iii) the amount of the payments is based on the amount or duration of the services performed. Otherwise, payments made pursuant to a registered License Agreement are subject to an effective rate of 24 percent.

In order to benefit from one of the lower rates, a certificate must be obtained from INTI. A registration fee that ranges from 0.15 percent to 0.25 percent, depending on the type of technology transferred, calculated over the amount of the consideration to be paid, or estimated to be paid, for the technology will apply.

Loan Agreements Between Related Parties

The Decree implicitly abrogated the powers of the Argentine Central Bank ("BCRA") to approve loan agreements executed between a local company and a foreign related company. These agreements were approved when they were executed on an arm's length basis and assessing the financial exposure of the borrower. Notwithstanding that such approval power has been implicitly abrogated, loan agreements between related parties should be executed on an arm's length basis. BCRA, through Communication A 2161 dated 15 November 1993, has acknowledged receipt of the abrogation of its powers.

Free Repatriation and Remittance of Investments and Profits

The Decree maintains the principle in force since 1989 that foreign investors are entitled to freely repatriate their investments and remit their profits abroad at any time.

1993, foreign companies had purchased nearly US$9.6 billion in asset value of privatized entities. Private capital inflow in 1992 almost reached US$8 billion and was slightly more than US$5 billion for 1993. With privatization largely completed, the massive capital inflows of the early 1990s are expected to subside. However, assuming continued growth and stability, foreign investment should remain in a surplus position for the remainder of the decade, although observers expect annual flows to level off at a figure around US$2 billion. Projects valued at more than US$16.5 billion have been announced or contracted for between 1994 and 2000.

Origin of Foreign Investment

The main sources of foreign investment in Argentina are the US, Europe, and its closest Latin American neighbors, Chile and Brazil. The US has been the leading foreign investor in Argentina, topping the list in 1991 through 1994; US investors' share of the country's total foreign investment over the past four years was more than 40 percent. Much of that participation has been in the form of the purchase of privatized assets (primarily infrastructure assets), with the next most prevalent form representing capital investments in the consumer products, and automotive industries.

Other principal foreign investors include those from Italy, Spain, France, Brazil, Chile, Germany, Switzerland, the Netherlands, and Canada. As noted, backing the overall foreign investment trend are bilateral agreements between Argentina and various countries, primarily those from Europe and the Americas. Typically, these bilateral trade agreements establish a government-to-government framework for channeling private investment and official financing and guarantees between firms from the participating nations. They also usually provide for international arbitration of investment disputes and grant foreign investors protection from uncompensated expropriation and full capital repatriation rights (even in the event of a currency crisis). The agreements and new reforms have gone a long way toward reducing Argentine sovereign risk for all investors, not just those covered under bilateral national agreements.

Sources of foreign capital are expected to diversify in the wake of the continued expansion of free market reforms around the world. Argentina's rich natural resource wealth, relatively high national income, open market economic policy, and historical international bent should continue to make it attractive to foreign capital in the years to come.

Based on announced projects scheduled for completion between 1994 and 2000, the US should remain the major investor in Argentina, being involved in 35 projects and 5 additional joint ventures with Argentine or third country firms. French firms are participating in 7 projects plus 4 multinational joint ventures; UK firms in 7, plus 3 joint ventures; and German firms in 7, plus 1 joint venture. Other investors include Chileans (6 projects and 3 joint ventures); Canadians (4 and 2); Italians (4 and 2); Japanese (2 and 1); Mexican (2 and 1); Dutch (2 and 1); Brazilian (2 and 1); Swiss (2 projects); Australian (1 project and 1 joint venture); and the Irish and Venezuelans with 1 project each.

Sectors of Foreign Investment

As noted, the largest share of recent foreign capital has gone towards the purchase of privatized state firms and their assets. The second largest share of foreign capital inflows has gone to the private sector through equity investments and credit. Foreign direct investment is occurring through direct purchase of assets, mergers and acquisitions, and new business formations, primarily from major multinational industrial corporations.

Infrastructure sectors such as telecommunications, sewer and water, oil and gas, transportation, ports and port services, and mining have received the greatest portion of the capital inflows. Other sectors that have participated to a significant degree include manufacturing, especially of automobiles and household durable and non-durable goods, and the construction and housing industries. Government policy is currently encouraging investment in a variety of sectors, including mining, construction, the auto industry, energy, forestry, fishing, processed agricultural products, and tourism.

For projects scheduled between 1994 and 2000, the greatest number are in food, beverage, and tobacco processing, while the next highest number—and highest dollar value—are found in the automotive sector, with 12 scheduled projects, mostly representing the expansion of existing operations. Some 12 projects represent various industrial and consumer manufacturing operations, while oil and gas production and distribution account for 8 projects; electric power generation and distribution for 5 projects; and mining operations for 3 projects. Other areas include various telecommunications and broadcasting projects; wood and paper products; and pharmaceuticals projects. Investment in services is also growing, with several investments in large-scale retail and wholesale ventures being particularly noteworthy, as are investments in financial and business services, and hotels.

INVESTMENT POLICY AND CHANGES

Foreign investment is legally defined as any contribution of capital belonging to foreign investors and/or the acquisition of shares of existing domestic enterprise using foreign capital. In general, any investment made by foreign individuals, companies, or unincorporated entities, as well as by Argentine companies with more than 49 percent foreign ownership control—or in which foreigners have the right to appoint and control the management of the entity—is deemed foreign investment. However, investments made by foreigners resident full time in Argentina are generally classified as domestic investment, while those made by Argentine nationals residing abroad are considered foreign investment.

Investment Authorization and Procedures— National Registry of Foreign Investment Foreign investors have the same rights and obligations that the Argentine Constitution and laws give to national investors involved in economic or productive activities within the country. At this time, foreign investment does not require formal approval and the registration on the Registro de Inversiones de Capital Extranjero (the Registry of Investment for Foreign Capital, or RICE) is optional, other than that decreed by specific legislation such as in the case of financial institutions and mass media. This does make for trouble in assembling accurate national investment statistics but does remove much of the red tape from the formerly cumbersome investment registration process. The Secretaría de Comercio e Inversiones (the Secretariat of Trade and Investments) of the Ministry of Economy constitutes the nation's foreign investment authority. Foreign entities wishing to invest in Argentina for the first time are encouraged to contact this agency for specific information on the rules and regulations regarding the type of investment contemplated.

Foreign investors may make investments using any foreign currency, capital goods, capital or profits from existing operations denominated in local currency, or intangible assets under certain conditions. They may also invest by means of capitalization of accounts payable to foreign creditors. In short, just about any assets can be used for investing in Argentina. Investment can also be made by the conversion of foreign debt into equity. This is usually accomplished when foreigners who desire to invest buy sovereign Argentine foreign debt at a discount on international markets, submitting this debt to the Argentine government for cancellation, and receiving official assets valued at a peso equivalent in return. The investor receives assets rather than cash, and usually must plan on making additional cash investments for upgrades and working capital. This option is generally available only for public assets, although it may be possible to invest in private operations through debt-equity conversion by negotiating with the authorities on a case-by-case basis.

An investor may voluntarily register with the RICE. No benefits accrue to firms choosing to register, although at times in the past registration was required in order to obtain foreign exchange to repatriate capital and earnings. Registration consists of a formal notification including the following:

- Name and address of the foreign investor.
- Name and location of the target firm.
- Description and purpose of investment activity.
- Currency used and the amount of the investment.

For transactions between a foreign-owned local company and its parent that involve a technology or trademark transfer, assignment, or license by foreign nationals in favor of Argentine residents or entities, the parties must submit a registration request to the Instituto Nacional de Tecnología Industrial (the National Institute of Industrial Technology, or INTI). Terms and conditions of the transaction and the consideration given should conform to standard market practices and have a reasonable relationship to the technology transferred. Such contracts between unrelated parties may be registered for informational and tax purposes. Patents, trademarks, and copyrights are protected in Argentina but, as is true worldwide, infringements can and do occur because effective enforcement is difficult. Investors are urged to familiarize themselves with local rules, customs, and practices in an effort to avoid infringement problems.

Foreign capital contributed in either portfolio or direct investments may be unconditionally repatriated at any time. Foreign investors have the right to remit earnings from their investments immediately, and registered foreign investors are allowed to use export proceeds for remittance abroad in the event that domestic foreign exchange controls go into effect that would otherwise restrict remittances. The federal government may suspend the rights of foreign investors only during a designated foreign payments emergency.

Reserved, Restricted, and Unrestricted Investment Activities Prior federal government approval was necessary under the 1976 Foreign Investment Law for investment in sectors such as defense, telecommunications, mass media, banking, publishing, insurance, and a number of other industries. Recent changes have eased this requirement. There are no special operating or performance requirements for foreign investors.

Barriers to entry may still exist in one form or another. Foreigners are barred from direct investment in uranium mining or nuclear power generation as a matter of national interest. Some restrictions also continue in mass media. Foreigners have reportedly been denied broadcasting licenses, although their participation is not officially prohibited either by law or government policy. Foreign investors may only enter the fishing and insurance industries through purchase of a controlling interest in an existing Argentine operation, as no new licenses are being issued in these sectors at this time. However, unlimited entry will likely be permitted in the insurance industry subsequent to ongoing restructuring and reform. Investments in banking and related services are not restricted, but foreign participation (ownership of local banks and the opening of branches or subsidiary operations of foreign banks) must be approved by the Banco Central de la República Argentina (the central bank, or BCRA). Such permission is decided on a case-by-case basis and depends on the nature of the investment and the investor, and the situation in Argentina at the time of the application.

Investments in non-mining activities in frontier areas require permission from the National Superintendent of Frontiers, a part of the Ministry of Defense, although investment in mining activities in these areas is unrestricted. The government is in the process of modernizing federal mining codes, and provincial governments are actively seeking to develop mineral resources in the western half of the country. Foreign investors are being actively encouraged to participate in this development. Chilean companies have already become heavily involved in mineral exploration in these areas.

Most of the past state monopolies—such as those that existed in communications, oil and gas exploration and production, airlines, railways, port operations, and distribution of water, power, and light—were disbanded by the government's prior privatization efforts. Foreign investors have been allowed to participate in privatization on an equal footing with national bidders, and foreigners accounted for nearly 40 percent of such investment.

Special Considerations and Arrangements for Foreign Investors As is the case with any foreign commitment, the investor should exercise extreme caution before proceeding with the investment. This means acquiring extensive knowledge of all applicable rules, regulations, and policies, as well as familiarity with the historic and current local market situation. Detailed study of the country's markets may protect against costly errors that could result from misunderstanding the foreign investment terms and conditions. In view of the recent, rapid change in the economy's structure and in Argentine commercial codes and rules regarding foreign participation, it is especially important for foreigners to familiarize themselves with the current environment and local market players.

Although generally allowed to own real estate directly in most of Argentina, foreign investors may face restrictions on land ownership near international borders (both land and coastal borders). Ownership of this type of property is subject to the prior approval of the Superintendent of Frontiers in the Ministry of Defense.

INVESTMENT INCENTIVES

All formal investment incentive programs requiring direct federal budgetary expenditures were suspended or eliminated by either the Economic Emergency Law of 1989 and the Deregulation Decree of 1991. Now, foreign investment incentive policy is based on the concept of national treatment for all investors, that is, treatment that is the same for both foreigners and nationals. In the past, a wide variety of industrial promotional programs existed giving tax breaks to specific industries or rewarding the establishment of industrial activity in certain geographic regions, usually to encourage development in neglected areas of the country. Foreign-owned firms generally had equal access to all such programs.

The main reason for the demise of such incentives was the government's decision to eliminate all subsidies that resulted in special treatment and economic distortion, as well as creating a costly addition to the national budget. Some companies still enjoy benefits from past promotional programs; however, these will soon expire—if they have not already done so—and are not expected to be renewed. It is still possible to obtain tax incentives under promotional schemes sponsored by various provincial governments. These usually take the form of a waiver of local taxes due or reduction in tax rates, and are negotiated on a case-by-case basis with the specific provincial governments based on the nature of the proposed investment.

At the moment, national investment incentive policies are almost more negative than positive: they are directed toward discouraging additional activity in heavily industrialized areas, in favor of creating industrial enterprises in less-developed geographic locations. For this purpose, the federal government divides Argentina into distinct geographic industrial zones in which certain types of industrial development are to be encouraged. An informal investment support and promotion program exists for this purpose under the direct responsibility of the Secretariat of Trade and Investment. Operationally, it is directed by the Undersecretariat of Investment.

Although no formal investment incentive programs are available at present, alternatives exist in the form of industry-specific tax and other special nontax incentives. Broad tax benefits exist in the manufacturing sector. No new promotional benefits are available, but items such as a tax refund on 15 percent of the sale price of new nationally produced capital goods for investment in economic activities (such as farm equipment, semiconductors, and other capital goods and approved intermediate products) are available for both foreign- and locally-owned producers.

FTZs Argentina has established a free trade zone (FTZ) in the Province of Tierra del Fuego in the far south. Products imported by approved high-priority industries are admitted duty-free to the zone; these firms may also be eligible for certain tax benefits. New legislation has been passed to authorize the creation of FTZs in each of Argentina's 23 provinces, as well as in four other areas of the country considered suitable for development as foreign trade ports. There is no schedule for the opening of these additional FTZs.

Tax Incentives Significant tax incentives exist in the mining sector under the Mining Investment Law (although foreigners are prohibited from investing in or owning operations involved in the production of certain minerals, including uranium). For eligible operations, the government guarantees taxes and tax rate stability for 30 years, as well as full tax deductibility for all prospecting and exploration costs for each project. Tax deductions may be taken for environmental conservation allowances. Profits on mines and mineral rights capital contributions are to be exempted from taxation entirely. In addition, accelerated depreciation can be used to account for investment in new mining operations and extensions of existing mining capacity.

In the oil and gas sector, entities may receive tax credit bonds in exchange for tax liabilities incurred during the first two years of a project's life. This allows for tax deferral, which in turn is intended to bolster the economic viability of new oil and gas projects. In addition, the overall tax regime for any industrial activity is generally attractive for multinational enterprises operating in Argentina. A 30 percent flat tax rate on income from subsidiaries or branches of foreign companies exists for all entities.

Nontax Incentives Various available nontax benefits take the form of accelerated procedures for government licensing and approvals. New concessions are expected to be offered to foreign entities to develop cellular telephone networks and infrastructure projects, including roads, bridges, and pipelines. In the fishing sector, transparency has been established for the procedures used to obtain new resource exploitation approvals and use permits for existing activities. In the automotive sector—in which the majority of manufacturers are foreign multinationals—entities operate with a highly protective import scheme that contains various tax and nontax barrier reduction incentives

determined by the amount of production exported and the specific destinations of the products. The government also actively encourages joint ventures between foreign and domestic firms, although this does not constitute official policy.

All in all, because foreign firms have essentially equal access to local loan funds, full currency convertibility, repatriation of capital and earnings, and virtually unrestricted access to almost all industrial sectors, the lack of official incentive programs is not likely to dampen foreign direct investment in the near future. Multinational industrial firms have typically used internally generated funds, funds representing intra-company transfers, or funds raised in international capital markets to make direct investments in Argentine projects.

INVESTMENT ASSISTANCE

Foreigners considering an investment in Argentina can draw on a variety of resources, both in Argentina and overseas. The main Argentine public and semipublic organizations offering basic information and consulting services include the Undersecretary of Investments—part of the Secretariat of Trade and Investment—and Fundación Invertir Argentina, an institution backed and managed by the private sector and also supported by the state. Invertir's primary function is to promote Argentine investment and assist investors interested in doing business in Argentina. These entities can provide a wealth of information and directions regarding what agencies and persons should be contacted, as well as where to find the required investment services and information.

In addition, numerous private organizations offer basic information and consulting services, usually on a fee basis, for virtually every aspect of investment in Argentina. Those organizations include management consulting firms, accounting firms, law firms, commercial banks, trading houses, and real estate agencies. Refer to the "Important Addresses" chapter for listings.

ECONOMIC DEVELOPMENT PROGRAMS

A massive public investment program is currently underway to develop and improve the nation's industry and infrastructure in the main segments of the economy. The main programs will focus on energy production, especially electric power generation and distribution, public works (roads, water, and sewers), and such transportation facilities as airports, railroads, waterways, and seaport and riverport facilities. Total investment in public goods and services in 1993-1995 should reach approximately US$30 billion. Two-thirds of these resources will come from the federal government and the proceeds from the privatizations of state entities, while the remaining one-third is expected to come from provincial and local governments. Running parallel to this ambitious list of activities are a host of specific economic development programs designed to encourage private investment and participation in these projects. Target sectors include agriculture and livestock, forestry, mining, and basic industry.

To diversify agricultural production and increase overall supply in Argentina, the Banco de la Nación Argentina (BNA) is increasing the financing available for firms that produce commodities for export. The BNA, an official development bank designed primarily to serve the needs of small- and medium-sized firms through direct loans to such businesses, has teamed up with the Agriculture Secretariat (SAGP) which, in turn, provides lines of credits to similar enterprises. Certain projects owned or operated by foreigners may be eligible for funds from these sources.

The forestry and mining sectors are assisted by programs from the BNA and the International Bank for Reconstruction and Development (IBRD, the World Bank). The BNA has also created a new industrial mining division that specializes in funding mining development, exploration, and operations. The IBRD provides assistance through subsidies for newly developed mining entities.

The general industrial sector is receiving development assistance through credit lines for financing investment and working capital, which are being extended primarily through the BNA and the Banco de Inversión y Comercio Exterior (BICE—set up to promote investment in and financial support of the import/export sector), as well as through other official and private financial sector institutions. In addition, Argentina is working in cooperation with the European Union (EU) to develop pilot programs in various industrial sectors and regions.

Most of these programs encourage (and to a certain extent provide funding for) foreign participation under specified terms and conditions. Foreign investors wishing to take advantage of these and other specific development programs are encouraged to contact the financial institutions or government agencies directly for more information.

AVAILABILITY OF LOANS AND CREDIT

Corporate financing in Argentina has traditionally been characterized by its heavy dependence on periodically hard to obtain external funding, particularly bank loans. But as the Argentine capital markets have been liberalized and internationalized

during the 1990s, investors in Argentina have been able to access internal, longer-term funding through local securities markets which are in turn increasingly tied to international capital markets. Financing is now available from a variety of private and public financial institutions both locally and foreign-owned. Among the most prevalent forms of loans are short-term credit facilities available from large, Buenos Aires-based, commercial banks, and longer-term loan funds available from the government-owned development banks.

Since the free market reform movement and internationalization of the local credit markets, a greater variety of loans at more favorable interest rates are available to qualified foreign borrowers. Public financial institutions still exist, but those foreign investors who may be eligible for public sector finance should find it relatively easy—and possibly less costly—to obtain financing from private sources.

Foreigners are allowed to borrow in both US dollars and Argentine pesos from domestic financial institutions, and they are often in a position (based on the creditworthiness of their international affiliates) to get better terms than domestic firms. US dollar-based loans are very common now that the country employs what is effectively a dual currency system. In fact, nearly half of all loan funds are US dollar-denominated. This situation may prove favorable to some foreign-invested firms, particularly those in export-related industries that conduct a large percentage of their business in US dollar-denominated products or commodities, such as petroleum products.

Credit has traditionally been scarce and costly in Argentina, much more so than in many other international markets, particularly in recent years, but rates have generally dropped and may in some cases be competitive with overseas funds.

Foreigners are now being encouraged to offer securities in the Argentine market. With the increased liquidity of these markets, it may make sense for multinational firms to list their Argentine operations on both the Bolsa and their home country exchanges. (Refer to the "Financial Institutions" chapter, beginning on page 241, for detailed discussions on securities markets in Argentina.)

REAL ESTATE—COMMERCIAL AND INDUSTRIAL SPACE

Real estate leasing or purchasing in Argentina, as is the case in many economies around the world, requires careful research and consideration before decisions can be made. The real estate market worldwide is still characterized by pricing inefficiencies, lack of procedural standardization, and localized variability in quality and supply. In Latin America as a whole—although to a lesser extent in Argentina—state-of-the-art commercial office and industrial space is harder to come by than in many other markets. The basics that many operators take for granted in Europe, North America, and the more developed Asian markets do not necessarily hold true in real estate markets in Argentina, even in the more highly developed Buenos Aires metropolitan region. In addition, the market is subject to volatility,

with reports indicating that some real estate prices in Buenos Aires fell by as much as 20 percent during early 1995 as a result of the economic crisis.

Difficulty in securing appropriate space usually goes beyond the initial lack of familiarity of local market terms and conditions. For example, in some areas, commercial projects may have been built under condominium-type laws. Here, tenants may have to deal with not one but multiple landlords, possibly on a floor-by-floor basis in some areas.

AVERAGE LEASE AND PURCHASE PRICES FOR VARIOUS REAL ESTATE TYPES IN BUENOS AIRES (as of March 1995)

Type	Price/Square Meter
Annual Quoted Downtown Office Rent	US$301.17
Asking rent in class A building in prime location for 1,000 sq m (10,000 sq ft) parcel. Includes all operating expenses plus taxes paid by tenant.	
Annual Quoted Suburban Office Rent	US$179.54
Asking rent in class A building in prime location for 1,000 sq m (10,000 sq ft) parcel. Includes all operating expenses and taxes paid by tenant.	
Annual Distribution Facility Rent	US$72.12
Distribution facility occupying 10,000 to 20,000 sq m (100,000 to 200,000 sq ft) with large bays and limited parking. Not including taxes, operating expenses, and insurance.	
Annual Warehouse Rent	US$72.12
Industrial space suitable for warehousing or light manufacturing for 2,000 to 4,000 sq m (10,000 to 20,000 sq ft) with 10 to 15 percent office space and 5 to 7 m (15 to 22 ft) ceilings. Does not include taxes, operating expenses, and insurance.	
Undeveloped Industrial Land Purchase Price	US$53.82–86.11
Price per sq m (10 sq ft) for commercially zoned industrial land located in the metropolitan area.	
Annual Retail Rent	US$718.50
Asking rent for retail space less than 1,000 sq m (10,000 sq ft) in a prime shopping area. Includes all expenses such as taxes and operating costs.	
Residential Monthly Rent	US$3,300–3,700.00
Two-bedroom apartment in a prestigious location.	
Residential Purchase Price	US$400,000–480,000.00
Two-bedroom apartment in a prestigious location.	

Information provided by Colliers Interamerica based in Miami, Florida working in conjunction with Badino Colliers in Buenos Aires, Argentina.

Asking prices are for class A properties in prestigious locations. Those actually seeking property in Argentina have a wide range of properties and locations to choose from. Prices can vary by as much as 40 percent from those mentioned. Recent reports from Argentina indicate that prices had fallen substantially in Argentina as of mid-1995.

Undeniably, it is important for the foreign manager or investor to heavily research the current market conditions. And because the real estate industry in Argentina is a closely held sector typically controlled by individuals and family groups, rather than arm's length corporate entities, it is also important to build key relationships with players in the local market in order to get a chance at fair and equitable treatment.

The typical way to find office space is with the assistance of a real estate agent. In the larger cities, particularly Buenos Aires, you will find real estate agents who specialize by property types and in serving foreign clients. They can often provide useful information such as where specific industrial activity occurs and which location will be most likely to provide the foreign operator with the right mix of services and resources. Large, multinational commercial property developers and managers operate in Argentina, and can often serve as good sources, consultants, and agents for foreigners. Some foreign businesses may be more comfortable with such an arrangement than they would be diving directly into the local agent market.

The outright purchase of property is complicated by inefficiencies in the valuation process. Valuing land is fairly difficult in general, but here it is compounded by the unique property appraisal process. Appraisals are generally considered to be somewhat unreliable given that appraisers' fees are usually based on a percentage of the property value rather than on a flat fee for service basis. Thus an upward valuation bias may be inherent in the system. Be diligent in your own valuation process by researching like-property prices and surrounding area values for comparison.

Construction of various commercial and residential facilities—from warehouses and retail space to office towers and multifamily housing—can be beset by time and expense overruns to a much greater degree than is recognized for similar projects in more developed economies. Plan for project completion schedules that are anywhere from 25 percent to 50 percent longer in Argentina than in the US, for instance. Also, development, construction, or rehabilitation expenses may be above average for certain contract labor and materials. To gain a realistic idea of the costs that should be involved, consult with local property development and construction consultants when planning a real estate project in Argentina.

In general, all property types are available for lease or can be built in Argentina. Buenos Aires has a good supply of top tier (Class A) office space, suburban office space, and retail space. Residential housing is relatively expensive to rent but relatively less expensive to purchase as compared to similar urban markets, such as Los Angeles. Land prices will vary widely by province and location (coastal and inland, urban and rural). The accompanying table reviews typical real estate rental and purchase prices in Buenos Aires.

USEFUL ADDRESSES

Subsecretaría de Inversiones
(Undersecretariat of Investments) I
Hipólito Yrigoyen 250, Piso 10, Of. 1010
1310 Buenos Aires, Argentina
Tel: [54] (1) 349-8515/6, 349-5037
Fax: [54] (1) 349-8522
(US mailing address: Miami Business Center, 3896 Biscayne Blvd., Suite 4046, Miami, FL 33137-9012)

Fundación Invertir Argentina
Bartolomé Mitre 326
Edif. Banco Nación, Piso 1, Of. 109
1036 Buenos Aires, Argentina
Tel: [54] (1) 342-7370
Fax: [54] (1) 342-7723

Inspección General de Justicia
San Martín 665
1004 Buenos Aires, Argentina
Tel: [54] (1) 312-2427, 373-7609

Instituto Nacional de Tecnología Industrial(INTI)
(National Institute of Industrial Technology)
Av. L.N. Alem 1067, Piso 7
1001 Buenos Aires, Argentina
Tel: [54] (1) 313-3013

Mercado de Valores de Buenos Aires S.A.
25 de Mayo 369, Pisos 8, 9 y 10
1002 Buenos Aires, Argentina
Tel: [54] (1) 311-1174

Secretaría de Industria
(Secretariat of Industry)
Av. Julio A. Roca 651
1322 Buenos Aires, Argentina
Tel: [54] (1) 334-5068, 342-7822
Fax: [54] (1) 331-3218

Secretaría de Energía
(Secretariat of Energy)
Av. Paseo Colón 171, Piso 8, Of. 803
1063Buenos Aires, Argentina
Tel: [54] (1) 349-8003/5
Fax: [54] (1) 343-6404

Subsecretaría de Comercio Exterior
Dirección de Promoción de las Exportaciones
(Bureau of Export Promotion)
Av. Julio A. Roca 651, Piso 6
1332 Buenos Aires, Argentina
Tel: [54] (1) 334-2975
Fax: [54] (1) 331-2266

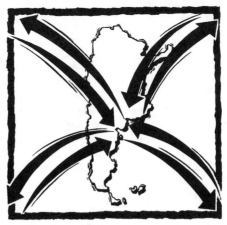

Foreign Trade

THE ROOTS OF ARGENTINE FOREIGN TRADE

During much of its modern history, Argentina has focused on the export of primary commodity agricultural products and the import of manufactured, high-value-added goods. This pattern was altered during the 1940s and 1950s with the advent of protective tariff and nontariff barriers, imposed to allow the development of domestic import substitution industries. For most of the 1960s through the 1980s, Argentina's national policy shifted back and forth between an open and a closed regime, to the detriment of both foreign and domestic interests.

After amassing large trade surpluses for most of the 1980s, during which time the government discouraged imports in an attempt to stabilize Argentina's finances, policymakers shifted again. In 1989 they adopted an open-market approach, allowing the economy to run up substantial trade deficits while encouraging the import of capital goods and other inputs to strengthen domestic production. While this deregulation allowed Argentine industries more access to the equipment needed to upgrade production, it also unfortunately hurt many local industries that were unable to compete with foreign goods that

flooded the domestic market. This was particularly true for manufacturers of consumer goods. Although roughly one-fifth of imports still consist of consumer goods—despite high import duties designed to restrict such trade in nonessentials—the vast bulk of imports are now made up of capital goods, parts for such goods, and intermediate inputs.

The Argentines remain somewhat distressed that the payoff in terms of higher-value-added exports has yet to be realized from allowing this import-driven trade deficit to swell. The trend is nevertheless positive, especially in contrast with the past, when imports were predominately for industrial inputs and domestic consumption. The current surge in investment in Argentina's industry should begin to pay off in the near future.

In line with its open-market policy, the Argentine government reduced and eliminated many barriers to international trade, resulting in the doubling of foreign trade between 1980 and 1994. The maximum import tariff was cut by more than half, from 50 to 20 percent, and the 15 percent surcharge (which constituted a minimum charge) was eliminated, allowing some goods to enter duty-free. In 1989 the average tariff was 39 percent; just five years later in January 1994 the average tariff had fallen to 9.1 percent. Today the tariffs on almost all imports have fallen even further, and as a signatory to the General Agreement on Tariffs and Trade (GATT), Argentina is pledged to reduce them even more. Discretionary import licensing, which had served to strictly limit imports, was also dropped. At the same time, the administration also eliminated most export tariffs and implemented a drawback system to rebate tariffs on inputs for products destined for export. Between 1980 and 1994, foreign trade grew at a compound annual growth rate (CAGR) of 4.75 percent.

Mercosur Influence The 1995 inauguration of the Mercado Común del Sur (Mercosur)—a customs union consisting of Argentina, Brazil,

Uruguay, and Paraguay that allows preferential trade to occur among these partners—has altered the trade situation for Argentina. Preferential trade among Mercosur members began in 1991, and free trade went into effect in January 1995. Argentina's 1993 trade with its Mercosur partners rose by nearly 30 percent, and has continued to grow—it was up by 26.6 percent in 1994. Although Argentina currently maintains a trade deficit with these countries, its exports to them are also rising rapidly. As the full provisions of the pact take effect, the mutual benefits among all the trading partners are expected to continue to multiply.

SIZE OF ARGENTINA'S FOREIGN TRADE

After taking a bit of a dip in the 1980s, Argentina's total foreign trade has more than tripled in the past eight years, rising from roughly US$11.6 billion in 1986 to US$37.3 billion in 1994. During these same years, the share of Argentina's gross domestic product (GDP) representing foreign trade has remained nearly level (12.5 percent in 1986, 11.7 percent in 1993, and 13.5 percent in 1994). This indicates that domestic production and foreign trade have been expanding at close to the same pace. The relative proportion of foreign trade to the total economy also graphically points up that the Argentine economy continues to be largely oriented toward the domestic sphere: more than 85 percent of the economy is focused on domestic markets. While the share of foreign trade relative to the economy appears to be growing, the overall proportional increase has been slight. Nevertheless, the focus is currently on export production.

In relation to other countries trading in world markets, the percentage of Argentina's GDP represented by foreign trade is fairly low. For example, in 1992 the following countries registered levels of foreign trade relative to their GDPs higher than the 11.8 percent posted by Argentina: Brazil, 15 percent; Mexico, 23.4 percent (37.3 percent with *maquila* trade); Japan, 15.2 percent; China, 40.2 percent; Taiwan, 76.9 percent; the US, 17.5 percent; Great Britain, 43.8 percent; France, 46.2 percent; and Germany, 60 percent. All these numbers point to the fact that Argentina continues to concentrate on its domestic markets to a greater extent than many other countries with more developed or rapidly expanding economies.

The emphasis on domestic markets in Argentina is a function of two factors. First, Argentina's economy is still relatively undeveloped when compared with the more developed economies of such nations as European Union (EU) members such as the UK, France, and Germany, which depend on foreign trade for a much greater proportion of their overall economic activity. Second, Argentina's proportionally large and important domestic markets constitute the core of its economy, as is also the situation in Brazil, the US, and Japan. Many domestic producers are just starting to enter the international trade sector, and it is a slow process because many of these producers need to invest heavily in imported capital goods and intermediate inputs to upgrade their production capabilities. The process is made even more difficult because the opening of Argentina's markets to increase the availability of those imports has also intensified the competition at home. Thus, domestic producers are having to become more competitive not only in international markets, but simultaneously in Argentine markets.

Prior to 1989 Argentina's markets were for the most part closed to imports, while exports were highly concentrated in a few sectors. When open markets were implemented, foreign trade performed as might be expected—that is, it surged rapidly. The overall numbers also camouflage a significant differential in the rate of growth of the various trade components. Imports have more than quadrupled (from US$4.7 billion in 1986 to US$21.5 billion in 1994), while exports have only doubled (from US$6.8 billion in 1986 to US$15.7 billion in 1994). This differential has arisen largely because of the need to import modern technology before domestic industries can supply exports in such quantity, quality, and diversity as to become competitive in global markets. This gap—between imports and exports—is likely to continue for some time, and narrowing it will require capital investment, modification of the management structure, and training of the workforce. Many Argentine businesses—and whole industries—are now engaged in this struggle. Those that find a way to persevere will begin to transform the current situation into a more balanced foreign trade.

EXPORTS

Until the 1990s, exports from Argentina remained at approximately the same level for decades, although tariff and nontariff barriers on imports allowed the country to post trade surpluses until 1981. The products exported were highly concentrated in three sectors: agriculture, industrial manufactures, and fuels. From 1980 through 1989 roughly two-thirds of Argentina's exports continued to be associated with agriculture (primary products averaged 38 percent; agricultural manufactures—processed and semi-processed products—averaged 37 percent). About one fifth of exports (21 percent) during the 1980s were industrial manufactures, consisting mainly of base metals (iron, steel, aluminum), some machinery, and chemicals. Only about 4 percent of the exports were fuels and fuel derivatives—production by the state-run monopoly was designed primarily to fill domestic need rather than to contribute to export revenues.

The country is still known primarily for its agricultural exports (grain, oilseeds, and meat products). According to statistics compiled by Argentina's Instituto Nacional de Estadística y Censos (INDEC) for 1994, exports of agricultural manufactures fell to a 29 percent share from a 37 percent share of total exports, while primary (agricultural) products dropped to a 24 percent share from a 38 percent share—or combined, from nearly three-quarters to about one-half. Meanwhile, industrial manufactures rose to a 37 percent share from a 21 percent share in 1994. Fuel exports rose as well, to a 10 percent share from a 4 percent share, but the real story was the surge in higher-value-added manufactured industrial products.

In 1994 exports were still heavily concentrated in a few sectors, but diversification was beginning to be visible. In that year INDEC reported that the top four exports—fuels, fats and oils, food byproducts, and cereals—together made up 37 percent of total merchandise exports. The top ten exports represented roughly 70 percent of all exports. Some of the highest growth in exports in 1994 came from higher-value-added goods, including transportation equipment (up 25.6 percent), chemical products (up 29.5 percent), and machinery and electrical products (up 13.2 percent).

For some, the shift in Argentine exports is occurring too slowly. Some analysts have voiced concern that the growth of nontraditional, higher-value-added exports needs to be further encouraged if they are going to supply the foreign exchange that is currently being supplied through foreign investment. Nevertheless, export rates have been growing steadily since 1992. In dollar terms, exports took a 3 percent dip in 1991, but then recovered, growing by 2.1 percent in 1992, by an even stronger 7 percent in 1993, and by 20 percent in 1994.

Agricultural and Related Commodity Exports

Agricultural products—both primary and processed (manufactured) products—have accounted for roughly 70 percent of Argentina's total export revenues for decades. To improve productivity and competitiveness in world markets, this sector is in need of capital investment for upgrading equipment and yields. Although crop yields have continued to increase marginally each year, the rate of growth is slowing, and production of some major commodities—wheat, sunflower seeds—has even declined. In 1994 exports of fresh vegetables and of oilseeds each

Product Category	1994 US$ Billion	%	± from 1993 (%)
Fuels	1.619	10.3	31.0
Fats and oils	1.533	9.7	12.1
Food by-products	1.341	8.5	8.2
Cereals	1.323	8.4	9.9
Oilseeds	0.953	6.1	36.7
Meat	0.912	5.8	21.9
Transportation	0.903	5.7	25.6
Machinery and electronic equipment	0.855	5.4	13.2
Base metals	0.786	5.1	12.0
Hides and leather	0.762	4.8	23.5
Chemicals	0.724	4.6	29.5
Seafood (fresh)	0.441	2.8	1.4
Seafood (processed)	0.278	1.8	2.2
Vegetables (fresh)	0.254	1.6	37.3
Mineral products	0.250	1.6	278.8
Other miscellaneous	2.805	17.8	28.8
Total	**15.739**	**100**	**20.0**

ARGENTINE EXPORTS BY CATEGORY

Source: INDEC

grew by 37 percent, while exports of hides and leather were up by 23 percent, meat by 22 percent, fats and oils by 12 percent, cereals by 10 percent, and food byproducts by 8 percent. Officials are actively promoting nontraditional agricultural crops and processed products for export.

Industrial and Manufactured Exports

Starting in 1993, the growth rate of industrial and manufactured exports began to surge. The 1994 exports of these products—including machinery, devices, electrical materials, transport materials, common metals, metal manufactures, chemicals, textiles, and clothing—increased by 57 percent over 1993 levels. Most of the increase is represented by growth in the export of transport equipment and chemicals, followed by exports of machinery and electrical devices. Base metals and mineral products also grew, with exports of mineral products jumping by more than 275 percent.

IMPORTS

Argentina has become a hot market for imports. Imports grew more than 20-fold between 1965 and

ARGENTINE IMPORTS BY CATEGORY

Product Category	1994 US$ Billions	%	± from 1993 (%)
Machinery and electronic equipment	7.415	34.4	27.5
Transportation	3.834	17.8	42.7
Chemicals	2.577	12.0	27.8
Base metals	1.272	5.9	32.5
Plastics	1.113	5.2	19.2
Textile products	0.828	3.8	2.1
Mineral products	0.801	3.7	41.9
Precision instruments	0.708	3.3	32.1
Paper products	0.694	3.2	18.2
Food products	0.593	2.8	30.3
Plant products	0.343	1.6	25.5
Live animals	0.251	1.2	3.5
Cement and glass	0.226	1.0	28.8
Other miscellaneous products	0.889	4.1	21.9
Total	**21.544**	**100**	**28.4**

Source: INDEC

1994, but the major growth has only been since 1991 when the more open policies of the Menem government began to go into effect. During much of the 1980s, the nation discouraged products from the outside, but Argentina is continuing to open its markets, reduce tariffs, deregulate government monopolies, and stabilize its exchange rate. End user demand is high for both consumer and industrial goods.

As noted, imports of capital goods, intermediate products, and parts and accessories represented 72.5 percent of imports by economic utilization category in 1994. In another listing by more specific categories, INDEC shows that machinery and electronic equipment represented the largest category of imports in 1994, accounting for 34 percent of all imports (up 27 percent from 1993). Imports of transportation equipment ranked second at 18 percent (up 43 percent), indicating the strength of the Argentine automotive industry, because much of this traffic represents trade in components with Brazil. Chemicals represented the third largest category with a 12 percent share of total merchandise imports (up 28 percent). Together these three categories accounted for nearly two-thirds of Argentina's 1994 imports, as well as for all import categories representing more than US$2 billion and 10

percent of the total. The top ten import categories account for 92 percent of all imports.

TRADE PARTNERS

Argentina's dominant trade partner is its largest neighbor, Brazil. Brazil achieved this standing in 1992 and so far has retained it in every year since then. In 1994 Brazil accounted for US$7.875 billion (21.1 percent) of Argentina's total trade. The nation's second largest partner was the US, with US$6.645 billion (17.8 percent) of total trade. Argentina conducts almost 39 percent of its trade with these two countries alone.

Aside from the two largest trading partners, eight other nations had trade with Argentina greater than US$1 billion in value in 1994. Individually, their shares of total foreign trade ranged from 5.5 percent to 2.9 percent, falling substantially below those of the top two partners. In order of their ranking, these trading partners are as follows: Italy (US$2.069 billion), Germany (US$1.988), Chile (US$1.812 billion), the Netherlands (US$1.528), Spain (US$1.442), Uruguay (US$1.430), France (US$1.286), and Japan (US$1.071 billion). When foreign trade with these eight traders is combined with the top two, the top ten trade partners account for almost 73 percent of Argentina's trade.

Argentina's trade relationships with its neighbors have been significantly affected by Mercosur. From 1975 to 1989, an average of only about 11 percent of Argentina's total foreign trade was conducted with Brazil. When the first step of preferential trade began at the start of the present

ARGENTINE IMPORTS BY ECONOMIC UTILIZATION

	1994 US$ Billion	%	± from 1993 (%)
Intermediate goods	6.211	28.8	22.8
Capital goods	6.038	28.0	47.2
Consumer goods	3.903	18.1	10.9
Parts and accessories for capital goods	3.385	15.7	21.0
Passenger vehicles	1.380	6.4	55.4
Fuels	0.583	2.7	51.4
Miscellaneous other	0.044	0.3	25.7
Total	**21.544**	**100**	**28.4**

Source: INDEC

decade, that figure jumped to 17 percent in 1990, and it has been rising steadily ever since. By 1992 Brazil had become Argentina's number one trading partner, and the amount and proportion of trade between the two countries continues to grow. To date Brazil has been the major purchaser of Argentina's new, nontraditional, higher-value-added exports.

Although relations with Chile periodically become strained, trade with it, alongside that with Mercosur partners Brazil and Uruguay, is expected to grow substantially in future years. In 1994 trade with Brazil grew by 23 percent over the level in 1993, that with Uruguay by 32 percent, and that with Chile—not a party to Mercosur—by 39 percent. Trade with Paraguay—the remaining Mercosur participant, but not a significant Argentine trade partner—grew by 31 percent to US$564 million in 1994.

Argentina is fairly well diversified in the markets for its products, although this is apt to change somewhat as it alters the mix of its exports to include more value-added items. In 1994 the major purchaser of Argentina's products was Brazil (US$3.595 billion, 22.8 percent), followed by the US (US$1.719 billion, 10.9 percent) and the Netherlands (US$1.176 billion, 7.5 percent). Together these three countries took 41 percent of all of Argentina's exports, representing all countries buying more than US$1 billion in Argentine exports. The top ten countries took 69 percent.

During 1994 among Argentina's top ten export markets, sales to Chile rose by 66 percent, to Paraguay rose by 38 percent, to the US by 34 percent, to Italy by 28 percent, to Brazil by 28 percent, to Uruguay by 27 percent, and to Spain by 17 percent. Sales also fell in several markets, although to a generally lesser degree: exports to the Netherlands dropped by 7 percent, to Japan by 5percent, and to Germany by 1 percent.

With the exception of its top two suppliers, Argentina gets its imports from a wide range of sources, none of which accounts for a particularly large percentage of its generally well diversified trade. In 1994 the major sources of Argentine imports were the US, with US$4.926 billion (22.9 percent) and Brazil, with US$4.280 billion (19.9 percent); together these two suppliers accounted for almost 43 percent of imports into Argentina. When the next three suppliers—Italy (US$1.422 billion, 6.6 percent of imports to Argentina), Germany (US$1.371, 6.4 percent), France (US%1.071, 5 percent)—are added, the top five represent slightly more than 60 percent of all imports.

During 1994 Argentina's imports from Belgium-Luxembourg grew by nearly 74 percent, while those from Spain grew by 70 percent; imports from Germany recovered, growing by 49 percent, from both Italy and France by about 45 percent, from Uruguay by 37 percent, from the US by 28 percent, from Brazil by 20 and from Chile by 17 percent. Among its top ten suppliers, Argentina reduced its purchases only from Japan, which saw its sales fall by 6 percent.

BALANCE OF TRADE

During the past 30 years, Argentina has maintained a balance of merchandise trade surplus in all

Leading Argentine Trade Partners

Exports—1994

Brazil 23%
Other 30 %
US 11%
Japan 3%
Paraguay 3%
Spain 4%
Germany 4%
Italy 4%
Uraguay 4%
Chile 6%
Netherlands 8%

Total 1994 merchandise exports: US$15.739 billion

Imports—1994

US 23%
Other 25%
Japan 3%
Uraguay 4%
Chile 4%
Spain 4%
France 5%
Germany 6%
Italy 7%
Brazil 20%

Total 1994 merchandise imports: US$21.544 billion

Note:Figures rounded to nearest whole percent. Totals may exceed 100% due to rounding.
Source: INDEC

but four years: 1981 and 1992 through 1994. During many of these years, Argentina actively managed its trade by using tariff and other barriers to artificially exclude imports. When open-market policies were introduced, imports began to outpace exports, causing deficits in the early 1990s. Based on improved export performance in early 1995, officials have projected break-even performance, or perhaps even a slight surplus in 1995. To regain its trade surplus, the country is focusing on diversifying its exports, stepping up production of high-value-added goods, and trading with its Mercosur partners.

Argentina's current accounts have been in deficit in 20 of the past 30 years, most recently showing a surplus only in 1990. In addition to merchandise trade, the current account deficit includes trade in invisibles (services), investment payments, and transfers. Argentina has generally maintained a deficit position in trade in services, and has historically paid out more investment income than it has received, keeping its finances on edge. Countries that generate substantial amounts of inbound investment and a high rate of growth in the domestic economy can sustain such disparities, but imbalances in current accounts pose more than the usual danger for Argentina, because its domestic economy could still be hurt by the loss of outside funds. Thus the development of exports, especially nontraditional ones, is taking on greater urgency. In 1994 nontraditional industrial products accounted for 40 percent of the growth in exports. In comparison, 40 percent of the increase in imports consisted of capital goods, which in turn are being used to increase productivity. Argentines point out that their current account deficit in 1994 was only 4 percent of its GDP, barely half the level of Mexico's deficit when it got into trouble at the end of that year.

As Argentines focus more and more on opportunities within Mercosur, the balance of trade situation is indicative of trends. Trade with Mercosur members posted a deficit of US$1.428 billion in 1992; however, this was reduced to US$530 million in 1993 and US$389 million in 1994.

ARGENTINE TRADE POLICY

The wide ranging reform programs introduced in 1989 have effected drastic changes in an economy that had reached an acute crisis stage in the late 1980s. Most of the statist controls imposed during prior decades have been removed, deregulation and restructuring of public and private sectors is well underway, and industries are being privatized. Argentina has adopted outward-looking trade policies in this early phase of economic recovery.

Even with the government's adoption of open-market trade policies, the process of becoming internationally competitive is proving to be difficult and slow, primarily because of the need to reform industry, management, and labor structures. Open-market policies have not eliminated the problems that Argentine businesses face in producing goods that can compete in both domestic and international markets. As a result, imports are likely to remain high for some time in order to meet domestic consumer demand, industrial investment in capital goods, and consumption of intermediate inputs for reexport production.

Some potential concerns regarding what appeared to be a developing overdependent on Brazil as a trade partner have largely been answered. Although Brazil accounted for the largest percentage of Argentina's trade—23 percent in 1994 and 30 percent in the first quarter of 1995—Argentina has also made progress in establishing stronger exports to the rest of the world. There are also indications that the overheating trade with Brazil will begin to settle down: Brazil is expected to slow down its rate of purchases to cut its own trade deficit, while at the same time becoming a more reliable partner. As a result of stabilization, Brazilian wagers are rising, reducing Brazil's cost of production advantage over Argentina and also increasing Brazilian purchasing power, thus providing a growing and steadier source of demand for Argentine goods.

The government has stuck with its open trade policies for the most part, backing off to allow for a transitional period only when protection of an important industry becomes necessary for its survival. Nearly all barriers to exports have been eliminated, and exports have been showing an increased growth rate—growth was particularly strong during the first six months of 1995—although growth has nevertheless been comparatively slow and occurs from a relatively low base level.

Some observers argue that 1995 has been the turning point for Argentina's exports. First, some see the domestic market as nearly saturated for a wide range of goods, even without the negative effects of the emerging markets downturn in early 1995 which have served to depress imports. Second, and more positively, the effects of investment appear to be kicking in: Argentine manufacturing activity—up 11 percent in 1994 from 1993—increased for the 19th consecutive quarter in the first quarter of 1995. Also, 1995 promises to be a record year of harvests of agricultural products, while international demand seems to be either growing or at least stable for the intermediate products that form the bulk of Argentina's exports.

The Argentine government is seeking to improve trading relationships and increase export access regionally—culminating in bilateral trade agreements and in the Mercosur pact—and on a global scale through GATT, potential ties with the EU, and possibly a future hemispheric free trade area.

MEMBERSHIP IN INTERNATIONAL ORGANIZATIONS

Argentina has long been a member of various international associations, even during its years of largely isolationist policies. As it opens its economy to foreign trade and encourages foreign investment, Argentina is also strengthening its ties with the global community. It has become a vocal participant in regional and international activities, reaching out and meeting with its neighbors to promote its own economic development and to resolve issues of concern—both directly and indirectly linked to foreign trade—on the international front.

Argentina was one of the 50 nations to join the United Nations (the UN, or in Spanish, the Organización de Naciones Unidas or ONU) when that organization was founded in 1945. It is a member of the International Monetary Fund (IMF), the International Bank for Reconstruction and Development (the World Bank or IBRD), the Inter-American Development Bank (IDB), the Organization of American States (OAS, or in Spanish, Organización de los Estados Americanos or

OEA), and the Latin American Integration Association (LAIA, or in Spanish, Asociación Latinoamericana de Integración or ALADI).

Argentina subscribes to most of the international trade pacts and commercial conventions, including GATT, its successor the World Trade Organization (WTO), the Berne and Paris Conventions on intellectual property, the International Chamber of Commerce (ICC), and the Customs Cooperation Council (CCC). Regionally, it has been a major force in the creation of Mercosur, a customs union among Argentina, Brazil, Uruguay, and Paraguay which went into full effect at the beginning of 1995. Argentina maintains bilateral trade treaties with various nations, including Brazil, Uruguay, Paraguay, Chile, and the US. It has also expressed an interest in joining the North American Free Trade Agreement (NAFTA) with the US, Mexico, and Canada and in negotiating a hemispheric free trade agreement.

Argentina's increasing participation in world, regional, and bilateral trade agreements and international organizations is serving not only to promote its foreign trade and economic expansion, but also to improve its relationships with other nations. As its foreign trade increases, so does its role in the global community. In turn, Argentina's trading partners are growing in number and importance.

Trade Agreements

INTRODUCTION

The most notable feature of Argentina's current trade policy is how thoroughly it embraces the notion of free markets. To encourage foreign investment and open Argentina's markets to the forces of competition, the administration in power since 1989 has employed unilateral market liberalization and stabilization measures in combination with multinational trade agreements. Having drastically reduced import tariffs and abolished much of its complicated structure of nontariff barriers, the administration then undertook a serious privatization effort, selling a collection of state-owned businesses that previously not only failed to operate profitably, but also had cost billions of dollars in subsidies. Finally, it implemented the Convertibility Plan, pegging the peso to the US dollar at a one-to-one ratio and making it virtually impossible for the government to finance a deficit. In short, the Argentine economy has moved from being one of the most controlled to one of the most liberal in the world.

In addition, in January 1995 Argentina put into effect the Common External Tariff (CET) approved by the Mercado Común del Sur (the Common Market of the South, or Mercosur) in 1994, fully

inaugurating the customs union formed by Argentina with Brazil, Uruguay, and Paraguay.

Documentation requirements are minimal, and the trade registry is open to all potential importers and exporters. In 1994 the maximum tariff dropped from 50 percent to 20 percent, reaching an average tariff of about 10 percent (down from 39 percent in 1989). Capital goods produced outside the country are subject to a 10 percent maximum tariff that is reduced to 2 percent or 0 percent for those not available from Mercosur member countries. Nontariff restrictions have been almost completely eliminated, persisting only in the protected car industry and, for security or environmental reasons, on a few other products. Quotas and a special regime are applied to automobile imports, and temporary quotas exist from time to time on paper products and a few other items. Other goods such as pharmaceuticals, foodstuffs, defense materials, and other specific items require governmental approval.

The liberalization measures have boosted production and caused the domestic economy to expand greatly. In an effort to encourage export opportunities, the country has aggressively pursued membership in a variety of multilateral trade agreements. Because participation in trade agreements is usually based on the reciprocal extension of trade privileges, such agreements generally serve to lower tariffs, eliminate quota restrictions, or otherwise remove protectionist barriers to cross-border trade between the nationals of member countries. The global and regional trade arrangements in which Argentina participates have contributed significantly to the current prosperity and freedom of its markets. The results of Argentina's commitment to free trade have been highly gratifying. Since 1991 the economy has grown by more than 30 percent, yielding a per capita gross domestic product (GDP) of more than $8,000 (double what it was as recently as 1989).

In only a few years, high growth and confidence in the economy have made Argentina—formerly largely isolationist in trade and political matters—a commercial ally of the US, the European Union (EU), and its Latin American neighbors. The full implementation of Mercosur should continue to encourage solid growth in all sectors. Argentina appears poised to pull itself permanently up from the ranks of the developing countries and take its rightful place among the major economies of the world.

GATT AND THE WTO

Known generally as GATT, the General Agreement on Tariffs and Trade is designed to provide a standard framework for global trade. Founded in 1947, GATT has passed through eight series of multilateral trade negotiations known as rounds; each round is named after the location in which the opening sessions were held, or after a prominent figure involved, such as the Dillon and Kennedy Rounds. The most recent was the Uruguay Round, begun in 1986.

Initially this round was to have been completed by 1990. It was extended as the agreement became more ambitious and more difficult to conclude. The Uruguay Round ended in December 1993 with compromises covering trade in goods and services. In the area of merchandise trade, the round resulted in an overall tariff reduction of 38 percent—higher than the less ambitious reduction originally targeted; the reduction of nontariff barriers; the integration of agricultural products under the multilateral system for the first time, reducing production support and export subsidies over a six year period; and the integration of trade in textiles to the multilateral rules through the gradual dismantling of the Multi-Fiber Arrangements (MFA) and the bilateral quota arrangements currently in force over a period of 10 years. In the area of trade in services, the round achieved a general agreement to liberalize and open specific markets.

The final agreement also covers intellectual property rights (IPR), and a new dispute settlement understanding (DSU) procedure. All of these elements of the Uruguay Round have been placed under the administration of the new World Trade Organization (WTO) created by the 124 signatory countries to implement and administer the agreements.

Argentina has ratified the Uruguay Round agreement, which was signed in December 1993 by 124 member countries. Since the agreement was signed, several other countries that were outside of GATT, before 1994, including China, Russia, and Taiwan, have applied for membership.

The agreement is expected to facilitate international trade through increased outsourcing of intermediate products and parts, allowing various producers to achieve greater economies of scale by removing artificial constraints to sources and markets. The Uruguay Round final agreement consists of more than 20,000 pages of text, so the actual extent of its provisions can be expected to remain unclear for some time.

GATT exists to promote international free trade. Its basic principles include the most favored nation (MFN) status, nondiscrimination, national treatment, and reciprocal tariff concessions. Regional trade blocs that may lead to preferential treatment among members are allowed in the form of customs unions and free trade zones on the condition that the members of such regional blocs agree to offer favorable treatment to members only by reducing existing tariffs, not by raising additional barriers to outsiders. This restriction theoretically applies to such integration processes as those established through Mercosur and the Asociación Latinoamericana de Integración (ALADI), of which Argentina is a member.

Other notable issues involve an agreement covering such trade related investment measures as local content requirements and agreements on safeguards to unify and regulate extraordinary import restrictions in a transparent fashion and prevent voluntary restraint agreements. Additional agreements exist to remove national health and safety regulations that serve primarily as barriers to international trade (although requirements deemed to apply to legitimate health and safety concerns with a scientific basis are exempted from this provision). The agreement also calls for limitations on voluntary restraint accords; changes the way that anti-dumping charges are calculated, assessed, and resolved; places limits on government subsidies to various industries and activities; and includes an agreement to revisit the area of free trade in services in the future with a view toward further liberalization of the existing provisions.

Tariff provisions require industrialized signatory countries to reduce tariffs on a variety of products, including beer, distilled spirits, construction equipment, farm machinery, medical devices, furniture, paper products, pharmaceuticals, steel, and toys. Tariffs on chemicals are to be phased out over a 15-year period, with some strategic exceptions allowed. Tariffs are to be lowered on electronic products (such as semiconductors) and pharmaceuticals, with both expected to receive added protection under IPR provisions. Under the new IPR rules, trademarks will be protected for 7 years, patents for 20 years, and copyrights for 50 years. (In early 1995 Argentina revised its copyright laws to provide explicit protection for computer software; it altered its patent laws to extend coverage to pharmaceuticals, previously excluded from such protection, largely in order to comply with the provisions of GATT. However, the patent law revisions include a waiting period of eight years before foreign pharmaceuticals receive full protection.) Official research and development (R&D) subsidies will also be limited to no more than 75 percent for basic research and 50 percent for applied research.

Areas of Disagreement Although GATT provides for the phasing out of some agricultural subsidies, Argentina has expressed concern that the agreement does not go far enough to force such exporters of competing products as the US and several EU countries to phase out their extensive production subsidy programs. To the contrary, Argentina has levied steep export tariffs on many agricultural products as a means of generating fiscal revenue, although these damaging policies have largely been eliminated in recent years. Of major concern to Argentina are the continued high protective tariff and nontariff barriers imposed by the US and other countries on Argentine agricultural exports, although for the most part, Argentina has resolved its disagreements over textile and garment imports, and the Argentine economy should benefit from the gradual deregulation of the items in question over the next 10 years.

Specific areas in which the major parties failed to reach agreement include aircraft, entertainment, financial services, shipping, steel, and telecommunications. The main antagonists over most of these issues have been the US and the EU. An agreement covering financial services was concluded in mid-1995, although the US refused to participate because of objections to the lack of immediate full reciprocity to granted for entry into less developed markets.

The WTO Designed along the lines of such independent international bodies as the World Bank and the International Monetary Fund (IMF), the WTO will be responsible for conducting future negotiations among GATT signatories and will adjudicate disputes. The WTO operates through a bureaucracy and three-judge panels which arbitrate specific disputes in secrecy. Unlike GATT—which required consensus and under which the loser could effectively veto an unfavorable ruling—WTO decisions may be appealed, but the final results will be binding. The WTO also has the broader responsibility of monitoring international trade and of ensuring the phaseout of barriers in banking, insurance, tourism, and telecommunications. It has final authority over all agreements concerning trade in goods and services, such as agricultural products, textiles, and apparel, as well as trade-related IPR issues that were negotiated under GATT. Nations failing to conform their practices and laws to WTO rules may have compensatory sanctions levied against them. Any signatory may withdraw from the WTO, but such behavior is expected to have major repercussions as the body becomes more established.

The Generalized System of Preferences

Under the terms of previous GATT Part IV agreement, many industrialized nations to assist developing nations set up a Generalized System of Preferences (GSP) to grant selective waivers or reductions of tariffs on imports of products from developing nations. In the US, Japan, Canada, and the EU countries, GSP programs promote growth in and exports from developing countries while also reducing the cost to national consumers of many imported products. Argentina is a beneficiary of the GSP programs of these countries; certain Argentine products can be imported duty-free or subject to reduced duties to these countries if they meet the GSP requirements.

Although many of its products are eligible for favorable treatment under the terms of many GSP programs, Argentina has also found that large importing countries use these programs in an attempt to impose tighter restrictions on certain other goods. For example, the US has been using GSP benefits to pressure beneficiary countries to adopt more stringent environmental, labor, and intellectual property rights policies. With implementation of the WTO, GSP eligibility remains just about the only unilateral trade sanction instrument available to the US and other industrialized nations. If tougher requirements are imposed, and if, as expected, many developing nations cannot meet them, then the only way for beneficiary countries to maintain preferential access to these markets without being subject to unilateral withdrawal, suspension, or limitation of benefits is to enter into free trade agreements (under which alleged violations are decided by consensus or panels, not unilaterally). Although the US has threatened to implement more restrictive requirements in its GSP program, to date no conclusive action has been taken toward modifying GSP requirements.

Basic Requirements Although specific programs vary in detail, the rules generally include the following provisions, which are taken specifically from the US GSP. Argentine goods must generally meet the following basic requirements to be imported duty-free under GSP:

- The product must be imported directly from Argentina to the country granting the preference;
- The product must be on the GSP eligible products list;
- The product must be either (i) entirely grown, produced, or manufactured in Argentina or (ii) primarily the product of Argentina, with a minimum of 35 percent of its value coming from the cost of materials or direct costs of processing in Argentina;
- Proper documentation, including a certified

United Nations Conference on Trade and Development (UNCTAD) Certificate of Origin Form A, must be submitted in addition to normal customs entry documentation;

- The exporter must formally request GSP status; and

- The product must meet the competitive needs limitations of the importing country, which can be used to limit preferential treatment of specific products from particular countries.

The GSP rules exist in addition to regular customs regulations and procedures, and GSP imports remain subject to all regular customs requirements such as those governing packing, marking and labeling, and restricted or prohibited imports. Products eligible for GSP treatment are identified in the tariff schedules of the countries sponsoring the programs. Those interested in this preference should consult the import regulations or a customs broker of the target market country.

MOST FAVORED NATION STATUS

Rather than representing the special preferential status the name implies, most favored nation (MFN) status has come to be seen as the norm in bilateral trade relationships between countries. Argentina, in fact, grants MFN status to every country with which it trades. Under MFN status both parties agree not to extend to any third party nation any trade preferences that are more favorable than those available under the agreement concluded between them unless they simultaneously make the same provisions available to each other. While MFN status is reciprocal—with each party agreeing to grant the status to the other—it must be negotiated separately with each country; each agreement includes additional and specific provisions relating to national security, dispute settlement procedures, trade promotion, and various other matters.

MERCOSUR: MERCADO COMÚN DEL SUR (SOUTHERN COMMON MARKET)

In December 1994 Argentina, Brazil, Paraguay, and Uruguay signed the Protocol of Ouro Preto, implementing the Southern Common Market, known widely as Mercosur. Mercosur was created in March 1991 by the Treaty of Asunción, which called for the signatories to establish a full common market arrangement among its members by January 1, 1995. The agreement calls for a gradual elimination of all tariffs on goods originating in and traded among the member states and the formation of a Common External Tariff (CET). It operates within the context

and terms of larger groupings, including ALADI and GATT, of which it is a part. During the transition period that ended December 31, 1994, tariff were reduced automatically, with a sharp initial cut and progressing in linear increments until all tariffs were eliminated. As of the inauguration of the customs union in January 1995, approximately 80 percent of all products traded—about 8,000 categories of goods—began to be traded duty-free within the bloc. Exceptions include textiles, steel, automobiles, and petrochemicals, which will remain protected by domestic tariffs for a period of four years.

Mercosur is still far from being a true common market, but the members have managed to achieve a customs union and continue negotiations aimed at full common market status by 2006. As a common market, Mercosur must do more than reduce and harmonize tariffs. It must also coordinate the economic, legislative, environmental, and infrastructure and technology policies of the various member countries. Members will be expected to harmonize their standards, establish a supranational bureaucracy with considerable power to affect the policy-making decisions of each country's government, and implement fully a common external tariff structure. They have a long way to go to achieve such goals. Nevertheless, trade among Mercosur countries has already increased fourfold—it approached US$11 billion in 1994—since the initial agreement was signed in anticipation of even greater cohesion. More importantly, Mercosur has helped to lock in the liberalizing changes already made by its members during the past few years. A momentum toward such change has been created that should prove very difficult to halt or reverse.

In Argentina, foreign trade with nations around the globe is growing by leaps and bounds, Mercosur has been especially important. The loss of import revenues from duties on goods originating within Mercosur countries has been more than compensated by the earnings generated by more competitive duty-free exports to these countries. While total Argentine exports grew 9.5 percent between 1991 and 1993, its exports to other Mercosur countries were up 86 percent, from US$2 billion to $3.7 billion. In 1993 Mercosur countries absorbed 28 percent of Argentina's exports; this figure rose to nearly one-third of all exports in 1994. Mercosur has especially improved Argentina's trade status with Brazil, its largest neighbor, the recovering economy of which gobbles up more than 20 percent of Argentina's total exports.

The effects of Mercosur will be felt beyond the Brazil-Argentina border. The combined population of the four member countries is 200 million—almost one-third of South America's population—with a total GDP of approximately US$600 billion.

Mercosur's territory covers nearly 12 million sq km (4.6 million sq mi), comprises 70 percent of the total land mass of South America, stretches from the tropical jungles of northern Brazil to the subantarctic zone of Argentina, and includes some of the world's most important agricultural and mineral resources. This wide variety of topographies, climates, and resources provides substantial opportunities for expansion and complementation in production.

Mercosur may be small compared to the North American Free Trade Agreement (NAFTA) with a GDP of $7.2 trillion or the EU with a GDP of $6.2 trillion, but it is still no small feat—and it has plenty of room left to grow.

Mercosur Principles and Provisions

Administrative Structure The governing body of Mercosur is the Common Market Council, consisting of the member states' ministers of foreign relations and economy. It is responsible for political leadership and decisionmaking to ensure compliance with the objectives and the time frames set within the agreement. The executive body of Mercosur is the Common Market Group, which is composed of 16 members and represents the foreign relations offices, the economic ministries, and the central banks of the member states. The Common Market Group has established an administrative headquarters in Montevideo, Uruguay, and has already appointed 11 working groups to deal with policy matters. A Mercosur Trade Commission will monitor trade regulations among members and be vested with the authority to review claims and mediate disputes. According to the terms of the Brasilia Protocol, final settlement of disputes among members will be through arbitration. This administra-

tive body will also serve as Mercosur's negotiating unit with other nations and trade blocs.

Elimination of Tariffs and Other Trade Barriers All nontariff restrictions and other limitations on trade between the member states were eliminated according to a gradual progressive automatic schedule, reaching zero duty and the removal of tariff restrictions of all kinds. These goals have already been achieved, leaving only a few sensitive products subject to limits based on national import policy.

Common External Tariff Member states further agreed to set a common trade policy toward third countries or groups of countries and to coordinate their individual positions in regional and international economic trade forums. Such a tariff is necessary to the creation of a common market in that once a CET is implemented, importers of finished goods for which the importer has paid the CET may sell the finished goods in the territories of other member countries without paying a second tariff. Until then, unless a product qualifies for preferential treatment under the rules of origin established by Mercosur, a trader must either pay the applicable tariff each time the product crosses a border of a member state or establish independent distribution centers in each member state.

To avoid running afoul of GATT requirements, the CET must not be higher than any member's individually negotiated MFN tariff rate. This has caused friction within Mercosur because Brazil, the economic heavyweight of the group, has insisted on maintaining the highest possible external tariff rates for some products, including capital goods and computers. The major sources of contention center around the tariff structures for capital

Percentage Growth in Argentine Exports to Mercosur vs. Total Exports

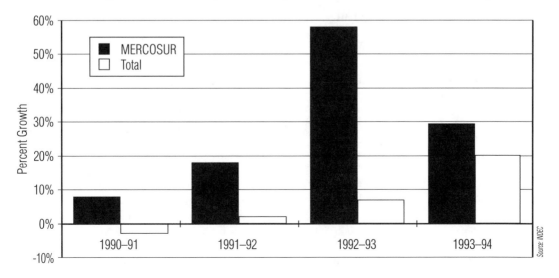

Source: INDEC

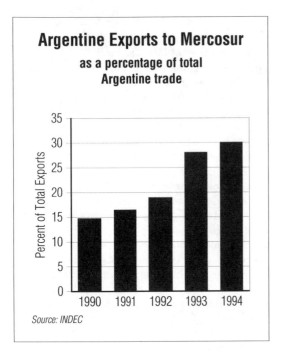

Argentine Exports to Mercosur

as a percentage of total Argentine trade

Source: INDEC

goods, computer equipment, and telecommunications. Brazilian tariffs range as high as 35 percent, while the other three countries have lowered or eliminated tariffs on these imports in order to build up their productive capabilities.

Mercosur members have had some difficulty establishing a CET. However, in August 1994, the Mercosur presidents ratified the formation of a CET structure—effective January 1, 1995—that sets CET rates of 0 to 20 percent. A CET of 14 percent on capital goods will be introduced only in 2001; even then, Paraguay and Uruguay will be given an additional five years to bring their external tariffs into line. A common levy tentatively set at 16 percent on informatics and telecommunications equipment will wait until 2006. The importation of chemicals has been partially resolved with a tentative agreement establishing a 0 to 16 percent tariff, but this is subject to modification in the future.

Current Tariffs The CET established January 1, 1995 imposes duties ranging from 0 to 20 percent. The CET initially will cover approximately 8,000 products. Tariffs on capital goods, informatics, and telecommunications equipment will gradually rise to meet the CET rate. The tariff for capital goods will come into force in 2001 at 14 percent through gradual linear convergence of each state's tariff level. The CET for informatics and telecommunications products will be implemented in 2006 at 16 percent, also through convergence.

Exceptions The parties agreed to keep lists of exceptions to the CET involving 300 products for Argentina, Brazil, and Uruguay, plus 399 for Para-

guay. For these products to circulate freely within Mercosur, they must have 60 percent local content for Argentina, Brazil, and Uruguay, and 50 percent for Paraguay (which must raise its level to 60 percent by 2001). The exclusion lists will remain in effect until 2001.

Transitions A special transition regime regarding a CET for motor vehicles and sugar remains to be established in future negotiations.

Rules of Origin Until a CET is fully implemented, member countries must apply rules of origin to determine whether some particular goods qualify for the preferential tariff rate. Importers and exporters alike need to understand these rules of origin before attempting to do business in any Mercosur market. Mercosur's rules of origin are straightforward:

1. Goods produced (for example, extracted, harvested, gathered, or born) within a member territory qualify as originating.

2. All goods manufactured wholly within the territory of one or more members from originating materials qualify as originating. Thus, if an Argentine company manufactures a telephone from plastic produced in Paraguay and audio components produced in Brazil, assembling the product in Argentina, the phone would qualify as originating. The manufacturer could export it to any member of Mercosur at the prevailing preferential tariff rate.

3. Depending on the product in question, this rule requires that either all non-originating components shift their tariff headings pursuant to the tariff nomenclature established under Mercosur; or all non-originating components shift their tariff headings and the finished product meets a regional value test. The Mercosur regional value test specifies that the value of originating goods may not be less than 60 percent of the free-on-board (FOB) value of the exported good.

4. A final rule applies if a particular product does not meet the requirements established by any of the other three rules, it permits a product to qualify as originating if the total value of non-originating materials incorporated into the finished product does not exceed 40 percent of the final export value of the finished product.

Sensitive Products Each country may maintain a list of sensitive products that enjoy extended protection from the complete elimination of tariffs on intrabloc trade. These products will be protected for an additional four years in Argentina and Brazil and five years in Paraguay and Uruguay.

Macroeconomic Policy Coordination Mercosur aims to harmonize fiscal, monetary, capital, and external trade policies in all sectors to guarantee adequate competitive conditions among member states. However, the reconciliation of pertinent laws in the individual member countries to make regulation compatible has so far not been a high priority issue in the various member countries. In fact, there are several substantial points of contention. An underlying problem has been the huge disparity in economic policy development among the members. Argentina, Uruguay, and Paraguay have achieved some semblance of stability through economic stabilization programs that seek to curb inflation, achieve fiscal balances, and open their economies. Brazil, the dominant economy in the group, has anti-inflation and privatization programs that are still in their infancy, and it maintains many export subsidies as well as tariff protections for key industries.

There are other gaps in coordination. As yet there has been no sign of any deal to coordinate member nation's policies regarding labor or the service industries, and social policies and programs differ vastly. Some steps have been taken toward coordinating the free movement of capital and the protection of foreign investment, but huge problems remain. Frontier bureaucracy has been one of Mercosur's leading practical enemies. At the twin-city interface of Uruguaiana (Brazil) and Paso de los Libres (Argentina), where 70 percent of Mercosur trade crosses the border, trucks in transit used to spend 12 to 24 hours awaiting customs clearance—excluding weekends, holidays, and frequent customs strikes. Train crews also used to lose a day clearing cargos at the border. This situation was changed as of January 1995, and Customs officials have agreed to make timely clearance a priority.

More mundane problems plague Mercosur's evolution into a full common market: for example, Uruguay's electrical system operates at 50 hertz while Brazil's is at 60; and transport companies have complained that the customs agents in the different countries had not yet learned to cooperate among themselves. These and many other issues will have to be resolved before true common market status can be achieved.

Expansion The Mercosur agreement provides that its membership base may be expanded and individual countries or other regional trading blocs allowed to join, after an initial period of five years and with the unanimous consent of the existing member states.

Automobiles Both Argentina and Brazil agreed to exempt their competing automobile industries from the free trade provisions of Mercosur.

Foreign Trade Zones Foreign trade zones in Tierra del Fuego (Argentina) and Manaus (Brazil) will continue to function with duty-free entry for nonbloc goods until 2013. Goods entering from all other foreign trade zones within Mercosur are subject to applicable CET duties.

Sectoral Agreements Adoption of interbloc agreements in various industries—such as services, transport, communications, and agriculture—is an integral part of Mercosur, necessary to accelerate the integration process and optimize the use of factors of production. These are designed to enable governments and private enterprise to take advantage of economies of scale; they favor intrasectoral specialization based on the respective comparative advantages, the intramarket complementation, and the formation of strategic partnerships so as to compete more efficiently in world markets. While government participation has so far been limited to a joint endeavor to build the Paraguay-Paraná Waterway, private enterprises are scrambling to merge and form joint ventures in order to take advantage of the huge Mercosur market more efficiently.

Conflict Resolution Controversies between member states are to be settled by direct negotiation. If no solution is reached, the controversy may be submitted for consideration by the Common Market Group, which must make its recommendations within 30 days. If either party disagrees with the recommendation the controversy will be submitted to an arbitration procedure established under the Brasilia Protocol. The panel will consist of three arbiters chosen from a list of 40 persons nominated by the four member countries. The arbiters' awards are binding on the parties. If disputes arise over trade policy matters and if no solution can be reached, the Ouro Preto Protocol allows the Mercosur trade commission to submit the question to the procedures established under the Brasilia Protocol.

Private Enterprise within Mercosur

Although most Latin American businesspeople list the US or the EU (or various of its member states) as their primary foreign markets, more and more acknowledge the growing importance of Mercosur to their companies' futures. By integrating the region's economies and creating a larger market, Mercosur potentially allows businesses to exploit economies of scale in serving such important sectors as agribusiness, electronics, aircraft and parts, chemicals, computers and peripherals, telecommunications, auto parts, and financial services.

Businesspeople have been quick to grasp this potential advantage. Indeed, they seem to be taking the lead in pushing for the harmonization of the participants' operations. Suppliers, faced with orders from different countries for similar parts, have been working with the various manufacturers to standardize specifications and production. Among the most popular common ventures to date have been automobiles and vehicle parts, beverages, furniture, ceramics, metal products, telecommunications services, and water and sewage service. More than 400 cross-border joint ventures and business associations have been agreed to so far, and projects include both commercial and manufacturing undertakings. In Argentina alone, more than 150 major domestic and multinational companies have entered into joint ventures or have merged their operations so as to serve the entire Mercosur market from one location.

Much of the trade increase has come from Brazilian companies. In the last four years, 320 Brazilian companies have set up offices in Argentina, investing a total of US$1.5 billion and accounting for a substantial percentage of total direct foreign investment in Argentina during the period. Their presence has also served to reassure—and stimulate the competitive interest of—other foreign and multinational investors, who do not care to be left behind. Brazil is also fast becoming Argentina's primary customer for its exports of natural resources and commodity products. More significantly, the Argentine pampas are becoming Brazil's breadbasket: Brazil absorbed almost half of Argentina's cereal grain shipments in 1994. These figures include almost 80 percent of Argentine rice exports, 70 percent of wheat exports, and 42 percent of its flour exports. Brazil also bought 55 percent of Argentina's dried fruit exports and 36 percent of its dairy products exports.

International automakers have been especially eager to jump into the Mercosur market using Argentina—with its growing emphasis on and installed capacity in automotive products—as a manufacturing base. Both General Motors and Chrysler left Argentina in 1982; both have now returned. Chrysler is negotiating to return in a partnership with a local manufacturer, while General Motors has already formed a joint venture with Ciadea, the Argentine assembler of and dealer in Renault products, to start up a US$100 million plant. Toyota plans to make 20,000 trucks a year for the Mercosur market by 1996, and Mazda and Mercedes Benz have also announced plans to build truck assembly plants in Argentina. Saab-Scania has gone even further—it now manufactures motors in its Argentine plant, builds transmissions in Uruguay, and performs final assembly of its trucks and buses in Brazil.

However, an important existing cross-border private industry joint venture, Autolatina, consisting of the Ford and Volkswagen operations in both Argentina and Brazil, broke up in late 1994, just as Mercosur was going into effect; the parties announced, rather abruptly, that their joint goals had been achieved and that their individual proposed future courses called for an independent rather than a concerted approach. Nevertheless, both companies will continue to operate in both markets.

Mercosur's Emerging Trade Agreements

Beyond surge in trade among member nations, Mercosur is becoming an important event around

which overall South American economic integration appears to be coalescing, auguring stronger economic ties across Latin America and beyond. The Mercosur agreement allows for—indeed expects—additional bilateral and multilateral agreements between the bloc and both individual countries and other trading blocs. The agreement stipulates that with the approval of all the member countries, any further country can join the bloc after a period of five years.

Chile Chile has been a keen and wary observer of the development of Mercosur, expressing its desire to associate with the bloc. No wonder: Brazil and Argentina are Chile's third and fourth largest trading partners, and about 40 percent of Chile's manufactured goods are sold to Mercosur states. However, Mercosur stipulates that members may not participate in other free trade areas—a problem for Chile, which has joined the Asia Pacific Economic Cooperation (APEC) and is actively seeking membership in NAFTA. However, APEC is at present only a formal agreement, with the inauguration of actual trade under its auspices not expected to begin until the next decade; Chile was also formally invited to join NAFTA late 1994, with negotiations expected to get underway in May 1995, although there is no expectation of an early admission to the pact.

Chile claims that it is not seeking full membership in Mercosur, but only desires to further economic cooperation and the creation of a free trade zone. However, the achievement of even these limited aims faces further difficulties: Chile's low (11 percent) tariff will be hard to reconcile with Mercosur's 14 percent average external tariff, and Brazil is not likely to agree to any further reduction in the CET. Chile's sophisticated financial economy will also be difficult to reconcile with Brazil's new *real* stabilization plan or Argentina's fixed exchange rate. On the other side, there is fear within Chile that products from Brazil's huge pulp, textile, and footwear industries and Argentina's powerful agricultural sector will invade tiny Chile and overrun its much smaller domestic industries. Nonetheless, talks continue, and many observers contend that Chile will associate in some form with Mercosur in the not so distant future.

Other Latin States Like Chile, Venezuela and Mexico are interested in negotiating agreements during 1995 to end customs and other barriers between themselves and the members of Mercosur. It is likely they will join Mercosur as full members when they are able to do so. Bolivia is currently conducting talks with Mercosur, although it is already a member of the Andean Pact (AP).

Most trade is already duty free among the Andean Pact nations of Venezuela, Colombia,

Ecuador, Peru, and Bolivia. On January 1, 1995, these five nations formed a separate customs union by adopting CETs averaging 14 percent. Negotiations on merging Mercosur and AP into a single bloc—tentatively called the South American Free Trade Association (SAFTA)—are already underway and could be completed as early as 1996.

NAFTA Mercosur has expressed guarded interest in joining with NAFTA toward forming a super-regional, New World free trade area. So far, this desire has not been enthusiastically received in the US, which has put off making any firm commitment to the bloc. Independently, the US has shown more interest in negotiating a bilateral trade treaty with Mercosur as an entity than in forming any type of trade agreement through NAFTA. However, Canada insists that any such agreements should be focused exclusively through NAFTA to avoid creating a maze of potentially contradictory trade treaties. Some observers worry that separate agreements would create more confusion for companies trying to sort out which arrangements apply to which country.

The Rose Garden—or "Four Plus One"—agreement was signed in 1991 to provide the US and Mercosur members with a structure within which to negotiate reciprocal trade and investment arrangements. Specifically, it provides the US with the means to negotiate with Mercosur members collectively rather than having to negotiate with each country individually, while it also allows the members of Mercosur to speak with a more powerful united voice than would likely be available to them separately.

The European Union The European Union (EU) has already enthusiastically opened talks with Mercosur officials and appears committed to drafting some sort of free trade agreement during 1995.

ASOCIACIÓN LATINOAMERICANA DE INTEGRACIÓN (LATIN AMERICAN INTEGRATION ASSOCIATION)

Established in 1980 to replace the Latin American Free Trade Associaton (LAFTA), Asociación Latinoamericana de Integración (ALADI)—or the Latin American Integration Association (LAIA)—was the dominant regional body dealing with Latin American trade prior to the development of Mercosur. It is a loose association of 11 Latin American countries with a flexible mandate to establish, in a gradual and progressive manner, a Latin American common market. In implementing this goal, ALADI has encouraged bilateral, subregional, and panregional trade and tariff agreements. This elastic manner of promoting economic integration reflects the vastly different political and economic climates of the member countries.

The members of ALADI are divided into three categories: most developed—Argentina, Brazil, and Mexico; intermediate—Chile, Columbia, Peru, Uruguay, and Venezuela; and least developed—Bolivia, Ecuador, and Paraguay—which enjoy a special preferential system. The differential benefits go to the less and least developed countries by application of the "principle of nonreciprocal treatment" when they sign their bilateral tariff arrangements with the more developed countries. The least developed countries receive MFN treatment, thereby receiving the same rights other ALADI countries obtain through their bilateral treaties. The Andean Common Market countries (Colombia, Peru, Venezuela, Bolivia, and Ecuador) function as a single trading nation and do not grant individual tariff concessions or tariff cuts on any item greater than those granted to other Andean Pact members. More than 23,000 tariff cuts have been implemented, although inter-ALADI trade still accounts for only about 11 percent of the member countries' total exports.

ALADI provides for and encourages multilateral links or agreements with Latin American nonmember countries or integration organizations, as well as with other developing countries or economic groups outside the continent. Indeed, most Central American countries, plus Cuba, Italy, Portugal, Russia, Spain, Switzerland, the EU, and the Organización de Estados Americanos (OEA)—the Organization of American States (OAS)—all participate in ALADI as observers.

As the development of Mercosur has gained momentum, ALADI has made independent attempts to strengthen its own role in Latin American integration. It has sought to expand intra-ALADI trade, provide additional support for less developed members, expand and diversify fields of cooperation, and harmonize macroeconomic policies among its members. However, little progress has been made in this regard due to the primary focus of the more powerful members on Mercosur (or NAFTA) commitments. ALADI may yet serve a strategic role in the region as a bridge between Mercosur and the Andean Pact (AP), as well as among Mercosur, AP, and NAFTA.

OTHER MULTILATERAL COOPERATION AGREEMENTS

Organización Latinoamericana de Energía (Latin American Energy Organization) Organización Latinoamericana de Energía (OLADE) was formed with the objective of providing a cooperative (but not a supranational) organization to provide a framework for the integration, conservation, sale, defense, and development of oil and other energy resources within the region. Its members include all the Latin American countries, except Belize and French Guyana, plus Barbados, Cuba, the Dominican Republic, Grenada, Haiti, Jamaica, and Trinidad and Tobago.

Sistema Económico Latinoamericano (Latin American Economic System) Sistema Económico Latinoamericano (SELA) was created in 1975 to formulate common economic strategies among member states, to encourage the formation of Latin American–based multinational companies, and to develop a code of conduct for transnational companies operating in the region. SELA determines and presents the collective position of its members in international forums; somehow the members have reached a consensus on their position with regard to such difficult issues as the restrictions that the US imposes on raw materials produced by underdeveloped countries and the provisions of US foreign trade law considered to be discriminatory against such nations.

Cairns Group Established in 1986 by major agricultural exporting countries that do not subsidize these exports, this organization strives to bring about reforms in international agricultural trade, including reductions in export subsidies, barriers to access, and internal support measures. It also represents its members' interests in GATT negotiations. Members include Argentina, Australia, Brazil, Canada, Chile, Colombia, Fiji, Hungary, Indonesia, New Zealand, the Philippines, Thailand, and Uruguay.

RELATED AGREEMENTS

Customs Cooperation Council Argentina belongs to and adheres to the policies and procedures of the Customs Cooperation Council (CCC), a multilateral body located in Brussels, through which participating countries seek to simplify and rationalize customs procedures. The CCC also examines technical aspects and related economic factors of customs systems; it develops policy positions designed to obtain harmony and uniformity and to simplify customs formalities.

Inter-American Development Bank The Inter-American Development Bank (IDB) was founded to promote the individual and collective development of regional developing member countries through the financing of economic and social development projects and the provision of technical assistance. Loans are made to governments or private entities for specific economic and social development projects and for sectoral reform programs. These loans are repayable in the currencies lent, and their terms range from 15 to 40 years. The Fund for Special Operations enables the IDB to make concessionary

loans for economic and social projects when circumstances call for special treatment, including lower interest rates and longer repayment terms.

International Chamber of Commerce The International Chamber of Commerce (ICC) is composed of various commissions made up of businesspersons and experts from various sectors. The commissions produce a wide array of specific codes and guidelines of direct use to the world business community and comment in detail on proposed actions by intergovernmental organizations, such as GATT, that are likely to affect business.

Intellectual Property Rights Argentina officially adheres to most treaties and international agreements on intellectual property rights, including the Paris Convention for the Protection of Industrial Property, the Brussels and Paris Texts of the Bern Convention, the Universal Copyright Convention, the Geneva Phonogram Convention, the Treaty of Rome, and the Treaty on the International Registration of Audiovisual Works. It is a member of the World Intellectual Property Organization (WIPO). The GATT Uruguay Round agreement specifically addresses patent protection, including pharmaceuticals, and Argentina has recently introduced changes in its intellectual property law to bring Argentina into compliance with these requirements.

Organización de Estados Americanos (Organization of American States) The Organización de Estados Americanos (OEA, or OAS in English)—the oldest international organization in the world—has recently begun to intensify its efforts to promote economic and trade cooperation among its members. Long considered a relatively weak body, it has recently attempted to take the lead in coordinating and integrating the many regional trade pacts between its members—including the participants in Mercosur, the Andean Group, and NAFTA—into the eventual creation of a free trade zone encompassing the entire North and South american continents.

United Nations Conference on Trade and Development and Economic Commission for Latin America and the Caribbean These UN agencies (known respectively as UNCTAD and ECLAC) strive to promote the international trade of developing countries in an effort to accelerate economic development. Like the OAS, they may have some value as a bridge in building a hemispheric free trade zone.

EMERGING TRADE AGREEMENTS

Free Trade Area of the Americas At the "Summit of the Americas," held in Miami in December 1994, all of the hemisphere's leaders except Cuba's Fidel Castro—who was not invited— agreed to set up a Free Trade Area of the Americas (FTAA) covering the entire western hemisphere by the year 2005. Some 23 pacts already exist among the various participants, and one goal is to harmonize these into a single agreement encompassing the hemisphere's combined US$13 trillion economy and 850 million people. The hemisphere is a large and growing market: US exports to Latin America more than doubled between 1985 and 1993, from US$30 billion to US$79 billion; Latin America and the Caribbean are experiencing sustained economic expansion and generally declining inflation; and foreign direct investment to Latin America doubled from 1990 to 1993, reaching almost US$15 billion in 1993. The conference agreed to pursue economic integration involving free trade along the lines of NAFTA, although Argentina held out the grander hopes of creating a "subsidy-free hemisphere" by 2005.

However, there are numerous major obstacles to the realization of such an ambitious partnership. Not least among these concerns is that many of the partners are currently competitors in important industries that remain protected domestically. The political difficulties of exposing these markets to foreign trade may prove too great for many governments. Widely differing levels of economic development and vastly different labor and environmental laws are also likely to slow the conclusion of any partnership among these countries. But perhaps the biggest threat to formation of an FTAA is the fear by many Latin American countries that the US will dominate the agenda. This does not sit well with many Latin countries (especially Argentina), because they do not strictly adhere to US policies and consider them to be intrusive. Although the US generally sees NAFTA as providing the working model for an FTAA, both Argentina and Brazil claim that they intend to stay focused on Mercosur and on building its contacts with the Andean Group, the EU, and the Asian regional blocs such as the Associ-

ation of Southeast Asian Nations (ASEAN). Argentina favors expansion of the freer, more liberal market provisions of Mercosur over what it considers to be the more limited liberalization offered under NAFTA.

The OAS, which has been given the lead in creating an FTAA, has been saying that it will concentrate on coordinating and integrating the many regional trade blocs already in existence. However, many summit participants have expressed doubt that the OAS is strong enough to manage the negotiations necessary to complete the overall unifying pact.

North American Free Trade Agreement The North American Free Trade Agreement (NAFTA) created an economic bloc consisting of the US, Canada, and Mexico, which in 1993 had a combined GDP greater than $6.5 trillion. NAFTA calls for the gradual elimination of tariff and nontariff barriers in a variety of areas and removes numerous impediments to investment, such as performance requirements and exclusionary approval procedures. Its scope is more limited than that of Mercosur, and it does not come close to creating a common market among its participants. Still, NAFTA has already had a major positive influence on trade among its member states.

Argentina is looking to integrate its markets with NAFTA, either individually or through Mercosur. Formal talks have not yet commenced, although the prospect has been a topic of discussion among officials of the countries involved. This market is extremely important to Argentina, and Argentina has expressed interest in negotiating a greater opening for its exports. The US response to Argentina's preliminary inquiries has been cautious. Officials in the US have indicated that Argentina must first open its own markets and improve its labor and environmental laws before it can gain the level of access to the US market that is now afforded to Canada and Mexico.

Import Policy & Procedures

INTRODUCTION

As a result of major changes beginning in mid-1989, Argentina's new liberal trade regime has virtually eliminated most nontariff barriers to imports. In response to problems in its domestic industries, it has reduced the level and application of import duties. On January 1, 1995, the Mercado Común del Sur (the Southern Common Market, or Mercosur) went into full effect. In March 1995 a new package of economic measures designed to increase revenues while further reducing expenditures was put in place in response to a worldwide financial crisis triggered by the December 1994 devaluation of the Mexican peso. As part of these measures, Argentina increased some tariff levels affecting goods included on its list of exceptions to the Mercosur Common External Tariff (CET), specifically capital goods, informatics, and telecommunications equipment.

Under the reforms begun in 1989, the highest tariff rate was reduced to 20 percent (from as high as 50 percent), although exceptions were made allowing higher special tariff rates on sensitive products such as automobiles, auto parts, and consumer electronics. Argentina's trade liberalization program has also eliminated many specific duties; substantially simplified document requirements; and opened the trade registry to all potential exporters and importers (listing on this registry—which was formerly used to limit entities allowed to operate in external trade—is required to officially engage in export and import business).

CONTENTS

This chapter discusses Argentina's policies and procedures for importing into the country. Such information is useful to persons seeking to sell goods and services to Argentina, firms deciding whether to establish a manufacturing facility or other operation in Argentina, foreign investors interested in investing in an entity located in Argentina, and persons in Argentina who are seeking to import from sources outside the country. (Refer to the "Marketing" chapter, beginning on page 177, for a discussion of the sales channels in Argentina and the "Business Entities & Formation" chapter, beginning on page 191, for information on establishing a company in Argentina.)

IMPORT POLICIES

Argentina has recently become one of the most open economies in the world, with a policy based on the idea of liberalized international trade and complementarity. By reducing high tariff rates and eliminating most nontariff barriers, Argentina has made major strides toward eliminating a discriminatory bureaucratic system. That system had enhanced the status of a relatively small number of local beneficiaries while serving to block the efforts of others, on both the inside and the outside, to participate in the economy.

With the creation of Mercosur, Argentina has become part of the largest market bloc in South America. This regional trade alliance with Brazil, Paraguay, and Uruguay seeks to eliminate all trade restrictions among the member states and to adopt a CET and trade policy towards other countries. (Refer to the "Trade Agreements" chapter, beginning on page 65, for a detailed discussion of Mercosur.)

Government Regulation

The principal authority governing trade policy is the Secretaría de Comercio e Inversiones (Secretariat of Trade and Investment). This body, in conjunction with the president and the Ministerio

IMPORTING GLOSSARY

ad valorem tariff A tariff assessed as a percentage of the value of the imported merchandise.

Asociación Latinoamericana de Integración (ALADI) An organization created to replace the Latin American Free Trade Association (LAFTA), ALADI includes Argentina, Bolivia, Brazil, Chile, Colombia, Ecuador, Mexico, Paraguay, Peru, Uruguay, and Venezuela. *See also* Mercosur.

cost, insurance, and freight (CIF) value The CIF value of goods includes the value of the goods plus the necessary costs and freight to bring the goods to the named port of destination, along with the cost of obtaining insurance and the cost of premiums paid to insure the goods during the carriage.

drawback The drawback regime provides a mechanism for refunding import duties on products destined for export. Duties and some taxes on imports that are directly used in exports are rebated under drawback, including tariffs, the 3 percent statistical fee on imports, and the value-added tax (VAT) of 21 percent. To benefit from the drawback system, the imported goods must be substantially transformed or directly used in the production of export goods.

General Agreement on Tariffs and Trade (GATT) A multilateral trade agreement aimed at expanding international trade. GATT's main goals are to liberalize world trade and place it on a secure, stable, regulatory basis. GATT is the only multilateral instrument that lays down agreed-upon rules for international trade. Implemented by the organization known as GATT and now called the World Trade Organization (WTO), it is the principal international body concerned with negotiating the reduction of trade barriers, applying the terms of the Uruguay Round agreements, and improving international trade relations.

Harmonized System (HS) A multipurpose international goods classification system designed to be used by manufacturers, transporters, exporters, importers, customs officials, statisticians, and others in classifying goods that move in international trade under a single commodity code. The system contains approximately 5,000 headings and subheadings of goods generally organized by industry.

legal kilo / legal weight The total weight of the merchandise and its own packaging, but excluding exterior containers or packing materials. For example, the legal weight of canned vegetables would include the vegetables and the can, but not the crate and wrappings for shipping.

Mercosur (Mercado Común del Sur or Southern Common Market) This regional trade alliance formed in 1991 seeks to create a free trade zone by 1995. Members are: Argentina, Brazil, Paraguay, and Uruguay. This alliance has the objective of establishing the free circulation of goods, services, and factors of production, achieving unified customs, coordinating fiscal and exchange policies, and setting a common external tariff and trade policy.

Project María A full-scale computerization of all areas of Argentina's customs service nationwide, which will establish a mechanism to expedite exporting and importing products in a matter of hours, provide daily information on foreign trade to improve control over unfair trading practices, and reduce the number of illegal acts by providing better valuation and control of imports.

Temporary Admission Regime (TAR) The TAR consists of duty-free admission of imported primary and intermediate goods and packaging to be used in export production. Exports must be completed within 180 days of admission.

value-added tax (VAT) An indirect tax on consumption that is assessed on the increased value of goods at each point in the chain of production and distribution, from the raw material stage to final consumption. The tax on processors or merchants is levied on the amount by which they increase the value of the items they purchase and resell.

de Economía (Ministry of Economy) sets broad trade and import policy. The Secretaría de Ingresos Públicos (the Secretariat of Fiscal Revenue of the Ministry of Economy) drafts customs rules, regulations, and tariffs, supervising the Administracíon Nacional de Aduanas (National Customs Administration). Customs is responsible for administering the Código Aduanero (Customs Code), which establishes specific policy and procedures governing foreign trade and the entry, exit, transport, and control of goods. Other agencies important to the importing process include the Ministerio de Salud y Acción Social (Ministry of Public Health and Social Action)—which handles the required registration of pharmaceuticals and other health products prior to importation—the Secretaría de Industria (the Industrial Secretariat)—which the automotive industry and imports of vehicles—and the Secretaría de Agricultura, Ganadería, y Pesca (Secretariat of Agriculture, Livestock, and Fishing, or SAGyP)—which regulates agricultural and livestock imports.

Tariffs and Other Import Charges

Argentine Customs uses the Harmonized Commodity Description and Coding System (HS) for classifying goods and assigning tariffs.

Rates of Tariffs Basic tariff rates—applied to the CIF (cost, insurance, and freight) value of imports—are:

- 0 (zero) tariff on some goods not produced domestically, as well as on some specific items such as newsprint, certain petroleum products, and others;
- 2.5 to 10 percent on raw materials, intermediate industrial materials, and primary products;
- 10 percent on capital goods, informatics, and telecommunications goods;
- 15 to 20 percent on consumer durable and non-durable goods; and
- 20 percent on finished automobiles.

Higher tariffs apply to a series of products included in the list exceptions established by Argentina within the framework of the Mercosur CET and in accordance with its Automotive Sector Regime in effect until the year 2000. This regime establishes higher tariffs for commercial importers and individuals, who are collectively authorized to import automobiles equivalent in value to a maximum of 10 percent of the value of domestic Argentine production of automobiles during the previous year. Quantitative limits—quotas—are applicable to products in sensitive sectors coming from Brazil at a zero tariff rate, including paper, steel products, and some home appliances, such as refrigerators and freezers. Special duty rates are also applicable to imports of textile fabrics and arti-

cles of apparel. Importation of used capital goods and equipment is restricted; such imports are subject to a 20 percent duty rate and customs inspection to certify that the goods have been adequately reconditioned and updated to be acceptable, as well as to verify the valuation used. Such used articles must carry certification from the supplier attesting to the type, degree, and quality of reconditioning of the equipment, confirmed by the Argentine Embassy in the country of origin of the goods.

Other Fees and Taxes

Additional fees and taxes that apply to imports to Argentina include:

- 3 percent statistical tax on the CIF value, except for capital goods, informatics, and telecommunications products;
- 21 percent value-added tax (VAT) on the CIF value plus tariff plus statistics tax (VAT is applied to all products regardless of whether they are imported or produced in Argentina);
- 6 to 8 percent advanced VAT on CIF plus tariff, plus statistics fee on all imports, depending on the frequency of importation (deductible from gross income tax);
- 3 percent anticipated profits tax on all consumer goods (deductible from gross income tax); and
- Excise taxes that may also be owed on specific products (these are levied regardless of whether the product is imported or produced in Argentina); these taxes range from 4 to 66 percent and are levied on such goods as cigarettes (66 percent); whiskey (50 percent); other hard liquor (30 percent); beer (4 percent); soft drinks (24 percent); tires (27 percent); lubricants (23–25 percent); and electronic products (10–24 percent).

Before customs grants clearance, all taxes must be paid and registered through the Certificado Unico de Impuestos y Tributos (Unitary Certificate of Taxes and Duties, or CUIT) document.

The Ministry of Economy has stated that it intends to announce any changes in tariffs and fees six months prior to their implementation. Under Mercosur the tariff schedules of Argentina and Brazil are to converge over time. However, given the economic crisis at the beginning of 1995, changes are likely to be made without this advance notice period being fully observed.

Fines and Penalties Customs law imposes fines and penalties for false declarations of quantity and quality. A false declaration of quantity or value can result in a fine of 2 to 10 times the difference between the falsely declared value and what is assessed as the normal CIF value, based on recent prices. For false declarations of quality or kind of merchandise, a fine of as much as twice the normal CIF value of the true quality or kind, as verified by appraisal, is applied against all merchandise falsely declared. If both quantity and quality are falsely declared, the maximum applicable fine is imposed.

Antidumping and Countervailing Duty Laws Argentina considers that dumping exists when the export price of imported merchandise is lower than the comparable sales price in normal commercial operations of identical or, failing that, similar goods destined for consumption in the domestic market of the country of origin or the country from which they are received. These issues are covered by Laws 24.176 and 24.425; GATT Regulations on Antidumping and Countervailing Duties; and Decrees 2121/94 and 106/95.

Drawback Argentina's liberal trade regime provides a mechanism for refunding various import charges on inputs used in production for export. The following charges are rebated: tariffs, the 3 percent statistical tax on imports, and the VAT of 21 percent. To benefit from the drawback system, the imported goods must be substantially transformed or incorporated in the production of export goods.

Restrictions and Prohibitions on Imports

Argentina's efforts to liberalize its economy have resulted in the lifting of many controls and restrictions on imports. Only a few remain in effect.

Import Licenses Argentina no longer requires import licenses, except for imports of automobiles.

Import Permits Certain hazardous or otherwise controlled items—such as explosives, arms, and ammunition—and certain foodstuffs—including artificial sweeteners—require an import permit.

Registration of Importers Importers must be registered with Customs. Imported goods must be cleared through customs by registered importers, using licensed customs agents. However, Argentina's liberal trade regime has opened the trade registry to essentially all potential importers, making this requirement more of a formality than the limitation that it was previously.

Quotas Permanent quotas remain on goods such as automobiles. Temporary quotas exist on paper, pulp, and a few other items.

Sanitary Certificates Many food-related imports require a sanitary certificate. In addition, Argentine law requires that all shipments of livestock, plants, bulbs, cuttings, rhizomes, roots, and tubers for propagation be accompanied by a sanitary certificate issued by a competent authority in the exporting country. The same requirement applies to grains and plant products (such as barley and peanuts) and all seeds—except coffee and cocoa beans imported without hulls for immediate roasting—unless they are accompanied by a "Certificate for Industrial Use

Only," signed by an official inspector in the exporting country and given a visa by an Argentine Consul. Salted and dried fish must also be covered by a sanitary certificate.

The import of small quantities—such as of vegetable seed weighing less than 500 gm (1 lb, 1 oz) and of forage seed weighing less than 200 gm (7 oz)—sent by mail or carried into Argentina in a passenger's baggage, of plants in transit, and of samples without value do not require a sanitary certificate. However, they will be inspected upon arrival.

Restrictions on Specific Products The importation of various products requires prior governmental approval:

Cottonseed and Seed Potatoes Potatoes for consumption or seed must conform to certain specifications and be labeled and packed in conformity with regulations.

Fresh Fruit Importation of fresh fruit in bulk is not allowed, with the exception of bananas. The exporting country must pack the fruit in specified containers, and some fruits must be wrapped individually in a certain type of tissue. Special labeling requirements also apply.

Barreled Apples These goods must be accompanied by an inspection certificate verifying that they are free from certain plant pests and diseases. Apples and pears must be shipped in refrigerated compartments.

Fresh Vegetables Special packing and labeling requirements apply to these goods.

Live Poultry, Dressed Fowls, Eggs (Both for Consumption and Reproduction) Special regulations cover these products. Dressed poultry must be processed in establishments in the exporting country approved by the General Administration of Animal Health of the Secretariat of State for Agriculture and Livestock (which maintains a registry of approved establishments).

Salted and Dried Fish In addition to being covered by a sanitary certificate from the country of origin, these products must be packed in boxes lined with either greased paper or tin, and the weight of the individual boxes must not exceed 50 kg (110 lb).

Insecticides and Veterinary Products These products must be registered with the Secretariat of Agriculture and Livestock. Insecticide registrations must be renewed every five years. Registration is the importer's duty, but the exporter is expected to supply required data on the commodity, samples, labels, and sanitary certificate.

Foodstuffs and Pharmaceuticals These products must be registered with the Argentine Ministry of Public Health. Pharmaceuticals registration must be renewed every five years. Registration is the responsibility of the importer, but the exporter is expected to supply necessary data on the product, samples, labels, and required sanitary certificates. Pharmaceutical imports may be entered but may not be sold until an authorization for sale is issued after a sample is analyzed from the shipment at customs. All pharmaceuticals labels must prominently display the following information:

- Laboratory's name, address, and name of contact point at laboratory;
- Product name and generic name (the lettering of both must be of equal size);
- Formula per pharmaceuticals unit;
- Expiration date;
- Instructions giving proper care for preservation and sale condition;
- Factory number, serial number, or both; and
- Logo clearly stating *Ministerio de Salud y Acción Social*, followed by its registration number.

Explosives, Arms, and Ammunition These products require an import permit from the Ministry of Defense.

Plants and Plant Materials These products must enter through certain specified ports and—except for preserved, pickled, or canned goods—are subject to inspection.

Dried or Preserved Fruit and Nuts Inspection certificates are not required for dried or preserved fruits, such as apples, damsons, figs, peaches, pears, plums, and raisins. However, they cannot be packed in bags of any kind. Almonds, carob beans, chestnuts, hazelnuts, pine kernels, walnuts, and other nuts must be packed in adequate standard type containers. Containers for both dried or preserved fruits and nuts must bear labels or inscriptions indicating the type of fruit or nut, country of origin, year of growth, grade, and net weight.

Tobacco (Raw and Cut) Importation of these products are allowed only through the ports of Buenos Aires, Rosario, Santa Fe, Paraná, and Bahía Blanca. A sanitary inspection must be completed before tobacco can clear customs.

Artificial Sweeteners Only persons or companies registered with the Ministry of Public Health may import items such as saccharine, and a special permit from the Ministry of Public Health is needed to clear each shipment through customs.

Imports Not Allowed to be Shipped by Mail Prohibitions on mail shipments to Argentina include the following products: coins; banknotes; currency; securities payable to bearer; traveler's checks; platinum, gold, or silver; precious stones; jewelry; other valuable articles except for insured packages; furs and skins of chinchilla and vicuña; radioactive material; radio and television receivers; phonographs and combination units (such as rack systems); ready-made clothes and fabric unless they are presents typical of those that would be given to individuals and having no commercial value; or perishable infectious biological substances.

Service Barriers to Imports

International Air Courier Tariff Rates The planned privatization and restructuring of the national mail system will streamline operations and bring currently existing high rates and fees into line with international levels.

Insurance Foreign insurance providers have not been able to directly enter major segments of Argentina's insurance market. However, the Argentine government actively encourages foreign companies to purchase existing national insurance companies.

Temporary Admission Regime

The Temporary Admission Regime (TAR) consists of a program for the duty-free admission of capital goods—such as machinery, equipment, instruments, molds, and patterns—and the materials, intermediate goods, and packaging to be used in export production. Exports using these products must also be completed and ready for export within 180 days from the admission of the inputs. This period of time may be extended for an additional 180 days. A bond must be posted in a value sufficient to cover the approximate amount of duty and other charges for regular import of the items; this will be canceled when the merchandise is reexported.

Argentina has not joined the Admission Temporair/Admisión Temporaria/Temporary Admission (ATA) Convention, which establishes the use of an international customs document known as the ATA Carnet for admission of products such as commercial samples. A carnet allows a person to bring merchandise temporarily into a member country for demonstration, show, and similar purposes without paying duties on it.

Free Trade Zones

Argentina has made provisions for duty-free foreign trade zones (FTZs), but has not yet developed these. Plans exist to develop FTZs in virtually every province as well as in La Plata (Buenos Aires Province), Rosario (Puerto Villa Constitución), and Concepción del Uruguay (Entre Ríos Province). Parties should check with the Secretariat of Industry to see whether an FTZ in question is actually functioning. Tierra del Fuego does have a Special Customs Area that allows duty-free imports of capital goods not produced in Argentina and planned for use in designated high-priority industries, as well as for goods to be assembled in local plants for sale in Argentina.

Samples

Sales Samples A traveling representative may bring samples into Argentina free of duty if they have no independent commercial value. If the samples have commercial value, a bond may be posted for the amount of duty that would be payable on such merchandise. Such bonds are good for 90 days and may be renewed for an additional 90 days. The bond is refunded upon exportation of the dutiable samples. Samples sent by parcel post or in other ways receive the same treatment as any other commercial shipment and are subject to the same documentary requirements. However, customs broker services are generally not needed to clear shipments of samples, with or without value. However, customs may charge storage fees.

Plant Samples With regard to plants and plant parts admitted, the weight of each sample must not exceed 200 gm (7 oz), and no more than two samples of the same species and origin, destined for a single consignee, may arrive at the same time via the same means of transportation. The phrase *Muestra sin Valor* (Sample without Value) must appear on inner containers, as well as outside wrappings. Application for inspection of seeds must be made prior to importation, and the importer or its agent may be present at the inspection. The combined sample weight from the same source, for the same consignee, arriving by the same means of transportation, may not be greater than 1 kg (2 lb, 3 oz) for flowers, forage crops, and vegetable seeds, and 3 kg (6 lb, 10 oz) for other seeds.

Advertising Matter

Customs assesses a duty on advertising matter imported into Argentina. However, in practice customs rarely assesses duty on single catalogs and price lists sent to individual addresses through the regular mail provided they are marked as *impresos* (printed matter) and are intended for informational purposes rather than for distribution. Items exempt from import duties include magazines and printed matter, pamphlets, posters, notebooks, calendars, photographs, records, and other articles for promotional purposes relating to merchandise sold by foreign companies when they are received free of cost. The value of these pieces may not exceed US$100 (or the equivalent in other foreign currencies). They must also carry fully visible, indelible printed or engraved copy or logos that prevent their sale.

The receipt of such duty-free shipments will be permitted only once per consignee in a given calendar year. A customs broker's services are generally not necessary to clear advertising matter received by parcel post from abroad, unless it is subject to other restrictions.

Standards for Product Quality and Safety

Argentina has signed the "Standards Code" negotiated and accepted during the Tokyo Round of Multilateral Trade Negotiations (MTN) under the General Agreement on Tariffs and Trade (GATT) (specifically the Uruguay Round Agreement on Technical Barriers to Trade). Generally, Argentine standards must be used, although, in some instances, foreign standards may be acceptable. To be safe, foreign exporters should request and follow any instructions from the Argentine importer. For further information, contact the Secretariat of Trade and Investments, Undersecretariat of Trade. (*See* "Useful Addresses" on page 88.)

Consumer Protection Measures

Argentine consumer protection law has been criticized for focusing on the preservation of individual rights without addressing marketplace abuses such as price fixing and monopolies. The Liga de Defensa del Consumidor (ADELCO), a consumer protection group formed in 1980, publishes several monthly reports on consumer research and information on how consumers can assert their rights. ADELCO also handles cases in which consumers seek redress for inferior goods or services.

Parties to an import transaction should check for regulations developed as a result of the 1993 Consumers Defense Law (No. 24,240), especially as they pertain to advertisements, warranties, repair, and after-sale services. Although consumer protection standards are not generally considered to be very strict, bias toward the individual consumer can result in problems for those introducing specific products into Argentine markets.

Environmental Protection Measures

Argentine environmental protection laws have been criticized as being relatively ineffectual. A central government environmental agency, the Secretaría de Recursos Naturales y Ambiente Humano (Secretariat of Natural Resources and Human Environment, SRNAH), has attempted to work with the provincial governments in creating a more effective environmental policy. However, until recently environmental concerns have been given a low priority, and the provinces continue to enjoy a great deal of autonomy in this area; most have passed their own environmental legislation, thus limiting the effectiveness of the SRNAH.

Similarly, Argentina's legislation on hazardous waste (No. 24,051) has had a limited impact. The law seeks to regulate production, handling, transport, disposal, storage, and other acts involving hazardous wastes, as well as to regulate the introduction of dangerous wastes generated in any foreign country into national territory, including into the air and maritime space claimed under Argentine jurisdiction. The penalty for violation of the law is imprisonment for up to 25 years. However, only some of the law's provisions are federal in nature. With the exception of Mendoza, which has ratified the law in its entirety, all other provinces have exempted themselves from specific provisions of the law.

Marking and Labeling

Retail Packages Numerous special rulings affect the marking of individual products, such as textiles and textile manufactures, hats, gloves, shoes, metal manufactures, sanitary articles and hardware, bricks, glazed tile or roof tile, glass and glass manufactures, furniture, cleaning articles, bazaar articles and toys, paper products and writing materials, rubber manufactures, hosiery, fertilizers, and gasoline pumps. To safeguard against fines, the exporter should request specific instructions from the importer as to how each product should be marked.

Argentine regulations provide that all imported goods should be inspected for country-of-origin marking while being cleared through customs. The general rules governing country of origin marking provide that if marks of any variety appear on the article itself, the country of origin must also appear in a visible place. If the article itself is too small for other marks to appear on it, the country of origin should be clearly indicated in a visible place on the container, wrapper, or principal label. If the principal label is too small, the country of origin may be shown on a supplementary label attached to the container on the same face as the principal label.

The label should also contain indications of quantity, quality, purity or mixture (when applicable), and the measurement or net weight in metric units. This information must be printed, lithographed, or painted on the label—size permitting—and on the retail wrapping, as well as on the general container. All packaged products must have metric labeling. For further information, refer to the provisions of Argentine Law 11.275 (Merchandise Marking Act); Law 22.802 (Commercial Loyalty Act); and Resolution 100/83 of the Secretariat of Trade.

Food and Beverages In the case of processed food, an exporter should make sure that a product's label and ingredients meet the requirements set forth by Argentine law. In the case of beverages shipped by casks, barrels, or demijohns which are subject to an Argentine internal revenue tax, the labels do not need to indicate volume because this information will appear on the internal revenue stamp.

Oils The name "edible oil" may be used only for oil extracted from a single basic material and mixtures of different comestible oils. To sell oil under the name of the basic material, such as "olive oil," it must be a pure edible oil, extracted solely from the substance indicated.

Electrical Products Argentine electric products use AC,1,3 phases, 2,4 wires, 50 cycle, 220/380 volts (220/440 volts DC, 2,3 wires).

Machinery The required markings should be shown in a visible place on a metal plate permanently affixed to the principal part of the machinery. The plate must be affixed by rivets, screws, bolts, or solder, or rendered immovable by some chemical substance.

Hazardous Materials Exporters to Argentina should ascertain from their importers whether the country currently adheres to the United Nations recommendations for the labeling and packing of hazardous materials, and how to conform to national standards to ensure the goods in question can be imported. For example, if the goods will be sent by air, the regulations of the International Air Transport Association (IATA), the International Civil Aviation Organization (ICAO), or both must be met. For goods going by boat, the latest International Maritime Organization (IMO) regulations should be consulted.

Credit and Payment Conditions

Argentina has eliminated all restrictions on import payments and has removed all foreign exchange controls. The Banco Central de la República Argentina (Central Bank, or BCRA) is required to buy or sell foreign exchange to maintain the fixed exchange rate.

Buyers and sellers usually use a letter of credit (L/C) to finance trade transactions, although they may negotiate other forms of payment, such as a sight draft with payment in 90 to 150 days. No minimum payment terms exist on L/Cs, and the private trading partners are free to negotiate payment terms on their own. L/Cs usually cost between 2 and 3 percent of the amount of the credit for first class firms having an established relationship with the issuing bank. For other firms, generally those that are smaller, represent new accounts, or are new to trade, the cost usually ranges from 4.5 to 5 percent. Letters of credit are generally valid for one year.

Open accounts may be established for long time customers with have proven payment track records. Forfaiting and other nontraditional payment transactions are relatively unfamiliar, but are beginning to be accepted in Argentina.

Countertrade

Generally, countertrade arrangements in Argentina have been limited to trade with the countries of the former Soviet Union, but these arrangements have not been used recently. Thus, Argentina has limited experience with barter and countertrade, with the exception of the payment arrangements under the bilateral clearing accounts with member countries of the Asociación Latinoamericana de Integración, or ALADI (the Latin American Integration Association—LAIA—in English). Under the current foreign exchange regime, there are no financial incentives to enter into countertrade arrangements. Moreover, only the government may operate countertrade transactions in traditional grain exports.

IMPORT PROCEDURES

In an international transaction, the seller and buyer must comply with two sets of requirements: the export regulations of the country from which the goods are shipped and the import regulations of the country to which the goods are delivered. This discussion focuses on the second step: bringing the goods into Argentina. Of course, shippers of goods must also abide by the export regulations of their own country, which may include export documentation, declarations, and licenses.

The customs procedures for entry into Argentina have traditionally been extensive and time consuming, making it costly to import into the country. In an effort to remedy this situation, Argentina's Customs Service has introduced Project María, an electronic data processing system, to allow for quicker, more efficient cargo clearance and payment of duties in the near future.

Argentine Customs has also hired and trained approximately 1,900 new officers, raising its personnel to approximately 5,100 agents. To reduce customs costs, Argentina has implemented a system for the selective control of merchandise in the case of imports. The use of unified *a posteriori* (after the fact) valuations and the simplification of regulations have minimized intervention by customs officials, thereby speeding the clearance of merchandise and reducing payments for extraordinary services.

On other fronts, Argentina has reorganized baggage control at the Ezeiza Airport. A system of red and green lights selects those persons subject to inspection on a random basis without participation by the individual customs agent.

Preshipment Stage

Preshipment Inspection Argentine Customs maintains no mandatory preshipment or postshipment inspection requirements.

Insurance Arrangements At the time the goods are shipped, a seller or importer may be required to present a certificate of insurance to the shipping company. The foreign exporter purchasing insurance should take care to follow the importer's instructions. Marine insurance can be obtained through virtually any insurance company, whether located in Argentina or abroad.

Sanitary Certificates For items requiring a sanitary certificate, the parties should make sure that the certificate states that the exporter has complied with all specified requirements. In addition, the exporter must ensure that all boxes, cases, divisions, and other packing components being used for the shipment are new.

Prior Authorization From Governmental Agency For products requiring prior authorization, the parties should contact the appropriate governmental agency for information on the authorization procedures. For more information, *see* "Restrictions on Specific Products" on page 80.

Marking and Packing

Shipping Cases Exterior packing cases should indicate shipping marks and numbers on at least two sides, showing gross and net weight in kilos. Brush or stencil marks are permissible. The shipping mark and the number of packages should be shown, although it is not necessary to number packages of uniform content, quality, weight, and size. If goods in the same shipment will be sent to different consignees, then appropriate marks should identify the goods. Parties should check special regulations covering the packing and marking of perishables, inflammables, and certain other goods.

Containers The Argentine government has passed regulations that apply specifically to shipments into Buenos Aires. All such cargos must be unitized, palletized, or containerized. Failure to comply with the regulations will subject the cargo to lightering or transfer to other port areas at the carrier's expense and delay to the vessel. These regulations provide that identification (markings) of all pieces must be identical to the documentation covering their import into Argentina, and that such markings must be legible and adhere to the specifications of the International Marine Organization (IMO).

All cargo that lends itself to containerization, unitization, or palletization must be presented to the carrier for shipment in the packaging system (containerized, unitized, or palletized) best suited for that particular commodity. Standard packaging requirements apply, namely that construction of all packages must adequately protect cargo subjected to normal cargo handling procedures; that material used to protect packaging must, when required, provide protection from dampness as well as temperature variation; and that bagged cargo not containerized, unitized, or palletized must be preslung in shipper-provided slings to facilitate handling and prevent damage. Consignees or shippers must also indicate on their sale or purchase documents the obligation to transport cargos as defined by these regulations.

Retail Packages Dealers and manufacturers in Argentina must send the Bureau of Commerce and Industry samples of labels, containers, wrappers, and advertising materials pertaining to packaged goods that are sold at retail, and must explain the source of any coined expressions serving as trademarks. In addition, they must legally justify their right to the use of the firm name or signature appearing on the labels or inscriptions. If the trademark has already been registered, they must submit proof of such registration.

When submitting labels used in their home country for approval, Argentine branches of foreign companies must submit a certificate from their home office, authenticated by the Argentine Consul serving that overseas area, stating that the accompanying label is an original that is actually in use in the sale of the product in the country of origin. This approval from the Bureau of Commerce and Industry of the Ministry of Agriculture seeks to prevent Argentine branches of foreign firms from using the label of a foreign concern on products that the foreign company does not actually manufacture or sell in its own country.

Documentation at Packing

Commercial Invoices An original and three copies, in Spanish, of the commercial invoice are required. Carbon, printed, or photocopied invoices may not be substituted for the original. Moreover, each copy of the invoice must be signed, manually, in ink, by a properly authorized member of the firm. The authorized member's name must be typed directly underneath the signature, followed by the member's title or position within the firm. A telephone number should also be included. If the shipper or agent is in charge of handling or completing the commercial invoice, a responsible agent should still sign the invoice.

The invoice should contain the following basic information:

- Place and date of execution;
- Full name and address of foreign exporter;
- Full name and address of consignee;
- Full name and address of agent (freight forwarder);
- Place or port from which the merchandise was exported;
- Means of transportation (ocean, air, or parcel post);
- Date of departure;
- Carrier's flag;
- Port or place of entry in Argentina; and
- Number of invoice.

In addition, the invoice should clearly display the following information:

- Origin of goods, and—if there are goods of various origins—the origin of each item;
- Marks and numbers on packages;
- Kinds of packages (such as wooden crates or steel barrels);
- Full and exact description of merchandise;
- Composition of the goods (for chemicals, cloth, or liquids), including purity, percentage of individual components in mixtures, and so forth;
- Quantity or number of packages;
- Gross and net metric weight of goods, including legal weight of goods;
- Exact identification marks on the shipping cases;
- Unit price per article, kilogram, or liter;
- Product prices by unit and totals according with the condition of the sale;
- Cost of freight and insurance; and
- In the case of FOB (free on board) prices, any expense incurred prior to loading on the vessel.

The invoice must contain the following declaration in Spanish:

"DECLARO BAJO JURAMENTO QUE LOS PRECIOS CONSIGNADOS EN ESTA FACTURA COMERCIAL SON LOS REALMENTE PAGADOS O A PAGARSE, Y QUE NO EXISTE CONVENIO ALGUNO QUE PERMITA SU ALTERACIÓN, Y QUE TODOS LOS DATOS REFERENTES A LA CALIDAD, CANTIDAD, VALOR, PRECIOS, ETC., Y DESCRIPCIÓN DE LA MERCADERÍA CONCUERDAN EN TODAS SUS PARTES CON LO DECLARADO EN LA CORRESPONDIENTE SHIPPER'S EXPORT DECLARATION."
(Translation: "I swear that the prices on this commercial invoice are those really paid or to be paid, and that no agreement exists that permits their modification, and that all data pertaining to quality, quantity, value, prices, etc., and description of the merchandise agree in all their parts with what was declared in the corresponding Shipper's Export Declaration.")

For shipments for which no payment will be made, the commercial invoice must still show the real value of goods for customs purposes. The same rule applies to regular invoices that show specific items for which no payment is involved.

Invoices must be clear and legible. No erasures or alterations are permitted. All originals must be typewritten. Photocopies are allowed, but must be signed—not merely initialed—in ink next to any photocopied signatures.

Commercial invoices that consist of more than one set must be properly stapled and well secured to prevent loss or substitution of any pages.

Pro-Forma Invoice Although not always necessary, the Argentine importer may request a pro-forma invoice for banking purposes or as the first step in negotiating an import contract. The pro-forma invoice or any other invoice that does not pertain to an actual shipment should include the following declaration, tailored to the purpose at hand, on each copy of the invoice:

"DECLARO BAJO JURAMENTO QUE LA PRESENTE FACTURA COMERCIAL SERÁ UTILIZADA PARA _____."
(Translation: "I swear that the present commercial invoice is to be used for _____.")

The pro-forma invoice need not be legalized by the consulate.

Bill of Lading The bill of lading should, at a minimum, be issued in one negotiable copy. Additional negotiable copies may be required by the importer, bank, steamship line, or other interested party. The bill of lading must include the following information:

- Name of the ship;
- Name of ship's captain;
- Port of registry;
- Registered tonnage;
- Name of the charterer or the shipper;
- Name of consignee (unless it is "to bearer" or "to order");
- Number of packages;
- Specific description of contents, quantity, quality, and marks of the goods;
- Port of loading and unloading, with declaration of port of call, if any;
- Amount of freight;
- Place, manner, and date of payment;
- Date of preparation of the document; and
- Signature of captain and of shipper (signature of shipping company and shipper should be signed manually, and not by facsimile).

Additionally, Circular RC-256 of the BCRA provides that all bills of lading must show the amount of freight and a statement "Freight Paid," or "Freight Payable at Destination" as appropriate.

Bills of lading covering general cargo must also indicate the weight and volume of each package, according to the manner in which freight charges are levied. Bills of lading covering other goods must indicate the total weight and volume of the shipment. In the case of "closed packages" of general cargo, the weight and volume should be shown for each package. However, this rule does not apply to casks, drums, or cases of wines or beverages; paints; lumber; or iron. In these instances, it will be necessary to show only the weight or the volume on which storage, slingage, or freight is payable.

Bills of lading made "to order" are generally recognized except for shipments of arms and munitions. Argentine regulations provide that an Argentine bank will be considered the owner of merchandise, and thus, liable for any charges incurred, such as storage costs, if the bill of lading is made out to its order. To avoid this situation, the exporter can have the bill of lading made "to order" endorsed in blank, and not list the bank as the "notify" party.

Customs does not allow the repetition of the number of packages shipped under one bill of lading.

Packing Lists In order to clear customs in Argentina, the packing list must describe the contents of each package. When parcels in the same lot contain the same contents, one description on the packing list will suffice. The packing list should be in Spanish; the original may be in English, French, Italian, or German; however, customs may require the importer to present a certified Spanish translation. The importer's instructions should be followed with regard to the number of copies needed.

No packing list is necessary for goods imported in bulk, such as coal, petroleum, or sand, or for articles identical in kind, characteristics, composition, or weight.

Certificates of Origin Although not generally required, certificates of origin may be requested by the Argentine importer or may be needed under terms of an L/C. A chamber of commerce can certify the certificate of origin. The certificates of origin should be presented in four copies (an original and three copies), together with other requisite documents.

Correction of Errors To correct steamship manifests as a result of errors in bills of lading, Argentine Customs Resolution No. 266 provides that the letter of correction must be signed within three days of the sailing of the vessel, or in any event, before the goods arrive at an Argentine port. The date of the signing the letter of correction must be certified by the maritime agent at the port of shipment, which for practical purposes is the vessel's steamship agent. This signature must be authenticated by the accredited agent of the vessel in Argentina. The letter of correction need not be legalized by the consulate.

Shipping and Transportation

Shipping documents should be filled out carefully and completely. To avoid fines and penalties, the shipping documents must accurately describe the exterior container used. For example, to describe a crate as a case may cause difficulties with Argentine Customs. In addition, case marks and numbers should correspond exactly with those appearing on the invoices and other documents.

Maritime Shipments The required documents for maritime shipments include: commercial invoice (original and three copies), bill of lading (minimum of one negotiable copy), and packing list (generally not required for bulk commodities or for articles identical in kind, characteristics, composition, or weight). Other documents that may be required include an insurance certificate (if the foreign exporter has purchased insurance), and a certificate of origin, if the terms of the importer, bank, or contract involved require it.

Air Cargo Shipments The required documents for air cargo shipments include: commercial invoice (original and three copies), air waybill (number of copies depends on requirements of importer and of airline used), and packing list.

Freight forwarding fees and agent fees cannot be shown on air waybills on a freight-collect basis, meaning that such fees must be prepaid.

Mail Service

Regular Mail Services Dutiable merchandise may be sent by regular mail to Argentina. However, Argentine Customs provides that in all cases the addressee must be present to authorize the opening, checking, and customs clearance of packages.

As an example, a US exporter must complete and attach US Customs labels and forms to send any of the following by regular mail to Argentina: letters and letter packages, postcards, printed matter, books (special rate), small packets, and direct sacks of prints. For each of the listed items, the US exporter must fill in a green customs label C1-Form 2976 (Authorization for Customs to Open International Mail) and attach it to the address side. With respect to nondutiable items of which the contents are valued at more than US$400, or if the US exporter does not want the contents of the nondutiable items to be described on the outside of the mailed package, the US exporter should attach the upper portion of the label on the outside and enclose a completed US Customs Declaration C2—Form 2976-A in the package. All packages containing dutiable items, irrespective of value, must have Form 2976 and two copies of Form 2976-A enclosed in the package. Additionally, the wrapper must be plainly marked, "Green Label Attached."

Parcel Post Services All parcels should be carefully packed and should bear the street addresses of the addressees and indicate the quantity and exact weight of each article enclosed in the parcel.

Parcels containing dutiable merchandise should be marked visibly *Sujeto a Derechos* (Subject to Tax or Duty). Argentine Customs regulations provide that, in all cases, the addressee must be present to authorize the opening, inspection, and customs clearance of packages.

In general, each commercial parcel must be accompanied by a consular invoice in duplicate. These invoices must include a signed declaration by the seller, similar to the one for commercial invoices (see above). The following items do not require consular invoices:

- Books, reviews, newspapers, printed papers, and scientific and literary periodicals, if no duty is payable;
- New or used effects or articles imported for noncommercial purposes or not of a salable nature or value, intended for personal use or consumption and which by reason of their quantity or type, give no grounds for indicating that they are intended for sale, and which do not exceed the value above which import duty would have to be paid;
- Goods in transit for other countries;
- Unused samples without salable value; brochures, posters, printed papers, diaries, almanacs, negatives, photographs, films, and other publicity articles advertising foreign goods or concerns, which are marked to prohibit their free sale;
- Spare parts and accessories for supplying or repairing foreign ships or aircraft in Argentina, if such are considered indispensable for the continuation of the journey;
- Costumes, properties, and other belongings of visiting theatrical companies;
- Goods returned to Argentina after definitive or temporary export unless a return invoice was explicitly requested when authorization for temporary export was granted; or
- Educational equipment or materials intended for schools or scientific research institutes, whether as purchases, gifts, loans, or technical or financial aid, on the condition that the Argentine Ministry of Foreign Affairs, International Trade, and Cult gives permission beforehand.

Parcels containing bees, plants, and seeds must be accompanied by an official sanitary certificate given a visa by an Argentine Consul. Parcels containing used linen and clothing must be accompanied by a certificate of disinfection issued by a competent authority in the country of origin and countersigned by an Argentine Consul. The wrapper must be marked "Disinfection Certificate Enclosed."

Express Mail International Service The Postal

Administration of Argentina has advised that express mail items must have the following endorsements or customs declaration. Business papers and documents should be labeled clearly next to the mailing label as BUSINESS PAPERS; no form is necessary. Merchandise samples, microfilm, microfiche, magnetic discs and tapes for computers, brochures with technical information on merchandise, and industrial plans and drawings require a form stating that the package may be opened. All merchandise and articles subject to customs duty require that the customs declaration form be included.

Entry of Goods

General Procedures The importer must initiate clearance of the goods within 15 days after the shipment arrives in Argentina. If, after 15 days the importer has not requested clearance, customs imposes a fine of 1 percent of the value of the merchandise and publishes the available information concerning the shipment. After 60 days without a request for clearance, customs puts the goods up for sale. The importer can retrieve the goods by paying the taxes and fines owed up to the time at which it is actually sold. After such a sale, customs deducts the amount of fines and duties owed at the time of sale, and rebates any excess to the importer, provider the importer can be located.

If the importer does not withdraw the merchandise within 15 days of requesting clearance, customs can authorize the sale of the merchandise upon request of the warehousing firm to cover storage costs.

Special Procedures Within 10 days of the arrival of a merchandise, the importer may present to customs an "Unknown Contents" statement, declaring that the importer does not know what is contained in the shipment. As a result, the importer requests an extended clearance period of 25 days to enable the importer to determine what is in the packages and arrange for clearance. If the merchandise is not cleared within the 25-day period, customs will impose a 1 percent fine and publish the available data, as per general procedures.

A request for "Suspensive Clearance" can be made 15 days after the packages arrive in Argentina. Such a request prevents customs from initiating the fine, publication, and sale procedures noted above for specified periods: three months, in the case of maritime transport and one month in the case of land transport. These periods can be extended once, by three months and one month, respectively. If the importer does not request clearance after these periods, customs sells the merchandise.

Transhipment Procedures All overseas merchandise in transit through Argentine ports to neighboring countries must be accompanied by a transshipment declaration. All documents should be clearly marked *mercadurias en tránsito* (merchandise in transit). These documents must be presented to Argentine Customs immediately upon the shipment's arrival.

Ports of Entry The main port of entry is Buenos Aires. Other ports include Quequén, Rosario, Bahía Blanca, La Plata, and Comodoro Rivadavia.

The main airport is Ezeiza Airport, which handles international flights. Other large airports include Jorge Newbery (mainly short distance internal flights), Córdoba, El Plumerillo, Jujuy, Resistencia, Río Gallegos, San Carlos de Bariloche, Corrientes, and Salta.

Inland Transportation

An important consideration for inland transport to the shipment's final destination is that most roads and railroads start at Buenos Aires, the country's main port of entry. Argentina has four main roads in its portion of the Pan-American Highway, as well as six railways.

To facilitate trade among Argentina, Bolivia, Brazil, Chile, Paraguay, Peru, and Uruguay, these countries signed an agreement in 1989 covering overland transportation. The agreement removes costly guarantees, especially in the areas of customs and insurance, the costs of which had been previously paid by the transport companies. Additionally, in 1990 Brazil and Argentina lifted restrictions on the transport of merchandise by truck across their borders.

USEFUL ADDRESSES

Secretaría de Comercio e Inversiones
(Secretariat of Trade and Investment)
Hipólito Yrigoyen 250
1310 Buenos Aires, Argentina
Tel: [54] (1) 331-2208

Secretaría de Agricultura, Ganadería, y Pesca
(Secretariat of Agriculture, Livestock, and Fishing)
Av. Paseo Colón 982
1063 Buenos Aires, Argentina
Tel: [54] (1) 362-2365, 362-5091, 362-5946
Fax: [54] (1) 349-2504

Ministerio de Salud Pública y Acción Social
(Ministry of Public Health and Social Action)
Av. 9 de Julio 1925
1332 Buenos Aires, Argentina
Tel: [54] (1) 381-8911, 381-8949

Cámara Argentina de Comercio
(Argentine Chamber of Commerce)
Av. L.N. Alem 36, Piso 8
1003 Buenos Aires, Argentina
Tel: [54] (1) 331-8051/5, 343-9423, 343-7783
Fax: [54] (1) 331-8055   Tlx: 18542

Cámara de Comercio, Industria y Producción de la República Argentina
(Chamber of Commerce, Industry, and Production)
Florida 410, Piso 1
1005 Buenos Aires, Argentina
Tel: [54] (1) 342-8252, 331-0813, 343-5638
Fax: [54] (1) 331-9116

Cámara de Importadores de la República Argentina
(Chamber of Importers)
Av. Belgrano 454, Piso 7
1092 Buenos Aires, Argentina
Tel: (1) 342-1101, 342-0523 Fax: (1) 331-9342

Cámara de Comercio Exterior del Centro de la República
(Chamber of Foreign Trade of Central Argentina)
Rosario de Santa Fe 231, Piso 4, Of. 9
5000 Córdoba, Argentina
Tel: [54] (51) 44-804

Cámara de Comercio de los Estados Unidos en la Argentina
(US Chamber of Commerce in Argentina)
Av. L.N. Alem 1110, Piso 13
1001 Buenos Aires, Argentina
Tel: [54] (1) 311-5420, 311-5126
Fax: [54] (1) 311-9076

Banco Central de la República Argentina (BCRA)
(Central Bank of the Argentine Republic)
Reconquista 266
1003 Buenos Aires, Argentina
Tel: [554] (1) 394-8411, 394-8119, 393-0021
Fax: [54] (1) 334-6489, 334-6468, 325-4860

Banco de Inversión y Comercio Exterior (BICE)
(Foreign Trade and Investment Bank)
25 de Mayo 526
1002 Buenos Aires, Argentina
Tel: [54] (1) 311-5596, 9546

Liga de Defensa del Consumidor
(Consumer Protection League)
Gral. J.D. Perón 1558
1037 Buenos Aires, Argentina
Tel: [54] (1) 375-3737, 3733

Secretaría de Recursos Naturales y Ambiente Humano (SRNAH)
(Secretariat of Natural Resources and Human Environment)
San Martín 459
1004 Buenos Aires, Argentina
Tel: [54] (1) 394-5161

Ministerio de Relaciones Exteriores, Comercio Internacional y Culto
(Ministry of Foreign Affairs, International Trade, and Cult)
Reconquista 1088
1003 Buenos Aires, Argentina
Tel: [54] (1) 311-0071/9, 312-1775, 312-3434
Fax: [54] (1) 312-3593, 312-3423 Tlx: 21194

Export Policy & Procedures

INTRODUCTION

Under its new open economy, free market approach, Argentina has made a great many positive changes to its previously cumbersome—and at times punitive—export regime. For many years, Argentina pursued counterproductive export policies, charging heavy export duties on its most prominent commodity products in an attempt to generate revenues to support the country's import substitution economic policy. The recent opening and deregulation of Argentina's economy has profoundly affected both domestic and external trade. For example, various decrees have deregulated the main Argentine agricultural and mining sectors and their respective internal wholesale and external export markets. Export tariffs ranging from 30 percent on wheat to as much as 41 percent on soybeans, in effect as recently as 1989, were converted to rebates of 2.5 percent on wheat exports and lowered to an export tax of 3.5 percent on soybeans at the end of 1993. The only export taxes remaining in June 1995 were those applied to soybeans and some types of leather.

Several measures have been adopted to make exporting easier, including the elimination of quantitative restrictions, permits, authorizations, and preshipment requirements on exports of goods and services. And the requirement that exporters register as such has become a statistical formality instead of a barrier favoring some at the expense of others. In order to ensure that traders will realize

the benefits of these reduced costs and prices, the authorities are taking measures to prevent intermediaries from capturing an inordinate share of the savings generated. This is designed to allow for real reductions of costs in international markets, making Argentine products more competitive.

Procedures have been simplified, and the Argentine Customs Administration has implemented a modern computerized system to speed processing. The collection of tax payments has been streamlined, and many of the taxes and fees themselves have been reduced or eliminated. Thus, taxes allocated to the merchant marine and the statistics tax on exports—the latter amounting to 3 percent of the FOB (free-on-board) value—have been abolished. Exports—especially those of nontraditional, high-value-added products—are being further encouraged through a scheme to reimburse domestic taxes on production for export, particularly within the agroindustrial and the manufacturing sectors. This scheme includes rebate of Argentina's hefty and newly increased 21 percent value-added tax (VAT) and also includes a drawback program to allow exporters of manufactured goods to recapture import duties paid on inputs transformed and later exported.

No charges are currently imposed for services provided by the various official bodies, such as the Shipping Authority and the Port Authority. Port costs on exports have been reduced substantially: by 11 percent on general and bulk cargos, by 8 percent on containers shipments, and by as much as 70 percent on fishing products. Significant reductions have also occurred in charges for pilotage on entry and exit, ship-handling on entry and exit, mooring and slippage, and general handling. The ongoing privatization of Argentine port activities is expected to result in more streamlined operations and greater cost reductions, further benefiting exporters as well as other users.

Entry restrictions have been eliminated for Argentine companies authorized to operate in international transport markets, while at the same time

EXPORTING GLOSSARY

despachante de aduana, corredor de aduana An Argentine customs broker or agent who is hired by an exporter or importer in Argentina to assist in clearing goods through Argentine Customs.

drawback The drawback regime provides a mechanism for refunding import duties on imported components of products destined for export. Duties and some taxes on imports that are directly used in exports are rebated under drawback, including tariffs, the 3 percent statistical tax on imports, and the value-added tax (VAT) of 21 percent. To benefit from the drawback system, the imported goods must be substantially transformed or directly used in the production of export goods.

Fundación Exportar An organization under the Ministry of Foreign Affairs which promotes and encourages Argentine exports.

Free Trade Zones Argentina has created a Special Customs Area in Tierra del Fuego allowing the duty-free import of goods not produced in Argentina for use in designated high-priority industries. In a further attempt to develop port and economic activity in this area, other imports entered through this zone receive a reduction of 50 percent on normal tariff rates. Other sites for free trade zones throughout the country are expected to be developed, with at least one to be designated per province, as well as others in strategic locations. Presently, Antarctica and the South Atlantic islands are also considered duty-free zones.

General Agreement on Tariffs and Trade (GATT) A multilateral trade agreement aimed at expanding and systematizing international trade. Its main goals are to liberalize and standardize procedures for world trade, placing it on a secure basis to contribute to economic growth and development. GATT is the only multilateral organization that lays down agreed-upon rules for international trade. The organization that oversees the agreement—now called the World Trade Organization (WTO)—is the principal international body concerned with negotiating the reduction of trade barriers and improving international trade relations. Argentina has been a member of the GATT since 1967.

Generalized System of Preferences (GSP) An international program under which developed countries allow, as a means of encouraging economic growth, imports of merchandise from developing countries to enter duty-free or at reduced tariff rates.

Latin American Integration Association (LAIA)—Asociación Latinoamericana de Integración (ALADI) An organization originally created to replace the Latin American Free Trade Association (LAFTA), LAIA involves Argentina, Bolivia, Brazil, Chile, Colombia, Ecuador, México, Paraguay, Perú, Uruguay, and Venezuela. It offers trade concessions on certain products obtained through bilateral negotiations.

legal kilo/legal weight The total weight of the merchandise and its own packaging, but excluding exterior containers or packing materials. For example, the legal weight of canned vegetables would include the vegetables, the can, and the label, but not the crate and wrappings for shipping.

Mercosur (Mercado Común del Sur or Southern Common Market) This regional trade alliance among Argentina, Brazil, Paraguay, and Uruguay was formed in 1991. The Common External Tariff and Customs Union of Mercosur went into effect in January 1995. This alliance, similar to the European Union (EU), seeks to establish the free circulation of goods, services, and factors, unify customs, and coordinate fiscal and exchange policies. Refer to the "Trade Agreements" chapter, beginning on page 65, for a full discussion of Mercosur.

most favored nation (MFN) A nondiscriminatory trade policy commitment on the part of one country to extend to another country the lowest tariff rates it applies to any other country. All contracting parties to GATT are obligated to apply such treatment with respect to one another.

Temporary Admission Regime (TAR) The TAR consists of duty-free admission of imported primary and intermediate goods and packaging to be used in export production. Exports must be completed within 180 days of admission.

rates on Argentine exports to Brazil and Paraguay have been reduced. As a result, the use of trucks is on the rise as a means of international transport among these neighboring countries, reinforcing the effects of more liberalized trade among these partners of Mercosur (the Mercado Común del Sur, or the Southern Common Market).

Developments have been overwhelmingly favorable, opening up what had been a complex and often anti-export-biased system. The sweeping nature and rapidity of change has often made it difficult to acquire hard information except on a case-by-case basis; this uncertainty is daunting, but also provides many opportunities for internationally oriented businesspeople.

The following section discusses Argentine export policy and the procedures for exporting from the country. This information is useful for those wishing to purchase goods and services from Argentina, expand current operations in Argentina to export markets, establish an enterprise in Argentina that will supply foreign markets, or invest in an export business located in Argentina.

EXPORT POLICIES AND GOVERNMENT REGULATION

Several official agencies are involved in setting export policy and procedures, as well as in administering the everyday process of exporting goods from Argentina.

The Secretaría de Comercio e Inversiones (Secretariat of Trade and Investment) sets Argentina's broad policies governing foreign trade. The Dirección Nacional de Impuestos (National Tax Administration) of the Ministry of Economy sets tariff and tax rates. However, it is the Exports Promotion Bureau and the Customs Administration, which actually implement and administer trade policies and procedures, along with the various agencies of the Program for the Modernization of Agricultural Services of the Secretariat of Agriculture, Livestock, and Fishing, which are prominent, given the role played by agricultural exports in Argentina.

Dirección de Promoción de las Exportaciones The Exports Promotion Bureau—one of several bureaus overseen by the Subsecretaría de Comercio Exterior (Undersecretariat of Foreign Trade)—has primary direct responsibility for formulating specific policies and drafting regulations regarding various aspects of trade, which involves the following:

- Drafting procedures to establish or revise standards related to the export of goods.
- Advising on export policy with a view toward defending local production.
- Certifying the origin of those exports eligible for

generalized system of preferences (GSP) benefits, as well as through other agreements, while monitoring compliance with any assigned quotas (such as those on textiles under Multi-Fiber Arrangements)

- Administering insurance programs on export credits.
- Setting and administering procedures related to refunds, drawbacks, and export duties.
- Developing programs to communicate Argentine foreign trade policy nationally and internationally.
- Advising the exporting sector and encouraging participation in international markets.
- Giving technical assistance at both the federal and regional levels by organizing seminars and courses on foreign trade.
- Organizing fairs, exhibitions, and shows designed to strengthen the country's position in international markets.
- Mediating claims from foreign countries involving noncompliance, failure, or default on export contracts by Argentine entities.

This responsibility is shared with the Subsecretaría de Relaciones Comerciales Internacionales (Undersecretariat of International Trade Relations) and the Ministerio de Relaciones Exteriores, Comercio Exterior, y Culto (Ministry of Foreign Affairs, International Trade, and Cults). The Dirección de Promoción Comercial (Bureau of Trade Promotion) is gathering market information to be used in preparing a database of trade opportunities and organizing trade missions to foreign markets.

Administración Nacional de Aduanas The National Customs Administration (referred to by its Spanish acronym, ANA) implements legislation, systems, and mechanisms to administer, standardize, and simplify customs procedures. It is responsible for day-to-day operations of Argentina's foreign trade activities. Among other things, ANA is involved in preparation for the computerization of its activities (Project María); establishing a special control division to monitor and combat such problems as underinvoicing and miscategorization of products; improving the gathering and processing of information on foreign trade; and monitoring instances of unfair competition between domestic manufacturers and importers.

The ANA administers the Código Aduanero (Customs Code), which contains the rules and regulations governing Argentine customs policies and procedures, including rules for specific incentives and rebate programs for exports, and federal tax incentives and other benefits available to the exporters of services. It also specifically addresses special import and export regimes, zones outside the general customs territory, prohibitions on imports and exports, trade reciprocity, and penalties for customs violations.

Programa de Modernización de los Servicios Agropecuarios The Program of Modernization of Agricultural Services (PROMSA) is designed to support the development of the important agricultural and fishing sectors. This entity is involved in the reorganization of the Secretaría de Agricultura, Ganadería, y Pesca (Secretariat of Agriculture, Livestock, and Fishing, or SAGyP), the operation of specialized, newly decentralized agencies, and the implementation of programs involving animal and vegetable quality, health, technological research, marine resource management and research, and foreign trade promotion for nontraditional agricultural products. PROMSA administers the following projects, all of which are designed to foster growth in the private sector and, consequently, of exports of agricultural and fishing products. Where certifications are required, it is these subagencies that are responsible for qualifying and certifying the specific products.

The Servicio Nacional de Sanidad Animal (the National Service of Animal Health, or SENASA) is responsible, together with provincial governments and private cattle breeders, for implementing plans to improve health and sanitation standards in the industry. It coordinates vaccination campaigns; maintains the animal quarantine station and a central laboratory in Ezeiza; and offers training programs for officers, professionals, and technicians.

The Instituto Argentino de Sanidad y Calidad Vegetal (Argentine Institute of Plant Health and Quality, or IASCAV) seeks to gain wider acceptance of Argentine plant products in international markets by setting up phytosanitary barriers— such as those to control the fruit fly in Patagonia and citrus canchrosis in the Northwestern region; constructing and installing a plant quarantine station in Ezeiza; developing a regional laboratory in Tucumán Province to deal with toxic agricultural wastes; and supplying and training staff to implement these functions.

The Instituto Nacional de Semillas (National Seed Institute, or INASE) seeks to promote the production and marketing of seeds of a graded and certified quality; creating new mechanisms for certification; speeding up the system to grant title of ownership for newly developed crop species; ensuring the identification and quality of marketed seeds bought locally and in foreign markets; training and supervising staff; and ensuring Argentina's presence and involvement in foreign special events in the field.

The Instituto Nacional de Investigación y Desarrollo Pesquero (National Institute of Fishing Research and Development, or INIDEP) operates programs that include research and evaluation of fish resources; the construction of two fishing development centers (one for warm water species in Corrientes Province and another for salmonid culture in Neuquén Province); the establishment of a centralized fishing information network; and the dissemination of technological knowledge and training to public and private sector operators.

The Sistema Integrado de Información Agropecuaria y Pesquera (Integrated System of Agricultural and Fishing Information) seeks to improve the collection and availability of information to simplify the planning and execution of policy in the sector.

The Promoción de Exportaciones No Tradicionales (Promotion of Nontraditional Agricultural Exports, or PROMEX) encourages the export of new agricultural products by serving as a clearinghouse for information on the operation and supply of foreign markets; requirements for entering foreign markets; tariff and nontariff restrictions in various foreign markets; seasonal requirements and future projections for various markets; and a database covering principal importers in particular markets, research centers, consulting firms, international specialists, and the major international fairs and exhibitions for such products. This project also provides training in the analysis of different markets and trade opportunities, the design and evaluation of export projects, and the management of international trade operations.

The Promoción de Exportaciones Cárnicas (Promotion of Meat Exports, or PROCAR) encourages the export of meat products by scheduling participation in international fairs and exhibitions, organizing promotional campaigns, building and maintaining a market information system, and providing assistance to exporters of meat products regarding quality and standards.

Credit and Financial System In 1992 the Argentine government created the Banco de Inversión y Comercio Exterior (Bank for Investment and Foreign Trade, or BICE). BICE concentrates on channeling funds from international organizations into export-related activities. Eventually, more domestic financial resources are expected to be available for the provision of medium- and long-term export-related financing. The system of prefinancing for producers and intermediate marketing agents operated through BICE is designed to offer finance terms to match those provided by other countries in order to make Argentine exports more competitive in international markets.

Export Registration and Licenses

All exporters must register as such, and registration is required to become eligible for export incentives. This registration, which formerly served to restrict exports, has largely become a formality designed specifically for statistical purposes. The export of a few sensitive materials requires advance approval. Exporters should contact their customs broker to confirm whether any such licensing requirements exist for the specific goods they want to export.

Export Tariffs, Duties, and Taxes

The Argentine government has reduced or eliminated export duties on grains, oils, and by-products that made these major Argentine exports less competitive in world markets. As of January 1995 the only export duties remaining in force were those affecting oilseeds and some types of raw leather.

The government has eliminated taxes and contributions affecting exports of grain, oils, and subproducts. These taxes and contributions included the merchant marine fund, the export promotion fund, the statistical tax on exports—which was 3 percent of the free on board (FOB) value—the fee for the Instituto Nacional de Tecnología Agropecuaria (INTA), and the tax on foreign currency transfers.

Quality Standards

Certain products, such as meat, seeds, fruit, and vegetables, must meet certain sanitary or safety standards before being deemed eligible for export. Information on quality standards for exports can be obtained from the appropriate governmental agency. Servicios al Comercio Exterior (Services to Foreign Trade) assists those interested in promoting foreign trade in the areas of seed, animal, and plant product health, safety, and quality through its own functions and those of other decentralized agencies, such as SENASA (animals), IASCAV (plants), and INASE (seeds) of the Program for the Modernization of Agricultural Services (PROMSA), which certify health, safety, and quality standards of Argentine agricultural and marine products.

Animal Product Health and Safety SENASA's duties include: keeping records about the premises where animals are slaughtered and animal products and by-products are prepared and stored; organizing and managing the sanitation and control of exports, imports, and inter-provincial trading of animals, animal products, and by-products, as well as biological pharmaceutical products and animal feedstock; granting the necessary certification required to export, import, or transport livestock, animal products, and animal by-products; approving the opening of plants to slaughter, process, store, or transport animals, products, and by-products; implementing programs to eliminate animal disease; and developing systems for the inspection of food products.

Plant Sanitation and Quality IASCAV's main activities include: defining, certifying, and monitoring areas as free of specific plant pests and diseases; establishing and organizing quarantine regulations for the importation of live plants and plant products; creating sanitation control systems for imports and exports; establishing and maintaining information systems and training centers; creating a system for the control and evaluation of chemicals used in relation to agriculture; overseeing commercial quality control and organic products systems; and issuing quality certificates for plant products to be exported.

Trade in Seeds INASE's services include: providing national certification of the varietal identity of vegetable products; providing international certification of the varietal identity of seeds according to the standards of the Organization of Economic Cooperation and Development (OECD); controlling trade in seeds; issuing title for new plant species; maintaining a national register of crop plant variety ownership (El Registro Nacional de la Propiedad de Cultivas); and controlling physicobotanical, physiological, sanitary, and genetic quality of seeds distributed in both domestic and foreign markets.

Policies Directed at the Private Sector

Encouragement of Investment Beginning in 1993, the government extended the reach of export prefinancing schemes to include all agricultural products. These schemes include new lines of credit from the Banco de la Nación Argentina (BNA), direct access for agricultural producers, extension of terms, greater flexibility, and guarantees (warrants).

Increasing Competitiveness Programs designed to encourage international representation and competitiveness in the agroindustrial sector include health and sanitary negotiations related to meat products, currently targeted at the Philippines, Korea, and Taiwan. Health and sanitation negotiations are also being held over gaining increased access to US and European Union (EU) markets for a wider range of agroindustrial products. Regional integration of standards on animal health, plant health, and classification are also being discussed with the objective of facilitating intraregional trade, particularly among Mercosur member nations.

Customs Benefits for Exporters The following are some of the main indirect tax benefits for exporters:

To help alleviate the tax burden on exports and make them more competitive internationally, Argentina's reimbursement policy has undergone significant reform. Reimbursement is designed to compensate more adequately for indirect taxes paid on the portion of value added domestically. The reimbursement rates are applied to the exported FOB value net of imported inputs, making them less than the full nominal rates.

All purchase value-added tax (VAT) amounts are returned to exporters. Import duties and statistics taxes on imported products used to manufacture exported goods are reimbursed or are excluded from direct taxation when mechanisms such as drawback and temporary import are used.

Argentina has several steps to increase the efficiency of obtaining insurance for export credits, one of its basic instruments of export policy. Exporters should consult either their customs broker or the Seguro de Crédito (Credit Insurance) office in the Dirección de Promoción de las Exportaciones (Export Promotion Bureau) for more information.

A US$300 million credit line provides prefinancing for agricultural and industrial sector exports. Credit agreements also exist with banks and governments in various nations, including specific arrangements with Germany, Spain, China, Japan, Finland, France, and Italy. This financing normally covers between 80 and 100 percent of the cost of capital goods, equipment, and turnkey plants (factories ready for use when delivered to the client) for terms of from 2 to 10 years at international interest rates. BNA has also instituted a wide range of credits for the agroindustrial sector as well as credit programs aimed at rebuilding working capital and investment for small- and medium-sized industrial and service companies.

Intra-Mercosur Trade Very few export incentives are authorized for trade within Mercosur. Export financing and credits are allowed only under terms, interest rates, and conditions prevailing in international markets, ostensibly to avoid the distortion of preferential treatment available to the exporters of one or more member countries. Reimbursement is available for indirect taxes paid by exporters or accumulated in the prior stages of production (according to the policies established by GATT). Other incentives include: drawback—or Temporary Admission Regime (TAR) facilities—allowing for suspension, exemption, or reimbursement of taxes on merchandise that is used for the purpose of perfecting, complementing, or conditioning a product for export; a customs deposit (common or extraordinary) that permits a trader to place merchandise in a designated location for up to one year (with extensions of up to a maximum of three years) during which time tax payments are suspended; and an industrial deposit regime (granted to a particular firm), which allows a firm to import merchandise, process it in Argentina, and export it, during which time tax payments are suspended so long as the goods remain under customs control and supervision. In addition, Argentina and Brazil may agree bilaterally that goods originating in either country will not pay any CET introduced by the other country.

Export Restrictions and Prohibitions

Export Quotas Products that are particularly competitive often face quotas that limit the amount of their sales to foreign countries. Quotas are usually fixed by the importing country or by multilateral or bilateral trade restraint agreements with other countries.

For example, quotas on GSP product benefits are established by importing countries on the basis of the GSP framework established under GATT. An importing country may limit the number of items that can be brought into the country under favorable GSP tariff treatment. Once the specified amount has been admitted, additional imports are charged higher rates if the quota is a tariff-rate quota, or forbidden entry for the remainder of the period stipulated—usually a calendar year—if covered by an absolute quota. One of the most commonly invoked quota agreements is the Multi-Fiber Arrangement (MFA), used by importing countries to restrict the entry of textiles and textile products from producer countries (MFA rules are scheduled to be phased out under the terms of the Uruguay Round of the GATT which went into effect in January 1995). Argentina is currently affected by quota limitations on textile products exported to some developed markets, exporters should consult with their customs broker about these matters beforehand.

Antidumping and Countervailing Duty Laws Under GATT, an importing country may assess antidumping and countervailing duties against Argentine exports when the importing country determines that its markets have been unfairly flooded by Argentine exports priced below the market value.

Import Regulations of Foreign Governments Import documentation requirements and other regulations imposed by foreign governments vary from country to country. Many governments require consular invoices, certificates of inspection, health certification, and various other documents. Although these requirements are usually the compliance responsibility of the buyer of the goods and the enforcement responsibility of customs officials in the importing country, Argentine Customs may on occasion refuse to approve export of goods that will not be admitted at their destination. Exporters should check with their buyers and customs broker to determine beforehand what materials are necessary to complete exit from Argentina as well as entry into the buyer's country.

EXPORT PROCEDURES

Parties to an export-import transaction must comply with two sets of requirements: the export regulations of Argentina (although a great deal of deregulation has simplified requirements in this area), and the import regulations of the country to which the goods will be delivered. This discussion focuses on the first step: sending the goods out of Argentina. Once this has been accomplished, the shipment must then comply with the import regulations in the buyer's country, which may include various import documentation, declarations, and licenses. This second step is generally the responsibility of the importer, although the exporter should be prepared to provide the buyer with any special documentation, labeling, or other special arrangements necessary for the importer to complete the transaction.

Export transactions are handled primarily through customs brokers (*despachantes de aduana*). For detailed rules and regulations governing customs procedures, consult an Argentine customs broker or the Argentine Customs Code.

Customs formalities were often lengthy and complicated procedures. A full-scale computerization of all areas of Argentina's Customs Administration has been implemented nationwide. This new system—known as María—permits traders to accomplish all export and import required submissions, clearances, informational filings, recordkeeping, and payment of fees to be carried out rapidly. The system is also designed to provide a running daily report on foreign trade to permit improved controls and to monitor unfair trading practices. The project is financed from a surcharge of US$15 imposed on each import and export transaction.

Customs Clearance

To avoid delay at Argentine Customs, the exporter should be aware of all current requirements and have all necessary documents in order. Because of the rapidity of ongoing change and the range of different product requirements, this can be difficult. Therefore, exporters may wish to select a customs broker (preferably based on evaluations, interviews, and recommendations from other exporters) and, if possible, arrange to route the shipment through a port which has good facilities and staff for handling the goods to be exported. The customs broker should have familiarity with the type of goods being exported, a good working relationship with the personnel at the port, and be able to advise the exporter on the types of documents required and the best method for preparing and submitting the necessary documentation.

Preshipment Considerations

Preshipment Customs Clearance To avoid outgoing delays at a port or border, the exporter should verify in advance if any preshipment clearances are required. Exporters may wish to consult a customs broker to see if advance clearance from customs may be obtained or if any preshipment requirements must be met.

Insurance Arrangements Exporters should strongly consider insuring the goods until the risk of damage or loss passes to the importer (usually upon transfer of title and entry overseas). The exporter should become familiar with Incoterms, which represent the codification of international terminology and rules for the uniform interpretation of common contract clauses in export and import transactions. The most common Incoterms include FOB (free-on-board), FAS (free alongside ship), CFR (cost and freight), and CIF (cost, insurance, and freight). Refer to page 274 in the "International Payments" chapter for a full listing of Incoterms.

Argentine companies that take advantage of any government benefits—such as tax forgiveness, release from import duties, or government contracts—must insure through an Argentine insurance provider.

Certification of Quality Only such plant and animal products as have been certified according to quality and safety may be exported. Some foreign countries also require such certifications for entry. (*See* "Quality Standards" on page 95 for further discussion, and "Useful Addresses" on page 99 for contact information.)

Export Registrations and Licenses

All exporters must be registered as such and maintain prescribed documentation regarding their activities. Such registration is required to receive any benefits available under export incentives. Registration as an exporter used to be rather difficult and exclusive, but under deregulation, such registration has largely become a formality (although registration does entail the collection and maintenance of specified records). For detailed rules and regulations on export registration, refer to the Customs Code.

Export Clearance and Request for Export Incentives To obtain export clearance and request benefits under an export incentive program, the exporter must file Customs Form OM-700A. Argentine Customs uses the information provided in this document to approve the export, determine whether the shipment qualifies for any incentives claimed, and decide whether the documentation is adequate. If deemed to be inadequate or otherwise unacceptable, customs will return the application to the exporter. Once customs approves the request, it will stamp the document with the date and time of approval. The approved form then serves as the embarkation permit. Photocopies of the approved form may be used to satisfy other documentation requirements. The exporter has 30 days after this approval is received in which to complete the documentation and the exportation.

Exporters can file amended documents without penalty within five days after the initial export permit is granted, provided they have cause and follow prescribed procedures. Exporters can avoid problems with documentation by being sure that they are actually eligible for the incentives they claim. Inquiries can be made through the División Normativa de Exportación (Division of Export Norms) or the Secretaría Técnica (Technical Secretary). (*See* "Useful Addresses" on page 99 contact information).

Clearance Requirements All goods must be cleared and—at least theoretically—inspected before final export clearance can be obtained. Some inspections of nonsensitive goods are nominal in practice. However, other goods—such as armaments, sensitive materials, nuclear material, and anesthetics—require actual physical inspection. Exporters must obtain permits from any regulatory authorities responsible for any restricted goods being exported prior to submission of this final request for clearance to customs. Depending on the nature of the product, customs will stamp the documentation *Canal Rojo, Canal Naranja*, or *Canal Verde* (Red, Orange, or Green channel).

Canal Rojo-Verificación Obligatoria (Red Channel-Obligatory Verification) applies to special restricted materials, which customs must physically inspect before loading and final clearance. Documents stamped *Canal Naranja* (Orange Channel) are for items requiring endangered species clearance from the designated authority, such as SENASA, IASCAV, or the Dirección de Flora y Fauna Silvestre (Bureau of Plants and Wildlife). Goods designated for *Canal Verde* (Green Channel) are subject only to general verification aboard ship prior to sailing.

Documentation at Packing

Clearance through customs will be more efficient if the exporter makes certain that all the necessary documents are completed and properly submitted through the María automated system, if such automated submission is available, or properly attached to the goods during the packaging stage for physical submission. Exporters should consult with their customs broker to ensure all documents are prepared correctly, submitted as required, and processed correctly without delay.

Commercial Invoice All commercial shipments require a commercial invoice. The exporter should insert one signed original into the package and

should provide further signed copies as advised by the customs broker. A signed copy should be sent directly to the importer, as well.

The commercial invoice—which must be made out in Spanish—should contain an acceptable translation if the regulations of the importing country require it.

With regard to the commercial invoice contents, the customs broker should be consulted to make sure that the importing country does not have additional requirements. Typically, most commercial invoices contain the following information:

- The name and address of the exporter and importer.
- The name and address of the consignee who will receive the goods for the foreign importer.
- A description of each product, including the quantity sold and the value of the goods in the currency in which they were sold.
- The product weight.
- The dimensions of the package.

The customs broker should be able to advise the exporter on which product weight—gross, legal, or net—should be declared in the invoice. Prices for exported goods are often quoted in US dollars; no restrictions exist on foreign currency exchange.

Packing List The exporter should ask the customs broker and the importer whether a packing list should be enclosed with the shipment. Usually, a packing list specifies the weight of each item shipped, the total weight of the shipment, the total number of packages shipped, the type of packages shipped, and the description of each product, if not included on the commercial invoice.

Certificates of Origin If a claim for GSP preference is to be made for the goods, the exporter should obtain a certificate of origin attesting to Argentina as the country of origin of the goods. A certificate of origin is a separate document consisting of the Argentine supplier's statement of where the goods originated. Exporters should verify if such documents are required and, if so, whether a specific format is necessary.

Documentation at Shipping

The documentation requirements for shipping goods from Argentina may vary depending on the mode of transport: land (truck or rail), sea, air, or mail. In addition to the usual bill of lading documents, a shipper may request to see insurance, health, and other certificates. The foreign importer or the bank handling payment for the goods may have additional documentary requirements that must be met before the shipper will accept the goods. The exporter should check with a customs broker about these matters beforehand.

Argentina's port operations are in flux, with privatization changing the way operations are conducted at many facilities. Many projects for improving Argentina's infrastructure are also either in the planning stage or actually underway. These are expected to have a huge future impact on the quality and timeliness of shipping service, as well as on the costs associated with shipping. However, this high degree of change can be expected to disrupt operations in the interim as new procedures and facilities are developed.

Air Freight The exporter should consult a customs broker to determine the specific documentation needed for shipment by air. Typically, the foreign importer and the air carrier will furnish information about their specific requirements for the contents of an air waybill and the number of copies to be enclosed. If so, the commercial invoice should indicate the number of the air waybill. A customs broker should also be able to advise regarding special rules for the transport of particular goods, including dangerous and restricted goods, should these apply. Most freight airlines will supply information on these rules, which may include national and international regulations, such as those of the International Air Transport Association (IATA) and the International Civil Aviation Organization (ICAO).

The Argentine government has levied a high fee on outbound traffic by international courier. However, the government has stated that it plans to remove this fee. The proposed privatization and restructuring of the national mail system may also serve to resolve this issue by lessening the need to protect the national monopoly. Argentina has also scheduled the privatization of many airports and their ancillary facilities and services by the end of 1995, which could further alter air shipping operations.

Shipments by Sea The exporter should consult with a customs broker to determine the type of documentation required for shipments by sea. Typically, the exporter must furnish a bill of lading that indicates the marks, serial numbers, quantity, and kinds of packages, and the gross weight in metric units.

Many ports have been privatized, with additional operations and services scheduled for privatization. A wide range of infrastructure projects designed to improve the movement of cargos by sea are also either planned or underway.

Overland Transport The exporter should consult with a customs broker to determine the type of bill of lading required for overland transport by truck, rail, or other mode of transport to the port of embarkation and through to the final buyer, if such is part of the contract. Over-the-road transport between Argentina and Brazil is becoming more common and thus more regularized, under Mercosur.

USEFUL ADDRESSES

Refer to the "Important Addresses" chapter for a list of customs brokers, transportation firms, and other organizations of use to the exporter.

Secretaría de Comercio e Inversiones
(Secretariat of Trade and Investments)
Hipólito Yrigoyen 250
1310 Buenos Aires, Argentina
Tel: [54] (1) 331-2208

Administración Nacional de Aduanas (ANA)
(National Administration of Customs)
Azopardo 350
1328 Buenos Aires, Argentina
Tel: [54] (1) 343-0661/9, 343-0101/9
Fax: [54] (1) 331-9881, 345-1778

Fundación Exportar
Reconquista 1098
1003 Buenos Aires, Argentina
Tel: [54] (1) 315-4125
Fax: [54] (1) 311-4334

Secretaría de Agricultura, Ganadería, y Pesca (SAGyP)
(Secretary of Agriculture, Livestock, and Fisheries)
Av. Paseo Colón 982
1063 Buenos Aires, Argentina
Tel: [54] (1) 362-2365, 362-5091, 362-5946
Fax: [54] (1) 349-2504

Subsecretaría de Comercio Exterior
Dirección de Promoción de las Exportaciones
(Bureau of Export Promotion)
Av. Julio A. Roca 651, Piso 6
1332 Buenos Aires, Argentina
Tel:[54] (1) 334-2975
Fax: [54] (1) 331-2266

Banco de Inversión y Comercio Exterior (BICE)
(Investment and Foreign Trade Bank)
25 de Mayo 526
1002 Buenos Aires, Argentina
Tel: [54] (1) 311-5596, 311-9546

Departamento de Asesoramiento
(Advisory Division)
Tel: [54] (1) 343-3906, 342-3399, 331-9357

Departamento de Regímenes
(Programs Division)
Tel: [54] (1) 343-3974/342-0740-2899-4754

División Normativa de Exportación
(Division of Export Norms)
Tel: [54] (1) 343-0661

Instituto Argentino de Sanidad y Calidad Vegetal (IASCAV)
(Argentine Institute of Plant Sanitation and Quality)
Av. Paseo Colón 982
1063 Buenos Aires, Argentina
Tel: [54] (1) 343-8311

Instituto Nacional de Investigación y Desarrollo Pesquero (INIDEP)
(National Institute of Fishing Research and Development)
Tel: [54] (1) 362-4284

Instituto Nacional de Semillas (INASE)
(National Seed Institute)
Av. Paseo Colón 982
1063 Buenos Aires, Argentina
Tel: [54] (1) 362-3988, 362-7111

Programa de Modernización de los Servicios Agropecuarios (PROMSA)
(Program for the Modernization of Agricultural Services)
Tel: [54] (1) 362-1866

Cámara de Exportadores de la República Argentina
(Argentine Exporters Association)
Av. Roque Sáenz Peña 740, Piso 1
1035 Buenos Aires, Argentina
Tel: [54] (1) 328-9583, 320-5944, 320-8556
Fax: [54] (1) 328-1603   Tlx: 22910

Secretaría de Relaciones Económicas Internacionales
(Undersecretariat of International Economic Relations)
Reconquista 1088
1003 Buenos Aires, Argentina
Tel: [54] (1) 331-7281, 331-4073
Fax: [54] (1) 312-0965

Promoción de Exportaciones Cárnicas (PROCAR)
(Promotion of Meat Exports)
Tel: [54] (1) 362-1311

Promoción de Exportaciones No Tradicionales (PROMEX)
(Promotion of Nontraditional Exports)
Tel: [54] (1) 362-0145

Servicio Nacional de Sanidad Animal (SENASA)
(National Animal Sanitation Service)
Tel: [54] (1) 345-3219

Industry Reviews

INTRODUCTION

This chapter describes the status of and trends in major Argentine industries. It also lists key contacts for finding sources of supply, for developing sales leads, and for conducting market research. For purposes of this chapter, Argentine industry has been grouped into nine categories. Some smaller sectors of commerce are not detailed here, while others may overlap into more than one area. If your business even remotely fits into a category, do not hesitate to contact several of the organizations listed; they should be able to assist you further in gathering the information you need. Here we have included industry-specific contacts only. We highly recommend that you peruse the "Trade Fairs" chapter, beginning on page 121, and "Important Addresses", beginning on page 315, where you will find additional resources, including a variety of trade promotion organizations, chambers of commerce, business services, and media outlets.

An entire volume could likely be devoted to each industry area, but such in-depth coverage is beyond the scope of this book; the intent is to give you a basis for your own research. Each section has two main segments: an industry summary and a list of useful contacts. The summary notes the range of products

available in a certain industry and that industry's ability to compete in worldwide markets. The contacts include government departments, trade associations, publications, and trade fairs that can provide information specific to the industry. All addresses and telephone numbers given are located in Argentina unless otherwise noted. The telephone country code for Argentina is [54]; other telephone country codes are shown in square brackets where appropriate. Telephone city codes appear in parentheses.

As you begin your review of Argentine industry, please note that all industry in the country must now be seen in terms of the reforms introduced by the Menem administration since 1989. The most important reforms include: the deregulation of industries, the privatization of many state-run industries (including transportation networks, electric power generation, telephone companies, and oil refineries), the opening of the economy to international competition, and the adoption of the convertibility regime. Since the introduction of these reforms, the Argentine economy has grown by 30 percent, its level of growth second only to China among world economies. The policies have been far-reaching and detailed in that they affect almost every aspect of industrial life in the country.

Argentina's manufacturing industry has an intermediate level of development, comparable to that of Brazilian industry. Although it does not match the sophistication and performance of European, North American, or Japanese manufacturing, Argentine technological capacity is more developed that of most other Latin American countries. Since the establishment of the current free market economic policy in 1989, Argentine businesses have been operating in an open and competitive environment similar to those of other free market economies. Survival under such conditions would be impossible without the attainment of a certain level of technological capability. The principal factors which have put Argentina at this level of development are its experience with manufacturing—Argentine firms have been involved in such production since the turn of the 20th century)—the generally high level of education of its population (especially its technicians and engineers), and the existence of a dynamic, demanding, and diverse internal market. As an example of its industrial capacity, Argentina possesses an important automotive industry, which currently produces 400,000 cars annually, supplying most of the needs of the internal market. Moreover, the domestic auto parts industry supplies most of the components for this production. Introduction of new models is just behind the schedule in Europe, with several European-introduced models having been recently produced in Argentina. The Argentine steel industry has also been a strong exporter of such high-quality products as seamless steel tubes for the oil industry, and Argentine engineering companies also export complex equipment such as electric power turbines and offshore platforms.

Even though manufacturing began in Argentina around the turn of the century, it did not become a significant activity until the 1930s. Between then and the mid-1970's, industry was widely protected against competition from imported goods. The most important manufacturing sectors prior to 1930 included midrange operations such as meat processing, milling, and brewing, with the textile industry also showing significant growth. Later, around 1940, the light metal-mechanical industry (particularly the production of finished goods) and some sectors of the specialty chemicals industry, became substantial contributors. Towards the end of the 1950s and the beginning of the 1960s, the automotive industry became increasingly important, and along with it evolved additional metal–mechanical and machine-tools industries.

During the 1970s the manufacture of certain value-added products—such as household appliances, machinery, and equipment—developed for export, in particular to other Latin American countries. In fact, several Argentine industrial companies set up branches in importer countries. However, after 1976 this expansion faded because of problems with the overvaluation of the national currency and high interest rates.

Since the establishment of the Argentine Convertibility Plan in 1991, manufacturing has recovered strongly. The basis for this recovery has mainly been the result of a boom in consumer spending following the establishment of economic stability. Consumer demand was supported by the reappearance of available credit—which had been unavailable during the previous decade—for consumption and for the purchase of consumer durables. However, it is unlikely that internal demand alone will be able to sustain this elevated rate of growth in the future, and the challenge for Argentine companies is to increase their exports, particularly those of higher-value-added goods. It is important to point out that since 1990, huge investments have been made in capital goods—most of them imported—resulting in annual manufacturing productivity gains of about 5 percent to 7 percent annually.

AGRICULTURAL PRODUCTS AND PROCESSED FOODS

Meat Processing

Meat processing is the oldest manufacturing activity in the country. Worldwide exports of beef underwrote Argentine prosperity during the early 20th century; and, although still important, this sector—representing almost 3 percent of the value of industrial production—is no longer dominant. Meat products now share export leadership among agricultural products with leather products, edible oils, and fish products.

The meat processing industry has maintained an estimated annual production valued at about US$10 billion annually, processing nine million head of livestock a year. The top three firms in the industry—Frigorífico Rioplatense, Quickfood, and the multinational Swift Armour—have each registered about US$200 million in annual sales in recent years. The next largest firms—Friar and Tres Cruces—post around US$100 million in sales. The next 10 largest companies gross between US$50 and US$20 million apiece. Together, these top 15 firms in the industry account for roughly one-eighth of the production in this well diversified sector.

Dairy

The dairy industry, which is largely oriented toward the domestic market, has experienced a notable transformation during the last decade. This can be characterized by both strong market concentration and increased diversity of products offered. The industry has aggregate annual sales of about US$4 billion. The leading dairy companies have made important efforts during this period to produce differentiated goods with greater added value (including yoghurt, dessert products, cheeses, and—increasingly—reduced calorie products). These developments have both followed and stimulated demand, while producing higher profits.

A key competitive factor has been the relation between suppliers and processors, because the quality of raw materials strongly affects the final product. This has resulted in increased processor competition to retain the best milk producers, leading the processors to offer technical assistance and quality control programs. The top firms in the industry are Mastellone Hermanos (with annual sales of US$850 million and a focus on milk and yoghurt) and SanCor (US$620 million, which specializes in cheese production). Other firms participating in this industry are Lactona (*dulce de leche*, jam, and yoghurt, US$50 million), Italy's Parmalat (liquid milk), and multinational Nestlé (powdered milk, desserts, ice cream, cheeses, and other high-value-added products, with US$400 million annual revenues, including nondairy food products). Together these large firms command nearly half of the market.

Lastly, the fresh cheese sector comprises many small and medium-sized companies that produce for local markets. Many have serious quality problems, which have inhibited growth. This group of dairy companies has a very small value of production when compared with the industry as a whole.

Edible Oils

The edible oils sector has experienced the highest rate of growth among agribusiness industries during the last decade. This has been based largely on strong export performance: during this period, it has become an export leader, racking up about US$3 billion in annual foreign sales. Current edible oil production is about three million tons a year. This industry is highly dependent on the price and quality of the oilseeds (mainly soybean and sunflower) available in the country. Yield and availability are generally good in Argentina, attracting the interest of some foreign firms, which are setting up oil processing plants in order to export to their countries of origin (currently, the industry remains dominated by local companies).

Argentine edible oil producing industrial plants are very capital-intensive, given the need for state-of-the-art technology to meet overseas quality standards. This sector is mainly composed of economic groups specifically dedicated to this niche activity. The main companies in the sector are Aceitera General Deheza (US$350 million in sales), Vincentín (US$300 million), Oleaginosa Moreno (US$220 million), and Buyatti, Guipeba, and Oleaginosa Oeste (US$200 million each). Additionally, Molinos Río de la Plata, a unit of Bunge & Born, with annual sales of US$900 million including other product lines, is a leader in edible oil for domestic consumption. In the production of corn oil—as well as of mayonnaise and related by-products—Refinerías de Maíz is the undisputed leader.

Milling

The Argentine milling industry annually produces 3.5 million tons of wheat flour. Such production of milled products is destined primarily for the domestic market, cereal exports usually being made in raw unprocessed form. Leading flour producing companies belong to groups that dominate both local and export cereals trading. The leading milling firm, Molinos Río de la Plata (with US$920 million in annual sales), belongs to transnational Bunge & Born. Smaller milling companies include Morixe, Lagomarsino, and Molino Cañuelas, each of which has sales of about US$100 million. Large cereal companies include Cargill, which has a lock on the production of cereal-based balanced feeds (US$960 million in annual sales), Nidera (US$540 million in sales), and La Plata Cereal (US$390 million).

Biscuits and Confectionery

The leading companies in the production of crackers and similar products include Bagley, a local company bought in 1994 by French firm Danone, and Terrabusi, recently bought by the US's RJR Nabisco; each does about US$300 million in annual sales. Between them, these two companies dominate the market. Other producers include Canale (US$80 million in sales), Panrek (of the Arcor group), Granix, Mayco, and Capri. The leaders in the confectionery market are the local affiliates of the transnationals Nestlé, Kraft-Suchard (with US$200 million in sales), Cadbury-Stani (US$90 million), and Georgalos, plus a great many smaller firms. Local group Arcor—one of the major powers in the Argentine food industry—also participates in the confectionery market. Arcor is vertically integrated, producing its own raw materials, from glucose to packaging. These characteristics allow Arcor to keep its costs competitive, sustaining its exporting activities. Arcor grosses about US$720 million annually and is a major exporter of foods such as jams and candies, as well as inputs for the food industry such as glucose.

Beer

The beer industry has experienced significant growth due to changes in Argentine consumer preferences, with a sharply increased demand for beer. In 1980 Argentine consumption was 2 million hectoliters; by 1990, this had grown to 6 million, while reaching 11.3 million hectoliters in 1994. The leading brewery is Cervecería y Maltería Quilmes, with US$345 million in annual sales. Other brewers include Río Paraná (also part of the Quilmes group, with US$70 million in sales), Cervecería Bieckert (US$40 million in sales), Cervecería del Cuyo y Norte Argentino (US$75 million a year), Compañía Industrial Cervecera (US$15 million), and Cervecería Santa Fe. As a result of the impressive growth in the domestic market, the Brazilian brewery Brahma has established its own operation in Argentina. Most recently, the German brewery Warsteiner joined the local market with a US$80 million investment for a new plant inaugurated in early 1995. Total sales for leading breweries reached US$600 million in 1994.

Wine

The Argentina wine industry—one of the oldest in the country—consists of two different markets: table wines, the so-called "common wines" (retailing for about US$1.50 per liter and generally considered to be of low quality), for which there is heavy demand; and premium, or "fine wines," (retailing for about US$5 or more per liter). The first market is dominated by large companies, such as Peñaflor (US$280 million in sales) and Resero (US$100 million). Several small and medium-sized companies—including the Catena group, Bodegas y Viñedos Santa Ana (US$65 million in sales), Bodegas Chandon (US$60 million), A. Etchart (US$16 million), Bodegas Navarro Correa (US$9 million), Bodegas Esmeralda (US$10 million), Finca Flischman, Orfila, Valmont, and a great many small premium vineyards—make up the second market. Total wine sales in 1994 were approximately US$1 billion.

It is important to point out that despite the high quality of Argentine wines, export volumes have been relatively insignificant. While Chilean wines of similar quality can be found on supermarket shelves worldwide, Argentine wines remain virtually unknown. This may be due partially to the inability to produce the necessary volumes demanded by international markets, as well as to strong local demand which has left little excess production for export. As far as common wines go, exports of unfermented grape juice and bulk wine have been growing, fueled by the reduced local consumption replaced by beer. In 1982 consumption of wine was 21 million hectoliters, while by 1994 consumption had fallen by one-third to 14 million hectoliters.

Soft Drinks

As is the case virtually everywhere in the world, the Argentine non-alcohol beverage market is dominated by US giants Coca-Cola and Pepsi-Cola. Their huge sales figures give an idea of the magnitude of the mass consumption market in Argentina: Coca-Cola grosses US$1.6 billion per year, while Pepsi-Cola affiliates gross US$800 million.

Fierce competition has resulted in sustained annual investments of approximately US$100 million by Coke and US$35 million for Pepsi for increasing manufacturing capacity and aggressive advertisement campaigns. Both bottlers have also recently launched new lines of carbonated drinks, including a carbonated grapefruit drink, new diet flavors, juices, and other products. Domestic consumption climbed to 22 million hectoliters in 1994.

Juice and Fruit Concentrates

The juice and fruit concentrate market (consisting primarily of citrus products) is a sector which has grown strongly during the last decade, based mainly on increased demand for exports (as has been the case with edible oils). Argentina's excellent conditions for growing citrus fruit have provided raw materials at low cost and of high quality by international standards. Most companies in the sector operate their own fruit plantations. The main companies are Pindapoy (with US$32 million in annual sales, specializing in orange juice), San Miguel (the main producer of lemon juice, almost all of it for export, with US$30 million in sales), Jugos del Sur (US$26 million), Zumos Argentinos (US$13 million), and Litoral Citrus (US$10 million).

Fish Processing

The fishing industry is among those areas most likely to show improved export performance in the intermediate to long term, because of growing demand for fish products (associated with growing global demand for healthier foods) and the abundance of exploitable species in Argentina's continental sea; these include hake, squid, and anchovy. Large fishing fleets from Russia, Japan, Spain, and South Korea, among others, are permanently operating under license in Argentine waters.

Because of its export potential, the fish processing industry has attracted the attention of foreign investors as well as of local groups whose primary operations are unrelated to the sector. Argentina's exporting experience in this sector is recent, going back only 15 years. Nevertheless, yield volumes are considerable. In 1994 the marketable catch was approximately 900,000 tons, of which 528,000 tons were exported, with 85 percent of this being destined for European markets.

Although the tendency among Argentine firms has been to rid themselves of satellite operations that do not fit with their core businesses, the fishing sector has maintained the interest of companies with no direct operations in the sector. For example, motorcycle-manufacturer Zanella has created Zanella-Mare, a fully equipped fishing company with the view towards exporting, while textile firm Alpargatas has invested US$50 million in its fishing subsidiary, Alpesca (which has US$31 million in annual sales). The largest companies in the sector are Harengus (US$42 million in sales), the already mentioned Alpesca, Pesantar (US$25 million), and Pescasur (US$20 million). The 20 companies which follow these largest firms gross about US$10 million each, and the overall market is highly fragmented. Given the abundance of fish resources existing in Argentine waters, the relatively low degree of exploitation by Argentine companies, and the growing world demand for fish products, there is still room both for new companies to enter this sector and for the expansion of existing ones.

Government Agencies

Secretaría de Agricultura, Ganadería y Pesca
(Secretariat of Agriculture, Livestock, and
Fisheries)
Av. Paseo Colón 982
1063 Buenos Aires
Tel: (1) 362-2365, 362-5091, 362-5946
Fax: (1) 349-2504

**Dirección de Mercados de Productos no
Tradicionales**
(Administration of Markets of Non-Traditional
Products)
Paseo Colón 922
Buenos Aires
Tel: (1) 362-1738 y 349-2280/2
Fax: (1) 349-2280

Dirección de Mercados Agrícolas y Agroindustriales
(Administration of Agricultural and Agroindustrial
Markets)
Paseo Colón 922, Piso 1, Of. 131
1063 Buenos Aires
Tel: (1) 349-2272/4
Fax: (1) 349-2272

Dirección de Mercados Ganaderos
(Administration of Livestock Markets)
Paseo Colón 922
1063 Buenos Aires
Tel: (1) 349-2287, 349-2294
Fax: (1) 362-5144

Dirección de Recursos Ictícolas y Acuícolas
(Administration of Fish and Marine Resources)
San Martin 459, Piso 2
1004 Buenos Aires
Tel: (1) 394-1869, 394-5961 x8557

Dirección Nacional de Pesca y Acuicultura
(National Administration of Fishing and
Aquaculture)
Av. Paseo Colón 982, Anexo Jardin, Piso 1
1063 Buenos Aires
Tel: (1) 349-2330/1
Fax: (1) 349-2332

Trade Associations

Asociación de Industria Argentina de Carnes
(Meat industry)
Paraguay 776
1057 Buenos Aires
Tel: (1) 393-8049, 322-0587

Asociación de la Industria Vitivinícola Argentina
(Wine producers)
Guemes 4464
1425 Buenos Aires
Tel: (1) 774-1887, 774-3370
Fax: (1) 776-2529

Cámara Argentina de Bebidas sin Alcohol
(Non-alcohol beverages)
Rivadavia 1823, Piso 3, Of. A
Buenos Aires
Tel: (1) 952-5375 y 953-7982
Fax: (1) 952-5375

Cámara Argentina de Consignatarios de Ganado
(Cattle brokers)
Lima 87, Piso 2
1073 Buenos Aires
Tel/Fax: (1) 381-7283, 381-8522, 382-6412, 383-9393

**Cámara Argentina de la Industria de los
Oleaginosos**
(Oilseeds industry)
Piedras 83
1070 Buenos Aires
Tel: (1) 342-5728

Cámara Argentina de la Industria Frigorífica
(Meat processing industry)
Lavalle 710
1047 Buenos Aires
Tel: (1) 322-6131, 393-5579

Cámara Argentina de Productores Avícolas
(Poultry producers)
Bouchard 454, Piso 6
1106 Buenos Aires
Tel: (1) 312-2000/9, 313-5666 x333, x334
Fax: (1) 312-2000/9 x333

**Cámara de Armadores, Pescadores, Congeladores
de Argentina (CAPECA)**
(Shipowners, fishing, and freezing companies)
Tucumán 731, Piso 3, Of. E
1049 Buenos Aires
Tel: (1) 322-1031

Cámara de Fabricantes de Refrescos y Afines
(Refreshments manufacturers)
Av. L.N. Alem 734, Piso 7
1001 Buenos Aires
Tel: (1) 311-4271, 311-2882

**Cámara de la Industria Aceitera de la República
Argentina (CIARA)**
(Edible oil industry)
Tucumán 637, Piso 6
1049 Buenos Aires
Tel: (1) 322-3990, 322-7908, 393-8322
Fax: (1) 393-7685

Cámara de la Industria Cervecera Argentina
(Breweries)
Av. Roque Sáenz Peña 637, Piso 5
1393 Buenos Aires
Tel: (1) 362-5767, 326-0125
Fax: (1) 326-5767

Cámara de la Industria Tabacalera
(Tobacco industry)
Reconquista 656, Piso 3
1003 Buenos Aires
Tel: (1) 313-7705/8, 312-8207
Fax: (1) 312-8205

Cámara Industrial de Productos Alimenticios
(Food products)
Av. L.N. Alem 1067, Piso 12
1001 Buenos Aires
Tel: (1) 312-1929, 312-3508
Fax: (1) 312-1929, 312-3508

Centro Azucarero Argentino
(Sugar industry)
Reconquista 336, Piso 12
Buenos Aires
Tel: (1) 394-0257, 394-0358, 394-0459
Fax: (1) 322-9358

Centro de Exportadores de Cereales
(Cereal exporters)
Bouchard 454, Piso 7
1106 Buenos Aires
Tel: (1) 311-1697, 311-4627, 312-6924

Federación Argentina de la Industria Molinera
(Milling industry)
Bouchard 454, Piso 6
1106 Buenos Aires
Tel: (1) 311-0898, 312-8717, 313-4185
Fax: (1) 313-4185

Instituto Nacional de Vitivinicultura
(National Viticulture Institute)
A. Julio A. Roca 651, Piso 5, Of. 22
1067 Buenos Aires
Tel/Fax: (1) 343-3846

Directories and Publications

Annual Buyers Guide
Top Latin American Processors Directory
(Annual; English)
Stagnito Publishing Company
1935 Shermer Rd., Suite 100
Northbrook, IL 60062, USA
Tel: [1] (708) 205-5660
Fax: [1] (708) 205-5680
Food and food industries

Latin American International Food Industry Directory
(Annual; English, Portuguese, Spanish)
Aquino Productions
Box 15760
Stamford, CT 06901, USA
Tel: [1] (203) 325-3138

Gaceta Agronómica
(6 issues/year)
Viamonte 494, Piso 2-6
1053 Buenos Aires
Agriculture

Industria Alimentaria
(Every 2 months)
Editora Técnica Integral S.R.L.
Av. Corrientes 2763, Piso 2, Of. 9 y 10
1046 Buenos Aires
Tel: (1) 962-6100
Published by the COPAL, the Argentine Federation of Food Industries

Industria Lechera
(Every 2 months)
Centro de la Industria Lechera
Mediano 281
1178 Buenos Aires
Dairy industry

Instituto Nacional de Investigación y Desarrollo Pesquero. Memoria
(Annual)
Instituto Nacional de Investigación y Desarrollo Pesquero
Casilla de Correo 175
7600 Mar del Plata
Fishing industry

Novedades de la Industria Alimenticia
(Every 2 months)
Stagnito Publishing Company
1935 Shermer Rd., Suite 100
Northbrook, IL 60062, USA
Tel: [1] (708) 205-5660
Fax: [1] (708) 205-5680
Food processing industry

Trade Fairs

Refer to the "Trade Fairs" chapter for complete listings, including contact information, dates, and venues. Trade fairs with particular relevance to this industry include the following, which are listed in that chapter under the headings given below:

Agriculture, Horticulture & Aquaculture
* Exposición de Ganadería, Agricultura e Industria
* CENIPA '95
* Expoferichaco
* Exposición Agroindustrial y Comercial
* Feria Internacional de Agro Alimentación

Food, Beverages & Hospitality
* AGRI FOOD '95
* Argentina Exposición Mundial de Alimentos, Bebidas y Tecnologías Afines
* CONAL '96
* Expogolosina '95
* SAIHEL '95—TECHNOPAN—TECHNOPASTAS
* Techno Bebiendo
* Techno Fidta

FORESTRY AND WOOD PRODUCTS

Lumber and Wood Products

The Argentine forestry industry has annual production estimated at around three million cubic meters of wood. The country has more than 20 million hectares (50 million acres) considered suitable for forestry operations. Forested wilderness currently occupies 780,000 hectares (1.95 million acres). Output per hectare is as follows: willows, 300 cubic meters in 10 years; pines, 500 cubic meters in 25 years; and eucalyptus, 400 cubic meters in 8 years. Costs per hectare of land are: US$80 in the Province of Córdoba, US$200 in the Province of Corrientes, and US$200 in the Province of Misiones.

Roughly 90 percent of the supply of raw wood is found in the Provinces of Misiones, Entre Rios, and Buenos Aires. Related processing operations are frequently located near the forests. Commercial activity is dominated by small to medium-sized companies (65 percent of which have no more than 10 employees). The construction of wood furniture is centered around items of traditional folk design made of *quebracho* wood. This folk style has been much appreciated by US and European consumers. However, because the industry is extremely fragmented, there are not enough standardized, large-scale manufacturers to produce in quantity for the export markets.

Paper

Argentina annually produces 750,000 tons of cellulose paste and 140,000 tons of newsprint. Pulp and paper producers—primarily large, integrated companies, producing 100 percent of paper pulp and 50 percent of paper—include Celulosa Argentina (with US$128 million in annual sales), Alto Paraná (US$113 million), Papel Prensa, (US$95 million), Papelera del Plata (US$87 million), Massuh (US$81 million), Papel Misionero, and Ledesma. The main producers of cardboard and cardboard boxes are Cartocor (a subsidiary of the Arcor group, with US$73 million in annual sales) and Zucamor (linked to the US company Union Camp, with US$63 million in sales). Many foreign firms have opened operations in Argentina recently: the already mentioned Union Camp bought 30 percent of Zucamor; Kimberly-Clark—manufacturer of Kleenex tissues—recently bought the diaper company Descartables Argentinos; and the Canadian firm Kruger is setting up a pulp production plant. Other foreign companies that recently entered Argentina are the Chilean CMPC, Inland Container from the US, the French Arjo Wiggins, and the German firm, Zellulpapier Waren.

Government Agencies

Dirección de Producción Forestal
(Administration of Forestry Production)
Av. Paseo Colón 982, Piso 1
1063 Buenos Aires
Tel: (1) 349-2101, 349-2103
Fax: (1) 349-2108

Dirección de Recursos Forestales Nativos
(Administration of Native Forestry Resources)
San Martin 459, Piso 2
1004 Buenos Aires
Tel: (1) 394-1869, 394-5961 x8-489

Instituto Forestal Nacional (IFONA)
(National Forestry Institute)
Julio A. Roca 651, Piso 7
1067 Buenos Aires
Tel: (1) 303-444   Tlx: 21535

Trade Associations

Asociación de Fabricantes de Celulosa y Papel
(Cellulose and paper manufacturers)
Belgrano 2852, Piso 1, Of. 04
1209 Buenos Aires
Tel: (1) 97-0051/4
Fax: (1) 97-0053

Cámara Argentina de Papeles y Afines
(Paper and related products)
Carlos Calvo 1247
1102 Buenos Aires
Tel: (1) 27-5671

Cámara de Empresarios Madereros y Afines (CEMA)
(Lumber)
Maza 578, Piso 5
1220 Buenos Aires
Tel: (1) 954-1111, 954-2046
Fax: (1) 97-1556

Cámara de Fabricantes de Muebles, Tapicerias y Afines (CAFYDMA)
(Furniture and rug manufacturers)
Manuel Ricardo Trelles 1961/87
1416 Buenos Aires
Tel: (1) 583-5606/7
Fax: (1) 583-5608

Directories and Publications

Argentina Forestal
(6 issues/year)
Cámara Argentina de Aserradores de Maderas, Depósitos y Afines
Alsina 440
1087 Buenos Aires
Tel: (1) 342-4389
Forestry

Trade Fairs

Refer to the "Trade Fairs" chapter for complete listings, including contact information, dates, and venues. Trade fairs with particular relevance to this industry include the following, which are listed in that chapter under the headings given below:

Agriculture, Horticulture & Aquaculture
• MADERA '95

Construction & Housing
• FITECMA '95

Furniture & Hardware
• AMOBLAR '95
• EXPOMUEBLE
• TECHNOMUEBLE '95

HOUSEHOLD APPLIANCES AND ELECTRONICS

The typical Argentine company in this industry sells a wide range of products, from appliances (including refrigerators, washing machines, dishwashers, and air conditioners) to consumer electronics (television sets, radios, and videocassette recorders—VCRs), depending heavily on recognized brand names and established distribution networks. For the most part, the technology used comes from abroad. A case in point is that of the local Aurora group. With US$260 million in annual sales and a wide line of products, it is the largest firm in the sector. A licensee of multinational Grundig, the company makes large expenditures on advertising and largely controls its main distribution channels. Another company with a similar profile is Philco (with US$252 million in annual sales), belonging to the local Macri group (which also owns carmaker Sevel). The local affiliate of Whirlpool (with US$211 million in annual sales) also specializes in appliances.

Another characteristic of this industry is its localization. Most electronics assembly plants, as well as some appliance plants, are located on the extreme southern island of Tierra del Fuego, which was established as a free trade zone to encourage this sort of development. Production of consumer electronics consists mainly of the assembly of imported parts and components. Other companies with plants in Tierra del Fuego include New San, the local branch of Sanyo (with US$162 million in annual sales), Radio Victoria, licensee of Hitachi (US$127 million), and Noblex (US$109 million), linked to Samsung. Another important firm, especially in air conditioning as well as in electronics, is BGH, with US$94 million in annual sales.

Government Agencies

Secretaría de Industria
(Secretariat of Industry)
Av. Julio A. Roca 651
1322 Buenos Aires
Tel: (1) 334-5068, 342-7822
Fax: (1) 331-3218

Trade Associations

Cámara de Industriales de Artefactos para el Hogar
(Housewares)
Paraguay 1855
Buenos Aires
Tel: (1) 813-2673, 812-0232
Fax: (1) 814-2650

Asociación de Industriales Metalúrgicos de la República Argentina (ADIMRA)
(Metallurgy industries)
Alsina 1609, Pisos 1 y 2
1088 Buenos Aires
Tel: (1) 40-0055, 40-4967, 40-5063, 40-5292, 40-5571
Fax: (1) 814-4407

Asociación de la Pequeña y Mediana Industria Electrónica y Eléctrica
(Electronic and electric industry)
Gascón 62
1181 Buenos Aires
Tel: (1) 981-2335

Asociación de Fabricas Argentinas de Terminales Eléctricas
(Electric terminals)
Av. L.N. Alem 690, Piso 10
1001 Buenos Aires
Tel: (1) 313-2552, 315-3050
Fax: (1) 313-2484

Cámara Argentina de Industrias Electrónicas (CADIE)
(Electronic industries)
Bdo. de Irigoyen 330, Piso 5, Of. 121
1072 Buenos Aires
Tel: (1) 334-4159, 334-5752, 334-6672, 334-7763
Fax: (1) 334-6672

Cámara de Fabricantes de Equipos y Máquinas de Oficina
(Office equipment manufacturers)
Alsina 1607, Piso 1
1088 Buenos Aires
Tel: (1) 371-5063, 371-5055, 371-5071

Directories and Publications

Técnica e Industria
(Monthly)
Rodríguez Peña 694, Piso 5
1020 Buenos Aires
Tel: (1) 46-3193
Technology and industry review

Trade Fairs

Refer to the "Trade Fairs" chapter for complete listings, including contact information, dates, and venues. Trade fairs with particular relevance to this industry include the following, which are listed in that chapter under the headings given below:

Computers & Communications
- Computación '95

Furniture & Hardware
- REGALA

Television, Radio, Video & Photography
- ELECTROSHOW '95
- EXPOFOTO

INDUSTRIAL PRODUCTS AND SERVICES

Plastics

This is a highly fragmented sector, with many small and medium-sized companies producing anything from household utensils to auto parts. The leading companies specializing in plastic containers are the local firm American Plast and the local affiliate of Dart Containers, each with annual sales of about US$30 million. The most important packaging companies are the affiliate of Tetra Pak (US$120 million in annual sales) and the national firm Vitopel (US$78 million in annual sales).

Steel and Aluminum

Argentina annually produces almost 3.3 million

tons of crude steel, 1.6 million tons of hot rolled flat laminates, 1.2 million tons of hot rolled non-flat laminates, 1 million tons of cold laminates, and 600,000 tons of seamless steel tubes. The undisputed leader in this industry is the Grupo Techint, owner of Siderca (with US$500 million in annual sales, a strong exporter of seamless steel tubes for the oil industry) and of the Siderar complex (US$700 million annually). Siderar was created by the merger of Propulsora Siderúrgica and the ex-state company Somisa-Aceros Paraná (an integrated producer of basic iron and steel commodity products). Following in importance is Acindar (US$450 millions in sales), a vertically integrated company, which manages the production of articles from the elaboration of primary steel through the fabrication of pipes, sheet-metal for construction, and nails. The five companies which follow these gross between US$25 and US$90 million annually, and specialize in different alloys and treatment of steel for special uses.

Aluar (US$257 million in annual sales) is the only local producer of primary aluminum. Aluar produces 173,000 tons annually, exporting about 100,000 tons of this output. Other smaller companies produce aluminum alloys and profiles for special purposes.

Construction and Engineering

An estimated 190,000 homes are being constructed in Argentina every year, and observers expect this number to increase to 275,000 by 1998. Since 1991 there has been an increase in activity in this industry as a result of both new state and private construction projects allowed by the reappearance of long-term credit and mortgages. Recent medium-scale constructions include hotels and convention centers (by Intercontinental, Hyatt, Ceasar Park, Sheraton Córdoba), the refurbishing of gasoline service station chains (YPF), and the construction of shopping centers (the Tren de la Costa complex) and supermarkets (Wal-Mart and Carrefour). Large-scale constructions include public works, especially in recently privatized services such as telecommunications (the upgrading of the Telefónica and Telecom networks), highways (Autopistas del Sol, north Greater Buenos Aires area), and hydroelectric power plants (including the installation of new turbines at Piedra del Aguila and Yaciretá).

The most important companies for construction and engineering are Techint (with annual sales of US$590 million), Benito Roggio (US$260 million), Sideco—part of the Macri Group (US$340 million), Impsa (US$134 million), Sade of the Pérez Companc group (US$130 million), and José Cartellone (US$85 million). Companies following in importance are Comercial del Plata Constructora (belonging to the Comercial del Plata group) and Gerlach Campbell. The 25 largest companies in the sector grossed a total of US$2.3 billion in 1994.

Cement

The main producer and distributor of cement in Argentina is Loma Negra (with US$260 million in annual sales in 1994), with nine production plants and 55 percent of the market. Cement production has been registering significant growth and improvement since 1991, as a result of the expansion in construction. Other major firms, in descending rank order, include Juan Minetti S.A., Corcemar, and Cementos Avellaneda, which together gross about US$305 million annually. Total cement production in 1994 was six million tons.

Government Agencies

Secretaría de Industria
(Secretariat of Industry)
Av. Julio A. Roca 651
1322 Buenos Aires
Tel: (1) 334-5068, 342-7822
Fax: (1) 331-3218

Trade Associations

Asociación Argentina de Hormigón Elaborado
(Concrete)
San Martín 1137
1004 Buenos Aires
Tel: (1) 312-3046/8

Asociación de Fabricantes de Cemento Portland
(Portland cement makers)
San Martín 1137
1137 Buenos Aires
Tel: (1) 312-1083, 315-2272
Fax: (1) 312-1700

Cámara de Fabricantes de Máquinas de Herramientas Portatiles y Afines
(Power tool manufacturers)
Alsina 1607, Piso 1
1088 Buenos Aires
Tel: (1) 371-5063, 371-5571, 371-6840

Asociación de Fabricas Argentinas de Terminales Eléctricas
(Electric terminals)
Av. L.N. Alem 690, Piso 10
1001 Buenos Aires
Tel: (1) 313-2552, 315-3050
Fax: (1) 313-2484

Asociación de Industriales Metalúrgicos de la República Argentina (ADIMRA)
(Metallurgy industries)
Alsina 1609, Pisos 1 y 2
1088 Buenos Aires
Tel: (1) 40-0055, 40-4967, 40-5063, 40-5292, 40-5571
Fax: (1) 814-4407

Cámara Argentina de Empresas Viales
(Road construction)
Piedras 383, Piso 3
1070 Buenos Aires
Tel/Fax: (1) 343-1122

Cámara Argentina de Ferroaleaciones y Aleaciones Especiales (CAFAE)
(Iron and special alloys)
Alsina 1607, Piso 1
1088 Buenos Aires
Tel: (1) 371-5063, 371-4967

Cámara Argentina de la Construcción
(Construction)
Av. Paseo Colón 823
1063 Buenos Aires
Tel/Fax: (1) 361-5036/7, 361-8778

Cámara Argentina de la Industria del Aluminio, Metales y Afines
(Aluminum, metals, and related activities)
Paraná 467, Piso 1, Of. 3 y 4
1017 Buenos Aires
Tel: (1) 40-1987, 371-1987, 371-4301

Cámara Argentina de la Máquina Herramienta
(Machine tools)
Av. Julio A. Roca 516, Piso 3
1067 Buenos Aires
Tel: (1) 343-1493, 343-3996, 343-9476
Fax: (1) 343-3996

Cámara de Fabricantes de Caños y Tubos de Acero
(Steel pipe and tube manufacturers)
Alsina 1607
1088 Buenos Aires
Tel: (1) 371-5063, 371-5571

Cámara de la Pequeña y Mediana Industria Metalúrgica
(Metallurgy industry)
Av. L.N. Alem 1067, Piso 14
1001 Buenos Aires
Tel: (1) 311-6555, 313-0638

Cámara de Productores de Metales
(Metal producers)
Alsina 1607, Piso 1
1088 Buenos Aires
Tel: (1) 371-5571, 371-4967

Cámara Argentina de la Industria Plástica
(Plastic industry)
J. Salguero 1939/41
1425 Buenos Aires
Tel: (1) 826-6060, 826-8498
Fax: (1) 826-5480

Centro Argentino de Ingenieros
(Engineers)
Cerrito 1250
1010 Buenos Aires
Tel: (1) 811-0570

Centro de Industriales Siderúrgicos
(Iron and steel industries)
Paulea 226, Piso 2
1001 Buenos Aires
Tel: (1) 311-6367, 311-6321/2
Fax: (1) 311-6367

Centro de Arquitectos y Constructores
(Architects and building contractors)
Tucumán 1539
1050 Buenos Aires
Tel: (1) 46-2664

Federación Argentina de la Construcción
(Construction)
Piedras 383, Piso 3
1070 Buenos Aires
Tel: (1) 343-1122

Unión Argentina de la Construcción
(Construction)
Av. L.N. Alem 896, Piso 6
1001 Buenos Aires
Tel: (1) 311-2864, 311-2739, 311-2692

Directories and Publications

Ideas en Arte y Tecnología
(3 issues/year)
Universidad de Belgrano
Teodoro García 2090
1426 Buenos Aires
Tel: (1) 774-2133
Covers architecture, engineering, and computer science

Técnica e Industria
(Monthly)
Rodríguez Peña 694, Piso 5
1020 Buenos Aires
Tel: (1) 46-3193
Technology and industry review

Trade Fairs

Refer to the "Trade Fairs" chapter for complete listings, including contact information, dates, and venues. Trade fairs with particular relevance to this industry include the following, which are listed in that chapter under the headings given below:

Construction & Housing
- CONSTRUMA
- EXPOVIVIENDA
- FEMATEC

Environmental & Energy
- ExpoSanitarios '95

Machinery & Tools
- Metalurgia '95

Industrial Materials
- Argenplas
- World of Concrete Expo '95

MINING

Argentina is considered "the world's last mining frontier." Its extensive mineral deposits, situated primarily along its Andean borders with Chile and Bolivia, have a geological structure similar to that found in those countries, both of which have long mining traditions. Since deregulation and the opening of the mining sector to private companies—along with the approval of the Mining Investment Law in 1993, which provides fiscal stability for 30 years and a series of tax exemptions—a number of large mining projects have gotten underway. Most have been made by foreign companies. Estimated investments over the next five years are on the order of US$2 billion. The current value of mining production—about US$600 million annually—is quite small compared with its potential.

The new Mining Investment Law offers a 100 percent deduction on income taxes for income made by investing in prospecting, exploration, and special mining studies. Additional special policies regarding tax deductions in extraction and industrialization exist. Moreover, royalties paid to the state may not exceed 3 percent of the mineral's value at the mine's mouth. In May 1993 provincial governments acceded to the Mining Agreement established between the nation and the provinces, further reducing tax burdens on mining activity. The five most important mining projects underway will involve a total investment of US$1.5 billion dollars from 1993 to 1998. The main project is "Bajo la Alumbrera" mine in the Province of Catamarca. A joint venture by Musto Explorations of Canada and Mount Isa Mines (MIM) of Australia will invest US$780 million to develop the mine. Annual production is expected to reach 180,000 metric tons of copper and 20,000 kg of gold. Other important mining projects include El Pachón (representing a US$220 million investment in copper production), Potasio Río Colorado (a US$280 million investment in potassium mining), Cerro Vanguardia (a US$150 million investment in a gold and silver mine), and Salar del Hombre Muerto (a US$95 million investment in a lithium mine).

Government Agencies

Secretaría de Minería
(Secretariat of Mining)
Av. Julio A. Roca 561, Sector 9
1322 Buenos Aires
Tel: (1) 349-3212, 349-3232
Fax: (1) 343-3525

Dirección de Desarrollo Minero
(Administration of Mining Development)
Av. Julio A. Roca 561, Piso 8
1322 Buenos Aires
Tel: (1) 349-3133

Dirección de Recursos Geológicos y Mineros
(Administration of Geological and Mining Resources)
Julio A. Roca 651, Piso 8
1322 Buenos Aires
Tel: (1) 349-3131

Instituto Nacional de Tecnología Minería (INTEMIN)
(National Institute of Mining Technology)
Parque Tecnologico Migueletes
Casilla de Correo 327
1650 San Martín
Tel: (1) 754-5151, 754-4141
Fax: (1) 754-4070, 754-8307

Servico Geológico
(Geological Service)
Av. Julio A. Roca 651
1322 Buenos Aires
Tel: (1) 541-3160/2

Trade Association

Unión Minera Argentina
(Mining)
Av. Roque S. Pena 615, Piso 4
1393 Buenos Aires
Tel: (1) 394-7369

Directories and Publications

Actividad Minera
(Monthly)
Minera Piedra Libre S.R.L.
Bolivar 187, Piso 4, Of. B
1066 Buenos Aires
Tel: (1) 343-6422
Fax: (1) 343-6138
Mines and mining industry

Latin American Mining Letter
(Twice a month)
M.I.I.D.A. Ltd.
PO Box 2137
London NW10 6TN, UK
Tel: [44] (181) 961-7407
Fax: [44] (181) 961-7487
Mines and mining industry

Fundación Bariloche: Publicaciones
(Irregular publishing schedule)
Fundación Bariloche
Instituto de Economía de la Energía
Casilla de Correo 138
8400 San Carlos de Bariloche
Pcia. de Río Negro
Mines and mining industry

Trade Fairs

Refer to the "Trade Fairs" chapter for complete listings, including contact information, dates, and venues. Trade fairs with particular relevance to this industry include the following, which are listed in that chapter under the heading given below:

Environmental & Energy
• International Mining Meeting

PETROLEUM AND CHEMICALS

Oil

Argentina extracts 38.6 million cu m of crude oil annually. Its refineries produce 18 million cu m of automotive fuels—gasoline and diesel. Fuel and oil by-product exports gross almost US$1.6 billion. According to recent estimates, fuel production represents almost 13 percent of the total value of industrial production. Argentina is self-sufficient in oil and gas, while producing excess amounts for export.

Argentina's petroleum industry had always been regulated by the state, and virtually all exploration activity was carried out by the state company Yacimientos Petrolíferos Fiscales (YPF). Following the passage of reforms in 1989, the natural gas and petroleum industry was demonopolized and deregulated. As a result of deregulation, this large state-owned company, including natural gas and petroleum exploration activity as well as both upstream and downstream operations, was privatized. This was accomplished through the sale of small volumes of stock shares in local and international markets (YPF is currently quoted on the New York Stock Exchange). YPF is now the largest private company in Argentina based on its value (estimated at US$4.5 billion), sales (US$4 billion in 1994), and profits (US$540 million in 1994).

Other important companies in the sector, in order of importance, are the local subsidiaries of Shell (with an annual US$1.7 billion in sales) and Exxon (with US$1.3 billion in 1994 sales). Further back, although still of importance, is Pérez Companc (US$424 million in sales), Astra (US$334 million), Bridas (US$296 million), and Isaura (US$226 million). Many other foreign firms also participate in exploration and oil production, including the US firm Amoco, France's Total, and Germany's Deminex, among others.

Petrochemicals

Argentina produces 285,000 tons of ethylene, 271,000 tons of polyethylene, and 91,000 tons of polyvinyl chloride (PVC) annually, among many other petrochemical products. This industry grew substantially during the 1980s, largely thanks to substantial investment and state support. Large plants were established under the government's reserved market policy, increasing production significantly. For example, ethylene production went from 47,000 tons in 1980 to 255,000 tons in 1984. During this period, the so-called "petrochemical-pole" was set up in Bahía Blanca, in the southern part of the Buenos Aires Province. Several companies, related by contracts to supply raw materials, were set up in a concentrated area with the aim of stabilizing prices and volumes in intraindustrial transactions (for example, the prices and volumes of ethylene sold to polyethylene plants). Privatization is ongoing, with the state selling its shares in different companies in the industrial complex, shares which had given the state considerable de facto operating control from its position "inside" the sector.

The main companies operating in the market are Pasa (with US$207 million in annual sales), Petroquímica Bahía Blanca (US$155 million), and Ipako (US$140 million). Other important companies include Tecpetrol, Petroken, and Petroquímica Cuyo. Today this industry operates in the context of a free trade competitive environment and is strongly oriented toward export production. During 1994 Argentina exported about US$700 million in petrochemical products.

Chemicals

Local branches of transnational corporations, particularly those of US- and German-based companies, play an important role in the Argentine chemical industry. The main manufacturer of chemical products in the country is the local subsidiary of Dupont de Nemours, with annual sales of US$260 million. Following in order of importance are the Argentine branches of Bayer and Hoeschst (US$260 and US$160 million in sales, respectively). All three top firms have highly diversified production, which they complement with imports from their home country operations. Dupont specializes in the production of plastic materials and synthetic fibers (such as Lycra); Bayer in pharmo-chemical products (although it is highly diversified); and Hoeschst in industrial chemicals. Of lesser importance is Atanor, from the Bunge & Born group, which specializes in fertilizers (US$140 million in annual sales).

Other transnational companies active in the industry include the local affiliates of Basf, Dow Chemical, ICI, Cyanamid, Unistar, Exxon Chemical, Air Liquide, Monsanto, and Liquid Carbonic. Production of resins, paint, and varnishes is led by Alba (a Bunge & Born subsidiary with annual sales of US$150 million), the local affiliate of Sherwin & Williams, and Colorín (a local firm with annual sales of US$70 million recently bought by the Venezuelan group Corimon).

Cleaning Products and Cosmetics

The leading company for household cleaning products and cosmetics is the Argentine subsidiary of the Anglo-Dutch firm Unilever (with annual sales of US$650 million), which places a great many brands and top-of-the-line products into various markets. In descending order of importance are Avon, the US direct sales company (with annual Argentine sales of US$280 million), S.C. Johnson & Son (US$140 million), and the local branch of Gilette (US$130 million). The 10 companies which follow have annual sales of between US$20 and US$50 million dollars. Recently arrived Procter & Gamble, which purchased Compañia Química (the local leader in detergents with its "Magistral" brand) from the Bunge & Born group and soapmaker Llauró.

Pharmaceuticals

Two aspects distinguish the Argentine pharmaceuticals industry from its counterparts in Latin America. One is its ability to meet domestic demand through local production, and the other is the dominance of non-multinational-affiliated domestic companies. Argentine patents law, which until recently did not effectively protect patents on pharmaceuticals products, allowed national firms to compete with transnational corporations by removing the need for extensive product development expenditure by the nationals. This key law has recently been changed, establishing intellectual property rights in line with the requirements established by the General Agreement on Tariffs and Trade (GATT). The two leading Argentine pharmaceuticals firms are Bagó and Roemmers, each with about US$150 million in annual sales. The next largest firm is Sidus (US$140 million in sales), which is also the leading company in biotechnology, an activity for which it has created a separate affiliate, Biosidus. Other important firms are the local affiliates of Roche, Schering Plough, and Pfizer. The local affiliate of Bayer (with US$260 million dollars in 1994 sales) participates in this industry, as well as in many other chemical sectors. The next 20 companies gross between US$100 and US$20 million, some using domestic and some foreign capital. Many of these produce veterinary pharmaceuticals; the leading firm in this sector is the local affiliate of Ciba-Geigy (with annual sales of US$200 million).

Government Agencies

Secretaría de Industria
(Secretariat of Industry)
Av. Julio A. Roca 651
1322 Buenos Aires
Tel: (1) 334-5068, 342-7822
Fax: (1) 331-3218

Secretaría de Energía
(Secretariat of Energy)
Av. Paseo Colón 171, Piso 8, Of. 803
1063 Buenos Aires
Tel: (1) 349-8003/5
Fax: (1) 343-6404

Dirección Nacional de Combustibles
(National Administration of Fuels)
Av. Paseo Colón 171, Piso 6, Of. 620
1063 Buenos Aires
Tel: (1) 349-8030/1

Trade Associations

Asociación Industrial Artículos de Limpieza, Personal del Hogar y Afines (ALPHA)
(Personal care products)
Av. L.N. Alem 1067, Piso 12
1001 Buenos Aires
Tel: (1) 312-4605

Cámara Argentina de Especialidades Medicinales (CAEME)
(Pharmaceutical laboratories)
Av. L.N. Alem 619, Piso 5
Buenos Aires
Tel: (1) 313-0489

Cámara Argentina de la Industria de Productos de Higiene y Tocador
(Personal care and toilet products)
Paraguay 1857
1121 Buenos Aires
Tel: (1) 42-5925

Cámara Argentina de la Industria Plástica
(Plastic industry)
J. Salguero 1939/41
1425 Buenos Aires
Tel: (1) 826-6060, 826-8498
Fax: (1) 826-5480

Cámara Argentina de Productores de Drogas Farmacéuticas (CAPDROFAR)
(Pharmaceutical drug producers)
Carlos Pellegrini 465, Piso 11, Of. 84
Buenos Aires
Tel: (1) 326-6209

Cámara Argentina de Productos Químicos (CAPQ)
(Chemical products)
Rodriguez Peña 426, Piso 3
1020 Buenos Aires
Tel: (1) 476-0534

Cámara de Empresas Petroleras Argentinas
(Oil companies)
Av. L.N. Alem 1067, Piso 2
1001 Buenos Aires
Tel: (1) 313-1544, 313-2589
Fax: (1) 313-1544

Cámara de Fabricantes de Detergentes
(Detergent manufacturers)
Av. L.N. Alem 1067, Piso 12
1001 Buenos Aires
Tel: (1) 312-4605

Cámara de la Industria de la Pintura
(Paint industry)
Av. L.N. Alem 1067, Piso 13
1001 Buenos Aires
Tel: (1) 313-0064, 313-7083

Cámara de la Industria del Petroleo
(Petroleum industry)
Av. Madero 1020, Piso 11
1106 Buenos Aires
Tel: (1) 312-0410, 312-0898, 312-9418
Fax: (1) 312-0898

Cámara de la Industria Química y Petroquímica
(Chemical and petrochemical industries)
Av. L.N. Alem 1067, Piso 14, Of. 58
1001 Buenos Aires
Tel: (1) 311-7732, 313-0944, 313-1059
Fax: (1) 312-4773

Cámara de Sanidad Agropecuaria y Fertilizantes
(Livestock health and fertilizer safety)
Av. Rivadavia 1367, Piso 7, Of. B
1033 Buenos Aires
Tel: (1) 381-2742, 381-6418, 383-0942
Fax: (1) 383-1562

Centro Industrial de Laboratorios Farmacéuticos Argentinos (CILFA)
(Pharmaceutical laboratories)
Esmeralda 130, Piso 5
1035 Buenos Aires
Tel: (1) 394-2963, 394-2978, 394-2981

Confederación Farmacéutica Argentina
(Pharmaceutic Confederaton)
Alsina 655, Piso 2
1087 Buenos Aires
Tel: (1) 343-5632

Federación de la Industria del Caucho
(Rubber)
Av. L.N. Alem 1067, Piso 16
1001 Buenos Aires
Tel: (1) 313-2009, 313-2140, 313-2192
Fax: (1) 312-9892

Instituto Argentino del Petroleo
(Argentine Petroleum Institute)
Maipú 645, Piso 3, Primer Cuerpo
Buenos Aires
Tel: (1) 322-3233, 322-3652, 322-3244
Fax: (1) 322-3233

Instituto Petroquímico Argentino
(Argentine Petrochemical Institute)
Av. Santa Fe 1480, Piso 5
Buenos Aires
Tel: (1) 813-3436, 813-6636
Fax: (1) 813-3436

Trade Fairs

Refer to the "Trade Fairs" chapter for complete listings, including contact information, dates, and venues. Trade fairs with particular relevance to this industry include the following, which are listed in that chapter under the headings given below:

Cleaning
• Expo-Clean

Environmental & Energy
• Argentina Oil & Gas Expo '95

Health & Beauty
• EXPOUTILISMA '95
• COSMESUR
• Expo Internacional de Cosmetología

Medical & Dental
• Expo Farmácia

Industrial Materials
• PINTURA '95

TELECOMMUNICATIONS

In 1989 Argentina began the deregulation and demonopolization of its telephone service with the privatization of the state-owned monopoly, ENTEL. The market was divided between two companies—Telecom and Telefónica de Argentina—which would be in charge of the trunk phone network and basic telephone service in, respectively, the Center-to-North and Center-to-South regions of the country. These companies will hold a monopoly in these markets until 1997. In return, the companies were required to invest heavily, pledging to meet certain quality standards and service expansion goals.

The Argentine telecommunications market involves approximately US$8.5 billion a year. The ratio of telephones to 100 inhabitants rose from 11 in 1991 to 13 in 1993, and both companies have plans involving the investment of about US$5 billion each during the next five years (1995–2000). The company Telintar took responsibility for supplying international service and value-added services, such as data package transmission, automated teller machine (ATM) communications, electronic mail, data banks, and similar services.

Two separate bands have been established to cover the entire country for cellular phone service, and two companies were allowed to compete in each area. In the Greater Buenos Aires and La Plata area, the operating companies are Movicom (operating since 1988) and Movistar (Miniphone), operating since 1993. In the provinces, service began in 1993 with the establishment of CTI, a company formed by US communications firms GTE and AT&T with the local Clarín and Benito Roggio groups. CTI was given a concession to supply cellular phone service in the two regions outside Buenos Aires and La Plata. These firms serve about 200,000 subscribers. In 1996 Telefónica de Argentina and Telecom will be able to operate the second band of cellular telecommunications, competing directly with CTI.

As noted, the telecommunications market will be fully deregulated in 1997, allowing the entrance of new companies to compete with previously established providers. Many foreign firms, from long distance service providers, such as AT&T, to cable network operators like TCI (owner of the local Cablevisión cable network) have announced their intentions to compete with Telefónica and Telecom after deregulation.

In 1994 Telefónica de Argentina grossed US$2.1 billion, while Telecom had revenues of US$1.8 billion, occupying third and fifth places, respectively, among Argentina's largest companies. Telintar had sales of US$520 million, while cellular phone company Movicom had sales of US$280 million.

Government Agencies

Secretaría de Obras Publicas y Comunicaciones
(Secretariat of Public Works and Communications)
Sarmiento 151
1041 Buenos Aires
Tel: (1) 49-9481, 312-1283

Comisión Nacional de Telecomunicaciones (CNT)
(National Commission of Telecommunications)
Sarmiento 151, Piso 4, Of. 435
1041 Buenos Aires

Trade Associations

Asociación Argentina de Televisión por Cable (ATVC)
(Cable television)
Av. de Mayo 749, Piso 2, Of. 10
1084 Buenos Aires
Tel: (1) 342-3382
Fax: (1) 343-1716

Cámara de Empresas de Obras Ferroviarias y Vias de Comunicación
(Railway works and communication networks companies)
Av. Córdoba 890, Piso 3
1054 Buenos Aires
Tel: (1) 322-0555, 322-6453

Consejo Profesional de Ingeniería de Telecomunicaciones, Electrónica y Computación
(Telecommuications, electronics, and computer engineers)
Perú 562
1068 Buenos Aires
Tel: (1) 30-8407, 30-8423, 34-6291, 34-7289

Directories and Publications

Comunicaciones: Telecomunicaciones, Comunicaciones de Datos, Computadoras y Satélites
(Quarterly)
Intercom Corp.
9200 S. Dadeland Blvd., Suite 309
Miami, FL 33156-2703, USA, USA
Tel: [1] (305) 670-9444
Fax: [1] (305) 670-9459
Distributed throughout Latin America for the telecommunication and computer technologies

Latin America Telecom Report
(Monthly; English)
International Technology Consultants
1724 Kalorama Rd. NW, Suite 210
Washington, DC 20009-2624, USA
Tel: [1] (202) 234-2138
Fax: [1] (202) 483-7922
Latin American telecommunications and information technology markets

Latin American Cable & Pay TV
(Monthly; English)
Kagan World Media, Ltd.
126 Clock Tower Place
Carmel, CA 93923, USA
Tel: [1] (408) 624-1536
Fax: [1] (408) 625-3225

Revista Telegráfica Electrónica
(Monthly)
Arbo S.A.C.E.I.
Av. Martín García 653
Buenos Aires
Telephone and telegraphic communications

Trade Fairs

Refer to the "Trade Fairs" chapter for complete listings, including contact information, dates, and venues. Trade fairs with particular relevance to this industry include the following, which are listed in that chapter under the headings given below:

Computers & Communications
- Argentina '95
- CLER '95
- COMEXPO/ARGENTINA
- EXPO Usaria
- INFOCOM '95
- INFOTEC

- TELECOMINICACIONES '95

Television, Radio, Video & Photography
- CAPER '95

TEXTILES AND APPAREL

Cotton and Synthetic Yarns

Argentina produces about 200,000 tons of cotton annually of a quality and at prices that are internationally competitive. Such privileged access to raw materials forms the basis for the various sectors of the domestic cotton spinning industry. On the one hand, Alpargatas and Grafa (with US$350 million and US$115 million, respectively, in annual sales), are both large, vertically integrated textile firms; between them, these firms operate most of the cotton spinning facilities. These firms use the product to weave fabrics in their own plants rather than selling it; this type of vertical integration is common among smaller textile companies as well. However, on the other hand, there are certain types of medium-sized to large companies dedicated solely to spinning, primarily for export. Such companies include Guilford Argentina (with US$50 million in annual sales), Algodonera San Luis (US$31 million), and Tiroití.

The local synthetic yarns industry—which is actually closer technologically to the chemical industry than it is to the textile industry—is under serious pressure from low-cost overseas competition. Consequently, Hisisa (with US$38 million in sales in 1993), a major fixture in the Argentine industry, had to close its doors, unable to compete without the tariff protections which it had enjoyed throughout its history. Other firms, such as Manufactura de Fibras Sintéticas (US$56 million), have been able to remain in the market, at least for the present.

Textiles

The most important textile companies are the previously mentioned Alpargatas and Grafa (with US$350 million and US$115 million in sales, respectively). Alpargatas holds 70 percent of the local denim market and dominates the market for canvas and other thick cotton fabrics. It also owns a sports footwear and sportswear factory producing Topper (the second most successful sports shoe brand in Argentina) and is the local representative for Nike sports shoes. Grafa dominates the local bed linen and towel markets, as well as the one for work clothes.

Other important firms in the sector are Tejeduría Argentina del Noroeste (US$42 million in sales), Inta (US$33 million), Tejimet (US$28 million), and Uzal (US$25 million). The 10 companies which follow these major firms gross between US$15 and US$20 million annually, making up a somewhat concentrated sector. Key leaders exist in markets for specific products (as in the cases of the denim, bed linen, and towels markets, as noted); other product lines are also subject to domination by a small number of producers. However, the traditional market power of some companies has been greatly altered by free trade, as imports—particularly from Brazil and Southeast Asia—have threatened markets throughout the industry. The serious difficulties faced by many firms in this sector have caused the government to reverse itself somewhat to provide some protection for the industry, one of very few exceptions made to the free trade policy now in force.

Apparel

The clothing manufacturing industry is extremely fragmented, with predominantly small to medium-sized companies (many producing through the *facón*, or independent job subcontractor, system). Such firms are responsible for more than 70 percent of production. The total value of sales in the apparel sector is estimated at US$6 billion. Difficulties in modernizing (through specialization, increasing scales of production, automation, and similar improvements) have placed the sector at a disadvantage in competing with low-cost imports from Southeast Asia and Brazil (as well as those from European out-of-season clearance sales). The barriers which had protected the sector from foreign competition—including strong consumer preference—are being eliminated by large differences in price and the flexibility being shown by foreign manufacturers (for example, Brazilian manufacturers are making clothing specially designed for Argentine markets). In fact, some companies which control brands and distribution channels are placing their orders in Southeast Asia using their own designs and patterns, thus replacing smaller local subcontractors. The situation is particularly serious for the small manufacturing companies that do not control brand names or distribution channels; many of these may disappear.

Sports Footwear and Sportswear

Argentina has been no exception to the surge in growth that this sector has experienced worldwide during the last two decades as consumer preferences have changed in favor of more informal sports apparel. This industry was practically nonexistent in Argentina as recently as 20 years ago. For instance, in 1970 there were only 10 sporting goods stores in the whole country, while today there are more than 2,500. In the sports shoe sector, concentration is much higher than in other textile or clothing industries. Competition prevails primarily among the few local licensees of foreign brands, with large sums being spent on advertising, innovation, and retooling

in order to maintain product differentiation. The leading firm is Gatic S.A., the local licensee for Adidas, as well as New Balance, Le Coq Sportif, Superga, L.A. Gear, Bata, Benetton, and Vibram. Gatic's annual sales have been US$285 million, and it controls about 55 percent of the market. In second place is Alpargatas, licensee and representative of Nike and owner of the Topper national brand, with 35 percent of the market. This leaves only 10 percent of the market for other licensees of international brands as well as for smaller firms manufacturing various local brands.

Leather Footwear

In contrast with the impressive growth in demand for sports footwear, the leather shoe industry has seen a systematic drop in demand: from 100 million pairs of shoes produced in 1970 to only 70 million produced today, representing annual sales of US$450 million. Imports, virtually nonexistent in the past, have risen to 15 million pairs a year, or nearly 20 percent of total national consumption. Within this context, many companies of all sizes have been disappearing. Many have attempted to convert to sports shoe manufacturing, although such conversion represents a tremendous cost for the many small firms that characterize this industry. Unlike the fragmented leather footwear industry which depended on a cadre of highly skilled shoemakers, the sports shoe industry requires more capital than skill, and the industry is dominated by large firms and requires large investments in equipment as well as in advertising in order to compete effectively.

Making matters worse, the largest sports shoe companies have recently entered the leather shoe industry (Gatic, with the license for the Bata and Ecco lines, as well as Alpargatas with its brand, Bull). Together with Grimoldi (with US$62 million in sales, the leading company in the sector, and the licensee for Hush Puppies), they have used competitive strategies from the sports footwear market: brands publicized through advertisement, licenses of foreign brands, and huge investments in new product and process technologies. As a result, a greater concentration is being produced and many small to medium-sized companies are going out of business.

Despite competitive advantages in Argentine shoe production (given the availability and low cost of high-quality leather), footwear exports are marginal. This may be largely the result of the difficulties that the small firms, which once prevailed in the industry, have had in reaching the scale and quality standards necessary to serve international markets. The current tendency towards conversion, with a greater degree of concentration, could be the basis for establishing the necessary economies of scale. If so, these companies could avail themselves of the cost advantages which Argentina enjoys to make significant entries into export markets.

Leather and Tanning

The leather processing industry is primarily oriented towards exports: of total annual revenues of US$700 million dollars, nearly two-thirds—US$450 million—is derived from exports. The most important company in the industry is Federico Meiners, with US$108 million dollars in sales in 1994. Following in order of importance are Yoma (US$66 million), Fonseca (US$65 million), San Luis (US$61 million), and Sadesa (US$58 million). The next 15 companies which follow gross between US$10 and US$50 million annually. The industry is hardly concentrated, and small and medium-sized companies represent the norm.

Government Agencies

Secretaría de Industria
(Secretariat of Industry)
Av. Julio A. Roca 651
1322 Buenos Aires
Tel: (1) 334-5068, 342-7822
Fax: (1) 331-3218

Trade Associations

Asociación Civil Fabricantes de la Industria del Calzado (ACFIC)
(Shoe industry)
Chilavert 6780, Piso 1
1439 Buenos Aires
Tel: (1) 601-9499

Asociación de Establecimientos Textiles con Proceso Industrial
(Textile establishments with industrial processing)
Av. L.N. Alem 1067, Piso 8
1001 Buenos Aires
Tel: (1) 311-0499

Asociación de Fabricantes de Tejidos de Algodón
(Cotton fabric manufacturers)
Av. L.N. Alem 1067, Piso 8
1001 Buenos Aires
Tel: (1) 311-0499

Asociación de Fabricantes de Tejidos de Lana
(Wool fabric manufacturers)
Av. L.N. Alem 1067, Piso 8
1001 Buenos Aires
Tel: (1) 311-0499

Asociación de Fabricantes de Tejidos de Punto
(Knitted fabric manufacturers)
Av. L.N. Alem 1067, Piso 8
1001 Buenos Aires
Tel: (1) 311-0499

Asociación de Hilanderías de Algodón
(Cotton spinning mills)
Av. L.N. 1067, Piso 8
1001 Buenos Aires
Tel: (1) 311-0499

Asociación de Industriales Textiles Argentinos
(Textile industries)
Uruguay 291, Piso 4
1015 Buenos Aires
Tel: (1) 373-2256, 373-2502, 373-2154

Asociación de Tintorerías de Establecimientos Textiles
(Textile dyeing establishments)
Av. L.N. Alem 1067, Piso 8
1001 Buenos Aires
Tel: (1) 311-0499

Asociación Peinadurías e Hilanderías
(Combing and spinning mills)
Av. L.N. Alem 1067, Piso 8
1001 Buenos Aires
Tel: (1) 311-0499

Asociación Texturizadores de Hilados Sintéticos y Afines
(Synthetic yarn texturizers)
Av. L.N. Alem 1067, Piso 8
1001 Buenos Aires
Tel: (1) 311-0499

Cámara Algodonera Argentina
(Cotton manufacturers)
25 de Mayo 347, Piso 2, Of. 200
1002 Buenos Aires
Tel/Fax: (1) 312-0246

Cámara Argentina de Indumentaria para Bebes y Niños
(Baby and children's clothing)
Junín 347, Piso 4, Of. B
1026 Buenos Aires
Tel: (1) 953-9540

Cámara de la Industria Curtidora Argentina
(Tanning industry)
Av. Belgrano 3978
1210 Buenos Aires
Tel: (1) 981-4393, 983-9623
Fax: (1) 981-5437, 983-8502

Cámara Argentina de la Industria del Calzado
(Shoe industry)
Av. Rivadavia 4323
1205 Buenos Aires
Tel: (1) 981-0732, 981-2303, 981-5992
Fax: (1) 981-3203

Cámara de la Industria de Fibras Manufacturadas
(Manmade fiber industry)
Av. E. Madero 1020, Piso 24
1106 Buenos Aires
Tel: (1) 313-6015
Fax: (1) 319-4258

Cámara Industrial Argentina de la Indumentaria
(Apparel industry)
Av. L.N. Alem 1067, Piso 13, Of. 41
1001 Buenos Aires
Tel: (1) 313-6006, 313-6107
Fax: (1) 313-6206

Cámara Industrial de la Seda y de las Fibras Sintéticas
(Silk and synthetic fiber industries)
Av. L.N. Alem 1067, Piso 8
1001 Buenos Aires
Tel: (1) 311-0499

Cámara Industrial de las Manufacturas del Cuero y Afines de la República Argentina (CIMA)
(Leather manufacturers)
Bernardo de Irigoyen 972, Piso 5
1034 Buenos Aires
Tel: (1) 304-5116, 27-1860
Fax: (1) 304-9448

Cámara Industrial del Deporte y Afines (CAMIDA)
(Apparel)
Alsina 1433, Piso 7, Of. B
1088 Buenos Aires
Fax: (1) 381-4757

Cámara Industrial Marroquinera Argentina
(Leather goods industry)
Bdo. de Irigoyen 972, Piso 5
1072 Buenos Aires
Tel: (1) 27-1860, 304-9448, 304-5116

Federación Industriales Textiles Argentinos (FITA)
(Textile industries)
Av. L.N. Alem 1067, Piso 8
1001 Buenos Aires
Tel: (1) 311-0499, 311-0599, 311-6899, 311-7776
Fax: (1) 311-7602

Directories and Publications

Latin American Textile Industry Directory
(Annual; English, Portuguese, Spanish)
Aquino Productions
Box 15760
Stamford, CT 06901, USA
Tel: [1] (203) 325-3138

Cleo en la Moda
(Every 2 months; English and Spanish eds. available)
Ediciones Ariadna
472 Suipacha
Buenos Aires
Leather and fur, shoes and boots, clothing trade, textiles and fabrics

Gaceta Textil
(Monthly)
Gaceta Editora Coop Ltda.
25 de Mayo 786, Piso 12
Buenos Aires
Textile industries and fabrics

Industria Textil Sud Americana
(Every 2 months)
Editesa S.A.
Av. Roque Saenz Pena 825
Buenos Aires
Textile industry

Mundo Textil Argentino
(Monthly)
25 de Mayo 267-218
Buenos Aires
Textile industry

Textiles Panamericanos: Revista para la Industria Textil
(Quarterly)
Billian Publishing, Inc.
2100 Powers Ferry Rd.
Atlanta, GA 30339, USA
Tel: [1] (404) 955-5656
Fax: [1] (404) 952-0669
Textile and fabric industries

Trade Fairs

Refer to the "Trade Fairs" chapter for complete listings, including contact information, dates, and venues. Trade fairs with particular relevance to this industry include the following, which are listed in that chapter under the headings given below:

Apparel, Jewelry & Textiles
- Expoferta y Segunda
- Feria de la Moda
- MABYN 20 Colección
- Moda Visión—Idea Textil—Muestra
- Mujer '95
- Salon Internacional de la Moda
- SERMAC '95
- SIMAT '96
- Textil Hogar '95

Footwear & Leather Goods
- CEMCA
- EFICA
- EXPOCAIPIC
- EXPOCALZADO
- Expocentro del Calzado

VEHICLES

In 1994 Argentina's automotive industry produced 408,000 units, marking a historical high in output and an impressive recovery from the recent low of 100,000 units produced in 1990. This notable increase is mostly the result of the return of credit to Argentina after the institution of the Convertibility Law. This allowed Argentines, after a long period of purchasing restraint, to buy consumer durable goods and begin to satisfy the pent-up demand built up over years during which they had to make do with outdated equipment. The controversial tariff and quota regime which protects this industry determines that consumer demand will be satisfied primarily from local production.

The main companies in the automotive sector are Sevel, the local licensee for Fiat and Peugeot, which belongs to the Argentine Macri group; CIADEA, the local licensee for Renault, owned by the Brazilian-Argentine auto parts group, COFAL; and the local affiliates of Ford and Volkswagen. Until the end of 1994, Ford and Volkswagen operated jointly as Autolatina in Argentina and Brazil; each now operates separately in both countries. In 1994, Sevel grossed US$2.2 billion, Autolatina US$1.9 billion, and

CIADEA US$1.6 billion, occupying respectively second, fourth, and seventh place among Argentina's largest companies.

The main weakness of the Argentine automotive industry is the dispersed production of a relatively large number of models, resulting in a lack of economies of scale in production for any given model or firm. The Car Industry Regime, currently in force, is a set of regulations aimed at compelling automakers to specialize in just a few models, thus producing at a level that allows competitive pricing and exports, while allowing them to import the models whose production has been discontinued under this plan. The best-selling car in 1994 was the Fiat Duna at 50,000 units, while the minimum production level to achieve economies of scale to become competitive in international markets is considered to be about 100,000 units per year. Other models produced include the Renault 9 with 40,000 units produced and the Renault 19, the Peugeot 504, the Ford Escort, and the Volkswagen Gol, each varying between 30,000 and 40,000 units per year. However, it is important to point out that despite its relative inefficiency, the Argentine industry is not merely an assembly line for foreign-made parts. Rather, the local autoparts industry supplies about 60 percent of all components used.

Truck and multipassenger transport vehicles production is about 15,500 units annually. The leader is the local subsidiary of Mercedes Benz (with annual sales of US$480 million), followed by the local branch of Scania (grossing US$220 million), and Fiat Iveco (US$126 million in sales).

Since 1994 Argentina has attracted subsidiaries of General Motors (which is installing a new plant in Córdoba Province), Chrysler (partnering with Fiat Iveco), and Toyota (which is also constructing a plant). All these new ventures will start production of pickup trucks and other light transportation vehicles.

Government Agencies

Secretaría de Industria
(Secretariat of Industry)
Av. Julio A. Roca 651
1322 Buenos Aires
Tel: (1) 334-5068, 342-7822
Fax: (1) 331-3218

Subsecretaría de Transporte Automotor
(Undersecretariat of Automobile Transport)
Hipólito Yrigoyen 250
1310 Buenos Aires

Trade Associations

Asociación de Fábricas Argentinas de Tractores
(Tractor manufacturers)
1015 Buenos Aires
Tel: (1) 49-8573, 49-8590
Fax: (1) 49-8573

Asociación de Fábricas de Automotores (ADEFA)
(Automobile manufacturers)
Marcelo T. de Alvear 636, Piso 5
1058 Buenos Aires
Tel: (1) 312-1306, 312-3483
Fax: (1) 315-2990

Cámara Argentina de Fabricantes, Equipos, Herramientas e Instrumentos para el Servicio del Automotor
(Automotive service)
Alsina 1607, Piso 1
1088 Buenos Aires
Tel: (1) 371-5063, 371-5571, 371-4967

Cámara Argentina de la Industria de Autocomponentes
(Car parts industry)
Viamonte 1167, Piso 2
1053 Buenos Aires
Tel: (1) 46-9516, 46-8993

Cámara Industrial de Fabricantes de Autopiezas (CIFARA)
(Autoparts manufacturers)
Viamonte 1393
1053 Buenos Aires
Tel: (1) 49-5784, 49-6029, 49-6889
Fax: (1) 49-6724

Directories and Publications

A.G.E.S.
(6 issues/year)
Asociación de Garajes y Estaciones de Servico
Hipólito Yrigoyen 2738
Buenos Aires
Automotive industry

Argentina Automotriz
(6 issues/year)
Av. Belgrano 1580, Piso 6
1093 Buenos Aires
Tel: (1) 381-8383, 381-9277, 381-9253
Automotive industry

Corsa
(Weekly)
Editorial Abril S.A.
Leandro N. Alem 896
Buenos Aires
Automotive industry

Trade Fairs

Refer to the "Trade Fairs" chapter for complete listings, including contact information, dates, and venues. Trade fairs with particular relevance to this industry include the following, which are listed in that chapter under the heading given below:

Automotive

• AUTOPAR

• Expo-Motors

Trade Fairs

INTRODUCTION

Argentina, because of active official attention aimed at promoting trade, is rapidly gaining a notable position in the trade fair field. This chapter focuses primarily on shows taking place in Argen-

tina, but some information regarding shows occurring outside Argentina might prove useful to a businessperson interested in Argentina. In particular, Brazil occupies a special place in the Argentine economy and is also the site of many important international trade fairs. Whatever your company's focus, you should find a number of exhibitions of interest in the following listing of trade fairs.

One can readily see the richness and complexity of Argentina and its business environment by reviewing the breadth of trade fairs taking place in Argentina today. Virtually every area—from traditional agricultural shows to high-tech fairs—is covered in some Argentine format. The listings in the following pages contain information that has been gathered from a number of different sources. However, the primary sources were Argentine government agencies and trade show organizers themselves. While the editors have made every attempt to verify that the entries are correct and current, it is always advisable to check with a trade show's organizer to ensure that the dates and location are firm.

The majority of Argentine fairs take place in Buenos Aires, the center of the nation's business. Córdoba—Argentina's second city—is host to an ever increasing number of shows, while Corrientes, Paraná, Salta, Santa Fe, and San Miguel de Tucumán host some international fairs as well. For information on shows in these other centers, contact the government trade promotion agency Fundación Exportar. (*See* "Useful Addresses" on page 123.)

The trade fair listings are organized first by product category, then alphabetically by name within a product category. (The product categories are provided in the table of contents, and cross-references to other categories are within the table.) Shows falling into the "Comprehensive" category comprises trade shows that exhibit goods bridging several categories, often from one particular region of Argentina or of the world. When reviewing these listings be sure to explore any related categories. Also included are other potential sources of trade show information: organizations, associations, and directories.

Each listing provides the name of a trade show, recent or upcoming dates, city, specific site, frequency, and contact information—however, available data varies in its completeness. If you find that a date given for a show has already passed, don't despair. Although some shows are single events most occur regularly, annually or every two or three years. Some, particularly fashion shows, occur more than once a year. Certain events are repeatedly held in the same location, but some move around from year to year. Remember that if the organizer of a particular show has changed since these listings were compiled, trade associations in your area of interest may be able to confirm an upcoming show. Note that show names are predominately in Spanish, thus most listings include a brief English description. You will almost invariably discover some variations in the names of the fairs; these exist at several different levels and for a number of possible reasons. Larger fairs may include smaller, associated congresses or conferences, and some of the fairs use only acronyms. In addition, Spanish names may be translated in a variety of ways.

EXHIBITING IN ARGENTINA

The available facilities and the procedures for exhibiting in Argentina are similar to those elsewhere in the region. Pay particular attention to any information you receive from show organizers. If possible, get names of exhibitors at previous shows so that you can interview them concerning any problems encountered in the past; find out how best to avoid or cope with such difficulties. Contacting past exhibitors will also give you an opportunity to get the general flavor of a show and perhaps to discover some key contacts.

The type of displays used and the size, shape, and location of the space available should be confirmed early in the process—then you can make decisions about what to bring from your headquarters and what to rent at the fair location. Some exhibitors have greater success renting displays locally rather than shipping them. Not only will you be spared the difficulty of clearing displays through customs, but you may also be better accommodated: locally rented displays are more likely to be designed specifically for the size and layout of that particular exhibition space. If you do decide to bring your own display materials, make sure that you allow adequate time—and then some—for all items to clear customs. If you will require assistance to set up your display, be sure to communicate that clearly to the show organizers well in advance so that the necessary assistance can be arranged. Faxes may be the most effective method of communicating with show organizers because it circumvents some of the problems inherent in operating across two languages and gives you a record of interchanges suitable for review with the organizers should any confusion arise.

Since trade fairs always cause a shortage of hotel rooms and rental cars, create a plan to guarantee that you and your staff will have adequate lodging, transportation, and other necessities. Plan ahead for contingencies, and you will have a much smoother experience in Argentina, and to your prospective suppliers and clients you will appear much calmer, confident, and in charge.

Trade Fair Venues in Argentina

The number of trade fairs in Argentina has been growing rapidly during the past few years, for a variety of reasons. The Argentine government has been a very proactive partner to its importers and exporters in order to heighten awareness of opportunities within the new Argentina. The recent increase in foreign investment in Argentina is proof of growing international confidence in the country's business climate. Additionally, with the establishment of Mercosur—the customs union including Argentina, Brazil, Paraguay, and Uruguay— observers are expecting to see a number of new trade shows that are specifically targeted at the concerns of the Mercosur members. As this regional trade increases, it may also prove worthwhile to monitor trade show activities in member and other neighboring nations.

There are more than 100 established trade fairs in Argentina, and the number, as mentioned earlier, is growing rapidly. Within Argentina approximately 80 percent of all trade fairs take place in Buenos Aires. The second most popular exhibition site is the inland city of Córdoba, with many of the shows taking place at the Predio Ferial Córdoba. While these two locations account for the majority of trade show activity in Argentina, you will also see that the cities of Neuquén, Salta, and Mar Del Plata are also represented.

In Buenos Aires the principal sites are: the Buenos Aires Sheraton Hotel; the Centro Costa Salguero; Centro de Exposiciones, Ferias y Congresos; the Centro Municipal de Exposiciones; and the Predio Ferial de Palermo. There are also many additional, smaller venues, which host specialized shows.

FOR FURTHER INFORMATION

Argentine consulates in your home country are often the best source of information about trade fairs in Argentina. For instance, the Argentine embassy in the US publishes a monthly newsletter,

Argentine Trade & Investment News, which includes listings of upcoming Argentine trade fairs; and embassies in other countries may also provide regular or occasional published listings. (Refer to the "Important Addresses" chapter, beginning on page 315, for listings of embassies, consulates, and trade offices.)

There are a several other strategies for researching information on trade shows that can help you market your product or service, or help you find suppliers in Argentina. If you are interested in exporting to Argentina, your country's embassy in Buenos Aires may be able to advise you about trade missions or participation in trade fairs in that city. A number of organizations used in researching this chapter are listed in "Useful Addresses" on page 123. Professional associations in Argentina in your area of interest are often excellent sources of information on trade fairs (refer to the "Important Addresses" chapter, beginning on page 315, for listings). Basic reference materials include *Exhibit Review* magazine and the *International Encyclopedia of Associations* and *Trade Fair Directory* (the latter two from Gale Publications).

FURTHER READING

Books and Periodicals

The Exhibit Review, 4620 SW Beaverton-Hillsdale Hwy., Suite B-1; Portland, OR 97221, USA; Tel: [1] (503) 244-8677 Fax: [1] (503) 244-8745.

Directory of Argentine Importers, 1994, Available from: Martin D. Garcia, 2626 11th Street #2, Santa Monica, CA 90405, USA; Tel: [1] (310) 452-0614

Ferias & Congresos, bimonthly periodical listing and reviewing trade fairs in Argentina. Available from: Ferias & Congresos S.A., Av. Córdoba 3580, 1188 Buenos Aires, Argentina; Fax: [54] (1) 862-2301, 88-7630, 865-8972.

How to Get the Most Out of Trade Shows, by Steve Miller; foreword by William W. Mee, Lincolnwood, IL, USA; NTC Business Books, 1990.

Marketing by Exhibiting in the Global Market: A Complete Handbook to International Exhibiting, by Michael S. Muribi and Carol A. Fojtik. Available from: Expressions International, Inc., 330 N. Garfield, Suite 110, Lombard, IL 60148, USA; Tel [1] (708) 495-8740.

Electronic Sources

There are four premier electronic sources covering international trade shows. While these online databases can be expensive to use, their advanced search capabilities allow the user to locate fairs by country, date, subject, and a number of other criteria in a very efficient and timely fashion. Some trade associations have the ability to search these databases for their clients.

Eventline and *Fairbase,* Available via Knight Ridder Information Services; Tel: (800) 334-2564 (toll-free in the USA only), or [1] (415) 858-3785 (non-US callers).

Global Meeting Online; Tel: [1] (615) 482-6451.

Trade Fair International, Inc., 1350 Connecticut Ave. NW, Suite 850, Washington, DC 20036, USA; Tel: [1] (202) 785-2209.

USEFUL ADDRESSES

Trade Fair Venues

Buenos Aires Art Center Loft
Herrera 541
1295 Buenos Aires
Tel: [54] (1) 300-1111, 300-2211
Fax: [54] (1) 300-1115

Buenos Aires Sheraton Hotel
San Martín 1225
1104 Buenos Aires, Argentina
Tel: [54] (1) 318-9000
Fax: [54] (1) 318-9353, 318-9346

Centro Costa Salguero
Jerónimo Salguero y Rafael Obligado
1425 Buenos Aires, Argentina
Tel: [54] (1) 807-3000
Fax: [54] (1) 371-9994, 803-2219

Centro de Exposiciones, Ferias y Congresos
Autopista Center
Juan Bautista Alberdi 4550
1407 Buenos Aires, Argentina
Fax: [54] (1) 683-4010, 683-4912

Centro Municipal de Exposiciones
c/o Centro Cultural General San Martín
Sarmiento 1551, Piso 3
1042 Buenos Aires, Argentina
Tel: [54] (1) 374-1251

Predio Ferial Córdoba
Av. Cárcano s/n
Bo. Chateau Carreras
5009 Córdoba
Tel: [54] (51) 81-0759
Fax: [54] (1) 89-0023

Predio Ferial de Palermo
Juncal 4431
1425 Buenos Aires, Argentina
Tel: [54] (1) 777-5501/6
Fax: [54] (1) 774-1072

Organizations

Fundación Exportar
Reconquista 1098
1003 Buenos Aires, Argentina
Tel: [54] (1) 315-4125
Fax: [54] (1) 311-4334

Center for Exhibition Industry Research
4350 East-West Highway, Suite 401
Bethesda, MD 20814, USA
Tel: [1] (301) 907-7626
Fax: [1] (301) 907-0277

TIPS FOR ATTENDING A TRADE FAIR

Trade fairs can be extremely effective for making face-to-face contacts and sales or purchases, identifying suppliers, checking out competitors, and finding out how business really works in the host country. However, the cost of attending or exhibiting at such fairs can be high. To maximize the return on your investment of time, money, and energy, you should be very clear about your goals for the trip and give yourself plenty of time for advance research and preparation.

You should also be aware of the limitations of trade fairs. The products on display probably do not represent the full range of goods available on the market. In fact, some of the latest product designs may still be under wraps. While trade fairs give you an opportunity to make face-to-face contacts with many people, both exhibitors and buyers are rushed, which makes meaningful discussions and negotiations difficult.

These drawbacks can easily be minimized if you have sufficient preparation and background information. Allow several months for preparation—more if you first need to identify the fair that you should attend. Even under ideal circumstances, you should begin laying the groundwork a year in advance. Don't forget that exhibiting at or attending a fair in a foreign country means more complex logistics: numerous faxes and phone calls involving you, the show operator, and local support people, plus customs and transportation delays.

Participating in international trade fairs, particularly at the outset, should be considered a means of fulfilling long-term goals. At domestic fairs, you may exhibit on a regular basis with short-term sales and marketing goals. But at a foreign fair, it is often best to participate as a way to establish your company, make contacts for the future, and learn more about a market, its consumers, and products. New exporters may not generate high sales, but they often come away with information that assists them with future marketing and product development.

Selecting an appropriate trade fair

Consult the listings of trade fairs in this book to find some that interest you. Note the suggestions in this chapter for finding the most current calendars of upcoming fairs. Once you have identified some fairs, contact the organizers for literature, including a show prospectus, attendee list, and exhibitor list. Ask plenty of questions! Be sure not to neglect trade organizations in the host country, independent show-auditing firms, and recent attendees or exhibitors. Find out whether there are "must attend" fairs for your particular product group. Fairs that concentrate on other, but related, commodities might also be a good match. Be aware that there may be preferred seasons for trade in certain products.

Your research needs to cover a number of points:

• *Audience* Who is the intended audience? Is the fair open to the public or to trade professionals only? Are the exhibitors primarily foreigners looking for local buyers or locals looking for foreign buyers? (Many trade fairs are heavily weighted to one or the other; others may be so oriented to local activity that they may not be equipped to cater to international businesspeople.) Decide whether you are looking for an exposition of general merchandise produced in one region, a commodity-specific trade show, or both. Are you looking for a "horizontal"—one that covers a wide range of products—or a "vertical" show—one that covers those involved in the production and marketing of a narrow range of products through all stages of the process?

• *Statistics* How many people attended the fair the last time it was held? What were the demographics? What volume of business was done? How many exhibitors were there? How big is the exhibition space? What was the ratio of foreign to domestic attendees and exhibitors?

• *Specifics* Who are the major exhibitors? Are any particular publications or organizations associated with the fair? On what categories of products does the fair focus? Does the fair have a general theme or a changing theme? How long has the fair been in existence? How often is it held? Is it always in the same location, or does it move each time? How much does it cost to attend? Are there any separate or special programs connected with the event, and do they require additional entrance fees? What does it cost to rent space?

Before you go

• If you have not already spoken with someone who attended the fair in the past, be sure to find someone who will give you advice, tips, and general information.

• Make your reservations and travel arrangements well in advance, and figure out how you are going to get around once you get there. Even if the fair takes place in a large city, do not assume that getting around will be easy during a major trade fair. If the site is in a small city or a less developed area, the transportation and accommodation systems are likely to become overburdened sooner than in metropolitan areas.

• Will you need an interpreter for face-to-face business negotiations? A translation service to handle documents? Try to line up providers well in advance of your need for their services.

• For printed materials, pay attention to language barriers and make preparations that will help you overcome them. Assess your literature and decide what should be available in translation or in bilingual editions. Have the translation work done by a true professional, particularly if technical terms are used. Consider having a bilingual business card, and add the country and international dialing code information to the address and telephone number. Find out from the show organizers which countries will be represented, and prepare information in the languages of those countries as well, if necessary.

• Do you need hospitality suites and/or conference rooms? Reserve them as soon as you can.

• Contact people you would like to meet before you go. Organize your appointments around the fair.

• Familiarize yourself with the show's hours, locations (if exhibits and events are staged at multiple venues), and the schedule of events. Then prioritize.

While you are there

• Wear businesslike clothes that are comfortable. Find out what the norm is for the area and the season.

• Immediately after each contact, write down as much information as you can. Do not depend on remembering it. Several companies now make inexpensive portable business card scanners with optical character recognition (OCR) software to read the information into a contact management program.

• Qualify your prospects before launching into a full presentation. Are you dealing with the right person? Ask open-ended questions to discover the person's true interests.

• Consider arriving a day early to get fully oriented, confirm appointments, and rest up.

• It is common sense: make sure you take breaks, even if you have to schedule them. You'll end up having far more energy and being more effective.

After the fair

• Within a week after the fair, write letters to new contacts and follow up on requests for literature. If you have press releases and questionnaires, send them out quickly as well. Even better, send these leads back to your office while you are still at the fair so that your new contacts receive literature when they return home.

• Write a report evaluating your experiences while they are still fresh in your mind. Even if you don't have to prepare a formal report, spend some time organizing your thoughts on paper for future reference. Aim to quantify the results. Did you meet your goals? Why or why not? What would you do differently? What unforeseen costs or problems arose?

• With your new contacts and your experiences in mind, start preparing for your next trade fair.

If you are selling

• Familiarize yourself with import regulations for products that you wish to exhibit at the fair.

• Set specific goals for sales leads, developing product awareness, selling and positioning current customers, and gathering industry information. For example, target the numbers of contacts made, orders written, leads converted into sales, visitors at presentations, brochures or samples distributed, customers entertained, and seminars attended. You can also set goals for total revenue from sales, cost-to-return benefit ratio, amount of media coverage, and amount of competitor information obtained.

- Review your exhibitor kit. Is there a show theme that you can tie into? Pay particular attention to the show's hours and regulations, payment policies, shipping instructions and dates, telephone installation policies, security, fire regulations, and extra-cost services.

- Find out about the labor situation. Is it unionized, and what are the regulations? Will you have to hire your own workers to set up and break down the booth, or can the organizer or showcase facility provide them for you?

- Gear your advertising and product demonstrations to the expected target audience. Should you stress certain aspects of your product line? Will you need brochures and banners in different languages? Even if you do not need to translate the materials currently in use into another language, will you need to rewrite them for a different culture? Consider advertising in publications that will be distributed at the fair.

- Plan the display in your booth carefully; you will have only a few seconds to grab the viewer's attention. Secure a location in a high-traffic area—for example, near a door, a restroom, a refreshment area, or a major exhibitor. For banners use copy that is brief and effective. Focus on the product and its benefits. Place promotional materials and giveaways near the back wall so that people have to enter your area, but make sure that they do not feel trapped. If you plan to use videotapes or other multimedia, make sure that you have enough space. Remember to ascertain whether you will need special equipment or equipment designed for different electrical current. Such presentations may be better suited to hospitality suites, because lights are bright and noise levels high in exhibition halls.

- Attend to the details. Order office supplies and printed materials that you will need for the booth. Have all your paperwork—order forms, business cards, exhibitor kit and contract, copies of advance orders and checks, travel documents, and so on—in order and at hand. If you ordered a telephone line, obtain your own host-country compatible telephone or arrange to rent one. Draw up a schedule for staffing the booth.

- Plan and rehearse your sales pitch in advance, preferably in a space similar to the size of your booth.

- *Don't:* sit, read, smoke, eat, or drink in the booth; bad-mouth your competitors or complain about the show; ignore prospects while chatting with colleagues; stand with your back to the aisle or lean on booth furniture.

- If you plan to return to the next show, reserve space while you are still on-site.

If you are buying

- Familiarize yourself with customs regulations on the products that you seek to purchase and import into your own country or elsewhere. Be sure to get such information on any and all products in which you might be interested.

- Set specific goals for supplier leads and for gathering industry information. For example, target the numbers of contacts made, leads converted to purchases, seminars and presentations attended, and booths visited. Other goals might be cost-to-return benefit ratio, amount of competitor information gathered, and percentage of projected purchases actually made.

- List all the products that you seek to purchase, their specifications, and the number of units you plan to purchase of each.

- Know the retail and wholesale market prices for the goods in your home country and in the country where you will be buying. List the highest price you can afford to pay for each item and still get a worthwhile return.

- List the established and probable suppliers for each of the products or product lines that you plan to import. Include addresses and telephone numbers and note your source for the information. Before you go, contact suppliers to confirm who will attend and to make appointments.

TRADE FAIRS OUTSIDE ARGENTINA

Many Argentine exporters will exhibit at trade fairs internationally. The following is a list of 1995 fairs with a significant Argentine presence. For more information on Argentine exhibitors at these fairs or on Argentine international trade missions, contact Fundación Exportar.

Country & City	Trade Fairs	1995 Dates
BOLIVIA		
Santa Cruz de la Sierra	EXPOCRUZ	Sept. 14–27
BRAZIL		
Curitiba	Exposición Industrial Argentina	June 7–11
Esteio	EXPOINTER	Aug. 26–Sept. 3
Río de Janiero	ABRAS *(Supermarkets)*	Sept. 17–20
	Salón Náutico *(Boats)*	May 18–23
São Paolo	BRASILPLAST *(Plastic)*	May 18–24
	EXPOSAUDE *(Hospital equipment)*	July 4–7
	FEIMAFE *(Machines and tools)*	March 20–25
	FENATEC and FENIT *(Textiles)*	June 6–9
	FISPAL *(Food)*	June 20–23
CHILE		
Santiago	EDIFICA *(Construction)*	Sept. 26–30
	FISA	Oct. 27–Nov. 5
Talca	Feria Internacionale del Maule	March 23–April 2
COLOMBIA		
Bogotá	AGROEXPO *(Agroindustry)*	July 17–23
	ASOPARTES'95 *(Auto parts)*	June 6–9
FRANCE		
Paris	EQUIPAUTO *(Auto parts)*	Oct. 13–19
Burdeos	VINEXPO *(Wine)*	June 19–23
GERMANY		
Cologne	ANUGA (Food)	Sept. 30–Oct. 5
	Herren-Mode-Woche/Inter-Jeans *(Men's fashion)*	Feb. 3–5; Aug. 4–6
	ISM *(Candy)*	Jan. 29–Feb. 2
Hannover	CEBIT '95 *(Computers)*	March 8–15
Frankfurt	Feria Internacional del Libro *(Books)*	Oct. 11–16
Düsseldorf	GDS *(Shoes)*	March 17–20; Sept. 15–18
Offenbach	Internationale Lederwarenmesse *(Leather goods)*	Feb. 18–21; Aug. 26–29
HONG KONG		
Hong Kong	INTER HANDBAGS *(Leather goods)*	Oct. 26–29
ITALY		
Cesena	AGRO-BIO-FRUT *(Fruit and horticulture)*	May 4–7
JAPAN		
Tokyo	FOODEX	March 7–10

SOUTH KOREA

Seoul	International Building and Construction Exhibition	Dec. 1–5

MEXICO

Guadalajara	Feria Internacional del Libro *(Books)*	Nov. 25–Dec. 3

PANAMA

Panama City	EXPOCOMER	March 8–13

PERU

Lima	Feria Internacional del Pacífico	Nov. 17–26

SOUTH AFRICA

Johannesburg	SAITEX	Nov. 30–Dec. 4

UNITED KINGDOM

London	London Wine Trade Fair	May 16–18

URUGUAY

Montevideo	Feria del Prado	Sept. 2–17

US

Las Vegas, NV	BIG I: International Auto Parts Fair	Oct. 24–26
	COMDEX (FALL)	Nov. 13–17
	International Leather Show	May 1995
Boston, MA	Boston Seafood Show	March 14–16
	Boston Wine Expo	Feb. 1995
New York, NY	Eastern Dairy Deli Bakery Association	Oct. 1995
	Hispanic Chamber of Commerce NY Show	
	International Fancy Food and Confection Show	July 1995
	Leatherwork Industry Mission	
	Long Island Global Business Show	July 9–12
		Sept. 1995
		May 1995
New Orleans, LA	Encuentro '95	Sept. 1995
Miami, FL	Food Pack of the Americas	Jan. 18–20
	Miami International Boat Show	Feb. 16–22
Chicago, IL	International Housewares Show	May 1995
	International Meat Industry Show	Sept. 1995
	International Mid West Wine Show	Oct. 15–18
	National Hardware Show	Aug. 1995
		Chicago, IL
New Hampshire	New Hampshire International Expo	Sept. 1995
Los Angeles, CA	Organic Produce Industry Show	June 1995
San Diego, CA	Produce Marketing Association	Oct. 21–24

VENEZUELA

Caracas	EXPO-CANIDRA *(Auto parts)*	May 25–28

TRADE FAIRS IN ARGENTINA

COMPREHENSIVE
Trade fairs exhibiting a wide range of goods

American Week in Buenos Aires	Buenos Aires Annual May 12–22, 1995	Argentine-American Chamber of Commerce Av. Leandro N. Alem 1110, Piso 13 1001 Buenos Aires Tel: (1) 311-5420, 311-5126 Fax: (1) 311-9076
Exposición de Productos de Hong Kong Hong Kong product exposition	Buenos Aires Hotel Inter-Continental March 27–28, 1995 July 31–August 1, 1995	Hong Kong Trade Development Council Reconquista 513, Piso 3, Of. B 1003 Buenos Aires Tel: (1) 314-2636, 314-8304
ESMIC '95 Exposición de San Martín Industrial y Comercial San Martín industrial and commercial exposition	San Martín, Bs. As. Predio Ferial San Martín Oct. 27–Nov. 5, 1995	Cámara Económica de San Martín Calle 81 No. 2051 1650 San Martín Pcia. de Buenos Aires Tel: (1) 755-0354, 754-6255 Fax: (1) 754-0619
EXPOARAB Exposición Industrial, Comercial y Cultural del Mundo Arabe con La Argentina Industrial, comercial, and cultural exhibits from the Arab world	Buenos Aires Centro Comercial de Exposiciones Sept. 26–Oct. 7, 1995	Cámara de Comercio Argentino-Arabe Montevideo 513, Piso 6 1019 Buenos Aires Tel: (1) 372-8167, 371-2561 Fax: (1) 372-8167
EXPOASIA "96 Exposición Internacional de Productos Asiáticos Asian products	Buenos Aires Centro Costa Salguero March 5–8, 1996	Viewpoint S.A. Rodriguez Peña 770, Piso 8, Of. 42 1020 Buenos Aires Tel: (1) 374-1320, 374-1543 Fax: (1) 371-9994
EXPOSERVICIO '95 Exposición para el Comercio Internacional International commerce trade show	Buenos Aires Palacio San Miguel August 7–11, 1995	Cámara de Exportadores de la Rep. Argentina Av. R. S. Peña 740, Piso 1 1035 Buenos Aires Tel: (1) 320-9583, 320-5944, 320-8556 Fax: (1) 328-1003
Expo Mar del Plata '95 Primera Exposición de la Producción de Movimiento del Sudeste Products of the Southeast	Mar del Plata Estancia la Trinidad January 2–15, 1995	Ricardo Bengolea y Asociados Estancia la Trinidad Km. 36 de la Ruta Nacional No. 2 7612 Camet Tel: (23) 79-0993 Fax: (23) 60-0363
Feria de las Naciones International general merchandise exhibition	Buenos Aires Predio Ferial de Palermo Oct. 25–Nov. 5, 1995	Cooperadora de Acción Social (COAS) Pte. Roque Saenz Peña 852, Piso 2 1035 Buenos Aires Tel: (1) 476-2305, 40-8573 Fax: (1) 328-7883, 328-8573
Feria Industrial, Comercial y de Servicios del Sur Argentino Southern Argentinian industrial and commercial Fair	Bahía Blanca Centro de Exposiciones y Congresos de Bahía Blanca November 1995	Corporación del Comercio y de la Industria de Bahía Blanca Alsina 19, Piso 2 8000 Bahía Blanca Tel: (91) 38-416, 22-112 Fax: (91) 51-7161
FERINOA Feria Intenacional del Norte Argentino Products of northern Argentina	Salta Coop. de Productores Tabacaleros de Salta October 19–29, 1995	Cámara de Comercio Exterior de Salta Alvarado 51 4400 Salta Tel: (87) 31-1003, 22-5293

FIA '95 **Feria Internacional Aconcagua** International fair of Aconcagua	Mendoza Centro Ferial de Mendoza Annual November 8–19, 1995	Unión Comercial e Industrial de Mendoza Patricias Mendocinas 1157, Piso 3, Of. 7 5500 Mendoza Tel: (61) 25-1335 Fax: (61) 26-1181
FICO **Feria Internacional de** **Córdoba** Industrial and commercial fair	Córdoba Predio Ferial Córdoba Every 2 years Aug. 31–Sept. 10, 1995 August/September 1997	Feriar S.A., Predio Ferial Córdoba PO Box 348 5000 Córdoba Tel: (51) 81-0759, 81-1293, 81-0769 Fax: (51) 89-0023

AGRICULTURE, HORTICULTURE & AQUACULTURE

CENIPA '95 **Exposición y Congreso** **Nacional e Internacional de** **Pesca, Acuacultura e Intereses** **Maritimos** Fishing and Aquaculture industries	Mar del Plata Estadio Ciudad de Mar del Plata Oct.30–Nov. 3, 1995	Fundación Bolsa de Comercio de Mar del Plata Olavarría 2464/68 7600 Mar del Plata Tel: (23) 86-1783 Fax: (23) 91-2444
Expo Fiesta Rural Rural festival and exhibition	Neuquén Hipódromo Ciudad de Neuquén March 3–12, 1995	Expo Fiesta Rural Sarmiento 809, Of. 109 Casilla de Correo 125 8300 Neuquén Tel: (99) 23-220, 20-772 Fax: (99) 23-3885
Expochacra '95 Farm expo	Capital Federal Establecimiento la Magdalena Ruta Nacional 188, km 94.5 March 9–12, 1995	Editorial Atlántida S.A. y Establecimiento la Magdalena Azopardo 579 1307 Buenos Aires Tel: (1) 331-4590 Fax: (1) 331-3272
Expoferichaco **Feria Internacional** **Agroindustrial, Comercial,** **Cultural y Artesanal** International agroindustrial, commercial, cultural, craft fair	Chaco Predio Ferial de UCAL March 16–26, 1995	Comisión Fiesta Nacional del Algodón Hotel Gualok San Martín 1198 Presidencia Roque Saenz Peña 3700 Chaco Tel: (714) 20-521, 20-715, 21-723
Exposición Agroindustrial y **Comercial de Verano** Agricultural industry show	Mar del Plata Base Naval de Submarinos (Playa Grande) Jan. 20–Feb. 12, 1995	Sociedad Rural Argentina Juncal 4431 1425 Buenos Aires Tel: (1) 777-5501 Fax: (1) 774-1072
Exposición de Ganadería, **Agricultura e Industria** **Internacional** Livestock, farming, and industry exposition	Buenos Aires Predio Ferial de Palermo Annual July 27–Aug. 16, 1995	Sociedad Rural Argentina Florida 460 1005 Buenos Aires Tel: (1) 322-3431, 322-3696, 322-2030 Fax: (1) 325-8231
Exposición de Otoño Autumn horse show	Buenos Aires Predio Ferial de Palermo April 2–11, 1995 April 1996	Asociación Criadores de Caballos Criollos Larrea 670, Piso 2 1030 Buenos Aires Tel: (1) 961-3387, 961-2305
Exposición Internacional de **Orquideas** Orchid growing supplies	Buenos Aires Palacio Lorenzo Raggio August 19–27, 1995	Winkler's Orchids Dr. Pedro I. Rivera 3750 1430 Buenos Aires Tel: (1) 795-5636, 543-5100 Fax: (1) 542-8339

Feri Fauna del Hogar Pet show	Buenos Aires Centro de Exposiciones, Ferias y Congresos (Autopista Center) May 1995	Full Line S.R.L. Lavalle 1634, Piso 1, Of. C 1040 Buenos Aires Tel: (1) 371-5877, 49-1178
Feria Internacional de Agro Alimentación Agricultural trade show	Buenos Aires Predio Ferial de Palermo September 13–18, 1995	Cfa. Argentina de Feria S.A. (CAF S.A.) Arroyo 894, Piso 3, Of. 5 1007 Buenos Aires Tel: (1) 327-2599, 327-2089 Fax: (1) 325-3742
Frutihorticola Fiesta Nacional de la Flor Flower and horticulture exhibition	Escobar Ciudad Floral de Escobar Sept. 29–Oct. 16, 1995	Sociedad Civil Fiesta de la Flor de Escobar M. Gelvus 1051 1625 Belén de Escobar Pcia. de Buenos Aires Tel: (488) 20596, 21936, 21935
MADERA '95 Exposición Internacional de la Foresto Industria International exposition of the forestry industry	Buenos Aires Centro Costa Salguero June 30–July 4, 1995	Cámara Argentina de Aserraderos de Madera Alsina 440 1087 Buenos Aires Tel: (1) 342-4389
MERCOFLOR '96 Exposición de Floricultura y Horticultura Floral and horticulture exhibit	Buenos Aires Predio Feria de Palermo May 30–June 2, 1996	Sea Air C. Pellegrini 979, Piso 6, Of. 22 1085 Buenos Aires Fax: (1) 668-1285

APPAREL, JEWELRY & TEXTILES

Expoferta y Segunda Fashion exhibit	Córdoba Predio La Vieja Usina March 2–15, 1995 July 28–August 6, 1995	Fura Producciones 25 de mayo 192, Piso 4, Of. 1 5000 Córdoba Fax: (51) 23-9235
Feria de la Moda Fashion show	Buenos Aires Predio Ferial de Palermo June 22–July 16, 1995	Ricardo A. Sabbag Producciones S.R.L. Av. Rivadavia 1815, Piso 2 1033 Buenos Aires Tel: (1) 952-2557, 952-3915, 952-2763 Fax: (1) 951-6421
MABYN 20 Colección Children's and baby clothing	Buenos Aires Palacio San Miguel August 1995	Cámara Argentina de Indumentaria para Bebés y Niños Junín 347, Piso 4, Of. B 1026 Buenos Aires Fax: (1) 953-9540
Moda Visión—Idea Textil— Muestra Fashion and textile exhibit	Buenos Aires Sheraton Hotel 2 times a year June 27–29, 1995 November 1995	Conjunto de Expositores Av. Córdoba 1513, Piso 7 1055 Buenos Aires Tel: (1) 812-1042
Mujer '95 Exposición Integral para la Mujer Women's clothing	Córdoba La Vieja Usina May 4–7, 1995	Juárez Tobal y Asociados 25 de Mayo 192, Piso 4 5000 Córdoba Tel: (51) 23-9235
Salón Internacional de la Moda Fashion exhibit	Buenos Aires Centro Costa Salguero 2 times a year March 15–18, 1995 August 16–18, 1995	Rossi Heinlein & Asociados S.A. Viamonte 494, Piso 2 1053 Buenos Aires Fax: (1) 311-9413, 311-9387, 312-4951

SERMAC '95 **Salón Internacional de** **Accesorios, Maquinarias y** **Servicios para la Confección** Textile industry exhibit	Buenos Aires Centro Costa Salguero May 4–8, 1995	Revista Informe Textil e Indumentaria y Laster Av. Entre Ríos 258, Piso 4, Of. H 1079 Buenos Aires Tel: (1) 372-6909, 375-1922 476-2923
SIMAT '96 **Salón Internacional de** **Maquinaria y Accesorios** **Textiles** Textile machinery and accessories	Buenos Aires Centro Costa Salguero May 23–27, 1996	Laster S.A. Av. de Mayo 1365, Piso 8 1085 Buenos Aires Tel: (1) 381-5104 Fax: (1) 381-9711
Textil Hogar '95 Textile Show	Buenos Aires Centro Costa Salguero April 9–12, 1995	Informática Textil Latinoamericana Corrientes 2835, Piso 1 1193 Buenos Aires Tel: (1) 961-6154, 962-2287, 961-8447
UHR '95 **Salón Internacional de la** **Relojeria y Joyeria** Jewelry and watch trade show	Buenos Aires Sheraton Hotel Aug. 30–Sept. 2, 1995	Rossi Heinlein & Asociados S.A. Viamonte 494, Piso 2, Of. 8 1053 Buenos Aires Fax: (1) 311-9413, 311-9837, 312-4951

AUTOMOTIVE

AUTOPAR **Feria Internacional del** **Automotor, Partes, Accesorios** **y Equipamiento para Servicios** Automobile parts and services	Córdoba Predio Ferial Córdoba July 4–9, 1995	Feriar S.A. Casilla de Correo 349 5000 Córdoba Tel: (51) 81-1293, 81-0759, 81-0769 Fax: (51) 89-0023
Expo-Motors **Auto Salón Internacional** International motor show	Buenos Aires October 6–16, 1995	EMIBA, Division de Grupo Comercial Argentina Av. Córdoba 669, Piso 1 1045 Buenos Aires Tel: (1) 311-1086/7 Fax: (1) 313-6975

BOOKS

EXPOLIBRERIA **Exposición Internacional de** **Artículos los de Librería,** **Papelería y Afines** Stationery exposition	Buenos Aires Centro Costa Salguero October 26–30, 1995	Emprendimientos Conjuntos Alsina 2178, Piso B, Of. A 1090 Buenos Aires Tel: (1)951-6277, 951-3001, 951-9021/5 Fax: (1) 952-9248
Feria del Libro Córdoba Book fair	Córdoba Cabildo Histórico y Teatro Real de la Ciudad de Córdoba September 14–24, 1995	Comisión Feria del Libro Córdoba Av. Gral. Paz 81, Piso 4 5000 Córdoba Fax: (51) 21-3558
Feria del Libro Infantil **y Juvenil** Children's book fair	Buenos Aires Centro Municipal de Exposiciones July 3–23, 1995	Fundación El Libro Av. Córdoba 744, P.B., Of. 1 1054 Buenos Aires Tel: (1) 322-2226, 322-2165 Fax: (1) 326-5681
Feria Internacional del Libro International book fair	Buenos Aires Centro Municipal de Exposiciones April 16–May 6, 1996	Fundación El Libro Av. Córdoba 744, P.B., Of. 1 1054 Buenos Aires Tel: (1) 322-2225, 322-2165 Fax: (1) 325-5681

BUSINESS & PROFESSIONAL SERVICES

ESE—Exposición de Servicios Para Empresas Business services exposition	Buenos Aires Centro Costa Salguero March 17–25, 1996	Pinchon Rivière Consultores Paraguay 866, Piso 9 1057 Buenos Aires Fax: (1) 374-8111, 374-2678, 374-1956
EXPOSEGUROS '95 Insurance industry	Buenos Aires Palacio San Miguel October 3–6, 1995	Asociación Argentina de Productores, Asesores de Seguros (AAPAS) Bolivar 332, Piso 4 1066 Buenos Aires Fax: (1) 382-3350, 382-0780, 382-3218
PUBLICITARIA "96 Exposición de la Industria Publicitaria Publicity industry exhibition	Buenos Aires Predio Ferial de Palermo May 21–27, 1996	Imfoc S.A. Tte. Gral. J.D. Perón 1610, Piso 2 1037 Buenos Aires Fax: (1) 382-3350, 382-0780, 382-3218

CLEANING

Expo Clean Exposición Intenacional de Limpieza y Mantenimiento Empresarial Industrial cleaning exposition	Buenos Aires Predio Ferial de Palermo September 6–9, 1995	Expotrade S.A. Reconquista 617, Piso 8 1003 Buenos Aires Tel: (1) 311-8636, 311-8447 Fax: (1) 312-1330

COMPUTERS & COMMUNICATIONS

Argentina '95 Telecommunications products and services	Buenos Aires Annual October 1995 October 1996	Latcom, Inc. 9200 S. Dadeland Blvd., #309 Miami, FL 33156, USA Tel: [1] (305) 670-9444 Fax: [1] (305) 670-9459
CLER '95 Information technology, telecom, data communications for electric companies	Buenos Aires Biennial October 1995 October 1997	Latcom, Inc. 9200 S. Dadeland Blvd. #309 Miami, FL 33156, USA Tel: [1] (305) 670-9444 Fax: (305) 670-9459
COMEXPO/ARGENTINA Computers and telecommunications equipment	Buenos Aires Sheraton Hotel Annual May 1995 May 1996	Marketing International Corp 200 N. Glebe Rd., Suite 900 Arlington, VA 22203, USA Tel: [1] (703) 527-8000 Fax: [1] (703) 527-8006
Computación '95 Computer industry exhibit	Buenos Aires Predio Ferial de Palermo April 21–30, 1995	Inforexco S.A. Hipólito Yrigoyen 1427, Piso 9 1089 Buenos Aires Tel: (1) 383-5399, 383-9964
EXPO Usuaria Exposición de Informática, Teleinformática y Telecomunicaciones Telecommunications and informatics exhibit	Buenos Aires May 10–13, 1995	Marketing International Corp 200 N. Glebe Rd., Suite 900 Arlington, VA 22203, USA Tel: [1] (703) 527-8000 Fax: [1] (703) 527-8006
INFOCOM '95 Exposición Int'l de Informática y Telecomunicaciones Telecommunications and informatics exhibit	Buenos Aires Predio Ferial de Palermo June 5–11, 1995	Cámara de Empresas de Software y Servicios Informáticos (CESSI) Cámara de Informática y Comunicaciones (CICOMBRA) Rincón 326 1081 Buenos Aires Tel: (1) 951-2855, 951-2631

INFOTEC **Feria Int'l de Informática,** **Ofimatica y** **Telecomunicaciones** Telecommunications and informatics exhibit	Córdoba Predio Ferial Córdoba October 17-22, 1995	Feriar S.A. Casilla de Correo 348 5000 Córdoba Tel: (51) 81-1293/0759/0769 Fax: (51) 89-0023
SOFTWARE Trade exposition featuring software and informatics services	Buenos Aires Annual September 1995 September 1996	Cámara de Empresas de Software y Servicios Informáticos (CESSI) Tucumán 1427, Piso 6, Of. 601 1050 Buenos Aires Tel: (1)373-0813, 371-1549 Fax: (1) 40-1549
TELECOMUNICACIONES '95 **Exposición Internacional y** **Congreso de** **Telecomunicaciones** Telecommunications expo	Buenos Aires Sheraton Buenos Aires August 14–18, 1995	Cámara de Informática y Comunicaciones de la República Argentina Av. Córdoba 744, Piso 2, Of. D 1054 Buenos Aires Tel: (1) 394-1130, 393-5810 Fax: (1) 325-9604
Windows World Argentina Microsoft Windows software exhibit	Buenos Aires Palacio San Miguél Nov. 28–Dec. 1, 1995	Mind Trainer S.A. Av. Roque S. Peña 651, Piso 8 1035 Buenos Aires Tel: (1) 326-6501, 326-3363, 326-2712 Fax: (1) 334-4605, 343-7020

CONSTRUCTION & HOUSING
See also Machines and Tools

Biel '95 **Exposición Internacional y** **Congreso de la Industria** **Electrica y Luminotécnica** Electrical and lighting industry	Buenos Aires Predio Ferial de Palermo September 11–17, 1995 Every 2 years	Cámara Argentina de Industrias Electromecánicas (CADIEM) 1428 F.D. Roosevelt 2445, Piso 11, Of. C Buenos Aires Tel: (1) 788-8501/2 Fax: (1) 788-8499
CONSTRUMA **Feria Internacional de la** **Construcción y Equipamiento** **del Hogar** House building and household equipment fair	Córdoba Predio Ferial Córdoba Annual August 1–6, 1995	Feriar S.A., Predio Ferial Córdoba Casilla de Correo 348 5000 Córdoba Tel: (51) 81-0759 Fax: (51) 89-0023
ExpoSanitarios '95 **Exposición de Artículos para** **la Instalación Sanitaria, Gas y** **Afines** Construction of housing	Buenos Aires Predio Ferial de Palermo October 16–22, 1995	Exposanitarios S.A. Av. Gaona 3316 1416 Buenos Aires Tel: (1) 583-7129 Fax: (1) 582-7221
EXPOVIVIENDA **Exposición Internacional de la** **Vivienda** Housing exhibition	Buenos Aires Centro Costa Salguero April 9–14, 1996	Asociación de Empresarios de la Vivienda Suipacha 207, Piso 1, Of. 116 1008 Buenos Aires Tel: (1) 327-2321, 327-0476
FEMATEC **Feria de Materiales y** **Tecnologías para la** **Construcción** Construction materials and technologies	Buenos Aires Predio Ferial de Palermo Annual May 8–13, 1995	Servi-Expo S.R.L. Arroyo 894, Piso 3, Of. 5 1007 Buenos Aires Tel: (1) 327-2599, 327-2089 Fax: (1) 325-3742
FITECMA '95 **Feria Internacional** **Tecnológica de la Madera** Wood technology trade show	Buenos Aires Predio Ferial de Palermo June 20-25, 1995	Asociación de Fabricantes y Representantes de Máquinas, Equipos y Herramientas para la Industria Madera (ASORA) Av. Belgrado 427, Piso 5, Of. B 1092 Buenos Aires Tel: (1) 345-7475/6

Salón de Máquinas para el Movimiento de Suelos, Gruas y Máquinas Viales Earthmoving and heavy equipment exhibit	Buenos Aires Predio Ferial de Palermo May 8–13, 1995	Servi-Expo S.R.L. Arroyo 894, Piso 3, Of. 5 1007 Buenos Aires Tel: (1) 327-2599, 327-2089 Fax: (1) 325-3742
Salón del Marmol y Afines Marble exhibit	Buenos Aires Predio Ferial de Palermo May 8–13, 1995	Servi-Expo S.R.L. Arroyo 894, Piso 3, Of. 5 1007 Buenos Aires Tel: (1) 327-2599, 327-2089 Fax: (1) 325-3742

ENVIRONMENTAL & ENERGY

Argentina Oil & Gas Expo '95 Exposición Intenacional del Petróleo, Gas y Productos Afines Gas and oil products	Buenos Aires Centro Costa Salguero October 16–20, 1995	Uniline Ferias y Exposiciones S.R.L. Paraná 123, Piso 5, Of. 121 1017 Buenos Aires Fax: (1) 374-2678, 374-5763, 374-8111
EcoIndustria '95 Feria Internacional de la Industria y el Medio Ambiente Environmental exposition	Buenos Aires Centro Municipal de Exposiciones November 15–19, 1995	Unión Industrial de Capital Federal México 628, Piso 5, Of. 6 1097 Buenos Aires Tel: (1) 361-7925, 383-5399, 383-9964
Expo Eco Residuo Exposición Internacional del Tratamiento de los Residuos Urbanos Urban waste treatment exhibition	Buenos Aires Predio Ferial de Palermo Aug. 25–Sept. 3, 1995	Banpaku S.A. y Pichon Riviere Consultores S.A. Paraguay 866, Piso 9 1057 Buenos Aires Tel: (1) 312-3306, 312-4667 Fax: (1) 312-4667
LATCOM '95 Latin rural electric companies conference	Buenos Aires Every two years October 1995 October 1997	Latcom, Inc. 9200 S. Dadeland Blvd. #309 Miami, FL 33156, USA Tel: [1] (305) 670-9444 Fax: [1] (305) 670-9459
WEFTEC '95 Exposición y Seminario de Agua Pura y Medio Ambiente Clean water/environmental show	Buenos Aires Predio Ferial de Palermo November 8–12, 1995	Asociación Argentina de Preservación del Agua y su Medio Ambiente Hipólito Yrigoyen 820, Of. 6 1086 Buenos Aires Tel: (1) 342-6835 Fax: (1) 331-1848
International Mining Meeting	Buenos Aires October 25–26, 1995	Secretaría de Mineria de la Nación Av. J. A. Roca 651, Piso 2 1322 Buenos Aires Tel: (1) 331-9954, 343-6314, 349-3262 Fax: (1) 331-4230

FOOD, BEVERAGES & HOSPITALITY
See also Agriculture, Livestock & Horticulture

AGRI FOOD '95 Feria Internacional Agro Alimentaria de la Argentina	Buenos Aires Predio Ferial de Palermo September 18-23, 1995	Compañía Argentina de Ferias S.A. y Sociedad Rural Argentina Arroyo 894, Piso 3, Of. 5 1007 Buenos Aires Fax: (1) 342-0635, 342-4438
Argentina Exposición Mundial de Alimentos, Bebidas y Tecnologías Afines International exposition of food and beverages and their technologies	Buenos Aires Predio Ferial de Palermo April 20–30, 1995	Exportable S.R.L. Humboldt 1967, Piso 2 1414 Buenos Aires Fax: (1) 777-1551/9

Catering '95 **Exposición Internacional de** **Proveedores a Empresas** **Elaboradoras de Comidas** Restaurant and catering trade show	Buenos Aires Centro Costa Salguero October 6–9, 1995	Banpaku S.A. Paraná 123, Piso 4 1017 Buenos Aires Tel: (1) 374-1320, 374-1543, 374-1848 Fax: (1) 371-9994
CONAL '96 **Salón de Expositores y** **Congreso Nacional de** **Mayoristas de Comestibles,** **Bebidas y Afines** Food and beverage wholesalers	Buenos Aires Sheraton Buenos Aires July 12–14, 1995	Federación Argentina del Comercio Mayorista de Comestibles, Bebidas y Afines Pte. Luis Sáenz Peña 310, Piso 6 1110 Buenos Aires Fax: (1) 381-8837, 381-6758
Expogolosina '95 **Salón Intenacional de la** **Golosina y Artículos Varios** Candy and confectionery show	Buenos Aires Sheraton Hotel March 27–30, 1995 April 1996	Asociación de Distribuidores de Golosinas y Afines e Imfoc S.A. Hipólito Yrigoyen 1178, Piso 6 1086 Buenos Aires Tel: (1) 381-0623, 381-0780, 381-3218
Hotel '95 **Salón Internacional de** **Productos, Equipamientos y** **Servicios para la Hotelería,** **Gastronomía y Catering** Hotel, restaurant, and catering show	Buenos Aires Sheraton Hotel November 21–24, 1995	Asociación de Hoteles de Turismo Av. Rivadavia 1157/9, Piso 9, Of. C 1033 Buenos Aires Tel: (1) 383-2039, 383-1160 Fax: (1) 383-0669
SAIHEL '95—TECNOPAN— **TECNO PASTAS** **Salón Internacional del** **Helado Artesanal** International food fair	Buenos Aires Centro Costa Salguero June 16–21, 1995	Editorial Publitec Honorio Pueyrredón 550 1405 Buenos Aires Tel: (1) 901-5141, 903-6082, 903-6934
Tecno Bebiendo **Exposición Internacional de** **Tecnologías para las Bebidas** Beverage industry technology	Buenos Aires Centro Costa Salguero May 9–12, 1995	Banpaku S.A. Paraná 123, Piso 4 1017 Buenos Aires Tel: (1) 374-1320 Fax: (1) 903-6082
Tecno Fidta **Feria Internacional de** **Tecnología Alimentaria** Food technology fair	Buenos Aires Centro Costa Salguero Annual October 1995	Banpaku S.A. Paraná 123, Piso 4 1017 Buenos Aires Tel: (1) 374-1320 Fax: (1) 903-6082

FOOTWEAR & LEATHER GOODS
See also Apparel, Textiles & Jewelry

CEMCA **Centro Expositor de las** **Manufacturas de Cuero y** **Afines** Leather and accessories exhibit	Buenos Aires Predio Ferial de Palermo 2 times a year March 10–12, 1995 August 11–13, 1995	Cámara Industrial de las Manufacturas del Cuero y Afines de la Rep. Argentina (CIMA) Bernardo de Irigoyen 972, Piso 5 1034 Buenos Aires Tel: (1) 304-5116, 27-1860 Fax: (1) 304-9448
EFICA **Exposición Feria Internacional** **del Calzado Argentino** Argentine footwear exposition	Buenos Aires Centro Costa Salguero March 10–12, 1995 August 11–13,1995	Cámara de la Industria del Calzado Av. Rivadavia 4323 1205 Buenos Aires Tel: (1) 981-5992, 981-0818, 981-9609 Fax: (1) 981-3203
EXPOCAIPIC **Exposición de los Industriales** **Proveedoras de la Industrial** **del Calzado** Footwear and leather industry suppliers exposition	Buenos Aires Centro de Exposiciones, Ferias y Congresos (Autopista Center) June 27–30, 1995	Cámara Argentina de Industriales Proveedores de la Industria del Calzado José Marmol 326 1183 Buenos Aires Tel: (1) 981-5689, 982-1124 Fax: (1) 981-5689

EXPOCALZADO Footwear exhibition	Buenos Aires Centro de Exposiciones, Ferias y Congresos (Autopista Center) 2 times a year April 8–10, 1995 September 9–11, 1995	Asociación Civil Fabricantes de la Industria del Calzado (ACFIC) Chilavert 6780, Piso 1 1439 Buenos Aires Fax: (1) 601-9499
Expocentro del Calzado Footwear exposition	Córdoba La Vieja Usina 2 times a year March 25–27, 1995 August 25–27, 1995	Cámara de la Industria del Calzado Ayacucho 72, Of. 601 5000 Córdoba Tel: (51) 22-9581 Fax: (51) 21-5825

FURNITURE & HARDWARE
See also Machines & Tools, Construction & Housing

AMOBLAR '95 **Feria Internacional del** **Mueble de Argentina** Argentine furniture exhibition	Buenos Aires Centro Municipal de Exposiciones August 16–21, 1995	Cámara de Fabricantes de Muebles, Tapicería y Afines (CAFYDMA) Manuel Ricardo Trelles 1961/87 1416 Buenos Aires Tel: (1) 583-5606/7 Fax: (1) 583-5608
ANTIQDECO **Exposición del Anticuario** **y la Decoración** Antiques and interior decoration show	Córdoba La Vieja Usina July 14–24, 1995	Juárez Tobal y Asoc. Rioja 1153 5000 Córdoba Tel: (51) 25-7086, 60-8966 Fax: (51) 24-5743
EXPOHABITAT **Exposición Central del** **Confort, el Mueble y el Habitat** Home and furniture show	Buenos Aires Centro Municipal de Exposiciones September 1995	Cámara de Empresarios Medereros y Afines (CEMA) Maza 578, Piso 5 1220 Buenos Aires Tel: (1) 954-1111, 954-2046 Fax: (1) 97-1556
EXPOMUEBLE **Salón Internacional del** **Mueble** Furniture exposition	Buenos Aires Centro Municipal de Exposiciones May 5-21, 1995 May 1996	Cámara de Fabricantes de Muebles, Tapicerías y Afines (CAFYDMA) Manuel Ricardo Trelles 1961/87 1416 Buenos Aires Tel: (1) 583-5606/7, 582-9582 Fax: (1) 583-5608
Ferreteria '95 **Exposición Internacional de** **Ferretería, Pinturería y Bazar** Exhibition of hardware, painting and houseware stores	Buenos Aires Predio Ferial de Palermo August 24–29, 1995	Asociación de Ferreterias, Pinturerías y Bazares 1646 Lavalle, Piso 3, Of. A 1048 Buenos Aires Tel: (1) 372-8876 Fax: (1) 372-6309
REGALA **Salón Internacional de** **Artículos para la Mesa,** **Decoración y el Regalo—** **Blanco—** **Electrodomésticos** Gifts for the home; home appliances	Buenos Aires Centro Costa Salguero March 23–27, 1995 August 16–21, 1995	Cámara de Fabricantes de Muebles, Tapicerías y Afines (CAFYDMA) Manuel Ricardo Trelles 1961/87 1416 Buenos Aires Tel: (1) 583-5606/7, 582-9582 Fax: (1) 583-5608
TECNOMUEBLE '95 **Salón Internacional** **Proveedores de la Industria** **del Mueble** Furniture trade show	Buenos Aires Centro Expositor CAFYDMA August 15–20, 1995	Cámara de Fabricantes de Muebles Tapicerías y Afines (CAFYDMA) Manuel Ricardo Trelles 1961/87 1416 Buenos Aires Tel: (51) 583-5606/7 Fax: (51) 583-5608

GIFTS & CRAFTS

Feria del Regalo Gift fair	Buenos Aires Centro Municipal de Exposiciones December 1995	Casa del Teatro Av. Santa Fe 1235/45 1059 Buenos Aires Tel: (1) 811-2932, 813-3941
Feria del Sol Art festival	Buenos Aires Salas Nacionales de Exposiciones Aug. 9–Sept. 3, 1995	Asociación Amigos del Museo Nacional de Bellas Artes Av. Figueroa Alcorla 2280 1425 Buenos Aires Tel: (1) 803-4062 Fax: (1) 806-5885
Feria Internacional de Artesanías International exhibition of Latin-American craftsmanship	Córdoba Predio Ferial Córdoba Annual April 13–141996	Feriar S.A., Predio Ferial Córdoba PO Box 348 5000 Córdoba Tel: (51) 81-0759, 81-1293, 81-0769 Fax: (51) 89-0023
Salón del Regalo Empresario y Promocional Business and promotional gifts	Buenos Aires Sheraton Hotel September 5–8, 1995	Imfoc S.A. Tte. Gral J.D. Perón 1610, Piso 2 1037 Buenos Aires Fax: (1) 382-3350, 382-0780, 382-3218

GRAPHIC ARTS

Exposición Latinoamericana de Diseño e Industria Industrial and graphic design show	Buenos Aires Patio de la Madera November 4–12, 1995	Asociación Latinoamericana de Diseño Industrial y Gráfico (ALADI) Virrey Olaguer y Feliú 2439 1426 Buenos Aires Fax: (1) 328-1358, 328-8640
Expo Sign Argentina '95 Exposición Internacional de Comunicación Visual Visual communications exhibition	Buenos Aires Predio Ferial de Palermo September 14–17, 1995	Expotrade S.A. Reconquista 617, Piso 8 1003 Buenos Aires Tel: (1) 311-8636, 311-8447 Fax: (1) 312-1330

HEALTH & BEAUTY

COSMESUR '95 Exposición Internacional de Perfumería, Cosmética, Estética y Belleza del Mercosur para el Mundo Perfume and cosmetics expo	Buenos Aires Centro Municipal de Exposiciones September 15–18, 1995	Mercoprof S.A. 25 de Mayo 252, Piso 7, Of. 72 1002 Buenos Aires Fax: (1) 342-0635, 342-4438
COSMOPROF Exposición Profesional de Cosmética & Belleza de la Argentina Cosmetic traders and suppliers	Buenos Aires Centro Municipal de Exposiciones September 15–18, 1995	Cosmoprof Latinoamérica S.A. 25 de Mayo 252, Piso 7, Of. 72 1385 Buenos Aires Tel: (1) 342-0635 Fax: (1) 342-4438
Expo de Peluquerías Beauty shop expo	Buenos Aires Centro Costa Salguero April 2–4, 1995	JC Producciones & Asociados S.R.L. Juan de Garay, Piso 2, Of. C 1153 Buenos Aires Tel: (1) 855-4683, 855-5093 Fax: (1) 855-4683
Expo Internacional de Cosmetología y Estética Aplicada Cosmotology exhibition	Buenos Aires Centro Costa Salguero Annual May 1996	Anxiuss S.R.L. Tte. Gral. J.D. Perón 1730, Piso 3, Of. 45 1037 Buenos Aires Fax: (1) 374-5405, 374-0338

EXPO PERFUMERIA '95 Perfume exhibition	Buenos Aires Palacio San Miguel October 19–22, 1995	Expositora S.R.L. Paraná 264, Piso 6, Of. 61 1017 Buenos Aires Tel: (1) 470-0867, 479-1234 Fax: (1) 374-7121
EXPOUTILISIMA '95 Health and beauty expo	Buenos Aires Predio Ferial de Palermo July 5–16,1995	Utilities S.A. Carlos Calvo 761, Piso B 1062 Buenos Aires Tel: (1) 26-6130, 304-8228 Fax: (1) 448-3602

INDUSTRIAL MATERIALS

Argenplas Thermoplastics, resins, transformers, converters, molds and dies	Buenos Aires Predio Ferial de Palermo Every 3 years in April April 18–24, 1996 April 1999	Cámara Argentina de la Industria Plástica Salguero 1939 1425 Buenos Aires Tel: (1) 821-9603 Fax: (1) 826-5480
EXPOCAUCHO **Exposición Internacional del** **Caucho** International rubber exposition	Buenos Aires Predio Ferial de Palermo September 5–10, 1995	Federación Argentina de la Ind. del Caucho Av. L.N. Alem 1067, Piso 16 1001 Buenos Aires Tel: (1) 313-2009, 313-2140 Fax: (1) 312-9892
PINTURA '95 **Exposición Internacional y** **Congreso de la Industria de la** **Pintura** Paint industry	Buenos Aires Centro Costa Salguero September 4–10, 1995	EFYC S.A. Emprendimientos Feriales y de Comunicación Estado de Israel 4791 1185 Buenos Aires Fax: (1) 854-6322, 855-5214
World of Concrete Expo '95	Buenos Aires Centro Costa Salguero September 20-23, 1995	Aberdeen Group Paraná 123, Piso 5, Of. 121 1017 Buenos Aires Fax: (1) 374-8111, 374-2678, 374-1956

MACHINERY & TOOLS
See also other categories which may include exhibitions with machines specific to those industries

EMAQH—Exposición **Internacional de la Máquina** **Herramienta** Machine and metalworking tools, analytical/scientific equipment	Buenos Aires Centro Internacional de Exposiciones Buenos Aires April 27–May 5, 1996	Asociación Expomahe Alsina 1609, Piso 5, Of. 21 1088 Buenos Aires Tel: (1) 371-1593, 374-1758 Fax: (1) 375-3150
FITAG Agrarian technology	Córdoba Predio Ferial Córdoba Annual May 17–21, 1995 May 1996	Feriar S.A., Predio Ferial Córdoba PO Box 348 5000 Córdoba Tel: (51) 810759 Fax: (51) 890023
Metalurgia '95 **Exposición Internacional de la** **Industria Metalmecánica** Metalworking exposition	Buenos Aires Predio Ferial de Palermo October 2–8, 1995	Asociación de Industriales Metalúrgicos Alsina 1609, Piso 1 1088 Buenos Aires Tel: (1) 371-5063, 371-5292, 371-5182 Fax: (1) 814-4407

MEDICAL & DENTAL
See also Health & Beauty

Expo Farmacia **Exposición Nacional de** **Farmacia y Productos Afines** Pharmacy exposition	Buenos Aires Predio Ferial de Palermo May 18-22, 1995	Expositora S.R.L. Paraná 264, Piso 6, Of. 61 1017 Buenos Aires Tel: (1) 470-0667 Fax: (1) 374-7121

EXPODENT '95 **Muestra de la Industria y** **Comercio Dental Argentino** Dental industry trade exhibit	Córdoba La Vieja Usina August 16–19, 1995	Cámara Dental de Córdoba Av. Gral Paz 79 5000 Córdoba Tel: (51) 24-4769, 24-4753
EXPOSALUD **Feria Internacional de** **Equipos, Insumos y Servicios** **para la Salud** International medical equipment exposition	Córdoba Predio Ferial Córdoba Annual October 18–22, 1995 October 1996	Feriar S.A. PO Box 348 5000 Córdoba Tel: (51) 81-1087, 81-1293, 81-0759 Fax: (51) 89-0023
Exposición Internacional de la **Asociación Odontológica** **Argentina** Dental equipment	Buenos Aires Sheraton Hotel Oct. 29–Nov. 4, 1995	Asociación Odontológica Argentina Junin 959 1113 Buenos Aires Tel: (1) 961-6062, 961-6063 Fax: (1) 961-1110
Hospitalar Argentina **Feria Internacional de** **Productos, Equipos y Servicios** **para el Sector de la Salud** Hospital supplies and services expo	Buenos Aires Centro Costa Salguero November 8–11, 1995	Mercoferias Corrientes 692 1636 Olivos Pcia. de Buenos Aires Tel: (1) 794-2802 Fax: (1) 799-8087

PACKING & PACKAGING

ENVASE **Exposición Internacional del** **Envase y Embalaje** Packaging equipment and supplies	Buenos Aires Centro Municipal de Exposiciones Every 2 years Oct. 30–Nov. 3, 1995	Instituto Argentino del Envase Av. Jujuy 425 1083 Buenos Aires Tel: (1) 957-0968 Fax: (1) 956-1368
Expoflexible '95 **Exposición de la Industria del** **Envase Flexible** Packaging exposition	Buenos Aires Centro Cosa Salguero June 26–July 2, 1995	Cámara Argentina de Productos de Envases Flexibles Bacacay 1789 1405 Buenos Aires Tel: (1) 825-4120 Fax: (1) 205-2276

RETAIL & FRANCHISING

EXPOESTACION '95 **Exposición Nacional de** **Proveedores de Estaciones de** **Servicio** Service station exposition	Buenos Aires Sheraton Buenos Aires August 22–25, 1995	Imfoc S.A. Tte. Gral. Juan D. Perón 1610, Piso 2 1037 Buenos Aires Fax: (1) 382-3350, 382-0780, 382-3218
Exposición Comercial de **Convenience Stores** Convenience stores	Buenos Aires May 3-4, 1996	Exposible S.R.L. Medrano 70, Piso 3 Buenos Aires Tel: (1) 981-5383, 981-2426, 981-0905
Ferimar Factory shops exhibition	Mar del Plata Centro de Exposiciones de Mar del Plata January 6–March 3, 1996 Annual	Ricardo A. Sabbag Producciones S.R.L. Av. Rivadavia 1815, Piso 2 Of. A 1033 Buenos Aires Tel: (1) 952-2557, 952-3915, 952-2763 Fax: (1) 951-6421
Franchising Conference & **Expo**	Buenos Aires Palacio San Miguél June 13–14, 1995	Mind Trainer S.A. Av. Roque S. Peña 851, Piso 8 1035 Buenos Aires Tel: (1) 326-6501, 326-3363, 326-2712 Fax: (1) 326-8178

Salón Nacional de Proveedores y Encuentro Latinoamericano de Supermercadistas Supermarket suppliers exposition	Buenos Aires Sheraton Hotel September 13–15, 1995	Cámara Argentina de Supermercados Viamonte 342, Piso 3 1053 Buenos Aires Tel: (1) 313-1812, 313-1822, 313-1835 Fax: (1) 313-1897

SPORTING GOODS, ENTERTAINMENT & TOURISM

ARMAS Feria Internacional de Armas Militares, Deportivas y de Caza—Pesca y Accesorios— Exposición Internacional de Tecnología Militar Military armament, hunting and fishing gear exposition	Buenos Aires Predio Ferial de Palermo Annual March 21–31, 1996	Organización M.C. S.R.L. Pte. R.S. Peña 720, Piso 2, Of. B 1035 Buenos Aires Fax: (1) 328-0890, 328-8679, 328-8640
BUCEO Salón Internacional de Actividades Subacuáticas International diving exhibition	Buenos Aires Predio Ferial de Palermo Oct. 27–Nov. 1, 1995	Federación Argentina de Activ. Subacuáticas Arribeños 1599, Piso 15 1426 Buenos Aires Fax: (1) 855-5214, 854-6322
EIDA Exposición Internacional de Artículos Deportivos y Afines Sports and leisure fair	Buenos Aires Centro Costa Salguero November 16-20, 1995	Cámara Industrial del Deporte y Afines (CAMIDA) Alsina 1433, Piso 7, Of. B 1088 Buenos Aires Fax: (1) 381-4757
Expo Todo Esqui '95 Ski equipment	Buenos Aires Sheraton Hotel May 19–25, 1995	Oscar Patiño y Asociados M.T. de Alvear 976, Piso 9 1058 Buenos Aires Tel: (1) 328-0270, 328-9780
EXPOJUEGOS '95 Toy exposition	Buenos Aires Centro Municipal de Exposiciones July 13–August 13, 1995	Fundación del Quemado Alberti 1093 1223 Buenos Aires Tel: (1) 922-5844, 922-2588 Fax: (1) 924-3978
Exposición Internacional de Gambling Gambling exhibition	Buenos Aires Centro Costa Salguero June 5-8, 1995	Congresos Interncionales S.A. Moreno 584, Piso 9, Of. A 1091 Buenos Aires Tel: (1) 922-1537, 342-3216, 342-3283 Fax: (1) 331-0223, 334-3811
EXPOTURISMO '95 Primera Exposición Internacional de Turismo al Público International tourism expo	Buenos Aires Predio Ferial de Palermo Oct. 27-Nov. 5, 1995	Expositora S.R.L. Paraná 264, Piso 6, Of. 61 1017 Buenos Aires Tel: (1) 470-0867, 479-1234 Fax: (1) 374-7121
IAE Expo Internacional de Entretenimientos Buenos Aires Entertainment exposition	Buenos Aires November 8–10, 1995	Monografie y Rossi Heinlein & Asociados S.A. Viamonte 494, Piso 2, Of. 8 1053 Buenos Aires Tel: (1) 311-9413, 311-9837
Juegos y Juguetes '95 Games and recreation expo	Mar del Plata Centro de Exposiciones y Congresos La Loma July 1–August 14, 1995	Impacto S.R.L. Juan B. Justo 630 7600 Mar del Plata Tel: (23) 89-3442, 89-3447
Juguete Feria Internacional de Buenos Aires International toy exhibit	Buenos Aires Centro Costa Salguero Annual May 4–8, 1996	Cámara Argentina de la Industria del Juguete Cochabamba 4067 1262 Buenos Aires Tel: (1) 922-1537, 922-0169 Fax: (1) 923-6658

SAGSE **Expo Sudamericana de** **Materiales para Juegos de** **Azar** Gambling exposition	Buenos Aires November 8–10, 1995	Monografie y Rossi Heinlein & Asociados S.A. Viamonte 494, Piso 2, Of. 8 1053 Buenos Aires Tel: (1) 311-9413, 311-9837
Salón Náutico '95 Nautical exhibition	Buenos Aires Predio Ferial de Palermo Sept. 22–Oct. 1, 1995	Cámara Argentina de Constructores de Embarcaciones Livianas (CACEL) Av. del Libertador 433 1646 San Fernando Tel: (1) 745-9581 Fax: (1) 744-3619
SIT—Salón Internacional de **Profesionales del Turismo** Tourism professionals conference	Córdoba Predio Ferial Córdoba September 27–30, 1995	Feriar S.A. Casilla de Correo 348 5000 Córdoba Tel: (51) 81-1293, 81-0759, 81-0769 Fax: (51) 89-0023

TELEVISION, RADIO, VIDEO & PHOTOGRAPHY

Bienal de Radioteledifusora Radio broadcast exhibition	Buenos Aires Centro Municipal de Exposiciones (Pabellones Anexos) June 1–4, 1995	Broadcasting S.A. Suipacha 760, Piso 7, Of. 38 1427 Buenos Aires Tel: (1) 855-4683, 855-5093 Fax: (1) 855-4683
CAPER '95 **Exposición y Jornadas de** **Televisión por Cable** Cable television exhibition	Buenos Aires Centro Costa Salguero November 19–23, 1995	Asociación Argentina de Televisión por Cable (ATVC) Av. de Mayo 749, Piso 2, Of. 10 1084 Buenos Aires Tel: (1) 342-3382 Fax: (1) 343-1716
ELECTROSHOW '95 **Feria Internacional de Audio,** **TV, Video, Iluminación e** **Instrumentos Musicales** Audio, TV, video, lighting and musical instrument exhibit	Buenos Aires Predio Ferial de Palermo August 24–27, 1995	Asociación Argentina de Audio y Video y Cámara Argentina de la Música Tucumán 1748, Piso 2, Of. 4 1050 Buenos Aires Fax: (1) 49-7874
EXPOFOTO **Exposición Internacional de** **Equipos y Sistemas** **Fotográficos y de Video** Video and photographic systems and equipment	Buenos Aires Centro Municipal de Exposiciones October 13–22, 1995	Cámara Argentina de Comerciantes e Importadores de Optica, Fotografía y Afines (CACIOFA) Pasaje del Carmen 716, Piso 8, Of. A 1019 Buenos Aires Tel: (1) 812-3893 Fax: (1) 812-2751
TECNOCINE **Primera Exposición y** **Seminario Internacional de la** **Industria y Producción de** **Cine y Video** Movie and video production	Buenos Aires Centro Costa Salguero April 20–23, 1995	Cámara de la Industria Cinematográfica Argentina Av. Callao 157, Piso 8 1022 Buenos Aires Tel: (1) 40-1378, 476-4148

TRANSPORTATION

Tecnovial **Exposición Internacional de la** **Industria y la Ingeniería Vial** Transportation engineering exposition	Buenos Aires Predio Ferial de Palermo November 1995	EFYC S.A. Emprendimientos Feriales y de Communicación Vidal 1886, Piso 2, Of. G 1428 Buenos Aires Tel: (1) 786-6290 Fax: (1) 781-8732
FITT **Feria Internacional del** **Transporte Terrestre** Ground transportation fair	Buenos Aires Centro Municipal de Exposiciones (Pabellones Anexos) Sept. 22–Oct. 1, 1995	Invol S.A. Sarmiento 1469, Piso 5, Of. C 1042 Buenos Aires Tel: (1) 49-1498, 49-1935

Business Travel

INTRODUCTION

For the first-time business traveler, it is easy to expect the Argentina of old films and dated newspaper headlines: tango dancers in smoky bars, colorful gauchos and endless herds of cattle on the limitless pampas, and hyperinflation. All three continue to be important to Argentina's image of itself, but much more is left out than is explained by such images. Argentina is a sophisticated, stylish, and cosmopolitan country. Annual inflation has dropped to less than 4 percent in 1994. And despite a reputation for staying up until dawn, the typical Argentine

businessperson spends more hours in the office than do counterparts in the US, Japan, or Europe.

Major airlines from around the world fly into Buenos Aires—known universally as BA. Air is also the best bet for domestic business travel. The road system is well developed, but distances can be vast. At 2,776,654 sq km (1,072,067 sq mi), Argentina is nearly as large as all of Western Europe combined, stretching over a distance equivalent to that from Labrador to Cuba. And like the US, Canada, and Australia, Argentina takes conscious pride in its immigrant history. Its people are mainly of Spanish and Italian descent, although the nation also includes people of many other national origins.

NATIONAL TRAVEL OFFICES WORLDWIDE

Most Argentine consulates around the world provide visitor information as well as more traditional consular services. Local representatives of Aerolíneas Argentinas can usually provide general tourist information as well as airline bookings and tickets. In general, Argentina has yet to capitalize effectively on its potential as a tourist destination. However, the government has named tourism as an area for development in the near future, and improvements in the availability of information may be forthcoming. Overseas offices providing tourist information are found in the following locations:

Australia & New Zealand

Auckland 11 Floor, Harbour View Bldg., 52 Quay St., PO Box 2320, Auckland, New Zealand; Tel: [64] (9) 309-1757 Fax: [64] (9) 373-5386.

Canberra 1st Floor, MLC Tower, Wooden, ACT 2606, Australia; Tel: [61] (6) 282-4555.

Sydney 100 Miller St., Suite 6, Level 30, North Sydney, NSW 2060, Australia; Tel: [61] (2) 922-7272 Fax: [61] (2) 923-1798.

ARGENTINE ADDRESSES & TELEPHONE NUMBERS

Addresses and telephone numbers listed in the "Business Travel" chapter are in Argentina unless otherwise noted. Country codes for international dialing appear in square brackets, i.e., [33] for France or [1] for the US and Canada. City codes appear in parentheses, i.e., (171) for London or (1) for Buenos Aires.

If you are calling Argentina from outside the country you will need to dial the local international access code, i.e., 011 from the US or 001 from Japan, then [54] for Argentina's country code, followed by the city code and the local telephone number. Some of the codes for major cities in Argentina are: (1) for Buenos Aires, (51) for Córdoba, (41) for Rosario, and (61) for Mendoza.

Argentine street addresses list the street name, followed by the building number. Postal codes are four digits and precede the city name. In listings where all addresses are in the same city, we write the postal code in parentheses following the street address, as in our hotel listings.

For telephone dialing codes and more information on Argentine address formats, refer to pages 315 and 316 in the "Important Addresses" chapter.

Europe

Belgium 225 Ave. Louise B.3, 1050 Brussels, Belgium; Tel: [32] (2) 647-7812 Fax: [32] (2) 467-9319.

France 6 rue Cimarosa, 75116 Paris, France; Tel: [33] (1) 45-53-33-00 Fax: [33] (1) 45-53-46-33.

Germany Wiesenhuettenplaz 26, 8th Fl., 60329 Frankfurt am Main, Germany; Tel: [49] (69) 923-1050 Fax: [49] (69) 923-6842.

Netherlands Herengracht 94, 1015 BS Amsterdam, Netherlands; Tel: [31] (20) 623-2323, 623-6242 Fax: [31] (20) 626-7344.

Spain Paseo de la Castellana 53, Madrid 1, Spain; Tel: [34] (1) 442-4500 Fax: [34] (1) 442-3559.

United Kingdom 53 Hans Place, London SW1X 0LA, UK; Tel: [44] (171) 589-3104 Fax: [44] (171) 589-3106.

Canada

Ontario Suite 620, 90 Sparks Street, Ottawa, ON, K1P 5B4, Canada; Tel: [1] (613) 236-2351 Fax: [1] (613) 235-2659.

Quebec Suite 605, 1010 Saint Catherine St. West, Montreal, PQ, Canada; Tel: [1] (514) 866-3810.

United States

Chicago 20 North Clark St., Suite 602, Chicago, IL, USA; Tel: [1] (312) 263-7435.

Houston Suite 1810, 2000 S. Post Oak Road, Houston, TX, USA; Tel: [1] (713) 871-8935.

Los Angeles Suite 1450, 3550 Wilshire Blvd., Los Angeles, CA, USA; Tel: [1] (310) 739-9977.

Miami Suite 722, 25 SE Second Ave., Miami, FL, USA; Tel: [1] (305) 373-1889.

New York 12 West 56th St., New York, NY, USA; Tel: [1] (212) 397-3523 Fax: [1] (212) 397-3523.

San Francisco Room 1083, 870 Market St., San Francisco, CA, USA; Tel: [1] (415) 982-3050.

Washington, DC 1600 New Hampshire Ave. NW, Washington, DC; Tel: [1] (202) 939-6400.

Argentina

National Tourism Office Santa Fe 883, P.B., Buenos Aires Tel: (1) 312-2232, 312-5550.

Secretariat of Tourism Suipacha 1111, Piso 21, 1360 Buenos Aires; Tel: (1) 312-5624, 311-2089; Fax: (1) 313-6834.

Argentine Chamber of Tourism Tucumán 1610, Pisos 5 y 6, Buenos Aires; Tel: (1) 40-5108, x13.

Buenos Aires Tourism Office Sarmiento 1551, Piso 5, Buenos Aires; Tel: (1) 46-1251.

Every province in Argentina—and many cities—has a tourist office; most of these also maintain offices in Buenos Aires.

VISA AND PASSPORT REQUIREMENTS

A valid passport is required for entry into Argentina, but visa policies are liberal. Tourists from Canada, the US, and most Western European countries do not need visas. Nationals from other countries need visas, available from the nearest Argentine embassy or consulate. In theory, nonvisa visitors must obtain a free tourist card, good for 90 days, at the port of entry. In practice, immigration officials issue tourist cards only at major crossings, including international airports and landing docks for the ferries from Uruguay. Travelers who are not given a tourist card can fill one out upon departure.

A visa is theoretically required of all business travelers, but most businesspeople who will be in the country for less than 90 days enter as tourists to minimize paperwork. Foreigners who will be in Argentina for longer than 90 days, or who might expect to draw official attention because of their business activities, should obtain valid business visas. Application for a business visa requires a letter from the traveler's employer stating the business reason for travel, the anticipated length of the visit, and acceptance of financial responsibility for the traveler. Multiple-entry business visas are valid for four years.

Long-term work and residence permits are also available. Permanent residents may engage in any profit-making activity. Temporary residents may also work, but must first obtain a work permit. The Dirección Nacional de Migraciones issues work permits on application by the traveler's employer in Argentina. Permits are valid from one to three years.

The country is very document oriented. Whether entering with a visa or a tourist card, it is important to carry a passport at all times. Police can, and occasionally do, demand identification at any time. A passport is usually required to check into a hotel, cash traveler's checks, and conduct other routine business.

Travelers who were born in Argentina but hold current citizenship in another country may experience legal difficulties. Under Argentine law, anyone born in Argentina (except the children of diplomats) is an Argentine citizen for life, and is subject to the military draft and other national obligations. Contact an Argentine embassy or consulate for assistance before entering the country.

Drivers need an International Driver's License as well as a national, state, or provincial license from home. If a driver is stopped for a traffic violation or at a checkpoint, police officers sometimes claim not to recognize the international license or claim that it is invalid. The best response is to politely refer them to the Spanish translation on the license.

IMMUNIZATIONS

Proof of vaccination against yellow fever or other diseases is not required unless you are arriving from an infected area. The most common requirement is yellow fever vaccination for travelers arriving from tropical South America and Africa. The World Health Organization (WHO) does not recommend vaccinations or preventive medication against any endemic diseases, although malaria is occasionally reported in the extreme northeast section of the country.

CLIMATE

Argentina is a long, narrow country stretching from the subtropics along the northeastern border with Brazil to the subpolar regions of Tierra del Fuego in the south. The western edge of the country runs along the Andes Mountains. The Central Andes include the highest mountain in South America, Aconcagua, 6960 m (21,100 ft), but elevations gradually fall toward the south.

The Andes are high, dry (nearly all the rain falls

AIR TRAVEL TIME TO BUENOS AIRES

- From Frankfurt nonstop: 14 hours
- From London nonstop: 14 hours
- From Los Angeles via Miami: 14 hours
- From Miami nonstop: 8.5 hours
- From New York via Miami: 11.5 hours
- From Paris nonstop: 14 hours
- From São Paulo nonstop: 2.5 hours
- From Santiago nonstop: 2 hours
- From Sydney via Los Angeles: 27 hours
- From Tokyo via Los Angeles: 26 hours

---

on the western slopes in Chile), and thinly vegetated in many places. The north (Chaco) is hot and subtropical; the northeast (Misiones) is tropical and wet. The south (Patagonia) is cool, windy, and dry all year, with snow in winter. The central portion of Argentina (Pampas), with the primary business cities of Buenos Aires, Córdoba, Mendoza, and Rosario, is temperate.

Because Argentina is south of the equator, the seasons are reversed from Europe, North America, and much of Asia. Buenos Aires has a climate similar to New York City, although its winters are considerably milder and without snow. Summer—the months of January and February—is quite hot and humid; the city seems almost deserted because everyone who can flees to nearby beaches or mountains to get away from the heat. Winter is damp and chilly. Rain falls throughout the year, from 100 cm per year (39 in) in Buenos Aires to less than 50 cm (20 in) in Mendoza in the foothills of the Andes.

The best months to visit are April and May (autumn) and October and November (spring). However, business goes on year-round, although December, January, and February are the least optimal because of the Christmas season and the summer vacation schedule. Average annual temperatures range from 24°C (75°F) to 11°C (51°F) in Buenos Aires (sea level) and Córdoba (420 m/1270 ft), and 24°C (75°F) to 8°C (46°F) in Mendoza (820 m/2484 ft).

BUSINESS ATTIRE

Buenos Aires is every bit as dressy and conscious of fashion as Milan, Paris, New York, or Hong Kong, although it tends to appreciate traditional formality rather than avant-garde experimentation. Initial business impressions for both men and women are based largely on dress, starting with the shoes and moving up. The casual dress codes that have become common in US offices are unlikely to spread to Argentina.

Men wear stylish medium weight wool suits during the winter months. In summer, men change to tropical weight woolens and cottons. For any season, dark, conservative colors are most appropriate for business occasions. If you are going out in the evening, it is standard to change to a darker suit. Black tie is common for visits to the opera, ballet, and some other functions, which may include business dinners. It is always better to ask in advance than to appear underdressed.

Women should follow similar guidelines. Wool or silk suits and dresses are most appropriate for business wear, preferably in conservative colors and styles. Medium heeled shoes are standard. In general, simple elegance is the impression to strive for. Trousers or pants suits are generally not acceptable business attire for women.

When dining in a formal restaurant, men should wear a coat and tie (or an ascot), women a skirt and blouse or a dress. Similar styles are appropriate if you are invited to a meal at someone's home. For an *asado* (an outdoor barbecue), casual but slightly dressy resort clothing is appropriate.

Casual wear for men is a sweater, shirt, and pants or a shirt and pants, depending on the weather. For women, a top with very chic pants or a skirt is appropriate. Nighttime attire remains somewhat more formal.

If visiting during the winter (June to August), both genders need warm clothes and topcoats. Central heating is uncommon in public buildings. Homes and offices are often equipped with electric space heaters, although central heating (and air conditioning) is the norm in business hotels.

Shorts are generally not worn in urban areas except on the way to participate in a sport such as tennis or football (soccer). At beaches and swimming pools, swimsuits are noticeably more conservative than those worn by either gender in Brazil.

AIRLINES

Argentina has three major airlines: Aerolíneas Argentinas, with domestic as well as international service; Austral, domestic only; and Líneas Aéreas del Estado (LADE), which serves Patagonia. Aerolíneas Argentinas' international routes as well as most other international airlines fly into Ezeiza International Airport, about 45 minutes southwest of Buenos Aires. Domestic flights usually use Aeroparque Jorge Newbery, just north of downtown Buenos Aires (BA) near the Río de la Plata.

Major international airlines include American, Air France, Aero Perú, Avianca, British Airways, Iberia, KLM, Ladeco, LAN-Chile, Líneas Aéreas Paraguayas, Lloyd Aero Boliviano, Lufthansa, Malaysia Air, Swissair, United Airlines, and Varig. (Refer to "Airlines and Air Cargo Carriers" on page 346 of the "Important Addresses" chapter for contact information.)

TIME CHANGES

Argentina is three hours behind Greenwich Mean Time (GMT) and two hours ahead of Eastern Standard Time (EST). When you are in Argentina, add or subtract the number of hours shown to determine the time in each of the cities listed below:

Amsterdam	+ 4
Cairo	+ 5
Chicago	- 4
Frankfurt	+ 4
Hong Kong	+11
Istanbul	+ 5
Johannesburg	+ 5
London	+ 5
Los Angeles	- 5
New York	- 2
Paris	+ 4
Perth	+16
Rome	+ 4
Singapore	+11
Sydney	+13
Taipei	+10
Tel Aviv	+ 5
Tokyo	+12
Toronto	- 2

CUSTOMS ENTRY (PERSONAL)

Argentine customs officials usually ignore foreign visitors, but expensive cameras, laptop computers, and similar electronic items may arouse interest. It's a good idea to have a prepared list of such equipment, including serial numbers, ready for authorities to inspect and stamp. Inspectors at Ezeiza Airport in Buenos Aires are particularly vigilant. Travelers are also subject to police inspection at internal checkpoints, usually at provincial borders and major highway junctions. Officials at international borders are usually efficient and helpful, but internal checkpoints tend to be more bureaucratic and formal in their approach.

Customs inspection follows the usual red and green lane approach: green for nothing to declare, red for dutiable items. Personal effects may be brought into Argentina without duty. Each adult traveler is also allowed two liters of alcoholic beverages, 400 cigarettes, 40 cigars, and 4 kg of foodstuffs duty-free. Travelers arriving by land or water from neighboring countries may bring one-half of the normal amounts, that is, one liter of alcohol, 200 cigarettes, 20 cigars, and 2 kg of food. There are no restrictions on the import or export of Argentine or foreign currency, bonds, securities, or letters of credit.

FOREIGN EXCHANGE (PERSONAL)

The unit of currency is the peso ($), set at an official exchange rate of one peso = one US dollar. Bills are 1, 2, 5, 10, 20, 50, and 100 pesos. Coins in circulation are 5, 10, 25, 50 centavos, and 1 peso. Exchange rates have been stable since the new peso was introduced in January 1992. There is no black market in currency exchange.

Traveler's checks and currency can be exchanged at banks, exchange shops (*casas de cambio*), and hotels, as well as both Buenos Aires airports. Hotels are convenient, but usually offer the lowest rate. Banks and *casas de cambio* offer similar rates, but cash, particularly US dollars, commands a better exchange rate and lower fee than traveler's checks. Bills of all denominations are accepted, but take only crisp, new notes. Wrinkled, soiled, or torn banknotes will probably be refused. For the most current information, look for *Ambito Financiero* or *El Cronista*—Argentina's equivalent to the *Wall Street Journal* or *Financial Times*—or the financial sections of other local papers.

Cashing traveler's checks can be difficult, especially in smaller towns. Commissions can run as high as 10 percent, but can usually be avoided by cashing checks at a branch of the issuing bank or company such as American Express or Thomas Cook. Cashing traveler's checks can be a lengthy process with innumerable forms to be completed. Any variation between the sample signature and the cashing signature can lead to refusal of the check.

Cash is also available from automated teller machines (ATMs), particularly in Buenos Aires, Córdoba, Mendoza, and Rosario. Credit cards (American Express, Diner's Club, MasterCard, and Visa) are widely accepted at business hotels, expensive restaurants, and upscale stores. It has been common in the recent past to find a 10 to 20 percent surcharge added for credit card payments—or a similar discount for cash—although this is becoming less frequent as interest and inflation rates fall and stabilize. US dollars may also be accepted at par value.

TIPPING

Tipping is neither widespread nor expensive, even in Buenos Aires. Airport porters get $1 per bag, while hotel porters get $1 for all bags. Taxi drivers near hotels are beginning to expect a 15 percent tip from foreigners, but the standard practice is to round the fare up to the nearest peso or 50 centavos to provide a small tip. Restaurant waiters expect a 10 percent tip. Ushers at concerts, plays, and films get 5 percent of the ticket price. Gas station attendants get $1 or $2 when they fill the tank, wash the windshield, and perform the usual services, such as checking the oil. Hotels add a service charge to all room bills.

AIRPORT ACCESS

Aerolíneas Argentinas and other domestic carriers usually operate bus service between the airport and a central downtown point. Bus schedules are coordinated with flight times.

Buenos Aires is the major exception. Aeroparque Jorge Newbery, just north of downtown, is best reached by taxi (about $10 to or from downtown). Ezeiza Airport, 35 km (22 mi) southwest of downtown, is 45 to 90 minutes away, depending on traffic. Taxi service is $40 one-way. Some observers note that travelers should be cautious with airport taxi drivers, some of who may try to cheat or rob passengers. Manuel Tienda León (Tel: 396-2078) runs an efficient door-to-door minibus service for $15 each way. Buses leave every half hour from 5:30 to 10 am, every 20 minutes until 5 pm, and then every half-hour until 10 pm.

The airport at Córdoba is located at Pajas Blancas 15 km (9 mi) from downtown; Plumerillo Airport is located 8 km (5 mi) from downtown Mendoza; and Fisherton Airport, serving Rosario, is 8 km (5 mi) west of the city center. If not using an airline bus, taxi is the best way to and from the airports in these cities.

ACCOMMODATIONS

Buenos Aires has a solid selection of international class business hotels with all the expected services: heating, air conditioning, satellite and local television, minibars, telephones, business centers, health clubs, swimming pools, bars, fine restaurants, and front desk clerks who speak English, French, Italian, and German as well as Spanish. Room service is both universal and universally slow. Hotel laundry tends to be expensive, and hotel telephone charges verge on extortion.

Expect to pay $250 per night—and up—for a top-end hotel, half that for a more moderate first class room. First class hotels offer the same level of service and comfort as the top-end hotels, but the furnishings and decor are likely to be a few years out of date and the prices lower.

Most hotels offer discounts for corporate guests as well as for repeat visitors. For the best rates and service, let the company's local office handle negotiations rather than booking from abroad or through a centralized hotel chain booking service.

Advance reservations are not needed during January and February because everyone who can leaves town to escape the heat and humidity. Advance reservations are essential any other time of the year, however. The summer vacation season begins December 15 and ends around March 15. Winter vacations begin around July 5 and end the middle of August. Travelers unlucky enough to arrive without a booking can try contacting the local tourist office. If traveling to the provinces, it is better to book ahead from Buenos Aires than to arrive in a provincial town without advance arrangements.

BUENOS AIRES

The majority of Buenos Aires business hotels are in or very near the downtown business area, although a few are as far away as Recoleta to the north of the main business district. The four-digit number in parentheses that follows the street address in the listings below is the postal code.

Top-End

Caesar Park Buenos Aires Posadas 1232 (1014), Recoleta; a very short taxi ride from downtown and a good selection of nonsmoking rooms—a rarity in Argentina. Health and fitness center, sauna, pool, business center, computer rentals, three restaurants. Rates: double $280. Tel: (1) 814-5150 Fax: (1) 814-5148.

Hotel Libertador Kempinski Av. Córdoba 698 y Maipú (1054), near Plaza San Martín; business center, computer rentals, extensive convention and meeting facilities with two excellent restaurants, El Portal and the Pergola. Rates: double $295. Tel: (1) 322-2095 Fax: (1) 322-9703

Park Hyatt Buenos Aires Posadas 1086/88 (1011), near Retiro; large business center and some of the most modern hotel meeting space in the city, computer rentals, fully equipped health club, sauna, spa, and swimming pool; incorporates an historic turn-of-the-century mansion. Rates: double $305. Tel: (1) 326-1234 Fax: (1) 326-3736.

Plaza Hotel Florida 1005 (1005), on the Florida pedestrian mall; very French, very formal, with superb service and some of the most exclusive jewelers, furriers, banks, and travel agencies in Buenos Aires on the ground floor. A favorite for visiting heads of state and for fashion shows. Rates: double $260. Tel: (1) 311-5011 Fax: (1) 313-2912.

Hotel Inter-Continental Moreno 809 (1070), is the newest—it opened in January 1995—most up-to-date major hotel in Buenos Aires. Located in the heart of the city, it has 310 rooms, health club, pool, sauna, meeting facilities, fully equipped business center. Rates: double $290. Tel: (1) 340-7100 Fax: (1) 340-7199.

Alvear Palace Hotel Av. Alvear 1891, in the Barrio Norte area—15 minutes north of the center and near shops and embassies—this beaux-artes grande dame would easily be at home in Paris. Some 254 recently renovated rooms, restaurants, lounges, night club, indoor pool, meeting facilities, business center, computer rentals, multilingual secretaries. Rates: double $250. Tel: (1) 804-4031 Fax: (1) 804-0034.

First Class

Buenos Aires Sheraton San Martín 1225/75 (1022), Retiro; business center, computer rentals, meeting and conference facilities, health club, tennis, heated pool, sauna, rooftop bar, several restaurants and top-notch entertainment. Rates: double $295. Tel: (1) 311-6311, 311-6326/7 Fax: (1) 311-6353, 312-0346.

Hotel Claridge Tucumán 535 (1049) near the Florida pedestrian shopping area; all the usual business facilities, but best known for its restaurant. Rates: double $150. Tel: (1) 322-7700, 322-8025 Fax: (1) 322-8022.

Hotel Continental Av. Roque Sáenz Peña 725 (1035), just off the Florida pedestrian mall. A stately, old-fashioned hotel with all the modern services, but well insulated from the maddening crowds. The avenue is lined with gorgeous jacaranda trees that bloom twice yearly—although anyone who is allergic should steer clear of the entire neighborhood. Rates: double $150. Tel: (1) 373-3251/9 Fax: (1) 322-1421.

Panamericano/Holiday Inn Crowne Plaza Buenos Aires Carlos Pellegrini 525 (1009); All the expected business facilities on Av. 9 de Julio in the heart of downtown near government and business centers. Driving is next to impossible, but taxis are plentiful. Rates: double $350. Tel: (1) 348-5000 Fax: (1) 348-5250/1.

CÓRDOBA

Most hotels in Córdoba are concentrated in the downtown area near Plaza San Martín. Prices are considerably lower than Buenos Aires, as are the level of facilities and services. Foreign language abilities are likely to be minimal, but the staff is also likely to try harder to help. Most hotels offer basic business services such as photocopying or sending and receiving faxes, but only during regular business hours. Advance bookings are a good idea year-round. If possible, make bookings through a local office or representative for the best service and lowest rates.

Hotel Crillon Rivadavia 85 (5000); a familiar favorite with long-time business visitors, very friendly, although the glory has faded slightly. Rates: $75. Tel: (51) 21-609316 Fax: (51) 24-0742.

Hotel Nogaró San Jerónimo 137 (5000); central location and reasonable prices for a new hotel. Rates: $75. Tel: (51) 2-24001/5 Fax: (51) 24-3661.

Hotel Sussex San Jerónimo 125 (5000); the most attractive, most comfortable, and most expensive hotel in town. Rates: $100. Tel: (51) 22-9071/5 Fax: (51) 229070.

MENDOZA

Business hotels in Mendoza are scattered around the Plaza Independencia, southeast of the railway station. Mendoza is farther from Buenos Aires than Córdoba or Rosario, thus hotel prices are even lower. Local wines are a bargain, with the reds generally better than the whites.

Gran Hotel Huentala Primitivo de la Reta 1009; a dependable address. Rates: $60. Tel: (61) 24-0766, 24-0136, 24-0664 Fax: (61) 24-0664.

Hotel Aconcagua San Lorenzo 545 (5500); the top-of-the-line hotel in the city for business. Rates: $70. Tel: (61) 24-2321, 24-3833, 24-2450 Fax: (61) 31-1085.

Hotel Plaza Chile 1124 (5500); the most stylish hotel in town, in a beautiful neocolonial building. Rates: $55. Tel: (61) 23-3248, 23-3000 Fax: (61) 23-3248, 23-3350.

ROSARIO

Rosario business hotels have gravitated toward the northeastern corner of the city, near the Plaza 25 de Mayo and the open bluffs above the Rio Paraná.

Hotel Libertador Córdoba and Av. Corrientes; the top hotel in the city. Rates: $75. Tel: (41) 24-1005.

Hotel Republica San Lorenzo 955; just around the corner from blufftop parks. Rates: $60. Tel: (41) 24-8580.

Nuevo Hotel Europeo San Luis 1364; slightly inland and slightly cheaper. Rates: $55. Tel: (41) 21-1514.

EATING

Runaway Spanish cattle long ago turned the Pampas into one huge cattle ranch, and Argentina has been famed for its meat ever since. However, the country's rich immigrant heritage has created more restaurant variety than the steak, steak, and steak menu that many first-time visitors expect. Italian dishes, from spaghetti to lasagna, canelloni, and ravioli are ubiquitous offerings. Ñoquis (gnocchi in Italian) are a traditional end-of-the-month meal and a common restaurant special on the 29th of each month. In addition, Argentina offers French, Spanish, and German restaurants—brasseries or cervecerías—that are top-notch according to international standards.

But Argentines still insist that no meal is complete without beef. In Argentina, the Spanish word for meat, carne, means only beef; lamb, pork, venison, wild game, and poultry all have their own words.

The parrillada, a mixed grill of steak and assorted entrails—achuras in Spanish—is a passion throughout Argentina. The usual accompaniments include chinchulines (small intestines), tripa gorda (large intestine), ubre (udder), riñones (kidneys), mollejas (sweetbreads), lengua (tongue), sesos (brains), morcilla (blood sausage), and chorizo (spicy sausage). Lungs are the only part of the cow not customarily eaten in some form. Other beef favorites are bife de chorizo (grilled steak), tira de asado (small chunks of barbecued beef served with fried potatoes), and lomo (sirloin steak), most often served with a small salad and red Argentine wine (vino tinto). Beer and mineral water are the other standard drinks while eating. But whatever the cut, portions are gigantic by European and North American—not to mention Asian—standards.

There are also a few distinctive regional cuisines. The Andean Northwest has spicy food that is closer to the Indian-influenced dishes from the central Andean highlands than to the relatively bland beef of the Pampas. Middle East and Arab dishes are common in Mendoza and areas north. Argentines are not big fish eaters, but seafood is generally excellent. River fish are excellent in the Northeast. Game dishes, including boar, trout, and venison are regional specialties in the Southern Andes. In the extreme South, look for lamb and mutton in place of beef.

Coffee is wildly popular and always served espresso strength. The most common way to buffer the caffeine jolt is to order a cortado: black coffee cut with a little hot milk. Sugar is served on the side.

Argentina produces excellent wines, especially the reds from the Mendoza area. And because almost all consumption is domestic, prices have remained extremely reasonable. A bottle of good wine at a local store costs about as much as a liter of Coca-Cola. Domestic beer, whiskey, and gin are also good and reasonably priced. However, brand-name imported drinks carry a hefty surcharge.

Argentines drink huge amounts of soft drinks, from Coca-Cola to the local tonic water, Paso de los Toros. Fruit juices are superb. Mineral water, both carbonated (con gas) and uncarbonated (sin gas) are common drinks at mealtime. Small towns without bottled mineral water always have soda, poured from huge siphon bottles. Tap water (and homemade soda water) is considered safe to drink throughout Argentina.

Breakfast is a minimal meal for most Argentines, usually nothing more than café con leche—a large cup of strong coffee laced with heated milk—and bread. Breakfast meetings are unpopular—though accepted—because so many businesspeople have worked late the night before.

Lunch starts around 1 pm and may stretch to two hours. Business lunches are still a relatively uncommon phenomenon. At home or in a restaurant, the typical lunch includes *picadas*—appetizers such as sausage, cheese, salami, and olives—followed by soup or pasta, then meat and salad, dessert, and espresso coffee. Salads, like the tap water, are usually safe.

Tea time—*la hora del té*—4 to 6 pm, is a quick break for coffee, tea, or *mate* (a heavily caffeinated herb tea that is the national drink, beloved by Argentines but seldom relished by outsiders), plus perhaps a pastry or other light snack. Do not ignore tea time: it may be the only way to survive all the way until dinner.

Argentines seldom start dinner before 9 pm. Top restaurants don't begin to fill until closer to 10 pm, and it is difficult to find a restaurant that even begins serving much before 8 pm. Some businesspeople finish work around 8 pm, change, attend a cocktail party, continue on to a business dinner about 10 pm, and then head out for early morning entertainment about 1 am, although such behavior is the exception rather than the rule. Dinner menus resemble those from lunch, with even larger portions and more time spent at the table. For an early dinner, look for a steakhouse or a hotel restaurant: both are usually open all day. Dining out is usually a dressy affair, with coat and tie for men and stylish suits or dresses for women. However, dress is becoming more relaxed in general.

There are several types of restaurants available. *Churrasquerías* are all-you-can-eat meat restaurants. Waiters circulate with huge skewers of grilled meats, and diners simply indicate what they want and how much. *Carritos* are basic steak restaurants, usually located on the riverside and open continuously from lunchtime until 2 am. *Picadas* specialize in hundreds of different appetizers, from seafood to beef, cheese, and, yes, nuts. Alcoholic and non-alcohol drinks are available. *Whiskerías* are low-key cocktail lounges offering sandwiches and other simple food. For light snacks, try a *confitería*, which serves small sandwiches, pastries, coffee, tea, and other drinks. *Heladerías* are ice cream shops, the best of which make their own ice cream (*elaboración propia* or *elaboración artesanal* are the key words to look for).

BUENOS AIRES

Beef is almost always the most reasonably priced choice. One person can eat enough beef for two or three at a local *carrito* along the riverfront Av. Costanera Rafael Obligado and easily spend less than $15, including wine. However, the popular business restaurants charge prices on a par with New York, London, or Hong Kong. The *Buenos Aires Herald* publishes a convenient *Guide to Good Eating*

in Buenos Aires, which includes a handy introduction to Argentine wines. Because restaurants—and telephone numbers—are constantly changing, be sure to check locally.

La Cabaña Steakhouse. Enduring since 1935, famous for its high-quality beef and Argentine fare; reputed as the best place to eat beef in Argentina. $50 and up; reservations not necessary. Lunch and dinner. Entre Ríos 436. Tel: (1) 383-2639.

Tomo Uno French-Italian cuisine. Quietly elegant, view of city lights, and some of the best dining in BA. $50 and up; reservations required. Dress: jacket and tie required. Lunch and dinner served. Carlos Pellegrini 521 (in the Crowne Plaza Panamericano Hotel); off Av. 9 de Julio. Tel: (1) 326-6310, 326-6698.

Au Bec Fin Classic French cuisine, best known for prawn mousse and filet mignon. One of the best—and most expensive restaurants—in Argentina. $60 and up; reservations required. Dress: jacket and tie required. Dinner only. Vincent López 1827. Tel: (1) 801-6894.

Refugio del Viejo Conde French cuisine, including profiteroles of king crab and caviar, and trout from the Bariloche lake district; located in a softly lit, antique-filled mansion. $60 and up; reservations required. Dress: jacket and tie required. Dinner only. Cerviño 4453, Palermo. Tel: (1) 773-1362, 773-6907.

La Bourgogne Changing menu of French cuisine, depending on availability of fresh produce; spacious, refined dining in quiet upstairs salon. Tea served in afternoon. $60 and up; reservations recommended. Dress: jacket and tie. Similar fare but less elegant atmosphere downstairs in La Cave. Prix fixe menu light fare $45, dinner $65. 2027 Ayacucho at 1891 Avenida Alvear Recoleta. Tel: (1) 805-3857.

Los Años Locos Beef, beef, and beef in one of the city's longest-lived *carritos*. The crowd is noisy, the portions immense, and good cheer seems to be included in every dish. $20; no reservations. Dress: informal. Lunch and dinner. Costanera Norte and Pampa, on the waterfront. Tel: (1) 784-8681.

Happening Another extremely popular *carrito*, offering a varied menu of grilled fish, chicken, and the ever present beef. Half-portions are enough for at least two healthy appetites from anywhere outside of Argentina. $25 and up; no reservations. Dress: informal. Lunch and dinner. Guide 1931. Tel: (1) 805-2633.

Babette Country French cuisine. Some of the simplest, finest, and cheapest French farm food in BA. Coq au vin and apple pie are perennial favorites. $10. No reservations. Dress: informal. Lunch and dinner. M.T. de Alvear 628, between Calle Florida and Plaza San Martín. No telephone.

Tsuru Japanese teahouse. Traditional Japanese meals, including sashimi and sushi, a rarity in beef-loving Argentina. A favorite with the local Japanese community. $40. Reservations recommended. Dress: jacket and tie. Lunch and dinner. San Martín 1225, in the Sheraton Hotel. Tel: (1) 311-6331.

Las Nazarenas Traditional steakhouse. One of the better steakhouses in Buenos Aires and one of the more expensive, but good for a long meal without too much business talk. $25. No reservations, but tends to fill up for lunch. Dress: jacket and tie. Lunch and dinner. Reconquista 1132, downtown. Tel: (1) 312-5559.

Colbeh Melahat Iranian cuisine. This may be the only place in Argentina to get traditional Iranian rice and lamb dishes. Well worth the trip to the northern suburbs. $50. Reservations recommended. Dress: jacket and tie. Lunch and dinner. Av. del Libertador 13030, Martinez. Tel: (1) 793-3955.

Mora X French and Argentine. A popular meeting place serving everything from light snacks to full meals; mostly traditional Argentine dishes, but with a light French accent. $25. No reservations. Dress: informal to jacket and tie. Lunch and dinner. Vicente López 2152, Recoleta. Tel: (1) 803-0261.

CÓRDOBA

There are a number of grill restaurants on the outskirts of town, especially in the Cerro de las Rosas area. The entire area is popular locally when the weather cooperates.

La Mamma Italian cuisine. Excellent Italian dishes. $15. Reservations recommended. Dress: jacket and tie. Lunch and dinner. Alcorta 270. Tel: (51) 22-8330.

Betos Argentine cuisine. Popular *parrillada* for business entertaining. $20. No reservations. Dress: jacket and tie. Lunch and dinner. San Juan 454.

Firenze Argentine cuisine. Very busy and very traditional cafe. $10. No reservations. Dress: informal to jacket and tie. All day. 25 de Mayo 220.

MENDOZA

The city has a good variety of restaurants, most of them clustered in the city center. Local wines are among the best in Argentina.

Al Arab Middle Eastern cuisine. A popular combination of Middle Eastern and Argentine food, with live entertainment. $20. No reservations. Dress: jacket and tie. Lunch and dinner. Perú and Rivadavia.

Vecchia Roma Italian Cuisine. Superb Italian dishes with good service. $20. Reservations recommended. Dress: jacket and tie. Lunch and dinner. Av. España 1619. Tel: (61) 25-1491.

Parrillada Arturito *Parrillada.* Extremely popular locally, can be crowded at lunch. $15. No reservations. Dress: jacket and tie. Lunch and dinner. Chile 1515.

ROSARIO

The better restaurants, like business hotels, are concentrated in the northwestern corner of the city. Italian or Italian-derived restaurants are the best choices.

Borgo Antico Argentine with Italian touches. Probably the most stylish restaurant in the city, with food and service to match. $35. Reservations recommended. Dress: jacket and tie. Lunch and dinner. Ricardone 131.

Il Nuovo Pavarotti *Parrillada.* A popular grill, despite the Italian name, often busy at midday. $15. No reservations. Dress: jacket and tie. Lunch and dinner. Laprida 988.

Café de la Paz *Confitería.* One of the most popular cafes in the city. $5 and up. No reservations. Dress: informal to jacket and tie. All day. Sarmiento and San Lorenzo.

LOCAL CUSTOMS OVERVIEW

Argentina sometimes seems like a European country that has somehow been misplaced in South America; certainly Buenos Aires is far more reminiscent of Paris or Madrid than it is of other Latin American cities. Argentina's people, including those of the business community, are extremely proud not only of the country's recent successes in recovering from repressive military governments and economic disaster, but also of its more distant, past glories, when the nation was one of the richest in the world. The Argentines and the business community may be compared with royalty, who, though temporarily down at the heels, fully expect to regain their rightful place in the world.

Travelers accustomed to moving quickly and finalizing details with a phone call will have to adjust; there is no way to push the pace of approvals. However, while Argentines may take their time, they are also capable of being quick, efficient, and straightforward. The work ethic is also alive and well in Argentina, and the business day usually begins by 9 am, come what may.

Contacts and introductions are helpful, especially when doing business with any level of government. Prior business dealings, professional organizations, chambers of commerce, common friends or acquaintances, even embassy referrals are more likely to be successful than a cold call. Expect to make a visit or two just to establish personal ties before concluding any negotiations. In the very recent past, political and economic uncertainties forced businesses to rely much more on relationships and mutual trust than on written contracts for success. Personal impressions and relationships remain a critical part of every business deal.

Argentine businesspeople tend to be formal. Manners and politeness are extremely important. Titles, whether academic or professional, are commonly used. Confrontation and threats, either real or implied, are frowned upon. Anyone who is seen as abrasive or uncooperative is unlikely to succeed. Argentine women seldom hold public positions of power in business, but may often exercise considerable control behind the scenes. Foreign women should experience few problems conducting business as long as they remain professional in manner and dress and sensitive to local norms.

To cut costs and increase efficiency, Argentine businesses are becoming avid users of technology, from computers to fax machines. The only technological problem travelers might encounter is the local telephone system, although this is improving rapidly; cellular phones are also coming into general use by businesspeople.

Promptness is important, particularly for foreign businesspeople. Appointments are equally important. Do not expect to see anyone without an appointment, and do not always expect to see them on time. Business cards are important as a clue to professional rank and standing. Business documents or proposals must be translated into Spanish to have any legal standing in Argentina.

Every business discussion opens with personal small talk. Sports are a favorite topic, especially the ups and occasional downs of Argentina's football (to North Americans, soccer) teams. Fishing, hunting, skiing, food, and wine are other good topics. Try to avoid recent history, especially the "dirty war" in which domestic dissent was brutally suppressed by a military regime. Everyone in Argentina has a strong opinion—often one opposed to official policies or actions—but (as is the case elsewhere) criticism from outsiders is not appreciated, and the wounds are still relatively raw. When asked for an opinion, it is best to give a polite nonanswer unless speaking to an acquaintance of reasonably long standing.

Business topics are always introduced indirectly and concluded the same way, even at a business gathering. Never finish a meeting by grabbing a briefcase and dashing out the door, which implies that some other engagement is more important than the present company. Allow the chief Argentine in the group to end the meeting and then leave gracefully after a few minutes of small talk. Business may be discussed at business meals, but meals are usually considered to be social occasions that are used to get to know each other better.

Top executives in large businesses usually speak English. Outside the boardroom, some knowledge of Spanish is useful. Secretaries and second tier personnel are likely to speak a little English.

DOMESTIC TRANSPORTATION

With 12 million people, more than one-third of Argentina's entire population, Buenos Aires—known universally as BA—has world class traffic jams morning and evening. City driving is best left to Argentines and Formula I competitors who are accustomed to aggressively picking their own path, regardless of lane markings, traffic lights, and other legal niceties. Fortunately, most business destinations and business hotels are clustered within a relatively small area downtown. The subway (Subte) provides excellent service in and out of downtown, but has only a single crosstown line. Taxis are plentiful (until it rains) and inexpensive by international standards. Traffic flows reasonably smoothly in the country's other cities.

Taxis are generally black and yellow and always carry a lighted "Taxi" sign while on duty. They can be flagged down in the street, found waiting at most major hotels, or called on the phone. Taxis in BA are metered and generally honest. Taxis in other cities are not metered; agree on the rate before getting in. Drivers know their cities extremely well, although BA drivers may occasionally take the long way around to inflate the metered price. Drivers working out of or near major BA hotels might expect a 10 percent tip, but local custom is simply to round the meter fare up to the next peso or 50 centavos. There is no tipping on top of bargained fares.

The Subte has five lines, four of them running from downtown to the western and northern outskirts of BA. The single crosstown line runs between the Retiro and Constitución railway stations. Buy a handful of tokens, or *fichas*, in advance to avoid the long lines during rush hours. Trains run from 5:30 am to 1:30 am seven days a week. Frequency is good during the week, but expect longer waits on weekends. The Subte is clean and reasonably safe, but pickpockets and purse-snatchers are becoming more common, especially during rush hours. Violent assault is extremely rare, but a favorite tactic is to grab a wallet or purse and jump off just before the doors close. The best defense is to keep a good grip on belongings and not to stand near the door just before the train leaves the station.

A common alternative to taxis and public transit is a *remise*, a car and driver hired by the day or the week; *remises* are also available for single trips, even short ones. *Remises* are metered, but charge lower rates than taxis. In BA, any hotel or travel agency can make the arrangements, or contact Manuel Tienda León (Tel: (1) 396-2078), which also provides airport coach service. Prices start about $60 per day. In other cities, the hotel front desk can make the arrangements.

Car rentals start about $40 per day, including

Argentina

Iquique •   Uyuni •   Villa Montes •

Bolivia   **Paraguay**

Presidente
Epitácio •

Pedro Juan
Caballero •

Maringá •

Antofagasta •   Rivadavia •

Jujuy

San Salvador
de Jujuy •

24°

Brazil

Salta •
Salta

Chaco

Formosa

☉ **Asunción**

Curitiba •

São
Francisco
do Sul •

Copiapó •

Tucumán •

San Miguel
de Tucumán •

*Santiago
del Estero*

Formosa •

Misiones

Catamarca

Resistencia •

Corrientes •
Santo Tomé •

Posadas •

Catamarca •

Santiago
del Estero •

*Santa
Fe*

Corrientes

São
Borja •

La Serena •

La Rioja •

La Rioja

Laguna Mar
Chiquita

Curuzú
Cuatiá •

Uruguaiana •

Pôrto
Alegre •

San Juan
San Juan

Santa Fe •
Córdoba •

*Entre
Ríos*

Pelotas •

Rio Grande •

Valparaíso •

Córdoba

Paraná •

Rosario •

San Luis •

Río Cuarto •

Uruguay

Santiago ✛
Chile

Mendoza •

*San
Luis*

**Buenos
Aires**

Colonia •

☉ **Montevideo**

Mendoza

Junín •

La Plata •

Concepción •

36°

Realicó •

La Pampa

Telén •

Santa
Rosa •

Buenos Aires

Mar del Plata •

Neuquén

Zapala •

Neuquén •

Bahía
Blanca •

Río Negro

Atlantic

Puerto Montt •

Viedma •

San Carlos de Bariloche •

Golfo San Matías

Ocean

Esquel •

Rawson •

Chubut

Golfo San Jorge

Comodoro
Rivadavia •

Colonia
Las Heras •

Puerto Deseado •

Santa Cruz

48°

Gobernador
Gregores •

Puerto
Santa Cruz •

Islas Malvinas
(Falkland Islands)

Stanley •

**Río
Gallegos** •

*Tierra del
Fuego*

Punta Arenas •

Porvenir •

Ushuaia

	International border
☉	Provincial border
☉	National capital
•	Provincial capital
●	Secondary city
	Railroad
	Primary road

0	200	400 km
0		300 mi

72°   60°   48°

Greater Buenos Aires

Río de la Plata

	District border
	Primary road
	River
●	Urban Area
✈	Airport

0 — 6 mi
0 — 8 km

To Tigre

San Fernando

Beccar

San Isidro

Hipódromo

Olivos

Vicente López

Villa José L. Suárez

Florida

Núñez

Saavedra

Aeroparque

General San Martín

Hipódromo Argentino

Parque Tres de Febrero

General Urquiza

Belgrano

Av. Del Libertador

Jardín Zoológico

Villa Devoto

Av. La Plata

Av. Juan B. Justo

Palermo

Av. Callao

Santa Fe

Villa Bosch

Av. de los Incas

Av. San Martín

Recoleta

Caseros

Av. de Mayo

Paseo Colón

Av. Segurola

Rivadavia

Once

Floresta

Av. San Juan

Av. Entre Ríos

Boca

To Morón

Flores

Av. Caseros

Barracas

Nueva Chicago

Nueva Pompeya

Av. A. Alcorta

DISTRITO FEDERAL

BUENOS AIRES

San Justo

Av. Juan B. Alberti

Parque Almirante Guillermo Brown

Riachuelo

Villa Diamante

Avellaneda

Sarandí

Villa Domínico

Avenida General Paz

Villa Lugano

27 de Febrero

Autódromo Municipal

Fiorito

Lanús

Av. Grat. Mitre

To Quilmes

Carmino de Cintura

Ingeniero Budge

Remedios des Escala

Av. Hipólito Yrigoyen

Camino General Belgrano

Matanza

Autopista Tte. General P. Riccheri

L. Santa Catalina

Lomas de Zamora

Cintura

Arroyo San Francisco

Arroyo de las Piedras

Matanza

Arroyo Santa Catalina

Arroyo del Rey

General

Boca

Camino de

Almirante Brown

Aeropuerto Internacional de Ezeiza

To Esteban Echeverría

N

Central Buenos Aires

Río de la Plata

Dársena Norte

Dique No. 4

Dique No. 3

Dique No. 2

12 Casa Rosada (Casa de Gobierno)	**3** Plaza Lavalle	
10 Cathedral	**5** Plaza Libertad	**Parks**
9 Correo Central (post office)	**7** Plaza San Martín	**T** Tourist Information Office
8 Estación Retiro (train station)	**4** Teatro Colón	
1 Congreso Nacional (Congress)	**H1** Bauen Hotel	
13 Parque Colón	**H2** Hotel Claridge	
6 Plaza de la República	**H3** Hotel Continental	
11 Plaza de Mayo	**H4** Hotel Libertador	
2 Plaza del Congreso	**H5** Marriott Plaza Hotel	

N

0   1 km

0   1/2   1 mile

Central Córdoba

3 Aerolíneas Argentinas	**12** Plaza de Justica
8 Austral (airline office)	**1** Plaza General Paz
9 Banco de Córdoba	**7** Plaza San Martín
15 Bus terminal (NETOC)	**4** Telecom
5 Cabildo	**10** Universidad
6 Cathedral	
2 Mercado Norte	**H1** Hotel Crillon
14 Mitre railroad station (FCNGBM)	**H3** Hotel Nogaró
13 Palacio Municipal	**H2** Hotel Sussex
11 Plaza de la Independencia	

Parks
T Tourist Information Office
Post Office
Hospital
Railroad

0   200 m

0   1/4 mile

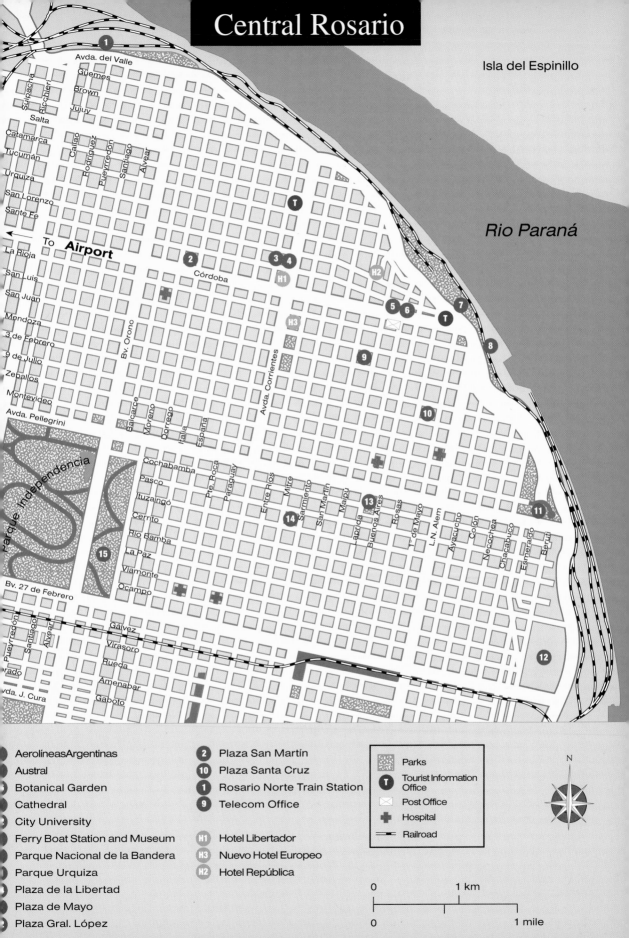

Central Rosario

Isla del Espinillo

Rio Paraná

To **Airport**

Parque Independencia

Legend

- AerolíneasArgentinas
- Austral
- Botanical Garden
- Cathedral
- City University
- Ferry Boat Station and Museum
- Parque Nacional de la Bandera
- Parque Urquiza
- Plaza de la Libertad
- Plaza de Mayo
- Plaza Gral. López

- **2** Plaza San Martín
- **10** Plaza Santa Cruz
- **1** Rosario Norte Train Station
- **9** Telecom Office

- **H1** Hotel Libertador
- **H3** Nuevo Hotel Europeo
- **H2** Hotel República

- Parks
- **T** Tourist Information Office
- Post Office
- Hospital
- Railroad

0   1 km

0   1 mile

N

Central Mendoza

Aerolíneas Argentinas — 9
Austral — 10
Bus terminal — 11
Club Regatta — 3
General Liceo Military School — 1
House of Government — 13
Municipal Aquarium — 12
Museum of Natural History — 5
Plaza España — 7
Plaza Independencia — 4
Plaza Italia — 6

Plaza San Martin — 8
San Martín railroad station — 2
Hotel Aconcagua — H4
Hotel Horizonte — H3
Hotel Penitentes — H1
Hotel Vecchia Roma — H5
Hotel Vigo — H2

Parks
T Tourist Information Office
Post Office
Hospital
Railroad

0   1/2 km

0   1/2 mile

N

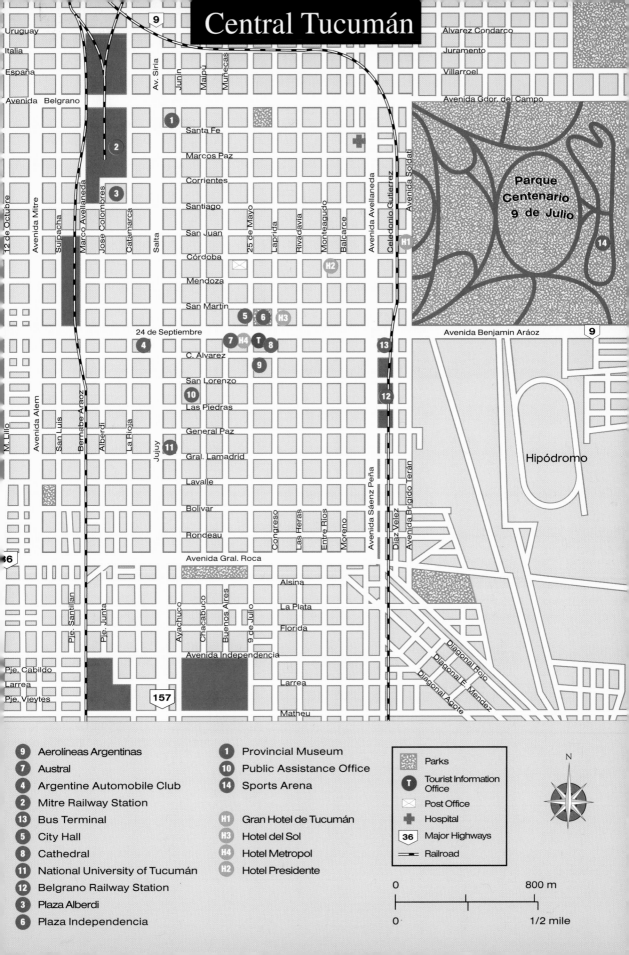

Central Tucumán

Uruguay
Italia
España
Avenida Belgrano

9

Av. Siria · **Junin** · **Maipú** · **Muñecas**

Álvarez Condarco
Juramento
Villarroel
Avenida Gdor. del Campo

Santa Fe
Marcos Paz
Corrientes
Santiago
San Juan
Córdoba
Mendoza
San Martín

12 de Octubre · **Avenida Mitre** · **Suipacha** · **Marco Avellaneda** · **José Colombres** · **Catamarca** · **Salta**

25 de Mayo · **Laprida** · **Rivadavia** · **Monteagudo** · **Balcarce**

Avenida Avellaneda · **Celedonio Gutierrez** · **Avenida Soldati**

Parque Centenario 9 de Julio

14

H1

H2

24 de Septiembre
C. Alvarez
San Lorenzo
Las Piedras
General Paz
Gral. Lamadrid
Lavalle
Bolivar
Rondeau
Avenida Gral. Roca

M. Lillo · **Avenida Alem** · **San Luis** · **Bernabé Aráoz** · **Alberdi** · **La Rioja** · **Jujuy**

Avenida Benjamin Aráoz · **9**

Hipódromo

Congreso · **Las Heras** · **Entre Ríos** · **Moreno** · **Avenida Sáenz Peña** · **Díaz Velez** · **Avenida Brigido Terán**

Alsina
La Plata
Florida
Avenida Independencia
Larrea
Matheu

Pje. Santillán · **Pje. Junta** · **Ayachuco** · **Chacabuco** · **Buenos Aires** · **9 de Julio**

Pje. Cabildo
Larrea
Pje. Vieytes

157

36

Diagonal Rojo · **Diagonal E. Mendez** · **Diagonal Agote**

- **9** Aerolíneas Argentinas
- **7** Austral
- **4** Argentine Automobile Club
- **2** Mitre Railway Station
- **13** Bus Terminal
- **5** City Hall
- **8** Cathedral
- **11** National University of Tucumán
- **12** Belgrano Railway Station
- **3** Plaza Alberdi
- **6** Plaza Independencia

- **1** Provincial Museum
- **10** Public Assistance Office
- **14** Sports Arena

- **H1** Gran Hotel de Tucumán
- **H3** Hotel del Sol
- **H4** Hotel Metropol
- **H2** Hotel Presidente

Parks
T Tourist Information Office
Post Office
Hospital
36 Major Highways
Railroad

N

| 0 | | 800 m |
| 0 | | 1/2 mile |

South America

Caribbean Sea

Neth. Antilles

Panama

Trinidad & Tobago

Barranquilla
Maracaibo
⊛ Caracas
Venezuela
San Cristóbal
Ciudad Guayana

Georgetown
Paramaribo
Guyana
Suriname
French Guiana
★ Cayenne

Atlantic Ocean

Medellín

Isla de Malpelo (Colombia)

⊛ Bogotá
Cali
Colombia

Boa Vista

Mitú

Macapá

Negro

Equator

0°

⊛ Quito
Ecuador
Guayaquil

Fonte Boa
Manaus
Amazon
Santarém
Belém
São Luís

Amazon

Iquitos

Piura

Marañón
Ucayali

Rio Branco

Pôrto Velho

Brazil

Fortaleza
Teresina

Natal
Recife

Trujillo
Huánuco
Peru
⊛ Lima

Cuzco

Ica

Arequipa

Lago Titicaca

Bolivia
Trinidad
La Paz ⊛
Cochabamba
Santa Cruz
Sucre ⊛

Pôrto Nacional

São Francisco

Aracaju
Salvador

Cuiabá

⊛ Brasília
Goiânia

South Pacific Ocean

Arica

Xingu

Tocantins

Belo Horizonte
Vitória

20°

Antofagasta

Tropic of Capricorn

Paraguay

Paraná

Rio de Janeiro
São Paulo

Isla San Felix (Chile) Isla San Ambrosio (Chile)

Chile

San Miguel de Tucumán
Resistencia

⊛ Asunción

Curitiba
Florianópolis

South Atlantic Ocean

Juan Fernández Islands (Chile)

Córdoba
Mendoza
Valparaíso
⊛ Santiago
Rosario
Buenos Aires ⊛
Argentina

Paraná

Pôrto Alegre
Salto
Uruguay
⊛ Montevideo

International border
⊛ National capital
★ Departmental capital
• Major city
River

Concepción

Mar del Plata
Bahía Blanca

0   500 kilometers
0   nautical miles   500

40°

Puerto Montt
San Carlos de Bariloche

Comodoro Rivadavia

Strait of Magellan

Stanley
Islas Malvinas (Falkland Islands)

Punta Arenas
Ushuaia
Cape Horn

South Georgia

80°   60°   40°   20°

insurance. All of the major international companies are represented in Argentina, plus local providers. Drivers must be 25 or older and show an International Driver's License in addition to their national, state, or provincial licenses. Credit cards are almost always required.

Argentina's highway system is well developed and well maintained, but roads are often narrow and filled with trucks. Mountain roads are usually steep, slippery, and filled with unmarked switchbacks. Most drivers sound the horn before rounding blind mountain corners to warn oncoming traffic. Rural drivers are every bit as aggressive as their urban counterparts, but highways sometimes offer a bit more room for maneuvering.

Domestic air transportation is excellent. The primary carriers are Aerolíneas Argentinas (AR), Austral, and LADE, plus a number of regional airlines. Service is generally frequent, punctual, and safe. With the exception of Buenos Aires, airlines normally operate coach service between airport and city center in conjunction with all flights.

Advance air bookings are essential for all flights. Flights during the summer—December, January, and February—are habitually overbooked. It is generally best to check in two hours before flight time during the summer, and one hour the rest of the year, to avoid being bumped from chronically overbooked flights. Baggage claim checks are always matched against claimed luggage on arrival.

Business travelers with predictable schedules may benefit from AR's "Visit Argentina" ticket. The discount ticket, available only outside Argentina in conjunction with an international ticket purchase, currently costs $450 for four flight coupons. Additional coupons are $150 each. Routing must be booked when the coupons are issued, but one change is allowed free of charge. Subsequent changes cost $50 each. Austral has a similar program called Jetpaq; its coupons are interchangeable with AR.

Argentina has long had an efficient, but heavily subsidized, train system. The federal government is in the process of cutting subsidies and turning the rail network over to the individual states, most of which cannot afford to operate their sections of the system. Rail service is improving, but because of the distances involved, rail travel is generally not a reasonable option for business travel except for commuter lines in the Buenos Aires area.

HOLIDAYS AND VACATIONS

Vacation time is January and February and the middle two weeks of July. Do not even consider trying to do business during vacation season. Many businesses close during some part of the vacation period, and nearly everyone is away from the office

NATIONAL HOLIDAYS

The entire country celebrates the following holidays:

New Year's Day	January 1
Maundy Thursday	Thurs. before Easter Sunday
Good Friday	Fri. before Easter Sunday
Easter	Late March or April
Labor Day	May 1
Anniversary of 1810 Revolution	May 25
Malvinas Islands Day	June 10
Flag Day	June 20
Independence Day	July 9
Death of General Jose de San Martín	August 17
Columbus Day	October 12
Immaculate Conception	December 8
Christmas	December 25

for at least a week or two. Courts are closed during the month of January and during Holy Week (*Semana Santa*), the week before Easter. A number of more localized patriotic and religious holidays are also celebrated across the country.

Holidays falling on Tuesday or Wednesday are celebrated on the previous Monday, while holidays falling on Thursday or Friday are celebrated on the following Monday.

BUSINESS HOURS

Business hours begin between 8 and 9:30 am and run until between 5:30 and 7 pm. Senior management usually comes to the office a little later and stays late. Some offices—especially those in the provinces—are closed between noon and 3 pm.

Banking hours are generally 10 am to 3 pm, Monday through Friday. It is usually possible to make appointments with bank officials outside normal banking hours. In addition to the normal holidays noted above, all banks are closed on November 6 (Bank Employee Day) and December 30.

Government offices are open from noon to 7 pm during the winter and 7 am to 2 pm during the summer, Monday through Friday.

COMMUNICATIONS

Telephones Argentina is improving its telephone system and international service is generally considered to be adequate. Domestic service is improving but is not yet world class. Business hotels offer international direct dial service from rooms, and

USEFUL TELEPHONE NUMBERS

Dialing from inside Argentina

International direct dial access	00
AT&T USA Direct	[1] (800) 200-1111
Police, fire, or ambulance (free call)	101
Taxi problems and complaints (BA)	(1) 343-5001
Visitor Information (BA)	(1) 312-2232, 312-6560
Visitor Information (Córdoba)	(51) 44-027
Visitor Information (Mendoza)	(61) 24-2800
Visitor Information (Rosario)	(41) 24-8382
Automóvil Club Argentino (ACA)	(1) 802-6061/9
Touring Club Argentino	(1) 392-6742

Airport and Flight Information

Ezeiza International	(1) 620-0271
Aeroparque Jorge Newbery	(1) 771-2071
Migraciones (Immigration)	(1) 312-3288, 312-7985

Lost or Stolen Credit Cards

(Call collect to the USA, regardless of where card was issued)

American Express	[1] (919) 333-3211
Diner's Club	[1] (303) 799-1504
MasterCard	[1] (314) 275-6690
Visa	[1] (410) 581-7931

domestic telephone service is somewhat better from hotels. Charges can be high.

The telephone companies have been privatized, and service is improving steadily. Public telephones are readily available. Most use cards, which can be purchased at streetside kiosks as well as at telephone company offices for $5. To dial local calls, simply dial the five-to-seven digit number. Many telephone exchanges and numbers are changing as the system is upgraded, so wrong numbers are likely to be common for several years.

To dial international calls, first dial 00 for international access, then the country code, area and city code, and telephone number. For example, to call World Trade Press direct, dial 00-1-415-454-9934.

Fax and Online Services Fax machines are widely used in Argentina. Hotels and many businesses have fax machines, as do most telephone company centers. A number of photocopying and business service centers can provide this service, and offices that send telegrams may also be able to transmit faxes and telexes. Fax surcharges vary widely. Connection to the Internet and other telephone-linked computer services is possible but still not common.

Post Office Outgoing airmail letters take about five days to reach the US, about a week to reach Western Europe. Letters can be sent from post offices, hotels, or streetside mail boxes. Inbound mail can take weeks to arrive.

Media Buenos Aires is an important Spanish-language publishing center. BA's three daily papers—*La Nación, Clarín,* and *La Prensa*—are well-known internationally. *Ambito Financiero* and *El Cronista* are the leading financial dailies, and *Mercado, Negocios,* and *Prensa Económica* are the top business magazines.

Publications in various foreign languages are available. US and British magazines and newspapers are sold widely in BA, less often in other cities. The English language *Buenos Aires Herald* provides football/soccer, boxing, basketball, baseball, cricket, rugby, and other sports scores from around the world. The country's most popular English-language magazine is the *Review of the River Plate,* which covers commercial and agricultural news. The most popular bookstores for English-language materials are the Acme Agency, Mackern's, Ateneo, Sarmiento, ABC, and Rodriguez. Publications may also be found in French, Italian, Portuguese, and German.

Local radio and television programming is almost entirely in Spanish, although English-language newscasts are available on radio. A large number of US, British, French, Italian, German, Spanish, Brazilian, Mexican, Venezuelan, and Chilean TV programs are broadcast on cable TV, all dubbed into Spanish. Local color TV and video uses the German PAL system. CNN, ITN, and other English-language satellite services are available in most business hotels.

LOCAL SERVICES

All of the familiar business services are available in Buenos Aires, most commonly through hotel business centers. Other business centers come and go; ask for current suggestions from embassies, consulates, and local business contacts. Several photocopying services are now available in downtown locations, many with the kind of fast service, high quality, and quick turnaround printing services found in metropolitan areas of Asia, Europe, and the US. Some of the services available in Buenos Aires are mentioned here.

Messenger Services

Within BA and the surrounding areas, a number of messenger companies are operating, many of them offering 24-hourservice.

Concorde, Av. Roque Sáenz Peña 825, Piso 1, Of. 16-17, El Centro, BA; Tel: (1) 394-0433, 854-8852, 449-7488 Fax: (1) 394-0438, 449-4408.

Mensajería Integral, Av. 25 de Mayo 316, El Centro, BA; Tel: (1) 325-6142.

Moto Wings, Herrera 1301, BA; Tel: (1) 21-7721.

Courier Services

International couriers include the following:

DHL Buenos Aires, Hipólito Yrigoyen 448, 1086 Buenos Aires; Tel: (1) 331-3217.

Federal Express, Maipú 753, 1006 Buenos Aires; Tel: (1) 393-6127, 393-6139, 393-6054.

UPS, c/o Airway Systems, Tacuarí 222, Buenos Aires; Tel: (1) 347-1000.

Computer Rentals

Computer Work Center, Avenida Cabildo 3081, BA; Tel: (1) 701-3022. Per hour rentals.

Integral Computación, Maipú 374, BA; Tel: (1) 386-6252, 327-2609. Per day IBM-compatible rentals.

Mid y Asociados SRL, Perú 457, BA; Tel: (1) 331-4870. Rentals and service on IBM compatibles.

Conference Areas

Most of the hotels that offer business services and the business service centers have conference rooms for rent and will provide services related to business meetings and informal gatherings. Rooms vary in size, style, and luxury, and rental rates are dependent on these factors.

Temporary Office Rentals

Alvear Palace Business Center, Marcelo T. de Alvear Recoleta 1891, BA; Tel: (1) 804-4031 Fax: (1) 804-9387.

On-Line, Rivadavia 5414, BA; Tel: (1) 903-3410, 901-7406, 4946.

Translation Services

Written translations and simultaneous and technical interpreters are available from a number of companies, many located in downtown BA. Some hotels and most business centers offer translation services, as well.

A Language Source ASS, Perú 428, Piso 4, BA. Tel: (1) 342-4229.

Interlingua. Alsina 521; BA; Tel: (1) 342-0161 Fax: (1) 343-8037.

STAYING SAFE AND HEALTHY

Buenos Aires is one of the safest large cities in the world, but crime is increasing. Violent attacks are rare, but pickpockets and purse/briefcase snatchings are on the rise. A favorite ruse is to spray mustard on the victim, then offer to wipe it off, quietly removing valuables in the process. Streets and sidewalks are well lit at night, and crowded with car and pedestrian traffic until after midnight. It is not necessary to remove jewelry

before leaving the hotel, but it is a good idea to avoid dark or deserted streets unless walking in a group. Women do not need a male escort to go to restaurants, cafés, films, or theater, although it is customary for women to go out in groups rather than alone.

Thieves often drop wallets and purses in mailboxes after removing the cash. If you are robbed, report the incident to the police. There is a good chance that credit cards, passports, and other items will be returned within a few days. Most business hotels have small safes in their rooms as well as safety deposit boxes.

Sanitary conditions in Argentina are generally quite good. Sewage disposal and water treatment facilities are modern and effective, especially in urban areas. Tap water is safe in the developed areas throughout the country, although it may taste strongly of chlorine in some locales. Argentines generally drink mineral water by habit, not necessity.

There should be no problem obtaining prescription drugs and toiletries. The largest *farmacia* (pharmacy) in the country, Franco Inglesa (corner of Florida and Sarmiento in BA), has a multilingual staff. BA pharmacies take turns staying open at night. Look in the window for a sign saying *"Farmacia de Turno,"* which gives the address of the nearest open drug store. Newspapers also list pharmacies open that night. Cosmetics and toiletries are sold in *perfumerías*, not *farmacias*.

EMERGENCY INFORMATION

Police, fire, or ambulance (free call from any telephone): 101

Police (nonemergency crime in Buenos Aires): 381-8041

Doctors and Hospitals

Argentina has more physicians per capita than the US, with similar standards of practice. Office visit fees start about $15; payment is expected at the time of service.

Buenos Aires British Hospital, Perdriel 74 (1280); Tel: (1) 304-1081, 304-1089.

Centro Gallego, Belgrano 2199; Tel: (1) 951-3061.

German Hospital, Pueyrredón 1658 (1118); Tel: (1) 821-7661.

Córdoba Hospital de Urgencias, Catamarca and Blvd. Guzmán; Tel: (51) 40243.

DEPARTURE FORMALITIES

Leaving Argentina is almost as easy as getting in. All it takes is a ticket and a completed tourist card or valid visa. There are no restrictions on the export of currency or other monetary instruments, or of other items except the usual firearms and other weapons not allowed on plane flights. Departure tax is $15, payable at the airport in pesos or US dollars.

BEST TRAVEL BOOKS

No travel book can keep up with changing prices, addresses, and telephone numbers, especially when the national telephone system is being rebuilt almost from the ground up. The books mentioned below are oriented toward leisure travelers, but are as practical as any on the market in any language.

Insight Guide: Argentina, edited by Deirdre Ball. Singapore: APA Publications (HK) Ltd., 1994. ISBN 0-395-66205-2. 331 pages, US$21.95. Beautifully illustrated with color photos and maps. Lots of history and cultural information; a good introduction to the people and the country.

Argentina, Uruguay & Paraguay: A Travel Survival Kit, by Wayne Bernhardson & Maria Massolo. Hawthorne, Vic., Australia: Lonely Planet Publica-tions, 1992. ISBN 0-00864421-40-0. 606 pages, US$16.95. Written for budget travel, but very strong on practical details.

South American Handbook, edited by Ben Box. London: Trade & Travel Publications Ltd., 1995. ISBN 0-900751-51-7. Also written primarily for budget travelers, but with solid details, especially on cities outside Buenos Aires.

Do's and Taboos Around the World, edited by Roger Axtell. New York: John Wylie & Sons, 1993. ISBN 0-47159-58-4. 196 pages, US$12.95. A comprehensive and humorous rendition of cultural do's and don'ts for the business traveler.

Fodor's, Frommer's, and Birnbaum's all publish guidebooks to South America, with substantial chapters on Argentina, as does the *South American Handbook.*

The Pirelli Guide, although somewhat dated (1991), it has a wealth of detailed information on Argentina, especially on the history and the provinces.

Business Culture

INTRODUCTION

Understanding Argentina's cultural heritage is necessary for understanding its people and how business is done in the country. A clearer picture of Argentina's business culture will smooth the way in business transactions and can make it not only beneficial, but also enjoyable to do business with an Argentine businessperson or company. The following discussion is designed to give a basic explanation of and a guide to Argentine social and business cultures so that visitors can manage their relationships with Argentine businesspeople more effectively and conduct business more productively. Many of the values, beliefs, and behaviors are outlined in general terms, which tends to suggest that Argentine culture is quite homogenous. However, there is a difference between the *porteños* who live in Buenos Aires—as well as the inhabitants of other large cities such as Córdoba and Rosario—and the residents of more rural parts of the country. Those living in the cities tend to be more modern and cosmopolitan in outlook and behavior, while those living in more rural provinces are generally more traditional and conservative.

Argentine culture, like its geography, is a dramatic combination of strikingly contrasting elements. It has a long history of soaring triumphs and crushing defeats. After a half-century of political instability and

many misguided economic policies, it has in the course of little more than a decade developed from a Third World nation to a world class player in the international economy. Its vibrant atmosphere today reflects its turbulent past as it maintains a unique blend of forward-thinking pragmatism and rich tradition. In general, Argentines adhere to the conventions and sentimentality of Latin America. However, while they are expressive, they are at the same time driven toward achievement and modernization.

THE PAST MAKES THE PRESENT

In 1816 the colonial Vice-Royalty of the River Plate—representing the area that would later become Argentina—formally declared its independence from Spain. A bitter political battle followed concerning the extent of central authority versus the retention of local autonomy. Finally, the country achieved national unity; a federal constitution was promulgated in 1853; and the Republic of Argentina was formally established.

The new nation was separated by distance and physical or political barriers from many of its neighbors. Its territory also had only a few organized Indian groups, so populating the vast land was left primarily to European immigrants. These immigrants arrived in droves, seeking their fortunes in this land of opportunity and abundant natural resources. Between 1837 and 1939 more than four million immigrants arrived from all over the globe. Argentina flourished, becoming a formidable world economy during its golden age from roughly 1880 to 1930.

Argentina's plentiful natural resources from which the country had hoped to make its fortune—including precious metals, fertile farmland, and the thriving and well situated port of Buenos Aires—generated an economy based on rents and a culture heavily influenced by the interests of large landowners. Early

Our thanks to Viviana Gaeta, who proudly shared her Argentine heritage with us. Consultant Gaeta is the owner of Horizons Travel, Marin County, California, which focuses on travel to South America today.

governments were never able to develop policies adequate to maintain, protect, and promote the ample opportunities the country's resources offered. Competing interests and a lack of focus among those in charge precluded steady growth in any sector.

Although Argentina escaped many of the harshest effects of the worldwide Great Depression in the 1930s, this era served as prologue to a sad period in the country's history, characterized by military coups d'états on one side and underground opposition on the other, escalating to include extralegal, terrorist, and guerilla activity. During this period of unrest, the economy deteriorated and corruption became rampant. Perhaps the most important element of this period was rise of Juan Domingo Perón. Perón ruled as president from 1946 until 1955 and again from 1973 to 1974; he left office in 1955 as the result of a coup, dying in office in 1974 shortly after returning to power. The Perón era was an extremely complex period in the nation's history, although Argentines are beginning to have the historical perspective to come to terms with its implications.

Peronist policies served largely to close the Argentine economy to the rest of the world, protecting its industries from foreign competition and allowing the government to intervene strongly in the economy. Following Perón's death, the already fragmented country began to crumble. In the name of preserving order and of cleansing the country of antisocial elements, successor military governments established an essentially closed society. The military finally yielded control in 1983, and constitutional civilian government returned under President Raúl Alfonsin. However, economic performance continued to be mediocre and volatile as the administration struggled to reassert civilian authority while simultaneously trying to restore the social fabric. The focus on social and political goals prevented the government from reconstructing the ailing economy from the bottom up.

To the surprise of many, Carlos Menem, a Peronist from the provinces, won the presidency in 1989. Spearheaded by its star Minister of Economy, Harvard Ph.D. Domingo Cavallo, the Menem administration has privatized and deregulated practically the entire economy while also opening it to the world. The Convertibility Law of 1991 made the new Argentine peso equal to the US dollar and pledged to back all domestic currency issued with hard foreign currency reserves. As a result, foreign investment funds and foreign businesses began to show new interest in Argentina, encouraged by growing success and prosperity.

This renewed economic success has not come without cost: unemployment has remained a stubborn problem. Moreover, Argentina was further threatened in early 1995 as the so-called "tequila effect" triggered by Mexico's economic problems set off a chain reaction that affected Argentina. Nevertheless, few in Argentina have seriously suggested that the government should retreat from its policies designed to maintain wage, price, and currency stability. This adherence to fiscally responsible policies was underscored by Menem's reelection in May 1995 with fully 50 percent of the popular vote, representing a strong mandate.

THE SEARCH FOR A NATIONAL CHARACTER

National Diversity

Argentina is, above all, a land of immigrants and ethnic diversity, although unlike much of the rest of Latin America, the diversity speaks with European rather than Indian accents. Argentina is one of the few societies in Latin America in which Europeans and North Americans can feel at ease and inconspicuous. It is far more accessible to US and European visitors than other Latin American countries because it so resembles western societies—at least on the surface. But at the same time, it is distinctly Latin American in many of its core values and traditions. Spanish is the national language, although visitors may hear English, German, Italian, and French on the streets of Buenos Aires and elsewhere. Many Argentine businesspeople speak English. With its vast array of ethnic heritages embedded in the matrix of a traditional Latin culture and its dramatic history of ups and downs, it is small wonder that Argentine culture sometimes strikes outsiders as somewhat odd, even surrealistic.

However, while many Argentines share traits that set them apart from other nationalities—their unique speech patterns, for instance, or their famously delicious beef, gaucho folklore, and love of the tango—these are insufficient to produce a sense of strong national commonality.

With that said, it is relatively safe to add that there are two recent events which have united all Argentines as one people: the 1986 World Cup in Football (equivalent to the soccer of North America) and the 1983 South Atlantic War (against Great Britain over the Islas Malvinas (Falkland Islands). Virtually all Argentines, regardless of ethnic heritage, social class, or geographic region, are passionately patriotic, supporting Argentina as a nation with respect to these two events, the one a victory, the other a defeat. A visitor will be on pretty safe ground in presuming a unified interpretation regarding the latter subject; however, it should be avoided unless the converser is prepared to knowledgeably support the Argentine position.

Regional Diversity Although Argentina can be divided into four main geographic regions—the Andes to the west and northwest, the lowlands to the north and northeast, the vast Pampas of the central part of the country, and Patagonia to the south—each with its own local variations, there is really only one clear distinction that needs to be made when speaking of Argentine culture: the difference between the residents of Buenos Aires, called *porteños*, and the rest of the nation—the interior.

With more than 12 million people, greater Buenos Aires is the 10th largest city in the world and home to more than one-third of the population of Argentina. It is the social, cultural, financial, economic, and political center of the country. *Porteños* are considered to be sophisticated, glamorous, and cultured; residents of the interior are thought to be traditional and in touch with the land. The frictions between the metropolis and the hinterland over who was to control the country started when Argentina was settled. The problems persist into the present.

Individuality

Argentines place a high value on individuality. One of the most vibrant symbols of the past which is supposed to represent the national character is the *gaucho*—that near-mythical legendary historical plainsman who is independent, brave, athletic, a bold warrior, loyal, and generous. The *gaucho* is the idealized version of a complex historical figure who has become etched into the Argentine consciousness. Modern Argentines believe that they have incorporated the values associated with the *gaucho* into their own system, and in Argentina, Latin *machismo* is colored by the special case of the *gaucho*.

Of all these idealized qualities, personal independence is perhaps the most important—acting solely of one's own free will and being willing to stand up and take the consequences. To take orders from somebody else is considered undignified and weak. Many Argentines, therefore, strive to get into a position to give orders rather than have to take them. Much admired in Argentina is the bold risk-taker and entrepreneur. But individualism is often expressed through *gauchadas*, gaucho-like acts of generosity, such as going out of one's way to help someone else solve a problem. Argentines take great pride in being in a position to offer a *gauchada*. Thus, while it may sometimes be difficult to get an official or employee to do something that is a normal and routine part of the job, that same person may readily perform the act if one asks for it as a favor: it becomes a *gauchada* and proves that the individual is acting selflessly and completely out of free will rather than under constraint. However, some blame the nation's chaotic and fractured development on this individualism, noting that many want to be leaders while few are willing to be led.

Creatures of Habit

The dramatic upheavals, violent shifts, and rever-sals in Argentina's economic and political life have infused its people and culture with a strong streak of formal traditionalism and conservatism. Argentines tend to be creatures of habit. Many will not try new things until they have been thoroughly tested and accepted. Traditionally many grew up eating meat at least twice a day, every day, and would not do otherwise. Although varied by the range of ethnic backgrounds represented, Argentine cuisine strikes many outsiders as lacking in variety, whereas the natives find it to be remarkably satisfying. Argentina produces many excellent wines, and while wine is a part of everyday life for many Argentines, drinking habits are moderate—it is considered undignified to drink to excess. Argentines do not like to draw attention to themselves, such as through loud and unusual behavior in public. Many tend to stick close to home; they even vacation in the same place year after year. However, Argentines love to hear tales of adventure and exotic locales and will often voice a desire to go there themselves—someday.

Candor

Argentines believe in being open, frank, and direct, but also take pride in being tactful and diplomatic. In both speech and writing, they may be indirect, elaborate, and complimentary. They can be almost poetic in the way they express themselves. They place a premium on not offending. This impressionistic approach to language is not meant to mislead, and they themselves are seldom confused; they are just trying to be polite and tactful. Even seemingly objective information is open for discussion and subject to heated dispute, which can become more heated as one descends the social pyramid. Don't bother offering to look up information or otherwise try to appeal to objective authority for verification in such cases; there would be little cultural need to resolve the apparently contradictory "facts" that arise in such instances. The matter can always be revisited another time.

It is a matter of pride for Argentines to know the correct response to any query, and they will offer detailed directions if asked for help in finding a destination. Both social and business invitations may be accepted, whether or not the invitee intends to attend. In this regard, business commitments and promises made in a social context need to be verified in a work environment, in which an accurate answer is more likely to be forthcoming.

Despite this picture of polite reserve, foreign women should be prepared to field personal and probing questions. Argentines are genuinely interested in family—the traditional domain of women—and will often ask directly about one's situation, age, marital status, and children.

Argentines are warm and effusive, seldom trying

to hide passion or sentimentality. They touch each other often when speaking, and they maintain little physical distance between speakers, much less than is customarily maintained in many other cultures. In their earnest desire to compliment and be warm and friendly, Argentines will lavish praise and compliment extensively even something that—from another point of view—could be considered an insignificant event or achievement. This is not insincerity, and a visitor would be making a grave mistake by deprecating these expressions or misinterpret them.

Argentines do have strong opinions on many issues, and although they can be circumspect and reserved, they can also voice their opinions forthrightly or publicly. Groups of gesticulating men can usually be found arguing sports, economic policy, or politics. On these subjects the Argentines' usual circumspection gives way to heated debates full of emotional displays. Football (soccer to a North American) is the national sport—far more so than track and field, boxing, basketball, rugby, tennis, or any other of the numerous sports to which Argentines give their attention. Team allegiances are formed early in life and remain strong. Some will readily tell you what political party they belong to and why, what party they voted for in the last election and why, and discuss the major (and minor) issues of the day in detail. Argentines are generally well-informed about politics and economic policies, and they take great interest and pride in discussing them.

Family

The family remains the centerpiece of Argentine life, commanding the individual's highest loyalty. Children are cheerfully welcomed, and it is customary to bring them to certain social occasions. Extended families are still quite common. Most young people live with their parents until they are married. Students do not usually leave home to attend college; if it is necessary to do so, they enjoy returning home. Children will often grow up with cousins as their best friends, and this closeness frequently carries on into adulthood. One of the great occasions in a family's life is still a girl's fifteenth birthday. The family may throw a big party to mark this rite of passage.

The heads of rich and powerful families command widespread respect, but this respect carries with it the responsibility to care for others and maintain personal and family honor. As a result, Argentine men, like other Latin American males, are much concerned not only about their ability to provide and protect, but also with their honor. Honor is as important as business success; it routinely affects day-to-day life at home, in the community, and in business. Females must protect

their reputation and that of their family in the same way that males protect honor.

Family relationships carry over into business as well. Nepotism is expected, and positions are filled with family members first and with close friends of the family second, especially in smaller firms. Argentines do distinguish between business and family more so than do other Latin American cultures, but the line is certainly less clearly drawn than in most North American or European and in some Asian cultures, where business and personal life are generally considered not to overlap. In all business dealings, foreigners should be prepared to talk about family and friends.

Religion

Along with the family, religion is one of the mainstays of Argentine life. More than 90 percent of the population is Roman Catholic; there is a small but active Protestant community, and a tight-knit Jewish community of about 350,000. Small pockets of several other religions can also be found, primarily in Buenos Aires. Argentines enjoy constitutional guarantees of religious freedom, although Catholicism is the official state religion. However, religion does not really seem to have a strong grip on the national psyche: only about 20 percent of the population are considered to be active, practicing Catholics. When traveling past a church, many Argentines will sometimes make the sign of the cross, but this is about the extent of daily religious observance, at least in Buenos Aires. Like all else Argentine, the church has many factions. In some cases, the farther one goes from the city, especially, the more that Catholicism diverges from official doctrine and takes on the characteristics of a folk religion. Still, official Catholicism has provided Argentina with some of its most impressive monuments, from the modest but picturesque churches of the Andean region to the Jesuit missions of Mesopotamia in the northeast to the many splendid churches of Córdoba and the capital.

The role of the Catholic church is much greater in political, civic, and governmental affairs than is the case in some other, more secular countries. Historically, it has been inextricably entwined with the workings of the state—for example, divorce was legalized only in 1987 after a long and bitter battle between church and state—and conflict exists between the dominant conservative wing of the official church hierarchy and the small but more militant populist-leftist liberation theology group. The church exerts considerable influence over government, but overall, relations between the two have been relatively free of the conflict found in other Latin American countries.

Women

Argentine women are the same time venerated and somewhat relegated to a secondary role. This assignment to a lesser position applies especially in some more traditional areas and segments of Argentine society. The Argentine woman is honored for her role at the center of the all-important family, where she tends to occupy an elevated position; and she is viewed as a precious object to be protected by her men (father, brother, and husband). The perceived role of women is therefore largely defined, circumscribed, and isolated by this cultural tradition. Actually, women bear considerable responsibilities in the family, in the community, and in the economy. The percentage of Argentine households headed by women has been growing steadily for the past decade.

Although nominally afforded equal rights at all levels under law, women still lag behind men in Argentine social and economic spheres. Generally well educated, women in Argentina—like women elsewhere—often find it difficult to reach decision-making roles or attain executive positions in business. In order to help support their families, many women who have professional educations and qualifications must accept low-paying jobs because of a lack of available opportunities. Paradoxically, foreign businesswomen do not generally meet the level of resistance they are likely to encounter in some other Latin American or Asian countries.

In general, Argentine women operate in a more restricted, and restrictive, sphere than do many of their North American and European sisters. Foreign women should try to dress conservatively—especially if traveling alone or with another woman—although casual wear is becoming more accepted. Women should also take care not to offend the spouse of an Argentine businessman with whom she is conducting business; jealousy or misunderstanding can quickly destroy an otherwise productive business relationship. In general, women do not go to bars, and certainly not alone (the exception to this rule would be the cocktail lounge of a first class hotel).

Women should be aware of *piropos*—verbal comments made by males in public regarding and directed at women. The *piropo* is not, however, a matter of a few crude words thrown out in passing; It is meant to be, and often is, truly poetic. The woman is not really expected to respond or to take the man up on his implied interest. It is usually best to simply ignore these comments; they are not intended to cause harm, and the situation is rarely dangerous. Avoiding eye contact, ignoring the comment, and coolly acting as if the incident did not occur usually does the trick. If the male perpetrator does not take the hint or becomes overly aggressive, it may be necessary to issue a clear and curt response to the effect that additional similar behavior is inappropriate and unwelcome. But be careful: this is a fine line that is readily open to misinterpretation due to cultural differences.

Psychoanalysis

The popularity and prevalence of psychoanalysis in Argentina warrants mention. Psychotherapy and traditional psychoanalysis is commonly undergone by a wide range of Argentines across all social and economic lines, although it is most common among the upper-middle class. Although most prevalent in Buenos Aires—where there are reportedly more psychotherapists per capita than anywhere else in the world—psychoanalysis is relatively common nationwide to the extent that specialized clinics have been established by many industries and trade unions as an integral part of the normal employee benefit package.

Other Latin Americans claim that Argentines go about life with a certain malaise that is distinctly Argentine. Some observers contend that the Argentines are still trying to figure out whether they are Europeans or Latin Americans, and other Latin Americans often chide them for not having yet made up their minds. Argentines, in general, would disagree—heatedly—although the sheer number of mental health professionals and the extent to which they find employment would seem to testify to a certain complexity in the Argentine psyche. Pessimism and cynicism have long been noted as strong recurrent themes in the social milieu of the country. Argentines claim that analysis helps to lessen the anxieties due to the constrictions and ambiguities of modernization.

THE BUSINESS ENVIRONMENT

Argentines combine a unique mixture of European efficiency and Latin American flexibility in their business style. Most industries are modernized or modernizing and in many—though not all—sectors, plant and equipment are up-to-date. Business is well within the range of international standards, and managers employ the latest techniques, operate using reliable accounting and reporting standards, and conduct sophisticated transactions. Many executives speak English or some other European language. Despite a liking for leisure, Argentines have a reputation for hard work.

Argentine business does not conform to the stereotypical Latin *mañana* model. For the most part Argentines are savvy, resourceful, ambitious, and, in general, highly educated. They have time and again made the most of the contradictory economic policies of successive governments in order to build industry and create wealth, succeeding where mere survival would have been a major accomplishment. They embrace free markets and welcome the resulting competition. Enormously competitive in the marketplace, Argentines do not subscribe to the cutthroat, win-at-any-cost competition prevalent in North America and some other business venues.

Competition in business is like competition in sports—you play the best you can, and the victor's spoils go to those who put forth the best effort. At the same time, Argentines have a generally healthy, relatively relaxed approach to their jobs.

Buenos Aires is a sprawling, international city, which every day welcomes numerous business visitors from all over the globe. Visitors are treated with courtesy, warmth, generosity, respect, and acceptance. No Latin backwater, Buenos Aires is an agreeable and easy place to do business. The familiarity of local businesspeople in some other parts of Argentina with cosmopolitan, international standards may not be as great, but they are little less sophisticated and no less shrewd than their *porteño* counterparts.

Business Style

Nowhere does Argentina's mixed heritage manifest itself so clearly as in its style of doing business. Argentines adhere to the traditional Latin American tenet that one works to live rather than lives to work, although they are at the same time intensely competitive and profit-driven. Although it is changing in response to the internationalization of Argentine markets, the perception currently remains that someone who is too eager to spend long hours at work or is overly preoccupied with a career is a bit odd and outside the accepted norm. Although organizational structures are sophisticated and business dress formal, Argentines approach business with a relaxed and friendly attitude. Argentines tend to create alliances in order to get the job done; they work well together in pursuit of common goals and readily share credit for achievements. Although argumentative, they avoid open conflict and direct opposition to viewpoints, especially those of their superiors. Overly aggressive "upstarts" who take unfair advantage of competitors or push fellow workers aside in a quest for advancement are frowned upon and are rarely rewarded for such behavior. However, foreign businesspeople should not underestimate their Argentine counterparts, who are quite competitive and committed to high returns and sustained growth. They are generally knowledgeable and very detail oriented, so it is best to be well prepared and ready to answer detailed questions about your business proposals.

Nevertheless, family and friends remain the top priorities for Argentine businesspeople, and a business associate must expect to wait if a relative or friend drops by or needs help unexpectedly. In any event, rarely will an Argentine adhere rigidly to a scheduled meeting time. Foreign businesspeople should expect to wait and should be prepared for the eventual meeting to proceed informally and at a leisurely pace. Social matters must be thoroughly disposed of before business issues are raised.

Foreign businesspeople should themselves be prompt, patient, and courteous no matter how unaccustomed they may be to such behavior: it is simply Argentine standard practice.

Especially in family-owned companies, jobs were often filled by family and friends, or at the very least by an acquaintance referred through the employer's network of contacts. Now, however, more arm's-length standards of professionalism generally prevail.

Unlike many other Latin Americans, Argentines do not generally bargain. Outside Buenos Aires, in the provinces, bargaining is still acceptable for many products and services, but within the international business community, it is simply not done. Deals are concluded after sophisticated and knowledgeable business negotiations.

Getting Started

Relationships are important in Argentine business; the closer the relationship, the better your chances of concluding a deal. Outside of a family relationship, personal friendships with their accompanying feelings of trust provide the strongest possible base for business success. However, Argentines will carefully evaluate the different alternatives in a very objective and businesslike manner. If your business style is fast-paced, you will need to adjust, because there is no way to push people to go faster. This is just the way they do things.

Argentines feel that they cannot know how others will react in a business situation unless they know who they are as people first. They will want to know your views on politics, culture, and the economy, both in your own country and in theirs. Thus you should, at the bare minimum, have a passing knowledge of Argentine culture and politics so that you can participate in a conversation on these subjects.

Contacts are essential to establishing relationships, especially when doing any kind of business with government agencies. Try to develop as large a network of contacts as possible. There are many subtle political changes occurring in Argentina, and contacts can often help you understand what is going on. International organizations such as Rotary Club International or Lions Club International are good starting points. It is easy to schedule general introductory meetings with members after you have attended a local Argentine meeting. In many instances, these can lead to valuable contacts in your specific areas of interest. Foreign embassies in Argentina—not only your own, but those of other countries as well—can also be helpful. As a foreign businessperson, you may be able to arrange an invitation to one of their commercial cocktail parties, often an excellent way to obtain information, and sometimes *gauchadas,* from local government officials. Such contacts can save you countless hours of waiting in offices to see the wrong people.

Personal relationships can be difficult to establish, especially if your business style does not readily lend itself to such interaction, but it is important to try to do so if you expect to establish a long-term and successful business relationship in Argentina. Take the time to build lasting personal ties; your chances of success will increase. Remember, being accepted as part of a network also entails reciprocity; you will be expected to use your own contacts and relationships to help others when called upon for assistance.

Time

It is often said that North Americans and Latin Americans will never truly understand each other because they do not share a common place in time. Latin Americans look first to the past, while North Americans live almost completely in the future. As for the present, it becomes the scene of constant misunderstanding, disappointment, and irritation. From the North American, Asian, or European point of view, Latins are always late. For the Latin Americans, these others never take the time to develop relationships or understand situations fully. Whereas one culture is driven by time, the other sees it as a resource to be enjoyed and experienced. One culture sees time as a commodity—to spend, gain, lose, waste, and invest. The other sees it as something not quite so tangible—there is plenty of it today, and if that's not enough, there will be more tomorrow; in time, everything will get done.

However, Argentina is not typically Latin American as far as time is concerned. Many Argentine businesspersons are very time-conscious and convinced that time is money. Nevertheless, in Argentina, there is always time for family and friends, for romance and politics, for a cup of coffee or a long lunch. A sense of urgency may be viewed with mistrust or as rudeness.

In short, Argentines have adopted some European concepts of timeliness, although things tend to move more slowly than in North America or Europe, and a foreign businessperson must be tactful.

Ethics

In Argentina, payoffs, kickbacks, and official corruption have long been a part of everyday life. If the definition of a corrupt society is one in which such unofficial payments are part of standard operating procedure, then Argentina is in trouble—at least by the standards of many in the US and Europe.

The practice of paying *propinas*—tips—and *coimas*—bribes (the equivalent of the Mexican *mordida*)—to "expedite" matters is widespread in Latin America (as it is in other areas of the world), and foreign businesspeople must be careful in how they

approach dealing with the "system." Foreigners must try to put aside their culturally biased views and dispassionately examine the realities of the situation if they expect to accomplish their goals, especially quickly and with a minimum of difficulty. Businesspeople from the US, in particular, should remember that under the provisions of the Foreign Corrupt Practices Act they are liable to criminal prosecution for attempting to bribe foreign officials. (Refer to "The US Foreign Corrupt Practices Act" on page 223 in the "Business Law" chapter for a discussion of this law.)

Further complicating an already bewildering system are the periodic anticorruption campaigns that occur in Argentina. In response to charges of corruption against high-ranking members of the administration, the Menem government instituted an anticorruption drive in late 1994 with a view toward the May 1995 elections. While the use of *propinas* and *coimas* remains widespread, official policy is set against their use, but enforcement ebbs and flows depending on the circumstances.

However, some observers note that with the deregulation, demonopolization, and privatization of many state-run and cartel-like businesses, the conditions that provided the opportunity for graft are being removed. Over time, these free market changes should do a great deal to eliminate many of these problems. Nonetheless, such payments remain a way of life, and are an important—and often pragmatically necessary—part of many business dealings. Foreign businesspeople must be careful to avoid the embarrassment of being made an example of the government's anticorruption dragnet. At the same time, some government officials and private businesspeople are becoming more sensitive to international standards and expectations, modifying the way they do business.

Some businesspeople treat such *propinas* and *coimas* as incentive payments: if the payment is not specifically illegal and is paid primarily to speed up what would (or should) be done anyway, then it can be seen as a means of expediting the underlying transaction. As such, it may not run afoul of specific Argentine or foreign legal prohibitions. If you are uncomfortable with or uncertain about how to proceed in a situation in which it seems a *propina* or *coima* is expected, you may consider employing local legal or accounting professionals during the negotiation stages. They will be more familiar with local business practices and may well be able to save your company unnecessary expense and legal problems. In any event, plans to initiate business dealings in Argentina must include a realistic evaluation of the uncertainty of such added costs. There should also be a clear-cut understanding regarding the payment of *propinas* and *coimas* between top management and on-site personnel.

Negotiations

After you have located the necessary contacts, cultivated the necessary relationships, and reached the stage of agreeing to pursue a business relationship, you must be prepared to make your presentation. Argentines prefer to conduct business face-to-face rather than by telephone. Therefore, all negotiations should be scheduled accordingly.

Ideally, your team will include someone with a good working knowledge and understanding of Argentine Spanish and customs. Local legal counsel may be able to help you interpret any finer points. Nevertheless, at the very least your team members should have a working knowledge of Spanish and a solid understanding of the business culture in which they are operating, as well as of their own business and the specific project. Ideally, the people you choose to accompany you will be the ones possessing the best "people" skills and management acumen.

Procedure When arranging negotiations with Argentine businesspeople, it is customary to give them as much detail as possible about the issues to be discussed, as well as a list of the delegation members attending. Attendees' titles, positions, and responsibilities should be clearly stated so that the Argentines can evaluate the seriousness of the negotiations and include the appropriate personnel on their own team. If there is any resistance from your negotiating counterparts, you may be able to come to agreement on structure and agenda even before you reach the table, thereby clearing more time for discussion of substantive issues.

It is important to be aware of the extent to which the persons across the negotiating table are authorized to exercise their own discretion in agreeing to terms. Because of the centralized nature of decision-making in Argentine firms, you will want to be absolutely sure that an agreed-upon contract draft can be immediately approved and signed. At the very least, you should be aware of which Argentine team member will be communicating with top management and how quickly approval can be obtained.

Formulating an Approach In Argentina a positional bargaining approach usually does not provide the most effective method of negotiating. Because your Argentine counterparts will have carefully assessed your character and interests before deciding even to enter into negotiations, it will prove to be that much more difficult for you to take an unreasonably hard-nosed positional approach. If you do pressure your Argentine counterparts into accepting an agreement on your terms because of your company's size, powerful financial position, or some other overwhelming advantage, you run the risk that the agreement will backfire. If you notice weakness on the other side, taking

undue advantage is likely to result in either the withdrawal of the Argentine team or the nonperformance of the contract, in which case you will have lost considerable time and other valuable resources. However, be aware that the other side may feel free to attempt to pressure you if it senses that it holds the advantage.

It is far more advisable to use a mutually beneficial, win-win approach that takes into account the satisfactory fulfillment of interests on both sides. Proving your goodwill during the negotiating process will go a long way toward ensuring a positive relationship with your Argentine colleagues. Remember, if you have come this far, you have already invested time and energy into developing a long-term relationship. Failure to keep in mind and cultivate the social aspects of the transaction will leave you unprotected. You need to be shrewd, but playing the game—fairly—is absolutely necessary in Argentina.

Beginning the Meeting Negotiations are likely to be held in a hotel, conference center, or meeting room near the Argentine place of business. In accordance with the idea of Argentine hospitality, the negotiating venues are usually comfortable and well equipped. Subordinates usually arrive early to attend to seating arrangements and other details. A higher status executive arrives later, with a personal secretary, interpreter, and any other necessary members of the entourage, although it is considered bad form to pack the gallery with nonessential retainers. This grand entrance gives both teams an indication of who the power brokers are.

It is important to be appropriately friendly. Efforts to begin dealing immediately with substantive issues are likely to be construed as rude and suspicious behavior. Remember that Argentines consider impatience one of the main cultural failings of non-Latins. Easing into substantive talks gives you and your counterparts time to settle down and get comfortable with each other.

Entering into Substantive Talks Following initial courtesies, the head of the host delegation usually opens the meeting with formal, general welcoming remarks and then turns the floor over to the head of the guest delegation. As noted, the structure of the session will usually have been decided earlier.

If your Argentine counterparts are not proficient in your language (though they may have some understanding or even fluency), the speaker should make every effort to speak slowly and clearly. However, speakers should resist the tendency to talk down to the audience or speak more loudly than necessary. Decisions in Argentina are made based on context as much as—and sometimes more than—on content (although Argentine businesspeople will certainly not approve a deal that is short on substance). There will inevitably be some bargaining, some give-and-take; this is all part of the social interaction.

Negotiators should not allow negotiations to reach the stage of confrontation. It is important to keep lines of escape open. Thus, negotiations should be allowed to stay open-ended, and if it becomes apparent that agreement cannot be reached on key issues, it is important to allow the talks to fade away rather than reach a dramatic conclusion. This allows everyone to save face and leaves open the possibility of future talks.

Argentine Negotiating Tactics Despite their penchant for outspokenness and independence in other contexts, Argentine negotiating teams usually present a united front, generally making it impossible to exploit differences among the individual members, who defer to the principal negotiator. This person is usually the main spokesperson. The rest of the team members may not even be allowed to discuss issues; perhaps they will not even be allowed to address your team except on some very narrow technical subject in which they possess specific expertise. In turn, the senior person present defers to the president or executive vice president for periodic advice, by absenting himself during breaks or by phone if absolutely necessary. As noted, it is crucial that you understand the chain of command and who is ultimately responsible for signing the deal.

The Argentine emphasis on "people" skills means that most principal negotiators are very experienced, adept, and persuasive. They will often try to play on friendship to obtain concessions. It is up to your team to separate personalities from the economic issues. Argentine negotiators may also use temper as a tool in an attempt to soften you up. Look for and recognize these age-old negotiating tricks, and prepare an appropriate counterplan to get the negotiations back on a principled and fair footing should these detours occur.

Argentine negotiators usually do not resort to such threats as suggesting that they have other interested competitors or breaking off talks abruptly over a point of contention. They will try to gauge how strongly your side wants the agreement and exert whatever pressure they feel is appropriate according to the situation. Many outsiders are inclined to rush through an agreement so they can get on with their business; if you exhibit impatience or a sense of urgency, Argentines might exploit this weakness. It is more effective to take matters slowly and methodically.

Argentine Approach to Contracts

Historically, Argentines have relied on somewhat simple and straightforward contracts that incorporate references to the specific Argentine laws covering the various points in detail. However, following all the complex privatizations involving foreign capital and the flood of international trade in recent years, business relationships in Argentina are changing. Contracts are becoming more complex—both to cover the needs of multinational transactions not completely provided for by Argentine law and to please foreign investors accustomed to lengthy contracts with detailed provisions for all conceivable contingencies. Although many Argentines consider lengthy, US-style contracts redundant and excessive in their length and level of detail, they are becoming far more accustomed to such documents and are even entering into the spirit. Legalistic foreigners largely have themselves to blame for this change.

Argentines are becoming detail oriented and will finalize an agreement only after it has been carefully scrutinized by legal and financial professionals at all levels. Visiting businesspeople should have their own local Argentine attorneys (and perhaps accountants) similarly scrutinize the deal before a contract is signed. It is important that all terms and conditions are set forth in detail and nothing is left open to interpretation or verbal agreement. There is the ever present difference between what may seem an honest verbal promise and the actual intention or ability of the contracting party to perform.

It is also important to keep in mind that you will not only be entering into a quantifiable, tangible, legally binding agreement, but will also become part of a larger, ongoing relationship that needs to be nurtured if you are to benefit from it. Therefore you should be comfortable before entering into something that is expected to be long-term and could well prove to be a very positive and beneficial relationship.

BUSINESS ETIQUETTE

Foreign businesspeople must carefully balance the modernized business environment of Argentina with the cultural traditions of its inhabitants. Despite their sophistication and high-tech business skills, Argentines are traditional and conservative, adhering to many Latin customs in their personal and business relationships. They do not generally look kindly on nonstandard behavior, especially in a business situation; rather such behavior is viewed with mistrust and distaste. Moreover, form is sometimes as important—and in a few situations even more important—than content, and that content can be very context-specific. Nuances in body language, facial expressions, and clothing can often tell you more about a person or situation than does direct verbal communication. It can also help you present yourself in the most favorable light.

Business Attire The general standard of dress among Argentines is high, and they are more likely to prefer the subtle, rich, understated style of London to the trendier style of Milan. If you are uncertain, it is best to err on the side of the conservative, the formal, and the elegant. Both men and women dress in business suits; changing into more formal evening wear for dinner or evening entertainment is customary. Argentines are quite conscious about dress and are said to evaluate someone's attire starting with the quality of the shoes.

The Business Day Argentines are generally night owls; the workday can extend until 10 pm, and some executives have been known to schedule meetings as late as 8 pm. While Argentines may schedule appointments as early as 8:30 am, some executives prefer to arrive around 9:30 am. Some businesspeople, especially in smaller firms and in the provinces, still adhere to the custom of going home for a midday meal and *siesta*, though this is becoming less common as employees' commute distances grow longer and less relaxed international business norms gain more of a foothold.

Greetings Argentines are generally quite warm and even effusive in their greetings, which, among friends, usually involve a lot of hugging and kissing. Even at a first meeting, unless one is introduced under highly formal business circumstances, greetings are especially friendly. Women kiss women, and women kiss men; only men don't kiss men, but after a friendship develops, even this restriction can be done away with. As in certain European countries, if the business setting is more formal and the greeting is accompanied by an introduction, a warm handshake is customary. Shake firmly; Argentines take a firm handshake as a sign of strength and sincerity. At large parties you are expected to introduce yourself; at smaller gatherings the host or hostess will take the initiative to introduce you.

Argentines do not follow the convention of other Spanish-speaking countries, in which a person's full name includes the family names of both parents. Many people use a single given name and a single family name. However, double family names do occur, as well as double given names, and if you do not know which a particular person prefers, try to follow the lead of someone who is not a close friend or relative of that person.

Academic and professional titles are sometimes used in business circles, and you should be careful to note it whenever this is the case. Great attention is given to rank and title, often simply as a matter of respect rather than as a reflection of accomplishment. Sometimes a prominent leader will be referred to as *Doctor* even though he might not have completed a graduate degree; follow suit. *Don*, *Jefe*, and *Licenciado* are also titles of respect used with people who might not really be patriarchs, chiefs, or licensed degreeholders. What is important is the appropriate show of respect to others and the gracious acceptance of it when granted by others.

Business cards can be exchanged upon introduction. You are not expected to make a fuss when receiving these cards, as is the case in some Asian countries. Be sure to have your own cards to give out.

Meetings Meetings will probably begin after the time for which they were scheduled. Be aware also that even though you have an appointment, it may not be kept. It is considered a sign of power to keep one's appointments waiting; the higher a person's status in an organization, the more likely that individual is to neglect an appointment or to keep you waiting. However, it will be taken as an insult if you fail to arrive at the scheduled time. Because time is such a flexible concept in Argentina, it is best to allow more of it than you think is necessary between appointments. If you do get behind and must arrive late, an apology with a simple explanation—"something came up"—should suffice.

Business, as noted earlier, is usually discussed only following social amenities. Meetings always begin gradually with discussions of extraneous topics, concluding in the same way. Never dash in and begin talking business or dash out at the end of a meeting without achieving closure through appropriate social small talk. Don't expect to conclude your business in one meeting, and don't pressure your host to do so. Patience and graciousness are imperative.

While your business host may ask personal questions of you, it is impolite to initiate such a conversation. If you must take the lead, talk about sports (football—or soccer to North Americans—especially), literature, movies, theater, music, or the Argentine economy (do not, however, pass judgment on it). Do not at a first meeting ask if the other person is married or has children. However, foreign women should be prepared to answer these questions from the very first. Avoid topics such as the South Atlantic War, the often touchy relations with Chile, or the *desaparecidos*—the "disappeared" victims of the painful "dirty war" of the 1970s and early 1980s. However, it seems that in 1995 the country is beginning to come to terms with this experience. Argentines are extremely fond of criticizing their country, but guests should not join in; it is one thing for Argentines to criticize, but quite another for them to hear it from a foreigner. Most important, keep in mind that Argentines pride themselves on their European heritage.

The foreign businessperson should always be alert for the nuances and hidden meanings in any conversation. Repeat details as you understand them, clearly, and make certain you are in agreement. Remember: Argentines will often tell you what they think you want to hear in an effort to be agreeable.

Business Meals and Entertaining Actual business may or may not be conducted over meals, but such business meals are an important aspect of establishing and developing a network of contacts and relationships. General business talk, gossip, and politics is also fit for mealtime discussion. However, any business issue—from specific data to an invitation to an agreement in principle or a firm deal—must be specifically revisited in a business setting. In sum, Argentine businesspeople are increasingly allowing business lunches to become a recognized institution.

A foreigner will rarely be invited to an Argentine's home for a meal, but if you are, it is a good idea to bring flowers—Birds of Paradise are considered classy—chocolates, or a gift for the children. Don't bring wine—it's too common. If you are invited for dinner at 9 pm (a common dinner hour), don't arrive before 9:30, unless the host has specified "American time" or "English time" (*hora Americana* or *hora Inglesa*), either of which means "promptly." When you enter, compliment the hostess on her home, her beautiful flowers, or the meal. However, do not overact. Argentines are very sensitive to false courtesy. After a meal, don't hurry off unless the other guests do so.

Gift-Giving Exchanging gifts and favors is common business practice in Argentina, and is a good way to get things done. Foreign businesspeople should participate in the custom, but it is important to do so appropriately and with style and grace. Here are a few things to remember:

- Never go empty-handed to anyone's home.
- Women should avoid giving gifts to male colleagues, as even the most innocuous present could be misconstrued as a personal overture.
- Do not bring a business gift until a friendly relationship has been established.
- Gifts for children are almost always appropriate and are greatly appreciated.
- Gift-giving should follow business, when the atmosphere has become more relaxed.
- If you plan another visit to the country, ask your Argentine colleagues if they would like you to bring them something from your home country.

Gestures

During conversation, Argentines tend to stand much closer to each other than many North Americans or Europeans, and an Argentine man may touch the arm or shoulder, or even finger the lapel of the man with whom he is speaking. Do not back away—you might be considered rude or snobbish. Argentines are effusive; gestures are an important part of their conversation. But be careful when using your hands in conversation. Gestures are very context-sensitive, and many do not translate well between different countries. Some points to remember regarding Argentine gestures:

- Brushing the top of the hand from under the chin outward means "I don't know" or "I don't care."
- Standing with the hands on the hips suggests anger or a challenge.
- Yawning in public is considered extremely rude.
- Never pour wine by grasping the neck of the bottle with the hand and rotating the hand backward so that the palm turns upward. Also, always pour with the right hand, never the left.
- The traditional Western gesture for "everything is OK"—thumb and index finger touching in a circle—is considered a very rude and offensive gesture, and Argentines will take it as such.
- If someone extends an arm to you, palm down, and makes a scratching motion with the fingers, the gesture is meant to beckon you.
- Whereas men often cross their legs knee-over-knee, this is considered improper for women.

If you do not smoke, try not to be offended when someone does—the habit is still common in Latin America. In fact, smoking is a very social undertaking in Argentina; if you pull out a pack of cigarettes, always offer one to every member in the group.

ADDITIONAL RESOURCES ON ARGENTINE CULTURE

Argentines are for the most part highly educated and well-read. There is no shortage of daily Spanish-language newspapers, and periodicals are also available in English, French, Portuguese, German, Greek, Hungarian, Italian, Japanese, Ukrainian, Polish, and Yiddish. The *Cronista Comercial*, *Mercado*, and *Ambito Financiero* are all good business publications. The English-language *Buenos Aires Herald* is published daily and may be found at some international newsstands in large cities worldwide. It serves the Anglophone expatriate community and publishes such trivia as US baseball and Commonwealth cricket scores, and it is known for its outspoken critiques of the Argentine government. The English-language *Review of the River Plate* magazine covers topics of commercial and agricultural interest. For shortwave radio enthusiasts, Radio Argentina Al Exterior broadcasts news reports from the provinces and the capital to Argentine expatriates worldwide.

Foreigners can get some insight into and gain a better feel for popular Argentine culture by seeking out national works of art, literature, theater, and music that have made their way throughout the rest of the world. Argentine writers, such as Jorge Luis Borges, Julio Cortázar, Ernesto Sábato, Manuel Puig, Osvaldo Soriano, and Adolfo Bioy Casares write powerfully about their Argentine heritage, and many of their works are available in translation. Some observers argue that one of the best ways to get the flavor of contemporary Argentine culture is through the work of Argentine cartoonist, Quino. Many Argentine movies and movies adapted from

TEN TIPS FOR FOREIGN NEGOTIATORS

A number of tactics may be helpful to foreign negotiators dealing with Argentine businesspeople:

1. Preparation is an essential part of the negotiation process. The successful negotiator will have a thorough knowledge of the Argentine personnel as well as of the project and issues. Interview other businesspeople who have dealt with the company you are negotiating with, research and study any existing contracts they may have with other companies, and know the professional history of as many of the negotiators as possible.

2. Put yourself in their shoes. Ask yourself, "If I were representing their team, what would I ask for? What would represent a fair agreement?" Such an exercise may give you fresh insight into their interests, strengths, and weaknesses.

3. Prepare a list of possible positions the other side may take. Then be sure to develop alternatives to these before coming to the negotiating table.

4. Use objective criteria in setting your standards and formulating your proposals. Market studies, government price indexes, and other independent objective measures will prove useful. It will become difficult for the other side to contest your position on more emotional and anecdotal grounds.

5. Develop and keep your best alternative position in mind throughout the negotiations. This represents your bottom line. Do not let your counterparts know up front what your best alternative is. If it turns out to be stronger, use the alternative as a tool to improve the terms of a possible agreement. Always give yourself the freedom to believe that you can walk out if you feel you aren't getting what you need.

6. Don't put all your cards on the table. Play them one at a time. This fits in well with the Argentine viewpoint of negotiation as a social transaction. It also avoids the take-it-or-leave-it approach—which is seen as insulting, a challenge, and not playing the game.

7. Use silence. Be prepared to sit quietly and impassively for what seems like an eternity to see what will ensue. This gives the appearance of deliberate consideration, avoids the appearance of overly hasty response, and may result in additional concessions or information from the other side.

8. Listen carefully and take copious notes. To dispel any confusion, repeat important points after they are stated. This also lets the other team know that you have been listening to them. You will thus flag points of contention, eliminate extraneous misunderstandings, and be better able to keep the talks on target. Use every occasion possible to assure the Argentine team that you are thinking long-term and therefore are interested in satisfying mutual concerns.

9. Build contingent agreements. The accords should include stipulating enforcement mechanisms and penalties for nonperformance. If the Argentine team objects, tell them that you in no way doubt their good intentions, but such addenda are formalities demanded by your lawyers.

10. Be prepared to walk away from the deal. Bad business is worse than no business, and if the terms and the all-important chemistry aren't right, it will be bad business. However, don't stalk out in a huff or tie up loose ends too tightly. After all, you have invested a considerable amount of time, money, and effort to get this far, and you don't want to burn your bridges. Besides, in the highly personalized world of Argentine business, if you leave those on the other side of the table with a bad impression, word will get around, thus closing off other potential avenues of business. Leave them with a good impression and it may open other doors in the future.

the works of native authors depicting important historical and cultural themes periodically play in US and European theaters. *Apartment Zero, Man Facing Southeast, The Official Story,* and *Kiss of the Spider Woman* are all feature films with Argentine themes.

Some Argentines may insist that the best way to learn about Argentine culture is to listen to the tango. Tangos relate the angst of life and offer more specific reflections on political, historical, and economic events. Tango recordings are often available in the international sections of large recorded music stores, and professional dance troupes tour the world offering interpretations of the tango.

However, with the modernization occurring in Argentina, the tango now belongs more to the realm of show business than to everyday life.

Refer to the "Important Addresses" chapter for additional contact information on publications, media outlets, organizations, and bookstores.

Demographics

STATISTICAL SOURCES

The statistics gathered in this section represent a variety of sources and varying timelines. The data may vary somewhat from source to source, but should provide the reader with a solid background on trends in Argentina. Most of the sources listed below are updated annually, and the most recent available were consulted for this chapter. As we go to press, a number of these statistical resources are coming on line electronically. Also refer to "Statistical Publications and Sources" on page 354.

Business Latin America Business Outlook, New York: Economist Intelligence Unit.

Demographic Yearbook, New York: United Nations, Statistical Office.

Economic and Social Progress in Latin America, Washington, DC: Inter-American Development Bank.

Economic Survey of Latin America and the Caribbean, Santiago, Chile: United Nations, Economic Commission for Latin America and the Caribbean.

Europa World Year Book, London, England: Europa Publications Ltd.

Statistical Abstract of Latin America, Los Angeles: University of California at Los Angeles.

Statistical Abstract of the United States, Washington, DC: US Department of Commerce.

Statistical Yearbook, Republic of Argentina, Buenos Aires: Instituto Nacional de Estadística y Censos

Statistical Yearbook/Annuaire Statistique, Paris: UNESCO.

World Development Report, New York: Oxford University Press (published for the World Bank).

World Economic and Social Survey, New York: United Nations.

World Factbook, Washington, DC: US Central Intelligence Agency.

World Resources, Washington, DC: World Resources Institute.

World Resources: A Report by the World Resources Institute and the International Institute for Environment and Development, New York: Basic Books.

Population

AVERAGE ANNUAL POPULATION CHANGE

1980–1985	1990–1995	2000–2005 (estimated)
1.43%	1.17%	1.07%

Source: United Nations Population Division and International Labour Office

AGE DISTRIBUTION

	1994	2000
Under 5 years	9.4%	9.1%
5–14 years	19.0	17.6
15–64 years	62.0	63.3
65 years and over	9.6	10.0

Source: U.S. Bureau of the Census, International Data Base

POPULATION PROJECTIONS
in millions

Year	Millions
2025	45.51
1995	34.26
1990	32.32
1950	17.15

Source: United Nations Population Division and International Labour Office

Population

POPULATION TRENDS

Population:	33,912,994
Population growth rate:	1.1%
Birth rate:	19.6 births/1,000 population
Death rate:	8.6 deaths/1,000 population
Net migration rate:	0.2 migrant(s)/1,000 population
Infant mortality rate:	29.4 deaths/1,000 live births
Life expectancy at birth:	
total population	71.3 years
male	68.1 years
female	74.8 years
Total fertility rate:	2.7 children born/woman
Density (per sq km)	12.2

Source: CIA World Factbook.   All figures are 1994 estimates.

TOTAL POPULATION BY GENDER AND AGE GROUP

Age	Total	Male	Female	% of Total
All Ages	32,615,528	15,937,980	16,677,548	100%
0–4	3,350,073	1,695,891	1,654,182	10.27%
5–9	3,277,937	1,657,514	1,620,423	10.05%
10–14	3,342,577	1,686,997	1,655,580	10.25%
15–19	2,850,105	1,417,619	1,432,486	8.74%
20–24	2,454,123	1,213,835	1,240,288	7.52%
25–29	2,304,242	1,137,361	1,166,881	7.06%
30–34	2,214,181	1,094,131	1,120,050	6.79%
35–39	2,119,168	1,043,202	1,075,966	6.50%
40–44	1,963,648	969,612	994,036	6.02%
45–49	1,690,055	832,386	857,669	5.18%
50–54	1,489,724	722,631	767,093	4.57%
55–59	1,361,547	652,436	709,111	4.17%
60–64	1,305,161	601,706	703,455	4.00%
65–69	1,064,115	481,562	582,553	3.26%
70–74	760,853	324,719	436,134	2.33%
75–79	556,333	222,793	333,540	1.71%
80–84	319,769	119,063	200,706	0.98%
85–89	138,422	48,207	90,215	0.42%
90–94	42,787	13,069	29,718	0.13%
95 +	10,708	3,246	7,462	0.03%

Source: INDEC, Censo Nacional de Población y Vivienda 1991

Labor

ECONOMICALLY ACTIVE POPULATION BY SECTOR—TOTALS

Agriculture, forestry, fishing	1,200,992
Mining	47,171
Manufacturing	1,985,995
Electricity, gas and water	103,256
Construction	1,003,175
Wholesale/retail trade, restaurants and hotels	1,702,080
Transport, storage and communication	460,476
Finance, insurance, real estate and business services	395,704
Community, social and personal services	2,399,039
Other	691,302
Total	9,989,190

Source: ILO, Year Book of Labour Statistics (mid-1990)

SCHOOLING RATES FOR VARIOUS AGE GROUPS

(% of age group attending formal school)

Age	1980	1991
5 years	60.0%	84.8%
6–12 years	93.5	97.5
13–17 years	52.8	66.7
18–22 years	13.9	26.8

Source: Secretaría de Programación Económica, EDPA-INDEC

ECONOMICALLY ACTIVE POPULATION BY SECTOR—PERCENTAGES

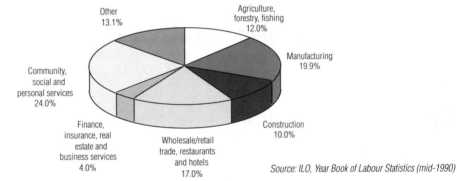

Other 13.1%

Agriculture, forestry, fishing 12.0%

Manufacturing 19.9%

Community, social and personal services 24.0%

Finance, insurance, real estate and business services 4.0%

Wholesale/retail trade, restaurants and hotels 17.0%

Construction 10.0%

Source: ILO, Year Book of Labour Statistics (mid-1990)

URBAN UNEMPLOYMENT

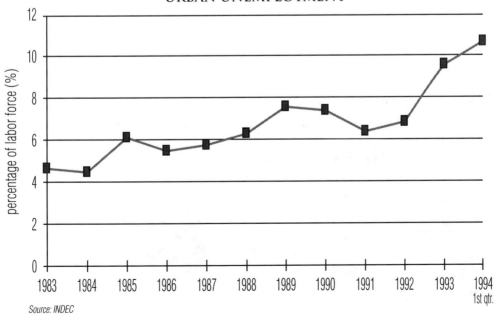

percentage of labor force (%)

1983 1984 1985 1986 1987 1988 1989 1990 1991 1992 1993 1994 1st qtr.

Source: INDEC

Inflation

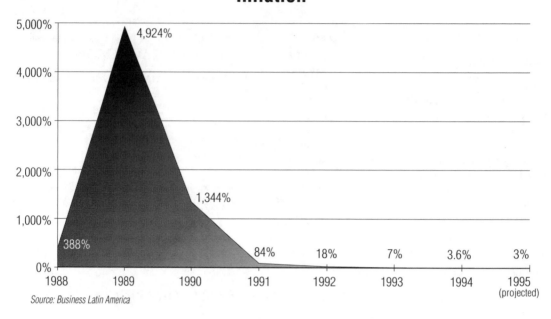

Source: Business Latin America

Media, Communications and Housing

MEDIA RECEIVERS

	1988	1989	1990
Radio Receivers (thousands in use)	21,000	21,500	22,000
Television Receivers (thousands in use)	6,850	7,000	7,165
Telephones (thousands in use)	3,694	3,922	4,622
Daily Newspapers	194	n.a.	159

Source: UNESCO, Statistical Yearbook

TELEPHONE SERVICE

	1990	1991	1992	1993
Lines Installed	3,471,283	3,629,939	4,256,643	4,967,588
Lines in Service	3,086,964	3,199,190	3,682,145	4,091,804
Lines in Service/100 persons	12	12	11	13
Digital Lines	460,284	559,000	1,189,499	2,270,390
Degree of network digitization (%)	13.3	15.4	27.9	45.7

Source: Comisión Nacional de Telecomunicaciones (INDEC)

HOUSEHOLDS BY TYPE OF HOUSING

Houses Type A:
no deficiencies in plumbing or electricity service.

Houses Type B:
some deficiencies in plumbing or electrical service.

Source: INDEC, Censo Nacional de Población y Vivienda 1991

Cities and Territorial Divisions

POPULATION OF MAJOR CITIES

Buenos Aires	11,382,002	San Juan	358,396
Córdoba	1,166,932	Salta	342,316
Rosario	1,096,254	Santa Fe	338,013
Mendoza	728,966	Resistencia	294,658
La Plata	644,155	Bahía Blanca	264,021
San Miguel de Tucumán	626,143	Corrientes	222,772
Mar del Plata	523,178	Paraná	194,452
		Santiago del Estero	190,863
		Posadas	188,642
		San Salvador de Jujuy	165,783
		Neuquén	135,464
		San Nicolás	131,079
		Río Cuarto	130,907
		Formosa	124,997

Source: INDEC, Censo Nacional de Población y Vivienda 1991

PRINCIPAL POLITICAL AND TERRITORIAL DIVISIONS

Province	Population	% of Total	Capital
Capital Federal	2,965,403	9.1%	
Buenos Aires	12,594,973	38.6%	La Plata
Catamarca	264,234	0.8%	Catamarca
Chaco	839,677	2.6%	Resistencia
Chubut	357,189	1.1%	Rawson
Córdoba	2,766,683	8.5%	Córdoba
Corrientes	795,594	2.4%	Corrientes
Entre Ríos	1,020,257	3.1%	Paraná
Formosa	398,413	1.2%	Formosa
Jujuy	512,329	1.6%	San Salvador de Jujuy
La Pampa	259,996	0.8%	Santa Rosa
La Rioja	220,729	0.7%	La Rioja
Mendoza	1,412,481	4.3%	Mendoza
Misiones	788,915	2.4%	Posadas
Neuquén	388,833	1.2%	Neuquén
Río Negro	506,772	1.6%	Río Negro
Salta	866,153	2.7%	Salta
San Juan	528,715	1.6%	San Juan
San Luis	286,458	0.9%	San Luis
Santa Cruz	159,839	0.5%	Río Gallegos
Santa Fe	2,798,422	8.6%	Santa Fe
Santiago del Estero	671,988	2.1%	Santiago del Estero
Tierra del Fuego	69,369	0.2%	Ushuaia
Tucumán	1,142,105	3.5%	San Miguel de Tucumán
Country Total	**32,615,527**		

Source: INDEC, Censo Nacional de Población y Vivienda 1991

* A dispute concerning sovereignty over the islands exists between Argentina which claims this sovereignty and the UK which administers the islands.

Paved Roads

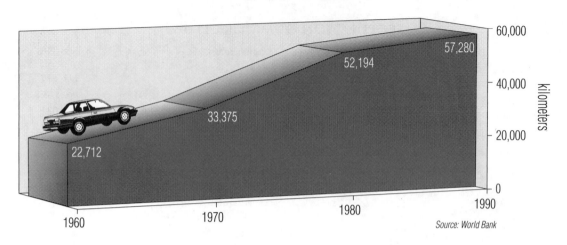

Source: World Bank

Energy

ENERGY USE PER CAPITA—
OIL EQUIVALENTS

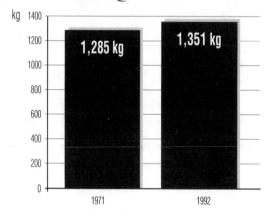

GDP OUTPUT PER KG—
OIL EQUIVALENTS

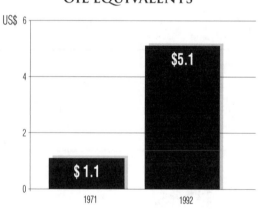

Source: World Bank

ELECTRICITY GENERATING CAPACITY VS. ACTUAL PRODUCTION

	1960	1970	1980	1990
Capacity (thousands of kilowatts)	3,474	6,691	11,988	17,128
Production (millions of kilowatt-hours)	10,460	21,730	39,679	50,904

Source: World Bank

Marketing

KEYS TO MARKETING IN ARGENTINA

Selling a product in Argentina can be as simple as signing a contract with a local sales agent or as complex as establishing a company or even a chain of distribution companies in the country. Argentina's markets are now more open to foreign imports and direct foreign investment than ever before. Inflation has fallen to near-insignificance, and the currency has stabilized. Price controls and many import and investment barriers have been lifted. Large state-run industries have already been privatized, and this process is continuing. Multinational companies have increased their investments in Argentina, while many small businesses have begun exporting into the Argentine market and are profiting from its new openness.

Although there is renewed optimism in the country, there are also some growing pains. A number of industries are being restructured, while others are finding survival to be difficult in the face of intensifying competition from more efficient sources, both foreign and domestic. Furthermore, restrictions concerning which markets are open, partially open, and which still closed continue to be in a state of flux,

and many distribution channels have yet to be even functionally, much less fully, developed. However, those interested in the new Argentina can gain an understanding of the new rules and regulations and anticipate many of the potential problems through adequate advance planning.

It is unnecessary to spend a fortune on research just to learn whether there is a market; that information is relatively easy to get from a variety of sources. This book is one. Your home country's embassy commercial service and Argentine trade associations and chambers of commerce are others. Along the way, you will find knowledgeable, experienced people whose job it is to help you wend your way through mazes constructed by knowledgeable, experienced people whose job it is to get you lost. One key to initial success is to keep costs as low as possible—possibly through direct sales—until you have established a toehold. Another is to go all-out to fill orders quickly and answer inquiries immediately. Above all, your company must make a genuine, explicit commitment to exporting, because otherwise the worst problems will come from within, rather than from the country or the competition. Export sales generate a momentum of their own that is difficult to stop, and they pull in repeat business, new accounts, and offers from persons eager to serve as your local representatives. But none of this occurs before you have taken the first step, which means: you must begin carefully to lay the groundwork.

The changes in Argentina's newly open economic system are already overwhelming many of Argentina's relatively undeveloped marketing channels. Over time, the increasing volume of foreign business is sure to introduce practices and standards that are even more international in nature, as well as to call forth greater capacity and new ways of approaching Argentine markets. However, in the interim, pioneering marketers will have to come up with answers to marketing problems largely on an ad hoc basis; this

CONTENTS

UTILIZING CUSTOMER INFORMATION

Once basic data has been accumulated, the next task is to learn how to sort and use it. Focus your marketing efforts by analyzing the data in terms of the needs and preferences of potential customers and then formulating an effective sales strategy that will reach and appeal to the most likely buyers. The basic theory is that consumers' purchasing behavior can be predicted from an analysis of their general characteristics.

Marketers may hire one of the Argentine information service companies to generate, process, and distribute customer information about a particular market. These companies commonly assist in developing information systems tailored to the needs of the particular marketing organization. By subscribing to such a system, a businessperson can review financial management, research, marketing, purchasing, and administrative information. Market research firms can even carry this analysis a step or two further, performing a professional review of the data and advising the trader about markets that appear to be most lucrative. For a full package of services—market research, analysis, and advertising development and placement—an advertising firm can be employed. Refer to page 345 for contact information on advertising agencies and page 346 for market research firms.

Regardless of whether one obtains the assistance of a professional in marketing, one should gain at least a general familiarity with, if not in-depth knowledge of, the types of customer information available and how to use them. Most of this information falls into four areas: demographics (customers' physical and environmental attributes), psychographics (what the customer thinks and values), buying patterns (what, where, and how often the customer buys and how much is spent), and media attraction (where consumers most often learn about what they buy). From a review of all of this data, a trader can begin to target the market for a particular product—but if any part of the picture is missing, the analysis becomes less accurate, and marketing is more likely to go wrong. Thus, to predict who will buy a product or service, analysis of customer information should generally proceed as follows:

1. Determine the demographics—the physical and environmental characteristics of potential customers: who they are in terms of such factors as age, education, geographic environment, earned income, family status, and household structure.

2. Add the psychographic data—as manifested by the customers' preferred lifestyles. Find out why they act the way they do; why they want a product or service; why they prefer one item over another; what they are likely to spend their money buying; and what will be most likely to influence their decisions.

3. Mix in buying patterns to figure out how much purchasing power the potential customers have: how often they purchase a product, how much they spend, and where they go to buy it.

4. Identify the types of messages and media channels that appeal most to the potential customers in order to penetrate the market most efficiently, that is, to "get the biggest bang for the buck."

Your research will ideally lead to an evaluation of the product itself to determine whether it is likely going to fit the intended market, that is, whether the product will satisfy the current needs of the primary buyers. This research should suggest whether customers might consider the product a necessity or a luxury (which in turn would indicate whether the product will sell regardless of its packaging and whether customers will make single or repeated purchases). Another factor that should become apparent is the frequency of purchases, which will help to determine how fast the customer base will have to grow to ensure the success of the business. The marketer should also look at the product in terms of trends in the market data in an effort to anticipate whether the product or product line would have to be modified in order to meet the changing needs and desires of the targeted customers (and if so, in what ways and how frequently).

makes for both huge frustration and opportunity. On the one hand, marketers will neither be able to rely on standard operating procedure nor be able to count on the support systems to which they have become accustomed. On the other hand, they will not be trapped by the straitjacket of traditional perceptions and ways of doing things; they will have the chance to create new ways of doing business.

Marketing in Argentina requires that you:

- Identify the customers most likely to purchase your product and evaluate the product for its appeal to that market.
- Learn the geographic markets.
- Learn the ways of structuring or doing business in Argentina.
- Determine the best marketing channels for your product.
- Determine the most effective means of advertising or otherwise promoting your product.
- Commit to exporting your product.

A review of the "Opportunities" chapter, beginning on "Opportunities" on page 27, will be helpful in highlighting opportunities for trading with Argentine businesses. Helpful contacts—particularly trade associations, chambers of commerce, and government agencies—are listed in the "Important Addresses" chapter, beginning on "Important Addresses" on page 315.

WHO WILL BUY?

In area, Argentina is about the size of that part of the US located east of the Mississippi River; its population numbers nearly 34 million. Argentina's markets are very diverse, with demands that range from the most basic to the most sophisticated products. The economy is expanding, and its prominent sectors include manufacturing, agriculture, forestry, and fishing; community, social, and personal services; wholesale and retail trade; and construction. Indeed, the question to ask is not so much "Is there a market?" but "What is the best market for our product or service in Argentina?" The answer to this latter question must be derived from an evaluation of the intended and potential uses of a product or service, which in turn leads to identification of the most likely users. To sell a product or service successfully in today's increasingly open and educated Argentine consumer market, one must identify the customers most likely to use the product, determine the product attributes most likely to appeal to those customers, and tailor the merchandise, quality, packaging, and presentation accordingly.

Finding Customer Information

Detailed, reliable information on Argentine markets is not nearly as voluminous or as easily accessible as similar information in more developed industrialized nations. This is not to say that market and demographic information does not exist, but rather that you just have to be more persistent—perhaps more creative—to obtain it.

For general demographic information (such as population statistics, age distribution, consumer prices, housing, educational levels, inflation, unemployment figures, and television, newspaper, and radio usage), the following sources provide fairly current and accurate information: US Bureau of the Census, International Data Base; International Monetary Fund; United Nations Population Division; World Bank; Republic of Argentina Statistical Yearbook; INDEC, Censo Nacional de Población y Vivienda; ILO Yearbook of Labor Statistics; UNESCO Statistical Yearbook; and Secretaría de Programación Económica. (Refer to the "Important Addresses" chapter, beginning on page 315, for contact information.)

Trends in Argentine Markets

A trader must keep current on developing trends when evaluating Argentine customer information: anticipating shifts in markets can be as important as knowing existing customer needs. Large-scale trends that affect Argentine markets include the following.

Population is concentrated in large urban centers. More than 80 percent of Argentines reside in urban areas, and more than one-third of the population lives in metropolitan Buenos Aires. With the highest percentage of population and consumption focused in the Buenos Aires area, there is no doubt that the capital city region leads the country in terms of purchasing power. Argentines residing in or near Buenos Aires generally represent the most sophisticated consumers in the country. These individuals receive more exposure to foreign goods—displayed in shops and advertised on cable television—and they have a long-standing taste for imports—particularly consumer goods with status appeal. Other major centers of business activity include Córdoba, Rosario, and Mendoza. The city of Córdoba—the second largest in the country—is a university town with a highly educated population and a relatively sophisticated consumer base; it is also the country's second ranking industrial and commercial center. Rosario—the next largest city, which in fact disputes the title of second city claimed by Córdoba—also has a strong industrial base; it is the largest grain and river port in Argentina. Mendoza is the fourth most populated region in Argentina, the nation's leading wine producer, and a gateway to Chile.

Population growth rate is slowing down. Argentina's population growth rate has been decreasing during the past 15 years and is expected to continue to be relatively slow through at least the year 2025. This slow growth rate has created a bulge in the 20-to-40 age group, as well as a growing population in the 50-plus age group. Today's average Argentine household has 2.7 children. The traditional family unit—that is, a father, mother, and children residing in the same home—still represents the norm in Argentina. However, more and more women are entering the workforce, particularly after children have reached school age, and more households are being headed by a single parent—usually a woman. Consumers in this age and social range typically purchase many household items and appliances, and with more women in the workforce, the need for more convenience items is expected to increase.

Most significant purchasing power is in the middle —in the 20-to-40 age bracket. With the largest percentage of the population in the middle age range, total gross purchases should be on the rise in Argentina, certainly as long as the economy continues to progress. Individuals between the ages of 20 and 40 are in the process of finishing or have already finished their education, are working full-time, and are starting families or already rearing children. Purchases of big-ticket items—homes, automobiles, furniture, and appliances—should become significant among this age group. The demand for general consumer goods—such as food, clothing, toys, and household items—should also be relatively high within this age range.

The percentage of the population that is educated is on the rise. More than 95 percent of Argentines are literate, and better than half have been to high school. The percentage of individuals attending and completing university degree programs is increasing. With an increase in the educational level of a population will come greater product awareness and sophistication in purchasing decisions. People will expect quality and will be quite knowledgeable about a product before deciding to buy. In general, the more education an individual receives, the more discerning that individual becomes regarding purchasing. Additionally, as education increases, so does receptivity to new products or services. This population segment should be particularly important to foreign businesspersons who are introducing new and different products into the Argentine market.

Customers and businesses are becoming increasingly aware of environmental concerns. Citizens and elected officials in Argentina are showing a growing awareness of environmental issues. Argentine companies are facing tougher regulations requiring them to control industrial emissions and properly dispose of hazardous wastes. Consequently, products that eliminate or decrease environmentally harmful residues and by-products are in greater demand. Environmentally friendly packaging is also becoming a popular alternative in Argentina.

Argentines are buying more. With renewed optimism about the economy and a more stable—and, some even argue, overvalued—peso making imports relatively cheaper, Argentines are buying more of everything, from high-tech equipment to necessities and luxury consumer goods, from audio and video equipment to camping gear.

Argentine end users look for quality, variety, and competitively priced products. Increasingly, Argentine consumers expect high-quality products and a large variety of styles, models, and features at competitive prices. These product attributes are particularly important for consumer goods because competition has intensified with the opening of domestic markets to imports.

The availability of consumer credit is also having a major effect in boosting consumption. Because of the high inflation that characterized much of the 1980s and the very early 1990s, there was virtually no credit available to businesses, much less to consumers. Since the Convertibility Law began to stabilize the peso, credit has once more become available, fueling increased consumption among growing numbers and categories of buyers for an ever-increasing range of goods and services. This in turn has given new importance to marketing designed to reach these newly empowered potential customers.

WHERE IS THE MARKET LOCATED?

After determining the primary applications of a product and its most likely customers, a marketer should review the various Argentine regions and identify areas where major users of the product are concentrated. From Argentina's rich temperate plains—the Pampas—to urban and urbane coastal Buenos Aires to the more traditional northwest and the rugged south, Argentina holds outstanding opportunities for marketing both standard and innovative products to business and personal customers. Geographically, Argentina is South American, but culturally, it is generally more European, in particular Spanish and Italian.

In researching Argentina's geographic markets, keep in mind that 80 percent of the population resides in urban areas (although "urban" may refer to a population center with as few as 2,000 residents). People are continually moving out of rural areas in hopes of finding greater opportunities in the country's urban centers. While Argentina's large cities are certainly easier to target and represent greater opportunity for consumer or high-tech products, traders should not overlook Argentina's enormous agricultural market, which is central to the economy and spills into both rural and urban areas nationwide. There is great potential for sellers and manufacturers of agricultural equipment and related products.

Trade in services is becoming an important market for foreign companies. For example, the liberalization and privatization of several industries in Argentina has created an enormous market for business consultants who can provide expertise to Argentine firms urgently needing to restructure their productive and managerial processes in order to become competitive internationally. There is also a significant ongoing franchising boom in Argentina. This growing interest has provided a new niche for franchising consultants, who not only help local franchisors set up their systems, but also carry out searches (on commission) to aid major foreign franchisors find reliable master franchisees in Argentina.

While Buenos Aires remains the industrial, financial, intellectual, and cultural center of the country, it is important to remember that Argentina is a vast country with 23 provinces. It is also important to recognize the diversity of these provinces, as well as to explore them, because they are developing significantly in their own right. Following is an outline of the Argentine provinces grouped into regional markets.

ARGENTINE REGIONAL MARKETS

Northwestern Andes (Región Andina del Noroeste)

(Provinces: Jujuy, Salta, Tucumán, Catamarca. Population: 2,785,000. Major Cities: San Salvador de Jujuy, San Miguel de Tucumán.) Located in northwestern Argentina, this region borders Bolivia on the north and Chile and the spine of the Andes on the west. Like much of Argentina, agriculture represents the economic backbone of this region. Sugar (along with its by-products, alcohol and paper) and tobacco are the predominant industrial crops. Citrus fruit, tomatoes, beans, cereals, oilseeds, grapes, olives, and nuts are also harvested. The primary industry is the processing of agricultural products; these are sugar refineries, tomato packing plants, and tobacco processing facilities. The largest sugar mill in the country is in Jujuy. Mines produce lead, silver, and zinc. The production of petroleum products has been the economic mainstay in Salta for the past 40 years.

Central Andes (Región Andina Central)

(Provinces: San Juan, Mendoza, La Rioja. Population: 2,162,000. Major Cities: Mendoza and San Juan.)

Though similar in topography to the North Andean Region, the Central Andean Region—also known as the Cuyo—supports a more Mediterranean-style agriculture. This region is the country's top producer of wine. With more than 1,000 winery operations, including some of the largest in the world, the region's wineries have helped Argentina become the fifth largest producer worldwide, although its wines have yet to reach international export markets in any significant volume. Grapes and olives are the region's main agricultural crops, with 90 to 95 percent of the grape harvest used for the production of wine. The processing of fruit juices and fruit and vegetable preserves is another important industry. Mendoza province is the leading producer of canned tomatoes, tomato sauce, puree, juice, and extract. La Rioja also has a long mining tradition. The most valuable minerals extracted there are gold and tungsten. Copper, iron, and lead are still mined in San Juan Province.

Chaco (Región Chaqueña)

(Provinces: Chaco and Formosa. Population: 1,238,000. Major Cities: Formosa, Resistencia.) Bordering Paraguay to the north and east, the great subtropical savannas of Chaco and Formosa support intensive agriculture and ranching. The Chaco is the country's leading producer of cotton, and production has grown significantly in recent years. In addition to cotton, which accounts for half of its cultivated area, Formosa Province specializes in the cultivation of citrus and other fruit, such as bananas. In the early 1980s, oil reserves were discovered and exploited in Formosa. Chaco Province has become the country's second largest producer of forestry products.

Central Region (Región del Centro)

(Provinces: Córdoba, San Luis, Santiago del Estero. Population: 3,725,000. Major Cities: Córdoba, Santiago del Estero.) Córdoba is a powerful agricultural and industrial center, and among the provinces it is second in terms of economic output. The agricultural and industrial sectors each contribute one-fourth of Córdoba's economy, with trade and services—including a strong tourist industry—accounting for the remaining half. Because of its developed foreign trade infrastructure, Córdoba is a major site for international exhibitions. The region's main crops are cereals, fodder, soybeans, and potatoes. Also known for dairy products, Cordoba's most important industry is metallurgy (machinery and equipment, such as engines, automobiles, car parts, tractors, trucks, and motorcycles). Agricultural processing plants (mills, cold storage, dairies, and canneries) are the second most important industrial activity in the region.

Pampas (Región Pampeana)

(Provinces: Buenos Aires, La Pampa. Population: 15,820,000. Major Cities: Buenos Aires, Mar de Plata, La Plata, Bahia Blanca.) The Federal Capital and the Province of Buenos Aires account for more than 50 percent of the national output of manufactured products, representing a diversity of industries: textiles, steel, wood products, chemicals, leather and leather goods, building materials, and—most importantly—the food industry (cereals products and meatpacking). Consumer durable items produced within the province include automobiles and parts, plastics, and home appliances. Nondurable consumer items include fiber knits, garments, pharmaceuticals, chemical products, and cosmetics. Tourism income also represents an important and growing contribution to the economy. The Atlantic beaches, inland lake districts, and the Paraná Delta area are all popular vacation areas.

The Pampas region traditionally symbolizes Argentina to the world. It is the center of cattle ranching in a country known for its beef. Farming is a significant economic activity, the most important harvests being corn, wheat, sorghum, and oilseeds. Potatoes, onions, tomatoes, garlic, pears, and apples are also grown in the Pampas. Salt was the only commodity mined in the Pampas until 1963, when an oil field was located. Since then, 300 wells have been drilled for the extraction of oil and gas.

With 200 sq km (77 sq mi) Buenos Aires itself—the district called in Spanish the Capital Federal—is the smallest national political unit by area; however, it is also the most densely populated. Buenos Aires is the seat of the national government. The securities and commercial markets are also in the Federal District (as it is known in English). The metropolis generates nearly one-quarter of the country's gross domestic product (GDP).

Patagonia (Región Patagónica)

(Provinces: Río Negro, Neuquén, Chubut, Santa Cruz, Tierra del Fuego, Islas del Atlántico Sur (South Atlantic Islands). Population: 1,482,000. Major cities: Neuquén.) Patagonia is the Argentine equivalent of Australia's Outback and in many ways Patagonia lives up to its image. The geography includes vast plateaux, the Andes Mountain Range, several islands located in the South Atlantic, and varied coastlines. Agriculture (ranching and farming) represents a significant portion of the economy of the region. Patagonia's apple and pear harvests account for approximately 70 percent of national production: one-third of the apple production is for export. Sheep and, to a lesser extent, cattle are bred extensively, the sheep (particularly Merino) for wool as well as for meat. Sheepherding is most extensive in the provinces of Chubut, Santa Cruz, and Tierra del Fuego. Oil and gas production is the primary economic activity in Neuquén Province, which is home to one-third of Argentina's petroleum reserves. The major industries of this region have developed in ways that complement its natural resources, with hydroelectric complexes, knitting mills and factories, cold storage plants, juice concentrating facilities, and agricultural equipment producers. Tierra del Fuego has been given special foreign trade status, allowing certain goods to be imported there at reduced rates in order to encourage industrial development. Patagonia is also a major player in the tourism industry. Bariloche, the country's most popular winter resort, is a recognized world class ski resort. Sport fishermen flock to the region's many lakes and rivers, and ecotourism is gaining a foothold in Patagonia.

Mesopotamia (Región Litoral)

(Provinces: Santa Fe, Misiones, Corrientes, Entre Ríos. Population: 5,403,000. Major Cities: Rosario, Santa Fe, Corrientes.) The "land between the Paraná and Uruguay Rivers" in the northeast abuts Paraguay, Uruguay, and Brazil. As is the case in much of Argentina, the economy of this region is a mix of agriculture and industrial production. Industrial crops such as rice, sugarcane, cotton, and tobacco predominate in this region, although citrus fruit production is also significant, especially in Entre Ríos Province. Tea is harvested in Misiones. Dairy farming is also a significant activity. Automotive assembly, the production of agricultural machinery, steel milling, petrochemicals, home appliances, and intermediate metal fabrication constitute the region's strong and growing industrial base. An improved road and railway network connecting Argentina with Brazil, Uruguay, and Paraguay, as well as various bridges and tunnels interconnecting the provinces have increased industrial development. This trend is expected to continue and strengthen as the Mercado Común del Sur (Mercosur) partnership increases trade among the four neighboring countries that touch this area. Some observers predict that the Litoral will become the fastest growing and most prosperous region in the country over the next few years.

FROM A TOEHOLD TO AN ESTABLISHED PRESENCE

Nine Steps into the Market

Entry into the Argentine market can be accomplished in a variety of ways: by using already established local distribution channels, such as agents and Argentine importers; through joint venture and licensing arrangements with Argentine firms; by direct marketing; or through the more substantial investment needed to open a branch or subsidiary in Argentina. Depending on such factors as overall intent, time frame, financial and physical size, product line, and potential Argentine markets, a company that wants to do business in Argentina might begin in any one of these ways or might decide to use a customized or combined approach. Although there are advantages to being physically close to the market—that is, located in it—it is certainly possible to attain a significant presence in Argentine markets at a relatively low cost without establishing any direct business presence there. The goal is to determine how to reach the primary users of the product or service through the most efficient, cost-effective means, then learn how to gain their repeat business.

Overall, a trader must weigh the advantages of using existing channels against the advantages of starting from scratch. Presumably, the locals know the markets—where they are, what they require, what they will buy, and how much and at what price. By doing business through an Argentine agent or distributor, an exporter can avoid having to wade through all of those details. Test-marketing through a few Argentina-based specialists can show the nature, location, and size of a market before a heavy investment is made. On the other hand, marketing through someone else will mean a loss of a percentage of the profits, of some control over the process, and learning the finer points of the process. The exporter will have to rely on the Argentine representative's investigation, marketing decisions, and general "smarts." The exporter's product will also probably be only one of many handled by the distributor, thus the level of attention paid to it will likely be limited. If the representative is skilled in the particular industry and type of product, this may not be a negative. However, the selection of a distributor must be made very carefully.

In contrast to the situation that prevailed as recently as a few years ago in which distribution was often fragmented, Argentina has been experiencing a dramatic change in the way that products are distributed. Before there were numerous small participants in the distribution chain and seemingly innumerable small outlets. This system is being consolidated, concentrated, and rationalized at an extremely rapid pace. On the one hand, this response has occurred largely to fill the needs of a rapidly growing consumer constituency that is demanding more, better, and less costly goods than could be delivered by the old system. On the other hand, it is also the product of the needs of the new, larger outlets, such as supermarkets and discount chains.

It is also important to distinguish between the means of marketing and distributing consumer and

AGENT/DISTRIBUTOR SERVICE (ADS)

This customized service of the US Department of Commerce is designed to help US businesses locate overseas representatives. A US government employee at an overseas location (often operating through the US embassy or consulate; usually a national of the host country) contacts prospects and reports their level of interest in your product.

This service works well for many companies. However, it has limitations: it can be used only by firms entering a new territory or after they have served notice of their intent to discontinue the relationship with an existing distributor.

The lead time necessary for processing and receiving a response to an ADS request is generally between 60 and 90 days. For this reason advance planning is necessary. One way to shorten the time required is to inform ADS that you will be visiting the target country shortly and need priority service. They will set the process in motion and send information overseas; you should be able to collect the results abroad personally about 30 days after submitting your application.

You can expect anywhere from zero to six leads, with three being the norm. The quality of the leads varies with the preparer, the specific market, and the specificity of the product. By all means request the names of those distributors who were contacted but did not show interest (as well as those who did). This will eliminate duplications as you contact firms on your own.

Contact the US Department of Commerce, Washington, DC for more information.

industrial products. More and more consumer goods are being sold through large outlets such as supermarkets. However, industrial products are sold differently, through such means as trade fairs and calls on buyers.

Listed below are several ways to enter the Argentine market. In considering each of these market penetration strategies, it is important to keep in mind the product involved and the most successful way of reaching your intended target market.

1. Hire a local agent, distributor, or importer. Agents have played a key role in placing foreign (particularly European and US) industrial products in Argentina because they provide a convenient, efficient link between potential end users and machinery manufacturers. Other products which typically reach Argentine end users through these channels may include health care equipment, consumer goods such as household appliances, and high-tech equipment.

In most cases, agents are responsible for introductions, consulting about market strategies for their market, arrangements for exhibitions at local fairs, and general promotional activities. They generally help in the negotiations and final sale of the product and then perform support services, helping with quotations, financing, import regulations, permits, arranging for warehousing of inventory, and collections. Agents are generally paid a fee plus a royalty or commission based on sales volume and receipts.

Importers and distributors, on the other hand, purchase goods directly for resale. They perform more functions and assume greater risk than an agent; by the same token, they tend to share less of the information they gain from the effort. Argentine importers generally warehouse and promote the products, processing and shipping the orders. They may even handle follow-up service. The distributor or importer's compensation is the profit margin, and they will want to negotiate a substantial discount from list price. Most distributorships are granted on an exclusive basis for the entire country, at least for particular products or product lines, if not for the contracting party's entire business.

Whatever responsibilities an agent or importer has must be spelled out precisely in the contract. It is imperative to adapt the contract to the following three areas: your product or service, your company, and the particular markets. Be sure to consult both home country and Argentine legal advisors to prevent or provide for potential problems.

Advantages These arrangements in general involve less commitment and less expense than virtually any other means of introducing a product into a foreign economy.

By using any of these established distribution channels, the exporter places the responsibility for handling the importation process in the hands of local Argentine businesspeople. Furthermore, these people are presumably more knowledgeable about the local market, culture, and language. Finally,

principal-agent relations are basically governed by the Civil Code and the Commercial Code, which permit the termination an agency agreement essentially at the discretion of the principal. However, keep in mind that agents may also withdraw essentially at will and that all agreements, whether for a definite or indefinite term, should include a notice of termination clause.

Disadvantages Problems can arise if a well planned and comprehensive contract is not signed from the start of the relationship. Strategic decisions such as export pricing or an international marketing plan, must be included in any agreement with agent or distributor. For example: is the agent or distributor expected to participate in trade shows? Is the agent expected to join you personally? Is the agent expected to pay part of the costs? Another concern is that middlemen are in business to maximize their own profits—not those of the manufacturer. They can be notorious for their "cherry picking": the practice of taking orders for products, brands, or manufacturers that are in demand and avoiding any real effort to sell manufacturers' products that may require "push."

2. Establish a franchise. Argentina is experiencing a franchising mini-boom; interest appears to be keen and growing. Franchise contracts are protected under the Argentine Commercial Code. Rights to servicemarks, commercial trademarks and names, know-how, and shared production aspects can be protected if covered by contractual provisions; such provisions become binding on both the franchisor and the franchisee. Elements of the contract include the license, methods, systems, or know-how transferred to the franchisee, the supply of needed inputs, methods of sales, quality standards, and ultimate control by the franchisor of the contract elements. Franchisors entering the Argentine market are doing so primarily by seeking out a local master franchisee to develop the local market for them. Furthermore, some of these master franchisees can then sub-franchise, as is the case with local owners of some foreign-based fast-food franchises (which have proved to be the most popular, fastest-growing area of franchising).

Franchising was neither common nor popular in Argentina before 1991. But by the end of 1992, approximately 50 local and foreign franchisors had signed up about 500 franchisees, employing roughly 5,000 workers and accounting for sales estimated at US$300 million. Franchises have attracted interest among growing categories of nontraditional franchisees: young people, women, and new entrepreneurs from among those displaced by economic restructuring. These people will often pool their resources or use severance payments to buy a franchise. Their usual lack of experience can often be offset to a large extent by the training, management, and support systems that are included in most franchising packages.

Advantages Franchising works well in Argentina for the same reasons it works well in any country. Franchisors benefit because they can expand business rapidly, with only a fraction of the capital that would otherwise be needed to open branches. However, the risks of losing control—such as those inherent in license arrangements—can generally be avoided. Franchisees benefit because they can be their own bosses, but do not have to create a name or develop their own support, supply, operational, or management systems. All of these elements have already been successfully established, and franchisees can use these existing strengths to leverage their own investments in capital and effort.

Disadvantages Franchises have been successfully used in Argentina, but the obligations of the franchisor must be clearly delineated in the contract to avoid the franchisor's bearing the legal obligations that should be assigned to the operator (for example, in case of labor disputes, default, or bankruptcy). In particular, Argentine law is somewhat unclear about franchisor obligations in case of bankruptcy, so attempts should be made to cover this possibility through contractual provisions.

It is necessary to seek legal advice prior to signing any contract. Another concern is the Argentine consumer's apprehension about trying new products. This is particularly true among lower income segments of the population. Therefore, aggressive marketing and extra support may be needed to attract this particular market segment, which is often targeted for small-ticket, frequent repeat purchases of many franchise products.

3. Negotiate a licensing arrangement. Licensing arrangements involve the transfer of know-how, technology, or other intangible property (such as patents or trademarks) from a foreign individual or company to an Argentine individual or firm. Such transfers are governed by Argentine Law No. 22,426, which establishes two categories of transactions: those between related companies and those with third parties. Transfers between related companies were subject to prior government approval. Transfers of know-how between nonrelated companies do not require approval, although the government requests that they be registered for informational purposes and they must be registered to obtain favorable tax treatment. (Withholding is at a 27 percent rate for unregistered contracts, while registered contract royalties are withheld at between 18 and 24 percent, based on the type of technology involved.)

Advantages Licensing can be especially advantageous for small companies lacking the capital, management, and other necessary resources and experience to expand internationally through direct investment. Licensing is a fairly economic way to test and develop a market that can later be exploited through a direct presence or investment. Licensing is also advantageous when opportunities exist for licensing auxiliary processes without having to license the basic product technologies. Finally, licensing may offer a means of getting around certain import barriers.

Disadvantages The licensor may in time lose its competitive edge to the licensee and be effectively if not legally barred in the future from direct expansion in the areas served by the licensee.

4. Establish a joint venture. Argentine legislation permits the establishment of temporary mergers equivalent to joint ventures. Such a "temporary union of enterprises," as it is known, may be formed by Argentine companies with branches of foreign companies and individuals residing in Argentina. Its purpose must be to perform work or render services within Argentina or outside of the country using Argentina as its domiciled base of operations. A temporary union of enterprises—neither a company nor a partnership—is not considered a legal entity.

The companies or individuals establishing the union are responsible for the actions performed jointly. A contract should be signed and registered with the Inspección General de Justicia (IGJ, or Inspection General of Justice) in Buenos Aires or a similar agent in the provinces. In order to be legal, the contract must contain a number of specific clauses and must also provide for the appointment of a legal representative in charge of managing the local operation.

Advantages The advantages of this strategy are the sharing of risk and the ability to draw upon the strengths of different firms to accomplish a specific project. Thus, a company with in-depth knowledge of the local market might combine with a foreign partner who lacks market knowledge but has considerable know-how in the area of technology and process applications. As with a licensing arrangement, a joint venture is a means of getting around some import barriers. For example, the automobile industry remains heavily protected in Argentina, and the best (and, in some cases, the only) means of entering the market may be through a joint venture.

Disadvantages A joint venture requires the sharing of rewards as well as risks, thus reducing potential returns. The danger also exists that one's partner of today may become one's competitor of tomorrow, using inside knowledge of your operation and capabilities against you in the future.

However, for most international operations the main disadvantages of the joint venture are the very significant costs associated with the long distance control and coordination needed to work with a partner.

5. Exhibit at trade fairs. Trade shows are a good way of getting market exposure; of looking for distributors, customers, or potential suppliers; and of learning about the competition, the market, and the way business is done in the area. Several venues in Argentina are sites of major international exhibitions. (Refer to the "Trade Fairs" chapter, beginning on page 121, for additional information.)

Advantages As an exhibitor, you can be approached on the spot by distributors or customers who are interested in your product. Often these potential business associates have exhibits at the show, as do potential competitors, so you can meet a large number of people in your industry all at one time. Contacts can be made on many levels, from the smallest businesses to the largest corporations, from local distributors and agents to foreign business representatives. Never underestimate the importance of the personal touch that can accompany such direct interactions.

Disadvantages Exposure is limited to only those companies and individuals attending the fair, and competition with other products targeted for the same industry may be intense. Immediate sales may not even cover the cost of attending. The benefit to the business can only be seen over time and depends on whether the contacts at the event are in fact appropriate to the business.

6. Open a branch office. To be able to operate legally as a branch in Argentina, it is necessary to furnish proof of the existence of the parent company abroad, register the parent's articles of incorporation or partnership contract with the office of the IGJ, and appoint representatives and likewise register them. Branches are treated as separate entities, independent from their parent firms, and must comply with all applicable rules and regulations and sustain all the legal obligations as nationally incorporated firms.

Advantages Establishing a branch in Argentina entails relatively low formation costs; not only are there no capital minimums, but assigned capital is not even mandatory. Capital and earnings may be repatriated immediately without restriction.

Disadvantages All of the foreign parent corporation's assets—and not only its Argentine assets—are potentially at risk, because the parent firm's capital is considered to back the local operation. Also, branches are taxed in full as an entity; consequently, branches pay a "distribution" of profits tax sooner than do separately incorporated firms. Foreign companies operating branch offices in Argentina may experience occasional difficulties in dealing with cultural differences, as well as problems associated with local competitors.

7. Establish a separately incorporated subsidiary. Foreign corporations frequently operate in Argentina through a separately incorporated subsidiary rather than through a branch. Although both forms are recognized, the separately incorporated subsidiary places at risk only its locally assigned capital rather than the full capital of the parent. Corporations are regulated by a law effective throughout Argentina. Foreign firms considering establishing a foothold in Argentina are encouraged to investigate the tax and legal aspects of incorporation with legal counsel prior to making any final decisions. Refer to the "Business Entities & Formation" chapter, beginning on page 191, for more specific information on establishing subsidiaries in Argentina.

Advantages Corporations may be wholly foreign-owned or have local participation, thus being more flexible than branches of foreign corporations, which are wholly owned by the parent. As is the situation with branches, foreign capital and earnings may be repatriated immediately without restriction. Unlike branches of foreign corporations, a foreign (or, for that matter, even an Argentine) subsidiary's liability is limited to the assets owned by that subsidiary and not those of the parent company.

Disadvantages Establishing a subsidiary is considerably more costly than entering the market through any sort of local representative and as an option is, therefore, generally effectively limited to larger companies who are willing and able to make a major commitment of time and funds.

8. Do direct marketing. The costs of intermediaries can be avoided by direct contact of likely business and consumer customers. This method can be chosen by firms that supply particular products to specific markets. In recent years, some success has been achieved in Argentine markets through direct sales of such products as insurance, used medical equipment, big-ticket health care equipment, and some luxury products such as pleasure boats. Goods can be transferred more directly from a producer to the intended customers without the additional delay, difficulty, and cost of operating through intermediaries.

Advantages Direct marketing is particularly easy for manufacturers of highly specialized, technical products, because they can target consumers directly. For example, five hospitals in Argentina set the standards within the industry. Therefore, a sale of equipment to one of those hospitals serves to establish the supplier substantially within the market, which is relatively small and easy to target.

Some fairly standard products, such as some financial and insurance products, may also be sold via direct marketing. Mailings are often done in conjunction with banks or credit card companies or offered through professional associations.

Disadvantages Direct marketing is usually not the best means of selling a complex product that requires explanation, requires the buyer to select from a variety of options, or sells better when the buyer can see the actual item. This type of marketing is also only as effective as the quality of the mailing lists used. Also, direct sales often require a great deal of customer service support, and direct marketers must expect a high incidence of returns for refund, because the customer cannot fully judge the product prior to delivery.

9. Bid on public projects or procurement contracts. National, regional, and local official and government agencies purchase millions of dollars' worth of supplies, equipment, and services annually, and a sizable portion of such procurement is now being opened to bids from overseas suppliers. (Refer to page 43 of the "Opportunities" chapter for a discussion of public procurement.)

Advantages A successful bid can advance a product's reputation in Argentine markets. It can also result in new contacts in the private sector if the goods and services are open to public view.

Disadvantages Significant price concessions may be required in order for the bidder to be chosen over the competition. Some preferences for Argentine bidders may be allowed, and foreign companies may be further hampered by having to show that they can meet registration and import requirements, offer strict product guarantees, post bonds, and provide costly on-site follow-up services.

GETTING THE WORD OUT— ADVERTISING AND PROMOTIONAL CHANNELS IN ARGENTINA

Advertising expenditures in Argentina have increased substantially in recent years. Between 1990 and 1993 expenditures grew a by a phenomenal 257 percent, to US$2.75 billion. Moreover, despite attention which varies disproportionately among internal markets—particularly comparing Buenos Aires with the rest of the country—Argentine annual spending on advertising is still relatively low at about US$75 per capita, versus US$380 in the US. And with deregulation and a stable currency, advertising is becoming far more dynamic. There are several media for marketing products and services in Argentina, including radio and television, print, and a number of other creative means of attracting the general public's attention.

Television accounts for more than half of all advertising expenditures (55 percent); however, this kind of coverage is disproportionately expensive relative to alternative media, and represents a much lower percentage of the count of actual billings. Radio and the print media are also considered effective means of reaching Argentine consumers, and are considerably less expensive than television advertising.

The leading products advertised in Argentina in order of coverage are: (1) foods, (2) household articles, (3) graphic and editorial arts, and (4) non-alcoholic beverages. The biggest new set of advertisers in Argentina includes the financial institutions offering private pension fund management.

The method of advertising chosen by an exporter to Argentina will be determined to a great extent by the product or service offered, the intended market, and the exporter's advertising budget. It is also important to keep in mind that, unlike in advertising strategies in the US and elsewhere, less attention is paid to regional markets. Additionally, there is considerable disinclination on the part of many Argentine consumers to try new products, particularly within the lower income populations. The majority believe it is too risky to try a new product, particularly if the consumer is reasonably happy with the existing brand. Therefore, whatever advertising medium you choose, the advertisement will have to be highly persuasive and perhaps aggressive in order to chip away at the consumer's brand loyalty.

Media and Channels

Newspapers One of the main advertising channels available in Argentina is newspapers. Newspaper advertising accounts for roughly 13 percent of total advertising expenditures in Argentina; it effectively reaches the entire population. About 45 percent of all copies of daily papers are sold in the provinces and 55 percent in metropolitan Buenos Aires. In the provinces, advertising is very important to local papers, which account for between 79 and 96 percent of the print advertising market, depending on location (national papers distributed countrywide account for the remainder).

There are approximately 160 daily newspapers in circulation. Argentina's major national dailies are *Clarín*, *La Nación*, *La Prensa*, and *Ambito Financiero*. (Refer to page 352 of the "Important Addresses" chapter for addresses and telephone numbers.) *Clarín* and *La Nación* are the largest general circulation newspapers, with print runs roughly three to four times those of the more specialized business press titles, such as *Ambito Financiero* (which has a press run of approximately 70,000).

Magazines Magazine advertising represents

approximately 7 percent of total advertising expenditures. The leading general interest magazines is *Viva*, with an average press run of 1.15 million copies. The next largest such magazines are *Nueva* (600,000), *Magazine Semanal* (300,000), and *Nuestra* (180,000). Advertising costs are fairly expensive: in magazines, running as much as US$17,500 per page for the largest circulation publications and between US$8,000 to US$10,000 per page in second tier publications.

Television Nearly three-quarters of all advertising in Argentina is via television and radio. Some 55 percent of revenues from billings come from television, with an additional 4 percent from the rapidly growing cable sector. Television advertising starts at about US$4,000 for a 30-second spot—about US$133 per second. However, it is possible to negotiate lower prices. For example, Channel 13 has quoted a rate of US$58 per second and Channel 11 US$77 per second. Because there is more competition, national channels and large channels serving the Buenos Aires area may actually charge less than some provincial stations having a local monopoly.

There are about 470 television stations broadcasting in the country with various levels of power output. Argentina has roughly 9 million homes have television set. The average Argentine family watches four hours of television each day. Although many rural areas are still without electrical power—and few of these areas would be reached by existing television broadcasts anyway, this unserved segment accounts for only about 15 percent of the population. Argentine television viewers are among the best served and connected in Latin America. Nationwide 54 percent of households with television also have cable, compared to 13.2 percent in Mexico and 0.6 percent in Brazil.

Both the public and private sectors may operate television stations. There are even cable programs aimed especially at farmers, and some regional newspapers are banding together to sponsor cable channels, extending their franchise to another media. In 1995 Argentina is expected to account for 70 percent of the nearly US$2 billion in projected pay-TV revenue for all of Latin American. This explosion in pay-TV is partially the result of the removal of barriers to foreign investment. As recently as 1992 Argentina did not allow foreign investment in cable television systems. Currently, Argentina is considering enacting new laws permitting as much as 49 percent foreign ownership.

Because most Argentines in the larger cities are exposed to US and European television programming through cable television, many foreign products are clearly seen and often recognized. As a result, advertising and promotion activities are increasingly adapting US presentation methods to build on this recognition factor. It is important to

keep in mind that although television advertising is a highly effective method of reaching the consumer—particularly in the Buenos Aires market—it is also the most costly. (Refer to page 358 of the "Important Addresses" chapter for television station contact information.)

Radio With approximately 22,000,000 radio receivers in use in Argentina (one for every 1.5 Argentines), radio advertising is considered to be an effective method of advertising. It is an especially good way to reach segments of the population that lack access to television. Because power and effective range is somewhat limited, there are no truly national radio networks. However, more firms are offering programming services to small local firms, leading to more homogenized programming and service standards nationwide. Nevertheless, radio advertising is still generally aimed at the Buenos Aires market.

The public and private sectors operate more than 160 AM stations and 10 shortwave stations. During the last 10 years, there has been a major increase in the FM radio audience at the expense of the AM radio audience. Radio accounts for about 13 percent of all Argentine advertising billings. Although not as expensive as television, radio advertising can nevertheless be costly. For maximum benefit, advertising must be carefully targeted through stations that broadcast to the regions where the product is most likely to sell and to the audience most likely to purchase it.

Other Types of Advertising The remaining 8 percent of advertising billings represents a broad range of channels. Of this, only about 1 percent represents traditional outdoor advertising—billboards, posters, and signage—suggesting that perhaps Argentina has less visual pollution than some more developed countries. Advertising using trailers on feature films is fairly common, and some firms are experimenting with putting ad footage on videocassettes for sale or rental.

As noted, direct marketing is beginning to be used in Argentina to a greater extent. However, it is still a minor factor in advertising, and there is as yet little solid data to suggest whether or not it is effective. However, it is growing rapidly from this small base and represents the hottest new idea (or at least it did some months back).

Some agencies and practitioners are also experimenting with more sophisticated means of designing advertising messages. These include the gathering of more fine-grained psychographic data to assess the needs of customers; how customers perceive products; and the ability of products to satisfy such customer needs. The use of semiotics—the study of meanings—is also being investigated as an aid in constructing advertising that optimally conveys the desired, nuanced message.

Professional Help—Advertising Agencies and Public Relations Firms

Argentina has a number of advertising agencies and many management consultants that can assist in preparing and placing advertisements in various media. Most of these firms also offer market research services. Although the use of advertising agencies is far more developed in Argentina than in some Latin American countries, those in the market for such services would also do well to investigate public relations firms, some of which are even better established. Given the relative lack of development in distribution, advertising, and media channels, firms skilled at promoting ideas or other firms (rather than specific products) may be able to offer some insights and creative ways of getting the word out about you and your product. The leading agencies are members of the Asociación Argentina de Agencias de Publicidad (Argentine Association of Publicity Agencies). There are also many foreign agencies that have opened Argentine offices primarily to cater to existing clients but which are now branching out to serve new and local clients as well. (Refer to page 345 of the "Important Addresses" chapter for a list of major advertising agencies, both Argentine and foreign.)

OVERCOMING TRADE BARRIERS

The government has done much to open the Argentine economy to international markets in recent years. Although Argentina has lowered tariff barriers and virtually eliminated nontariff barriers, foreign businesses will still encounter some tariffs, fees, taxes, and restrictions—not to mention linguistic and cultural differences. Thus it is important to familiarize yourself at least with the few surmountable hurdles that all companies interested in participating in the global marketplace must face.

Import Regulations The government divides tariffs into three categories, which it applies to the CIF (cost, insurance, freight) value of the goods in Argentina. The maximum rate of 20 percent is applied on all consumer goods; 5 percent to 15 percent on most industrial imports and raw materials; and 5 percent to 10 percent on agricultural products. No tariff is levied on capital goods, but some automotive products must pay a 22 percent tariff. In addition to the tariffs, various fees and taxes are applied. Now that the 10 percent statistics fee has been removed, the main additional item is the value-added tax (VAT)—which was recently raised to 21 percent from 18 percent. A variety of other specific fees and levies may apply. The only remaining substantive nontariff barrier is a quota system applicable to auto and auto parts imports,

as well as to certain paper products.

The Argentine Merchandise Marking Act requires that imported goods be inspected for country-of-origin marking during customs clearance. Argentine regulations require metric labeling for all packaged products. Samples brought into Argentina are admitted free of duty, provided that they have no commercial value. If the samples do have value, bond must be posted to cover the implied duty. Such bonds are usually for a period of 90 days. Upon reexportation of dutiable samples covered, the bond is refunded. Advertising materials—except for individual specimens—is subject to duty when imported to Argentina. (Refer to the "Import Policy & Procedures" chapter, beginning on page 77, for more information.)

Linguistic and Cultural Differences Although English has become the dominant language of international business and many Argentines operate quite comfortably in at least one European language other than Spanish, Argentina remains a Spanish-speaking country. It is therefore, imperative that foreign businesspeople expect and prepare to conduct business in Spanish, and it is to their advantage to become at least functional in that language. It is also important for the foreign businessperson to learn something about the history, culture, and contemporary situation in Argentina. They must remember that the Argentine market is not just a generic extension of Latin America. Rather, Argentina is a complex mixture of both Latin American and European influences that has developed its own unique tradition, one that must be dealt with and respected on its own terms.

HELPING YOUR COMPANY LEARN TO LOVE EXPORTING

Eight In-House Rules

1. Adopt a global strategy. Most companies become international by a haphazard evolutionary process rather than according to strategic choice. Some companies are first attracted to foreign markets by unsolicited export orders; others respond to specific opportunities. Yet others consciously plan to develop supplies of resources, acquire foreign technology, achieve greater production efficiency or lower cost through foreign operations, or boost sales by entering international markets.

The basic reasons for having a global strategy are: most markets extend beyond the often arbitrary boundaries of a single country; and the competition that ultimately determines performance is not confined to individual locations and country markets. To remain—or become—competitive, the strategic horizon for most companies must, therefore, be set to take in both domestic and foreign threats and opportunities.

2. Eliminate as much guesswork as possible. You cannot become successful at exporting if you arbitrarily pick an overseas market, and limit your business possibilities to your company's existing products or services, just to "see what will happen." Instead, a company must seek to identify areas of probable demand (within Argentina or other foreign markets) where its capability for performance against existing or potential competitors is greatest, even though the specific customer needs that are to be met may differ from those the company has been meeting in the past.

Some important questions you must answer before taking the plunge into international marketing are:

- Do you need to make changes to your product?
- Who are the potential buyers, and how do you find them?
- How will your buyer find you?
- Do you need to advertise; exhibit at a trade fair; take some other specific action?
- How many different products can you sell?
- How much can you expect to sell?
- At what price and what margin can you expect and can you afford to sell?

3. Get management support, and stick with the program. It is imperative that your company have a long-term commitment to export marketing. Successful export marketing is not realized as quickly as successful domestic sales. Additionally, there are many hurdles to overcome—personal, political, cultural, and legal, among others. It will be at least six, maybe nine months before you and your overseas associates can even begin to expect to see glimmers of success; in some cases, it may be even longer. Remember to be patient and keep a close, but not suffocating, watch on your international marketing efforts. Above all else, give the venture a chance to develop. More than a few companies have cut their international marketing and advertising budgets because of premature and misunderstood evaluations of international marketing results and potential. Again, you must commit at least to the medium term, if not the long haul.

4. Avoid an internal tug-of-war. Consultants report that one of the biggest obstacles to successful export marketing in larger companies is internal conflict between divisions within a company. Domestic marketing battles international marketing, and each is also warring with engineering; moreover, everybody fights with the bean counters (accounting people). All the complex strategies, relationship building, and legal and cultural accommodations that export marketing requires mean that support and teamwork are crucial to the success of the venture.

5. Stick with export marketing even when business booms at home. Exporting is not something to fall back on when your domestic market falters. Nor is it something to put on the back burner when business is booming at home. It is difficult to ease your way into exporting. All the complex strategies, relationship building, legal and cultural accommodations, financial and management investment, and general blood, sweat, and tears that export marketing requires means that a clear commitment is necessary from the beginning. Any other attitude as good as dooms the venture from the start, and you may as well forget it. We can not overstress this aspect: take the long-range view or don't play at all. Decide that you are going to export and that you are in it for the long haul as a viable, moneymaking, full-fledged strategic division within your company.

6. Become personally familiar with your customers and distributors. Whoever is responsible for export sales within your company must become personally familiar with customers and distributors to be successful in the long run. Anything that acts as filter between you and your customers is negative.

7. Get expert assistance and advice. Getting expert assistance is very important, and it doesn't need to come from expensive consultants. An exporter can find out from their own client information about competitors and complementary producers. The real challenge is knowing how to ask the right questions.

8. Respect your overseas market. No matter what product or service you are exporting, you must respect your overseas customers and their culture. Once this is accomplished you may realize that your product needs to be further fine-tuned or tailored to truly serve the local market. This may involve altering the product itself or simply repackaging it. Whatever changes need to be made, the benefits usually outweigh the costs.

Business Entities & Formation

TYPES OF BUSINESS ENTERPRISES

Argentina's Commercial Companies Law, Civil Code, and Code of Commerce provide for a variety of business forms, all of which are available to foreign investors under Argentina's liberal foreign investment laws. Investors are free to structure their business activities using corporations, partnerships, joint ventures, branch offices, franchises, sole proprietorships, or simple agency or licensing agreements. An investor's choice of entity will hinge on numerous factors and circumstances, such as the required degree of control over the business, the acceptable amount of government supervision, the anticipated duration of an investment, the acceptable degree of exposure to liability, and preferred tax treatment. (Refer to the "Taxation" chapter for a discussion of tax treatment.)

The most common organizational forms that foreign investors use are the stock corporation (*sociedad anónima,* or S.A.), and the branch office (*sucursal*). Use of joint ventures and franchise agreements has also become increasingly common in recent years. Other business forms, including the limited liability company (*sociedad de responsabilidad limitada,* or S.R.L.), the general partnership (*sociedad colectiva*), the limited partnership (*sociedad en comandita*), and the sole proprietorship (*empresa unipersonal*), are usually less desirable because they do not offer owners or investors desired tax treatment or optimal limits on liability.

CONTENTS

Sociedad Anónima (Corporation)

An Argentine corporation, or S.A., is defined as a combination of individuals or entities contributing capital for the purpose of producing or exchanging products or services, then dividing the profits and losses among themselves. The corporation's most salient feature is limitation of liability—once a business is properly incorporated, it has a legal existence separate from its investors, and those investors are not liable for the obligations of the business beyond the amounts they have invested. Corporations are formed in accord with Argentina's Commercial Companies Law, No. 19,550.

The S.A., preferred by most large and medium-sized businesses contemplating substantial or long-term investment in Argentina, is the only business form that can offer shares of capital to the public. Any S.A. that does not offer shares to the public is referred to as being "closed."

An S.A. may engage in any legal activity; however, its purpose must be clearly stated in the S.A.'s articles of incorporation.

Capital Ownership interests are represented by shares of stock ("share deeds"). At least two shareholders are required to form an S.A. The minimum amount of capital required to start an S.A. is US$12,000. Although there is no maximum limit on capital contributions, if capitalization exceeds US$2,100,000, an S.A. faces greater government supervision than does a smaller S.A. Capital stock must be fully subscribed prior to formation of an S.A., and a minimum of 25 percent of the capital value must be paid in concurrently with corporate formation. Subscribers must pay for the rest of their share of subscribed capital within two years. If a subscriber uses assets other than cash to pay for stock, the subscriber must contribute the entire amount when the corporation is formed. Stockholders who default on payments for initial capital face liability for interest and damages arising from such defaults.

KEY REGULATORS AND REGISTRIES

Inspección General de Justicia (IGJ, or Office of the Inspector General of Justice) This agency is the chief government body regulating corporations and branches incorporated or otherwise established in the Federal Capital. Administrative or judicial agencies approve commercial formations at the provincial level elsewhere in the country. The IGJ, or its provincial equivalent, approves applications for the formation of corporations and the establishment of branches. Approval is usually a formality, absent some glaring oddity or illegality about a proposed entity. Technically, the IGJ retains the authority to request any information about a regulated entity, examine any books, attend any meetings, and—should it find improprieties—file accusations with administrative authorities and courts. In practice, the IGJ only exercises its monitoring authority when it approves initial articles and revisions of these, approves changes in capital, and requires filing of annual financial statements.

The IGJ, as well as other regulatory agencies, may monitor a corporation more closely if (1) corporate capital exceeds US$2,100,000, (2) the corporation's shares are publicly traded, (3) the corporation is controlled by the state, (4) the corporation operates a financial business, (5) the corporation operates a government concession or public utility, or (6) the corporation is controlled by a corporation falling within any of these categories.

The functions formerly performed by the Public Registry of Commerce—that is, the registration of all businesses, including sole proprietorships—for businesses located in the Federal Capital have been performed by the IGJ since 1980.

Public Registries of Commerce (Commercial Registries) These registries are maintained by commercial courts located in each province. The filing of documents—such as articles of incorporation, branch licenses, powers of attorney, partnership deeds, and joint venture agreements—in these registries usually constitutes the final step in the formation of a business entity located outside the Federal Capital.

Comisión Nacional de Valores (CNV, or National Securities Commission) The CNV authorizes and regulates public offerings of capital shares and other corporate securities, and maintains regulatory authority over mergers and acquisitions.

Banco Central de la República Argentina (BCRA, or Central Bank) The BCRA oversees the financial and banking industries.

During its existence, an S.A. can increase its authorized capital by as much as five times the original amount without altering its bylaws. To receive approval for a higher increase in capital, all previous stock issues must have been fully subscribed, the S.A.'s bylaws must allow for the increase, and the S.A. must meet various publication and registration requirements. The S.A. must first offer the new shares to existing stockholders before any outside parties are eligible to buy. If a new offering is not fully subscribed, those who did subscribe may incur liabilities for obligations connected with the offering.

An S.A. can also reduce capital, provided stockholders convene an extraordinary meeting and vote to do so for cause. To reduce its capital, an S.A. must comply with auditing requirements and other measures intended to protect creditors, unless the S.A. has excess profits or cash reserves sufficient to repurchase its shares. Reductions in capital are required by law if the losses of the S.A. amount to more than 50 percent of its stated capital, and the shareholders refuse to subscribe enough new capital to raise the existing capital above the 50 percent level.

Although the Commercial Companies Law authorizes the issuance of corporate debentures, these have never been a popular means of raising funds among Argentine corporations. An S.A. is more apt to issue negotiable corporate bonds, which can be denominated in any currency. Bonds can carry floating, specific, or general guarantees and can be guaranteed by banks and financial institutions. Such bonds do not require specific authorization in the bylaws—except for certain convertible issues—but can be issued based on a resolution voted at a stockholders' meeting, either as publicly offered or privately placed securities. Many of these bonds are listed on the Argentine Stock Exchange (Bolsa de Comercio de Buenos Aires).

An S.A. is required by law to pay 5 percent of its annual profits into a special reserve until the total reserve fund equals 20 percent of the corporation's stated capital.

Share Characteristics Although different classes of shares or share deeds are allowed, all shares must have the same par value, stated in Argentine currency. Shares may be either nominative—registered and issued in the name of the holder—or issued in bearer form; shares may be either negotiable or nonnegotiable. Stock certificates may represent more than one share of stock. Each share of common stock typically entitles its holder the right to one vote in stockholders' meetings. In a "closed" S.A., bylaws can provide for classes of stock in which each share carries as many as five votes. An S.A. can also issue preferred stock, which usually entitles holders to first rights on dividends or first rights to distributions of assets on liquidation, although preferred stock usually has no voting rights. An S.A. must keep a stock book, or "Registry of Shares," recording all shares issued, names of subscribers, and all stock certificates transfers.

Under Argentina's liberal foreign investment laws, which guarantee foreigners equal treatment with local investors, virtually no limits are imposed on the extent of foreign ownership of an S.A.'s shares.

Management Provisions for the corporate governance of an S.A. are set forth in the articles of incorporation, a draft of which is approved by shareholder vote at the initial organizational meeting. (*See* "Formation and Registration of Business Operations" on page 197.)

Directors Shareholders elect a board of directors, who manage the general business affairs of the corporation. Directors may serve for terms of up to three years and can be reelected indefinitely. Directors do not have to be shareholders, but they do have to give a guarantee—the amount of which can be nominal—pledging that they will fulfill their duties as set forth in the S.A.'s articles of incorporation. While directors do not have to be Argentine nationals, the majority of directors on an S.A.'s board must be Argentine residents, and all directors must maintain a legal Argentine domicile.

A quorum of the board (50 percent plus one of its members) must meet every three months. The directors appoint corporate officers, and may themselves serve as officers. Directors face personal liability to shareholders if they commit illegal acts or acts that are ultra vires (beyond the scope of the authority stated in the corporation's charter), or if they fail to comply with legal duties of loyalty and diligence.

Directors' total compensation cannot exceed 25 percent of the S.A.'s profits in any year in which the rest of the profits are distributed as dividends. This limit is reduced to 5 percent of the corporate profits in years in which no dividends are distributed. Amounts exceeding these percentages, as well as any compensation in years when an S.A. sustains a loss, may be paid only if specifically approved by shareholders at a general meeting.

Shareholders Ordinary shareholder meetings are held annually to consider directors' reports and performance, financial statements, supervisory committee reports designed to monitor corporate management and finances, and any other pertinent matters. Meetings must be preceded by the publication of an official notice, including an agenda—and description—of matters to be considered at the meeting. The notice must be given at least ten days in advance of the meeting and must be published for at least five days. Extraordinary shareholder meetings may be requested by shareholders controlling more than 5 percent of the S.A.'s capital, or by the board of directors or a supervisory committee if either deems it necessary.

Directors, members of supervisory committees, and other managers are required to attend shareholder meetings. During meetings shareholders typically determine the distribution of profits, elect directors, determine directors' fees, and elect members of other supervisory committees. Shareholders may send proxies to meetings to speak and vote in their stead (directors and other S.A. employees are not allowed to serve as proxies). At an ordinary meeting, shareholders controlling 50 percent of the capital of the S.A. constitute a quorum; at an extraordinary meeting, the quorum requirement is raised to 60 percent.

In either type of meeting, resolutions can pass by a simple majority of those present and voting. In some circumstances—such as when an S.A. contemplates a fundamental change in its purpose or a dramatic expansion of the company's business—minority shareholders disagreeing with the decisions of the majority are entitled to withdraw from the S.A. and to take payment for their equity. Such payments are based on the most recent certified balance sheet for the S.A.

Dividends Shareholders have the authority to determine the distributions of the profits of the S.A. by majority vote at the corporation's annual meeting. No profits can be distributed until all reserve requirements have been met and all prior losses covered. Directors and supervisory committees face personal liability for improper distribution of dividends. A corporation cannot recover dividends that were improperly distributed to shareholders if the shareholders received the dividends in good faith.

Statutory Auditors Articles of incorporation usually provide for company auditors, who are appointed by shareholders at ordinary annual meetings. Members of the committee of auditors (*síndicos*) must be lawyers or accountants who are residents of Argentina. Every S.A. with capital exceeding US $2,100,000, as well as banks and other financial institutions, must appoint a committee of at least three *síndicos* and alternate *síndicos* (*comisión fiscalizadora* or *sindicatura*).

The *síndico* examines and verifies the corporation's books and documents; verifies its liquid assets; monitors its compliance with laws, regulations, articles of incorporation, bylaws, and shareholder resolutions; attends and voices opinions in shareholders' and directors' meetings; prepares written reports on the corporation's financial condition, presenting these to shareholders at annual meetings; calls extraordinary shareholders' meetings whenever necessary; and may have other duties as well. *Síndicos* may be liable to shareholders if they fail to discharge their duties conscientiously and may also be liable to directors if such a failure results in the directors taking improper actions that otherwise would have been avoided.

Shareholders may additionally elect a surveillance committee (*consejo de vigilancia*) consisting of from three to fifteen shareholders to monitor corporate management. If such a committee is appointed in place of *síndicos,* the committee must appoint independent outside auditors to prepare the required annual financial reports for the shareholders' meetings (and to comply with reporting requirements).

In smaller corporations that choose not to appoint *síndicos* or surveillance committees, shareholders must elect alternate directors to perform similar functions. Shareholders in all corporations retain the right to examine the corporation's books and documents, and are entitled to access any records.

Books and Records All forms of business in Argentina, including the S.A., must keep two account books: a Journal, containing summary entries covering all official transactions, and an Inventory and Financial Statements Book, containing official detailed, itemized, annual income statements, balance sheets, and other financial statements. An S.A. must also keep books containing the minutes of directors' and shareholders' meetings, a Registry of Share Ownership, and a Record of Attendance at Shareholders' Meetings. The exact format of these books is important: they must be bound and "rubricated" (marked) by the Inspección General de Justicia (Inspector General of Justice, or IGJ) if the firm is located in the Federal Capital or a local commercial court if located in the provinces. All official records must be kept in Spanish. An S.A. must prepare annual financial statements, which must be certified by an independent auditor qualified under Argentina's professional accounting standards.

Government Supervision All corporations face some degree of government supervision, in that applications for approval of corporate formation, initial and revised articles of incorporation, annual financial statements, and other documents must be filed with various agencies. (*See* "Formation and Registration of Business Operations" on page 197.) The IGJ is the chief administrative body regulating corporations in Federal Capital; other important regulators include the Comisión Nacional de Valores (National Securities Commission or CNV), and Banco Central de la República Argentina (Argentina's Central Bank). Corporations with capital in excess of US$2,100,000, corporations whose securities are sold to the public, state-controlled corporations, corporations involved in financial businesses, and corporations operating utilities or government concessions face heightened government regulatory requirements.

Liquidation The law requires that a corporation liquidate its assets and distribute them to shareholders when its losses are equivalent to its capital. Shareholders can also initiate voluntary liquidation of a corporation and distribution of its assets by passing a resolution at an extraordinary shareholders' meeting.

Shareholders' rights during liquidation are prescribed in the corporation's articles of incorporation. Typically a majority of the shareholders can appoint a liquidator, or get a court to do so, and are given some specified time period during which they can file with the court any objections to the liquidator's distribution of any corporate assets. During liquidation shareholders are entitled to inspect various financial statements and other disclosures of the corporation's assets and liabilities. Any residual assets are generally distributed to shareholders in proportion to their holdings.

Sucursales (Branch Offices)

After the stock corporation, the *sucursal* (or branch office) is probably the most popular form used by foreigners doing business in Argentina. Although the formation of a branch office requires a number of formalities (*see* "Formation and Registration of Business Operations" on page 197), it generally involves less expense than formation of an S.A. Unlike an S.A., a branch is governed primarily by the laws of its home country, which set most of the rules governing its business operations. Many foreign businesses with significant presences in Argentina prefer to incorporate a subsidiary S.A. rather than establish a branch office, because the only assets exposed to liability in Argentina are those of the separately incorporated Argentine subsidiary. Where the branch form is used, the assets of the entire foreign business, both in and outside of Argentina, could potentially be at risk.

To establish a branch, a foreign company must prove its good standing in its home country, have a domicile in Argentina, and assign capital to the Argentine branch, although no minimum amount of capital is required. The management of a branch is vested in a representative who must be appointed in the branch's deed of formation, a document formally recorded by the IGJ if located in the Federal Capital or a commercial court if located in the provinces. This representative must have full authority to transact all business and handle all affairs for the branch, including receipt of legal papers. A broad power of attorney granting such authority must be filed along with the branch's deed of formation.

The parent company must keep separate accounting records for its Argentine branch operations, and the branch must file annual accounting statements, prepared in the same manner as those required for corporations, with the pertinent Argentine government agencies (usually the IGJ). These statements must be certified by an Argentine public accountant.

Sociedad de Responsabilidad Limitada (Limited Liability Companies)

The limited liability company, or *sociedad de responsabilidad limitada* (S.R.L.), is essentially a limited partnership, involving a minimum of two and a maximum of fifty partners who subscribe and pay for capital, which is divided into equal "quotas." A partner's liability for the obligations of an S.R.L. is limited to the amount the partner paid for the quotas held. Because it is considered to be an association of natural persons, the S.R.L. form is available only to individuals; an S.A. or foreign corporation—which is a legal but not a natural person—cannot be a quotaholder in an S.R.L.

An S.R.L. with assets of less than US$2,100,000 is easier to form and administer than an S.A., and, generally speaking, an S.R.L. of this size faces less regulation and government supervision than an S.A. However, quota transfers or other interests in these entities are typically subject to onerous bylaw restrictions, such as unanimous consent of the partners, which can make any changes in ownership or management extremely unwieldy. While smooth operation of any business entity is contingent on harmony among the partners, an S.A. can arguably weather changes in personnel among investors and management far more easily. In Argentina, S.R.L.s have historically been most popular as vehicles for smaller, family-owned enter-prises. S.R.L.s are taxed as partnerships (that is, the entity itself is not taxed, and all revenues and expenses flow through to the individual partners for tax reporting). Thus an S.R.L. may be the entity of choice for foreign investors who wish to have income taxed in their home country as income derived from a foreign partnership in order to avoid double corporate taxation.

The words *"sociedad de responsabilidad limitada"* must always follow the name of an S.R.L.; otherwise the entity's managers may incur full liability for the entity's actions.

Capital No specific minimum amount of capital is required to form an S.R.L. However, the capital must be fully subscribed as of the time the S.R.L. is formed. At least 25 percent of the capital must be paid in by the partners at formation, and the rest of the capital must be paid up within two years. If quotaholders contribute their share in some form other than cash, this must be paid in full at the time the S.R.L. is formed. The incorporation contract between the S.R.L. partners can authorize the company to issue additional capital quotas in the future, with the condition that a majority of the partners approve the issue.

Quotas are of equal value and entitle quota-holders to equal voting rights; their transfer is regulated by the partnership contract recorded in the deed of incorporation and bylaws of the S.R.L. In the absence of specific alternate provisions in the partnership contract governing quota transfers, any transfer will require the approval of three-quarters of the partners. Dissenting partners are entitled to judicial review of any transfer.

Management The details of S.R.L. governance are set forth in the partnership contract. As partners, quotaholders hold ultimate authority over the entity. Typically, partners appoint a manager or managers, who have roughly the same duties as S.A. directors.

Quotaholder meetings, both ordinary and extraordinary, are governed either by the partnership contract or, in the absence of special provisions in that document, by the same set of rules as S.A. stockholder meetings in the Commercial Companies Law. Quotaholders typically meet annually to review financial statements and deal with such issues as the profit distribution, quota transfers, manager appointments, and partnership contract changes. Usually more than a simple majority vote is required to change the partnership contract. Minority quotaholders who dissent from certain fundamental changes in business operations usually have rights similar to dissenting minority shareholders in an S.A., that is, to withdraw and receive a distribution of their share of the S.R.L.

Statutory Auditors, Books, and Records
Syndics and surveillance committees are appointed by quotaholders and serve as in-house auditors. Books and records of S.R.L. meetings and transactions must be kept in the same form and manner as corporate books and records (*see* "Books and Records" on page 194). If the capital of an S.R.L. exceeds US $2,100,000, the company becomes subject to all the rules and government supervision faced by an S.A. of similar size.

Liquidation An S.R.L. must liquidate its assets if its losses equal its capital. Absent liquidation in these circumstances, the quotaholders become jointly and severally liable for any of the obligations of the S.R.L.

Sociedades (Partnerships)

In addition to the S.R.L., Argentine law recognizes four other types of partnerships: the *sociedad colectiva,* a general partnership that engages in commercial activities; the *sociedad civil,* a general partnership that does not conduct commercial activities; and two types of limited partnerships, the *sociedad en comandita por acciones* and the *sociedad en comandita simple.*

In general, foreign investors do not generally use partnerships because they offer fewer protections from liability than does an S.A. or S.R.L.; they also require a high degree of cooperation and unity among the partners. Moreover, because partnerships are considered associations of natural persons, an S.A. or foreign corporation cannot serve as a partner.

Limited partnerships may be preferable to general partnerships because only the former offer some limitation of liability. For foreign investors, limited partnerships are the favored vehicles to take advantage of foreign partnership tax treatment in their home country on income derived from an Argentine entity. The *sociedad civil,* or civil partnership, is governed by the Civil Code, and is generally used by associations of Argentine professionals, such as lawyers and accountants. This form is not used by businesses engaged in commercial activities.

Sociedad Colectiva In a general partnership, governed by the Commercial Companies Law, all partners are jointly and severally liable for all of the partnership's liabilities. Provisions governing capital contributions, management of the partnership, changes in its members, and liquidation of the partnership are usually recorded in a partnership agreement. The Commercial Companies Law establishes standard rules governing partnerships that fail to provide for such matters in an agreement.

In the absence of a provision in the agreement specifying arrangements for management responsibilities, any partner can conduct business on behalf of the entire partnership. If an agreement designates several partners as managers without specifically enumerating their duties, they can similarly take any action for purposes of administering the partnership's business. The Commercial Companies Law provides for the removal of any manager or partner at any time for any reason by a majority vote of the partners, but in general partnership agreements require more than a simple majority to unseat a partner. The Commercial Companies Law also provides that modifications to a partnership agreement require the unanimous approval of the partners. The approval of the holders of a majority of the partnership's capital is required for other resolutions. A partner cannot take any action that involves competition with the partnership without the express unanimous consent of the remaining partners.

Sociedad en Comandita Limited partnerships have two kinds of partners: *comanditarios* (limited or silent partners), whose liability is limited to the amount of their capital contribution; and *comanditados* (general or active partners), who face unlimited liability.

Two types of *sociedades en comandita* exist. The first, the *sociedad en comandita por acciones* (S.C.A.), mirrors the S.A. in that the capital held by the limited partners consists of shares with equal par value. The second type, the *sociedad en comandita simple* (S.C.S.), is similar to the S.R.L. in that the limited partner's capital consists of equal portions that are not issued as shares. In general, the same rules that govern an S.A. govern *sociedades en comandita por acciones*, while the rules that govern an S.R.L. cover *sociedades en comandita simples.*

Capital The partnership agreement—recorded in a partnership deed—stipulates the amounts of capital to which limited and active partners subscribe. In the S.C.A., all shares of capital must have an equal par value. An S.C.A. can offer shares having different classes and status, similar to preferred and common shares, but only limited (never active) partners can own such shares. An S.C.A. must comply with the same reserve requirements established for an S.A.

Management As in all partnerships, provisions for management should be set forth in the partnership agreement. Generally, only the active or general partners handle the administration of the partnership's affairs, although the agreement may call for a third party manager. Limited partners cannot play any active role in management without losing their silent partner status and thus their shield from liability. However, they are allowed to inspect partnership records and to voice opinions on partnership business at meetings of the partners.

The partnership agreement governs procedures for partners' meetings and voting rights. Meetings are held annually to consider financial statements, distribution of profits, management performance, and other business. Both active and limited partners are entitled to vote in meetings. For purposes of establishing a quorum and voting rights, active partners are considered to have designated amounts of capital divided into shares similar to those held by the limited partners.

Statutory Auditors, Books, and Records An S.C.A. must appoint *síndicos* in the same manner as an S.A., complying with the same strictures for the books, records, and annual financial statements of an S.A. An S.C.S. must follow the rules applied to an S.R.L.

Liquidation The partnership agreement should provide a mechanism that allows the partnership to survive the loss of a partner, whether through death, insolvency, or voluntary departure. The agreement usually also sets forth conditions under which liquidation is mandatory, such as when a partnership's losses equal its capital, as well as processes for voluntary liquidation. In the absence of a specific provision in the agreement, liquidation can be achieved only through the unanimous approval of the partners.

Agrupaciones de Colaboración and Uniones Transitorias (Joint Ventures)

With the liberalization of Argentina's foreign investment laws, many outside investors have focused their attention on gaining alliances with Argentine businesses that have ongoing operations and in-place infrastructure. Joint ventures of temporary partnerships between foreign companies and existing Argentine companies have become increasingly common. This type of organization is also playing an important role in the massive privatizations that have been occurring in Argentina in recent years. Such ventures provide a convenient form in which various companies can cooperate in making joint bids for projects available from the Argentine government.

Argentine corporate law explicitly recognizes two kinds of joint venture: *agrupaciones de colaboración* (temporary partnerships) and *uniones transitorias de empresas* (temporary unions of companies or U.T.E.s). The temporary partnership usually involves a contemplated longer term relationship between participants who wish to develop continuing mutual business activities. The temporary union is a joint venture designed for a specific task of limited duration.

Although provisions in the Commercial Companies Law specifically address rules governing these organizations, neither form is considered a legal entity separate from its members. Thus members face unlimited liability for the venture's obligations, and they must operate in their own names. Participants in joint ventures are subject to some registration requirements (*see* "Formation and Registration of Business Operations" on page 197), and they must establish a domicile in Argentina. On the other hand, joint ventures are subject to few formal requirements concerning capitalization, management, and dissolution. Contractual agreements among the participants govern these matters.

Franchises

Argentina's Commercial Code recognizes and protects franchise contracts. Argentine contract, licensing, and trademark laws (refer to the "Business Law" chapter, beginning on page 215, for a discussion of Argentine commercial law) govern most aspects of such arrangements, including transfers of knowledge to franchisees, supply of equipment, sales methods, trade names, and degrees of franchisor control over franchise operation. Foreign franchisors should draft franchise agreements carefully to clarify all of the rights and obligations of both parties. Special care should be taken with respect to agreement provisions in anticipation of the bankruptcy or other commercial failure of either party because Argentine law does not clearly cover the rights, responsibilities, and liabilities of parties in such situations.

Empresa Unipersonales (Sole Proprietorships)

In an *empresa unipersonal* (sole proprietorship) all business assets are owned by an individual, who is wholly liable for business obligations. While this form is available to foreigners who reside in Argentina, and involves few formalities, it is usually of minimal interest because of the unlimited exposure to liability. If a nonresident foreigner wishes to establish a sole proprietorship in Argentina, the foreigner must appoint a resident representative. Such an appointment requires a clear agency agreement, as well as the observation of all relevant Argentine labor laws.

FORMATION AND REGISTRATION

Formation and Registration of Business Operations

At a minimum, businesses in Argentina must register with the appropriate authorities before commencing business operations. The formation of many business entities also requires prior government approval, although under the government's liberal investment regime such approval is usually given as a matter of course. This section outlines the procedures and documentation required to form and register most types of business entities in Argentina. Legal provisions covering formation and registration are contained in Argentina's Commercial Companies Law, No. 19,550, and Foreign Investment Law, No. 21,382.

Argentina's permissive foreign investment laws are premised on the basic concept that foreign investors are entitled to the same treatment as that given Argentine nationals, and this guarantee includes foreign investors' rights to establish any form of business available to Argentines for nearly any commercial purpose. The Argentine government takes this guarantee seriously, and it has solicited vast amounts of foreign capital to support its economic programs during recent years. Thus foreign investors considering the establishment of Argentine business entities are relatively unlikely to encounter administrative resistance, invisible barriers, or biased treatment— as has been the case at times in the past—as they establish commercial entities in Argentina.

Although the rules and regulations governing formation and registration include streamlined procedures designed to encourage foreign investors to establish businesses in Argentina, investors should bear in mind that formal entry in local commercial registries can nevertheless be a complicated process. Notaries and local judges, whose approvals are required, play large roles in the authentication and acknowledgment of necessary documents. (Refer to "Notaries Public (Escribanos Públicos)" on page 234 of the "Business Law" chapter for a discussion of notaries and their importance in Argentina.) Investors' activities will also require contact with government agencies, and, given Argentina's complex federal structure and the extent of organizational changes in Argentine administrative bodies during recent years, it may not always be clear which agencies, courts, or registers play a role in regulatory approval and supervision of particular businesses and types of business entities. Setting up a business in Argentina could require that an investor go beyond simple compliance with stated procedures, as well as require interpretation of Argentine laws and regulations.

Thus it is essential to obtain legal and accounting advice from professionals in Argentina who are familiar with the federal and local government structure and who know what the regulatory requirements and procedures are and how they are implemented. With such assistance, investors can structure their companies to maximize compliance with laws and regulations while minimizing exposure to regulatory agencies.

(Refer to the "Important Addresses" chapter, beginning on page 315, for partial listings of government agencies and legal and accounting firms in Argentina.)

With some knowledge of formation and registration procedures, investors establishing businesses in Argentina should be able to monitor the progress and status of required agency approvals and filings, ensure that the process is not sidetracked, and identify any additional requirements in a timely manner. Note that all submissions must be in Spanish, and any original documents not in Spanish must be accompanied by a Spanish translation made by a public translator.

Procedures—Argentine Corporations A minimum of two founders, or promoters, both of whom must have a legal Argentine domicile for purposes of the organization of the S.A., must complete the following steps:

- Call an organizational meeting, at which agreed-upon capital is subscribed and paid, and during which a majority of subscribers approve a board of directors, a syndic, and articles of incorporation. The articles must include:
  — identification of all shareholders;
  — the corporation's name and domicile;
  — indication of the corporation's specific purpose;
  — the amount of the corporation's capital, and each shareholder's capital contribution;
  — the organization of management and inhouse auditing committees, and rules for shareholder meetings;
  — rules for distributions of profits and losses;
  — provisions establishing shareholder rights and obligations to each other and third parties; and
  — such other provisions, such as those governing operation, dissolution, and liquidation, as are desired.
- Record the minutes of the organizational meeting and the articles in a deed of the inaugural meeting. This deed must be notarized.
- Publish a summary of the articles of incorporation in Argentina's official gazette (the *Boletín Oficial*).
- Submit for approval the deed of the inaugural meeting, together with a copy of the publication of the articles, to the Inspección General de Justicia (IGJ), the government agency responsible for regulating corporations.

If the corporation's shares are to be offered to the public, the promoters must follow the same steps, but must also take the following actions prior to the organizational meeting:
- Prepare and sign a prospectus, which contains

proposed articles and bylaws, amounts of capital to be subscribed and paid in, share characteristics, the corporation's object, and any other information required by the Commercial Companies Law. (Refer to the "Business Law" chapter, beginning on page 215, for a more detailed description of prospectus contents).

- File the prospectus with the IGJ and obtain that body's approval.
- Submit to the Comisión Nacional de Valores (National Securities Commission, or CNV) the application to offer its shares to the public.
- Establish a contract with a bank, which will send an agent to the inaugural meeting as an official representative of future capital subscribers.
- Arrange for an IGJ official to preside at the inaugural meeting.

Most of the important documents referred to above, including the deed of the inaugural meeting, the prospectus, and the articles of incorporation, must be formalized by a notary public.

Corporate existence is deemed to begin as soon as subscribers have paid in 25 percent of the capital and the publication and registration are complete. During the interval between the inaugural meeting and final registration with the IGJ, a corporation can operate as long as the words en formación are appended to its name. However, limitations on the liability of directors and shareholders will not apply until registration is complete.

The formation process can take from two weeks to two months for a "closed" corporation and about a month longer for a corporation offering shares to the public. The cost of formation consists of publication charges (about US$200), notarial fees (charged at scaled rates, approximating 0.5 percent of subscribed capital), other professional fees (accountants and attorneys), and a stamp tax assessed on subscribed capital (this tax varies by jurisdiction; in the Federal District of Buenos Aires, the tax is 1 percent of subscribed capital). Total fees, including statutory books, but excluding the stamp tax and professional fees, approximate US$1,000 to US$2,000.

During its existence, an S.A. pays annual registration fees to the IGJ. The amount of these fees depends on the amount of the S.A.'s capital, but usually does not exceed US$600.

Procedures—Branches A foreign corporation that intends to establish a branch office in Argentina must take the following actions:

- Submit to the IGJ an application for registration of the branch. The application should include the following documents, all authenticated by a notary in the corporation's home country, recognized by an Argentine consul, and translated by an Argentine public translator:
  - A copy of the articles of incorporation and bylaws that created and govern the foreign corporation;
  - A copy of the portion of the minutes of the board of directors authorizing the establishment of the branch, assigning capital to the branch, and appointing a local legal representative;
  - A copy of the minutes of a shareholder's meeting at which the board of directors was elected; and
  - A power of attorney allowing the applicant to represent the corporation.
- Publish the minutes of the board of directors stating the establishment of the branch, its capital, and its representative, in the Boletín Oficial.
- Register the above documents with the IGJ if located in the Federal Capital or the Public Register of Commerce maintained by the local Commercial Court in provincial jurisdictions.

As a practical matter, foreign companies will find establishment of branches in Argentina much easier if they can demonstrate to the IGJ that their home government has reciprocal arrangements with Argentina recognizing branches of Argentine companies (however, such reciprocity is not an absolute requirement for the operation of a foreign branch in Argentina).

Procedures—Limited Liability Companies To form an S.R.L., an investor need only:

- Prepare and execute (either in private or before a notary public) a deed of incorporation. This deed contains the partnership contract among quotaholders, typically including provisions governing capitalization, exercise of management responsibility, changes in membership, in-house audit requirements, and liquidation procedures.
- Publish a prescribed summary of the deed in the Boletín Oficial.
- Register the deed with the IGJ if located in the Federal Capital or with the Public Registry of Commerce if located in the provinces.

These formalities usually require about two months to complete. Costs involved are approximately the same as those for forming a corporation (see "Procedures—Argentine Corporations" on page 198). Until all formalities have been completed, limited liability does not apply for quotaholders.

Procedures—Partnerships Investors who wish to enter Argentine partnerships must do the following:

- Prepare and execute a partnership deed containing the partnership agreement. This deed must be executed before a notary public for a *sociedad en comandita por acciones*; private execution is sufficient for a *sociedad en comandita simple.*
- Publish a summary of the deed in the *Boletín Oficial.*
- Register the deed with the IGJ if located in the Federal Capital or with the Public Registry of Commerce if located in the provinces.

Until all steps have been completed, limited partners are not entitled to limited liability.

Procedures—Joint Ventures To enter a joint venture, an investor need only do the following:

- Execute a private or public deed containing the joint venture agreement.
- Register the agreement with the IGJ if located in the Federal Capital or with the Public Registry of Commerce if located in the provinces. The registered agreement must include a list of financial contributions to the venture, a description of the object of the venture and the length of its term, and the names of its members and their responsibilities,

Additional Reporting Requirements

As noted above, an S.A. must pay an annual registration fee to the IGJ, and every S.A., branch office, S.R.L., and certain types of partnerships must file annual financial statements with the IGJ. These statements must be certified by independent public accountants in accordance with accepted Argentine accounting practices.

An S.A. or S.R.L. with capital in excess of US$2,100,000 may face additional reporting requirements, and an S.A. that offers securities to the public must comply with reporting regulations promulgated by Argentina's National Securities Commission (Comisión Nacional de Valores, or CNV). If securities are listed on Argentina's stock exchange (Bolsa de Comercio), an S.A. may also be subject to additional exchange rules.

Argentina's Central Bank may require financial businesses to comply with additional reporting regulations.

TEN REMINDERS, RECOMMENDATIONS, AND RULES

1. The stock corporation, or S.A., and the branch office are the business forms most popular with foreign investors. A subsidiary S.A. incorporated in Argentina limits a foreign owner's exposure to liability to the subsidiary's assets. A branch office could expose a foreign owner's assets outside of Argentina to liability. However, the costs of forming a branch in Argentina are usually less than costs of incorporating an S.A. in Argentina.

2. Argentina's liberal foreign investment regime hinges on the principle that foreign investors are entitled to an equal footing with Argentine nationals. Thus all business forms recognized by Argentine law are available to foreign investors, and there are no limits on the extent of foreign ownership of Argentine entities. Nevertheless, some forms may be inappropriate for foreign investment in the country.

3. Although foreign investors are unlikely currently to encounter either official or unofficial resistance to their commercial activities, establishing and fostering personal relationships with individuals in Argentine agencies that handle the registration and regulation of businesses can be important to success in Argentina.

4. Argentina has privatized and is deregulating its industries rapidly, which has led to some lack of clarity as to what rules apply and what government agencies play what roles in the establishment of business entities. Therefore, foreign investors should consider seeking professional assistance from consulting, legal, and accounting firms experienced in forming new business operations in the industry and locality in question.

5. Foreign individuals and entities that establish businesses in Argentina must in most cases obtain prior government approval—although this is routinely granted unless some problem is involved—and must register the entity through a formal filing of documents.

6. Although Argentina encourages new business ventures through streamlined formation and registration procedures, the formalities required may be more elaborate than those that many foreign investors are used to, and usually require the employment of an Argentine notary public.

7. Business entities are generally regulated by the Commercial Companies Law, No. 19,550. Foreign investors establishing Argentine businesses are also regulated by the Foreign Investment Law, No. 21,382.

8. The Inspección General de Justicia (IGJ) is the chief regulatory agency monitoring corporations and branches incorporated or established in the Federal Capital. The IGJ approves formation of these entities, approves changes in capital, and receives the required annual filing of financial statements.

9. Filing of notarized documents in a Public Registry of Commerce, maintained by a local

commercial court in the provinces, is typically the final step in the formation of a business entity.

10. Foreign investors who are able to show Argentine officials that Argentine businesses are entitled to reciprocal treatment in the investors' home countries may have an easier time dealing with the administrative steps required to form and register a business.

FURTHER READING

The preceding discussion is provided as a basic guide for those interested in doing business in Argentina. The resources described in this section provide additional information on business law, investment, taxation, accounting, and procedural requirements.

The Price Waterhouse and Ernst & Young guides are particularly notable, but other similar firms, such as Arthur Andersen, Coopers & Lybrand, and Deloitte Touche, also publish information on business operations in Argentina.

Boletín Oficial de la República Argentina. The official records publication of Argentina. Published daily, Monday through Friday. Available from: Suipacha 767, 1008 Buenos Aires, Argentina; Tel: [54] (1) 322-4164.

Price Waterhouse: Doing Business in Argentina. Available from a Price Waterhouse office near you or from: Price Waterhouse, Casilla de Correo Central 896, 1000 Buenos Aires, Argentina; Tel: [54] (1) 381-8181, 382-3005, Fax: [54] (1) 383-6339, 382-2793.

Ernst & Young's International Business Series: Doing Business in Argentina. Available from an Ernst & Young office near you or from: Henry Martín y Asociados, Ernest & Young Consulting, Maipú 942, P.B., 1340 Buenos Aires, Argentina; Tel: [54] (1) 313-8162, Fax: [54] (1) 313-1528.

USEFUL ADDRESSES

In addition to the government agencies listed here, individuals or firms should contact chambers of commerce, embassies, banks, and other financial service firms, local consultants, legal and accounting firms, and resident foreign businesses for assistance and information. (Refer to the "Important Addresses" chapter, beginning on page 315, for more complete listings.)

Inspección General de Justicia (IGJ)
(Office of the Inspector General of Justice)
San Martín 665
1004 Buenos Aires, Argentina
Tel: [54] (1) 312-2427, 313-7609

Banco Central de la República Argentina (BCRA)
(Central Bank of the Argentine Republic)
Reconquista 266
1003 Buenos Aires, Argentina
Tel: [54] (1) 394-8411, 394-8119, 393-0021
Fax: [54] (1) 334-6489, 334-6468, 325-4860

Bolsa de Comercio de Buenos Aires
Sarmiento 299, Piso 1
1353 Buenos Aires, Argentina
Tel: [54] (1) 311-5231/3, 311-1174, 313-4812
Fax: [54] (1) 312-9332

Comisión Nacional de Valores (CNV)
(National Securities Commission)
25 de Mayo 175
1002 Buenos Aires, Argentina
Tel: [54] (1) 345-2887 to 2897

Labor

THE LABOR ECONOMY

Free market reforms have changed Argentina's economic and labor landscape dramatically since their introduction in the early 1990s. Even though reverberations from the Mexican peso crisis in late 1994 have put a crimp in the expansion, the Argentine economy has responded vigorously to the reforms. Between 1990 and 1994, Argentina had the world's second fastest-growing economy (behind that of China). Hyperinflation, which set world records in the late 1980s, was also vanquished.

However, this shift to a market oriented economy has also had its downside, mainly in the form of unemployment, which has been on the rise: the privatization of state-owned firms, the introduction of laborsaving technologies, and trends toward a freer labor market have resulted in massive layoffs. Also, the newly developing economy has to date been unable to provide jobs for many of these displaced workers. Government austerity measures in the wake of the financial crisis in early 1995 have exacerbated the unemployment problem and exerted a downward pressure on wages, especially for Argentina's traditionally large and relatively handsomely paid middle class.

Despite signs of backlash in the face of economic liberalization, the country appears to be solidly embarked on a course toward a free market economy. Although real wages are still lower than they were in 1980, Argentine workers remain the best paid in Latin America. The percentage of people earning salaries below the poverty line has dropped after rising sharply in the 1980s. In the meantime, Argentina's massive, centralized unions are losing some of their once formidable political and economic clout.

Major labor law reforms were put in place beginning in 1991, and more are on the way. The reforms are intended to eliminate rigidities and distortions in the labor system, making it more responsive to market conditions. In an attempt to put it on a sounder financial footing and reduce the high cost to the state and employers of providing retirement benefits, the social security system has also been reformed. So far, the reforms in both areas may be considered to be only partially successful. But the Argentine government continues to regard these issues as essential components of its ongoing liberalization efforts.

A development that bears even closer observation concerning its impact on the labor market is the Mercado Común del Sur (Mercosur), the common market trade association emerging among the countries of the Southern Cone (Argentina, Brazil, Paraguay, and Uruguay). The free movement of labor is one of the features envisioned in the Mercosur single market, although actual implementation of this provision is considered to be some years off.

Some economists predict that Mercosur will lead to an economic division of labor, especially between Brazil and Argentina, its two largest economies. Because of its more skilled labor force, they expect Argentina to attract investments requiring technical skill, while Brazil—with labor costs 50 percent below those in Argentina's—is expected to attract investments that require more labor-intensive work.

Population

Argentina is a vast land, roughly the size of that part of the US located east of the Mississippi River. Despite enormous rural expanses, 84 percent of the country's population is urban (defined broadly as

CONTENTS

towns with more than 2,000 persons). More than one-third of Argentina's roughly 33 million people reside in greater metropolitan Buenos Aires. The society is unique in Latin America because more than half the population is considered to be middle class, although this middle class has been struggling to maintain its status in the face of the repeated economic and social shocks that have battered it during the past 20 years. Nevertheless, much of the population, especially in the capital and other large urban areas, enjoys a relatively high standard of living, comparable to that found in some of the smaller European countries and some of the industrializing countries of Asia.

The vast majority of Argentines are of European—mostly Spanish or Italian—extraction. But Buenos Aires is highly cosmopolitan, home to, for instance, half a million more recent Syrian, Lebanese, and other Middle Eastern immigrants. Community newspapers are published in English, French, German, Greek, Hungarian, Italian, Japanese, Polish, Ukrainian, and Yiddish.

More than 90 percent of the population is Roman Catholic (although only about 20 percent of the population professes to be actively Catholic). Argentine Protestants and Jews are roughly equal in number, each accounting for about 2.5 percent of the population. Spanish is the official language, but English, Italian, German, and French are also widely spoken. English is the most common second language that people speak—especially for business—followed by French. Managerial, clerical, and technical employees with a working knowledge of at least one language other than Spanish are readily found, especially in the Buenos Aires area. More middle and upper level workers have spent time overseas, increasing the availability of managers who are familiar with international business practices and who have second language capabilities.

Argentina's 1.4 percent birth rate is among the lowest in Latin America. At 74 years, the life expectancy of Argentine women exceeds that of men by 6 years. The portion of the population older than 65 years of age is growing rapidly. In 1960 the percentage of Argentines older than 65 years of age was 5.5 percent; by 1990 this had grown to 9 percent and is expected to continue growing until into the next century.

Labor Force

Unionization in government and manufacturing is widespread within Argentina's workforce of 13.2 million people. However, small businesses account for 60 percent of total employment. In greater Buenos Aires, men outnumber women in the workforce by about two to one.

Argentina is known for the high skills—and high wages—of its workforce relative to those of its Latin neighbors (Argentine wages are generally considered to be about twice as high as in neighboring Brazil, but half of those in Europe and North America). This so-called *"costo Argentino"*—the additional high labor and overhead cost structure of doing business in Argentina—has been a lingering issue for the country. The traditionally high standard of living has reduced Argentina's competitiveness in some areas, while its industry sector has been largely unable to capitalize on its strengths. Recent governments have tried to address the issue through efforts to reduce employer payroll costs.

A notable phenomenon in Argentina is black market labor, especially in the lower-skilled areas, such as construction. By some estimates, between 25 and 30 percent of workers receive under-the-table wages. Such employees earn low wages, work long hours, and receive no benefits, although they do not pay taxes. With benefits adding an amount equal to 30 to 50 percent of base wages, employers have been eager to use black market workers, and the tradition of evading taxes and regulation has tacitly supported them in this. However, the government has been cracking down on such scofflaws, and the public, which previously had turned a deaf ear to this sort of behavior, is now becoming more outraged by the perception—which apparently is accurate—that many black market workers are illegal aliens from the neighboring countries of Bolivia, Perú, Paraguay, and Brazil. The government has pledged to reduce the black market labor force and now has the backing of the union movement in this effort. Nonetheless, few companies seem to have taken advantage of a 1992 government offer to "regularize" their black market workforce by exempting employers from back payroll taxes provided that they put their people on the books in the future.

In the past few years, the participation rate—the percentage of working-age persons, defined as those 14 or older who are seeking or holding jobs—has climbed somewhat, reaching more than 40 percent in 1992. But their hold on these jobs is increasingly precarious. Economic reforms have ended the days of what had been, in effect, lifetime employment. In the Buenos Aires metropolitan area the vast majority of people work without written contracts. Some 16 percent are temporary workers. Nationwide, 11 percent are classified as domestic employees and one-fifth consider themselves to be self-employed—which, in many cases, may be a polite way of saying unemployed.

Labor Availability and Distribution by Sector

Companies setting up operations in Argentina should be able to find ample supplies of both skilled and unskilled labor, although the market for highly skilled workers remains tight. Because of structural changes in the economy, there is considerable disparity between existing worker skills and the skills needed for new industries or those companies that are updating their operations and technological infrastructure. Managerial personnel—one of the fastest-growing sectors of labor—are in high demand. In fact, the full costs of hiring skilled, middle to upper level managers may be greater in Argentina (calculated on the basis of purchasing power) than they are in the US.

Although the agricultural sector has traditionally been strong, directly and indirectly accounting for perhaps 30 percent of Argentina's gross domestic product (GDP) and as much as 70 percent of its foreign exchange earnings, its overall employment rate—around 9 percent—is falling. The industrial sector is substantial and growing: nationwide, manufacturing employs about one-third of the workforce. The rural provinces have benefited least from Argentina's recent economic reforms and have remained heavily dependent on state employment.

The service sector employs more than half of Argentina's workforce of 13.2 million persons and is growing more rapidly than the rest of the economy combined. The burgeoning service sector—led by growth primarily in the retail and personal services areas—employs the largest number of workers of any sector in metropolitan Buenos Aires; this dominance is only slightly less pronounced elsewhere in the country. Service industries such as finance and insurance have shown relatively little employment growth. Work in construction—which is notoriously cyclical—has likewise shown little overall growth, although workers in the skilled construction trades are considered difficult to find.

Manufacturing is the second largest employer in the capital city area, occupying more than a quarter of the workforce. Although the actual number of persons working in manufacturing has been rising only slowly, a recent survey of newspaper "help wanted" advertisements showed a sharp increase in demand for industrial workers. In part this surge reflects structural changes in the economy. As established industries acquire up-to-date equipment and new, more efficient industries open their doors, job requirements for industrial work are changing.

Foreign Workers

Argentina places no restrictions or quotas on the employment of foreign workers beyond compliance with standard immigration regulations. Expatriates may work in foreign-owned businesses as long as they hold a valid resident permit. In recent years, a growing number of workers from neighboring countries have entered the Argentine work force. Most are unskilled or, at best, semiskilled; many of them work in the country illegally.

Argentina maintains totalization agreements with Uruguay, Brazil, Chile, Italy, Paraguay, Greece, Portugal, and Spain: foreign professionals employed in Argentina are exempt from contributing to the otherwise obligatory Argentine pension program if they are covered by comparable plans in their home countries. Companies that have foreign scientists, professionals, or technicians under contract may apply for an exemption from most employer social security contributions, but only for contracts of less than two years' duration. Such exemptions considerably reduce payroll costs.

Unemployment and Underemployment

Despite a strong economy that is providing jobs in record numbers—nearly one million new jobs have been created since reforms began—more people are either entering or reentering the job market than there are available positions. Exacerbating the problem, the privatization of state-owned enterprises—generally consisting of bloated, inefficient major utilities—has been accompanied by radical downsizing of the workforce, as the new owners try to come to grips with low productivity and excessive labor costs. Before privatization, the public sector employed approximately 40 percent of the workforce, but downsizing has eliminated thousands of these positions. For example, privatization of the railroad system alone caused its workforce to shrink from 130,000 to just 20,000. Moreover, as part of the austerity program adopted in response to the financial crisis in early 1995, the government announced a new wave of privatizations. Although this will of necessity be among the last rounds of such government privatizations—virtually all state-run industry has been privatized—it comes at an awkward time as more workers are chasing fewer jobs in an already anxious economy.

As a result, official unemployment has been rising sharply, leaping from roughly 7 percent in 1991 to nearly 11 percent in 1994. In May 1995 this unemployment reached a record 18.6 percent. Because state-owned enterprises previously were proportionally more important employers in the provinces, unemployment rates outside Buenos Aires have risen even more dramatically; some observers place the real unemployment rate at more than 20 percent.

A similar rise has taken place in the rate of underemployment—that is, among workers who are seeking full-time positions, but who are able to find work for fewer than 35 hours per week. In 1993 and 1994 the unemployment rate surpassed the rate of underemployment for the first time in recent history.

Adding to the unemployment problem is the high cost of terminating employees, who are generally eligible for hefty severance payments if dismissed for reasons other than gross misconduct. Hence, employers are unwilling to hire additional full-time employees, leading to more overtime worked by harried employees because management does not wish to obligate itself long-term for what may only be a short-term upturn in product demand. Reducing the cost of termination is one of the reforms being considered in order to encourage the opening of new positions.

On the bright side, downsizing has been accompanied by the introduction of new technologies and a dramatic growth in productivity. Productivity in manufacturing rose 42 percent between 1991 and 1993. However, productivity still has a long way to go before it reaches the level found in developed, industrialized countries. Bank workers, for instance, cost as much to employ in Argentina as in the US, but are only 20 percent as productive.

Because the labor unions are key backers of the Menem government, the administration has been somewhat more sensitive to the unemployment issue than might otherwise have been the case. The government's backers in the unions recognize the need for economic reforms, but they are unhappy with the government's sluggishness in developing programs to address accompanying job losses. In November 1992 the Confederación General del Trabajo (General Confederation of Labor, or CGT) mounted a one-day general strike which led to a government pledge worth US$1.5 billion to be used to fight poverty and create new jobs.

However, in general the government's efforts to address unemployment have been confined to large-scale, short-term, public works programs. As an incentive to create new job openings, the new National Labor Law that went into effect in 1991 offered total or partial exemption from social security taxes for certain categories of work: positions filled by young professionals up to the age of 24, short-term training positions (of six to eight months), and positions created by companies engaged in new ventures.

Retraining

As the economy modernizes, retrenchment has left many without either work or directly applicable skills—or both. This has been true even among the ranks of skilled workers who were previously in great demand. The new economy needs a different mix of skills than the one reflected in the preexisting labor force. The government recognized this problem fairly early in the process of liberalizing the economy, but to date, it has been able to do little to remedy the situation.

However, since 1994 an ambitious retraining program has been in operation. With support from the Inter-American Development Bank (IDB), US$350 million has been earmarked for retraining 200,000 workers over a four-year period, including paid on-the-job training in advanced manufacturing techniques. Legislation is also planned to give incentives for apprenticeship arrangements that provide practical training in skilled operations. Nevertheless, to date, employers have not taken on the responsibility for worker training, nor have the unions pushed for it, putting the burden primarily on the shoulders of the government.

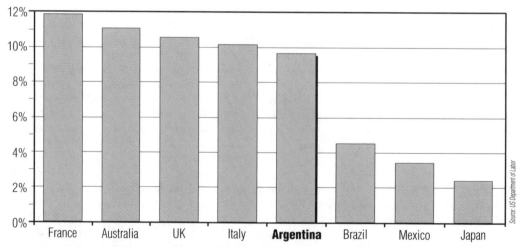

Comparative Unemployment–1993

Source: US Department of Labor

Note: The figures given are derived from official sources and should be viewed primarily as a relative guide. In virtually all cases actual unemployment is greater than official figures, which tend to understate this measure. This is particularly true of emerging nations, although developed, industrial nations are not immune.

HUMAN RESOURCES

Education and Attitudes Toward Learning

With a 96 percent claimed literacy rate, Argentina's is a highly articulate workforce—the most literate in all of Latin America. Education is free and compulsory from the ages of 5 to 12. Secondary and high school education is generally both affordable and available, although attendance falls by nearly half among those older than 14. The country's university system is also free. The university system has 53 institutions, divided equally between national—including a few provincially sponsored—public and private schools. For students on a nonacademic track, Argentina maintains a system of vocational schools.

Given the social and economic disruptions of the 1970s, 1980s, and 1990s, concerns have arisen about the state of the educational system. About half of Argentina's youth enroll in secondary schools, but only about half of those complete the program. In a recent survey of Buenos Aires students, 82 percent of them scored below 50 percent on a mathematics test, while 22 percent gave the wrong answer to every question. The university system is also ailing; it lacks real admission standards and essentially operates on a "no-fail" basis. One distortion of the system has been a surplus of professionals such as doctors and lawyers in a society strongly oriented toward middle class, white-collar values.

The government has been increasing its spending on education—which already stands at 5 percent of GDP—but the use of the new funds has become embroiled in long-standing jurisdictional conflicts between the central government and the provinces. The impact of increased spending on educational quality is thus expected to be minimal.

Traditionally, Argentines have placed considerable emphasis on education and taken great pride in their society's literacy and other educational achievements. Many Argentines recognize the link between educational attainment and success in an increasingly demanding economic environment. Nevertheless, the high dropout rate—due partially to a deteriorating educational system and partially to economic necessity as more students leave to seek employment to help out their desperate families—is an indication of the strength of the countervailing pressures.

Women in the Workforce

Women's rights are officially protected by the Argentine constitution and various laws and regulations. Women constitute roughly 37 percent of the overall workforce. Their participation in the labor market declines substantially after the age of 30, at least in metropolitan Buenos Aires (and probably even more significantly in the provinces, although specific data is lacking). This participation rate has been climbing, especially in recent years during which many single wage earners have been unable to support families and when single-parent households—usually headed by females—have also been on the rise. The situation of working women has also been disproportionally affected in a negative fashion by the changes wrought by economic reforms. Generally, Argentine women tend to take low-wage, relatively low-skill service sector jobs, although many aspire to and attain professional status.

Argentina has traditionally been a male-dominated society in which women have generally been expected to maintain the household while men operated in the workplace. Women in Argentina continue to experience difficulties in gaining acceptance and advancing in the workplace, although their situation is generally considered to be better than that of women in many other societies in Latin America or elsewhere in the world. Despite various attitudinal and structural barriers, increasing participation by women in virtually all sectors at all levels is having the effect of eroding traditional prejudices.

CONDITIONS OF EMPLOYMENT

With its long tradition of strong labor organization, Argentina maintains labor conditions and standards comparable to those in more developed, industrialized countries. As in many highly unionized countries, layoffs can be complicated and costly to employers. Because the rapid economic changes resulting from free market reforms require less rigidity in labor arrangements to succeed, efforts are underway to simplify termination requirements and lower such costs to employers. The unions have largely accepted this as inevitable, but they are pressing the government to pay greater attention to the problems of economic restructuring as it affects working people.

Working Hours, Overtime, Holidays, and Vacations

Workweek The 48-hour workweek is standard in Argentina, although there is considerable variation in the number of hours and how they are apportioned. Traditionally, workers planned to be on the job all day Monday through Friday, plus half of Saturday. Saturday work—though still common in some areas and industries—has generally been eliminated for office and government workers. Workers in occupations specified as hazardous or "unhealthy" are limited by law to a six-hour day. The standard urban office workday is seven hours (as is work on the night shift), with standard hours from 8:30 or 9 am to 5:30 or 6 pm, with a one-and-one-half-hour lunch break (women and employees less than 18 years of age must be given two hours off, although specific operations allows employers to seek exemptions from the longer period for women and minors). Workers must have a minimum of 12 hours off between consecutive workdays.

Legislative efforts are afoot to reduce the work-week; however, the proposed revision would also allow employers to demand a 10-hour day when called for by production requirements, as long as the average number of hours worked during the period was no more than nine, the current official maximum for number of hours worked. Overtime work beyond the usual number of hours per week must be compensated at one-and-a-half times the standard pay rate on weekdays and Saturday morn-ings; for Saturday afternoon, Sunday, or holiday work, overtime must be paid at double the standard rate.

Most businesses close after 1 pm on Saturday, except for service businesses such as supermar-kets, restaurants, and drugstores. By law, only essential services have been permitted to remain open on Sundays, although this restriction is being eroded, with more businesses remaining open.

Vacation Paid vacation ranges from 14 to 35 days, depending on the worker's length of service with the employer. New employees who have worked for the employer for less than six months receive one paid holiday for every 20 days of full-time work or its equivalent. Workers are not entitled to paid holiday time unless they have worked at least half the calendar year, although many employers prorate vacation time after a short probationary period. Argentines generally prefer to take their vacations during the summer months of January and February. Mid-July is another favorite period for vacations, largely because it, like the summer, coincides with school holidays. Some busi-nesses even close for various periods during these times. For this reason, the months of April through November (after Easter and before Christmas) are considered the best months to travel to Argentina on business.

Holidays In Argentina there are 11 days that by national law are paid holidays: January 1 (New Year's Day); Good Friday (before Easter Sunday, in March or April); May 1 (Labor Day); May 25 (Anni-versary of the 1810 Revolution); June 10 (Malvinas Day); June 20 (Flag Day); July 9 (Independence Day); August 17 (Anniversary of the Death of General José de San Martín); October 12 (Columbus Day); December 8 (Immaculate Conception); and December 25 (Christmas). In addition, banks are closed on November 6 (Bank Employee Day) and December 30.

With few exceptions, all businesses must close on national holidays, and many—especially busi-nesses in industries with strong unions—have established additional paid holidays. Some common ones include: Carnival Monday and Fat Tuesday before Ash Wednesday (in February or March); all or part of Easter week (but especially Maundy Thursday before Good Friday), when much of Argentina is on holiday. Locally, there are a number of additional patriotic or religious holidays that fall into this category.

Employment of Minors

Generally, employment of persons under the age of 14 is forbidden by law. The law does make some exceptions for those employed in a family business or farming. The workday for such minors, as well as for those between the ages of 14 and 18, is legally limited to 6 hours per day and 36 hours per week. But recent economic crises and current high unem-ployment have led to both increased instances and an unofficial relaxation in enforcement of child labor laws as families try to make ends meet by putting as many family members to work as possible.

Hiring Policies

In theory, firms are allowed to hire whomever they please. In actual practice, some hiring is either restricted or directed to union members, and much hiring, especially in smaller operations, is done among—or on the recommendation of—relatives or friends. Arm's-length hiring—including using the services of executive search firms—is at a fairly rudimentary level in much of Argentina except among larger, more sophisticated, internationally oriented firms. Nevertheless, Argentina operates more as a meritocracy—especially at more skilled and managerial levels—than many other traditional societies, especially those of Latin America.

Termination of Employment

In general, employers must follow a fairly strict standard procedure and fulfill a variety of require-ments in order to terminate an employee. In fact, many observers argue that Argentina's rigid rules for dismissing and compensating a dismissed employee are preventing the expansion of employ-ment. Rather than commit to hiring additional employees and incurring the future responsibilities, many firms are reportedly operating by using mandatory overtime. The rules are also contrib-uting to the widespread use of workers—often illegal immigrants—from the informal sector.

Employees have the right to receive written notice of dismissal, effective on the last day of a calendar month and served at least a month in advance. In lieu of notice, the employer may make a cash payment equal to the salary the employee would have earned during the period between the serving of notice and termination (in addition to any severance owed). During this period, a worker may be absent for two hours during each workday in order to seek other employment.

Severance pay is calculated at one months' salary per year of service, within upper and lower limits on the total payout: the minimum is two months' salary; the maximum is three times the average annual salary or quarterly average for a fraction of a year, as per the collective bargaining agreement in effect. Where a reduction in business activity or lack of work can be officially documented as the cause of the layoff, the worker is entitled to half of the severance payment that otherwise would be owed.

Recent Law 24.465 raised the 30-day employee probationary period during which dismissal can occur without the employer's obligation to give the worker either severance pay or prior notice.

Employees eligible for retirement benefits may be dismissed; however, the company must maintain such employees on the payroll until they can actually begin to collect pension (but for no longer than one year after they become eligible). Surviving dependent spouses and children can collect half of the imputed severance benefits for employees who die while employed, and they may be eligible for additional payments if the death resulted from a work accident.

Workplace Safety and Environmental Conditions

Occupational health and safety laws in Argentina are generally comparable to those in industrialized nations. The unions and government share enforcement responsibilities. By law, workers in hazardous or "unhealthy" occupations work a maximum of six hours per day. However, enforcement of such provisions has traditionally been somewhat lax, occupying a relatively low-priority position. This is especially true in certain industries and localities. Economic hardships have provided a climate that has not been conducive to improvement in such conditions.

WAGES AND BENEFITS

Minimum Wages

In August 1993 Argentina doubled its minimum wage to US$200 per month and US$1 per hour. Minimum wages—as well as prevailing wages—also vary from province to province. Most jobs in Argentina pay substantially more than minimum wage, with women working to supplement the family income representing the largest subgroup of those

actually working for minimum or near-minimum wages. Little skilled labor is available at such rates, although the large numbers of workers displaced by economic reorganization are exerting downward pressure on wages in many areas.

Wage and Salary Rates

In the formal economy, Argentina's workers—and in particular its skilled blue-collar and numerous white-collar workers—are the highest paid in Latin America. (The wages of those working in the country's substantial black market economy are, of course, much lower.) And according to some measures, those holding executive positions can actually earn more than comparable executives in the US.

Monthly salaries in 1993 averaged US$884, up from US$382 in 1985. In 1993 average monthly manufacturing wages were US$606.50, with projections using preliminary 1994 data yielding an average monthly rate of US$636.75, with a projected 1994 year-end figure of US$652.50.

Because of an inadequate supply of workers with the skills needed in modernizing sectors of the economy, wages are rising for such scarce employees, even as the wages of many others are either stagnating or falling. Salaries of the highest paid category of white-collar workers are more than three times greater than those of the lowest level managers; there is a comparable disparity between high- and low-wage industrial sector salaries.

Wages and salaries in manufacturing vary widely. Among white-collar workers, the three best paid categories of work are in the food processing, electrical goods, and petroleum products industries, in that order. The best paid blue-collar jobs are in the chemical, electrical goods, and petroleum products industries. The lowest salaries for white-collar workers are earned in the leather goods; ready-to-wear apparel; and the stone, glass, and ceramics industries. Blue-collar production workers' wages are lowest in leather goods, forest products, and ready-to-wear apparel. Wages of production workers in the depressed leather goods sector were about US$285 per month in 1994, 45 percent below the average manufacturing wage; those of manufacturing workers in the high-demand electrical goods sector were about US$825, (30 percent above average), while wages of commercial (white-collar) workers were about US$700 and those in the financial sector US$1,210.

The average wage declined in real terms by about one-third between 1985 and 1993, although purchasing power fell by less—about 25 percent. During the same period, real costs of labor rose by 50 percent. One of the key accomplishments of the Menem labor reform program has been to mandate the linking of wage hikes to increases in productivity, rather than to inflation, as was the case in the past. To avoid Mexican-style devaluation of its currency, the government began deflating the economy—rather than the currency—through higher taxes and wage cuts. Government salaries above US$2,000 per month have been reduced and frozen, and a pledge has been obtained from industry to cut executive salaries by roughly 20 percent.

Allowances, Bonuses, Sick Leave, and Other Benefits

Allowances Workers receive a monthly family allowance funded by a 9 percent employer paid payroll tax. (Rates are a substantially lower 3 percent in Patagonia.)

Bonuses All regular workers receive a mandated annual bonus equal to one month's salary, based on the highest monthly amount paid to the worker during the period. This bonus is payable in two installments at the end of June and the end of December.

Sick Leave Workers are entitled to paid sick leave of as much as six months, depending on length of service. The period of compensation is extended as much as six more months if the employee has dependents. If a worker is still unable to work because of illness after the expiration of this compensated period, the employer is required to keep that worker's position open for another year.

Argentine workers enjoy a range of other benefits, largely because of the country's traditionally strong labor union movement. The benefits are generally financed through employer and employee payroll contributions. Altogether, employer contri-

butions for these benefits (including family allowance contributions) amount to 33 percent of basic compensation. Workers contribute a minimum of 17 percent of their wages for such benefits (more if they cover dependents).

Health Benefits Medical care is provided to workers with funding that comes from a 9 percent payroll tax—6 percent contributed by the employer and 3 percent by the employee (plus an additional 1.5 percent per dependent paid by the employee). Generally, Argentines receive their health care through union-managed programs. Although private health plans are available, they are widely considered to be unreliable. While there is widespread discontent with health care delivery in terms of quality and access, the system has not been faced with the kinds of financial problems that have confronted the crippled Argentine pension system. As part of their pension contributions, employers pay 2 percent and employees 3 percent of wages for retiree health benefits.

Disability and Death Benefits In case of death or total disability, employers pay an indemnity equivalent to 1,000 average workday salaries multiplied by 65 and divided by the worker's age, up to a maximum amount of US$55,000 for death or total disability. For partial disability, the indemnity falls based on the determined percentage of disability. In cases of temporary disability, employers pay for medical treatment and drugs. Employers must also pay for prostheses or orthopedic appliances for workers with total or partial disabilities. For a worker killed in the course of work activities, employers also pay burial expenses amounting to

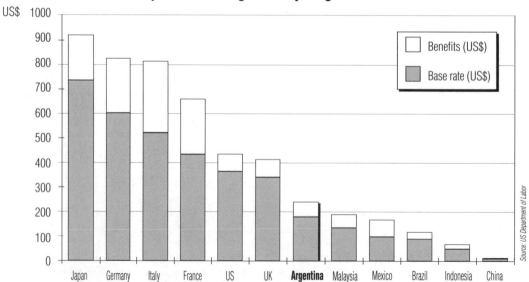

Comparative Average Weekly Wages—1992

THE ARGENTINE SOCIAL SECURITY AND BENEFITS SYSTEM

Argentina's social security system was substantially revised in 1994. Not only are employees allowed to direct their contributions to one of the 25 privately managed pension funds rather than the essentially bankrupt state retirement system, but the basis on which both employer and employee contributions are assessed has been revised as well.

Under Law No. 24,241, employees can opt between the parallel government and private pension systems. Employer contributions—or, for self-employed workers, that portion of contributions designated as the employer contribution—will continue to be channeled into the government system, and benefits owed to workers based on these contributions will still come from the government. However, employees—and self-employed persons—can elect to put their separate contributions into either the government system or the private system. All contributions made to nonretirement social service portions—retiree and current medical benefits—of the social security system will be held and administered by the government.

The government system—a defined benefit system in which payouts are based on a set percentage of worker earnings—makes payments to retirees from the contributions of current workers; future benefits are to be paid by later contributors. Because the number of employees contributing is falling relative to the growing number of retirees, the system is in an actuarial bind. Pensions are a liability of the government, but one the government has inadequate funds to satisfy; this led to the existing crisis in the social security system.

Under the new private pension system—a defined contribution plan in which retirement benefits are based on the principal and earnings of the actual funds contributed by the worker to an individually owned account—employees can cut themselves loose from the problems of the governmental system. However, they also lack the certainty of a predetermined payout, and their retirement payouts will be dependent on the investment results of the private pension management firm selected.

Under the new law, employers must contribute 16 percent of the wages paid to the employee towards retirement benefits, an additional 2 percent towards retiree medical benefits, and 6 percent towards the employee's current medical benefits. Employees contribute 11 percent of their wages towards retirement benefits, 3 percent towards retirement medical benefits, and 3 percent towards current medical benefits for themselves, plus an additional 1.5 percent for each dependent covered for current medical benefits. Self-employed workers must contribute 27 percent of wages towards retirement benefits, 5 percent towards retiree health benefits, and 9 percent towards current medical benefits. These percentages apply up to ceiling of US$3,780 per month of income.

In addition to the above, employers must contribute 9 percent of a worker's wages (calculated on the same basis as for social security) towards a family allowance payment to the worker. Operations in Patagonia, however, pay at reduced rates: 3 percent (as of January 1, 1995). Employers also pay for life insurance coverage for their workers at a rate of 0.039 percent on the total insured capital (capital was set at US$2.10 per worker as of April 1991). Workers who belong to a union have union dues deducted from their wages and forwarded to the union by the employer.

Altogether, employers pay 33 percent of basic wages to social security and family allowance, while employees pay a minimum total of 17 percent (more if dependents are covered or if union dues are withheld). Employers pay additional amounts for life insurance, disability insurance, workers' compensation, and unemployment benefits. The amounts paid are based on various measures other than payroll, as are directly mandated benefits.

as much as 75 times the worker's daily salary.

Workers' Compensation The costs of worker injury claims have been rising steadily, with some indication that an increasing incidence of questionable claims is an important factor in the increase. Reforms are in the works to improve the workers' compensation system. The anticipated reforms stress accident prevention, the provision of medical care and rehabilitation, subsidies to those undergoing medical treatment, and indemnities paid for disabling accidents. The new system would operate through employer associations, with participants sharing in the benefits and costs of maintaining it.

Unemployment Under the new National Employment Law, unemployment payments are fixed at an average of 80 percent of the employee's most recent salary, with a payment floor of US$120 per week and a ceiling of US$400. Generally unemployment benefits run from 4 to 12 months and include the continuation of medical care benefits.

Retirement Benefits Argentine employers contribute 16 percent and employees 11 percent of wages for retirement benefits. Even though the state-run pension program provides only a modest monthly income—typically around US$150 to US$170—the system has been in a precarious financial situation for some time. In part, the problem has been demographic, as Argentina's aging population increases the proportion of retirees to active contributors in the workforce has increased. Evasion of pension fund payments and the rise in pensions granted for questionable disability claims have added to the problem. A number of lawsuits filed to obtain back pension payments have further threatened the financial viability of the system.

In 1993 the government instituted reforms designed to address pension fund problems. These allowed employees the option of enrolling in competing, privately managed pension programs instead of with the state pension agency. The hope was to emulate the highly successful Chilean model, under which private pension funds have now become major institutional investors, boosting the country's capital markets and improving the benefits available to retirees. About 25 private pension fund groups have registered under the new program. However, the response to date has been disappointing, as a suspicious public waits to see if the newly inaugurated system will prove viable. Only about half of those eligible to enter the privatized system did so when the option first became available. The private funds have also come under criticism for selling company "image" rather than explaining what they offer. As both investors and providers become more familiar with the concept and operation of such vehicles, private funds are expected to relieve much of the current burden on governments at all levels.

Other Benefits Argentine employers generally do not provide many additional benefits to their workers. Larger firms—usually those located away from readily available services—may offer subsidized meals, transportation, or even housing for workers. However, most social welfare and enhancement programs are customarily offered by labor union *obras sociales* organizations (although these may be indirectly paid for in large part by employers).

As is the case in large centers elsewhere in the world, executive compensation customarily includes a wider variety of benefits; these can rapidly bring the costs of retaining executive talent up so that they are in line with (or even above) those in other world business centers.

LABOR RELATIONS

Unions and the Labor Movement

Large, centralized labor unions in Argentina have been a major force in the country's politics. They became the backbone of Juan Perón's populist-corporatist state of the 1940s and have since continued to play a critical role in shaping the direction of government policies into the present. They continue to be strongest in the metallurgical, the automotive, the banking, and the (shrinking) state sectors. Although union membership is technically voluntary, union shops are in effect exclusive. Many observers have also considered Argentine unions to be concerned with rigidly protecting the position of their existing members, often at the expense of workers outside the specific unions. At the high point of Argentine organized labor—in the mid-1950s—about 50 percent of workers belonged to unions. By 1992 participation had fallen to about 28 percent.

The election of Carlos Menem as Argentina's president in 1989 is widely seen as marking a major turning point in the history of the labor movement. Although backed by the unions and partly dependent on them for executing his policies, the *Justicialista* (Peronist) administration has carried out reforms that have weakened union power. For instance, the Menem government has pushed to replace industrywide collective bargaining with labor-management negotiations at the individual company level, thus depriving labor of its power to disrupt entire sectors. Also, traditionally, much of the country's social welfare system—*the obras sociales*—has been managed by the unions, and recent reforms are lessening labor's role while strengthening that of government and even of private agencies. The number of labor leaders elected to the Chamber of Deputies in the 1991 election was only half the number elected in 1983, following the collapse of the military regime.

Opposition from the unions has nonetheless been fragmented, largely because there is broad public support for the administration's economic reforms. Many unions—aware that job growth depends on an economy that is more export-driven and thus more competitive—recognize the need for reforms aimed at improving the economy. Rather than being hostile to international companies, Argentine unions generally welcome the interest of foreign investors and approach them in a manner more cooperative than many outsiders would expect. Nevertheless, Argentine labor is jealous of its prerogatives and is buffeted by contradictory forces. On the one hand, it has a history of importance and control that it is loath to surrender; on the other hand, however, it is faced with harsh economic realities dictating that it must relinquish power in order to survive.

Strikes and Disputes

Although the unions wield less power than in the past, conditions for organized labor are nonetheless better than they were under the repressive military regime that reigned between 1976 and 1983. Not only has direct suppression of labor activity and personnel ceased, but the military government's restrictions on the right to form labor groups were lifted in 1987–1988.

Politically-motivated labor actions have been common in Argentina's history. Strikes were an important contributor to the fall of Menem's predecessor, but the unions have been hesitant to challenge the current administration directly in this way. A one-day general strike in November 1992 did produce greater attention by the government to labor issues, but worker absenteeism was lower than the unions had hoped for—a sign of labor's declining influence over workers.

Some unions—mainly public sector unions affected by privatization and led by a younger generation of union leaders unhappy with the closed circle of the old guard Peronist labor bosses—have broken away from the dominant Confederación General de Trabajo (General Labor Confederation, or CGT). These more militant unions are the main source of labor opposition to government reforms. The leftist opposition parties they support are growing in strength, but appear unlikely to displace more traditional political groups from power.

Labor disputes in Argentina are subject to compulsory conciliation and arbitration by the Ministry of Labor. Workers have the right to pursue a strike until such time as the Labor Ministry decrees compulsory arbitration. Because of the long history of labor organization, dispute resolution mechanisms are highly developed in Argentina.

Business Law

CONTENTS

INTRODUCTION

During the past decade, Argentina has instituted numerous reforms of its business laws, primarily in an effort to encourage foreign investment. Current laws allow foreign businesses to operate in Argentina in essentially the same manner as Argentine businesses. Argentine laws protecting foreign owners' property are clear and compatible with international business standards. At the same time, the Argentines are recognizing a need for legal protections to control and guide new uses of the country's resources; areas of particular concern include labor, consumer, and environmental protections and procedures. Although Argentina's business laws are generally quite liberal, foreign traders and investors must carefully investigate all current legal requirements that apply to their business activities before commencing any transaction.

The information in this chapter is intended to emphasize the important issues in Argentine commercial law, but in no way should it be considered to constitute legal advice or to replace the advice of a licensed attorney. Foreign investors should always review their business activities with attorneys who are familiar with international transactions, with Argentine law and supplementary regulations, and with the laws of their own countries. Refer to page 345 of the "Important Addresses" chapter for a list of law offices in Argentina.

BASIS OF THE LEGAL SYSTEM

Argentina is a civil law country, meaning that its courts rely on laws compiled in codes, such as the Commerce Code and the Civil Code. Judicial decisions are typically based on code provisions rather than on precedents set by past judicial decisions.

Argentina established its independence from

This introduction is based in part on interviews with Osvaldo Agatiello, Latin American Regional Coordinator of Baker & McKenzie, Miami office; Pablo Rueda of Marval, O'Farrell & Mairal, New York City office; and Alberto Gonzalez of White & Case, Miami office.

LEGAL GLOSSARY

acceptance An unconditional assent to an offer or one conditioned on minor changes that do not affect material terms of the offer. *See also* counteroffer, offer.

agency The relationship between an agent and a principal. The agent represents and acts on behalf of the principal, who instructs and authorizes the agent to act.

attachment A legal process for seizing property before a judgment to secure the payment of damages if awarded. Attachment may be sought before or during the court action. This process is also referred to as sequestration. Example: a party who claims damages for breach of contract may request a court to issue an order freezing all transfers of specific property owned by the breaching party pending resolution of the dispute.

authentication The act of conferring legal authenticity on a written document, typically made by a notary public, who attests and certifies that the document is in proper legal form and that it is executed by a person identified as having authority to do so.

bailment A delivery of personal property by one person (the bailor) to another (the bailee) pursuant to a contract that requires the bailee to do something with the property—such as repair or transport it—and afterwards redeliver it to the bailor or otherwise dispose of it in accordance with the bailor's instructions. Example: a bailment arises when a seller delivers goods to a shipping company with instructions to transport them to a buyer at a certain destination.

capacity to contract Legal competency to make a contract. A party has capacity to contract if he or she has attained the age required by law and has the mental ability to understand the nature of contract obligations.

chattel An item of personal property.

counteroffer A reply to an offer that materially alters the terms of the offer. Example: a seller who accepts a buyer's offer on condition that the goods will be made of a different material has made a counteroffer.

domicile The place where a party is living or located with no definite, present intention of moving away.

good faith A legal standard implying honesty in the conduct or transaction at issue, honesty of intention, or freedom from an intention to defraud, depending on the circumstances.

injunction A court order that either requires a party to do a specific act or prohibits that party from doing an act. Injunctions can be granted on a permanent or temporary basis, pending resolution of a dispute.

joint and several liability The liability of two or more persons who are responsible together and individually, allowing the person harmed to sue all or any of the wrongdoers.

juridical act An action intended to have, and capable of having, a legal effect, such as the creation, termination, or modification of a legal right. Example: The signing of a power of attorney is a juridical act because it gives legal authority to an agent.

juridical person An individual or entity recognized under law as having legal rights and obligations. Example: limited liability companies, corporations, and partnerships are entities recognized as juridical persons.

negligence A failure to act with reasonable care, possibly resulting in legal liability for harm to others.

offer A proposal that is made to a specific individual or entity to enter into a contract. The proposal must contain definite terms and must indicate the offeror's intent to be bound by an acceptance. Example: a buyer's order to purchase designated goods on certain delivery and payment terms is an offer. *See* acceptance, counteroffer.

pledge A bailment or delivery of property to a creditor to secure a debt. Also, a recorded security interest in a chattel.

power of attorney A written document by which one individual or entity (the principal) authorizes another individual or entity (the agent) to perform stated acts on the principal's behalf. Example: a principal may execute a special power of attorney (authorizing an agent to sign a specific contract) or a general power of attorney (authorizing an agent to sign all contracts for the principal).

reasonable care The level of care that an ordinary, prudent person would be expected to exercise under the same circumstances.

warranty An affirmation of fact regarding the characteristics, safety, or suitability of a product.

Spain in 1816, and its current population includes a large percentage of citizens with Spanish and Italian ancestry. Argentina's laws are derived from various sources, including Roman law, the French Napoleonic Code, and Spanish and Portuguese laws; Italian law is an important source for Argentina's Commercial Code. Argentina's constitution, first passed in 1853 and revised in 1994, has provisions similar to those of the US Constitution.

STRUCTURE OF GOVERNMENT AND LAWS

Argentina is a federal republic consisting of 23 autonomous provinces and a federal district. An elected president, who appoints a cabinet composed of ministers, holds the country's executive power. Legislative power is exercised by a bicameral legislature, including a lower chamber (currently with 254 elected Deputies of the Nation, although the number may vary) and an upper chamber (composed of 72 elected Senators of the provinces). The highest federal court is the Supreme Court, made up of nine judges. In the past, the executive branch was generally the strongest, with the president being allowed a great deal of independence to operate by executive fiat. However, recent trends point toward a more empowered legislature and judiciary. Argentina's Supreme Court occasionally overrules the legislature, invalidating laws it deems unconstitutional.

Each of the provinces has its own government and courts that mirror the federal system. While substantive law is largely the same at both the federal and provincial levels, procedure may vary in provincial courts. Under Argentina's constitution, the provinces delegate to the federal legislature the power to enact laws of national scope governing civil, commercial, and other matters. Individual provinces may also enact their own specific provisions.

Argentina is a party to numerous bilateral and multilateral treaties and conventions. (Refer to the "Trade Agreements" chapter, beginning on page 65.)

LAWS GOVERNING BUSINESS

Foreign Investment and Companies Law No. 21,382 governs foreign investment. It was revised extensively in 1989, again in 1993, and now essentially provides foreign investors with the same status and rights as local investors. Investment in some industries, such as banking, insurance, mass media, and mining, may require government approval, but no prior approval is required for most types of investments (where applicable, requirements for approval apply equally to nationals).

Currency exchange for foreign investors is covered by Law 21,382 and Decree 1,853/93; there are currently no government regulations or limits on foreign exchange activity. The laws impose no time limits or currency requirements for remittance of profits or repatriation of investments.

If foreign companies wish to establish branches or other permanent representation in Argentina they must comply with the Commercial Companies Law, No. 19,550. In some circumstances, this law mandates certification of a foreign company's legal existence in its home country, maintenance of separate audited accounts in Argentina, registration of documents with a local commercial registry, and similar requirements. (Refer to the "Business Entities & Formation" chapter, beginning on page 191, for more information.)

Foreign citizens who travel to Argentina on business must comply with immigration laws codified in Law 22,439.

Local Companies The Commercial Companies Law governs the formation and operation of Argentine business entities. It sets forth the requirements and formalities for applications for government approval of company formation and company registration with a commercial registry, as well as rules governing such aspects as investor liability, company management, issuance of stocks and bonds, reporting, and audit requirements. Commercial registries and other key filing agencies are described in the Code of Commerce, Articles 34–42. Some types of companies are governed by industry-specific laws, such as the Mining Code, Law 1,919, and Law 21,526, which regulates the banking industry.

While Argentina does not have a separate labor code, companies that employ Argentine workers must afford them certain labor rights guaranteed in the constitution and codified in miscellaneous legislation addressed to specific types of work. If a foreign principal employs an agent in Argentina, the principal must observe Argentine labor laws. This means, among other things, that the principal must provide advance notice to an agent before terminating the agency relationship and may be liable for substantial severance benefits on termination.

Commercial Activities The legal requirements of most ordinary business transactions are detailed in the provisions of contract, agency, and remedy laws set forth in the Civil Code, the Code of Commerce, and the Code of Civil Procedure. The Code of Commerce supplements and modifies the Civil Code in its coverage of commercial contracts, which often require less formality than contracts governed exclusively by the Civil Code. Business customs are usually relevant in the interpretation of commercial contracts.

Certain financial aspects of transactions are governed by specific legislation, such as Decree-Laws 5,965/63 and 4,776/63, which set forth the requisites for the use of various types of commercial paper, such

THE INTERNATIONAL TRANSACTION: BASICS OF A ONE-TIME SALE

When dealing internationally, you must consider the business practices and legal requirements of the country where the other party to your contract is located. Parties generally have the freedom to agree to any contract terms that they desire, but the laws of your country or the other country may require a written contract. In some transactions, the laws may even specify all or some of the contract terms. Whether a contract term is valid in a particular country is mainly of concern in case you have to seek enforcement. Otherwise, you have fairly broad flexibility in negotiating contract provisions. However, you should always be certain to come to a definite understanding with the other party on four basic issues: the goods (quantity, type, and quality); the time of delivery; the price; and the time and means of payment.

For a small, one-time sale, an invoice or a simple contract may be acceptable. For a more involved business transaction or an ongoing relationship, a formal written contract is preferable in order to define clearly the rights, responsibilities, and remedies of all parties. Contracts that involve capital goods, high credit risks, or industrial or intellectual property rights will require special protective clauses. In preparing such contracts, it is essential to obtain legal advice from a professional who is familiar with the laws and practices of both countries involved.

For a simple, one-time deal, you need to consider at least the following clauses:

Contract Date

Specify the date when the contract is signed. This date is particularly important if payment or delivery times are fixed in reference to it—for example, "shipment within 30 days of the contract date."

Identification of Parties

Name the parties, describe their relation to each other, and designate any persons who are authorized to act for each party. The persons designated should also be the ones who sign the contract. If a person is signing on behalf of a company, you should be certain of that person's authority—request a written statement or corporate resolution if you are uncertain.

Goods

Description Describe the type and quality of the goods. You may simply indicate a model number, or you may have to attach detailed lists, plans, drawings, or other specifications. This clause should be clear enough

that both parties fully understand the specifications and have no discretion in interpreting them.

Quantity Specify the number of units, or other measure of quantity, of the goods. If the goods are measured by weight, you should specify net weight, dry weight, or drained weight. If the goods are prepackaged and are subject to weight restrictions in the end market, you may want to ensure that the seller will provide goods packaged to comply with those restrictions.

Price Indicate the price per unit or other measure, such as per pound or ton, and the extended price.

Packaging Arrangements

Set forth packaging specifications, especially for goods that could be damaged in transit. At a minimum, this provision should require the seller to package the goods in such a way as to withstand transportation. If special packaging requirements are necessary to meet consumer and product liability standards in the end market, you should specify them also.

Transportation Arrangements

Carrier Name a preferred carrier for transporting the goods. You should designate a particular carrier if, for example, a carrier offers you special pricing or is better able than others to transport the product.

Storage Specify any particular requirements for storing the goods before or during shipment, such as security arrangements, special climate demands, and weather protection needs.

Notice Provisions Require the seller to notify the buyer when the goods are ready for delivery or pickup, particularly if the goods are perishable or fluctuate in value. If your transaction is time-sensitive, you could even provide for several notices to allow the buyer to track the goods and take steps to minimize damages if delivery is delayed.

Shipping Time State the exact date for shipping or provide for shipment within a reasonable time from the contract date. If this clause is included and the seller fails to ship on time, the buyer may claim a right to cancel the contract, even if the goods have been shipped, provided that the buyer has not yet accepted delivery.

Costs and Charges

Specify which party is to pay any additional costs and charges related to the sale.

Duties and Taxes Designate the party that will be

responsible for import, export, and other fees and taxes and for obtaining all required licenses. For example, a party may be made responsible for paying the duties, taxes, and charges imposed by that party's own country, since that party is best situated to know the legal requirements of that country.

Insurance Costs Identify the party that will pay the costs of insuring the goods in transit. This is a critical provision because the party responsible bears the risk if the goods are lost during transit. A seller is typically responsible for insurance until title to the goods passes to the buyer, at which time the buyer becomes responsible for insurance or becomes the named beneficiary under the seller's insurance policy.

Handling and Transport Specify which party will pay shipping, handling, packaging, security, and any other costs related to transportation, and enumerate those costs.

Terms Defined Contracts for the sale of goods most commonly use Incoterms—as defined by the International Chamber of Commerce in Paris—to assign responsibility for the risks and cost of transport. (Refer to page 274 of the "International Payments" chapter for explanations of the Incoterms.)

Insurance or Risk of Loss Protection

Specify the insurance required, the beneficiary of the policy, the party who will obtain the insurance, and the date by which it will have been obtained.

Payment Provisions

In a one-time transaction, the seller will typically seek the most secure form of payment before committing to shipment, while a buyer will want the goods cleared through customs and delivered in satisfactory condition before remitting full payment. If payments cannot be made in advance, parties most often agree to use documentary credits. (Refer to the "International Payments" chapter for an explanation of such payments.)

Method of Payment State the means by which payment will be tendered—for example, delivery of a documentary letter of credit or documents against payment; prepayment in cash or traveler's checks; or credit for a specified number of days.

Medium of Exchange Designate the currency to be used—for example, Argentine pesos, the currency of the other party's country, or the currency of a third country.

Exchange Rate Specify a fixed exchange rate for the price stated in the contract. You may use this clause

to lock in a specific price and ensure against fluctuating currency values.

Import Documentation

Designate the documents for exporting and importing that each party will be responsible for obtaining, completing, and presenting to customs. Shipment of the goods, and even the contract itself, may be made contingent on a party's having obtained in advance the proper licenses, inspection certificates, and other authorizations. (Refer to the chapters "Import Policy & Procedures" and "Export Policy & Procedures" for further discussion of these requirements.)

Inspection Rights

If the buyer will be given a right to inspect the goods before taking delivery, specify the party who will make the inspection—for example, the buyer, a third party, or a licensed inspector; the location where the inspection will occur—for example, at the seller's plant, the buyer's warehouse, or a receiving dock; the time at which the inspection will occur; the presentation of a certified document of inspection, if needed; and any requirements related to the return of nonconforming goods, such as payment of return freight charges by the seller.

Warranty Provisions

Limit or extend any implied warranties, and define any express warranties on property fitness and quality. The contract may, for example, state that the seller warrants that the goods are of merchantable quality, are fit for any purpose for which they would ordinarily be used, or are fit for a particular purpose requested by the buyer. The seller may also warrant that the goods will be of the same quality as any sample or model that the seller has furnished as representative of the goods. Finally, the seller may warrant that the goods will be packaged in a specific way or in a way that will adequately preserve and protect the goods.

Indemnity

Agree that one party will hold the other harmless from damages that arise from specific causes, such as the design or manufacture of a product.

Enforcement and Remedies

Time Is of the Essence Stipulate that timely performance of the contract is essential. In the US, inclusion of this clause allows a party to claim breach merely because the other party fails to perform within the time prescribed in the contract. Although common in US

THE INTERNATIONAL TRANSACTION: BASICS OF A ONE-TIME SALE (cont'd)

contracts, a clause of this type is considered less important in other countries.

Modification Require the parties to make all changes to the contract in advance and in a signed written modification.

Cancellation State the reasons for which either party may cancel the contract and the notice required for cancellation.

Contingencies Specify any events that must occur before a party is obligated to perform the contract. For example, you may agree that the seller has no duty to ship goods until the buyer forwards documents that secure the payment for the goods.

Governing Law Choose the law of a specific jurisdiction to control any interpretation of the contract terms. The law that you choose will usually affect where you can sue or enforce a judgment and what rules and procedures will be applied.

Choice of Forum Identify the place where a dispute may be settled—for example, the country of origin of the goods, the country of destination, or a third country that is convenient to both parties.

Arbitration Provisions Although not yet a common remedy in Argentina, arbitration can be used as an alternative to litigation for the resolution of disputes that arise. You should agree to arbitrate only if you seriously intend to settle disputes in this way. If you agree

to arbitrate but instead file suit, the court is likely to uphold the arbitration clause and force you to settle your dispute as initially agreed in the contract. This means you will have to arbitrate before you can have your day in court.

An arbitration clause should specify whether arbitration is binding or nonbinding on the parties; the country where arbitration will be conducted (which should be a country that has adopted the UN Convention on Recognition and Enforcement of Foreign Awards or a similar convention); the procedure for enforcement of an award; the rules governing the arbitration, such as the UN Commission on International Trade Law Model Rules; the institute that will administer the arbitration, such as the International Chamber of Commerce (Paris); the law that will govern procedural issues or the merits of the dispute; any limitations on the selection of arbitrators (for example, a national of a disputing party may be excluded from being an arbitrator); the qualifications or expertise of the arbitrators; the language in which the arbitration will be conducted; and the availability of translations and translators if needed.

Severability Provide that individual clauses can be removed from the contract without affecting the validity of the contract as a whole. This clause is important because it provides that, if one clause is declared invalid and unenforceable for any reason, the rest of the contract remains in force.

---

as bills of exchange, notes, and checks. Limitations on interest rates are found in the Commercial Code.

Types of documents required for various transactions, as well as the formalities of documentation, are listed in contract law provisions in the Civil and Commercial Codes; the Notarial Law, No. 12,990; the Civil Code, Articles 997-1,011; and Law 1,184 governing Acknowledgments.

The Civil Code contains laws governing sales of real and personal property. Some sellers use a bailment device called a *deposito* to approximate the terms of the otherwise unrecognized conditional sale. Argentina subscribes to the United Nations Convention for the International Sale of Goods.

The Code of Civil Procedure establishes attachment procedures and executory actions for the legal collection of a judgment or other property. Pledges of property to secure debts are recognized under Law 9,644, Decree/Law 15,348/46 (later enacted as Law 12,962), and related legislation.

Prescription laws in the Civil and Commercial Codes establish time periods within which actions must be brought to avoid loss of legal rights. Argentina subscribes to the Convention on the Limitation Period in the International Sales of Goods.

The Argentine constitution provides for the free circulation of goods. Laws 22,262, 18,875, 20,852, and 22,802, and the related regulations disapprove of unfair or restrictive business practices. The Directorate for Commercial Loyalty and Consumer Protection (the DCLP) polices business practices. Recognition of individual consumer rights is increasing, but the government has not yet focused on unfair trade practices. A new statute, Law No. 24,240, is expected to bolster legal protections for consumers and businesses against malicious or comparative advertisements, products sold without warranties, or sales contracts that cancel consumer rights.

The right of Argentine citizens to a healthy environment has been codified in a recent amendment to the constitution, and the government has been increasing its focus on environmental laws and standards. In addition to joining several international treaties on environmental matters, the government recently passed laws prohibiting the import of hazardous wastes, requiring registration of companies that produce hazardous wastes, and providing severe criminal penalties for environmentally hazardous behavior. The Argentine government created the Secretariat of Environmental Protection and Environmental Audit Procedures—soon to be granted ministerial status—to enforce these laws. In general, the government has emphasized prevention of future environmental hazards over punishment for past problems.

Intellectual and Industrial Property Argentina's constitution recognizes that authors and inventors have valuable rights to their works and inventions. The Copyright Law, No. 11,723, protects literary and artistic works which have been registered with the Argentine Copyright Office. A recent decree specifically includes computer software within the scope of copyright protection. Industrial models and designs are protected if they have been registered with the Patent Office; it is also possible to cover such property under the copyright law. However, models and designs must choose one or the other route: they cannot receive the combined and overlapping protections of both regimes.

The Trademark Act, No. 22,362, provides protection for trademarks registered with the trademark office. Argentina is a party to international agreements protecting intellectual property—including the Paris Convention for the Protection of Intellectual Property—and has ratified the Uruguay Round of the General Agreement on Tariffs and Trade (GATT), which includes an intellectual property chapter.

Licensing agreements involving technology transfer are governed by Law 22,426. Transfers of technology between related parties, such as foreign companies and their Argentine subsidiaries, should be registered with the National Institute of Industrial Technology (INTI) in order to obtain favorable tax treatment. Such transfer agreements should conform with normal market practices.

Although Argentina does not have legislation specifically covering trade secrets, such secrets are protected under contract, labor, and property laws.

GEOGRAPHICAL SCOPE OF ARGENTINE LAWS

This chapter describes Argentina's federal laws, which are national in scope and apply in the Argentine provinces. However, each province also has its own laws and courts. While these laws are generally substantively similar to federal laws, they do vary, and there may be differences between federal procedure and procedure in provincial courts. Thus foreign investors or businesspeople should always check the laws of the particular provinces where they plan to do business.

PRACTICAL APPLICATION

Significant Legal Considerations Probably the most salient aspect of Argentine business law for outsiders is its generally favorable stance toward foreign investors. In 1989 and subsequent years, Argentina's foreign investment statute, Law No. 21,382, was amended and restated in a progressively liberal fashion designed to implement a single fundamental principle: foreigners investing in or engaging in economic activities with Argentina should enjoy the same status and have the same rights, constitutional and otherwise, as local investors. In general national treatment means that regulations apply to nationals and foreigners alike. With the exception of a sparse handful of industries that still face meaningful government regulation—such as the broadcasting and mining industries—this means that foreign investors can use any business form available in Argentina; can own any percentage of an Argentine business or property up to and including 100 percent; can have free access to any Argentine or international financing; and are eligible for any government incentive or program. Most foreign investments require no prior government approval at all, and an investor is subject to few, if any, reporting obligations. While some government approval and regulation is usually involved when a foreign business establishes an Argentine entity, such approval is usually given perfunctorily and the regulation is minimal; no discrimination exists between foreign and domestic operations. Any substantial regulation or legal hindrance to a foreigner's business activities is the exception—and equivalent to that faced in similar circumstances by other Argentine national firms—not the rule.

Foreign exchange laws are also designed to make life easy for foreign businesses: at present, investors can use any currency they prefer, can freely transfer foreign exchange in and out of Argentina; and can remit profits or repatriate investments at any time. Argentine law even offers to foreign investors who make deposits in Argentine banks some guarantees against currency conversion, and has in the past provided for an optional registration system designed to insure foreign investors against risks related to fluctuations in exchange rates (although such registration is currently considered to be for statistical purposes only and carries with it no benefits or guarantees).

The encouragement of foreign investment is taken very seriously by the government, and foreigners can expect little or no unofficial bias and few invisible barriers to their activities in Argentina. During recent waves of privatization of state-run industries, the Argentine government solicited vast amounts of foreign capital and the international business community has established a thriving, solid, and important base in the Argentine economy.

If there is a significant legal problem involved in doing business in Argentina, it is related to Argentina's federal structure, which is complex; it became even more complicated when Argentina's constitution was revised in 1994. Given the overlap of federal, provincial, and local laws, administrative agencies, and courts, the task of finding a path through Argentine bureaucracy can be somewhat cumbersome. However, this is not significantly different from the situation found in most other countries.

Delays in consummating business deals or establishing business ventures may be caused by the kind of confusion that is inevitably encountered in any country changing as rapidly as Argentina. Recent privatizations have led to the abolition of many old government agencies and the institution of new agencies, and to foreign businesspersons it may be unclear which government agencies play what roles in the supervision of particular business activities.

Role of Legal Counsel There is a large, sophisticated pool of lawyers in Argentina. The country's 80,000 lawyers are not just litigators; Argentine businesses routinely solicit their lawyers' opinions and advice during all stages of a transaction, requiring their assistance in structuring, negotiating, and consummating deals. Some Argentine businesses even have in-house attorneys who review all company transactions.

As Argentina has undergone waves of foreign investment and privatizations involving foreign capital, the role of Argentine attorneys in (and their familiarity with) international transactions has expanded. Many Argentine attorneys have not only Argentine but foreign law degrees, are multilingual, and are at least as experienced in international business law as lawyers elsewhere in the world.

Argentine lawyers must graduate from public or private accredited universities in Argentina. Foreign lawyers can practice in Argentina if they pass national licensing examinations. This procedure is sometimes simplified for attorneys from other Latin American countries. Generally foreign businesses must retain Argentine lawyers to deal with matters related to Argentine law. Of course, foreign attorneys are still used extensively by foreign businesses for advice on the international aspects of commercial transactions and investments, and foreign attorneys can usually refer their clients to Argentine lawyers as needed. Some foreign law firms have formed official alliances with Argentine firms.

Most of Argentina's lawyers who are experienced in international transactions are located in the country's largest cities—Buenos Aires, Córdoba, and Rosario. Firms tend to be sizable by South American standards, with the largest having 25 to 70 attorneys. Attorneys can be contacted through referrals from foreign law firms and "Argentina" listings in Martindale-Hubbell's *International Lawyers*, as well as through embassies, consulates, and chambers of commerce. (Refer to the "Important Addresses" chapter, beginning on page 315.)

Contracts Historically, written contracts in civil law countries are short, with few detailed clauses, instead referring to Civil Code provisions for an explanation of the specifics. Rather than emphasizing a single transaction, many contracts in Argentina serve to define a general, continuing relationship between the parties, and the norms set forth in the codes are presumed to form the framework of the relationship.

However, after all the complex privatizations involving foreign capital and the flood of international trade that followed the government's liberalization of foreign investment laws, business relationships in Argentina are changing. Contracts are becoming more complex—both to cover the needs of multinational transactions not completely covered by Argentina's Codes and to please foreign investors accustomed to lengthy contracts with detailed provisions for all conceivable contingencies. Although many Argentines consider lengthy, US-style contracts to be redundant and excessive in their length and level of detail, they are becoming far more accustomed to such documents.

Each party to a business contract should retain separate legal counsel. In order to avoid conflicts of interest, Argentine attorneys will refuse to advise both parties.

Role of Notaries The notarial profession is extremely important in Argentina, where the government and commercial community both emphasize the formalities of documentation to a degree to which many foreign businesspeople may be unaccustomed. A notary public, or *escribano público*, verifies documents and places them in a "protocol," an official registry. Notarization is required for many commercial documents—including contracts regarding real property, powers of attorney, incorporation papers, and partnership contracts—in order for them to be considered to have legal effect.

Notaries are highly qualified, with law degrees and specialized coursework in notarial law, two years of service accredited by Argentina's College of Notaries, and an appointment from the executive branch of the

THE US FOREIGN CORRUPT PRACTICES ACT

US business owners are subject to the Foreign Corrupt Practices Act (FCPA). The stiff penalties imposed under this act may make a US business owner reluctant to deal with a foreign company if there is even a hint of corrupt practice related to the transaction. The FCPA makes it unlawful for any US citizen or firm (or any person who acts on behalf of a US citizen or firm) to use a means of US interstate commerce (examples: mail, telephone, telegram, or electronic mail) to offer, pay, transfer, promise to pay or transfer, or authorize a payment, transfer, or promise of money or anything of value to any foreign appointed or elected official, foreign political party, or candidate for a foreign political office for a corrupt purpose (that is, to influence a discretionary act or decision of the official) for the purpose of obtaining or retaining business.

It is also unlawful for a US business owner to make such an offer, promise, payment, or transfer to any person if the US business owner knows, or has reason to know, that the person will give, offer, or promise directly or indirectly all or part of the payment to a foreign government official, political party, or candidate. For purposes of the FCPA, the term "knowledge" means both "actual knowledge"—the business owner in fact knew that the offer, payment, or transfer was included in the trans-action—and "implied knowledge"—the business owner should have known from the facts and circumstances of a transaction that the agent paid a bribe, but failed to carry out a reasonable investigation into the transaction. A business owner should make a reasonable investigation into the transaction, for example, if the sales representative requests a higher commission on a particular deal for no apparent reason, if the buyer is a foreign government, if the product has a military use, or if the buyer's country is one in which bribes are considered customary in business relationships.

Legal Payments

The provisions of the FCPA do not prohibit payments made to facilitate routine government action. A facilitating payment is one made in connection with an action that a foreign official must perform as part of the official's job. In comparison, a corrupt payment is made to influence an official's discretionary decision. For example, payments would not generally be considered corrupt if made to cover an official's overtime if such overtime is necessary to expedite the processing of export documentation for a legal shipment of merchandise or to cover the expense of additional crew to handle a shipment.

A person charged with violating FCPA provisions may assert as a defense that the payment was lawful under the written laws and regulations of the foreign country and therefore was not for a corrupt purpose. Alternatively, a person may contend that the payment was associated with demonstrating a product or performing a preexisting contractual obligation and therefore was not for obtaining or retaining business.

Enforcing Agencies and Penalties

Criminal Proceedings The US Department of Justice (DOJ) prosecutes criminal proceedings for FCPA violations. Firms are subject to fines of up to US$2 million. Officers, directors, employees, agents, and stockholders are subject to fines of up to US$100,000, imprisonment for up to five years, or both.

A US business owner may also be charged under other federal criminal laws. On conviction, the owner may be liable for one of the following: (1) a fine of up to US$250,000; or (2) if the owner derived pecuniary gain from the offense or caused a pecuniary loss to another person, a fine of up to twice the amount of the gross gain or loss.

Civil Proceedings Two agencies are responsible for enforcing the civil provisions of the FCPA: the DOJ handles actions against domestic concerns, and the Securities and Exchange Commission (SEC) files actions against issuers. Civil fines of up to US$100,000 may be imposed on a firm, or on any officer, director, employee, agent, or stockholder acting for a firm. In addition, the appropriate government agency may seek an injunction against a person or firm that has violated or is about to violate FCPA provisions.

Conduct that constitutes a violation of FCPA provisions may also give rise to a cause of action under the federal Racketeer-Influenced and Corrupt Organizations Act (RICO), as well as under similar state statutes if such exist in a state with jurisdiction over the US business.

Administrative Penalties A person or firm that is held to have violated any FCPA provisions may be barred from doing business with the US government. Indictment alone may result in suspension of the right to do business with the government.

government. Notaries ensure that documents are appropriately formalized and filed in proper registries, but they do not advise parties as to the substantive aspects of the law or of business transactions.

Dispute Resolution Neither Argentines nor foreigners favor litigation in Argentine courts as a vehicle for dispute resolution, not because of the judicial environment so much as because of the court process itself. Foreigners and Argentines alike generally agree that Argentine laws are compatible with international business standards and offer a good framework for resolving business differences. They also usually find that Argentine courts treat foreigners and locals with equal consideration. Nevertheless, parties tend to avoid the courts because lawsuits are protracted and lengthy and can be unpredictably costly.

The average commercial, civil, or administrative proceeding takes 1 to 6 years to litigate; appeals are available and may take an additional year. Business lawsuits against the Argentine government, including tax disputes, take even longer, because all procedures in these cases require written documents. Costs of litigation may be high and are subject to little control by the litigants because attorneys' fees, as well as experts' fees, are fixed by the courts—not by agreements between attorneys and clients—based on a percentage of the amount of the claims. The losing party must pay not only its own fees, but also those of the other side's attorneys.

Aside from the inefficiencies and costs involved in litigation, many Argentines are reluctant to go to court for cultural reasons. Argentine society expects parties to make a sincere effort to work out their differences, and a lawsuit is viewed as a last resort—even as a failure. On a per capita basis, Argentina's litigation rate is less than half that in the US. Some foreign businesses have been reluctant to resort to Argentine courts for fear of judicial corruption, although there is little indication that such corruption is common.

If any residual biases in Argentine courts remain from the days when state control over the economy was strict, they tend to appear in labor disputes. Foreign businesses that have differences with Argentine employees may want to resolve these outside the courts, because the courts may show a pro-labor bias. This reflects a labor law regime that is somewhat antiquated and that may be the subject of considerable reform in coming years.

In view of the difficulties often encountered in using the Argentine court system, common sense applies: parties should concentrate on drafting agreement terms that are as clear and precise as possible. Parties would be wise to pay particular attention to contract provisions that establish their rights and obligations in the event that perfor-

mance of the contract becomes impossible, the terms are breached (by either or both parties), or the agreement is mutually terminated. Other key provisions should address the way in which goods will be stored or returned, whether equipment and machinery can be dismantled and retrieved, and whether business operations must be suspended during disputes.

Alternative dispute resolution (ADR) processes—such as mediation and arbitration—are relatively new to Argentina, and Argentines seldom use them. The constitution unequivocally guarantees Argentines their day in court, and this guarantee obviously dampens the spirit of binding arbitration, despite the national tendency to shrink from the adversarial nature of open court battles (which ADR is designed to avoid). Nonetheless, arbitration tribunals are beginning to appear in Argentina.

Argentina is a member of the New York Convention on Arbitration and is pledged to enforce foreign arbitration awards. Arbitration of disputes involving multinational agreements is becoming more common as the government of Argentina signs more international trade and investment guarantee agreements, which typically include provisions calling for international arbitration of disputes. Argentina adheres to the provisions of the World Bank's Multilateral Investment Guarantee Agreement (MIGA) and US Overseas Private Investment Corporation (OPIC) which recognize international arbitration. Argentina is also a member of the International Center for the Settlement of Investment Disputes (ICSID). Moreover, Argentina has signed bilateral agreements providing for arbitration with the US, Italy, France, and Belgium.

Property Infringement Concerns Argentina has long recognized the need for property protection rights as a necessary incentive to encourage foreign investment. Strong federal laws protect intellectual and industrial property rights—including patents, copyrights, trademarks, and trade names—and Argentina has signed many international treaties and agreements—including MIGA, the OPIC agreement, and the Uruguay Round of the GATT—that secure these rights for foreign owners with property in Argentina. The Argentine constitution itself contemplates protection of intellectual property, stating in Article 17 that every author or inventor is the exclusive owner of the work, invention, or discovery produced for the period established by law. Although Argentina is a party to the Paris Convention for the Protection of Intellectual Property, some of the provisions of Argentine law appear to be inconsistent with that convention. However, Argentina is ameliorating many of these problems as it becomes more and more integrated in the international market.

Copyrights, governed by Law 11,723, are typically granted for 50 years from the time a work is first published and can be transferred through written assignments. Unpublished works are also protectable for three-year periods, renewable indefinitely. Article 13 of the Copyright Law extends protection to foreign works that are protected under foreign law, as long as authors can prove their rights to the works are recognized in their home countries. Copyright registrations, records of assignments, and other related documents are recorded in Argentina's National Copyright Register (NCR), or Registro Nacional del Derecho de Autor. Argentina is a member of several international copyright conventions, including the Berne Convention for the protection of literary and artistic work. Fees for registration of items such as trademarks are relatively minor, usually amounting to less than US$1,000, including professional fees.

In 1994 Argentina implemented an executive decree explicitly stating that computer software is protected under the Copyright Law. While software was technically protected under this law even before this decree, Argentina has had its problems with software piracy. Some government agencies have estimated that as much as 90 percent of the software market is held by pirates. As recently as a few years ago, infringers brazenly advertised their wares in Argentine newspapers. However, during the past two years, civil and criminal courts in Argentina have taken some highly publicized and aggressive measures to enforce copyright laws, seizing bootleg software, and imprisoning some of the more flagrant pirates. While the government appears to be taking its role in copyright enforcement with a new seriousness, its actions against infringers have been hampered by the slow pace of the Argentine court system.

Argentina has similarly stepped up its efforts to prevent infringement in the videocassette, compact disc, and audiocassette markets. Regulations now require the use of coded stickers on legitimate copies of such products; this allows police to identify illicit wares more easily. In some instances when the government has failed to act quickly enough to prevent infringement, the affected industries have formed trade associations to police their own markets.

Argentina's former patent regime, established by Law 111 of 1864, was the weakest area of the nation's guarantees of intellectual property rights. While most inventions, whether invented in Argentina or abroad, could be patented, pharmaceuticals were excluded. Argentina has now ratified GATT, which contemplates protection for pharmaceuticals traded in member countries. In early 1995, the Argentine Senate passed a bill that will substantially strengthen patent protection, addressed infringement, and extended patent duration from 10 to 20 years. In its original passage, this bill also authorized patents on pharmaceuticals after an eight-year transitional period. (*See* "New Patent Legislation" on page 236.)

To prevent problems over property rights, whether intangible or tangible, foreign businesspeople should insist on protective contract provisions that clearly establish the ownership of such rights and provide for apportionment of such rights in case the business relationship is dissolved.

RELATED SECTIONS

Refer to the "Taxation" chapter for a discussion of tax issues in Argentina; "Business Entities & Formation" for a description of the business forms recognized in Argentina and organizational procedures; "Foreign Investment" for a discussion of provisions and regulations; "Labor" for employment rules and standards; and "Import Policy & Procedures" and "Export Policy & Procedures" for discussions of rules involved in trade.

LAW DIGEST

[*Editor's note:* Because laws were enacted at various times, references are made to specific monetary amounts using different currencies—such as pesos, pesos moneda nacional (m$n), and australes, all of which have different relative equivalent values. Persons interested in operating in Argentina should check with legal counsel in Argentina to determine any specifically required amounts in terms of current pesos.]

ACKNOWLEDGMENTS

(Law 1,184)

Contracts, deeds, and other documents that require authentication by a public official are prepared in Argentina by a notary or other authorized public official, and made a part of the protocol. That is, the original documents are kept in an official register in the office of the notary or official. (*See* "Notaries Public"; "Public Instruments.") Instruments executed in foreign countries, however, are given full recognition in Argentina if duly acknowledged in the manner required in the country where they are executed, authenticated by a consular or diplomatic agent of Argentina, and the authentication certified by the Minister of Foreign Affairs of Argentina.

ALIENS

Foreigners enjoy the same civil rights in Argentina as Argentine citizens. They may do business, follow their trade or practice their profession and buy and sell real property.

Naturalization is granted to residents over 18 years of age after two years of continuous residence who meet the requirements set forth in Art. 2 of Law 346.

Foreigners may be allowed in the country as permanent, temporary or transitory residents. National identity cards will only be issued to foreigners who prove their permanent residency.

ATTACHMENTS

(Code of Civil Procedure for Federal Courts)

In order to attach property in an ordinary civil action, one of the following conditions must exist: (1) that the debtor is not domiciled in the Republic; (2) that the debt is evidenced by certain written instruments; (3) that in case of an action on a bilateral contract, the contract is in writing and complies with certain requirements as to its execution; (4) that the debt is evidenced by mercantile books kept in due form; or (5) if the debt is subject to a condition, that the plaintiff proves that the debtor tried to alienate, hide, or remove the property or that the responsibility of the debtor has decreased after the obligation was contracted.

An attachment will also issue against specific property that is the object of a possessory action. In an ordinary action, an attachment will issue at the request of any of the parties when facts are admitted that make out a prima facie case in their favor, or when a favorable judgment has been obtained.

The party who obtains an attachment must give security for costs and damages. Attachments will also issue in the summary actions known as "executory actions."

CHATTEL MORTGAGES

Two kinds of chattel mortgages are recognized: the so-called agrarian pledge (*prenda agraria*) and the registered pledge (*prenda con registro*). Both permit the debtor to retain possession of the article pledged, require the recording of the contract, provide a summary procedure for foreclosure, and forbid stipulations waiving such procedure, except that when the creditor is a government or banking institution, it may itself make the sale. The pledges are effective as towards third parties only from the date of recording. No subsequent pledge affecting the same property may be executed by the debtor, except with the consent of the creditor.

Agrarian Pledges Law 9,644 may affect: (a) machines in general, automobiles, agricultural implements, and tools; (b) animals and their products, and personal property devoted to rural operations; (c) fruits and crops corresponding to the year in which the pledge is made,... and timber, mining products, and products of national industries. The lien subsists for two years from the date of registration.

Registered Pledges Law 12,962 and Decree 8572/60 may cover chattels of any nature as well as growing crops, but may be made only in favor of: (a) the State, (b) co-operative societies and associations of farmers, stockmen, and industrialists; (c) warehousers of country products to guarantee credits; (d) merchants and industrialists to guarantee price of merchandise sold; and (e) registered loan establishments. A pledge may be of two kinds: (a) a specific pledge, covering specific articles of any nature, or (b) a floating pledge, covering merchandise and raw material in general to guarantee obligations of not more than 180 days; this

---

pledge covers the original articles and also those manufactured from them. A pledge contract may be assigned by endorsement, which to be valid against third persons must be recorded.

CONTRACTS

The nature, form, objects, and obligations of contracts are governed generally by the Civil Code. Nevertheless there is a definite class of contracts known as commercial or mercantile contracts, concerning which the provisions of the Civil Code are supplemented by the Commercial Code. The Civil Code, except as modified by the Commercial Code, however, governs mercantile contracts. (Civil Code, Art. 1137–1216).

To constitute a contract there must be an offer and acceptance, express or implied. The offer is void if the offeror dies or becomes incapacitated before the acceptance is received. Offers may be retracted any time before acceptance if the offeror has not renounced the right to retract. Verbal offers must be accepted immediately. A modification of the offer in the acceptance constitutes a new offer. The offeree may retract an acceptance any time before it reaches the offeror. If the offeree has accepted without knowledge of a retraction by the offeror or of the offeror's death or incapacity, the offeree is entitled to reimbursement for all losses suffered and expenses incurred.

Only those persons having legal capacity may enter into contracts, but only the incapacitated person, that person's representative, and any third parties affected may have a contract nullified because of incapacity. Ratification of a contract made in one's name has the same effect as previous authorization.

The objects of a contract must be definite or subject to definite determination.

The form of a contract is determined by the place where it is executed. If executed by various parties in different places, the formalities are governed by the law of whichever place is most favorable to its validity. According to the Civil Code the following contracts, except when executed at public auction, must be in the form of public instruments (*see* "Notaries Public" and "Public Instruments"): contracts regarding real property;... contracts of incorporation or partnership and extensions of the same, or such contracts whenever part of the capital is real property;... general and special powers of attorney for use in court, for the administration of property, or related to a public instrument or the execution of one; and contracts related to the performance of certain actions with respect to public instruments.

A contract that should be in the form of a public instrument, but that is drawn up as a private document, carries an obligation to reduce the same to a public instrument. The same rule applies to verbal contracts. Penalty clauses in contracts are enforceable.

Civil contracts involving more than 10,000 pesos must be in writing and cannot be proved by evidence other than the terms included in the writing. (See below with regard to modification in mercantile contracts).

Contracts made in Argentina that violate the laws of a foreign country are void. The validity, nature, and obligations of contracts to be carried out in Argentina are governed by Argentine laws, whether made in Argentina or in a foreign country, but if they are to be carried out in a foreign country, they are governed by the laws of that country. Contracts referring to real property in Argentina and executed in a foreign country, are valid if in the form of public instruments and properly legalized. If they are for the purpose of transferring title to real property the contracts must be protocolized by order of a competent judge.

As stated above, the Civil Law is supplemented by the Commercial Code in respect to mercantile contracts. In general the law of contracts set forth above is generic and applies to all contracts whether mercantile or otherwise. Matters falling within the scope of the Commercial Code are those relating to the transfer of personal property for the purpose of obtaining a profit from the same, whether in its form when transferred or after changing its form; operations of exchange, banking, or brokerage; negotiations with regard to bills of exchange, checks, or other endorsable paper; operations of factories, commercial agents, warehouses, and transportation; suretyship and corporate transactions, freight, construction, the purchase or sale of vessels, their equipment, and provisioning, and everything relative to maritime commerce; operations of factors, bookkeepers, and other employees of merchants concerning their employers; agreements with regard to the salaries of clerks and other employees of merchants; letters of credit, bonds, pledges, and similar documents; and other matters especially treated in the Code of Commerce. (Art. 8).

If a contract is commercial as to one party it is deemed commercial as to all parties. Commercial contracts may be evidenced by public instruments; by notations of mercantile agents and certificates of the contents of their books; by private documents signed by the parties or a witness in the contractor's name; by correspondence, telegrams, books of merchants, or admission of the parties; by witnesses; and by presumptions. Witnesses may not be used to prove a mercantile contract in matters involving more than mn$200 unless there is some written evidence of the contract. All blank

NEW REGULATIONS FOR REGISTRATION OF SOFTWARE

On 8 February 1994 the Executive Branch passed Decree No. 165/94 (the "Decree") which regulates the Intellectual Property Law No. 11,723 (the "IPL") with respect to registration of software. It should be noted that the IPL was enacted in 1933 and thus did not contemplate software. However, the Copyright Office has allowed the registration of software for protection purposes.

The Decree provides for the registration of published and unpublished works. This allows for the application of a reduced withholding tax rate of 10.5 percent on payments of royalties for software to foreign licensors.

Section 93(b) of the Argentine Income Tax Law provides that 35 percent of copyright royalty payments made to a foreign beneficiary are considered to be taxable income of the foreign beneficiary. Consequently, the effective income tax withholding rate for the foreign beneficiary of copyright royalty payments will amount to 10.5 percent of the gross royalty payments (30 percent on 35 percent). In order to be eligible for this tax benefit, several requirements should be met:

(a) The intellectual property or work should have been registered with the Argentine Copyright Office;

(b) The taxable income should derive from the exploitation of the author's rights and the applicable tax should directly affect the author/s and successor/s; and

(c) The taxable income should derive from the publication, performance, representation, exhibition, sale, translation, and other means of reproduction of the copyrighted materials, and should not derive from works completed by request or originated in the rendering of works or services agreed upon by contract.

If these conditions are not met, payments are subject to 27 percent income tax withholding. [*Editor's note:* because as of June 1995 the law had yet to be registered, the actual withholding rate was 30 percent based on the presumed payment rate.]

The Decree provides that:

(i) A software product or data base has been published when it has been put at the disposal of the general public, either by means of its reproduction in multiple copies which are commercially distributed or through the general offer of its transmission on an arm's-length basis with purposes of exploitation;

(ii) A software product or data base has not been published when its author, titleholder, or successor maintains it in confidence or negotiates the assignment of the intellectual property rights therein under an agreement with the interested parties.

Section 2 of the Decree provides that the registration of published databases should be made by means of a deposit of sufficient excerpts thereof and a brief indicating its structure, organization, and its main characteristics which may allow, in the opinion and at the risk of the applicant, for the individualization of the work and give the most accurate notion of its contents.

No indications are contained as to the way in which published software should be deposited. However, the Copyright Office has confirmed that its deposit in the form of a diskette, tape, or written document will be appropriate.

Section 3 of the Decree provides that in case of unpublished works or databases, the applicant should include in a wax-sealed and signed envelope, all the "expressions" of the work he deems appropriate and sufficient to identify his creation and guarantee the confidentiality of its secret information.

This sidebar is reproduced from Baker & McKenzie's Latin American Legal Developments Bulletin, vol. 2, no. 3 (April 1994); author Pablo Dukarevich of the Buenos Aires office. Copyright © 1994 Baker & McKenzie. Reprinted with permission of the law firm.

spaces and amendments in mercantile contracts must be authenticated by the signatures of the parties. Telegrams have the same force as letters. Words are understood in their general sense. In case of ambiguity, the intention of the parties must be sought and, when found, outweighs the literal sense. The customs of a business are taken into account in interpreting the contract. In general it may be said that contracts governed by the Commercial Code are made with much less formality than those that depend solely on the Civil Code, and the methods by which their existence and scope are proved are more numerous. Moreover, in many of the classes of commercial contracts, such as bills of exchange, checks, and partnership agreements, special rules are provided in the Commercial Code to govern their effect and operation.

COMMERCIAL COMPANIES

(Commercial Companies [Sociedades Comerciales] Law 19550) *See* "Partnerships."

Under Argentine law, stock companies (Sociedades Anónimas) are classed as mercantile companies even if not formed for commercial purposes. They are defined as two or more persons contributing capital for the purpose of producing or exchanging assets or services and dividing the profits and losses among themselves.

Corporate Name A firm name may include the name of one or more persons actually associated with the corporation and must contain the expression *sociedad anónima,* its abbreviation, or "S.A." Use of the words "of Argentina" or "Argentina," suggesting ties between the nation and a foreign corporation requires special authorization.

Articles of Incorporation should contain: (1) Information identifying all of the shareholders; (2) the firm name and domicile; (3) a precise indication of its purposes; (4) the amount of capital, expressed in Argentine currency, setting forth each shareholder's contribution; (5) the corporation's duration; (6) the organization of its management, the supervisory and accounting procedures, and the requirements for shareholders' meetings; (7) the rules regarding distribution of profits and losses; (8) the rights and duties of shareholders with respect to each other and to third parties; and (9) any provisions regarding operation, dissolution, and liquidation.

Liability of Stockholders and Directors During the process of incorporation, the promoters and directors are jointly and unlimitedly responsible for any debts. Directors are only authorized to carry out activities related to the incorporation and other activities authorized by the articles of incorporation. Once the company is constituted, it assumes all responsibilities undertaken in its name, and the promoters and directors are released from responsibility to third parties, although they may still be held liable to the company.

Stockholders who have fully paid for their stock are not liable for the obligations of the company. All stockholders with interests contrary to that of the company have a duty to abstain from voting in any such related matter or they could be responsible for resulting damages or injury from a vote on the matter. All stockholders voting in favor of a resolution subsequently declared null shall be unlimitedly and jointly responsible for any consequences resulting from that resolution.

Stockholders have a preemptive right with respect to all subsequent stock issues and can sue the company and directors if this right is violated.

Directors, supervisors, and overseers are unlimitedly and jointly liable for irregularities in public stock offerings and the distribution of dividends.

All administrators and representatives of the company are subject to a standard of loyalty and diligence and incur joint and unlimited liability for damages caused by noncompliance. A director of a company has a duty: (1) to reveal any conflict in interest to the board of directors and supervisors; (2) to abstain from any related deliberation; and (3) to refrain from competition with the company. Directors and supervisors are unlimitedly and jointly liable for negligent performance of their offices, or for violations of law or the rules of the company. A director can become exempt from this liability by filing a protest or a proceeding against the rest of the board, and stockholders may later vote to exonerate a director or manager from liability. A majority of directors must be domiciled in Argentina, and all directors must have special domicile in Argentina.

A company may censure any director, which will result in removal of that director from office.

Limited Liability Companies may be formed for any commercial purpose. The number of members cannot exceed 50; they are liable for the amounts stipulated next to their names in the company contract. The name of the company must be preceded or followed by the words "*sociedad de responsabilidad limitada*" or the letters "S.R.L.". The capital is divided into quotas of equal value. Twenty-five percent of the subscribed quotas must be paid within two years. A transfer of quotas requires a favorable vote of the quotaholders holding three-quarters of the capital of the company. Quotaholders who oppose a transfer are entitled to a judicial review of it.

A company is managed by one or more managers who have the same rights and duties as the directors of a corporation. A company may form a supervisory body or a committee of overseers that will be governed by the same provisions that are established for corporations. A committee of overseers is compulsory when the company's capital is more than 100,000 australes [now revised to 2,100,000 pesos]. Modifications of purpose, extensions of duration, transformations, mergers, splits, and all modifications that result in quotaholders having greater responsibilities may only be adopted by a vote of three-quarters of the company's capital. All other resolutions, such as the appointment of managers, may be adopted by a majority vote of the capital present. Each quota gives its holder the right to one vote.

Joint Stock Company (*sociedad en comandita por acciones*) is an entity in which the active partners incur liability to the same degree as the active partners of a general partnership and the silent partners limit their liability to the extent of their subscribed capital. Only the capital contributions of silent partners are represented by shares. Unless otherwise provided, joint stock companies are subject to provisions governing stock companies, and, in addition, to provisions governing general partnerships. The firm name must include the words "*sociedad en comandita por acciones*" its abbreviation, or the letters "S.C.A." The administrator shall become jointly liable with the company for failure to include these words. If the firm name does not contain the names of all the partners, the words "*y compañía*" or its abbreviation must also appear therein. Administration may be by a single person and undertaken by an active partner or a third party, whose term of office shall not have any maximum duration. Removal of the administrator is governed by the same rules pertaining to a general partnership, although a silent partner representing at least 5 percent of the capital may legally request removal with cause. An active partner who is removed as administrator has a right to withdraw from the company or to become a silent partner. If administration ceases, it must be reorganized within three months, during which time a provisional administrator is appointed. Meetings of the company shall include the active and silent partners and the administrator shall have a voice, but no vote. An assignment of any active partner's share of capital requires a favorable vote of a majority of the shares with a right to vote for which purpose any multiple vote rights attached to particular shares are disregarded.

Foreign Companies (Law 19550, Art. 118–124, and Law 8867) A company formed abroad and having only occasional dealings in Argentina is governed as to its existence and form by the laws of the country in which it is legally constituted. It is thus authorized to perform isolated acts in Argentina and to participate in lawsuits. In order to habitually engage in business as authorized by its charter, or to establish branches or any other type of permanent representation in Argentina, a foreign company must comply with following: (1) certify its existence in accordance with the laws of its domicile; (2) establish domicile in Argentina by complying with all local publication and registration requirements; and (3) justify its decision to create such representation and designate a representative to represent it in all civil and commercial matters. Branches must state the amount of capital assigned to their operations. If the laws of the country where the business is formed are dissimilar to Argentina laws, a judge of registry will establish the formalities to be completed by that business in Argentina. It is mandatory that the foreign company maintain separate accounts in Argentina and that it submit to administrative inspection. Normally, corporate papers, bylaws, and other documents related to the organization of the company must be registered in the Commercial Registry of the place where the office or agency has been established. In the nation's capital, registration is through the Inspección General de Justicia. Papers to be forwarded to Argentina should include certified copies of the certificate of incorporation and bylaws of the parent company and a broad power of attorney authorizing registration of the company and empowering a representative to conduct the business of the company in Argentina. If a company has a large capitalization, it should add a certified copy of a resolution of the board of directors that indicates the amount of capital to be employed in Argentina. This is for the purpose of reducing taxes and fees. All of these papers should be authenticated by an Argentina consul. (*See* "Acknowledgments"). A company should also add certified translations of all documents if practicable to avoid the expense of translation in Argentina.

Service of process on a foreign company may be accomplished as follows: (1) if related to an isolated act, personally on the agent who took part in the act or contract resulting in the litigation; (2) if there exists a branch or other representation, personally on the designated representative.

COPYRIGHT

(Law No. 11723) *See also* "Patents" and "Trademarks."

Copyrights may be obtained for scientific, literary and artistic works, including literary, dramatic and musical compositions, moving picture films, paintings, sculptures, maps, and phonograms. Privilege pertains to an author for life and to the author's heirs and assigns for 50 years after the author's death. It is subject to assignment, a record of which must be entered in the National Copyright Registry. For posthumous works the copyright period begins at the death of the author and continues for 50 years. If there are no heirs or assigns the privilege belongs to the state. Heirs or assigns cannot object to republication of a work if they permit 10 years to elapse without publishing it, nor to its translation 10 years after the author's death; but in such cases they may demand compensation to be determined by experts. Copyrights of anonymous works belonging to corporations last for 50 years. For photographic works, the copyright period runs for 20 years from first publication and for moving picture films 30 years.

Copyrights may be obtained for foreign works with the same rights as for native works, except that the privilege does not continue for a longer period than provided in the law of the country where the work was published; if such a period is longer than that designated in the Argentine law, the latter prevails.

In order to obtain a copyright, three copies of the work must be deposited within three months after its appearance in the National Copyright Registry. For foreign works the period runs from the day the work is offered for sale in Argentine territory. In the case of paintings, sculptures, and similar works, a sketch or photograph must be deposited along with data to permit identification. For moving picture films, the deposit consists of an account of the plot and dialogue and photographs of the principal scenes. The National Copyright Registry publishes a daily report in the official newspaper of the works filed, and if no objection is received within one month, the copyright is granted.

A national license for translating foreign nontranslated works may be granted to Argentine residents seven years after publication.

Works that become public domain shall nevertheless earn dues for exhibition, performance, reproduction, edition, and other uses.

Industrial Models and Designs Decree-Law 6,673/63 grants five-year protection to registered industrial models and designs, including foreign ones filed within six months of registration in the foreign country. Protection for foreign industrial models and designs is available to the extent that similar Argentine intellectual property is protected under reciprocal provisions available in the home country of the foreign investor seeking protection in Argentina.

DEEDS AND REGISTRATION

(C.C. Art. 997–1011)

Contracts involving the conveyance, alienation, or encumbrance of real property must be in the form of public documents or documents duly authenticated and registered. (*See* "Acknowledgments"; "Notaries Public"; "Public Instruments"; "Records.")

FOREIGN JUDGMENTS

(C.C.P. Art. 517–519)

Foreign judgments have the force provided by treaty. In the absence of a treaty, a foreign judgment may be enforced if the following circumstances exist: (1) the judgment was obtained in an action in personam; (2) the judgment was not entered by default against a defendant who was a resident of Argentina; (3) the obligation with regard to which the judgment has been issued is valid according to

the Argentine law; and (4) the judgment was issued in compliance with all the legal requirements of the country where issued and is properly authenticated according to the laws of Argentina. A petition for the execution of the judgment must be presented to the judge of first instance. The judgment will be translated if it is in a foreign language, and the judge will then hear the parties and the District Attorney and will decide whether it should be enforced. Foreign judgments are enforced in the manner provided for the enforcement of local judgments. The decision of the court of first instance may be appealed.

INTEREST

Obligations may bear interest at any rate that contracting parties stipulate (C. C. Art. 621), but in practice, courts will not enforce interest rates above those that Argentine banks are permitted to charge, on the ground that usury is against public policy. Interest may not be compounded, except when parties make an agreement after interest is due to authorize the addition of interest to the capital, or when a judgment is obtained for principal and interest and the debtor defaults in payment. If a debt is past due, interest must be paid at the agreed rate or in absence of an agreement, at the interest rate established by law, or if no interest rate is established by law, at such rate as a court may determine. (C.C. Art 622). A debtor is not in default until a demand is made judicially or extrajudicially, except when a contract provides that default shall occur if the debt is not paid at a certain time or when the nature and circumstances of the obligation indicate that time is of the essence.

An interest rate established by a court in a case of default may vary in different parts of the Republic. The Code of Commerce (Art. 565) provides that in case interest is stipulated but the amount is not set, the rate established by public banks is intended, and then only in case of default. It also provides that if the law or contract provides for interest at the current rate, the rate intended is that being charged by the National Bank. Art. 569 of the Code of Commerce provides that by means of a judicial proceeding or by private agreement, interest may be earned on arrears of interest. In the case of a judicial proceeding, the interest must be in arrears for at least one year. Interest is likewise earned on a balance due at end of a year pursuant to settlements.

The Penal Code provides that if a person takes advantage of the inexperience or necessity of another and induces the other to promise or to give in any way interest or other pecuniary gains that do not reasonably relate to the services promised or rendered, or to grant deposits or guarantees that can

FOREIGN INVESTMENT

FOREIGN INVESTMENT ACT

The Foreign Investment Act, as codified September 8, 1993 by Executive Order 1,853/93, provides as follows:

Article 1 Foreign investors who invest capital in Argentina using any form established in Article 3 for promoting economic activities, or expanding or enhancing existing ones, will have the same rights and duties that the Constitution and the laws accord to domestic investors, subject to the terms of this law and special or promotional regimes.

Article 2 The following definitions are used in this law:

(1) Foreign capital investment: (a) all capital contributions belonging to foreign investors and used in economic activities in Argentina; and (b) all or part of an existing domestic company's capital acquired by foreign investors.

(2) Foreign investor: all natural and legal persons domiciled outside Argentina; the holder of a foreign capital investment; and domestic companies of foreign capital (defined in the next section) that invest in domestic companies.

(3) Domestic company of foreign capital: all companies domiciled in Argentina in which natural or legal persons domiciled outside the Republic directly or indirectly own more than 49 percent of the capital, or directly or indirectly control the number of votes necessary to prevail in stockholders' or partners' meetings.

(4) Domestic company of domestic capital: all companies domiciled within Argentina, in which natural or legal persons also domiciled within the Republic directly or indirectly own not less than 51 percent of the capital and directly or indirectly control the number of votes necessary to prevail in stockholders' or partners' meetings.

(5) Domicile: as defined in Civil Code, Articles 89 and 90.

Article 3 Foreign investments can be made in: (1) freely convertible foreign currency; (2) capital goods, their parts, and accessories; (3) earnings or capital in domestic currency belonging to foreign investors, whenever lawfully transferable abroad; (4) capitalization of foreign credits in freely convertible foreign currency; (5) intangible assets, in accordance with specific laws; and (6) other types of contributions established in special or promotional regimes.

Article 4 Regulations pursuant to this law will be issued by an administrative agency within the Ministry of Economy and Public Works and Services, with a rank not inferior to Undersecretariat which, acting as the Enforcement Authority, will establish its structure, functions, and faculties.

Article 5 Foreign investors may remit abroad any net and realized profits as a result of their investments and may also repatriate their capital.

Article 6 Foreign investors are entitled to utilize any of the corporate structures recognized by Argentine laws.

Article 7 Domestic companies of foreign capital may access the domestic credit market with the same rights and conditions as domestic companies of domestic capital.

Article 8 Temporary contributions of foreign capital made pursuant to contracts for the provision of goods, works, services, or other activities are not subject to this law. They are instead governed by the terms of the respective contracts in accordance with applicable laws, notwithstanding which the owners of such contributions may choose to have their investment governed by this law.

Article 9 Legal deeds entered into between a domestic company of foreign capital and the company (or a subsidiary thereof) that directly or indirectly controls it are considered, for all purposes, to have been created between independent parties when the terms and conditions conform to usual market practices among independent entities.

Article 10 Prior laws relating to foreign investment and general rules issued pursuant to them are repealed. This law will apply to all proceedings pending under the repealed laws.

EXECUTIVE ORDER 1,853/93

Executive Order 1,853/93 of September 8, 1993, which approved the Foreign Investment Act codified on that same date, provides as follows:

Article 1 The codified text of the Foreign Investment Act as revised by the Economic and Administrative Reform

Acts is hereby approved as enclosed with this executive order.

Article 2 Foreign investors may invest in Argentina without prior approval, under the same conditions as investors domiciled within the country.

Article 3 The legal definition of foreign investor also includes Argentine natural or legal persons domiciled outside the national territory.

Article 4 Economic or productive activities include all industrial, mining, agricultural, commercial, financial, service, and other activities related to the production or exchange of goods and services.

Article 5 Foreign investors may exercise at any time their rights to repatriate their capital and to remit their earnings abroad.

Article 6 Except for the reserve mandated by law, the proportion of voluntary or statutorily constituted reserves owned by foreign investors in a domestic company, or those resulting from reappraisals or accounting updates, will not be considered as reinvestment of foreign capital.

Article 7 The prior approval required by the Technology Transfer Act is hereby repealed.

Article 8 For purposes of the Technology Transfer Act, all legal deeds entered into between independent companies, plus any made between a domestic company with foreign capital and the company (or a subsidiary) that directly or indirectly controls it, must be registered with the National Institute for Industrial Technology for informational purposes.

Article 9 The Secretariat of Commerce and Investment of the Ministry of Economy and Public Works and Services will be the Enforcement Authority of this law.

Articles 10, 11 The Enforcement Authority will have the following duties: (1) To gather statistical information on foreign investments; and (2) to issue general interpretive rules and take other action necessary to enforce the Foreign Investment Act (as codified September 8, 1993) and the rules approved in this Executive Order.

Article 12 Executive Order 1225 on foreign investment of November 14, 1989 is repealed.

be deemed extortion, the person taking such advantage shall be penalized by imprisonment and fine. The same penalty is applicable to a person who in bad faith acquires, transfers, or claims credit bearing usurious interest. These penalties are increased if a person is a professional lender or a commission merchant who commits acts of usury frequently.

LICENSES

Law 22,362, Decree 580/81, and Decree 1,853/93 govern the transfer of technology agreements. The Law applies to juridical acts that are intended to transfer technology or trademarks by persons domiciled outside the country to natural or legal persons domiciled in the country, when said acts produce effects in Argentina. License Agreements between related parties (such as parent-subsidiary) must be registered at the National Institute of Industrial Technology (INTI) to obtain tax preferences. License agreements between unrelated parties may, but need not, be registered at INTI for informational purposes only. Agreements covering "military secrets" need not be filed at all. Agreements between related parties must conform to usual commercial practices between independent parties. Failure to register the application at INTI does not invalidate the agreement, but any royalty expenses by the licensee become nondeductible and fees received by the licensor will be taxed at the full rate.

MONOPOLIES AND RESTRAINT OF TRADE

(Constitution 1994 Art. 10; Law 22,262; Law 18,875; Law 20,852; and Law 22,802)

The Argentine Constitution guarantees free circulation of goods. Since 1919 Argentina has had laws that regulate the monopolization of trade and abuse of economic power. Present law for the defense of competition covers monopoly practices in one or more branches of production, industry, or transport, or in domestic or foreign trade, throughout the national territory. The law is framed to prevent monopolization of the market rather than to cure it. The law defines "dominant position" as a question of fact. There is a "dominant position" when a person is the only one who offers or demands a specific product in the national market or when a specific good or service has no effective competition. The law also refers to a "dominant position" as one in which two or more persons do not compete between themselves or with a third party.

Acts of monopoly include those intended to fix prices, to limit or control technical development of production of goods or services, to limit distribution, to make exclusive rights agreements to tied-purchasing agreements, to fix resale prices below or over cost, and to destroy production in order to increase prices. The law is a flexible policy instrument that the government can modulate according to the needs of the market. For this purpose the law has created a public agency to study and repress monopolization and restrictive business practices.

NOTARIES PUBLIC (ESCRIBANOS PÚBLICOS)

(Notarial Law 12990; C.C. Arts. 997–1011) *See* "Pubic Instruments."

A notary must be an Argentine citizen, hold a degree in notarial services, and be a member of a national association. A notary may not be employed for a salary, nor engage in commerce, banking, or legal practice. The number of notarial offices is limited; notaries are appointed by the Federal Executive and they are subject to the supervision of the courts and the national association.

All important documents that are referred to in this digest as notarial documents (*escrituras públicas*) and that are a class of public instruments (*see* "Public Instruments") will have legal effect only if prepared by a notary or other competent official, and preserved in the record or protocol, which is an official registry.

Notarial documents must be in Spanish. If the person executing the document does not know Spanish, the document should be made in the form of a memorandum signed by the parties in the presence of and authenticated by the notary. If not signed in the notary's presence the genuineness of the signature must be certified to by the notary. It is then translated by an official interpreter. The memorandum and the translation are then placed in the notary's protocol.

A notarial document must state its nature, its object, the names and surnames of the persons executing it, whether they are of age, their family status, domicile or residence, and the place, day, month, and year when it was signed, which may be a holiday or Sunday. The notary must certify to knowing the persons executing the document, and when the certification is completed, it should be read it to the parties, and should at the end certify in handwriting to any interlineations or amend-

ments in the document. The document containing a complete statement of all the conditions, clauses, periods of payment, and the sums delivered in the presence of the notary is then signed by the parties in the presence of two witnesses whose names must be stated in the body of the document, and is then authenticated at the end of the document by the notary. If the notary does not know the parties, two witnesses must identify the parties, and the document must include their names, residence, and a certificate that the notary knows the witnesses. If the parties are represented by agents, the document must state that the power of attorney has been presented, and it must be transcribed in the notary's register along with the document. If the power has been executed in the notary's office, the notary need only refer to its place of record. Notarial documents that do not state the place and date of execution, the names of the persons signing, and their signatures, and that do not include the power of attorney (when executed by an agent) and the statement of the presence of two witnesses and their signatures, are void. The absence of other formalities does not vitiate the document, but renders the notary liable to fine. Documents are also void if not found in their proper place in the notary's protocol.

The notary must give any parties who request it an authenticated copy of the document. Subsequent copies may be given also, but a party who is required by the document to do any act is entitled to have a subsequent copy only by order of the court. Copies may only be given on citation of the parties in order to give them an opportunity to compare the copy with the original, and in case of their absence, a public official is appointed by the court for that purpose.

PARTNERSHIPS

(Law 19550)

A general partnership (*sociedad colectiva*) is a partnership of two or more persons with unlimited and joint responsibility, which is formed for commercial purposes under a firm name that must include the words "*sociedad colectiva*" or an abbreviation thereof. If the firm name does not contain the names of all partners, the words "*y compañía*" or its abbreviation must also appear therein. A partnership agreement regulates administration of the company, and in the absence of a contrary provision, any partner may indiscriminately administer the company. If certain partners are charged with administration of the company but no roles are specifically stated and no actions are expressly required to be taken jointly, the partners may indiscriminately undertake any administrative act. An administrator may be removed at

ENVIRONMENTAL LEGISLATION—HAZARDOUS WASTE

Decree No. 831/93 was published in the Official Gazette on 5 May 1993. The government has implemented, by means of this decree, the Hazardous Waste Law No. 24,05 1 of December 1991 ("HWL"). Substantially, this decree has a technical content. The local business community and legal advisors are still assessing its impact.

In brief, HWL regulates, at the federal level, the handling, transport, and final disposal of hazardous waste. HWL is applicable in the following situations:

(i) When waste is produced or located in places of federal jurisdiction;

(ii) When, although the waste is located within a provincial territory, it is intended to be transported outside of the province;

(iii) When, in the opinion of the Secretariat of the Environment, said waste could affect individuals or the environment beyond the territorial limits of the province in which it was produced; and

(iv) When the health or safety measures to be taken may have such an important economic incidence that it would be advisable to make such measures uniform in the whole of the federal territory.

Hazardous waste is defined in HWL as any residue that may cause harm, directly or indirectly, to human beings, or that may pollute the soil, the water, the atmosphere or the environment in general. Hazardous waste, radioactive waste, and spillage resulting from ordinary operations of ships are excluded from the definition of hazardous waste and will be governed by special laws and existing international treaties on these specific matters.

The enforcing authority, the Secretariat of the Environment, is in charge of the Federal Registry of Producers and Operators of Hazardous Waste. All the individuals and legal entities responsible for the production, transport, treatment, and final disposal of hazardous waste must register with said authority.

The individuals or companies involved in tasks that are regulated by the law must obtain an environmental certificate, issued by the enforcing authority. This certificate furnishes proof that the systems of handling, transport, treatment, or disposal to be applied to the hazardous waste by those individuals or companies registered, have been duly approved. This certificate shall be renewed each year.

HWL includes criminal provisions that punish with imprisonment for up to 25 years when hazardous waste provokes the death of a person.

Liability

In this regard, HWL establishes strict liability by reason of damage to third parties. This liability cannot be avoided by invoking transfer or abandonment of ownership of the hazardous waste. Likewise, the owner or custodian of hazardous waste cannot avoid being held liable by furnishing proof of a third party's fault whose action could have been avoided by acting with due diligence. The transformation, specification, development, evolution, or treatment of hazardous waste does not prevent its producers from being held liable for the damages caused by said hazardous waste with the exception of the damages caused by a more dangerous characteristic that a certain waste acquires as a result of a defective treatment made at a treatment or disposal facility.

The law includes lists of substances and products subject to control, of materials with dangerous features, and of operations that can or cannot lead to resource recovery, recycling, regeneration, direct reutilization, or other uses.

This sidebar is reproduced from Baker & McKenzie's Latin American Legal Developments Bulletin, vol. 1, no. 2 (July 1993); authors Miguel Menegazzo Cane and Marcelo Slonimsky of the Buenos Aires office. Copyright © 1993 Baker & McKenzie. Reprinted with permission of the law firm.

any time without cause by a majority vote of the partners, unless otherwise provided. If the partnership agreement requires removal with cause, any partner may request a judicial determination thereof. An administrator may resign at any time unless otherwise provided, but will remain responsible for any damages resulting from a fraudulent or untimely resignation. All modifications of a partnership agreement require the unanimous approval of the partners, unless otherwise provided, and all other resolutions shall be adopted by majority vote. A partner may not undertake acts for self-interest or for third parties that in any way compete with the partnership, except with the express and unanimous consent of the other partners.

Limited Partnership (*sociedad en comandita simple*) is a partnership formed for commercial purposes with two or more persons. Active partners have the same responsibilities as the partners of a general partnership, while silent partners are liable to the extent of their capital contribution. The firm name must include the words "*sociedad en comandita simple*" or its abbreviation and the names of all active partners should appear therein. The administration of a limited partnership is undertaken by active partners or third parties and is subject to the same norms as general partner-

ships. If silent partners interfere in the business or act as agents of the partnership, they become unlimitedly liable for all such acts, although they may examine books, give opinions, and advise in matters undertaken by partnership without incurring such liability. Resolutions are adopted in the same manner as in a general partnership. Silent partners have a right to vote on accounting matters and on the appointment of administrators. In event of bankruptcy, death, or incapacity of all active partners, a silent partner may undertake all urgent acts of the partnership until the situation stabilizes, without incurring liabilities otherwise applicable. A partnership is dissolved if it is not stabilized within three months. If the silent partners do not comply with all legal provisions, they shall be unlimitedly and jointly liable for their conduct.

NEW PATENT LEGISLATION

The Argentine Congress approved a new Patent Law on 30 March 1995.

One of the major differences from old Patent Law No. 111 of 1864 is that the new law does not exclude the patentability of pharmaceutical compositions. Some of the most important aspects are:

(i) "Invention" means any human creation that transforms matter or energy for human exploitation.

(ii) For an invention to be patentable, it must be new, imply an inventive activity, and be capable of having an industrial use.

(iii) The duration of a patent is 20 years from the filing date of the application.

(iv) The holder of a patent is obliged to work the patented invention, by itself or through third parties in the territory of the Argentine Republic. "Working" includes manufacturing, adequate distribution, and marketing, in a way sufficient to meet the demand of the domestic market.

(iv) Compulsory licenses are provided for in case of lack of exploitation.

(v) Protection is available for utility models for a 10-year term.

(vi) The National Institute of Industrial Property is made an autonomous agency, operating within the scope of the Ministry of Economics and Public Works and Services. It has jurisdiction over trademarks, industrial models and designs, and technology transfer laws.

In order to have the new law adapted to the GATT/TRIPS Agreement, which was approved by the Argentine Congress by Law No. 24,225 of 5 January 1995, President Menem on 18 April 1995 returned the new Patent Law to Congress after having "observed" 16 of its articles.

Among the most controversial "observed" provisions are Article 42, which requires working the patent in Argentina (importation is not sufficient), and Article 104, which establishes that pharmaceutical products will not be patentable before 1 January 2003. Congress, however, insisted, and on 23 May 1995 finally passed the patent bill into law with only a few changes.

Under the bill as finally passed, a patent holder is not required to manufacture the product in Argentina, thus accepting importation of the product to comply with the exploitation requirement. The 8-year transition period (a pharmaceutical product will be patentable only as from 1 January 2003) was ratified by Congress.

Joint Venture Another class of partnership is *"sociedad accidental o en paticipación,"* which is formed for one or more specific, temporary commercial transactions. It is not a juridical entity, and members may operate in their own names without a firm designation. It has no special form and does not register with the Public Commercial Registry. It is subject to the general law of contracts. If members knowingly allow their names to be used in the business, they incur unlimited and joint liability. Otherwise, third parties only have recourse against the member with whom they acted. Unless otherwise specified, members have the same rights of inspection as silent partners, and a member not engaged in a transaction is liable only to the extent of the contributed capital. Dissolution and liquidation are governed by the rules applicable to general partnerships.

Since 1983 joint ventures have been eligible to be organized as temporary partnerships or unions of companies. Other types of partnerships include the partnership of capital and industry (*sociedad de capital e industria*), and the cooperative society (*sociedad cooperativa*).

PRESCRIPTION

(C.C. Art. 3947–4043; C. Com. Art. 846–855)

The acquisition and loss of real and personal rights through the lapse of time is called "prescription".

Argentina has become a party to the Convention on the Limitation Period in the International Sale of Goods, of 1980.

Actions In any kind of actions, mere inaction of a creditor for the period designated by law, without the necessity of a presumptive title or good faith, frees the obligee from all obligations. The period of prescription varies according to the type of action. Chapters of both the Civil Code and Code of Commerce on prescription should be consulted, in addition to any provisions of law with respect to the particular subject.

An action of a debtor to demand restitution of a pledge given as a security of a credit prescribes in 20 years if the pledge has remained in the possession of the creditor or his or her heirs.

The obligation to pay the fees of arbitrators, lawyers, employees in the administration of justice, and notaries, and the salaries of agents prescribes in two years.

The action of creditors to revoke agreements made by debtors in fraud or prejudice of their rights, prescribes in one year.

The action of a purchaser to rescind a contract prescribes in six months.

In mercantile matters the period of prescription is 10 years unless a shorter period is provided by the Code of Commerce, the Civil Code, or other laws. (C. Com. Art. 846). Certain commercial actions prescribe in less than 10 years Art. 847–855. These include actions related to the recission of a judicial act of a commercial nature, which prescribes in four years unless a different period is specifically provided; related to the improper operations of a company or regarding certain classes of endorsable documents or of documents payable to bearer, which prescribe in three years; and related to maritime freight contracts, contracts of surety, and the provisioning of vessels, which prescribe in one year.

PRINCIPAL AND AGENT

(C. C. Art. 1869–1985; Com. C. Art. 221–281)

Agency may be conferred by a public or private instrument or orally. Acceptance may be express or implied. A general power of attorney only confers a power of administration, even though that power gives authority to do any act that the grantee deems convenient in the course of administration (C.C. art 1880). Special powers are necessary for the following purposes (C.C. Art. 1881): to make payments that are not in the ordinary course of administration; to make contracts extinguishing obligations that existed at the time the power was granted; to compromise a suit; to arbitrate; to waive jurisdiction; to renounce rights that have been acquired by prescription; to renounce a right to appeal; to renounce or remit debts gratuitously, except in the case of a bankruptcy of a debtor;... to make any contract for the purpose of obtaining or transferring real property; to make gifts, except in cases of small sums given to employees; to loan or borrow money unless the business of administration consists of loaning or borrowing, or unless it is absolutely necessary to borrow money to conserve property that is being administered; to lease real property for more than six years; to shift the status of a grantee to that of a bailee, unless the power refers to bailments or bailment is made as result of administration of the property; to require a grantee to perform any sort of personal services; to form a company; to give the grantee surety status; to create encumbrances on real property;... and to admit obligations existing prior to the granting of the power.

As general rule anyone capable of contracting may exercise a power of attorney. Unless specifically provided to the contrary, when a power is given to more than one person, it is understood that it is to be accepted by one of them only.

A grantee is required to carry out a power within the limits of authority given. For instance, a special power to sell does not include the power to mortgage nor to receive deferred payments, and a power to collect debts does not include the power to sue nor to modify a contract or remit a debt. A grantee must prefer interests of the grantor to any self-interests and must account for all operations and deliver to the grantor everything received as a result of exercising the power. A grantee may not sell property to the grantor or purchase the grantor's property without express authority. {Power may be delegated to another, but the grantor remains responsible for the substitute unless given express authority to substitute. A grantee may revoke a substitution at any time.

Powers of attorney that are to be presented in court, those for administration of property, and those that concern public instruments or matters that should be in the form of public instruments, must themselves be in the form of public instruments. (*See* "Notaries Public" and C. C. Art. 1184).

A power is terminated by revocation, renunciation on the part of the grantee, death of the grantee or grantor, or incapacitation of either party. The grantee and any third persons affected must know or should have known of the termination of the power in order to make it ineffective with regard to them. Everything that a grantee does while justifiably ignorant of a termination of the power binds the grantor. (C. C. Art. 1964–1966).

A revocation of a power may be express or implied. It is implied when a grantor gives a new power for the same purpose and the former grantee has knowledge of the subsequent power. (C. C. Art. 1971). The grant of a special power revokes a general power insofar as it affects matters dealt with in the special power.

An agent must act within the limits of the power but should not do less than what has been so entrusted. The nature of a business determines the extent of the powers needed to achieve the purpose of agency. An agent is not considered to have acted beyond the limits of a power if the result has been more advantageous than what was expected in granting the agency.

The functions of an agent are bestowed on various persons including those holding the necessary representation; on corporate representatives; and on representatives for the administration or liquidation of companies.

An agent is obligated, by virtue of acceptance of the agency, to comply with terms of the agency, and is liable for damages incurred by the principal due to partial or total noncompliance. However, an agent who finds it impossible to follow instructions is not obliged to act without further instructions, it being sufficient to take whatever conservation measures are indicated by the circumstances. An agent is required to render an account of the operations and to deliver to the principal everything received under the agency, even though it was not owing to the principal. The principal can even demand any gains resulting from abuse of the agent's powers, provided the agency was lawful, but the principal is not entitled to the benefits of an unlawful agency.

An agent's acts within the limits of the authority are deemed to have been done by the principal; the agent cannot enforce them, nor is the agent liable for them. An agent may sign contracts in the agent's own name or in name of the principal. If an agent exceeds the authority and the act is not ratified by the principal, such act is void, provided the other contracting party was aware of the true extent of the agent's authority. Neither would the agent be liable in such a case, unless the agent took on a personal obligation or committed to obtaining ratification. An agent would be personally liable if the other party was ignorant of the agent's actual authority. Ratification by the principal may be tacit, as by a manifest action or silence after being advised of the agent's act. Ratification is retroactive to the date of the agent's act.

With respect to third parties, an act is deemed to have been performed within the limits of an agency if its terms have been carried out, even though the agent may have actually exceeded the limits of the powers. A third party may not claim that powers have been exceeded or that terms of an agency have not been observed once the principal has ratified an action or has expressed a desire to ratify whatever has been done by the agent.

An agency may be gratuitous or onerous. It is presumed to be gratuitous if there has been no agreement that the agent is to receive remuneration for the work. It is presumed to be onerous if it consists of powers or functions conferred on the agent by law or when it consists of work connected with a lucrative profession or occupation of the agent. If an agency is onerous, the principal must pay the agent for services. The amount of fees may consist of a proportion of money or of goods that the agent, in carrying out the agency, has obtained or administered, except as provided in codes of procedures concerning lawyers and procurators. A principal must also compensate an agent for losses incurred in carrying out the agency but without fault on the agent's part.

PUBLIC INSTRUMENTS

(C. C. Art. 979–996) *See* "Notaries Public (Escribanos Públicos)."

Public instruments include all notarial documents ("*escrituras públicas*"), prepared by notaries in their registries ("*protocolo*") or by other public officers who have the same powers, together with copies of the same made in the manner provided by law, as well as many other documents, such as judicial documents and authorized shares of company stock.

Public instruments must be signed by the interested parties. Some classes of people, such as bankrupts, clergy, nonresidents of the place, and minors, may not be witnesses to public documents.

RECORDS

Registry of Real Property Real property registries exist in each province. The following documents shall be registered: (a) those that constitute, transmit, declare, modify, or extinguish rights on real estate; (b) those that impose attachments and any other injunctions; and (c) those required by other national or provincial laws.

To register these documents, certain formalities are required, such as acknowledgment by a notary public or by an administrative or judicial resolution.

These registries are public. Anybody with a legitimate interest can investigate the legal status of real estate therein registered, and any deeds, limitations, and attachments recorded. Registration fees usually depend on the value of the real property registered, the amount of the capital in a mortgages, and so forth. Fees also vary in each town or province according to their respective laws.

Commercial Register A public register is maintained by each commercial court for registration of all the merchants under its jurisdiction who are required to register their business license and other documents, such as articles of incorporation and bylaws in the case of a corporation, powers of attorney for managing the enterprise granted by merchants to factors or agents, and revocation of the same. (C. Com. Arts. 34–42). Registration in the federal capital is through the Inspección General de Justicia.

Industrial Register All natural or juridical persons, whether public or private, national or foreign, that engage in any kind of industrial activity in the country must register within 30 days of obtaining administrative authorization. Registration must be made for each separate industrial activity on an annual basis.

SALES

(Civil Code, Art. 1363–1407)

Sales of real property may be made subject to whatever conditions the contracting parties desire to make. A general provision not to resell is void, but a contract not to resell to a specific person is valid.

The law of conditional sales of personal property as known in Anglo-Saxon countries is not developed in Argentina. It is specifically forbidden to sell

---

COMPARATIVE ADVERTISING

Argentina's legislation does not specifically prohibit comparative advertising. But in 1971 Chamber II of the Federal Court of Appeals in Rolex S.A. vs. Orient S.A. ruled that using a competitor's trademark without its consent in an advertising campaign is an act of unfair competition.

In a more recent case, Axoft Argentina S.A. vs. Megasistemas S.A. (case No. 6,275/91 of 30 December 1993) Chamber II of the Federal Court of Appeals ruled that, while in principle only the owner of a trademark registration has the right to use the trademark, and thus a third party cannot use it without the owner's authorization, if a third party mentions the other party's trademark or refers to it in advertising, it is not allowed to discredit it.

In this case the defendant had used the competitors' trademark when comparing an old version of the competitor's software program with its own new version. The Court ordered the publicity to stop.

When Pepsi launched the "Pepsi Challenge" campaign (which compares Pepsi and Coke), at Coke's request Chamber II of the Federal Court of Appeals, by decision dated 22 October 1993, (published on 1 June 1994, in *La Ley*) preventively ordered Pepsi to stop the publicity holding that the campaign appeared to be contrary to honest practices in commerce, and that in view of section 10 bis (1) of the Paris Convention the court is bound to ensure effective protection against unfair competition. This case is now before the Supreme Court.

This sidebar is reproduced from Baker & McKenzie's Latin American Legal Developments Bulletin, vol. 3, no. 1 (January 1995); author Bernard W. Malone of the Buenos Aires office. Copyright © 1995 Baker & McKenzie. Reprinted with permission of the law firm.

---

personal property with a condition that title shall not pass until the price is paid, or that the vendor may reclaim the property on returning the purchase price. Nor may personal property be sold on condition that the sale is void if a purchaser can be found who offers a better price.

International Sale of Goods The United Nations Convention for the International Sale of Goods is in force.

TRADEMARKS

(Law 22362; Decree 558/81)

The ownership and exclusive right of a trademark is obtained by registration. To have a legitimate interest is a legal requirement for owning a trademark or opposing applications filed by third parties. Protection of a trademark lasts for 10 years and may be renewed indefinitely for periods of 10 years if the trademark has been used within a period of five years prior to each renewal. The rights to a trademark may be transferred freely to third parties, provided the transfer is recorded in the National Bureau of Industrial Property.

A petition for trademark registration must specify the name, address, and domicile of the petitioner; a description of the mark; and an indication of the products or services to be identified. Once an application for registration has been filed, it is published officially. The National Bureau of Industrial Property must make a decision within 30 days. An application for renewal of a trademark must be accompanied by a sworn statement declaring that the trademark has been used within five years prior to renewal, and for at least one of the classes in the Classification of Products and Services (adopted by Decree 558/81), or as a tradename. The product,

service or activity for which the trademark was used must also be stated.

The right of ownership of a trademark expires by waiver of the holder, termination of the term of duration, or court order nullifying or canceling the registration. A right of action for nullification prescribes after 10 years. An order of nullification can be obtained against a registration holder who knew or was in a position to know that a trademark belonged to a third party or when a trademark has been registered for the purpose of selling it to a third party. Judicial cancellation can be requested by a legitimately interested party for the nonlocal use of a trademark in any of the classes in which it was registered, within five years prior to the date of filing such a request.

Misuse of trademarks or commission of acts made illegal by the trademark law is punishable by fine and arrest. Those who commit punishable acts will be liable for from three months to two years imprisonment plus a fine. Attachment may be obtained by an owner of a trademark against articles that bear the trademark illegally.

Financial Institutions

INTRODUCTION

The overhaul of the nation's economic and financial system has launched Argentina on a trajectory toward current recovery and future growth. These actions manifested themselves primarily through an emergency economic reform package, including such sweeping reform legislation as the Economic Emergency Law of 1989, the Reform of the State Law of 1989, and the 1991 Convertibility Law (tying the Argentine peso to the US dollar at parity). These policies—coupled with commercial deregulation, labor and trade reforms, wholesale privatization of Argentina's bloated state-run industrial sector, financial market liberalization, set the stage for the recovery and stabilization of Argentine financial markets and systems, repositioning the economy for greater capacity utilization and growth.

There has been a long history of foreign financial institutional participation in the Argentine banking system, dating back to the 19th century, but full participation in the domestic market has been hampered by political expediencies and economic realities in the past. However, foreign banks and other financial institutions are operating in Argentina in a variety of guises. With annual inflation now lower than that found in many European countries and a more level playing field for foreign companies (foreign banks now operate on the same

regulatory and supervisory basis as local private institutions), entry barriers and operational constraints have eased, if not fallen outright. Domestic Argentine commercial banks, investment banks, cooperative banks, finance companies, credit card companies, and credit companies still provide the bulk of the financial services to the economy. As of the end of 1994, foreign banks controlled only approximately 15 percent of the nation's deposit base and held approximately 17 percent of all loans outstanding. Provided the crisis in early 1995 is weathered, financial stability is maintained, and economic expansion resumes, opportunities for foreign-owned financial institutions should proliferate in both commercial and retail markets.

Economic growth and financial stability aside, recent regulatory and monetary measures have made Argentina a far more attractive place for foreign businesses. The "new" Argentine economy has encouraged a repatriation of national capital held abroad, reversing the massive capital outflows of the past (as indicated by the huge increase in foreign currency time deposits held by Argentine banks). Greater financial solvency, transparency, and security of the financial system now offer a more solid market for foreign banks and broker-dealers.

Monetary indicators have performed positively since 1991, adding further evidence to real stability and growth. Significant real growth of the money supply and the increasing use of the peso as both a store of value and means of exchange have helped restore credibility to the financial system. Since 1991 the financial system has more than doubled its lending to the economy, with private sector borrowing now accounting for more than 80 percent of all loans in Argentina. In addition, the domination of domestic capital formation by public sector borrowing and the resultant "crowding out" of private borrowers seems to have been reduced considerably as a problem, although the crisis of early 1995 could reduce the capital available to the private sector as the government scrambles to shore up the system. Nevertheless, the net effect has been to make a greater amount of credit available at lower cost to both local and foreign operators.

Argentina's emerging securities market has boomed in the past few years. Market growth as measured by the total return indices for the Bolsa de Comercio de Buenos Aires (known as the Bolsa) was nearly 400 percent in 1991, the fastest of any market in the world during that period. Since then, growth has eased, but the market index generated a 30 percent net return from 1991 through year end 1994. Although many foreign investors continue to lump Argentina's debt and equity markets together with other, more fragile Latin American markets—making the Argentine markets more susceptible to ancillary global market swings—this linkage is starting to lessen as investors begin to evaluate Argentina as a separate entity. In time, with continued market growth, the absence of mandatory registration and ownership barriers to foreign operators, and a de-linkage of its markets from less developed, more volatile emerging markets, the Argentine market should become a more significant and stable source of capital and investment for local and foreign companies.

Even with all these new monetary and regulatory reforms in place, Argentina is still a speculative credit in the global debt market. However, as the government continues its efforts to clear up the external debt problem and as banking reforms take hold, access to international capital markets is expected to increase. Participation in the US-sponsored Brady debt reduction plan is widely believed to have been of great importance in increasing Argentine access to long -term credit. Already, large Argentine companies and the government have accessed the Eurodollar and international bond markets, borrowing billions of dollars through these intermediaries.

Despite its troubles in the past, the Argentine financial system at large is rather sophisticated and dynamic compared with those of most of other Latin American countries. The system offers a fairly wide range of financial services, administered by skilled personnel following international operating standards. Growth and stability in the Argentine financial system should allow it to continue with its reforms and improve its ability to withstand periodic short-term financial and economic shocks.

THE BANKING SYSTEM

During the period of low inflation and steady growth that began in the early 1990s, the banking system has strengthened and flourished. Bank liquidity and lending capacity have increased, the loan and deposit base have expanded, and access to international capital markets has opened up. Nevertheless, the sector remains somewhat fragile and continues to be vulnerable to volatility in global capital markets. Capital inflows are still highly variable and the high rate of credit growth could eventually lower economic growth due to poor credit decisions and inefficient loan monitoring capabilities. Despite a continuing shakeout—the total number of Argentine financial institutions fell from 220 in 1990 to 204 as of mid-1994, and more recent events have reduced the roster by even more—Argentina has too many weak small and medium-sized financial institutions. Despite free-market reforms, weak standards in certain areas remain a problem. In addition, a dual currency system—with wages and taxes paid in pesos, but larger commercial financial transactions and savings accounts and loans denominated in US dollars—may pose problems for banks in the future because they remain dependent on the ability of their customers to repay debt in US dollars (despite the assurances of the convertibility law that the peso and the dollar will remain on an equal footing). On the other hand, the high bad debt levels in Argentina—around 8 percent of total assets were classified as nonperforming at the end of 1993—were generally considered manageable, the top banks well capitalized, and the new rules and regulations imposed on the system adequate to bring the industry greater stability in the long term.

Argentina's banking system consists of the Banco Central de la República Argentina (BCRA), its central bank; private and publicly held commercial banks, including foreign banks; development banks and a network of official provincial banks; and a host of smaller institutions such as finance companies and credit unions.

Central Bank—The Bank of Argentina

Established in 1935, the BCRA is charged with regulating and controlling the banking and credit systems as well as the money supply and foreign exchange system. Specifically, the BCRA enforces exchange rate policies and manages foreign exchange reserves, supervises financial markets, administers the Financial Entities Law No. 21,596 of 1977 (which updated the structure of the financial system), acts as Argentina's financial agent, and also is depositary and agent for the nation in the international financial and banking organizations to which it is a party.

The 1991 Convertibility Law limits the BCRA's economic function to some extent, making it into a monetary control board (buying and selling foreign exchange in the market) rather than the powerful monetary policy maker it once was. The domestic money supply is now tied to the country's external reserves (the principal instrument of monetary policy), and the bank is prohibited from using monetary tools, such as buying or selling government securities to manage liquidity in the system. Thus, the central bank cannot independently increase the money supply and, as a result, monetary policy as a tool for managing Argentine economic growth no longer exists. Under the provisions of Article 19 of Law No. 24,444, the BCRA is no longer allowed to finance central or provincial governments (except under certain emergency conditions). As a result, the government must finance itself through its own means: credit and the taxation of businesses and individuals. This new arrangement ultimately decreases the enormous power the central bank previously held over the nation's broad economic affairs and allows domestic price levels, borrowing costs, and the availability of credit to be determined to a greater extent by market forces instead of by policy. There now exists greater independence between monetary and fiscal policy in Argentina. Foreign investors and operators in Argentina should benefit from this reduced political control over key macroeconomic variables such as local interest rates, loan availability, and politically led inflation. However, these strictures on the BCRA's freedom to act also pose risks by eliminating the institution's ability to respond in the near term.

Under Decree 445/95, the BCRA was granted authority to intervene to safeguard deposits and the financial system from bank failures. It was already trying to shore up troubled banks by reducing reserve requirements, allowing banks to have access to more funds, an activity that some observers viewed as violating the prohibition against serving as a lender of last resort. The new legislation allowed the BCRA to have a more direct role, overseeing a special fund—the Fondo Fiduciario de Capitalización Bancaria—to be used to restructure troubled banks. The new operation, with an estimated US$4 to US$5 billion in capital to be provided from domestic and foreign capital borrowing, is to be administered by a committee of officials and private bankers. Known as the "bank hospital," the operation will actually be divided into two separate segments: one to cover private and the other official provincial banks. Also, the fund can buy, sell, or hold shares of financial entities, at its discretion to regulate the financial system. The unit is empowered to funnel funds to troubled banks, convert debt from such loans into equity in the banks, and deal in the securities of such institutions. It can buy, sell, merge, or liquidate the securities and the underlying institutions, reducing the total number of financial institutions while strengthening those that remain. The goal is to accomplish this using market mechanisms and funds without

burdening the federal treasury with the direct costs of such restructuring. However, observers worry that poor sale prospects for many of the more marginal institutions could leave the government with a significant liability which it would have to cover to avoid a wholesale loss of confidence in the banking system.

The BCRA retains control of and supervises the banking system and financial entities through a number of policies and procedures. These include:

- Setting rules and regulations regarding lender credit risk limits, debt-to-equity ratios, and liquidity and minimum capital adequacy;
- Establishing and monitoring minimum cash reserves on deposits banks are required to maintain;
- Reviewing required institutional reporting by financial entities;
- Authorizing the establishment of entities and branches;
- Setting accounting and audit standards; and
- Performing audits.

The central bank is governed by a board of directors. The chair, a vice chair, and eight directors—each serving six-year terms—are appointed by the executive branch; all must be native or adopted Argentine citizens with at least 10 years standing. Board membership typically consists of industry specialists with knowledge and experience in legal, monetary, and banking and financial issues. Appointments are subject to confirmation by the Argentine Senate.

In addition to the BCRA board of directors, a superintendency of Financial and Exchange Entities exists to monitor financial and exchange activities. The president chooses and installs the superintendent and vice superintendent from among the BCRA's directors. The superintendent's powers and main duties include:

- Qualifying financial institutions and entities;
- Revoking authorizations to operate in exchange transactions;
- Approving plans designed to solve the problems submitted by financial entities;
- Applying financial regulations;
- Mandating orders to entities to protect their financial solvency;
- Establishing accounting, auditing, and financial reporting rules and regulations for financial entities;
- Enforcing regulations on credit cards and electronic cash transactions; and
- Monitoring the publication of monthly and other periodic balance sheets and other required financial reports.

At present the BCRA is considered to have greater legal and political independence from the federal government than before. This autonomy can benefit businesses by decoupling official monetary policy from an often more politically motivated fiscal policy, although, as noted, the BCRA now has fewer direct means of managing that monetary policy. While the risk of periodic rapid inflation may never be fully eliminated, this separation of powers may provide for greater balance in macroeconomic policy making.

Commercial Banks

Recent reforms have gone a long way toward restoring confidence in Argentina's financial system. However, the need for capital continues to define and dictate banking services. In general, domestic bank loan funds are available to only the most creditworthy companies and are usually obtainable at very high interest rates and for shorter terms than is customary in international capital markets. Still, the situation is considerably improved from the 1970s and 1980s. Funding for the intermediate- and long-term commercial loan market remains thin, thus forcing most commercial borrowers to look to the local capital market, Euro-markets, or foreign entities for their long-term financing needs.

The Argentine commercial banking industry is highly concentrated. By the end of 1994, there were 162 banks, with the top nine entities controlling approximately half of all domestic deposits, while the top 39 banks held nearly 80 percent of all deposits. Furthermore, public sector banks, discussed under the heading of development banks, controlled approximately 46 percent of all deposits.

The commercial banking industry can be divided into three main sectors: large, full-service, official and private institutions operating nationwide; smaller private-sector and rural-cooperative banks; and provincial and municipal banks. Of the 162 banks operating in 1994, 5 were national official banks, 28 were state-owned provincial and municipal banks; 61 were domestic private banks; 29 were foreign owned private banks, and 39 were coopera-tive institutions. Most commercial banks offer a broad range of banking services from credit and deposit operations and collateralized personal lending, to specialized fee-based services such as private retail investment advice and corporate finan-cial consulting. They are also active in areas such as leasing, factoring, and debt placement. All of these banks, as well as the official banks, offer the typical mix of retail services generally offered by multina-tional banks, such as checking accounts, draft issu-ance, and operations in the interbank market.

The larger commercial banking institutions account for the majority of Argentina's roughly $100 billion in assets. They are generally considered, by both international public- and private-sector banking officials, to be financially sound according to interna-tional operating standards. This is evidenced through healthy capitalization ratios, strong required reserve positions, and strong profitability performance. The largest private commercial banks, such as Banco Galicia, Banco Francés, Banco Río de la Plata, and a few others, offer a wide variety of services and are typically the most experienced in handling international firms' needs.

Consolidation Among the Smaller Banks The smaller private-sector and rural-cooperative banks play a lesser role in the banking system than they did 15 years ago. Consolidation among Argentina's numerous smaller banks is underway, resulting in even greater concentration of capacity and assets among the remaining larger financial institutions. In addition, this sector's deposit base is shrinking as customers shift funds to other financial vehicles and to larger, more stable banks. These small insti-tutions have traditionally served the limited needs of local small-scale industry and retail markets. In March 1995, following the crisis initiated by Mexico's devaluation of its peso, roughly one-third of Argentine banks—typically the smaller, local operators—were considered to be effectively out of business by observers. Because of some portfolio weakness as well as limits on capital of local banks, foreign entities seeking banking relationships in Argentina are generally advised to make a full credit assessment of the banks they plan to use.

Financial Regulation The two most important banking statutes in Argentina are the Financial Enti-ties Law (FEL) and the Charter of the BCRA, both of which were overhauled in 1989 to update financial institutions' role within the structure of the newly created market oriented system. These two statutes establish a licensing, regulatory, and supervisory structure for the banking industry, as well as for the broader financial sector. No financial entity in Argentina, either foreign or domestic, may operate without the authorization of the BCRA. Mergers of financial institutions must also be authorized by the central bank. The authorization procedure entails a BCRA evaluation of the project's economics and characteristics, the general and specific market conditions, and the managerial and financial experi-ence of the applicants. Commercial banks, invest-ment banks, mortgage banks, financial companies, housing and real estate savings and loan associa-tions, and all unlisted intermediation entities are included under these provisions.

In early 1994 new BCRA regulations governing financial institution approval required that appli-cants demonstrate appropriate prior experience and

GLOSSARY OF FINANCIAL TERMS

actuarial techniques Statistical research and management techniques used by the insurance industry to estimate the level of risk the company is exposed to for each policy type (liabilities). This risk is compared with the composition of the company's assets to match the flow of income with claims payments.

capital adequacy A financial measurement of a financial institution's equity capital in comparison with the level of its liabilities. This ratio is used extensively by regulators and financial managers to measure the level of inherent solvency of a particular entity. In general, the higher the capital adequacy measure, the lower the level of risk to the company's stock and bondholders. Most countries have adopted the Bank for International Settlements (BIS) recommendations on required capital.

crowding out In financial and lending markets, the phenomena of one borrower or borrowing sector dominating a market to such an extent that other borrowers must either borrow at higher than normal rates or, in the extreme case, may not be able to borrow at all.

custodial services The management and safekeeping of securities or other negotiable instruments owned by an individual or company by a financial institution providing this service.

debt-to-equity ratio The level of an entity's debt divided by its equity capital. This ratio measures the degree of financial leverage of an entity's balance sheet. High ratios—relatively more debt than equity—tend to reflect a more aggressive management style than lower ratios.

derivatives Financial instruments and investments whose repayment or underlying collateral base is comprised of related assets or third-party contracts. These include index options, interest rate swaps, and asset-backed securities, among others. This market has grown tremendously over the past decade. These instruments are used in financial instrument structures and for investment hedging and speculation.

exchange-traded A description for a financial instrument bought and sold on a formal stock, futures, or options exchange.

foreign exchange reserves The amount of foreign currency (typically US dollars, German marks, Japanese yen, or other "hard" or "reserve" currency) held by a nation's banking system as a reserve base, or financial backstop, for its international transactions and payments. The level of foreign exchange reserves is critical to the level of financial solvency for a nation's financial system.

hyperinflation A term describing a huge increase in an economy's price level over a short period of time. Hyperinflation is typically measured by a several-times increase in the average level of inflation. This rapid price increase can lead to insolvency of the economy's banking system, devaluation of its currency on global markets, and national economic collapse.

intermediation A term used to describe the role of a financial entity in conducting and completing a transaction between two distinct parties. These functions include the lending of deposits, brokering of securities, and creation of interest rate swaps, among others.

letter of credit A document issued by a bank stating its commitment to pay a party (supplier/exporter/seller) a stated amount on behalf of a buyer (importer), so long as the seller meets specified terms and conditions.

liquidity (a) A company's ability to meet its financial obligations at all times. (b) The availability of liquid funds in an economy. (c) The measure of a company's short-term assets with its short-term liabilities.

monetary policy A state-controlled economic and financial tool used to manage an economy's price level, activity, and solvency. Typically relegated to the central bank, monetary policy is instituted through the bank's manipulation of the money supply and lending environment by various means such as changing interbank interest rates, printing new money, changing bank rules and regulations, and altering the level of the nation's reserve base.

offshore banking Refers to banking operations transacted outside the country in question. In a host country, this would refer to a foreign entity's ability to bank at a host country's financial institution without

GLOSSARY OF FINANCIAL TERMS (cont'd)

regard to the foreign nation's rules and regulations. Entities typically utilize offshore banking facilities to escape more restrictive domestic banking operations, rules, taxes, and regulations in force.

over-the-counter market A marketplace for financial securities transactions conducted away from operating exchanges. Most transactions here take place electronically as opposed to under the open-outcry system on a stock exchange.

reciprocity The "mutuality of benefits," "quid pro quo," and "equivalence of advantages". In international transactions, the practice by which governments extend similar concessions to each other, as when one government allows certain financial practices or activities by foreign institutions within its borders in exchange for equivalent concessions from that foreign nation.

reinsurance A practice in the insurance industry of selling part of one insurance company's risk to another insurer specializing in such transactions to reduce the total risk of the first firm. Reinsurance is essentially a secondary market for insured risks, where the company's primary risk exposure to the public is transferred to another insurance company for the purpose of risk diversification and mitigation.

retail banking Banking functions provided to the public at large (retail consumer market). These services include deposit taking, checking accounts, residential mortgages, and other individual products and services.

transparency The extent to which laws, regulations, agreements, and practices affecting transactions are open, clear, measurable, and verifiable.

wholesale banking Banking functions provided to the business or industrial economy (wholesale market). These services include commercial lending, factoring, securities underwriting, and export financing, among others.

---

minimum capitalization of US$15 million in order to obtain a license to operate. In addition, authorities have instituted a dual rating system, with one system designed to classify borrowers according to previous payment record and current viability, and another to classify lenders according to capital, assets, management, earnings, and liquidity. Both are to operate nationally using comparable procedures in an effort to eliminate inefficiencies and misrepresentations in financial transactions.

Banking Sector Results The combination of aggregate national economic growth, increasing financial system stability, free market reforms, and the expansion of banking activities have bolstered the banking sector's recent economic performance and earnings. Since 1991 banks have had to access global capital markets, both through the issuance of debt securities and through increased intermediation activities. Activities such as electronic banking services (including automated teller machines—ATMs) and credit card operations have added to their capabilities in retail markets. This activity not only increases the type and level of services that banks can offer to customers, but also expands revenues and deposits to increase funding. On the wholesale side, rapid loan growth has increased the sector's asset base and potential for earnings growth in the future. However, there is strong disintermediation pressure in this segment.

Bank stocks declined in 1994 in step with the general stock market trend. Equity infusions from have given the industry a larger capital base from which to operate. Increased competition between domestic and foreign banks have pressured managements to increase operating efficiency and thus bolster earnings growth. The growing trend toward consolidation among the smaller, poorly capitalized banks will ultimately create stronger, more efficient and profitable survivor entities in the years to come.

Loan portfolio growth and a renewed access to global capital markets increased bank performance and earnings potential during the early 1990s. The sector's use of a dual currency deposit base (the US dollar as well as the Argentine peso) has grown by nearly 300 percent from a base of US$15 billion at the end of 1991 to US$45 billion at the end of 1994 (based on monthly averages for December). Deposit growth was matched on the liability side of the industry's balance sheet with a doubling of bank loans outstanding from US$23 billion in 1991 to more than US$50 billion in 1994. Adding to this growth was an increase in portfolio diversification, which will ultimately lead to more stable future earnings. Public sector loans as a percentage of total bank loans outstanding fell from approximately 40 percent in 1991 to approximately 22 percent in 1994. Private borrowing increased rapidly in the primary production (natural resources), commercial—both retail and whole-sale—and industrial sectors. Banks have also developed an important mortgage portfolio, driven by consumer demand. The interest rate spread—the difference between a bank's cost of funds and the interest earned on its loans—has stabilized. The new loan portfolio allocation mix and more stable net interest rate spread strengthens bank balance sheets and contributes to stronger and more stable earnings performance. Argentine banks have improved their profitability by charging high fees for services. However, operating costs are very high compared with international standards. The Argentine commercial banking entities with the highest visibility are Banco Galicia, Banco Francés, and Banco Río de la Plata. Other notable institutions include Banco del Sud, Banco Crédito Argentino, and Banco Roberts. All issue actively traded debt securities, and Banco Galicia, Banco Francés, and Banco del Sud list their stocks on the Bolsa. Banco Galicia and Banco Francés also list their stocks in the US—with the National Association of Securities Dealers Automated Quotation system (Nasdaq) and the New York Stock Exchange (NYSE), respectively.

Foreign Banks

Foreign bank operations have a long history in Argentina dating back to early natural resource and agricultural development efforts during the 19th century. Foreign-owned banks currently participate in both the retail and wholesale markets, accounting for approximately one-sixth of banking sector deposits. With the removal of operating and ownership restrictions, and the boom Argentina experienced during the early the 1990s, the national banking market has become more attractive to foreign-based and foreign-owned Argentine financial institutions.

The number of foreign banks in Argentina has remained relatively steady over the past 15 years. Currently, 31 foreign banks conduct a broad range of credit, deposit, and loan origination functions through more than 500 branches located throughout the country (although the vast majority are located in the greater Buenos Aires area). Nearly all perform wholesale functions while a smaller group offer retail services. Of the foreign banks presently licensed, the majority are European-based, followed by US and Asian banks. Nine US-based banks hold more than US$2 billion in deposits through more than 75 branches. Of these operators, only two—Citibank and Bank of Boston (which are among Argentina's oldest banks)—are currently active in retail operations; others are developing specializations in custodial activities. All US-based banks and most other foreign banks

offer wholesale—business lending and related—services to varying degrees.

Competition for depositors is fierce in Argentina, as is true in most retail banking markets around the world. However, foreign banks do have an advantage here that is lacking in other Latin American countries. The long-term presence of foreign banks and a population largely made up of people of European descent eases the way for foreign bankers doing business in Argentina. Foreign bankers are less likely to be limited by discriminatory rules and treated as second class corporate citizens as is often the case in other countries, an important distinction in a relationship-based industry.

Licenses Prior to 1994 foreign banking licenses were granted under a strict regime of central and local government approvals and regulations. More specifically, foreign capital and branches of foreign financial entities had to present evidence of reciprocity for Argentine banks in their country of origin according to the BCRA's then current criteria. In addition, those entities were also subject to National Executive Branch approval and had to comply with discriminatory local rules and regulations. Now, financial institutions and operations formed as foreign capital companies and the local branches of foreign entities are accorded treatment equal to that given to local firms—and because they typically have greater available capital and deeper expertise, they may be at a slight advantage to many domestic competitors. The reciprocity clause has not been revoked, but is not currently being enforced. Foreign banks can open or buy local branches without any legal restrictions.

The existing foreign banking community in Argentina consists of operations licensed decades ago, and has been left largely untouched by the recent market and regulatory reforms. However, new market oriented regulations opening the sector to a greater degree is expected to attract additional foreign capital and new competitors in the years to come. Generally licenses are granted for a specific term and have mandatory minimum capital adequacy, operational, and audit and reporting requirements similar to those required for domestic Argentine commercial banks. At this time, foreign banks may do business in Argentina only as commercial and investment banks and must be authorized by the BCRA before commencing operations. Offshore banking and trust operations are not permitted in Argentina.

Development and Other Specialized Banks

The government of Argentina operates several development and specialized state-owned commercial banks primarily designed to finance projects and support the industrial and agrarian sectors on a policy basis, although they offer many standard individual and business banking services as well. In addition, the World Bank and the Inter-American Development Bank (IDB) serve as official lenders and conduits for international funding for development projects in Argentina. As for the aforementioned "official" banks, the largest and most influential of these are the Banco de Inversión y Comercio Exterior S.A. (BICE), the Banco de la Nación Argentina (BNA), and the Banco Hipotecario Nacional (BHN). Provincial and municipal banks, such as the Banco de la Provincia de Buenos Aires (BPBA) and Banco de la Ciudad de Buenos Aires (BCBA)—the largest and best known of the non-national official banks—generally operate locally

Banco de Inversión y Comercio Exterior S.A. BICE began operating in 1992. The purpose of this bank is to finance investment projects and foreign trade. More specifically, the bank provides the public sector with an institution designed to support investment and the domestic accumulation of capital and export finance, as well as to funnel medium-term loan funds to industrial borrowers at competitive, international market rates.

Banco de la Nación Argentina BNA is the largest bank in Argentina. A state-owned commercial bank, it is assigned to the financing of development in approved economic sectors. Domestically, the BNA finances broad agricultural, industrial, and commercial sectors through short- and medium-term credits. It finances up to 80 to 90 percent of FOB value for agricultural and industrial exports on terms from 10 days to up to four years for certain capital goods. Overseas, the bank serves as an agent of the Argentine government in attracting foreign investment.

Domestically, the BNA also supports regional agricultural activity. For example, it supports bean farmers in the northeast; fruit growers in Río Negro; cotton growers in the Chaco; peanut farmers in Córdoba; and the general development of agriculture and agro-industry in Patagonia. The BNA offers a variety of credit lines to independent farmers, cooperatives, and companies for capital investment and working capital, and for preexport financing for larger companies. The bank has recently been successful in floating debt issues in the international markets to raise funds to finance exports of capital goods by small and medium-sized Argentine companies.

The bank was recently restructured to compete more effectively with privately owned commercial banks and to offer customers more comprehensive and useful services. Over the past several years, operating and administrative cost savings have been achieved through branch closings, staff cuts, decentralization of management functions, and an upgrade of bank systems with new technologies.

Banco Hipotecario Nacional In Argentina, as is the case throughout Latin America, funding is scarce for residential home construction and mortgage lending. The BHN was established to assist in developing financing for housing construction and purchase money mortgages. Refocused strictly as a wholesale bank in 1990, the BHN now operates through some 20 nonbanking agencies located nationwide. These groups act as intermediaries for housing construction companies seeking development and construction financing and consumers seeking mortgage financing. Lines of credit for home construction companies are made available through co-participation agreements with private, mixed, and public sector banks. The BHN offers its services primarily to domestic companies and residents. Foreign firms involved in housing construction generally finance their operations either with internally generated funds or through foreign-based banks or capital markets.

Provincial and Municipal Banks With the exceptions of Banco de la Provincia de Buenos Aires and Banco de la Ciudad de Buenos Aires, the provincial banks (and municipal local banks) are playing a relatively minor role in Argentina's banking market. Historically, they have functioned primarily as payment and collection agents for local government entities and sources of patronage (collectively they account for 60,000 workers, giving them disproportionate political influence). As with the smaller private banks, the provincial banking sector is changing rapidly. In early 1995, the International Bank for Reconstruction and Development (IBRD, the World Bank) estimated that 40 percent of loans held by Argentine provincial banks were unrecoverable. Some provincial banks are to be privatized. Because of their problems, one incentive being considered to encourage potential buyers is the promise that the provincial governments will guarantee to route all official financial business through the successor entities for a period of five years. These banks typically do not serve foreign firms operating in Argentina.

Other Banks and Financial Institutions

Commercial banks in Argentina have a strong hold on the bulk of retail and wholesale banking services. At present, only commercial banks may offer checking accounts with high fees, issue drafts, and make intermarket transfers, limiting the viability of such competing entities such as finance companies and credit unions. Even though they are mentioned in the banking law, there are no remaining savings and loan companies and only a few credit unions and finance companies.

Commercial banks may also underwrite securities, create medium- and long-term credit facilities, deal in securities, operate in the foreign exchange markets, and deal in equipment leasing and other financial activities.

NONBANK FINANCIAL INSTITUTIONS

Argentina has a few, mostly small to medium-sized financial institutions that serve as alternatives to the larger commercial banking institutions. As in most other economies supporting specialized financial firms, each of these operations focuses on a specific niche. Most have existed for long time, but the financial system overhaul in the early 1990s has drastically changed the financial landscape, and added new competitors to the financial services picture. Many of the existing operations are wholly owned subsidiaries of large banking companies. These institutions include factoring companies (receivables finance), financial warehouses, foreign exchange houses, and credit card companies.

Specialized Commercial Financial Institutions Factoring companies are essentially short-term lenders who provide liquidity by taking over a company's receivables for a fee (actual purchase of such receivables at a discount is forfaiting).

Financial warehouses cover a broad range of commercial applications such as: bonded warehousing for imported goods, deposit of inventory, and the storage of loan collateral, among other activities; they can also issue negotiable securities collateralized by the goods held in their facilities, adding a source of liquidity to markets.

Foreign exchange houses offer currency exchange and currency hedging services, profiting from the spreads and fees charged, as well as from trading for their own accounts.

Mutual unions are cooperative financial institutions organized to serve their members, usually small enterprises or individuals. The members' pooled funds create a source of loan capital for sectors that generally are underserved or not served at all by commercial banks and other outlets. In addition, investment clubs, although less formal in nature, exist to provide similar services to business and individual members.

There are no specific limitations on foreign participation or ownership in these and other specialized commercial services.

Leasing is regulated by banking Law No. 21,526 (Article 22), which allows banks to hold assets and lease them directly to customers. The greatest amount of activity is found in automobile, truck, and computer leasing, primarily because leasing allows clients to gain access to a car or other vehicle

without having to make a substantial downpayment or obtain a formal loan for the entire amount. Yet, of all major South American economies, Argentina's has the least developed leasing industry, despite leasing's potentially important role in financing capital purchases. A lack of tax and financial incentives to leasing seems also to be a factor in the lack of development.

Specialized Consumer Financial Institutions The primary consumer financial institution is the credit card company. Banks operate most of the ancillary consumer financial services and institutions, such as mortgage and car loan companies and credit card companies, as subsidiaries or separate departments. The credit card industry has experienced high growth in Argentina as in the rest of Latin America. Large US-based operators dominate the market here with MasterCard and Visa as the dominant players and Diner's Club, long the leader in Argentina, a close second, followed by American Express and have a significant market share. The growing availability of advance credit approval terminals and credit card vendor satellite links that bypass the historically erratic local telephone switches to provide credit authorizations and settlements, as well as the more stable inflation rates that make purchases on credit more viable options, will greatly add to credit card usage among foreign operators in Argentina and those Argentines eligible for credit.

After a long absence from the market, commercial banks are beginning to provide residential mortgages again, enabled by renewed access to long-term funds in global capital markets. Previously, the mortgage origination market was virtually nonexistent, with most home purchases made with cash or financed through short-term, secured personal loans, which hampered the development of the real estate industry. All mortgage lending in Argentina is denominated in US dollars, most of it for 10-year terms. Other terms and conditions available include such options as the "12/16" mortgage: a 12-year mortgage loan at 16 percent per year with an initial loan-to-value maximum of 50 percent. Some foreign-based banks offer 20 year terms as well. In general, the residential mortgage market is improving along with national economic growth and stability, but the rates are still very high compared with international standards.

A type of investment club known as the *circulo cerrado* (closed circle), was prevalent in Argentina during the late 1980s. Under this arrangement, a group of consumers banded together to buy certain big-ticket, durable consumer goods, such as large appliances or even automobiles. These consumers pooled their funds, making monthly (or other periodic) payments, until the capital needed to purchase an example outright was accumulated. The group members then draw lots to see who gets the item. All members continued to make their payments whether they get their turn in the first period or the last. Many such clubs were initially organized and sponsored by retailers of the goods to be purchased as a means to move their products.

Insurance Companies

Argentina's insurance market has been severely hampered over the years by overregulation, protectionism, and a mismanaged state reinsurance monopoly. The future success and growth of the industry depends heavily on the market response to broad insurance market reforms put in place since 1990. The market is slowly responding to reforms designed to reorganize a market known for its fragmentation, underdevelopment, overregulation, high premium costs, and financial weakness. In light of the state of the market, the reforms do offer significant opportunity for foreign companies wishing to do business in the Argentine insurance industry.

The liquidation of the state-owned reinsurer, the Instituto Nacional de Reaseguros (INDER) eliminated an enormous drain on the entire sector by eliminating INDER's right to 60 percent of all reinsurance premiums placed by the company issuing the policy (INDER was effectively bankrupt for several years and had been unable to pay large claims). The Argentine government is now encouraging foreign reinsurance companies to establish subsidiaries in Argentina, with some having already done so. Unfortunately for domestic insurers, the liquidation of INDER has triggered a massive shakeout, such that many Argentine companies may have to sell, merge, or liquidate. Already the number of insurance firms licensed in Argentina has gone from 258 in 1983 to 195 in 1993 to a reported 185 or so in late 1994, largely due to new capital rules and an onslaught of new competition.

The reforms went beyond liquidation of the state-owned reinsurer. Massive deregulation of insurance rates and policy offerings, elimination of restrictions on insurance practices for companies with foreign capital (and equal treatment for foreign firms), and tighter solvency requirements will combine eventually to create a more robust and financially sound insurance industry. The Superintendencia de Seguros governs industry practices, sets reference prices by policy type, and monitors the financial solvency of insurance companies (rather than working to keep them profitable).

Industry ownership is led by locally owned mutual or publicly held firms with almost half of the market, 40 percent being smaller, independent operators, and the remaining 15 percent to 20

percent being foreign-owned. A few large, well managed, and reputable Argentine firms do exist, but overall, the industry is fighting its poor image born of past company failures and widespread problems with nonpayment of claims. Here Argentine firms are at a slight disadvantage compared with well capitalized foreign competitors in terms of technology, management, and actuarial skills. Despite past problems, market growth since 1992 has ranged 12 percent to 15 percent annually. The automotive insurance market accounts for about half of the premiums in the total market, with life insurance accounting for about 15 percent; workers' compensation is about 11 percent and fire insurance is approximately 6 percent. Remaining categories are small to negligible contributors. Total premiums for 1994 were US$4.7 billion, with life insurance representing the most promising segment.

At present, the government is not granting new licenses because of the large number of insurance companies already operating in Argentina. However, the government encourages foreign companies to buy or to contract joint ventures with existing Argentine firms. Thus, foreign companies interested in the Argentine insurance market can capitalize on this combination of market growth, government encouragement, and industry structural inefficiency opportunities.

Pension Funds

The Argentine social security system is another beneficiary of the broad-based privatization and decentralization reforms. After running a deficit for most of the 1980s, the nearly bankrupt state system was scrapped and the government opened up the pension plan management market to private companies for the first time. The past 30 years saw a near doubling of the 65 and older age group, while the 1980s brought a drop in productivity and participation among the working population. In a financing structure designed to be sustained by a pensioner-to-worker ratio of 4 to 1, a drop in that ratio to 1.6 to 1 by 1990 meant that the old system simply could not satisfy demand. As a result of this financial strain, the average pension benefit dropped to US$150 per month, just a quarter of the average Argentine worker's monthly salary at the time. It was only a matter of time before changing demographic forces coupled with a mismanaged pension delivery system forced the implementation of the new system.

Workers are required to contribute 11 percent and employers 16 percent to each worker's retirement account. Workers now have a choice between a modified government social security package or one of various private schemes known by their

Spanish acronym AFJP (Administradoras de Jubilaciones y Pensiones). The new system is designed to emulate the highly successful Chilean privatized pension model begun in 1981, and which became so successful that Chilean private pension funds are now the nation's most powerful institutional investors. In Argentina, the progress toward that goal has just begun. It is projected that in the near future just 20 percent of the working population will remain in the modified government scheme, with another one-third subscribing to an AFJP administered by a large Argentine public commercial bank. The balance—nearly half of all workers—are expected to join one of the more than two dozen private plans. Because the newer, private plans are just emerging, a market opportunity exists for the many prominent foreign-based firms who have an edge over the local competition in many aspects of plan operations and administration.

Because these private pension funds are only just now beginning operations, observers expect that it will be years before the plans become a net supplier of credit to the economy. However, pension funds will ultimately generate substantial reservoirs of medium- and long-term credit (which have been largely unknown in Argentina) as the market reaches as much as US$50 billion over the next 10 years. Small to mid-sized companies, both foreign and domestic, should benefit by the creation of this market. In addition, pension reform will help boost economic recovery through increased domestic savings.

Underground Financial Operations

With a long history of financial and political and general inefficiency, Argentina has been accustomed to operating with an important underground economy. The frequent evasion of taxes has abetted the formation of sub rosa investment and transaction channels. Because of historically high interest rates, inflation, and the lack of available credit in the formal sector, underground financing has been common. Those individuals or businesses unable to get credit often apply to local individuals or investment circles for credit. Credit is offered from either a community service perspective (investment clubs) or as part of a usually unofficial business enterprise.

FINANCIAL MARKETS

Argentine financial market development has shown positive growth thus far during the 1990s. Although the markets remain relatively small and exhibit signs of inefficiency and volatility, they operate on the basis of a well organized and capitalized infrastructure, fed by the prospects of even greater growth and stability in the future. Argentine markets, like other emerging markets, have attracted a great deal of attention from international investors, driving local indices to new heights during the past several years. The growth in securities activity, fueled by huge inputs of foreign and returning Argentine flight capital, brought these markets to center stage as a major force in domestic capital formation.

The Securities Industry

Equities Markets The stock market in Argentina dates back to the 1850s with the founding of the Bolsa de Comercio de Buenos Aires (Bolsa). The Mercado de Valores de Buenos Aires (MVBA) accounts for 90 percent of all securities trading volume in Argentina. The remaining 10 percent of the exchange-traded market operates through 11 smaller exchanges. Each of these local market affiliates is run as an independent corporation whose stockholders are individual exchange members with full trading privileges. Local markets exist in Córdoba, Mendoza, Río Negro, Rosario, Santa Fe, and La Plata. In addition to the aforementioned exchanges, a highly developed and active over-the-counter (OTC) market exists. This Mercado Abierto Electrónico (MAE) now has daily trading volume exceeding that of the Bolsa. At one time a competitor to the exchanges, trading through the MAE, whose members are primarily banks, now largely deals in corporate and government bonds, while most equities trading occurs on the MVBA stock exchanges.

Mostly because of its well developed infrastructure, the Argentine equity markets have dealt well with the large surge in trading activity in recent years. Market capitalization, down to a low of about US$1 billion during the 1980s, had risen to nearly US$45 billion at its height in 1994. The annual volume of new shares grew from approximately US$25 million in 1985 to more than US$1 billion in 1994. However, the number of companies listed on the Bolsa has declined over the past decade from 227 in 1985 to around 100 at the end of 1994. The decline in listed entities is primarily the result of consolidation among competing firms, and the delisting of relatively inactive firms which had remained listed on the exchange, many of which had sustained no activity in years.

The Bolsa can be characterized as a fairly liquid, highly concentrated, emerging market. The top four companies listed comprised 58 percent of the market's capitalization and accounted for up to approximately 85 percent of all exchange trading volume on both the Bolsa and the over-the-counter markets. Moreover, the top nine listed companies account for just under 75 percent of total market capitalization and just under 90 percent of total trading volume. The top four listed companies consist of the two telecommunications companies privatized by the government, Telefónica and Telecom (sold by the government to the public in 1991 and 1992, respectively), Yacimientos Petrolíferos Fiscales (YPF), and Pérez Companc, a conglomerate. YPF is the largest company on the market, representing a market capitalization equal to nearly one-quarter that of the entire market. Once the state-owned oil company, YPF, was partly privatized in mid-1993 when the government sold 45 percent of its holdings in the company to domestic and international investors through a public offering and subsequent listing on the Bolsa and the New York Stock Exchange. (More of the remaining government stake in YPF is slated to be sold or used as a guarantee as part of the refunding operation announced to combat the financial crisis in early 1995.) Other leading listed firms include Citicorp Equity Investments, Banco de Galicia, Banco Francés, Baesa, and CIADEA. By industry, the leading sectors include oil and gas producers and telecommunications, followed by banks, food and beverage companies, automobile manufacturers, and electric utilities.

Three widely used stock indices currently exist. The most popular is the Bolsa Indice General (the Bolsa Index), and is comprised of all listed shares weighted by their market capitalization on the Bolsa. The Merval Index is representative of the Mercado de Valores de Buenos Aires, S.A., and is comprised of a theoretical portfolio of issues adjusted quarterly. A third index, the Burcap Index, is run by the Argentine Institute of Capital Markets and is weighted by stock market capitalization.

Overall, Bolsa performance since 1990, as represented by the annual change in the Bolsa index, has been an outstanding success despite its continuing susceptibility to global emerging market conditions and lingering market volatility—in early 1995 some issues were fluctuating by as much as 25 percent daily, despite exchange rules designed to dampen such movements. From year-end 1990 to year-end 1991 the market index jumped a whopping 710 percent, ending the year at 17,856. Global market volatility and profit taking contributed to a market reversal in 1991 in comparison to the phenomenal growth the year earlier.

Between 1992 and early 1994, the drop in international interest rates, coupled with the fall in inflation rates in Argentina, led to a substantial rise in the Argentine stock market (conversely, the rise of interest rates in early 1994 led to a down year, marked by increasing weakness as the year progressed). In 1993, listed companies posted significant earnings growth (earnings increased by more than 50 percent for the top 20 companies), reflecting both improving macroeconomic trends and the successful implementation with which exchange-traded companies increased productivity (which rose by 40 percent during this period). In addition, this growth was complemented by several new equity issues—mostly privatized companies—that increased market capitalization by almost one-third, accounting for about half of the increase in market value, as well as by the additional, although more limited, effect of mergers and acquisitions activity among medium- and small sized Argentine companies.

By the end of 1993, total market capitalization reached a new record of approximately US$44 billion, with trading volume more than doubling by year end. The Bolsa Index stood at 20,607, a 53 percent increase for the year. In early 1994, the market saw a correction of nearly 25 percent by the end of the first quarter. This downward movement was primarily a value adjustment, bringing the average price/earnings multiple down to the previous year's level of about 17. By year-end, the market rebounded somewhat, but the overall 20 percent decline in prices was mostly a function of the weak global equity markets than an erosion in Argentine economic fundamentals.

Approximately 60 percent of Bolsa listed shares are held by controlling groups, with the remaining 40 percent free floating and available for public trading; the percentages can be larger for individual company issues. Individuals constitute the controlling constituency in Argentina's equity markets, whereas institutional investors have been few. Banks and insurance companies have had little interest in the market, but that is expected to change as the value of privately administered pension system assets grows.

There are currently no direct or indirect restrictions on foreign ownership of exchange-traded or over-the-counter stocks, warrants, options, or debt instruments in Argentina. Foreign participation in the stock market is heavy. Foreign entities own more than half of all free floating shares (those available for public trading). In addition, the elimination of all capital gains taxes and income taxes on securities transactions applies to foreign as well as domestic owners, making Argentine securities even more attractive. These developments coupled, with an absence of restrictions on capital inflows and outflows of foreign and domestic currencies, make the Argentine financial markets very attractive to multinational investors and traders. The public offering of foreign shares on Argentine exchanges has been allowed since June 1992.

Regulation The Comisión Nacional de Valores (CNV) has functioned as Argentina's independent governing body for the capital markets since 1968. It is designed to function along much the same lines as the US Securities and Exchange Commission (SEC). The CNV's main responsibilities are to supervise authorized public offerings, to preserve transparency and investor safety, and to impose sanctions on market participants. The CNV also approves the rules of control, and penalize other stock and securities exchanges and members; it also keeps a register of brokers, open market, and mutual fund operators. Futures and options markets are also regulated by this governing body.

As noted, during 1992 changes to financial market operating rules made it easier to finance working capital and investments, increase trading transparency, increase safety for domestic and foreign investors, and modernize trading operations and practices. Daily price floors and ceilings have been instituted to control price volatility and protect investors. Trading is suspended for one-half hour if an issue's price moves more than 10 percent from its opening quote, and is suspended for the entire day if the price movement is 15 percent or greater. Additional structural enhancements have added greater stability and credibility to the Argentine financial markets such as the standardization of stock information and disclosure requirements, and mandatory credit ratings on bonds from at least one credit rating agency. Broker commissions rates now float instead of being fixed, and the abolition of stamp and transfer taxes on shares, as well as the removal of taxes on capital gains for both foreign and domestic investors, have made these markets immensely more attractive than in the past.

Securities and Market Operations Clearing is handled through the Caja de Valores S.A. (Stock Clearing Corporation), a subsidiary of the Bolsa de Comercio de Buenos Aires. The Caja de Valores clears trading, holding about 80 percent of publicly traded securities in registered book entry form. The remaining 20 percent of equity issues, as well as government securities, are in bearer form and are also cleared through this entity.

A mutual fund industry is beginning to emerge in Argentina. To date, limited activity has been seen in stock and money market type funds. Currently, approximately 50 or so mutual funds exist; however, these represent less than 1 percent of the market. Mutual funds are expected to become more prevalent due to regulatory reform and a growing institutional asset base.

As the Argentine market becomes more sophisticated, it is acquiring similar types of activities as developed markets. Short selling is still not allowed. However, in 1993 block trading was allowed for blocks of a minimum value of US$200,000 with prior exchange approval.

Several of the large capitalization companies are listed on overseas exchanges in New York (YPF, Telefónica, Telecom, BAESA, Banco Galicia, and Banco Francés), Zurich (Astra and Comercial del Plata), and Geneva (Astra); options on YPF stock are also handled in New York. Recent privatizations and subsequent new issue listings for firms such as the US$3 billion YPF allow foreign entities to invest in Argentine companies locally through such vehicles as American Depository Receipts (ADRs). Foreign investors may also participate in Argentine stocks through the purchase and sale of equity warrants (option-style instruments) available on overseas exchanges and issued from major international broker/dealers, such as Merrill Lynch, Morgan Stanley, Paribas Capital Markets, and Bankers Trust. One such popular composite security, the Argentine Basket, is a warrant comprised of the Telefónica, Telecom, Pérez Companc, Banco de Galicia, Cidea, Banco Francés, Baesa, and Astra.

Debt and Money Markets

Prior to 1991, given Argentina's high inflation, liquidity crisis, and economic problems of the recent past, there was effectively no market, either internally or externally, for long-term Argentine debt. However, this situation has changed, enabling the Argentine debt markets to expand and mature along with the country's growing economy and improved financial stability. Both government and corporate debt now trade freely, locally and overseas, and markets have opened up to allow its financial, industrial, and primary product sectors to finance their activities at more internationally competitive rates.

The Argentine debt and money markets generally operate separate from each other. The money market consists primarily of short-term government paper dominated by treasury bills, but also includes commercial paper, bankers' acceptances, and promissory notes. The debt market is comparatively modest in size—although it is growing—but has a long operating history in government and corporate bonds. Approximately US$67 billion in government debt was outstanding at the end of 1994. Of the nearly US$233 billion in government bond transaction volume occurring in Argentine markets in 1993, only about 3.5 percent of trading in government bonds was conducted on the Bolsa, while trading on the MAE was almost exclusively— 96 percent—in government debt. Issuance of new corporate bond debt rose from US$41 million in 1989 to US$5.297 billion in 1994.

Actively traded government debt instruments include the US dollar, denominated External Bonds of the Argentine Republic (Bonex), the most actively traded securities, Treasury Bonds (Bote), and Pension Debt Consolidation Bonds (Bocon). In addition, there are other debt instruments such as

PROPOSED NEW LEGISLATION ON CAPITAL MARKETS

A proposed bill prepared by the National Securities Commission ("NSC") is currently being debated in Congress. The purpose of this law is to guarantee transparency in the public offerings market. If approved, it will place Argentina's legislation at an advanced international level in this field. The issue of handling information is already regulated by Resolution NSC No. 190, as amended. However, this is the first time that a law emanating from Congress will deal with this matter.

A brief explanation of the proposed bill follows.

Disclosure Duties

The managers of entities that make public offerings of securities or the statutory auditors, as the case may be, will report, in writing, to the NSC, in a true and complete way, about any event or situation, positive or negative, which might impact the development of the entities' activities or the course of trading of their securities in the market. This information shall be supplied directly to the NSC immediately after said event or situation has occurred or immediately after knowing about said event or situation, as the case may be.

The entities which quote their securities in stock exchanges, over-the-counter markets or self regulated entities authorized by the NSC, shall fulfill the same reporting obligations by sending similar communications to said institutions. These reports shall be published immediately in their respective bulletins.

Waiver

Notwithstanding the foregoing, with the approval of three fourths of the members of the Board of Directors and also with the approval of the statutory auditor, the issuer may request to the NSC a waiver limited to a specific duty, if the disclosure of said information could seriously impact the company's interest.

Obligation to Make Public Holdings of Shares

1. The bill provides that the directors, managers and statutory auditors of entities that make public offerings of their shares shall have to inform to the NSC, within 10 days of commencing their duties, on the quantity and type of shares, debt bonds or purchase options they possess or administer, directly or indirectly, of the entity to which they are related, the period of time their duties will last, as well as the number and name of the entity, depository agent and subaccount in which said securities are registered.

   This information must be updated annually, whether changes have been operated or not, before 1 March.

2. They shall have to perform that initial communication even in the event of not possessing or administering the above-mentioned securities.

3. The aforementioned persons shall communicate to the NSC, before the 15th day of every month, any change in their holdings of the securities and purchase options pointed out above. The same information shall be supplied by those persons during the following 6 months after they have ceased their functions.

4. The same disclosure duty is also imposed on the managers of the entities that make public offerings of their shares. If there are different managerial levels, only the first level shall have to fulfill it, without prejudice of the power of the NSC to request the same information from other officers of the company, when it deems it suitable.

5. The members of the risk analysis council, directors, managers and statutory auditors of risk analysis companies are also reached by the obligation to communicate to the NSC their holding of securities of companies authorized to make public offerings in the same manner as explained in 3. above.

6. Any individual or legal entity which, directly or through other individuals or legal entities, or any group of persons who, acting in an agreed way, purchase or sell shares of a company which makes a public offer of its shares, in such quantity that it implies a change in the holdings which represent the controlling group or groups, shall inform about this transaction to the NSC within the 5 days

following the operation.

7. Those operations in which shares of an issuing company authorized to make public offerings of its shares are purchased or sold and grant more than 5 percent of the voting rights shall also be reported, within 5 days after the transaction.

The above information shall also be sent to the stock exchange, the over-the-counter market or self-regulated entity in which they quote their shares, and shall be published in their respective bulletins.

All the above information given to the NSC, shall have, for purposes of the law, the effect of a sworn statement.

Tender Offerings

The bill provides that the procedure governing tender offerings will be subject to the regulations issued by the NSC. If the tender offer is not carried out pursuant to said regulations, the purchasers of the shares shall not be permitted to exercise the voting rights which emanate from the acquired shares, without prejudice to, the application of the penalties foreseen in this bill. The agreements executed without complying with the foregoing will be considered void and null.

The current procedure to which takeovers are subject to by virtue of Resolution 227 of the NSC is as follows:

1. Any individual or legal entity which, directly or through third parties, intends to acquire a quantity of shares which enables him to reach the corporation's control must comply with the following rules:
   a. Previous report to the NSC of the features of the tender offer.
   b. Complete and suitable publication of the bid's terms.
   c. Determination of how long the bidding will last, which shall not be less than 10 days and not more than 20 working days, computable as from the date of the publication of the bid.
   d. Firm acquisition commitment with the exception of the offered price, which might be increased up to 5 percent.
   e. Proportional acquisition in the event that the sellers' offers exceed the quantity of shares the bidder intends to acquire.

2. The bidder shall notify in detail to the issuing company the terms of the bid. Once this is complied with, a publication in the Stock Exchange or the self-regulated entity's bulletin and in a national newspaper of important circulation is required.

3. Once the bidding period has ended, the bidder and the intervening brokers will have to inform its result to the NSC.

The proposed law seems to create a mandatory procedure, established through a new NSC resolution, for those engaged in a takeover, as opposed to current Resolution 227 procedure, which is voluntary.

Insider-Trading—Use of Privileged Information

1. In this respect, the bill stipulates that members of the board of directors, managers, statutory auditors and any individual who, by reason of his functions, position or activity, possesses information related to the development or the business activities of a company subject to the public offerings regime, which has not been made public and which is capable of having any influence on the price of its shares, shall keep this information secret. The above-mentioned people shall not be able to use this "price-sensitive" information with the aim of obtaining any advantage for themselves or for third persons.

2. The same obligation will apply to directors, officers and employees of risk-analysis companies and of public and private entities with supervisory powers, including the NSC, depositories of securities, stock exchanges and over-the-counter markets, who, by reason of their activities, have access to this information, even after cessation of their functions.

The bill provides that any benefit obtained by the individuals mentioned in 1. as a result of the purchase and subsequent sale, or vice versa, of securities of the company to which they are related, if carried out in a period of less than 6 months, will be considered as property of the company, which could claim it through a judicial action.

The obligation to keep secret and the limitations to trading imposed on the individuals mentioned in 1. and 2. are also imposed on those people who, by virtue of a temporary or accidental relationship with the company

PROPOSED NEW LEGISLATION ON CAPITAL MARKETS (cont'd)

or with the individuals mentioned in 1. and 2., have had access to the privileged information.

Fraud and Market Manipulation

The issuers, brokers, investors or any other participants in the markets of securities options and futures, commodities, financial assets, currencies, precious metals, other assets or their representative indexes shall have to abstain: (1) from developing practices or courses of action which imply or intend price or volume manipulation of securities, rights, products, or subproducts traded and (2) from defrauding any participant of those markets.

The bill makes an illustrative enumeration of actions which could be included in this category as follows:

1. To artificially affect the quotation, liquidity or traded volume of one or more securities, commodities, or other assets or their representative indexes.

2. [To induce to mistake] To mislead any participant of the market by means of false statements or the omission of essential information when there is an obligation to make that information available.

In order to make the law enforceable, the NSC is granted broad powers to punish these practices. Though the bill does not include criminal penalties since it only punishes these practices from an administrative point of view, these penalties are still very harsh. The bill sets forth the following sanctions:

1. In the case of companies that make public offerings of securities:

   - Fines that range from US$1,000 to US$5,000,000.

This figure may be increased up to three times when the benefit is unduly obtained or the avoided damage is higher than that amount.

The current maximum amount of this fine is US$7,000.

- Suspension for a maximum of 5 years of the right to make public offerings of securities.

- Permanent prohibition from making public offerings of securities.

2. In the case of stock exchanges, self-regulated entities over-the-counter market, brokers, its officers and employees or directors, managers, statutory auditors or any other individual who has engaged in these misconducts:

   - Fines that range from US$1,000 to US$5,000,000. This figure may be increased up to five times when the amount of the benefit unduly obtained or the avoided damage is higher than such amount.

   - Inability to carry out duties as directors, managers, or statutory auditors of corporations. This penalty may be imposed from 3 to 10 years.

   - Suspension for up to 5 years or prohibition to develop activities in the sphere of public offerings of securities.

The proposed law represents another step towards an improvement of the Argentine Capital Market's legal framework in order to provide legal protection, certainty and confidence to foreign and domestic investors.

---

government agency debt. Of particular importance for international traders are the three issues of US dollar denominated Brady bonds, including Par, Discount, and Floating Rate (FRB). These last are designed to pay a floating rate of return on capitalized, unpaid interest of prior foreign debt. At the end of 1993 Argentina issued its longest-term security in recent years, a 10-year, fixed rate Global bond.

Publicly held corporations, limited partnerships, civil associations, and cooperatives and corporations formed under article 118 of Law No. 19,550 may issue debt securities. Obligations may be issued in pesos or in any foreign currency, although non-peso bonds are almost invariably issued in US dollars.

Debt may be secured by the issuer's assets, by chattel mortgage, or by other means such as financial guarantees from insurers, banks, or corporations. These bills, notes, or bonds can be straight debt or have conversion or put-and-call features. Commercial paper—short-term securities (less than one year in maturity) issued directly by private corporations—is popular in the Argentine capital market, where borrowing at longer terms is much more difficult. Companies wishing to use commercial paper as a substitute for either bank lending or longer-term debt financing typically reissue (roll over) the security as a new issue when the previously sold paper is due for repayment.

Securities lending for short-term financing is permitted and is generally regulated through the Argentine Commercial Code. The most common of these practices is on the "deposit of government debt securities." Most of these operations use Bonex securities and are generally referred to as Bonex leasing.

Argentine entities have been allowed to issue securities, called closed investment funds, that consist of securitized corporate receivables—such as mortgages, auto loans, and other payments owed. This adds another type of security to Argentine capital markets, as well as another means for firms to get liquidity.

The improved business climate should encourage the development of new debt securities offerings from both privatized and conventional corporate issuers locally. Tax barriers have been reduced to encourage the issuance of short- and medium-term debt, known as "obligaciones negociables." Argentina's participation in the Brady plan, the restructuring of US$36 billion in debt, and the resumption of debt service has allowed the government and large, creditworthy corporations to raise money on the international debt markets. This opens the way for Argentine companies to issue debt with longer maturities. Bank capital formation has mushroomed under the new credit climate. Local banks have raided several billions of US dollars in the Eurobond markets at relatively low cost, enabling them to lend to local wholesale and retail customers.

Argentina's debt is still rated below investment grade. However, recent reforms and sound economic fundamentals have maintained access to foreign debt markets. Indeed, the interest rate spread for Argentine government debt and corporate debt has shrunk—from 3190 basis points above the London Interbank Offering Rate (LIBOR) for Bonex in early 1990 to only 280 basis points above LIBOR at the end of 1994—to levels that generally make this funding source feasible for all issuing sectors. In addition, greater financial system stability and financial management sophistication should lead to the development of new products such as the securitization of debt.

Specialized Financial Markets

Forward contracting on agricultural commodities in Argentina dates back to the beginning of the 20th century. Forwards have been traded on the Mercado de Cereales a Término ("forward") in Buenos Aires since 1907. Similar trading was also conducted on the Mercado a Término de Rosario in Rosario, Argentina's second largest city. A more modern futures contracts market now exists, trading primarily in agricultural and livestock prod-

ucts. Products available for trading activity include grains, oilseeds, and meats, as well as cattle and hogs. The two leading commodities markets are now the Mercado de Hacienda de Liniers and the Mercado de Cereales de Buenos Aires—the Liniers Livestock Market and the Buenos Aires Grain Market, respectively.

Only call options were traded on individual stocks, such as Pérez Companc, YPF, and Acindar, and these only on the major equity exchanges. Trading volumes remain modest, but interest has been growing.

Settlement procedures for all futures and options contracts are handled by each individual exchange. The CNV assumes regulatory duties on trading of forwards, futures, and options contracts unless otherwise specified. Foreign entities may participate in any and all derivative markets. Those interested in participating in these markets are encouraged to contact the CNV or any major local broker for more information on current rules, regulations, tax issues, and other requirements.

FURTHER READING

This discussion has provided a basic guide to money, finances, financial institutions, and financial markets in Argentina. Because the economic situation is changing so rapidly in Argentina, authoritative, up-to-date sources on the structure and function of the financial sector are limited. Those interested in current developments may wish to consult *Ambito Financiero* and *Cronista Comercial*, the two leading business newspapers. These periodicals cover economic and financial developments in Argentina. All publications are in Spanish unless otherwise noted.

Ambito Financiero   Daily financial newspaper. Available from: Paseo Colón 1196, 1063 Buenos Aires, Argentina; Tel: [54] (1) 349-1500, Fax: [54] (1) 349-1505.

Business Latin America   English-language weekly newsletter. Available from: Business International Corp., One Dag Hammerskjold Plaza, New York, NY 10017, USA; Tel: [1] (212) 750-6300.

El Cronista Comercial   Daily financial newspaper. Available from: Honduras 5663, 1414 Buenos Aires, Argentina; Tel: [54] (1) 775-4476.

Memoria Anual and *Boletín Estadístico* Annual and monthly statistical publications, respectively, from the Banco Central de la República Argentina. Available from: BCRA, Reconquista 266, 1003 Buenos Aires, Argentina; Tel: [54] (1) 394-8411, 394-8119, 393-0021; Fax: [54] (1) 334-6489, 334-6468, 325-4860.

Mercado Monthly magazine on Argentine markets. Available from: Perú 263, 1067 Buenos Aires, Argentina; Tel: [54] (1) 342-3613, 342-3322,

342-3475, Fax: [54] (1) 343-7826, 343-0639.

Prensa Económica Monthly magazine on Argentine economic news. Available from: Av. Rivadavia 926, Piso 5, 1002 Buenos Aires, Argentina; Tel: [54] (1) 345-4419, 345-0936.

The Review of the River Plate Leading English-language publication on Argentine economy. Three issues per month. Available from: Virrey Liniers 71, PB, Of. A, 1174 Buenos Aires, Argentina; Tel: [54] (1) 862-2624

USEFUL ADDRESSES

Refer to the "Important Addresses" chapter, beginning on page 315, for a list of Argentine embassies, consulates and trade offices, as well as various business organizations. Those organizations listed below may be of particular interest.

Banking

Banco Central de la República Argentina (BCRA)
(Central Bank of the Argentine Republic)
Reconquista 266
1003 Buenos Aires, Argentina
Tel: [54] (1) 394-8411, 394-8119, 393-0021
Fax: [54] (1) 334-6489, 334-6468, 325-4860

Banco de la Nación Argentina (BNA)
Bartolomé Mitre 326
1036 Buenos Aires, Argentina
Tel: [54] (1) 342-4041, 334-5355
Fax: [54] (1) 334-8700

Secretaría de Hacienda
(Secretariat of Finance)
Hipolito Yrigoyen 250
1310 Buenos Aires, Argentina
Tel: [54] (1) 331-0731, 342-2937, 341-8900
Fax: [54] (1) 331-0292

Insurance

Asociación Argentina de Compañías de Seguros
(Argentine Association of Insurance Companies)
25 de Mayo 565
1002 Buenos Aires, Argentina
Tel: [54] (1) 313-6974
Fax: [54] (1) 312-6300
Telex: 23837

Asociación de Aseguradores Extranjeros en la Argentina
(Association of Foreign Insurance Companies)
San Martín 201, Piso 7
1004 Buenos Aires, Argentina
Tel: [54] (1) 394-3881

Superintendencia de Seguros de la Nación
(Superintendent of Insurance)
Avda Julio A. Roca 721
1067 Buenos Aires, Argentina
Tel: [54] (1) 331-8733, 331-9821

Financial Markets

Bolsa de Comercio de Buenos Aires
Sarmiento 299
Buenos Aires, Argentina
Tel: [54] (1) 313-7084
Fax: [54] (1) 313-4472

Mercado de Valores de Buenos Aires S.A.
25 de Mayo 367, Pisos 8 y 9
1002 Buenos Aires, Argentina
Tel: [54] (1) 313-4522
Fax: [54] (1) 329-6499

Currency & Foreign Exchange

INTERNATIONAL PAYMENT INSTRUMENTS

Argentina maintains no official restrictions on payment arrangements and generally follows international standards and procedures in the execution of payments. It abolished existing minimums and other requirements and conditions for international payment instruments and arrangements as part of its deregulation of the foreign exchange regime. Terms may be freely negotiated.

The main mechanism used for international payments in Argentina is the letter of credit (L/C), although documents against acceptance (D/A) and documents against payment (D/P) are also used infrequently. Open account terms are seldom extended or accepted. Countertrade arrangements are uncommon, although a framework exists to implement such transactions, primarily with other South American member nations of the Asociación Latinoamericano de Integración (ALADI).

Some observers have noted that with the pressures of tight money found in early 1995, coupled with Argentina's lack of legal prohibitions against checks drawn on insufficient funds, some firms caught in the liquidity crisis have resorted to a "check is in the mail" ploy. Payees may incur costs and extended delays in collecting funds due. Those involved in international transactions may wish to insist on an L/C arrangement.

CONTENTS

CURRENCY

The currency used in Argentina is the peso, denoted in Argentina by the symbol "$." The peso replaced the previous currency, the austral, on January 1, 1992. Pesos come in notes of 1, 2, 5, 10, 20, 50, and 100 pesos, and coins are 1, 5, 10, 25, or 50 centavos or 1 peso (there are 100 centavos to the peso).

Although vending machines, telephones, and fareboxes on public transportation may be coin operated, tokens (*fichas* or *cospeles*) obtained from kiosks and retail stores are often used in place of coins.

THE CONVERTIBILITY LAW

The Convertibility Law of 1991 forms the core of Argentina's foreign exchange regime. It pledges that Argentina will maintain the peso at a one-to-one exchange rate with the US dollar and make the peso freely and fully convertible at market rates. (Actual rates have been slightly less than a full US dollar, largely reflecting transaction costs and usually resulting in a discount of only a few thousandths of a percent; effective parity is maintained and assumed and is not a factor except in larger wholesale transactions.) Under the Convertibility Law, Argentines and foreigners in Argentina are allowed to hold and use any currency.

Revisions in Argentina's foreign investment laws have removed prior approval and other restrictions from such investment and allow unrestricted entry, conversion, repatriation of capital and earnings at market rates. The Convertibility Law, in tandem with financial and business deregulation in general and liberalization of foreign investment law in particular, has revolutionized Argentina's international financial system and standing, restoring the currency to a degree of stability unknown for more than two decades.

The Convertibility Law also transformed the Banco Central de la República Argentina (BCRA, the

ARGENTINA'S FOREIGN EXCHANGE RATES

1980–1991: australs to US dollars
1991–1994: pesos to US dollars

	Year average	Year-end
1980	0.000184	0.0002
1981	0.000574	0.001073
1982	0.002594	0.004603
1983	0.01054	0.02138
1984	0.068422	0.1684
1985	0.6011	0.801
1986	0.9442	1.2129
1987	2.31	4.53
1988	10.85	15.82
1989	407.1	1220.0
1990	4,876.8	5,119.3
1991	9,541.5	9,917.8
1992	0.9915	0.9921
1993	0.9995	0.99
1994 (partial year)	0.9996	0.9999

Source: Banco de la República Argentina (BCRA)

central bank) into a currency board, preventing it from issuing more currency than can be backed by foreign currency reserves. This prevents the government from creating unbacked currency—"running the printing press"—or monetizing deficits and thus limits inflation, contributing to the stability and integrity of the monetary system.

Despite the panic shown by international investors in response to Mexico's devaluation of its peso in late 1994—which resulted in extreme pressure on Argentina to devalue its own currency in early 1995—the government remained steadfast in following the terms of peso convertibility. This adherence to law and policy came at the cost of considerable internal economic pain as the economy contracted and unemployment soared. A severe cash flow and liquidity problem developed as nervous depositors withdrew funds from the banking system, credit dried up, and the government scrambled to shore up the weakened financial system, while attempting to meet the goals established by international lenders as prerequisite for extending interim aid.

Nevertheless, the Argentine government has shown remarkable firmness of purpose in sticking to its stated policies. The resounding victory of President Menem and the strengthening of his party's hand in the legislature in the May 1995 elections have generally been viewed as a popular endorsement of this stringent government policy.

FOREIGN EXCHANGE OPERATIONS

Exchange Rates

In the past exchange rates have been volatile. However, as noted, the peso is now set at parity with the US dollar. Exchange rates of currencies other than the US dollar are based on the buying and selling rates for the US dollar in international markets. Swap transactions and forward exchange operations have been permitted in any currency since December 1989, although the market remains thin. Rates on such transactions may be freely negotiated.

Foreign Exchange Outlets

Virtually any authorized financial outlet can deal in foreign exchange, and major banks and foreign exchange houses specialize in the exchange business. Cash receives a better rate than traveler's checks (although notes must be new, clean, and crisp, or dealers may refuse them altogether). Banks and exchange booths at international airports offer good rates, and many hotels, travel agencies, and some fancier retail shops and restaurants will also exchange currency as a convenience to clients. Because of free convertibility, there is currently no black market operating in Argentina.

Credit Cards

Credit cards are generally accepted in urban areas. The most common are bank cards—Visa and MasterCard, and their international affiliates—followed by Diner's Club (its prevalence is linked to the long-term presence of its parent, Citicorp, in Argentina) and American Express. Until recently, many merchants added a surcharge (*recargo*) to purchases made using credit cards. With the stabilization of exchange and inflation rates in 1993–1994, this practice had largely died out. However, concerns reignited by the financial markets crisis in early 1995 could lead to a renewal of this practice or even a refusal to accept credit cards.

Purchases made using credit cards will be converted at the prevailing exchange rate at the time of processing, which may not be on or even near the date of the actual transaction (although the efficiency of processing is improving). Users should be aware that although the exchange rates offered by credit card firms are usually reasonable, fees and other charges can result in a less favorable final rate.

ELEMENTS OF THE FOREIGN EXCHANGE REGIME

Administration of Control

All exchange transactions must be carried out through entities authorized expressly for this purpose with no restrictions on the purchase or sale of foreign exchange at market prices. These authorized entities include banks, exchange agencies, exchange houses, exchange offices, and financial companies; each type of institution is subject to separate regulations.

Resident and Nonresident Accounts

Since January 1, 1993, both residents and foreigners have been allowed to hold checking accounts denominated in US dollars for use in both domestic and international transactions. Authorized banks may open accounts in pesos or foreign exchange in the name of residents or nonresidents who have met certain identification requirements that are aimed at, among other things, preventing money laundering. Accounts in foreign exchange must be denominated in convertible currencies and may be credited only with cash or with remittances from abroad. Both resident and nonresident holders of demand or time foreign currency accounts may use their credit balances freely in Argentina or abroad. Transfers between accounts may be made freely.

International Transactions

Import and export payments may be effected in convertible currencies. Payments may be freely settled by authorized financial entities.

Neither payments for invisibles nor the exportation of domestic and foreign bank notes is restricted. Proceeds from invisible transactions of the private sector need not be repatriated. The importation of domestic and foreign bank notes is not subject to exchange control.

Capital

All private sector loans may be transacted in the free exchange market without restriction. Authorized banks may accept foreign currency deposits, subject to certain conditions. Foreign borrowing by the public sector is regulated by Law No. 24.156 of October 29, 1992. In accordance with Article 5 of Decree No. 1853/93, foreign investors may, at any time, exercise their right to repatriate capital and remit earnings abroad. Local enterprises based on foreign capital may borrow domestically with the same rights and on the same terms as local enterprises based on domestic capital. Swaps of bonds for eligible debts agreed to under the Brady Plan by Argentina and foreign creditor banks began to take place in April 1993 in accordance with the debt- and debt-service-reduction operations. (The debt-equity swap and most of the interest swaps were completed by late April 1994.)

Gold

Residents may hold gold coins and gold in any other form in Argentina or abroad. Financial institutions, exchange houses, and exchange agencies may buy or sell gold in the form of coins or good-delivery bars among themselves and may buy such gold from their clients. The importation of gold coins and good-delivery bars is not restricted. Gold exports must be paid for in convertible currencies. Institutions may carry out arbitrage operations with their clients in gold coins or good-delivery gold against foreign bank notes. Authorized institutions may export gold to entities abroad.

Accessing Funds

Some travelers may be able to access funds from home by obtaining a cash advance on a credit card or with a personal check along with an American Express card through that company's offices. Some may even be able to obtain cash through an automated teller machine (ATM) debit card, provided that the issuing bank is a participant in an international network connected with an Argentine bank; an interested traveler should verify affiliations, procedures, and the ATM personal identification number (PIN) access code with the issuing bank prior to leaving for Argentina.

A foreigner may arrange fund transfers through the home bank either through an Argentine affiliate or through an Argentine correspondent bank. Such transfers may take some time to complete, because transfers into and out of Argentina are subject to delays (the efficiency of these transfers is improving as financial institutions become more accustomed to them).

Use of Foreign Currency

Under the Convertibility Law, a peso-dollar bimonetary system is in effect. Banks can and do accept deposits and checks in dollars and the law allows contracts and payments to be made in other currencies as well. Although residents and nonresidents may hold foreign currency, no foreign currency is in general use in Argentina. Although not legal render, there is some limited negotiability of other currencies in Buenos Aires and in some border areas. The US dollar is the most popular and commonly used foreign currency because it serves as an international reserve currency as well as the currency of Argentina's second largest trading partner. Chilean and Uruguayan pesos are relatively common near the borders with those neighboring countries. The weakness and volatility of the Brazilian real and the Paraguayan guarani make them less common or acceptable, although the increased interchange under the Mercosur trade agreement may alter this situation to some extent in the future. Because of a lack of familiarity with them, European or Asian currencies are not generally accepted, except in a few outlets in Buenos Aires.

FOREIGN RESERVES

Under the terms of the Convertibility Law, Argentina must back every peso issued with an equivalent amount of hard currency reserves. Not only is the Banco Central de la República Argentina (BCRA) prohibited from issuing additional funds without such backing, but the logical obverse of this policy is that if foreign currency reserves become severely depleted, the BCRA would withdraw pesos from circulation. Because Argentina has been running a trade deficit as it has raised its imports to upgrade the capacity of its domestic industries, it has relied heavily on foreign capital. Much of this inflow came in as portfolio investment, which can just as easily flow out (as was the case in early 1995). Some direct investment has also been accomplished by means of debt conversion, through which little or no actual cash enters the system (although a liability is canceled, relieving officials of the need to service it).

Argentina's foreign reserves (total reserves minus gold) grew steadily from US$82 million in 1964 to US$9.388 billion in 1979, before falling to a low of US$1.172 billion in 1983. This reserve position fluctuated throughout the 1980s, averaging US$2.3 billion between 1981 and 1989. With the economic reforms inaugurated in 1989, reserves began to grow as the overall economy improved. Reserves grew to US$4.592 billion in 1990, US$6.005 billion in 1991, US$9.99 billion in 1992, and US$14.089 in 1993. Total international reserves (a more inclusive measure than foreign currency reserves) were US$12.5 billion at the end of 1992, growing to US$17.6 billion at the end of 1994. The monetary base—equal to 88 percent of total international reserves at the end of 1992—had risen to 91.5 percent of such reserves by year-end 1994.

International Payments

International transactions add an additional layer of risk for buyers and sellers that are familiar only with doing business domestically. Currency regulations, foreign exchange risk, political, economic, or social upheaval in the buyer's or seller's country, and different business customs may all contribute to uncertainty. Ultimately, however, the seller wants to make sure he gets paid and the buyer wants to get what he pays for. Choosing the right payment method can be the key to the transaction's feasibility and profitability.

There are four common methods of international payment, each providing the buyer and the seller with varying degrees of protection for getting paid and for guaranteeing shipment. Ranked in order of most security for the seller to most security for the buyer, they are: cash in advance, documentary letters of credit (L/C), documentary collections (D/P and D/A Terms), and open account (O/A).

Cash in Advance

In cash in advance terms the buyer simply prepays the seller prior to shipment of goods. Cash in advance terms are generally used in new relationships where transactions are small and the buyer has no choice but to prepay. These terms give maximum security to the seller but leave the buyer at great risk. Because the buyer has no guarantee that the goods will be shipped, he must have a high degree of trust in the seller's ability and willingness to follow through. The buyer must also consider the economic, political and social stability of the seller's country, as these conditions may make it impossible for the seller to ship as promised.

Documentary Letters of Credit

A letter of credit is a bank's promise to pay a seller on behalf of the buyer so long as the seller meets the terms and conditions stated in the credit. Documents are the key issue in letter of credit transactions. Banks act as intermediaries, and have nothing to do with the goods themselves.

Letters of credit are the most common form of international payment because they provide a high degree of protection for both the seller and the buyer. The buyer specifies the documentation that he requires from the seller before the bank is to make payment, and the seller is given assurance that he will receive payment after shipping his goods so long as the documentation is in order.

Documentary Collections

A documentary collection is like an international cash on delivery (COD), but with a few twists. The exporter ships goods to the importer, but forwards shipping documents (including title document) to his bank for transmission to the buyer's bank. The buyer's bank is instructed not to transfer the documents to the buyer until payment is made (Documents against Payment, D/P) or upon guarantee that payment will be made within a specified period of time (Documents against Acceptance, D/A). Once the buyer has the documentation for the shipment he is able to take possession of the goods.

D/P and D/A terms are commonly used in ongoing business relationships and provide a measure of protection for both parties. The buyer and seller, however, both assume risk in the transaction, ranging from refusal on the part of the buyer to pay for the documents, to the seller's shipping of unacceptable goods.

Open Account

This is an agreement by the buyer to pay for goods within a designated time after their shipment, usually in 30, 60, or 90 days. Open account terms give maximum security to the buyer and greatest risk to the seller. This form of payment is used only when the seller has significant trust and faith in the buyer's ability and willingness to pay once the goods have been shipped. The seller must also consider the economic, political, and social stability of the buyer's country as these conditions may make it impossible for the buyer to pay as promised.

DOCUMENTARY COLLECTIONS (D/P, D/A)

Documentary collections focus on the transfer of documents such as bills of lading for the transfer of ownership of goods rather than on the goods themselves. They are easier to use than letters of credit and bank service charges are generally lower.

This form of payment is excellent for buyers who wish to purchase goods without risking prepayment and without having to go through the more cumbersome letter of credit process.

Documentary collection procedures, however, entail risk for the seller, because payment is not made until after goods are shipped. In addition, the seller assumes the risk while the goods are in transit and storage until payment/acceptance take place. Banks involved in the transaction do not guarantee payments. A seller should therefore only agree to a documentary collection procedure if the transaction includes the following characteristics:

- The seller does not doubt the buyer's ability and willingness to pay for the goods;
- The buyer's country is politically, economically, and legally stable;
- There are no foreign exchange restrictions in the buyer's home country, or unless all necessary licenses for foreign exchange have already been obtained; and
- The goods to be shipped are easily marketable.

TYPES OF COLLECTIONS

The three types of documentary collections are:
- Documents against Payment (D/P)
- Documents against Acceptance (D/A)
- Collection with Acceptance (Acceptance D/P)

All of these collection procedures follow the same general step-by-step process of exchanging documents proving title to goods for either cash or a contracted promise to pay at a later time. The documents are transferred from the seller (called the remitter) to the buyer (called the drawee) via intermediary banks. When the seller ships goods, he presents documents such as the bill of lading, invoices, and certificate of origin to his representative bank (the remitting bank), which then forwards them to the buyer's bank (the collecting bank). According to the type of documentary collection, the buyer may then do one of the following:

- With Documents against Payment (D/P), the buyer may only receive the title and other documents after paying for the goods;
- With Documents against Acceptance (D/A), the buyer may receive the title and other documents after signing a time draft promising to pay at a later date; or

- With Acceptance Documents against Payment (Acceptance D/P), the buyer signs a time draft for payment at a later date. However, he may only obtain the documents after the time draft reaches maturity. In essence, the goods remain in escrow until payment has been made.

In all cases the buyer may take possession of the goods only by presenting the bill of lading to customs and shipping authorities.

In the event that the prospective buyer cannot or will not pay for the goods shipped, they remain in the legal possession of the seller; however he may be stuck with them in an unfavorable situation. Also, the seller has no legal basis to file claim against the prospective buyer. At this point the seller may:
- Have the goods returned and sell them on his domestic market; or
- Sell the goods to another buyer near where the goods are currently held.

If the seller takes no action the goods will be auctioned or otherwise disposed of by customs.

PROCEDURE

The documentary collection process has been standardized by a set of rules published by the International Chamber of Commerce (ICC). These rules are called the Uniform Rules for Collections (URC) and are contained in ICC Publication No. 322. (*See* "Further Reading" on page 277 for ICC addresses and a list of available publications.)

The following is the basic set of steps used in a documentary collection. Refer to the illustration on the following page for a graphic representation of the procedure.

① The seller (remitter, exporter) ships the goods.
② and ③ The seller forwards the agreed upon documents to his bank, the remitting bank, which in turn forwards them to the collecting bank (buyer's bank).
④ The collecting bank notifies the buyer (drawee, importer) and informs him of the conditions under which he can take possession of the documents.
⑤ To take possession of the documents, the buyer makes payment or signs a time deposit.
⑥ and ⑦ If the buyer draws the documents against payment, the collecting bank transfers payment to the remitting bank for credit to the seller's account. If the buyer draws the documents against acceptance, the collecting bank sends the acceptance to the remitting bank or retains it up to maturity. On maturity, the collecting bank collects the bill and transfers it to the remitting bank for payment to the seller.

DOCUMENTARY COLLECTION PROCEDURE

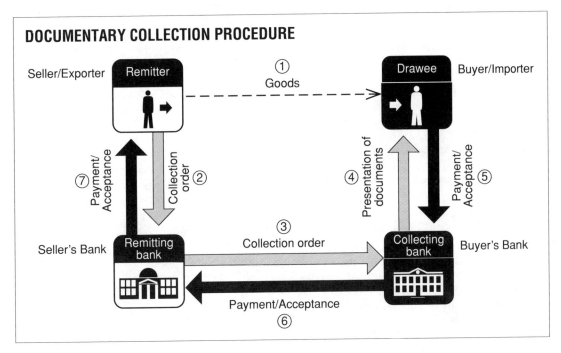

TIPS FOR BUYERS

1. The buyer is generally in a secure position because he does not assume ownership or responsibility for goods until he has paid for the documents or signed a time draft.

2. The buyer may not sample or inspect the goods before accepting and paying for the documents without authorization from the seller. However, the buyer may in advance specify a certificate of inspection as part of the required documentation package.

3. As a special favor, the collecting bank can allow the buyer to inspect the documents before payment. The collecting bank assumes responsibility for the documents until their redemption.

4. In the above case, the buyer should immediately return the entire set of documents to the collecting bank if he cannot meet the agreed payment procedure.

5. The buyer assumes no liability for goods if he refuses to take possession of the documents.

6. Partial payment in exchange for the documents is not allowed unless authorized in the collection order.

7. With documents against acceptance, the buyer may receive the goods and resell them for profit before the time draft matures, thereby using the proceeds of the sale to pay for the goods. The buyer remains responsible for payment, however, even if he cannot sell the goods.

TIPS FOR SELLERS

1. The seller assumes risk because he ships goods before receiving payment. The buyer is under no legal obligation to pay for or to accept the goods.

2. Before agreeing to a documentary collection, the seller should check on the buyer's creditworthiness and business reputation.

3. The seller should make sure the buyer's country is politically and financially stable.

4. The seller should find out what documents are required for customs clearance in the buyer's country. Customs brokers may be of help.

5. The seller should assemble the documents carefully and make sure they are in the required form and endorsed as necessary.

6. As a rule, the remitting bank will not review the documents before forwarding them to the collecting bank. This is the responsibility of the seller.

7. The goods travel and are stored at the risk of the seller until payment or acceptance.

8. If the buyer refuses acceptance or payment for the documents, the seller retains ownership. The seller may have the goods shipped back or try to sell them to another buyer in the region.

9. If the buyer takes no action, customs authorities may seize the goods and auction them off or otherwise dispose of them.

10. Because goods may be refused, the seller should only ship goods which are readily marketable to other sources.

Letters of Credit (L/C)

A letter of credit is a document issued by a bank stating its commitment to pay someone (seller/exporter/supplier) a stated amount of money on behalf of a buyer (importer) so long as the seller meets very specific terms and conditions. Letters of credit are often called documentary letters of credit because the banks handling the transaction deal in documents as opposed to goods. Letters of credit are the most common method of making international payments, because the risks of the transaction are shared by both the buyer and the seller.

STEPS IN USING AN L/C

The letter of credit process has been standardized by a set of rules published by the International Chamber of Commerce (ICC). These rules are called the Uniform Customs and Practice for Documentary Credits (UCP) and are contained in ICC Publication No. 500. (*See* "Further Reading" on page 277 for ICC addresses and list of available publications.) The following is the basic set of steps used in a letter of credit transaction. Specific letter of credit transactions follow somewhat different procedures.

- After the buyer and seller agree on the terms of a sale, the buyer arranges for his bank to open a letter of credit in favor of the seller.
- The buyer's bank (the issuing bank), prepares the letter of credit, including all of the buyer's instructions to the seller concerning shipment and required documentation.
- The buyer's bank sends the letter of credit to a correspondent bank (the advising bank), in the seller's country. The seller may request that a particular bank be the advising bank, or the domestic bank may select one of its correspondent banks in the seller's country.
- The advising bank forwards the letter of credit to the seller.

- The seller carefully reviews all conditions the buyer has stipulated in the letter of credit. If the seller cannot comply with one or more of the provisions he immediately notifies the buyer and asks that an amendment be made to the letter of credit.
- After final terms are agreed upon, the seller prepares the goods and arranges for their shipment to the appropriate port.
- The seller ships the goods, and obtains a bill of lading and other documents as required by the buyer in the letter of credit. Some of these documents may need to be obtained prior to shipment.
- The seller presents the required documents to the advising bank, indicating full compliance with the terms of the letter of credit. Required documents usually include a bill of lading, commercial invoice, certificate of origin, and possibly an inspection certificate if required by the buyer.
- The advising bank reviews the documents. If they are in order, they are forwarded to the issuing bank. If it is an irrevocable, confirmed letter of credit, the seller is guaranteed payment and may be paid immediately by the advising bank.
- Once the issuing bank receives the documents it notifies the buyer who then reviews the documents. If the documents are in order the buyer signs off, taking possession of the documents, including the bill of lading, which he then uses to take possession of the shipment.
- The issuing bank initiates payment to the advising bank, which pays the seller.

The transfer of funds from the buyer to his bank, from the buyer's bank to the seller's bank, and from the seller's bank to the seller may be handled at the same time as the exchange of documents, or under terms agreed upon in advance.

PARTIES TO A LETTER OF CREDIT TRANSACTION

Buyer/Importer   Seller/Exporter/Supplier

Buyer's bank   Seller's bank

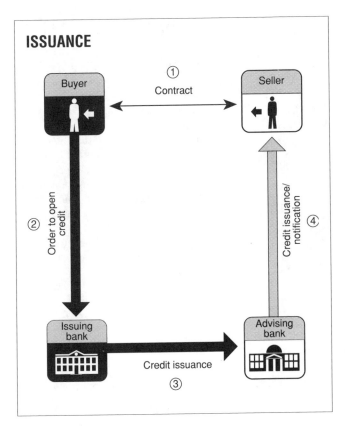

ISSUANCE OF A LETTER OF CREDIT

① Buyer and seller agree on purchase contract.
② Buyer applies for and opens a letter of credit with issuing ("buyer's") bank.
③ Issuing bank issues the letter of credit, forwarding it to advising ("seller's") bank.
④ Advising bank notifies seller of letter of credit.

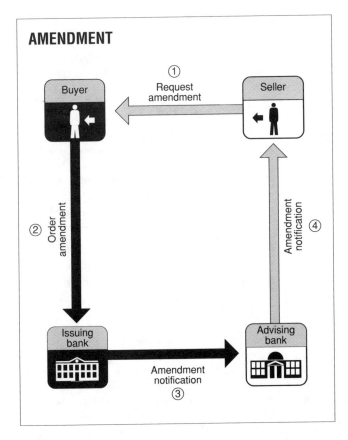

AMENDMENT OF A LETTER OF CREDIT

① Seller requests (of the buyer) a modification (amendment) of the terms of the letter of credit. Once the terms are agreed upon:
② Buyer issues order to issuing ("buyer's") bank to make an amendment to the terms of the letter of credit.
③ Issuing bank notifies advising ("seller's") bank of amendment.
④ Advising bank notifies seller of amendment.

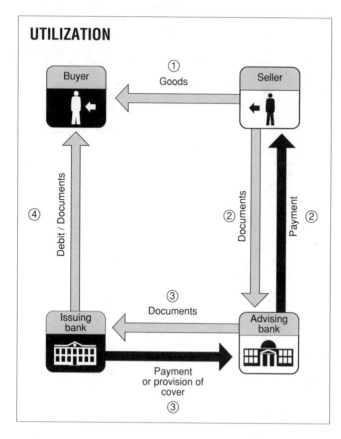

UTILIZATION

Buyer — ① Goods — Seller

④ Debit / Documents

② Documents

Payment ②

③ Documents

Issuing bank — Advising bank

Payment or provision of cover ③

UTILIZATION OF A LETTER OF CREDIT

(Irrevocable, confirmed credit)

① Seller ships goods to buyer.

② Seller forwards all documents (as stipulated in the letter of credit) to advising bank. Once documents are reviewed and accepted, advising bank pays seller for the goods.

③ Advising bank forwards documents to issuing bank. Once documents are reviewed and accepted, issuing bank pays advising bank.

④ Issuing bank forwards documents to buyer. Seller's letter of credit, or account, is debited.

COMMON PROBLEMS IN LETTER OF CREDIT TRANSACTIONS

Most problems with letter of credit transactions have to do with the ability of the seller to fulfill obligations the buyer establishes in the original letter of credit. The seller may find the terms of the credit difficult or impossible to fulfill and either tries to do so and fails, or asks the buyer for an amendment to the letter of credit. Observers note that as many as half of all letters of credit are amended or renegotiated entirely. Since most letters of credit are irrevocable, amendments to the original letter of credit can only be made after further negotiations and agreements between the buyer and the seller. Sellers may have one or more of the following problems:

- Shipment schedule stipulated in the letter of credit cannot be met.
- Stipulations concerning freight cost are deemed unacceptable.
- Price is insufficient due to changes in exchange rates.
- Quantity of product ordered is not the expected amount.
- Description of product to be shipped is either insufficient or too detailed.
- Documents stipulated in the letter of credit are difficult or impossible to obtain.

Even when sellers accept the terms of a letter of credit, problems often arise at the stage in which banks review, or negotiate, the documents provided by the seller against the requirements specified in the letter of credit. If the documents are found not to be in accord with those specified in the letter of credit, the bank's commitment to pay is invalidated. In some cases the seller can correct the documents and present them within the time specified in the letter of credit. Or the advising bank may ask the issuing bank for authorization to accept the documents despite the discrepancies found.

Limits on Legal Obligations of Banks

It is important to note once again that banks deal in documents and not in goods. Only the wording of the credit is binding on the bank. Banks are not responsible for verifying the authenticity of the documents, nor for the quality or quantity of the goods being shipped. As long as the documents comply with the specified terms of the letter of credit, banks may accept them and initiate the payment process as stipulated in the letter of credit. Banks are free from liability for delays in sending messages caused by another party, consequences of Acts of God, or the acts of third parties whom they have instructed to carry out transactions.

TYPES OF LETTERS OF CREDIT

Basic Letters of Credit

There are two basic forms of letters of credit: the Revocable credit and the Irrevocable credit. There are also two types of Irrevocable credit: the Irrevocable credit not confirmed, and the Irrevocable confirmed credit. Each type of credit has advantages and disadvantages for the buyer and for the seller. Also note that the more the banks assume risk by guaranteeing payment, the more they will charge for providing the service.

Revocable Credit This credit can be changed or canceled by the buyer without prior notice to the seller. Because they offer little security to the seller, revocable credits are generally unacceptable to the seller and are rarely used.

Irrevocable Credit The irrevocable credit is one the issuing bank commits itself irrevocably to honor, provided the seller complies with all stipulated conditions. This credit cannot be changed or canceled without the consent of both the buyer and the seller. As a result, this type of credit is the most widely used in international trade. Irrevocable credits are more expensive because of the issuing bank's added liability in guaranteeing the credit. There are two types of irrevocable credits:

- **The irrevocable credit not confirmed by the advising bank (unconfirmed credit)** This means that the buyer's bank which issues the credit is the only party responsible for payment to the seller, and the seller's bank is obliged to pay the seller only after receiving payment from the buyer's bank. The seller's bank merely acts on behalf of the issuing bank and therefore incurs no risk.

- **The irrevocable, confirmed credit** In a confirmed credit, the advising bank adds its guarantee to pay the seller to that of the issuing bank. If the issuing bank fails to make payment the advising bank will pay. If a seller is unfamiliar with the buyer's bank which issues the letter of credit, he may insist on an irrevocable confirmed credit. These credits may be used when trade is conducted in a high risk area where there are fears of outbreak of war or social, political, or financial instability. Confirmed credits may also be used by the seller to enlist the aid of a local bank to extend financing to enable him to fill the order. A confirmed credit costs more because the bank has added liability.

Special Letters of Credit

There are numerous special letters of credit designed to meet specific needs of buyers, sellers, and intermediaries. Special letters of credit usually involve increased participation by banks, so financing and service charges are higher than those for basic letters of credit. The following is a brief description of some special letters of credit.

Standby Letter of Credit This credit is basically a payment or performance guarantee. It is used primarily in the United States because US banks are prevented by law from giving certain guarantees. Standby credits are often called non-performing letters of credit because they are only used as a backup payment method if the collection on a primary payment method is past due.

Standby letters of credit can be used, for example, to guarantee the following types of payment and performance:

- repayment of loans
- fulfillment by subcontractors
- securing the payment for goods delivered by third parties.

The beneficiary to a standby letter of credit can draw from it on demand, so the buyer assumes added risk.

Revolving Letter of Credit This credit is a commitment on the part of the issuing bank to restore the credit to the original amount after it has been used or drawn down. The number of times it can be utilized and the period of validity is stated in the credit. The credit can be cumulative or noncumulative. Cumulative means that unutilized sums can be added to the next installment whereas noncumulative means that partial amounts not utilized in time expire.

Deferred Payment Letter of Credit In this credit the buyer takes delivery of the shipped goods by accepting the documents and agreeing to pay his bank after a fixed period of time. This credit gives the buyer a grace period, and ensures that the seller gets payment on the due date.

Red Clause Letter of Credit This is used to provide the seller with some funds prior to shipment to finance production of the goods. The credit may be advanced in part or in full, and the buyer's bank finances the advance payment. The buyer, in essence, extends financing to the seller and incurs ultimate risk for all advanced credits.

Transferable Letter of Credit This allows the seller to transfer all or part of the proceeds of the letter of credit to a second beneficiary, usually the ultimate producer of the goods. This is a common financing tactic for middlemen and is used extensively in East Asia.

Back-to-Back Letter of Credit This is a new credit opened on the basis of an already existing, nontransferable credit. It is used by traders to make payment to the ultimate supplier. A trader receives a letter of credit from the buyer and then opens another letter of credit in favor of the supplier. The first letter of credit is used as collateral for the second credit. The second credit makes price adjustments from which come the trader's profit.

OPENING A LETTER OF CREDIT

The wording in a letter of credit should be simple but specific. The more detailed an L/C is, the more likely the seller will reject it as too difficult to fulfill. At the same time, the buyer will wish to define in detail what he is paying for.

Although the L/C process is designed to ensure the satisfaction of all parties to the transaction, it cannot be considered a substitute for face-to-face agreements to do business in good faith. It should therefore contain only those stipulations required from the banks involved in the documentary process.

L/Cs used in trade are usually either irrevocable unconfirmed credits or irrevocable confirmed credits. In choosing the type of L/C to open in favor of the seller, the buyer should take into consideration generally accepted payment processes in the seller's country, the value and demand for the goods to be shipped, and the reputation of the seller.

In specifying documents necessary from the seller, it is very important to demand documents that are required for customs clearance and those that reflect the agreement reached between the buyer and the seller. Required documents usually include the bill of lading, a commercial and/or consular invoice, the bill of exchange, the certificate of origin, and the insurance document. Other documents required may be copies of a cable sent to the buyer with shipping information, a confirmation from the shipping company of the state of its ship, and a confirmation from the forwarder that the goods are accompanied by a certificate of origin. Prices should be stated in the currency of the L/C, and documents should be supplied in the language of the L/C.

THE APPLICATION

The following information should be included on an application form for opening an L/C.

① **Beneficiary** The seller's company name and address should be written completely and correctly. Incomplete or incorrect information results in delays and unnecessary additional cost.

② **Amount** Is the figure a maximum amount or an approximate amount? If words like "circa," "ca.," "about," etc., are used in connection with the amount of the credit, it means that a difference as high as 10 percent upwards or downwards is permitted. In such a case, the same word should also be used in connection with the quantity.

③ **Validity Period** The validity and period for presentation of the documents following shipment of the goods should be sufficiently long to allow the exporter time to prepare the necessary documents and ship them to the bank. Under place of validity, state the domicile of either the advising bank or the issuing bank.

④ **Beneficiary's Bank** If no bank is named, the issuing bank is free to select the correspondent bank.

⑤ **Type of Payment** Availability Sight drafts, time drafts, or deferred payment may be used, as previously agreed to by the seller and buyer.

⑥ **Desired Documents** Here the buyer specifies precisely which documents he requires. To obtain effective protection against the supply of poor quality goods, for instance, he can demand the submission of analysis or quality certificates. These are generally issued by specialized inspection companies or laboratories.

⑦ **Notify Address** An address is given for notification of the imminent arrival of goods at the port or airport of destination. Damage of goods in shipment is also cause for notification. An agent representing the buyer may be used.

⑧ **Description of Goods** Here a short, precise description of the goods is given, along with quantity. If the credit amount carries the notation "ca.," the same notation should appear with the quantity.

⑨ **Confirmation Order** It may happen that the foreign beneficiary insists on having the credit confirmed by the bank in his country.

SAMPLE LETTER OF CREDIT APPLICATION

Sender American Import-Export Co., Inc. 123 Main Street San Francisco, California ——— Our reference AB/02	**Instructions** **to open a Documentary Credit** San Francisco, 30th September 19.. Place / Date

Please open the following

[X] irrevocable   [ ] revocable documentary credit

Domestic Bank Corporation
Documentary Credits
P.O. Box 1040
San Francisco, California

Beneficiary	Beneficiary's bank (if known)
① Argentine Trading Company Lavalle 1716, Piso 2 1048 Buenos Aires Argentina	④ Banco de la Nación Argentina Bartolomé Mitre 326 1036 Buenos Aires Argentina

(left margin, vertical text) This credit is subject to the »Uniform customs and practice for documentary credits« fixed by the International Chamber of Commerce / It is understood that you do not assume any responsibility neither for the correctness, validity or genuineness of the documents which will be remitted to you / nor for the description, quality, quantity and weight of the goods thereby represented

② **Amount**
US$70,200.--

Please advise this bank
[ ] by letter
[X] by letter, cabling main details in advance
[ ] by telex / telegram with full text of credit

③ **Date and place of expiry**
25th November 19.. in San Francisco

Partial shipments	Transhipment	Terms of shipment (FOB, C & F, CIF)
[X] allowed [ ] not allowed	[ ] allowed [X] not allowed	CIF San Francisco

Despatch from / Taking in charge at For transportation to	Latest date of shipment	Documents must be presented not later than
Mexico, DF San Francisco	10th Nov. 19..	③ 15 days after date of despatch

Beneficiary may dispose of the credit amount as follows ⑤

[X] at sight upon presentation of documents
[ ] after ....days, calculated from date of ....

[ ] by a draft due ....
drawn on [ ] you   [ ] your correspondents
which you / your correspondents will please accept

---

against surrender of the following documents ⑥

[X] invoice   (....3....copies)

Shipping document
[X] sea: bill of lading, to order, endorsed in blank
[ ] rail: dublicate waybill
[ ] air: air consignment note
[ ]

[X] insurance policy, certificte   (............ copies)
    covering the following risks:
"all risks" including war up to
[ ] Additional documents final destination in
the USA
[X] Confirmation of the carrier that the
    ship is not more than 15 years old
[X] packing list (3 copies)

Notify address in bill of lading / goods addressed to ⑦	
American Import-Export Co., Inc. 123 Main Street San Francisco, California	Goods insured by [ ] us [X] seller

Goods ⑧
1'000 "Record players ANC 83 as per pro forma invoice
       no. 74/1853 dd 10th September 19.."

       at US$70.20 per item

Your correspondents to advise beneficiary [ ] adding their confirmation [X] without adding their confirmation ⑨

Payments to be debited to our U.S. Dollars account no 10-32679150

NB. The applicable text is marked by [X]

American Import-Export Co., Inc.

E 6801 N 1/2 3.81 5000

Signature _____

For mailing please see overleaf

TIPS FOR PARTIES TO A LETTER OF CREDIT

Buyer

1. Before opening a letter of credit, the buyer should reach agreement with the seller on all particulars of payment procedures, schedules of shipment, type of goods to be sent, and documents to be supplied by the supplier.

2. When choosing the type of L/C to be used, the buyer should take into account standard payment methods in the country of the seller.

3. When opening a letter of credit, the buyer should keep the details of the purchase short and concise.

4. The buyer should be prepared to amend or renegotiate terms of the L/C with the seller. This is a common procedure in international trade. On irrevocable L/Cs, the most common type, amendments may be made only if all parties involved in the L/C agree.

5. The buyer can eliminate exchange risk involved with import credits in foreign currencies by purchasing foreign exchange on the forward markets.

6. The buyer should use a bank experienced in foreign trade as the L/C issuing bank.

7. The validation time stated on the L/C should give the seller ample time to produce the goods or to pull them out of stock.

8. The buyer should be aware that an L/C is not fail-safe. Banks are only responsible for the documents exchanged and not the goods shipped. Documents in conformity with L/C specifications cannot be rejected on grounds that the goods were not delivered as specified in the contract. The goods shipped may not in fact be the goods ordered and paid for.

9. Purchase contracts and other agreements pertaining to the sale between the buyer and seller are not the concern of the issuing bank. Only the terms of the L/C are binding on the bank.

10. Documents specified in the L/C should include those the buyer requires for customs clearance.

Seller

1. Before signing a contract, the seller should make inquiries about the buyer's creditworthiness and business practices. The seller's bank will generally assist in this investigation.

2. The seller should confirm the good standing of the buyer's bank if the credit is unconfirmed.

3. For confirmed credit, it should be determined that the seller's local bank is willing to confirm credits from the buyer and the buyer's bank.

4. The seller should carefully review the L/C to make sure these can be met: specified schedules of shipment, type of goods to be sent, packaging, and documentation. All aspects of the L/C must be in conformance with the terms agreed upon, including the seller's address, the amount to be paid, and the prescribed transport route.

5. The seller must comply with every detail of the L/C specifications; otherwise the security given by the credit is lost.

6. The seller should ensure that the L/C is irrevocable.

7. If conditions of the credit have to be modified, the seller should contact the buyer immediately so that the buyer can instruct the issuing bank to make the necessary amendments.

8. The seller should confirm with the insurance company that it can provide the coverage specified in the credit and that insurance charges in the L/C are correct. Insurance coverage is often for CIF (cost, insurance, freight) value of the goods plus 10 percent.

9. The seller must ensure that the details of goods being sent comply with the description in the L/C and that the description on the invoice matches that on the L/C.

10. The seller should be familiar with foreign exchange limitations in the buyer's country that could hinder payment procedures.

GLOSSARY

DOCUMENTS IN INTERNATIONAL TRADE

The following is a list and description of some of the more common documents importers and exporters encounter in the course of international trade. For the importer/buyer this serves as a checklist of documents he may require of the seller/exporter in a letter of credit or documents against payment method.

bill of lading A document issued by a transportation company (such as a shipping line) to the shipper that serves as a receipt for goods shipped, a contract for delivery, and may serve as a title document. The major types are:

- **straight (nonnegotiable) bill of lading** Indicates that the shipper will deliver the goods to the consignee. The document itself does not give title to the goods. The consignee need only identify himself to claim the goods. A straight bill of lading is often used when the goods have been paid for in advance.
- **order (negotiable or "shippers order") bill of lading** This is a title document which must be in the possession of the consignee (buyer/importer) in order for him to take possession of the shipped goods. Because this bill of lading is negotiable, it is usually made out "to the order of" the consignor (seller/exporter).
- **air waybill** A bill of lading issued for air shipment of goods, which is always made out in straight non-negotiable form. It serves as a receipt for the shipper and needs to be made out to someone who can take possession of the goods upon arrival—without waiting for other documents to arrive.
- **overland/inland bill of lading** Similar to an Air Waybill, except that it covers ground or water transport.

certificate of origin A document certifying the country of origin of the goods. Because a certificate of origin is often required by customs for entry, a buyer will often stipulate in his letter of credit that a certificate of origin is a required document.

certificate of manufacture A document in which the producer of goods certifies that production has been completed and that the goods are at the disposal of the buyer.

consular invoice An invoice prepared on a special form supplied by the consul of an importing country, in the language of the importing country, and certified by a consular official of the foreign country of origin.

dock receipt A document/receipt issued by an ocean carrier when the seller/exporter is not responsible for moving the goods to their final destination, but only to a dock in the exporting country. The document/receipt indicates that the goods were, in fact, delivered and received at the specified dock.

export license A document, issued by a government agency, giving authorization to export certain commodities to specified countries.

import license A document, issued by a government agency, giving authorization to import certain commodities.

inspection certificate An affidavit signed by the seller/exporter or an independent inspection firm (as required by the buyer/importer), confirming that merchandise meets certain specifications.

insurance document A document certifying that goods are insured for shipment.

invoice/commercial invoice A document identifying the seller and buyer of goods or services, identifying numbers such as invoice number, date, shipping date, mode of transport, delivery and payment terms, and a complete listing and description of the goods or services being sold including prices, discounts, and quantities. The commercial invoice is usually used by customs to determine the true cost of goods when assessing duty.

packing list A document listing the merchandise contained in a particular box, crate, or container, plus type, dimensions, and weight of the container.

phytosanitary (plant health) inspection certificate A document certifying that an export shipment has been inspected and is free from pests and plant diseases considered harmful by the importing country.

shipper's export declaration A form prepared by a shipper/exporter indicating the value, weight, destination, and other information about an export shipment.

INCOTERMS 1990

Incoterms are a codification of international rules for the uniform interpretation of common contract clauses in export/import transactions. Incoterms were developed by the International Chamber of Commerce (ICC) in Paris, France.

CIP—carriage and insurance paid to (... named place of destination)

"Carriage and insurance paid to..." means that the seller has the same obligations as under CPT, but with the addition that the seller has to procure cargo insurance against the buyer's risk of loss of or damage to the goods during the carriage. The seller contracts for insurance and pays the insurance premium. The buyer should note that under the CIP term the seller is only required to obtain insurance on minimum coverage. The CIP term requires the seller to clear the goods for export. This term may be used for any mode of transport including multimodal transport.

CPT—carriage paid to (... named place of destination)

"Carriage paid to..." means that the seller pays the freight for the carriage of the goods to the named destination. The risk of loss of or damage to the goods, as well as any additional costs due to events occurring after the time the goods have been delivered to the carrier, is transferred from the seller to the buyer when the goods have been delivered into the custody of the carrier.

"Carrier" means any person who, in contract of carriage, undertakes to perform or to procure the performance of carriage, by rail, road, sea, air, inland waterway or by a combination of such modes. If subsequent carriers are used for the carriage to the agreed destination, the risk passes when the goods have been delivered to the first carrier. The CPT term requires the seller to clear the goods for export. This term may be used for any mode of transport including multimodal transport.

CFR—cost and freight (... named port of destination)

"Cost and Freight" means that the seller must pay the costs and freight necessary to bring the goods to the named port of destination but the risk of loss of or damage to the goods, as well as any additional costs due to events occurring after the time the goods have been delivered on board the vessel, is transferred from the seller to the buyer when the goods pass the ship's rail in the port of shipment. The CFR term requires the seller to clear the goods for export. This term can only by used for sea and inland waterway transport. When the ship's rail serves no practical purpose, such as in the case of roll-on/roll-off or container traffic, the CPT term is more appropriate to use.

CIF—cost, insurance, freight (... named port of destination)

"Cost, Insurance, Freight" means that the seller has

the same obligations as under CFR but with the addition that he has to procure marine insurance against the buyer's risk of loss of or damage to the goods during the carriage. The seller contracts for insurance and pays the insurance premium.

The buyer should note that under the CIF term the seller is only required to obtain insurance on minimum coverage. The CIF term requires the seller to clear the goods for export.

This term can only be used for sea and inland waterway transport. When the ship's rail serves no practical purpose such as in the case of roll-on/roll-off or container traffic, the CIP term is more appropriate to use.

DAF—delivered at frontier (... named place)

"Delivered at Frontier" means that the seller fulfils his obligation to deliver when the goods have been made available, cleared for export, at the named point and place at the frontier, but before the customs border of the adjoining country. The term "frontier" may be used for any frontier including that of the country of export. Therefore, it is of vital importance that the frontier in question be defined precisely by always naming the point and place in the term. The term is primarily intended to be used when goods are to be carried by rail or road, but it may be used for any mode of transport.

DDP—delivered duty paid (... named place of destination)

"Delivered duty paid" means that the seller fulfils his obligation to deliver when the goods have been made available at the named place in the country of importation. The seller has to bear the risks and costs including duties, taxes and other charges of delivering the goods thereto, cleared for importation. While the EXW term represents the minimum obligation for the seller, DDP represents the maximum obligation.

This term should not be used if the seller is unable directly or indirectly to obtain the import licence. If the parties wish the buyer to clear the goods for importation and to pay the duty, the term DDU (delivered duty unpaid) should be used.

If the parties wish to exclude from the seller's obligations some of the costs payable upon importation of the goods (such as value added tax (VAT)), this should be made clear by adding words to this effect: "Delivered duty paid, VAT unpaid (... named place or destination)."

This term may be used irrespective of the mode of transport.

DDU—delivered duty unpaid (... named place of destination)

"Delivered duty unpaid" means that the seller fulfils his obligation to deliver when the goods have been made available at the named place in the country of importation. The seller has to bear the costs and risks involved in bringing the goods thereto (excluding duties, taxes and other official charges payable upon importation as well as the costs and risks of carrying out customs formalities). The buyer has to pay any additional costs and to bear any risks caused by his failure to clear the goods for import in time.

If the parties wish the seller to carry out customs formalities and bear the costs and risks resulting therefrom, this has to be made clear by adding words to this effect.

If the parties wish to include in the seller's obligations some of the costs payable upon importation of the goods (such as value added tax (VAT)), this should be made clear by adding words to this effect: "Delivered duty unpaid, VAT paid (... named place or destination)." This term may be used irrespective of the mode of transport.

DEQ—delivered ex quay (duty paid) (... named port of destination)

"Delivered Ex Quay (duty paid)" means that the seller fulfils his obligation to deliver when he has made the goods available to the buyer on the quay (wharf) at the named port of destination, cleared for importation. The seller has to bear all risks and costs including duties, taxes and other charges of delivering the goods thereto.

This term should not be used if the seller is unable directly or indirectly to obtain the import licence.

If the parties wish the buyer to clear the goods for importation and pay the duty the words "duty unpaid" should be used instead of "duty paid."

If the parties wish to exclude from the seller's obligations some of the costs payable upon importation of the goods (such as value added tax (VAT)), this should be made clear by adding words to this effect: "Delivered ex quay, VAT unpaid (... named port of destination)." This term can only be used for sea or inland waterway transport.

DES—delivered ex ship (... named port of destination)

"Delivered Ex Ship" means that the seller fulfils his obligation to deliver when the goods have been made available to the buyer on board the ship uncleared for import at the named port of destination. The seller has to bear all the costs and risks involved in bringing the goods to the named port of destination. This term can only be used for sea or inland waterway transport.

EXW—ex works (... named place)

"Ex works" means that the seller fulfills his obligation to deliver when he has made the goods available at his premises (i.e. works, factory, warehouse, etc.) to the buyer. In particular, he is not responsible for loading the goods on the vehicle provided by the buyer or for clearing the goods for export, unless otherwise agreed. The buyer bears all costs and risks involved in taking the goods from the seller's premises to the desired destination. This term thus represents the minimum obligation for the seller. This term should not be used when the buyer cannot carry out directly or indirectly the export formalities. In such circumstances, the FCA term should be used.

FAS—free alongside ship (... named port of shipment)

"Free Alongside Ship" means that the seller fulfills his obligation to deliver when the goods have been placed alongside the vessel on the quay or in lighters at the named port of shipment. This means that the buyer has to bear all costs and risks of loss of or damage to the goods from that moment. The FAS term requires the buyer to clear the goods for export. It should not be used when the buyer cannot carry out directly or indirectly the export formalities.

This term can only be used for sea or inland waterway transport.

FCA—free carrier (... named place)

"Free Carrier" means that the seller fulfills his obligation to deliver when he has handed over the goods, cleared for export, into the charge of the carrier named by the buyer at the named place or point. If no precise point is indicated by the buyer, the seller may choose within the place or range stipulated where the carrier shall take the goods into his charge. When, according to commercial practice, the seller's assistance is required in making the contract with the carrier (such as in rail or air transport) the seller may act at the buyer's risk and expense.

This term may be used for any mode of transport, including multimodal transport.

"Carrier" means any person who, in a contract of carriage, undertakes to perform or to procure the performance of carriage by rail, road, sea, air, inland waterway or by a combination of such modes. If the buyer instructs the seller to deliver the cargo to a person, e.g. a freight forwarder who is not a "carrier," the seller is deemed to have fulfilled his obligation to deliver the goods when they are in the custody of that person.

"Transport terminal" means a railway terminal, a freight station, a container terminal or yard, a multipurpose cargo terminal or any similar receiving point.

"Container" includes any equipment used to unitise cargo, e.g. all types of containers and/or flats, whether ISO accepted or not, trailers, swap bodies, ro-ro equipment, igloos, and applies to all modes of transport.

FOB—free on board (... named port of shipment)

"Free On Board" means that the seller fulfills his obligation to deliver when the goods have passed over the ship's rail at the named port of shipment. This means that the buyer has to bear all costs and risks of loss of or damage to the goods from that point. The FOB term requires the seller to clear the goods for export.

This term can only be used for sea or inland waterway transport. When the ship's rail serves no practical purpose, such as in the case of roll-on/roll-off or container traffic, the FCA term is more appropriate to use.

INTERNATIONAL PAYMENT TERMS

advice The forwarding of a letter of credit or an amendment to a letter of credit to the seller, or beneficiary of the letter of credit, by the advising bank (seller's bank).

advising bank The bank (usually the seller's bank) receiving a letter of credit from the issuing bank (the buyer's bank) and handling the transaction from the seller's side. This includes: validating the letter of credit, reviewing it for internal consistency, forwarding it to the seller, forwarding seller's documentation back to the issuing bank, and, in the case of a confirmed letter of credit, guaranteeing payment to the seller if his documents are in order and the terms of the credit are met.

amendment A change in the terms and conditions of a letter of credit, usually to meet the needs of the seller. The seller requests an amendment of the buyer who, if he agrees, instructs his bank (the issuing bank) to issue the amendment. The issuing bank informs the seller's bank (the advising bank) which then notifies the seller of the amendment. In the case of irrevocable letters of credit, amendments may only be made with the agreement of all parties to the transaction.

back-to-back letter of credit A new letter of credit opened in favor of another beneficiary on the basis of an already existing, nontransferable letter of credit.

beneficiary The entity to which credits and payments are made, usually the seller/supplier of goods.

bill of exchange A written order from one person to another to pay a specified sum of money to a designated person. The following two versions are the most common:

- **draft** A financial/legal document where one individual (the drawer) instructs another individual (the drawee) to pay a certain amount of money to a named person, usually in payment for the transfer of goods or services. Sight drafts are payable when presented. Time drafts (also called usance drafts) are payable at a future fixed (specific) date or determinable (30, 60, 90 days etc.) date. Time drafts are used as a financing tool (as with documents against acceptance D/P terms) to give the buyer time to pay for his purchase.
- **promissory note** A financial/legal document wherein one individual (the issuer) promises to pay another individual a certain amount.

collecting bank (also called the presenting bank) In a documentary collection, the bank (usually the buyer's bank) that collects payment or a time draft from the buyer to be forwarded to the remitting bank (usually the seller's bank) in exchange for shipping and other documents which enable the buyer to take possession of the goods.

confirmed letter of credit A letter of credit containing a guarantee on the part of both the issuing and advising bank of payment to the seller so long as the seller's documentation is in order and terms of the credit are met.

deferred payment letter of credit A letter of credit by which the buyer takes possession of the title documents and the goods by agreeing to pay the issuing bank at a fixed time in the future.

discrepancy The noncompliance with the terms and conditions of a letter of credit. A discrepancy may be as small as a misspelling, an inconsistency in dates or amounts, or a missing document. Some discrepancies can easily be fixed; others may lead to the eventual invalidation of the letter of credit.

D/A Abbreviation for "documents against acceptance."

D/P Abbreviation for "documents against payment."

documents against acceptance (D/A) *See* documentary collection.

documents against payment (D/P) *See* documentary collection.

documentary collection A method of effecting payment for goods whereby the seller/exporter instructs his bank to collect a certain sum from the buyer/importer in exchange for the transfer of shipping and other documentation enabling the buyer/importer to take possession of the goods. The two main types of Documentary Collection are:

- **documents against payment (D/P)** Where the bank releases the documents to the buyer/importer only against a cash payment in a prescribed currency; and
- **documents against acceptance (D/A)** Where the bank releases the documents to the buyer/importer against acceptance of a bill of exchange guaranteeing payment at a later date.

draft *See* bill of exchange.

drawee The buyer in a documentary collection.

forward foreign exchange An agreement to purchase foreign exchange (currency) at a future date at a predetermined rate of exchange. Forward foreign exchange contracts are often purchased by buyers of merchandise who wish to hedge against foreign exchange fluctuations between the time the contract is negotiated and the time payment is made.

irrevocable credit A letter of credit that cannot be revoked or amended without prior mutual consent of the seller, the buyer, and all intermediaries.

issuance The act of the issuing bank (buyer's bank) establishing a letter of credit based on the buyer's application.

issuing bank The buyer's bank which establishes a letter of credit in favor of the seller, or beneficiary.

letter of credit A document stating commitment on the part of a bank to place an agreed upon sum of money at the disposal of a seller on behalf of a buyer under precisely defined conditions.

negotiation In a letter of credit transaction, the examination of seller's documentation by the (negotiating) bank to determine if it complies with the terms and conditions of the letter of credit.

open account The shipping of goods by a seller to the buyer prior to payment for the goods. The seller will usually specify expected payment terms of 30, 60, or 90 days from the date of shipment.

red clause letter of credit A letter of credit which makes funds available to the seller prior to shipment in order to provide him with funds for production of the goods.

remitter In a documentary collection, an alternate name given to the seller who forwards documents to the buyer through banks.

remitting bank In a documentary collection, a bank acting as an intermediary, forwarding the remitter's documents to, and payments from, the collecting bank.

revocable letter of credit A letter of credit which may be revoked or amended by the issuer (buyer) without prior notice to other parties in the letter of credit process. It is rarely used.

revolving letter of credit A letter of credit which is automatically restored to its full amount after the completion of each documentary exchange. It is used when there are several shipments to be made over a specified period of time.

sight draft *See* bill of exchange.

standby letter of credit A letter of credit used as a secondary payment method in the event that the primary payment method cannot be fulfilled.

time draft *See* bill of exchange.

validity The time period for which a letter of credit is valid. After receiving notice of a letter of credit opened on his behalf, the seller/exporter must meet all the requirements of the letter of credit within the period of validity.

FURTHER READING

For more detailed information on international trade payments, refer to the following publications of the International Chamber of Commerce (ICC).

How to Order ICC Publications

ICC Publications are available from ICC National Committees and Groups, which exist in 64 countries, or from:

ICC Publishing S.A.
38, Cours Albert 1er
75008 Paris, France
Tel: [33] (1) 49-53-29-23, 49-53-29-56
Fax: [33] (1) 49-53-29-02

ICC Publishing, Inc.
156 Fifth Avenue, Suite 308
New York, NY 10010, USA
Tel: [1] (212) 206-1150
Fax: [1] (212) 633-6025

Documentary Credit Rules Publications

Uniform Customs and Practice for Documentary Credits (1993 Revision) This sixth edition from the ICC came into force on January 1, 1994. The 49 articles of the new *UCP 500* are a comprehensive and practical working aid to bankers, lawyers, importers and exporters, transport executives, educators, and those involved in international trade transactions worldwide. Also available in bilingual English-Spanish and English-Russian editions. Order ICC No. 500, 1993 edition, 60 pages, US$9.95.

UCP 500 and 400 Compared An article-by-article comparison study between the 1993 revision and the 1983 revision to the *UCP*. This study also incorporates commentaries on the rationale for rewrite of the articles. Order ICC No. 511, 1993 edition, 135 pages, US$39.95.

ICC Guide to Documentary Credit Operations, by Charles del Busto. Offers a complete explanation of the documentary credit process including: international trade considerations; a list of political, legal and economic issues; documentary requirements; roles of the issuing and advising banks; types and uses of documentary credits. Contains graphs, charts and sample documents to illustrate and highlight important points as well as a suggested checklist for documentary preparation and examination. Also available in bilingual English-Spanish edition. Order ICC No. 515, 1994 Edition, 122 pages, US$34.95.

Standard Documentary Credit Forms Source-book of forms to use with *UCP 500*. Gives precise instructions about how the revised forms should be filled out. These standard forms have been developed on the basis of the UN's layout key and this alignment with other documents in international trade makes this publication an invaluable aid to all parties to a documentary credit. Order ICC No. 516, 1994 edition, 80 pages, US$29.95.

UCP 500 and Standby Letters of Credit: Special Report, by Brooke Wunnicke, Esq. and Diane B. Wunnicke. Focuses on sections of ICC's 1993 revision to *UCP 500* that relate to standby letters of credit. A John Wiley publication, distributed by ICC Publishing, Inc. Order ICC No. 938, 1994 edition, 100 pages, US$75.00.

Documentary Credits Insight A quarterly newsletter designed to keep you on top of worldwide letter of credit developments, which impact directly on your business. Published four times a year, DCI contains analytical commentary and up-to-the-minute information from the experts who drafted *UCP 500*. DCI also offers you a country-by-country update on documentary credit developments from correspondents in more than 25 countries. Must be ordered directly through ICC Publishing S.A. in Paris. Tel: [33] (1) 49-53-29-56 Fax: [33] (1) 49-53-29-02.

Incoterms Publications

Incoterms 1990 Defines the thirteen 1990 trading terms and specifies the respective rights and obligations of buyer and seller in an international transaction. Also available in bilingual Spanish-English and Russian-English editions. Order ICC No. 460, 1990 edition, 216 pages, US$27.95.

Guide to Incoterms 1990 Contains the full text of *Incoterms 1990* plus commentary illustrating how each Incoterm is interpreted in law and everyday practice. Order ICC No. 461/90, 1991 edition, 150 pages, US$49.95.

Taxation

CORPORATE TAXATION

AT A GLANCE

Corporate Income Tax Rate (%)	30
Capital Gains Tax Rate (%)	30
Branch Tax Rate (%)	30
Withholding Tax (%)	
Dividends	0
Interest	12*
Royalties from Patents, Know-how, etc.	24*
Branch Remittance Tax	0
Net Operating Losses (Years)	
Carryback	0
Carryforward	5

* Final tax applicable only to payments to nonresident

TAXES ON CORPORATE INCOME AND GAINS

Corporate Income Tax Resident corporations are taxed on worldwide income. Any profits, including capital gains, are taxable. Resident corporations are those incorporated in Argentina. Nonresident corporations are subject to tax on Argentine-source income only.

Rates of Corporate Tax Corporate tax is payable at the rate of 30 percent.

Capital Gains Capital gains are included in the taxable income of a corporation and taxed at the regular corporate rate.

Administration The tax year for a corporation is its accounting year. Corporations are required to make 11 advance payments, each in the amount of 8.5 percent of the previous year's tax. The payments are due monthly beginning in the sixth month after the end of the accounting year. The due dates in the months depend on the corporation's taxpayer registration number.

Corporations must file their tax returns and pay any balance due by a specified date in the fifth month after their accounting year. If the payment is late, interest is charged.

Dividends Dividends and branch remittances are not subject to tax.

Foreign Tax Relief Resident corporations may credit foreign income taxes against their Argentine tax liability, up to the amount of the increase in that liability resulting from including foreign-source income in the taxable base.

DETERMINATION OF TRADING INCOME

General Tax is applied to taxable income, which is the accounting profit earned in the tax period after adjustments provided for by tax law

RECENT TAX REFORMS

On 17 August 1993, Decree No. 1684/93 repealed the 1 percent CAT effective for fiscal years ending after 30 June 1995. However, on 30 August 1993, Decree No. 1802/93 established that the repeal shall be effective as from 1 September 1993 for assets located in the Argentine Provinces ("Provinces") provided that (i) the Provinces had adhered to the Federal Tax Treaty, as discussed below; (ii) such assets are used in agricultural, mining, industrial and construction activities, and that (iii) the Provinces in which such assets are located have eliminated the Provincial Stamp Tax on or before 27 October 1993, for financial and insurance transactions relating to such activities. For those Provinces in which the Provincial Stamp Tax repeal is enacted after 27 October 1993, the CAT abrogation will take place as from the first day of the month following the month on which the Provincial Stamp Tax abrogation is enacted.

Pursuant to the Federal Tax Treaty executed between the National Government and the Provinces on 12 August 1993, the Stamp Tax, the Gross Revenue Tax and, *inter alia*, the Provincial Tax on the Transfer of Oil, Gas and Electricity are in the process of being repealed with respect to certain specific taxable events. Initially, such repeal will encompass certain taxable events and, at a later stage, it will extend to most of the taxable events. The first stage should be completed on or before 30 June 1995, and the second stage should be completed on or before 12 August 1996. This tax repeal program is part of the National Government initiative to reduce the incidence of such taxes on the economy of the country. In addition, the Federal Tax Treaty is intended to promote the elimination of the local taxes imposed on the same taxable events as the provincial taxes. The Gross Revenue Tax is intended to be replaced by a Retail Tax on or before 12 August 1996. The Federal Tax Treaty also establishes that, as from 1 January 1994, the Provincial Land Tax rate and the taxable basis on which such rate applies should not exceed certain percentages established by the National Government. Until now, the compliance with the above-mentioned objectives has not been uniform among the Provinces.

and after adjustment for inflation. Exemptions are usually insignificant. Expenses are deductible to the extent incurred in producing taxable income.

Inventories Stock is valued according to procedures established by tax law, which result in values nearly equivalent to market value at the end of the tax period.

Provisions Provisions for bad debts and severance pay are allowed. They must be computed according to methods prescribed by tax law.

Depreciation Tangible assets may be depreciated using the straight-line method over the assets' expected lives. A method based on effective use may also be acceptable. In general, buildings are depreciated at an annual rate of 2 percent. However, a higher rate may be acceptable if it is established that, because of the materials used to construct the building, the expected useful life is less than 50 years. The law does not specify rates for movable assets. Intangible property may be depreciated, with exceptions such as goodwill and trade names.

Relief for Losses Tax losses may be carried forward for five tax periods. Losses from foreign sources may offset only foreign-source income. Loss carrybacks are not permitted.

OTHER SIGNIFICANT TAXES

The table below summarizes other significant taxes.

Nature of Tax	Rate (%)
Value-added tax	21
Various local taxes on gross receipts, real estate, and so forth	Various
Tax on assets, excluding certain assets as well as assets (other than land and automobiles) acquired within two years; does not apply to assets used in the agriculture and cattle raising, manufacturing, mining, and construction industries that are located in the Federal District or in provinces that adhere to the elimination of the tax; income tax creditable against this tax (effective for fiscal years ending on or after June 30, 1995, this tax will be completely eliminated)	
General tax rate	1
Banks and other financial institutions	0.4
Social security taxes, on salaries and wages, paid by the employer	33

MISCELLANEOUS MATTERS

Foreign-Exchange Controls Foreign-exchange controls have been eliminated. Consequently, transactions are carried out in a free market at prices set by supply and demand.

Debt-to-Equity Rules Argentina has thin capitalization principles under which a limit is established for interest expense if the debt-to-equity ratio is excessive. If a corporation is thinly capitalized, funds loaned to it by a related party may be recharacterized as equity. Under tax regulations, the interest on the recharacterized debt may be treated as a deductible expense in computing the corporation's tax, but the interest is also taxed separately at a rate of 30 percent. The effect of this procedure is different from disallowing the interest expense deduction if net operating losses are incurred by the corporation.

Transfer Pricing Income from exports of a company in Argentina is subject to tax. If the price of the export from Argentina is less than its wholesale price at the location of the buyer, such wholesale price is considered the price for tax purposes. Imports into Argentina are not subject to tax. However, if the import price is more than the sum of the wholesale price at the location of the seller, plus freight and insurance, the excess is subject to tax. These transfer-pricing rules do not apply if the taxpayer provides evidence that the transaction was between unrelated companies or if it establishes that there were reasons for not using the wholesale price.

TREATY WITHHOLDING TAX RATES

Some of Argentina's tax treaties establish maximum tax rates lower than those under general tax law, as shown in the table below.

	Dividends %	Interest %	Royalties %
Austria	15	12.5	15
Bolivia	0	12	24
Brazil	0	12	24
Canada	10/15	0/12.5	3/5/10/15
Chile	0	12	24
France	15	12	18
Germany	15	10/12	15
Italy	15	20	18
Spain	10/15	0/12.5	3/5/10/15
Sweden	0	12	15
Nontreaty countries	0	12	24

TAX ISSUES

Taxation of Revenues on Intellectual Property

The tax rate of 24 percent levied on revenues payable to foreign entities derived from the use in Argentina under contract of trademarks, designs, patents, licensing royalties, and other similar earnings represents an effective rate. The nominal rates on such earnings—based on presumed legal net revenues—range from 30 percent to 80 percent. However, revenues for activities including technical assistance, engineering, and other consulting involving the transfer of specialized know-how, are taxed at nominal rates of from 30 percent to 60 percent, resulting in an effective rate of 18 percent.

Export and Import Taxes

Revenues paid by resident Argentine importers on goods brought into the country are not taxable under Argentine law to the exporter who receives them in another country. However, the importer in Argentina is liable for payment of IVA (VAT) taxes on the value of the goods imported. However, the later payment of this tax affects the prices that can be charged by the exporter, and thus acts as an indirect tax or limit on the exporter's total earnings.

Source: Editors' notes

PERSONAL TAXATION

AT A GLANCE—MAXIMUM RATES

Income Tax Rate (%)	30
Capital Gains Tax Rate (%)	0
Personal Assets Tax Rate (%)	1*
Estate and Gift Tax Rate (%)	0

*Editor's note: the Argentine Senate has ratified legislation that cut the personal assets tax rate to 0.5 percent.

INCOME TAX—EMPLOYMENT

Who Is Liable

Residents are subject to tax on worldwide income. Nonresidents are taxed only on Argentine-source income.

The tax statutes do not contain a specific definition of "resident." Individuals who reside permanently in Argentina usually are considered resident. The permanent residence of an individual is determined by reference to such matters as location of home, location of spouse and dependents, personal property, economic interests, and social ties.

Taxable Income

Taxable income from employment includes all salaries, regardless of the taxpayer's nationality or the place where the compensation is paid or the contract is entered into. In general, taxable compensation also includes most employer-paid items except employee education expenses and, for resident foreigners and nonresidents only, home leave expenses and moving expenses.

Income Tax Rates

The progressive tax rates applied to Argentine residents for 1994 range from 11 percent to 30 percent, and nonresidents are taxed at a flat rate of 30 percent (see "Nonresidents" on page 284).

The table below presents 1994 individual income tax rates in Argentine pesos ($).

Taxable Income Exceeding	Not Exceeding	Tax on Lower Amount	Rate on Excess $
$	$	$	%
0	39,000	0	11
39,000	60,000	4,290	20
60,000	120,000	8,490	25
120,000	—	23,490	30

Married couples are taxed jointly; however, a wife is taxed separately on her income from personal activities (such as employment, self-employment, and business), assets acquired before marriage, and assets acquired during marriage with income from personal activities.

Deductible Expenses

When computing tax to be withheld from an employee's salary, employers are authorized to deduct certain allowable expenses, including:

- Social security contributions;
- Medical insurance payments for employees and their families;
- Expenses incurred by traveling salesmen based on estimates established by the tax authorities;
- Donations to the government and certain institutions (generally of a charitable or nonprofit nature);
- Burial expenses;
- Life insurance premiums; and
- Pension plan contributions.

In addition to receiving a deduction for social security contributions to the Pension Fund (see "Social Security Taxes" on page 283), employees receive a tax credit for these Pension Fund contributions up to the lower of $4,290 or 11 percent of net taxable income.

Personal Deductions and Allowances

Standard deductions are permitted in amounts established by law. The deductions and their estimated 1994 amounts in Argentine pesos include family allowances equal to $2,363 for a spouse and $1,182 for each child and other dependent. To qualify, the dependents must reside in Argentina for more than six months in the tax year and must not have income in excess of the amount of the personal exemption.

INCOME TAX—SELF-EMPLOYMENT/ BUSINESS INCOME

Who Is Liable

Residents are subject to tax on their worldwide self-employment and business income. Nonresidents are subject to tax on self-employment and business income only from Argentine sources.

Taxable Income

Self-employment or business income is taxable regardless of the recipient's nationality, the place of payment, or where the contract was concluded.

Income Tax Rates

Individuals are subject to tax on self-employment and business income at the rates described in the subsection "Income Tax Rates" on page 282.

Deductible Expenses

Expenses incurred in producing income are deductible. Additionally, certain expenses not primarily incurred for business purposes are deductible, including:

- Social security contributions;
- Medical insurance payments for taxpayers and their families;
- Donations to the government and certain institutions (generally of a charitable or nonprofit nature);
- Burial expenses;
- Life insurance premiums; and
- Pension plan contributions.

In addition to receiving a deduction for social security contributions to the Pension Fund (*see* "Social Security Taxes" on this page), individuals with self-employment or business income receive a tax credit for these Pension Fund contributions up to the lower of $4,290, 11 percent of net taxable income, or 40.74 percent of the amount contributed.

Personal Deductions and Allowances

Individuals with self-employment and business income also receive the standard deductions described previously in the subsection "Deductible Expenses" on page 283.

Directors' Fees

Directors' fees are taxed as self-employment income, as explained in the "Income Tax—Self-Employment/Business Income" section on page 282. Directors' fees paid by Argentine companies are considered Argentine-source income regardless of where services are performed.

INVESTMENT INCOME

Dividends from Argentine corporations paid to residents are not taxable.

Royalties and income from renting real property are taxed as ordinary income. Interest is taxed as ordinary income, except that interest from bank deposits and Argentine government bonds is tax exempt.

RELIEF FOR LOSSES

Business losses of self-employed persons may be carried forward for five years. Foreign-source business losses may offset only foreign-source income.

CAPITAL GAINS AND LOSSES

Capital gains are exempt from income tax. However, real estate is subject to a 1.5 percent transfer tax on the sale price.

PERSONAL ASSETS TAX

For 1994, individuals domiciled in Argentina are subject to the personal assets tax on their worldwide assets that exceed a value of $102,300 at the rate of 1 percent. If domiciled in a foreign country, individuals are taxed only on Argentine assets, but the $102,300 exclusion does not apply. Exempt assets include stock in domestic corporations, local government bonds, and deposits with local banks. Liabilities, other than mortgages on the taxpayer's home, are not deductible. [*Editor's note:* in March 1995, the Argentine Senate ratified legislation that cuts this tax to 0.5 percent and removes the exemption for stocks and bonds, which will now be included in the calculation.]

Expatriates residing in Argentina on work assignments for a period that does not exceed five years are considered domiciled abroad and are taxed only on personal assets located in Argentina.

SOCIAL SECURITY TAXES

Contributions are paid by employers, employees, and self-employed persons in accordance with the following schedule:

	Employer %	Employee %	Self-Employed Persons %
Pension Fund*	16.0	11.0	27.0
Retiree Health Benefits	2.0	3.0	5.0
Current Medical Benefits	6.0	3.0**	—
Family Allowance Fund*	9.0		
	33.0	17.0	32.0

[*Editor's notes:* the rates of these contributions were increased to the amounts stated as of July 1, 1994. **Employees pay an additional 1.5 percent for each dependent covered. Contributions are based on a maximum monthly wage of US$3,780. Employers pay additional amounts calculated on different bases for unemployment, life, disability, and workers' compensation insurance.]

Self-employed individuals pay social security taxes not on actual earnings, but on amounts established by law, depending on the type of activity.

ADMINISTRATION

Employees are not required to register with the tax authorities or file tax returns. Required information is submitted by employers, who also withhold taxes when paying salaries.

Self-employed taxpayers must register with the authorities. Tax returns are filed annually in June, declaring earnings for the previous calendar year.

Individuals with nonwage income, such as self-employment income, must make advance tax payments monthly from July to May, based on the previous year's tax. There is also a withholding system for payments to resident individuals. Withholding is imposed at various rates on income exceeding a minimum threshold. Amounts withheld are treated as advance payments.

NONRESIDENTS

Nonresidents residing in Argentina more than six months in a calendar year must file income tax returns and claim the actual deductible expenses incurred and exemptions available to residents, as described previously in the subsections "Deductible Expenses" on page 283 and "Personal Deductions and Allowances" on page 282. Nonresidents residing temporarily in Argentina, that is, for six months or less, are subject to withholding taxes after a deduction of 30 percent of their compensation to reflect expenses incurred in earning income. The remaining 70 percent is taxed at a flat rate of 30 percent, with no other deductions or exemptions, giving an effective withholding tax rate of 21

percent. Withholding tax is a final tax, and nonresidents subject to withholding tax are not required to file tax returns.

Dividends from Argentine corporations paid to nonresidents are not taxable.

Interest from bank deposits paid to nonresidents is only exempt from Argentine tax if the income is also exempt from foreign tax. Social security taxes are collected as outlined previously in section "Social Securities Taxes" on page 283. However, both an employer and employee may be exempt from contributions to the Argentine pension fund provided certain conditions are met.

DOUBLE TAX RELIEF/ DOUBLE TAX TREATIES

A tax credit is allowed for income taxes paid abroad, up to the increase in Argentine tax resulting from inclusion of the foreign-source income.

Argentina has tax treaties with Austria, Bolivia, Brazil, Chile, France, Germany, Italy, and Sweden. Under tax treaties signed with Austria, Italy, and Sweden, directors' fees for services performed in these countries for corporations established in Argentina are taxable only in Argentina.

Transportation & Communications

INTRODUCTION

Argentina's rapid move toward an open, internationally oriented economy based on free markets is reflected in the nation's push toward the modernization of its transportation and communications networks. In an effort to promote additional future activity while developing the capacity to handle the influx of the trade it is already getting, Argentina has privatized its ponderous, state-run transportation and communications monopolies and largely deregulated investment in these previously restricted sectors. The country's vital transport links—seaways, riverways, roadways, railways, and airways—are being restructured and updated. The country is also preparing feverishly for the arrival of the modern electronic and satellite communications age. However, the expanding Argentine economy has been both a blessing and a curse for carriers. With increased activity and the flow of products, there are many profitable new opportunities. However, shipping congestion and delays have been unavoidable, because the growth in domestic and international trade has quickly outpaced the rate at which Argentina's capacity can be expanded and improved to meet the demand.

Of all of the South American countries, Argentina has the most extensive air navigation, railway, and communications infrastructure. However, many of these systems were built decades ago and, because of a scarcity of funds, most have limped

along with minimal maintenance ever since. The major problem that many of these systems have faced is that they have been owned and operated by the government. Management decisions were often made based solely on politics, government priorities, and expediency; mismanagement and corruption also took their toll. These sectors supported bloated workforces while de-emphasizing investment, not to mention research and development. By the late 1980s, the operating subsidies required to keep these services running at even a marginal level had climbed into the millions annually. Restrictions on imports, technology transfer, and foreign investment further contributed to the decline of the Argentine infrastructure.

In 1989 Argentina took a huge step toward upgrading its dilapidated transportation and communications sectors. In that year, it began to privatize its infrastructure industries, beginning with its much-maligned telephone system. Next came some of the railroads. In the mid-1990s, the government concentrated on the roads and highways, and in 1994 the first private concessions were offered to operate terminals at the port of Buenos Aires. In the crisis atmosphere of early 1995, privatization schedules were speeded up to complete deregulation of the nation's airports. While these efforts are allowing the government to shed its responsibility for staggering operating deficits and infusing these systems with much-needed capital improvements, there is a harsh downside: the privatization process has caused the displacement of thousands of workers for whom as yet no alternative jobs exist.

AIR TRANSPORT

As one of the last transportation industries to be privatized, air transportation in Argentina is in an expansion mode as new investment is being funneled into both cargo and passenger operations. Since the country began to open its markets, not only are imported goods arriving in waves, but so

TRANSPORTATION GLOSSARY

bill of lading A document issued by a carrier to a shipper, signed by the captain, agent, or owner of a vessel, furnishing written evidence regarding receipt of the goods (cargo), the conditions on which transportation is made (contract of carriage), and the engagement to deliver goods at the prescribed port of destination to the lawful holder of the bill of lading. A bill of lading is, therefore, both a receipt for merchandise and a contract to deliver it as freight.

bulk cargo Cargo that consists entirely of one commodity and is usually shipped without packaging. Examples of bulk cargo are grain, ore, and oil.

charter A charter party or charter agreement is a lease or agreement to hire an airplane, vessel, or other means of conveyance to transport goods on a designated voyage to one or more locations.

consolidation The combining of less than a container load (LCL) of cargo from a number of shippers at a centrally located point of origin by a freight consolidator, and transporting them as a single shipment to a destination point. Consolidation of cargo often results in reduced shipping rates.

containerization The practice or technique of using a boxlike device (container) in which a number of packages are stored, protected, and handled as a single unit in transit. Advantages of containerization include: less handling of cargo, more protection against pilferage, less exposure to the elements, and reduced cost of shipping.

customs broker An individual or firm licensed by a government to act for importers or exporters in handling the sequence of customs formalities and other details critical to the legal and speedy exporting and importing of goods.

freight forwarder A person engaged in the business of assembling, collection, consolidating, shipping and distributing less-than-containerload or less-than-truckload freight. Also, a person acting as agent in the trans-shipping of freight to or from foreign countries and the clearing of freight through customs, including full prepa-ration of documents, arranging for shipping, warehousing, delivery and export clearance.

Incoterms 1990 A codification of international rules for the uniform interpretation of common contract clauses in export/import transactions. Developed and issued by the International Chamber of Commerce (ICC) Paris. Refer to page 274 of the "International Payments" chapter for a complete list of Incoterms.

intermodal transport The coordinated transport of freight, especially in connection with relatively long-haul movements using any combination of freight forwarders, piggyback, containerization, air-freight, ocean freight, assemblers, and/or motor carriers.

reefer container A controlled temperature shipping container, usually refrigerated.

roll-on, roll-off (Ro-Ro) A broad category of ships designed to load and discharge cargo which rolls on wheels. Broadly interpreted, this may include train ships, trailer ships, auto, truck and trailer ferries, and ships designed to carry military vehicles.

unitization The practice or technique of consolidating many small pieces of freight into a single unit for easier handling.

Warsaw Convention The informal name for The Convention for the Unification of Certain Rules Relating to International Carriage by Air, signed in Warsaw in 1929. An international multilateral treaty which regulates, in a uniform manner, the conditions of international transportation by air. Among other things it establishes the international liability of air carriers and establishes the monetary limits for loss, damage, and delay.

waybill A document prepared by a transportation line at the point of a shipment, showing the point of origin, destination, route, consignor, consignee, description of shipment and amount charged for the transportation service, and forwarded with the shipment, or direct by mail, to the agent at the transfer point or waybill destination.

Definitions in this glossary are excerpted from the Dictionary of International Trade, copyright © 1994 World Trade Press.

are traveling investors, businesspersons, and tourists. Of particular importance to Argentina is the inflow of technically advanced equipment needed by domestic industries—including the air transport sector—to modernize operations.

This rapid expansion of international air traffic is putting pressure on the air transport system—its infrastructure, equipment, and procedures. Argentina has the most extensive air navigation system of any South American country; nevertheless, its systems require upgrading to match current state-of-the-art international standards. The airport infrastructure throughout the country also needs investment to handle the new volume of international flights.

Privatization of the air transport sector has been slow in part because of the continuing need for government approvals. Historically, the Fuerza Aérea Argentina (the FAA, or Argentine Air Force) has operated and monitored the country's air transportation. Cutbacks in funding for the FAA have meant minimal investment in civil aviation, which has always suffered from being treated as secondary to military aviation. Although privatization is underway today, the private, civil air sector remains tied to the FAA, which continues to have the responsibility for all aviation. Even private concessions are still offered through the FAA, which must also approve the import and purchase of air transport equipment. The FAA retains primary responsibility for overseeing the operation of airport facilities, regulating air traffic safety and pilot training, and investigating accidents.

An additional difficulty with privatization has been the involvement of several competing interests. In the two largest airports, the baggage handling and warehousing services are already under contract to three companies. Successful privatization of the airports must include at least some agreement about the provision of—if not full control—over these essential services. To this end, the government has stepped up negotiations with these companies.

In late 1994 the Argentine government turned its full attention to the air transport industry in an attempt to reconcile the various interests and promote immediate privatization. The intent was to offer airport concessions to private investment consortia to get final privatization underway by late 1995. The government is also deregulating the import of modern navigational aids—classifying them as exempt capital goods—to ease imports in this sector (which must depend heavily on foreign manufacturers for state-of-the-art equipment because no local producers offer ground or airborne navigation aids). As a result, competition for Argentine air transport equipment contracts is

intensifying among foreign suppliers of high-tech air traffic control radar, avionics ground support, and takeoff and landing aids. Improvements can already be seen; outdated airport technology is being slowly replaced, and cargo handling facilities are being upgraded.

A giant step forward in automating the import process has been the implementation of a new computerized customs system, which tracked more than US$30 billion in imports and exports crossing the border in 1994. This system was purchased from France and initially installed at Ezeiza International Airport (outside of Buenos Aires) to process air cargo imports. By the end of 1995, all customs brokers and all border crossings with Chile, Brazil, Paraguay, Uruguay, and Bolivia will be linked with the central customs office.

Airports

Argentina has an inventoried 1,702 landing strips, with 1,473 considered to be minimally usable. The country has a network of more than 416 airfields. Of these, about 140 have permanent surface runways; just one has a runway longer than 3,659 m (2.25 mi); 31 have runways of from 2,440 to 3,659 m (1.5 to 2.25 mi); and 326 have runways of from 1,220 to 2,439 m (0.75 to 1.5 mi). Altogether about 200 airfields can handle small, domestic, commercial flights. With the exception of Jorge Newbery Airport in Buenos Aires, none of these airfields handle a significant volume of traffic. The federal government is considering either closing its operations at some of the smaller fields or offering them to the provinces.

Only 10 Argentine airfields are currently capable of handling international jet flights; they are: Ezeiza, Jorge Newbery, Córdoba, Jujuy, Resistencia, Rosario (Fisherton), Río Gallegos, San Carlos de Bariloche, Corrientes, and Salta. To a lesser extent, traders may fly goods into El Plumerillo outside of Mendoza. Most of these service an average of 250,000 passengers a year, except Córdoba—Argentina's second city in terms of population and industry—which typically handles about 750,000 travelers. Plans call for Ezeiza and Jorge Newbery to be privatized in 1995, and five others are being considered for privatization in 1996.

Buenos Aires The airports of Ezeiza International and Aeroparque Jorge Newbery work in tandem to serve the country's largest market, Buenos Aires; these are the only self-supporting airports in the country. Together they account for 65 percent of the nation's air traffic, each serving about 4 million passengers annually. Privatization and the resulting capital improvements are expected to increase capacity to 12 million passengers annually within the next 10 years.

Ezeiza International is the largest airport in the country. Its three operating runways can handle large jets and international cargo and passenger traffic. Situated approximately 35 km (30 mi) outside of Buenos Aires, its location is both accessible from the inland and a relatively short 45- to 60-minute drive to the city center.

Aeroparque Jorge Newbery, the second largest airport, handles mainly domestic air traffic or short flights to neighboring countries (primarily Uruguay). Owing to its limited runway length, only propeller planes and medium-sized jets (such as Boeing 727s or 737s) can land there. The airport is located about 7 km (4 mi) from downtown Buenos Aires. One runway is fully operational, as is one (albeit relatively large) terminal.

Regional Airports Regularly scheduled domestic and international flights serve several of Argentina's inland commercial centers. The Jujuy International Airport—Argentina's third largest—is capable of handling international traffic, although on a much smaller scale than the two airports that service Buenos Aires. Located 32 km (20 mi) outside of Jujuy, the airport has one operating runway and a single cargo terminal. Other important commercial and manufacturing centers are served by the airport at Pajas Blancas, located 15 km (9 mi) from downtown Córdoba; Fisherton Airport just 8 km (5 mi) west of Rosario's city center; and Plumerillo Airport 8 km (5 mi) outside of Mendoza, an important cargo stopover and the country's primary gateway to Chile.

Air Carriers

Aerolíneas Argentinas—the national carrier and the largest cargo carrier serving the nation—was sold to a consortium of public and private investors led by Spain's Iberia Airlines in 1990. The airline now controls Argentina's international routes and the internal routes of the nation's other major domestic airline, Austral. Internationally, it flies scheduled service to Madrid, Paris, Canada, and several points in the US; it also has routes operating to the Pacific Rim in East Asia and New Zealand. In the past year, Aerolíneas (as it is commonly called) has added new planes to its domestic fleet and augmented its international fleet with three new Airbus A310-300 aircraft. Three more weekly flights between Buenos Aires and Montreal, New York, and Los Angeles have been added, giving the carrier 17 weekly flights connecting Argentina with the US and Canada. Additionally, Aerolíneas has forged cargo-sharing alliances with LADECO, Air France, and other international carriers in anticipation of future growth.

Airlines of other nations also provide flights to Argentina's Ezeiza International Airport. Cargo and passenger service is provided by a variety of foreign carriers, including Canadian Airlines (CP Air) with scheduled service from various points in Canada as well as from Chicago and New York. KLM Royal Dutch Airlines and Lufthansa German Airlines count Buenos Aires as a port of call. Cargo-only service is provided by Ecuatoriana Jet Cargo and LanChile Airlines from Miami, New York, and Los Angles/Long Beach; Lloyd Aéreo Boliviano (LAB) offers similar service from Miami.

As aging airport technology is replaced and the privatization process improves, international cargo and passenger transporters are deepening their commitment to Argentina. For example, in late 1994, US-based FedEx announced the initiation of same-day courier and cargo service to Argentina from its hub in Memphis, Tennessee. To date, nearly all of the leading international cargo integrators have a presence in Argentina. In addition to FedEx, traders can rely on service from Airborne Express, Burlington Air Express, DHL Worldwide Express, Emery Worldwide, United Parcel Service, and TNT Express Worldwide. Additionally, LTH International Courier Service provides scheduled runs from Los Angeles/Long Beach, San Francisco/Oakland, New York, and Washington, DC.

WATER TRANSPORT

Water transport is Argentina's most important transportation sector. Nearly nine-tenths of Argentina's foreign trade passes by water through its seaports and river ports. Argentina has 3,500 km (2,200 mi) of navigable waterways, and the country is expected to become more focused on its river trade with Brazil, Paraguay, and Uruguay—its increasingly important Mercosur trading partners. The port of Buenos Aires, along with several ports along the Atlantic coast—La Plata, Bahía Blanca, Quequén-Necochea, and Comodoro Rivadavia—connect Argentina to ports around the world. However, while Argentina has good port access, the shallowness of the continental shelf off its Atlantic coast means that it lacks additional deepwater ports, and existing facilities are becoming somewhat crowded.

The dynamic potential of Argentina's marine and river shipping industry has yet to be fully realized. Under state ownership, the port industry's reputation was one of inefficiency, poor service, substantial delays, frequent and costly labor stoppages, and high port costs. Domestic customers were lost to the trucking industry, while international shippers cut back or eliminated their Argentina operations. Nevertheless, Argentine firms offer a variety of choices in serving international ports, including general, refrigerated (or reefer), liquid bulk, dry bulk, and containerized cargo handling capabilities.

Privatization of the Argentine ports, including Buenos Aires, was begun in 1994, and millions are being invested to increase port capacity and improve operations. Operations have been streamlined, management has been restructured, and the workforce has been reduced by three-fourths. Customers are already beginning to return, lured by the new open-market policies and persuaded by the visible signs of improvement in port equipment, labor conditions, and automation of cargo handling procedures. Argentina's move to revamp its marine terminals and waterways promises to bolster the country's increasing important waterborne trade.

Although Argentina's ports have been hard-pressed to deal with the surge in the country's foreign trade, the trend in Argentina toward diversification of exports into manufactured goods—coupled with port modernization and expansion—is expected to resolve many of the shipping industry's woes. Improvements to other aspects of the transportation infrastructure promise to secure better access to the ports and thus reduce the burdens and costs shouldered by importers and exporters. Road and railway privatization is expected to create better access conditions, as well as reducing transport costs for both traditional and nontraditional goods exported by Argentina. The same applies to port facilities and shipping on the Paraná and the River Plate, where deeper channels will allow the navigation of larger vessels. The growing number of international shipping lines calling at Argentine ports reflects the interest and faith of the international shipping community in the nation's infrastructure development.

Ports

Buenos Aires Argentine importers and exporters move approximately 480,000 20 ft equivalent units (TEUs) per year through Buenos Aires ports, and cargo traffic is on the rise. More than 90 percent of Argentina's container cargo passes through this port. The well protected Buenos Aires port area is working fast to overcome several obstacles to the rapidly expanding foreign trade. Complaints about congestion and delays—often a problem in the past—continue to be heard, but extensive changes are being made in an attempt to ease the problem of getting a berth.

For the Buenos Aires ports, one focus of the improvements underway is safety in navigation upriver. Buenos Aires, located at the mouth of the Río de la Plata, is accessible from the Atlantic Ocean only through a host of channels that must be continuously dredged to remove the silt deposited in the delta below the confluence of the Paraná and Uruguay Rivers. Analysts report that buoys and markers—essential to safe navigation—are once

again in place following several years of neglect. However, the largest remaining problem is the shallowness of the delta area—at least as far as larger oceangoing vessels are concerned.

In early 1994 the privatization of Buenos Aires' new half-dozen terminals caused an international stir. The initial award of five concessions excluded the port's largest stevedore company, Murchison-Román, which launched an appeal against the award of Terminals 1 and 2 to the winning consortium. Transport analysts report that progress at the site is being made at an acceptable rate. Ships are currently being unloaded using their own gear or with the aid of mobile cranes. In 1995 the new terminals plan to install a trio of quayside gantries, while seven container cranes will come into full operation. There are reports that four more modern cranes are on order from Spain and are to be installed in 1996.

The most sweeping changes at the Buenos Aires port will come about as a consequence of an anticipated US$110 million to be invested in 1996. Another US$91 million has been pledged for 2004 by the consortia that won the rights to operate the six port terminals. The investment will boost Buenos Aires' capacity to one million TEUs a year, which should improve efficiency and reduce port charges.

The Buenos Aires port is facing competition from neighboring ports. The newly developed port of Santos in Brazil could siphon as much as one-quarter of Buenos Aires' traffic. However, Argentine shippers are quick to point out that the cranes in Santos are unreliable and that the waterfront labor situation is more unsettled that in Argentina.

The main concern at the Buenos Aires port is not so much with the facilities side of the equation as with the labor factor. "The yoke of labor" is an expression often invoked in the region when addressing the historical record of work stoppages and wildcat strikes. Exporters to Argentina have been hurt in the past by carrier-imposed surcharges during stoppages and strikes, and the Argentine government and port authorities are becoming increasingly sensitive to this issue. Congestion at the port of Buenos Aires may have reached its upper limit in recent times during October 1994 when a slowdown action against terminal operators ran into a third week before being settled. The result was predictable: delayed vessels waiting for berths were moved to Campana, a small port approximately 65 km (40 mi) upriver from Buenos Aires. According to industry experts, vessel operators have been willing to pay the trucking fees incurred in such cases rather than wait 24 hours for a berth.

Many of these labor problems stem from Argentina's difficult privatization process. Each of the terminal operators in Buenos Aires had promised to employ a portion of the 1,300 dockworkers affected during the changeover, but terminal management subsequently claimed that many of the workers are ill prepared for modern mechanization. Additionally, conflicts have continued over working conditions. Labor wanted six-hour shifts plus overtime to continue, whereas management imposed three eight-hour shifts instead. Management also wants to require each worker to master multiple tasks rather than stay restricted to a single specific duty.

Facilities available at the Buenos Aires port are as follows:*

Transportation Service—Truck, rail, and barge.

Cargo Storage—Covered: 1,085,000 sq m (11,678,000 sq ft). Open: 290,000 sq m (3,121,000 sq ft). Refrigerated: storage is available.

Special Cranes—Heavy lift: 20 with maximum 2,000 metric ton (2,204 short ton) capacity. Container: one with 27 metric ton (29.75 short ton) capacity.

Cargo Handling—Port equipment is available to handle containerized liquid and dry bulk and general cargo. Major imports include chemicals, machinery, and fertilizers. Three ore and bulk, one liquefied gas, and two tanker terminals are available. Ro-Ro service is also provided from the three ramp facilities.

General—Although security is considered good, expensive chemicals, finished products, and electronics are susceptible to pilferage. Temperatures range from 3˚C to 40˚C (37°F to 104°F), with the average between 10˚C to 24˚C (50°F to 75°F). Early morning fog can be problematic in April and October, and humidity is high year-round. Average annual rainfall is 110 cm (43 in). The container facilities at the port are to be upgraded. Warehousing and cargo services at the airport have been privatized. A majority of imported containerized shipments are stripped inside the port and travel "LCL" (less than container load). Export packaging is a must to reduce loss or damage potential.

La Plata Argentina has big plans for the little port of La Plata, located 60 km (38 mi) southeast of Buenos Aires. The port currently handles small shipments and oil products from nearby Yacimientos Petrolíferos Fiscales (YPF) refinery. Argentina is seeking foreign investment to revive this port as a grain export terminal and to develop it as a container port. Plans call for the complex to come on line at the end of 1996, given sufficient funding. It would initially handle 100,000 containers a year—more than twice what Argentina's chief gateway can accommodate now. The province expects La Plata container traffic to increase

sharply after a free trade zone begins operating there in the near future.

Argentine shipping industry experts suggest that La Plata port container handling and storage costs will be as much 30 percent lower than corresponding rates in the Buenos Aires port because of reduction in the vessel turnaround time: the port is closer to the Atlantic Ocean, offers more efficient rail and truck access, and has a shorter, less complicated approach channel to navigate. The province began to dredge the principal "No. 9 sector" of the port in December 1994 to achieve a depth of 11.5 m (38 ft). The port officials have also replaced the approach channel buoys and lighting to conform with regulations set by the International Association of Lighthouse Authorities.

Shipping Firms

Some 12 major domestic shipping lines serve the Argentine market. The government's measures for upgrading its marine infrastructure are expected to enhance overall port operations, including the alleviation of much of the congestion that has previously plagued Argentina's gateways. The enormous surge in trade has prompted a number of ocean carriers that call there to expand their existing operations. Since the government's regulatory grip has been loosened, ocean service to the US East and Gulf Coasts, to other South American ports, to the Caribbean, and to northern Europe has been consistent and of sufficient capacity to meet demands. Likewise, reliable ocean service is now being provided between the Río de la Plata and Pacific Rim destinations by several well-known carriers, as well as by a few newcomers. As a consequence, traders need no longer use the US as a point of transshipment for goods being moved between Argentina and East Asia.

International shippers that call at Argentine ports include—among others—Columbus Line, Pan-American Independent Line of Uruguay, Crowley American Transport, Alianca, and Sea-Land Service, Inc. With the introduction of Maersk and Zim Container Line in 1994, traders now have additional options for shipping containerized goods. Most of these companies offer weekly sailing schedules to and from Argentina. The largest shippers have extensive satellite communications and computer networks that work with customs in Argentina and other countries to speed the import-export process at the borders.

Competition in Argentina's shipping industry is intensifying as more international shippers enter the fray. What was once considered an expensive route is becoming more reasonable in cost, because shipping rates are decreasing as the field becomes more crowded and freight and port capacity and

*Port facility information in this section is excerpted from Ports of the World (15th ed.), copyright © 1994 CIGNA Property and Casualty Co., reprinted with permission from CIGNA Property and Casualty Companies.

efficiency expand. The downside to this increased activity has been that several Argentine carriers have been forced out of business by the tougher competition.

OVERLAND TRANSPORT

Solving the surface transportation woes of this Southern Cone nation will be more difficult than upgrading other areas of the country's infrastructure. Argentina stretches 4,000 km (2,500 mi) from north to south, an expanse crossed by only a few major highways. Transportation analysts have expressed guarded optimism that some of the foreign companies bidding on and investing in the private management and operation of the 35,000 km (22,000 mi) of Argentina's national railroads will prevail in reforming this policy. For the time being, most traders must opt for either road or rail to reach the interior. Most choose trucking because railroad gauges are largely incompatible across international borders. However, trucking has drawbacks as well. Trucks are not inspected regularly, and most fleets use old and poorly maintained vehicles.

Six years ago, the transport and public works ministers of seven South American countries—Argentina, Bolivia, Brazil, Chile, Paraguay, Perú, and Uruguay—signed an agreement to facilitate overland transportation in an effort to promote trade among their countries. The agreement removed a variety of costly guarantees—especially in customs bonds and insurance—that transport companies had previously paid. The ministers also agreed to create uniform, bilingual forms to cover nearly all the paperwork required for the transport of goods.

At the current time, this transportation sector needs another boost—both to eliminate competing interests between nations that create invisible barriers to efficient foreign interchange and to improve the domestic physical and procedural infrastructures—to enable it to handle the growing influx of foreign trade and travelers. In fact, transit systems and roads are high on the government's list of projects needing funding and promotion. Several projects currently under construction are expected to enhance interregional trade within the next decade. These include: a projected new rail tunnel through the Andes to connect Argentina and Chile; a 2414 km (1500 mi) highway linking Buenos Aires with São Paulo, Brazil. A bridge has also been designed to connect Buenos Aires and Colonia, Uruguay.

Trucking An estimated 87 percent of passenger and 85 percent of domestic freight traffic is carried by road. Approximately 655,000 km (409,000 mi) of roads cross Argentina. At last reckoning, Argentina had about 208,350 km (130,000 mi) of national (partially privatized) and provincial highways; of this, 40,000 km (25,000 mi) were paved, 19 percent were gravel, and the remaining 62 percent were improved or unimproved dirt roads. About 38,000 km (23,750 mi) may be considered trunk roads. Argentina's portion of the Pan-American Highway consists of four main roads. The Dirección Nacional de Vialidad (National Highway Board, or DNV), in conjunction with the Secretaría de Obras Públicas y Comunicaciones(Public Works and Communications Secretariat), administers the national road system and is charged with shifting the construction and maintenance of the roads to provincial governments and private sector firms.

The most highly traveled sections of more than 30 national highways have become privately operated toll roads. Beginning in 1990, the government granted concessions to major Argentine construction firms for maintenance of highways in the country's interior in return for the right to charge tolls. Firms such as Roggio, Techint, Sade, Sideco, and a score of others have since taken over more than 9,300 km (5,800 mi) of inland highways. Although improvements on these highways have come slowly, they are gradually taking shape. For example, Techint Industrial Group's toll concession division, Camino del Oeste, has a 12-year contract covering 1,203 km (752 mi) of highway. Since the firm signed on in late 1990, it has repaved more than 150 km (94 mi), repaired another 275 km (172 mi), and installed a system including 63 emergency telephones for the use of drivers in distress.

At the beginning of 1994, the Argentine government put out an international call for bids on the construction, improvement, maintenance, and administration of the three main access routes to Buenos Aires. The plan was for the successful companies to operate the roads on a concession basis and collect tolls from the highway users. These 232 km (145 mi) of major access roads tend to be traveled heavily by commuters and vacationing suburbanites. Despite problems and delays caused by competing international and domestic political and commercial interests, environmental concerns, and public outcries over toll charges, construction on these roads has gotten underway. Nearly US$400 million has been invested in the expansion, and another US$300 million has been pledged toward finishing the improvements and building parallel free-access lanes.

Traffic managers have stressed that while traders have to swallow hard when paying these tolls, the preexisting road conditions actually made operations much more costly. Today, truckers can maintain their vehicles at much more reasonable cost and move goods more efficiently. Moreover, with the major highways in the hands of private contractors, the government has been able to apply road taxes where needed most: to repair secondary routes, pave dirt roads, and construct new roads. Indeed, in 1994 the DNV spent US$350 million on road improvements, improvements that will open new routes and new opportunities for Argentina's trucking industry.

In addition to improving road conditions, the Argentine trucking industry has received several additional incentives during recent years. These include the deregulation of freight insurance and the reduction or elimination of taxes on the import of transportation-related products—vehicles, parts, tires, and fuel. A few standards for the trucking industry have also been introduced, including a requirement that operating commercial freight vehicles must be less than 10 years old. The industry has also been opened to competition from foreign trucking firms, with the condition that the foreign-operated vehicles must be registered in Argentina.

Railroads Originally built between the 1860s and the 1930s—primarily by British and French investors—the Argentine rail system is one of the most extensive in the world. Until the early 1970s, the country could boast that all its cities of a population of 10,000 or more (with the exception of Ushuaia in Tierra del Fuego) were served by rail. Since then, population growth—and the deterioration of the rail system—have made that boast obsolete. Like its highways, much of Argentina's 35,000 km (21,875 mi) of railroads tend to branch out from Buenos Aires into the country's interior. Little more than a decade ago, the railroads were in even worse shape than the highways—run-down, inefficient, and inconvenient. Six independent state-owned companies operated various inland, intercity, and metropolitan passenger and freight services—each running up an annual deficit of several million dollars that the federal government was obliged to cover.

Since 1992 all but one of Argentina's railways have been privatized, resulting in a radical restructuring and bringing in more than US$1.5 billion in foreign investment for the freight network plus a similar amount for the passenger lines. The half-dozen independent, formerly state-owned railroads, each having trackage of at least 2,500 km (1,600 mi), were combined with the Buenos Aires urban rail system comprising subway and commuter lines. An existing 385 km (240 mi) passenger corridor that carries more than 1.8 million passengers annually runs between Buenos Aires and Mar del Plata.

During the privatization process, several major hurdles had to be overcome. Track gauges varied among the different independent operations—at least four gauges (1.435 m standard, 1.676 m broad,

1.000 m narrow, and 0.750 m narrow) are in use—preventing the sharing of track and equipment. An even greater management problem was poor service on most lines converging on a single hub: Buenos Aires. Transition of the labor force also proved to be an immense undertaking. Most of the railway lines have been so poorly maintained that service had become sporadic and undependable, causing the railroads to lose substantial business to the trucking industry. Privatization could only be accomplished by reshaping the railway system.

In the course of this reshaping, the government implemented a series of concessions, or franchises. Rather than following one preestablished model, planners decided to consider the practical operating differences among the three distinct economic and social regions being served. As a consequence, Argentina now features six separate but interrelated units, comprising approximately 25,920 km (16,200 mi) of track. Together they transport 14 million tons of freight per year, with freight moving an average of 575 km (360 mi). Additionally, some 7,680 km (4,800 mi) of track deemed unessential to the concessions was offered to the provincial governments, with the understanding that track segments not accepted would be abandoned. In turn, the concessionaires accepted the risk that they might not be able to improve the volume of freight traffic without rationalizing (and expanding) the systems on their own.

When it came to privatizing rail passenger service, the authorities took a different tack. Drawing upon experience elsewhere in Latin America, planners recognized that the social obligation had to be met by the use of some sort of subsidy. Three passenger rail network franchises were created: intercity passenger services; passenger service in the Buenos Aires–Mar del Plata corridor; and the commuter and subway services in the metropolitan Buenos Aires area. In creating these franchises, the government formed a new agency—Ferrocarriles Metropolitanos (FEMESA, or MetRail)—which presides over the commuter lines. Under the arrangement to be used, the government retains ownership of the right-of-way, equipment, stations, and other facilities. However, all property not required for direct operation of the services, including downtown terminals, has been separately franchised to real estate developers, who provide the government with a source of financing for the metropolitan service subsidies.

The passenger loads on the commuter railroads out of Buenos Aires are still immense, at least by US standards. For example, the Sarmiento Line—with a 38 km (24 mi) route and 15 stations—serves 80 million passengers annually. As one might imagine, use has declined in recent years due to cramped and uncomfortable service, while fare evasion has increased markedly. To make matters worse, the nation's taxpayers are footing the bill for operating the system, and capital for improvements has still to be found; the line has been operating at an annual deficit of approximately US$200 million during recent years. However, analysts hope that the combined talents of the foreign investors in the new privatization consortium will bring this line up to international transit standards in the near future.

The first freight railroad to be fully privatized, the Ferro Expreso Pampeano, bypasses Buenos Aires altogether. This line links the northern Paraná River port of Rosario with the main Patagonian coastal port of Bahía Blanca. It runs north-south some 320 km (200 mi) west of Buenos Aires and operates connecting branch lines throughout the Pampas region. Its approximately 4,800 km (3,000 mi) of track are primarily dedicated to the movement of grain exports. The first operational change that this franchise put into play was a switch from radio and fax communication to satellite linkup between Bahía Blanca and Buenos Aires. The satellite network deals mainly with shipment tracking and market and financial data: the business of clients, including tonnage moved and types of commodity and share of market by the railroad.

Ferrosur Roca is now recognized as one of the pivotal railroads in Argentina's new network. Like its predecessor—called the "Roca"— it is identified with two major connecting trunklines. One is the direct 615 km (385 mi) route linking Buenos Aires with Bahía Blanca; the other connects Bahía Blanca with Zapala in the Andes via the Río Negro Valley. Cement, agricultural products, minerals, and petroleum provide this 3,680 km (2,300 mi) broad gauge system with a solid, steady base of freight revenue. Although the seasonality of the cement business brings the greatest volumes in September and October, a number of businesses on the line provide balanced traffic during the rest of the year. Higher volumes of grains maturing between December and June add a year-round mix, as does the steady flow of minerals to the industrial areas of La Plata and Bahía Blanca from the western region of Neuquén.

The franchise companies face a major challenge in upgrading and maintaining trackage, the condition of which continues to be somewhat poor and inconsistent throughout the country. A lack of adequate maintenance over a protracted period has led to various infrastructural problems. Another problem is the rapid rate at which right-of-way and track becomes overgrown on the grassy plains. While these problems are being addressed on all track sections, priority is being given to the areas used by light tonnage trains (50 tons per car) that operate at relatively low speeds (32 kph or 20 mph). Private operators intend to expand the system to provide links that come closer to its customers in more remote regions of the network. For example, within the next 10 years, the capacity of the Buenos Aires subway and commuter lines is expected to double. Since privatization, use of the railways has already increased by nearly 20 percent. Freight traffic is also rising, and a 15 percent increase in such traffic is expected by the end of 1995.

Besides infrastructure enhancements, the railroad industry is trying to reestablish its relationship with ports and to persuade traders that rails can serve them as well as trucks. To date, word-of-mouth confirmation of more reliable service and the introduction of marketing campaigns to promote awareness are having an impact in returning to the rails some of the cargo traffic captured by motor carriers.

COMMUNICATIONS

Argentina's communications industries offer substantial opportunities for foreign trade and investment—and for good reason. Argentina's expensive, unreliable communications system has long been the source of ire among Argentines and frustration among foreign businesspeople. Much of what is envisioned for the telecommunications sector is now being built from scratch. Just four years after the nation began an extensive program of deregulation, as demand for new equipment, wireless systems, and telephone lines skyrockets, the 1995 communications industry budget is projected at US$1.6 billion.

Telecommunications

Local Telephone Services Argentine telephone services, both within and outside of the Buenos Aires area, were state-owned until the 1990s. Service was notorious and rates were high. During the 1980s, more Argentines subscribed to cable television than to telephone service: it was easier to get.

However, the state of local telephone services has begun to change. The single, state-owned company—ENTEL—was privatized in 1990, when it was split and sold to groups of foreign firms: Telefónica and Telecom. By 1993 these companies together invested US$1.9 billion in upgrading and expanding their systems. They have been replacing old lines at the rate of 400,000 lines per year as well as adding 500,000 new ones. Waiting time for installation of a new line has been decreased from months and years to a few weeks. Private lines now reach about 15 percent of the Argentine population, giving Argentina the highest telephone line density in South America.

Nevertheless, only approximately 7,500 automatic public telephones are operated by Telecom; about 4,100 of these are located in Buenos Aires and its northern environs, while the remaining 3,400 are thinly spread throughout the nation's interior. Competing Telefónica has about 7,000 units in and around Buenos Aires and approximately 14,500 scattered about the country. Demand still exceeds supply by a large margin, although the situation is improving rapidly. Travelers may have difficulty locating functioning public telephones available; travelers will find that the cities of Córdoba and Rosario have a greater concentration of usable public telephones. Telecom plans to add 1,000 public telephones in 1995, 2,000 more in 1996, and 3,000 in 1997. Telefónica de Argentina has yet to announce its investment plans.

Long Distance and International Services Argentina's long distance telephone service provider, Telintar, is generally considered to offer reasonably good service within the Buenos Aires area. Many sections of Buenos Aires have direct international dialing, and most Argentine cities can be direct dialed from within Argentina. Service elsewhere in the country may be more problematical. Argentina is served by two INTELSAT earth stations and a domestic satellite network with 40 ground stations. Microwave technology is widely used to transmit calls.

Mobile Telecommunications Services For more than a decade, the Argentine government has been strongly promoting the growth of cellular telephone systems, particularly in greater Buenos Aires. Given the government's support, the growth rate of the cellular telephone market has been astronomical— but not surprising, considering the inadequacy of the preexisting telephone service within this metropolis. Nationwide, Argentina's cellular phone density is the highest of any South American country. According to analysts, the average utilization per subscriber has been around 400 minutes per month, a rate far above the US and European standards of about 150 minutes per month. The usage cost of the cellular system for subscribers is 50 cents per minute (including taxes).

Privatization and deregulation of the telephone industry in general has made modern equipment more accessible and has provided the funds for capital investment to improve the system. In 1989 the Argentine government awarded the rights to install and operate the first cellular system—an advance model system (AMTS) band—in Buenos Aires to the consortium Compañía de Radiocomunicaciones Móviles (CRM). The CRM joint venture included Bell South and Motorola (of the US); Motorola and Socma and BGH (of Argentina), the latter a Motorola licensee. Known as Movicom, this first cellular telephone system serves the Buenos Aires and the surrounding metropolitan area with 12 cell sites. Geographically, this service area stretches from the City of La Plata (south of Buenos Aires) to Zárate (north of BA), and from Ezeiza International Airport (southwest of the city) to roughly 30 km (19 mi) offshore (east of BA). At last report, CRM had a total of 30,000 Movicom customers.

When the government awarded the first cellular band for Buenos Aires, it also imposed rigid local content and technical requirements on the equipment to be used, this had the practical effect of keeping out imports. To enter the market, a few foreign firms—Motorola, for example—licensed the partial manufacture and assembly of its cellular units to local companies. These restrictions have since been lifted, and the current requirement is simply that any mobile cellular unit used in Argentina must conform to the Argentine technical standards. A unit may be used in Argentina if approved by a recognized government agency of another country—such as the US Federal Communications Commission—that requires the same standards as those in Argentina.

In early 1994 another foreign consortium was awarded a cellular telephone contract to serve 1,600 cities and towns in the nation's interior. The consortium plans to invest a minimum of US$600 million to offer this service to 22 million people spread over great distances throughout Argentina. The system will consist of stationary telephones connected by wireless equipment.

USEFUL ADDRESSES

Government Agencies

Comisión Nacional de Telecomunicaciones (CNT)
(National Telecommunications Commission)
Sarmiento 151, Piso 4, Of. 485
1041 Buenos Aires, Argentina
Tel: [54] (1) 331-1203, 49-9481/2

Secretaría de Transportes
(Secretariat of Transportation)
Av. 9 de julio 1925
1332 Buenos Aires, Argentina
Tel: [54] (1) 381-1435, 381-4007

Subsecretaría de Transporte Aéreo, Fluvial y Marítimo
(Undersecretariat of Air, River, and Maritime Transport)
Hipólito Yrigoyen 250
1310 Buenos Aires, Argentina
Tel: [54] (1) 349-7205
Fax: [54] (1) 342-6365

Trade Associations

Cámara de Empresas de Obras Ferroviarias y Vías de Comunicación
(Railway works and communication networks companies)
Av. Córdoba 890, Piso 3
1054 Buenos Aires, Argentina
Tel: [54] (1) 322-0555, 322-6453

Cámara Argentina de Industrias Electrónicas (CADIE)
Bdo. de Irigoyen 330, Piso 5, Of. 121
1072 Buenos Aires, Argentina
Tel: [54] (1) 334-4159, 334-5752, 334-6672, 334-7763
Fax: [54] (1) 334-6672

Cámara Argentina de Telefonía y Afines (CATYA)
Av. Paseo Colón 588, Piso 5
1063 Buenos Aires, Argentina
Tel: [54] (1) 30-8853, 30-7956

Cámara de Informática y Telecomunicaciones de la República Argentina (CICOMRA)
(Computers and telecommunications)
Av. Córdoba 744, Piso 2, Of. D
1054 Buenos Aires, Argentina
Tel: [54] (1) 393-7352, 325-8839
Fax: [54] (1) 325-9604

Publications

Comunicaciones
(Monthly)
Editorial Comunicación Profesional
Av. Corrientes 2565, Piso 5, Oficina 3
1046 Buenos Aires, Argentina

Comunicaciones: Telecomunicaciones, Comunicaciones de Datos, Computadoras y Satélites
(Quarterly)
Intercom Corp.
9200 S. Dadeland Blvd., Suite 309
Miami, FL 33156-2703, USA
Tel: [1] (305) 670-9444
Fax: [1] (305) 670-9459
Distributed throughout Latin America for the telecommunication and computer technology industries

Revista Telegráfica Electrónica
(Monthly)
Arbo S.A.C.E.I.
Av. Martín Garcia 653
Buenos Aires, Argentina
Covers the telephone and telegraphic communications industries

Business Dictionary

PRONUNCIATION GUIDE

Spanish is the language of Argentina, although many of its cosmopolitan urban citizens speak various European languages. There are certain differences between the Spanish spoken in Argentina and the language as used in Spain as well as in the remainder of Latin America. Mexican pronunciation is softer, and the intonation more drawn out. Argentines and other Spanish-speakers generally have little or no difficulty in understanding each other, but differences of accent, vocabulary, and idiomatic expressions used in each of these countries can immediately pinpoint the nationality of the speaker. Once you have listened for a while, you realize that Spanish is a phonetic language with fairly logical pronunciation and spelling. Also note that business usage in Argentina includes a variety of English terms—such as "marketing," "packaging," and "joint venture."

Notes on Pronunciation

The five vowels of the alphabet (a, e, i, o, u) are always pronounced in the same way, regardless of what consonants they appear with. An 'a' is pronounced somewhere between the 'a' sound of back and that of father, 'e' as in get, 'i' as in police, 'o' as in hotel, 'u' as in rule.

In Argentina there is no 'lisping' sound on the 'z' as there is in Spain. Letters 'c' (only before 'e' and 'i') and 'z' are pronounced like an 's' as in sail. Note than when 'c' appears before an 'a', 'o' or 'u', it is pronounced like a 'k' as in kit.

'g' before 'e' and 'i' it sounds like 'h'; when it appears before the other three vowels, it sounds like hard 'g' as in gate or hug.

'gue/gui' pronounced as hard 'g' but 'u' is silent as in guitar.

'h' is always silent.

'j' sounds like 'h' as in hide or hall.

'll' sounds like 'y' as in yoyo.

'ñ' sounds like 'ny' as in canyon.

'qu' sounds like 'k' as in duck.

'r' is rolled, 'rr' doubly so.

'v' sounds more like 'b'; *vino* sounds somewhat like beano.

Stress

In general, if a word has a letter with an accent marked over it, that letter should be pronounced with greater stress. Unless otherwise accented, the stress falls on the next to last vowel. For pronunciation purposes, in this dictionary the letters underlined in a pronunciation are the ones that carry the stress of the word, as in <u>oh</u>-la for hola (hello).

Forms of Address

In Spanish there are two forms of address: one formal (singular—*usted*, plural—*ustedes*) and one informal (singular—*vos*, plural—*ustedes*, the same as in the formal), each to be used where appropriate. As a general rule, the formal address should be used when speaking with someone you've never met before, with an older person, with someone of higher rank, and so forth, unless the person addressed expresses his or her wish to the contrary. (Note that expressions in this mini-dictionary are suited for formal address, giving priority to the business context.)

Gender

Nouns in Spanish are either masculine or feminine. Nouns ending in 'o', 'e', or 'ma' are usually masculine. Nouns ending in 'a', 'ión', or 'dad' are usually feminine. Some nouns have both a masculine and a feminine form, depending on the ending, as in *viajero* (male traveler), *viajera* (female traveler). An adjective usually comes after the noun it describes, and must take the same gender form.

English	*Spanish*	*Pronunciation*

GREETINGS AND POLITE EXPRESSIONS

Hello	Hola	Oh-lah
Good morning	Buenos días	Bwehn-ohss dee-yahss
Good afternoon	Buenas tardes	Bwehn-ahss tahr-dehs
Good evening	Buenas noches	Bwehn-ahss noh-chehss
Good night	Buenas noches	Bwehn-ahss noh-chehss
Hello (on the telephone)	¿Sí?, ¿Hola?	Ssee, Oh-lah
Goodbye		
(more final)	Adiós	Ah-dee-yohss
(less definite)	Hasta pronto/Hasta Luego	Ahss-tah prohn-toh/Ahss-tah lweh-goh
See you tomorrow	Hasta mañana	Ahss-tah mahn-yah-nah
How do you do?	¿Cómo está usted?	Koh-moh eh-stah oo-stehd?
Please	Por favor	Pohrr fah-vohrr
Pleased to meet you	(1) Mucho gusto	Moo-choh goo-stoh en
	(2) Encantado	Ehn-Kahn-tah-doh
Please excuse me	Con permiso	Kon perr-mee-ssoh
Congratulations	¡Felicidades! ¡Felicitaciones!	Feh-lee-ssee-dah-dehss
		Feh-lee-ssee-tah-ssee-oh-neés
Thank you	Gracias	Grah-ssee-yahss
Thank you very much	Muchas gracias	Moo-chas grah-ssee-yahss
Thank you for your gift	Gracias por su regalo	Grah-ssee-yahss pohrr soo rreh-gah-loh
You are welcome	De nada/No hay porqué	Deh nah-dah/Noh ay pohr kay
I don't speak Spanish	No hablo español	Noh ahb-loh eh-spahn-yohl
I don't understand	No entiendo	Noh ehn-tee-ehn-doh
I understand	Entiendo	Ehn-tee-ehn-doh
Do you speak English?	¿Habla usted inglés?	Ah-blah oo-stehd in-glehss?
My name is John Smith	Mi nombre es John Smith	Mee nohm-breh ehss John Smith
I am John Smith	Yo soy John Smith	Yoh ssoy John Smith
I am called John Smith	Me llamo John Smith	Mee yah-moh John Smith
Is Mr./Miss Smith there?	¿Me puede comunicar con el	Meh pweh-deh ko-moo-nee-kahrr
(on the telephone)	Señor/la Señorita Smith?	kohn el Ssehn-yohrr/la
		Ssehn-yohrr-ee-tah Smith?
	¿Puedo hablar con...?	Pwed-doh ah-blar con...
Is Mr./Miss Smith there?	¿Está el Señor/la Señorita	Eh-stah el Ssehn-yohrr/la
	Smith?	Ssehn-yohrr-ee-tah Smith
Who may I say is calling?	¿De parte de quién?	Day pahrr-tay day kee-in?
Can we meet tomorrow	¿Nos podemos ver mañana?	Nohss poh-deh-mohss ver
		mahn-yah-nah?
Would you like to have	¿Podríamos cenar juntos/as?	Poh-dree-yah-mohs seh-nahr
dinner together?		hoon-tohs/tahs?
Yes	Sí	Ssee
No	No	Noh
Could you please	¿Sería tan amable de	Sseh-rree-yah tahn ah-mah-bleh
(get me a taxi?)	(llamarme un taxi)?	deh (yah-mahr-meh oon tahk-ssee?
	¿Me puede llamar un taxi?	Mee pweh-deh yah-mahr oon tahk-ssee?
I'm sorry Excuse me	Lo siento/Disculpe	Loh ssee-yehn-toh/Dis-kuhl-peh

English	*Spanish*	*Pronunciation*
I'm sorry (how sad)	Que lástima/Que pena	Kay lahss-tee-mah/Kay peh-nah
At your service	A sus órdenes	Ah soos or-dehn-ayss
Of course	Por supuesto	Pohrr soo-pwehs-toh
It is not important	No importa	Noh eem-pohrr-tah
How do you say?	¿Cómo se dice?	Koh-moh say dee-say?
Slower, please	Más lento por favor	Mahs len-toh pohrr fah-vohrr
Again	Otra vez	Oh-trah vayss
At what time?	¿A qué hora?	Ah kay oh-rrah?
Who	Quién	Kee-ehn
Where	Dónde	Dohn-day
Which	Cuál	Kwahl
When	Cuándo	Kwahn-doh
How many	Cuánto	Kwahn-toh
What	Qué	Keh
Why	Por qué	Pohrr-keh
Because	Porque	Pohrr keh

DAY/TIME OF DAY

morning	mañana	mahn-yah-nah
noon	mediodía	meh-dee-yoh-dee-yah
afternoon	tarde	tahrr-deh
evening	tarde	tahrr-deh
night	noche	noh-cheh
today	hoy	oy
yesterday	ayer	ah-yehrr
tomorrow	mañana	mahn-yah-nah
Monday	lunes	loo-nehss
Tuesday	martes	mahrr-tehss
Wednesday	miércoles	mee-yehrr-koh-lehss
Thursday	jueves	hoo-eh-vehss
Friday	viernes	vee-yehrr-nehss
Saturday	sábado	sah-bah-doh
Sunday	domingo	doh-meen-goh
holiday	feriado	fehrr-ee-yah-doh
New Year's Day	Año Nuevo	ahn-nyoh nweh-voh
time (hour)	hora	oh-rrah
place	lugar	loo-gahrr
early	temprano	teem-prah-noh
late	tarde	tahrr-deh

English	Spanish	Pronunciation
		NUMBERS*
one	uno	oo-noh
two	dos	dohss
three	tres	trehss
four	cuatro	kwah-troh
five	cinco	sseen-koh
six	seis	seh-eess
seven	siete	see-yeh-teh
eight	ocho	oh-choh
nine	nueve	noo-weh-veh
ten	diez	dee-yehss
eleven	once	ohn-sseh
twelve	doce	doh-sseh
thirteen	trece	treh-sseh
fourteen	catorce	ka-tohrr-sseh
fifteen	quince	keen-sseh
sixteen	dieciseis	dee-yehs-ee-sehss
seventeen	diecisiete	dee-yehss-ee-ssee-yeh-teh
eighteen	dieciocho	dee-yehss-ee-oh-choh
nineteen	diecinueve	dee-yehss-ee-noo-weh-veh
twenty	veinte	veh-yeen-teh
twenty-one	veintiuno	veh-yeen-tee-yoo-noh
thirty	treinta	treh-yeen-teh
forty	cuarenta	kwah-rehn-tah
fifty	cincuenta	sseen-kwehn-tah
sixty	sesenta	sseh-ssehn-tah
seventy	setenta	sseh-tehn-tah
eighty	ochenta	oh-chehn-tah
ninety	noventa	noh-vehn-tah
one hundred	cien	ssee-ehn
two hundred	doscientos	doh-ssee-yehn-tohs
three hundred	trescientos	treh-ssee-yehn-tohs
one thousand	mil	meel
one million	un millón	oon mee-yohn
first	primero	pree-meh-rroh
second	segundo	seh-goon-doh
third	tercero	tehr-seh-rroh

---

*The Dictionary of the *Real Academia Española* (Royal Spanish Academy) defines one billion as being equal to one million millions. However, the business community has adopted the standard US-derived international business usage of one billion as being equal to one thousand millions. Standard Spanish numeric notation also reverses that found in English numeric notation, using a comma (,) the way English notation uses the decimal point (.) to separate whole numbers from decimal fractions. Spanish uses the decimal point to separate the hundreds position from the thousands, thousands from millions, and so forth, whereas English notation uses the comma for this. For example, the Spanish "55.555,55" is equivalent to the English "55,555.55."

English	Spanish	Pronunciation

GETTING AROUND TOWN

Where is (the railway station)?	¿Dónde está (la estación del tren)?	Dohn-deh eh-stah (lah eh-stah-ssee-yohn de trehn)?
Does this train go to Buenos Aires	¿Este tren va a Buenos Aires?	Eh-steh trehn vah ah Bweh-nohs ay-rehs?
Please take me to Buenos Aires	Por favor, lléveme a Buenos Aires	Pohr fah-vohr, yeh-veh-meh ah Bweh-nohs ay-rehs
Where am I?	¿Dónde estoy?	Dohn-deh eh-stoy?
airplane	avión	ah-vee-yohn
airport	aeropuerto	ay-eh-rroh-pwehr-toh
bus (public)	colectivo	koh-lek-tee-voh
taxi	taxi	tahk-ssee
train	tren	trehn
train station	estación del tren	eh-stah-ssee-yohn dehl trehn
ticket	boleto	boh-leh-toh
one-way (single) ticket	boleto de ida	boh-leh-toh deh ee-dah
round trip (return) ticket	boleto ida y vuelta	boh-leh-toh ee-dah ee vwehl-tah
subway	subte	soob-teh

PLACES

airport	aeropuerto	ay-eh-rroh-pwehrr-toh
bank	banco	bahn-koh
barber shop	peluquería	peh-loo-keh-rree-ya
beauty parlor	salón de belleza	sah-lohn deh beh-yehss-ah
business district	zona comercial	zoh-nah ko-mehrr-ssee-yahl
clothes store	tienda de ropa	tee-ehn-dah deh rroh-pah
exhibition	exposición	eks-poh-ssee-ssee-yohn
factory	fábrica	fah-bree-kah
hotel	hotel	oh-tehl
hospital	hospital	oh-spee-tahl
market	mercado	mehr-kah-doh
post office	oficina de correos	oh-fee-ssee-nah deh koh-rray-ohss
restaurant	restaurante	rreh-sta-oo-rrahn-teh
restroom/toilet		
women's	baño de damas	bah-nyoh deh dah-mahss
men's	baño de caballeros	bah-nyoh deh kah-bah-yeh-rohs
seaport	puerto	pwehrr-toh
train station	estación de tren	eh-stah-ssee-yohn deh trehn
town square	plaza principal	plah-ssah preen-ssee-pahl

At the Bank

What is the exchange rate?	¿Cuál es el tipo de cambio?	Kwal ehss ehl tee-poh deh kahm-bee-oh?
I want to exchange (dollars)	Quiero cambiar (dólares)	Kee-eh-rroh kahm-bee-ahrr (doh-lah-rehss)
peso	peso	peh-ssoh

English	*Spanish*	*Pronunciation*
Brazilian real	real brasileño	ray-<u>ah</u>l brah-ssee-<u>leh</u>n-yoh
Chilean peso	peso chileno	p<u>eh</u>-ssoh chee-<u>leh</u>-noh
US dollar	dólar americano	d<u>oh</u>-lahrr ah-meh-ree-<u>kah</u>-noh
Can you cash a personalcheck?	¿Puede cambiarme un cheque personal?	Pw<u>eh</u>-deh kahm-bee-y<u>ah</u>rr-meh oon ch<u>eh</u>-keh pehr-sso-n<u>ah</u>l?
Where should I sign?	¿Dónde debo firmar?	D<u>oh</u>n-deh d<u>eh</u>-bo feer-m<u>ah</u>rr?
traveler's check	cheque de viajero	ch<u>eh</u>-keh deh vee-yah-h<u>eh</u>-roh
bank draft	giro bancario	h<u>ee</u>-roh bahn-k<u>ah</u>-rree-oh

At the Hotel

I have a reservation	Tengo una reserva	T<u>eh</u>n-goh <u>oo</u>-nah rreh-ss<u>eh</u>r-vah
Could you give me a single (double) room?	¿Tiene una habitación simple (doble) libre?	Ty<u>eh</u>-neh <u>oo</u>-nah ah-bee-tah-ssee-y<u>oh</u>n ss<u>eem</u>-pleh (d<u>oh</u>-bleh) l<u>ee</u>-breh?
Is there...	¿Tiene...	tee-<u>eh</u>-nee...
air conditioning?	aire acondicionado?	<u>a</u>-ee-rreh ah-kohn-dee-ssee-oh-n<u>ah</u>-doh?
heating?	calefacción?	kah-leh-fahk-sy<u>oh</u>n?
private toilet?	baño privado?	b<u>ah</u>n-yoh pree-v<u>ah</u>-doh?
hot water?	agua caliente?	ah-wa kah-lee-y<u>eh</u>n-teh?
May I see the room?	¿Puedo ver la habitación?	Pw<u>eh</u>-doh vehr lah ah-bee-tah-ssee-y<u>oh</u>n?
Would you mail this for me please?	¿Puede mandarme esto por correo por favor?	Pw<u>eh</u>-deh mahn-d<u>ah</u>rr-meh <u>eh</u>-sstoh pohrr koh-rr<u>heo</u> pohr-fah-v<u>oh</u>rr
Would you mail this for me?	¿Puede mandarme esto por correo?	Pw<u>eh</u>-deh mahn-d<u>ah</u>r-meh <u>eh</u>-sstow pohrr koh-rr<u>ay</u>-oh?
Do you have any stamps?	¿Tiene estampillas?	Ty<u>eh</u>-neh eh-stahm-p<u>ee</u>-yass
May I have my bill?	La cuenta por favor	Lah koo-<u>eh</u>n-tah pohr fah-v<u>oh</u>r
Do you accept credit cards?	¿Aceptan tarjetas de crédito?	Ah-ss<u>eh</u>p-tahn tar-h<u>eh</u>-tahss deh kr<u>eh</u>-dee-toh

In the Shop

Do you sell (books)?	¿Vende (libros)?	V<u>eh</u>n-deh (l<u>ee</u>-brohss)?
Do you have anything cheaper?	¿Tiene algo más barato?	Tee-y<u>eh</u>-neh <u>ah</u>l-goh mahss bah-rr<u>ah</u>-toh?
Do you have anything less expensive?	¿Tiene algo menos costoso?	Tee-y<u>eh</u>-neh <u>ah</u>l-goh m<u>eh</u>-nohs kos-t<u>oh</u>-sow
I would like (three books)	Quiero (tres libros)	Kee-hy<u>eh</u>-rroh (trehss l<u>ee</u>-brohss)
Give me three	Deme tres	D<u>eh</u>-meh trayhs
I'll take it	Lo llevo	Loh y<u>eh</u>-voh
I want this one	Quiero este	Kee-y<u>eh</u>rr-oh <u>eh</u>-steh
When does it open?	¿A qué hora abren?	Ah keh <u>oh</u>-rrah <u>ah</u>-brehn?
When does it close?	¿A qué hora cierran?	Ah keh <u>oh</u>-rrah see-y<u>eh</u>r-rahn?
How much?	¿Cuánto cuesta?	Kw<u>ah</u>n-toh kw<u>ay</u>ss-tah?

English	Spanish	Pronunciation

COUNTRIES

Argentina	Argentina	Ahrr-hehn-<u>tee</u>-nah
America (USA)	Estados Unidos	Eh-st<u>ah</u>-dohss Oo-n<u>ee</u>-dohss
France	Francia	Fr<u>ah</u>n-ssee-yah
Germany	Alemania	Ah-leh-m<u>ah</u>n-yah
Great Britain	Gran Bretaña	Grahn Bray-t<u>ah</u>n-yah
Mexico	México	M<u>eh</u>-hee-koh
Venezuela	Venezuela	Veh-neh-sw<u>eh</u>-lah
Colombia	Colombia	Koh-l<u>ohm</u>-bee-ah
Brazil	Brasil	Brah-ss<u>eel</u>
Chile	Chile	Ch<u>eeh</u>-leh
Peru	Perú	Peh-rr<u>oo</u>
Bolivia	Bolivia	Boh-l<u>ee</u>-vee-yah
Uruguay	Uruguay	Oo-r<u>uh</u>-gway
Paraguay	Paraguay	Pah-r<u>ah</u>-gway

EXPRESSIONS IN BUSINESS

General Business-Related Terms

accounting	contabilidad	kohn-tah-bee-lee-d<u>ah</u>d
additional charge	cargo adicional	k<u>ah</u>rr-goh ah-dee-ssee-yoh-n<u>ahl</u>
advertise	publicitar	poob-lee-see-t<u>ah</u>rr
application	solicitud	soh-lee-ss<u>ee</u>-tood
appointment	cita	ss<u>ee</u>-tah
bankrupt	quebrado	kay-b<u>rah</u>-doe
brand name	marca	m<u>ah</u>rr-kah
business	negocio	neh-g<u>oh</u>-ssee-yoh
buyer	comprador	kohm-prah-d<u>oh</u>rr
commercial affairs (business)	negocios	neh-g<u>oe</u>-see-yohss
capital	capital	kah-pee-t<u>ahl</u>
cash	efectivo	eh-fehk-t<u>ee</u>-voh
change (from a purchase)	vuelto	vw<u>el</u>-toh
charge	cargo	k<u>ah</u>rr-goh
check (draft)	cheque	ch<u>eh</u>-keh
check (examine)	revisar	rray-v<u>ee</u>-ssahrr
claim	reclamo	rreh-kl<u>ah</u>-moh
collect (payment)	cobrar	koh-br<u>ah</u>rr
collect (items)	recoger	rreh-k<u>oh</u>-hehrr
commission	comisión	koh-mee-ssee-y<u>oh</u>n
company	compañía	kohm-pah-n<u>yee</u>-yah
complain/inquire	reclamar	rreh-kl<u>ah</u>-mahr
complaint/inquiry	reclamo	rreh-kl<u>ah</u>-moh
copyright	derechos de autor	deh-rr<u>eh</u>-chohss deh ah-oo-t<u>oh</u>r
corporation	sociedad anónima	soh-see-yeh-d<u>ah</u>d ah-n<u>oh</u>-nih-mah
cost	costo	k<u>oh</u>-stoh

English	*Spanish*	*Pronunciation*
credit	crédito	krreh-dih-toh
on credit	a crédito	ah krreh-deetoh
credit card	tarjeta de crédito	tahrr-hay-tah deh krreh-dee-toh
currency	moneda	moh-neh-dah
customer	cliente	klee-yehn-teh
customs duties	aranceles de aduana	ahrr-ahn-seh-lehss deh ah-dwah-na
D/A (documents against acceptance)	documentos contra aceptación	doh-koo-mehn-tohss kohn-trah ahk-sehp-tah-ssee-yohn
D/P (documents against payment)	documentos contra pago	doh-koo-mehn-tohss kohn-trah pah-goh
deferred payment	pago a plazos	pah-goh ah-plah-ssohs
deposit (n)	depósito	deh-poh-ssee-toh
design	diseño	dee-ssehn-yoh
discount	descuento	dehss-kwehn-toh
distribution	distribución	dee-stree-boo-ssee-yohn
dividends	dividendos	dee-vee-dehn-dohss
documents	documentos	doh-koo-mehn-tohss
due date	fecha de vencimiento	feh-chah deh vehn-ssee-mee-yehn-toh
exhibit	exhibir (v) exhibición (n)	ehk-ssee-beerr (v) ehk-see-bee-ssee-yohn (n)
facsimile (fax)	fax	fahks
finance	finanzas	fee-nahn-ssass
firm	empresa	ehm-preh-ssah
foreign businessman	empresario extranjero	eem-preh-sahr-yoh ehk-strahn-heh-rroh
foreign capital	capital extranjero	kah-pee-tahl ehk-strahn-heh-rroh
foreign currency	moneda extranjera	moh-neh-dah ehk-strahn-heh-rrah
foreign exchange	cambio de divisas	kahm-bee-yoh deh dee-vee-sahs
foreign trade	comercio exterior	koh-mehrr-ssee-yoh ehk-steh-rree-yohrr
goods	bienes	bee-ehn-ehs
government	gobierno	goh-bee-yehrr-noh
industry	industria/sector	een-dooss-tree-yah/sehk-tohrr
inspection	inspección	een-spehk-ssee-yohn
insurance	seguro	seh-goo-rroh
interest	interés	een-teh-rrehss
international	internacional	een-tehr-nah-ssee-yoh-nahl
investment	inversión	een-vehr-ssee-yohn
invoice	factura	fahk-too-rrah
joint venture	inversión conjunta	een-vehr-ssee-yohn kohn-hun-tah
label	etiqueta	eh-tee-keh-tah
letter of credit	carta de crédito	kahrr-tah deh kreh-dee-toh
license	licencia (n) autorizar (v)	lee-ssehn-ssee-yah (n) a-oo-toh-rree-ssahr (v)
loan	préstamo	preh-stah-moh

English	Spanish	Pronunciation
mergers and acquisitions	fusiones y adquisiciones	foo-ssee-yohn-ayss ee ahd-kee-ssee-ssee yohn-ehss
model (of a product)	modelo	moh-deh-loh
money	dinero/moneda/plata	dee-nehr-oh/moh-neh-dah/plah-tah
monopoly	monopolio	moh-noh-poh-lee-yoh
office	oficina	oh-fee-ssee-nah
owner	dueño	dwayn-yoh
patent	patente	pah-tehn-teh
pay (v)	pagar	pah-gahrr
payment of goods	pago de mercancías	pah-goh deh mehrr-kan-ssee-yahss
payment by installment	pago a plazos	pah-goh ah plah-ssohss
payment in cash	pago en efectivo	pah-goh ehn eh-fec-tee-voh
payment in advance	pago adelantado	pah-goh ah-deh-lahn-tah-doh
permit	permiso	pehrr-mee-ssoh
principal	capital	kah-pee-tahl
private (not government)	privado	pree-vah-doh
product	producto	proh-dook-toh
profit margin	margen de utilidad	mahrr-hehn deh oo-tee-lee-dahd
range of goods	inventario	een-vehn-tah-ree-oh
receipt	recibo	rray-ssee-boh
register	registro(n)	rreh-heess-troh (n)
	registrar (v)	rreh-hees-trahrr (v)
report	informe (n)	een-fohr-meh (n)
	informar (v)	een-fohr-mahrr (v)
research and development (R&D)	investigación y desarrollo	een-veh-stee-gah-ssee-yohn ee deh-ssah-roh-yoh
return on investment/yield	rendimiento	rrehn-dee-mee-yehn-toh
sample	muestra	mweh-strah
sale	venta	vehn-tah
savings	ahorros	ah-ohrr-rrohss
seller	vendedor	vehn-deh-dohrr
settle accounts	liquidar cuentas	lee-kwee-dahrr kwehn-tahss
service charge	cargo por servicio	kahrr-goh pohrr sehrr-vee-ssee-yoh
sight draft	giro a la vista	hee-rroh ah lah vee-stah
tariffs	tarifas	tah-rreef-ahss
tax	impuesto	eem-pwehs-toh
telephone	teléfono	teh-leh-foh-noh
telex	telex	teh-lehks
trademark	marca registrada	mahrr-kah reh-hee-strah-dah
visa	visa	vee-ssah

Labor

compensation	compensación	kohm-pehn-sah-ssee-yohn
employee	empleado	ehm-pleh-ah-doh
employer	empleador	ehm-pleh-ah-dohrr

English	*Spanish*	*Pronunciation*
employment	empleo	eem-play-yoh
fire, dismiss (v)	despedir	deh-sspeh-deerr
foreign worker	trabajador extranjero	trah-bah-hah-dohrr ehk-strahn-heh-rroh
hire (v)	contratar	kohn-trah-tahrr
immigration	inmigración	een-mee-grah-ssee-yohn
interview	entrevista	ehn-treh-vee-stah
job	puesto	pwehss-toh
laborer	obrero	oh-breh-rroh
skilled laborer	obrero calificado	oh-breh-rroh kah-lee-fee-kah-doh
unskilled laborer	obrero no calificado	oh-breh-rroh noh kah-lee-fee-kah-doh
labor force	mano de obra	mah-noh deh oh-brah
labor shortage	falta de mano de obra	fahl-tah deh mah-noh deh oh-brah
labor surplus	excedente de mano de obra	ehk-sseh-dehn-teh deh mah-noh deh oh-brah
minimun wage	sueldo mínimo	swehl-doh mee-nee-moh
profession/ occupation	profesión/ocupación	proh-feh-ssee-yohn/ oh-kuh-pah-ssee-yohn
salary	salario	sah-lah-rree-oh
strike	huelga	hwehl-gah
training	capacitación	kah-pah-ssee-tah-ssee-ohn
union	sindicato	seen-dee-kah-toh
wage	sueldo	swehl-doh
work	trabajo (n)	trah-bah-hoh (n)
	trabajar (v)	trah-bah-hahrr (v)

Negotiations (Buying/Selling)

agreement	acuerdo	ah-kwehrr-doh
arbitrate	arbitrar	ahr-bee-trahrr
brochure, pamphlet	folleto	foh-yeh–toh
buy (v)	comprar	kohm-prahrr
confirm (v)	confirmar	kohn-feer-mahrr
contract	contrato (n)	kohn-trah-toh (n)
	contratar (v)	kohn-trah-tahrr(v)
cooperator	cooperador	koh-oh-peh-rah-dohrr
cost	costo	koh-stoh
counteroffer	contraoferta	kohn-trah-oh-fehrr-tah
countersign	contraseñar	kohn-trah-sehn-yahrr
deadline	plazo límite	plah-ssoh lee-mee-teh
demand	exigencia (n)	ehk-ssee-hehn-ssee-yah (n)
	exigir (v)	ehk-ssee-heerr (v)
estimate (v)	estimar	eh-stee-mahrr
guarantee (v)	garantizar	gah-rrahn-tee-ssahrr
label	etiqueta	eh-tee-keh-tah
license (n)	licencia	lee-ssehn-ssee-yah

English	*Spanish*	*Pronunciation*
market	mercado	mehrr-<u>kah</u>-doh
market price	precio de mercado	pr<u>eh</u>-ssee-yoh deh mehrr-<u>kah</u>-doh
minimum quantity	cantidad mínima	kahn-tee-d<u>ah</u>d m<u>ee</u>-nee-mah
negotiate	negociar	neh-goh-ssee-y<u>ah</u>rr
negotiate payment	negociar el pago	neh-goh-ssee-y<u>ah</u>rr ehl p<u>ah</u>-goh
order	pedido	peh-d<u>ee</u>-doh
packaging	packaging	peh-k<u>ay</u>-jeeng
place an order	hacer un pedido	ah-ss<u>eh</u>r oon peh-d<u>ee</u>-doh
price	precio	pr<u>eh</u>-ssee-yoh
price list	lista de precios	l<u>ee</u>-stah deh pr<u>eh</u>-ssee-yohss
product features	características del producto	kah-rrahk-teh-rr<u>ee</u>-stee-kahss dehl proh-d<u>oo</u>k-toh
product line	línea de productos	l<u>ee</u>-neh-ah deh proh-d<u>oo</u>k-tohss
quality	calidad	kah-lee-d<u>ah</u>d
quantity	cantidad	kahn-tee-d<u>ah</u>d
quota	cuota	kw<u>oh</u>-tah
quote (offer)/proposal	presupuesto	preh-ssoo-pw<u>eh</u>-stoh
sale	venta	v<u>eh</u>n-tah
sales confirmation	confirmación de venta	kohn-feer-mah-ssee-y<u>oh</u>n deh v<u>eh</u>n-tah
sell	vender	vehn-d<u>eh</u>rr
sign	firmar	feer-m<u>ah</u>rr
specifications	especificaciones	eh-speh-see-fee-kah-ssee-y<u>oh</u>n-ehss
standard (quality)	(calidad) estándar	(kah-lee-d<u>ah</u>d) eh-st<u>ah</u>n-dahr
superior (quality)	(calidad) superior	(kah-lee-d<u>ah</u>d) soo-peh-ree-<u>oh</u>r
trade	comercio (n)	koh-m<u>eh</u>rr-ssee-yoh (n)
	comerciar (v)	koh-mehrr-ssee-y<u>ah</u>r (v)
unit price	precio unitario	pr<u>eh</u>-ssee-yoh oo-nee-t<u>ah</u>-ree-yoh
value	valor	vah-l<u>oh</u>rr
value added	valor agregado	vah-l<u>oh</u>rr ah-gray-g<u>ah</u>-doh
warranty (and services)	garantía (y servicios)	gah-rrahn-t<u>ee</u>-ah (ee ssehr-v<u>ee</u>-ssee-yohss)
The price is very high	El precio es muy alto	Ayl pr<u>eh</u>-ssee-yoh ehss m<u>oo</u>-ee <u>ah</u>l-toh
The price is too high	El precio es demasiado alto	Ayl pr<u>eh</u>-ssee-yoh ehss deh-mah-see-y<u>ah</u>-doh <u>ah</u>l-toh
We need a faster delivery	Necesitamos una entrega más rápida	Neh-sseh-ssee-t<u>ah</u>-mohss <u>oo</u>-nah ehn-tr<u>eh</u>-gah mahss rr<u>ah</u>-pee-dah
We need it by (tomorrow)	Lo necesitamos (para mañana)	Loh neh-sseh-ssee-t<u>ah</u>-mohss (p<u>ah</u>-rrah mahn-y<u>ah</u>-nah)
We need a better quality	Necesitamos una mejor calidad	Neh-sseh-see-t<u>ah</u>-mohss <u>oo</u>-na meh-h<u>oh</u>rr kah-lee-d<u>ah</u>d
We need it to these specifications	Lo necesitamos con estas especificaciones	Loh neh-sseh-see-t<u>ah</u>-mohss kohn <u>eh</u>-stah-speh-ssee-fee-kah-ssee-y<u>oh</u>n-ehss
I want to pay less	Quiero pagar menos	Kee-<u>eh</u>-rroh pah-g<u>ah</u>rr m<u>eh</u>-nohss

English	*Spanish*	*Pronunciation*
I want the price to include…	Quiero que el precio incluya…	Kee-yehrr oh keh ehl preh-ssee-yoh een-kloo-yah…
Can you guarantee delivery?	¿Puede garantizarme la entrega?	Pweh-deh gah-rrahn-tee-ssahrr-meh lah ehn-treh-gah?
Can you guarantee the delivery date?	¿Puede garantizarme la fecha de la entrega?	Pweh-deh gah-rrahn-tee-ssahr-meh lah fay-chah deh lah ehn-treh-gah?

Products/Industries

aluminium	aluminio	ah-loo-mee-nee-yoh
automobile	automóvil	ah-oo-toh-moh-veel
automotive accessories	repuestos/accesorios de automóvil	rehy-pues-tohss/ahk-sseh-ssoh-rree-ohs deh ah-oo-toh-moh-veel
biotechnology	biotecnología	bee-oh-tehk-noh-loh-hee-ah
brick	ladrillo	lah-dree-yoh
carpets	alfombras	ahl-fohm-brahss
cement	cemento	sseh-mehn-toh
ceramics	cerámica	sseh-rrah-mee-kah
chemicals	productos químicos	proh-dook-tohss kee-mee-kohss
clothing…	ropa…	rroh-pah…
for women	de mujer	deh moo-hehr
for men	de hombre	deh ohm-breh
for children	de niños	deh neen-yohss
coal	carbón	kahr-bohn
computer	computadora	kohm-poo-tah-doh-rrah
computer hardware	hardware de computadora	hardware deh kohm-poo-tah-doh-rrah
computer software	software de computadora	software deh kohm-poo-tah-doh-rrah
concrete	cemento	sseh-mehn-toh
construction	construcción	kohn-strook-ssee-yohn
electrical equipment	maquinaria eléctrica	mah-kee-nah-ree-yah eh-lehk-tree-kah
glass	vidrio	vee-dee-yoh
gold	oro	oh-rroh
handicrafts	artesanías	ahrr-teh-sah-nee-ahss
minerals	minerales	mee-neh-rrah-lehss
mining industry	industria minera	een-doo-stree-yah mee-neh-rrah
musical instruments	instrumentos musicales	een-stroo-mehn-tohss moo-ssee-kah-lehss
paper	papel	pah-pehl
petroleum	petróleo	peh-troh-leh-oh
pharmaceuticals	productos farmacéuticos	proh-dook-tohss fahrr-mah-seh-oo-tee-kohss
plastics	plásticos	plahss-tee-kohss
pottery	cerámica	seh-rrah-mee-kah
rugs	alfombras	ahl-fohm-brahss
silver	plata	plah-tah
spare parts	repuestos	rreh-pweh-stohss
sporting goods	artículos deportivos	arr-tee-koo-lohss deh-pohr-tee-vohs

English	Spanish	Pronunciation
steel	acero	ah-ss<u>eh</u>-roh
telecommunications	telecomunicaciones	teh-leh-koh-moo-nee-kah-ssee-<u>yohn</u>-nehss
television	televisión	teh-leh-vee-ssee-<u>yohn</u>
television set	televisor	teh-leh-v<u>ee</u>-sohrr
textiles	textiles	tehk-st<u>ee</u>-lehss
tobacco	tabaco	tah-b<u>ah</u>-koh
tools	herramientas	eh-rrah-mee-y<u>eh</u>n-tahss
hand tool	herramienta manual	eh-rrah-mee-y<u>eh</u>n-tah mah-noo-<u>ahl</u>
power tool	herramienta mecánica	eh-rrah-mee-y<u>eh</u>n-tah meh-k<u>ah</u>-nee-kah
tourism	turismo	too-rr<u>ee</u>ss-moh
toys	jugu etes	hoo-g<u>eh</u>-tehss
watches/clocks	relojes	rreh-l<u>oh</u>-hehss
wood	madera	mah-d<u>eh</u>-rrah

Services

accounting service	servicio de contabilidad	sehr-v<u>ee</u>-ssee-yoh deh kohn-tah-bee-lee-d<u>ah</u>d
advertising agency	agencia de publicidad	ah-h<u>eh</u>n-ssee-yah deh poob-lee-ssee-d<u>ah</u>d
agent	agente	ah-h<u>eh</u>n-teh
customs broker	despachante de aduanas	dehs-pah-ch<u>ah</u>n-teh deh ah-dw<u>ah</u>-nahss
distributor	distribuidor	dee-stree-bwee-d<u>oh</u>rr
employment agency	agencia de empleo	aa-h<u>eh</u>n-see-yah deh ehm-pl<u>eh</u>-oh
exporter	exportador	ehkss-pohrr-tah-d<u>oh</u>rr
freight forwarder	agente de fletes	eh-h<u>eh</u>n-tay deh fl<u>eh</u>-tehss
importer	importador	eem-porr-tah-d<u>oh</u>rr
manufacturer	fabricante	fah-bree-k<u>ah</u>n-teh
packing services	servicios de empaque	sehr-v<u>ee</u>-ssee-yohss deh ehm-p<u>ah</u>-kay
printing company	imprenta	eem-pr<u>eh</u>n-tah
retailer	minorista	mee-noh-rr<u>ee</u>-stah
service(s)	servicio(s)	sehr-v<u>ee</u>-ssee-yoh(ss)
supplier	proveedor	proh-veh-eh-d<u>oh</u>rr
translation services	servicios de traducción	sehr-v<u>ee</u>-ssee-yohss deh trah-dook-ssee-<u>yohn</u>
wholesaler	mayorista	mah-yoh-rr<u>ee</u>-stah

Shipping/Transportation

bill of lading	conocimiento de embarque	koh-noh-see-mee-y<u>eh</u>n-toh deh ehm-b<u>ah</u>rr-keh
freight and insurance paid to	flete y seguro pagado a	fl<u>ay</u>-teh ee say-g<u>uh</u>-roh pah-g<u>ah</u>-doh ah
freight paid to	flete pagado a	fl<u>ay</u>-teh pah-g<u>ah</u>-doh ah
cost and freight	costo y flete	k<u>oh</u>-stoh ee fl<u>ay</u>-teh
cost, insurance, freight (CIF)	CIF	seh ee <u>eh</u>-fay

English	Spanish	Pronunciation
customs	aduana	ah-dwah-nah
customs duty	derechos aduaneros	deh-rreh-choss ah-dwah-neh-rrohs
date of delivery	fecha de entrega	feh-chah deh ehn-treh-gah
deliver (delivery)	entregar (entrega)	ehn-treh-gahr (ehn-treh-gah)
delivered at frontier	entregada en frontera	ehn-tray-gah-dah ehn fron-tehr-ah
delivered duty paid	entregada con impuestos pagados	ehn-tray-gah-dah kohn eem-pwehs-tohs pah-gah-dohs
delivered duty unpaid	entregada impuestos pendientes de pago	ehn-tray-gah-dah eem-pwehs-tohs pehn-dee-ehn-tehs deh pah-goh
delivered ex quay	entregada en el desembarcadero	ehn-tray-gah-dah ehn ehl dehss-ehm-barr-kah-deh-rroh
delivered ex ship	entregada en el barco	ehn-tray-gah-dah ehn ehl bahr-koh
export	exportación (n) exportar (v)	ehkss-pohrr-tah-ssee-yohn (n) ehkss-pohrr-tahrr (v)
ex works	en fábrica	ehn fah-bree-kah
free alongside ship (FAS)	franco en el muelle	frahn-koh ehn el mweh-yeh
free carrier	franco transportador	frahn-koh trahns-pohrr-tah-dohrr
free on board (FOB)	FOB	eh-fay oh bay
import	importación (n) importar (v)	eem-pohrr-tah-ssee-yohn (n) eem-pohrr-tahrr (v)
in bulk	a granel	ah grah-nehl
mail (post) (n)	correo postal	koh-rray-oh poh-stahl
country of origin	país de origen	pah-ees deh oh-rree-hehn
packing	embalaje	ehm-bah-lah-hay
packing list	lista de empaque	lee-stah deh ehm-pah-kay
port	puerto	pwehrr-toh
ship (to send)…	enviar…	ehn-vee-yahr…
by air	por avión	pohrr ah-vyohn
by sea	por barco	pohrr bahrr-koh
by train	por tren	pohrr trehn
by truck	por camión	pohrr kah-mee-yohn

WEIGHTS, MEASURES, AMOUNTS*

barrel	barril	bah-rreel
centimeter	centímetro	sehn-tee-meh-troh
dozen	docena	doh-sseh-nah
foot	pie	pyeh
gallon	galón	gah-lohn
gram	gramo	grah-moh
gross (144 pieces)	gruesa (144)	grweh-ssah (ssyehn-toh kwah-rrehn-tah ee kwah-troh)
gross weight	peso bruto	peh-ssoh broo-toh
hectare	hectárea	ehk-tah-rreh-ah
hundred (100)	cien	ssee-yehn
inch	pulgada	pool-gah-da

English	Spanish	Pronunciation
kilogram	kilogramo	kee-loh-grah-moh
meter	metro	meh-troh
net weight	peso neto	peh-ssoh neh-toh
mile (English)	milla	mee-yah
liter	litro	lee-troh
ounce	onza	ohn-ssah
pint	pinta	peen-tah
pound (weight–measure avoirdupois)	libra	lee-brah
quart (avoirdupois)	cuarto de galón	kwahr-toh deh gah-lohn
square meter	metro cuadrado	meh-troh kwah-drah-doh
cubic meter	metro cúbico	meh-troh koo-bee-koh
square yard	yarda cuadrada	yahrr-dah kwah-drah-dah
size	tamaño	tah-mah-nee-yoh
ton (metric)	tonelada	toh-neh-lah-dah
yard	yarda	yahrr-dah

* The system used in Argentina is the Unified International Weights and Measures (Metric) System.

ARGENTINA-SPECIFIC ORGANIZATIONAL TITLES

board of directors	directorio	dee-rrehk-tohrr-eeh-oh
chairman	presidente	preh-ssee-dehn-teh
deputy director	subdirector	ssoob-dee-rrehk-tohrr
manager	gerente	hehr-rrehn-teh
assistant manager	subgerente	ssoob-heh-rrehn-teh
president	presidente	preh-ssee-dehn-teh
vice president	vicepresidente	veess-preh-ssee-dehn-teh
company secretary	secretario	sseh-kreh-tah-rree-yoh
auditor (syndic)	síndico	seen-dee-coh
supervisor	supervisor	ssoo-pehr-vee-ssohrr
marketing director	director de marketing	dee-rrehk-tohrr deh mahrr-keh-ting
sales manager	jefe de ventas	heh-feh deh vehn-tahss
accountant	contador	kohn-tah-dohr
attorney	abogado	ah-boh-gah-doh

COMMON SIGNS

Entrance	Entrada	ehn-trah-dah
Exit	Salida	ssah-lee-dah
Men (restroom)	Caballeros	kah-bah-yeh-rrohss
Women (restroom)	Damas	dah-mahss
Up	Arriba	ah-rree-bah
Down	Abajo	ah-bah-ho

English	*Spanish*	*Pronunciation*

ARGENTINA-SPECIFIC EXPRESSIONS AND TERMS

Greetings

Hello (on the phone)	¿Hola?	oh-lah?
How do you do?	¿Cómo está?	Koh-moh eh-stah?
See you later	Hasta luego	Hahss-tah lweh-goh
Are you ill?	¿Está enfermo?	Eh-stah ehn-fehrr-moh?
How are you doing?	¿Cómo te va?	Koh-moh teh vah?
How is your business going?	¿Cómo van los negocios?	Koh-mo vahn lohss neh-goh-ssee-ohss
Is your family well?	¿Qué tal su familia?	Keh tahl soo fah-mee-lee-yah?
Did you sleep well?	¿Durmió bien?	Duhr-mee-oh bee-ehn?
What did you say (pardon)?	¿Cómo dijo?	Koh-moh dee-hoh?
It's very hot (weather)	Hace mucho calor	Ah-sseh moo-cho kah-lohr
It's very cold (weather)	Hace mucho frío	Ah-sseh moo-cho free-oh
Would you like a drink?	¿Le gustaría tomar algo?	Ley goo-stah-rree-yah toh-mahrr ahl-goh?
Welcome to Argentina	Bienvenido a Argentina (man)	Byehn-veh-nee-doh ah ahrr-hehn-tee-nah
	Bienvenida a Argentina (woman)	Byehn-veh-nee-dah ah ahrr-hehn-tee-nah
It's a beautiful country	Es un país muy hermoso	Ays oon pah-eess moo-ee ehr-moh-ssoh
It's a very interesting country	Es un país muy interesante	Ays oon pah-eess moo-ee een-tehrr-ay-sahn-teh

At the Restaurant

Waiter	Mozo	Moh-ssoh
Please bring me a menu	Tráigame el menú, por favor	Trah-ee-gah-meh ehl meh-noo, pohrr fah-vohrr
We want to order	Queremos pedir, por favor	Keh-rreh-mohs peh-deerr, pohrrfah-vohrr
The check	La cuenta, por favor	Lah kwehn-tah, pohrr fah-vohrr
Is it spicy?	¿Es picante?	Ehss pee-kahn-teh?
meal (main meal)	comida	koh-mee-dah
breakfast	desayuno	deh-ssah-yoo-noh
lunch	almuerzo	ahl-mwehr-ssoh
supper	cena	sseh-nah
appetizer	aperitivo	ah-peh-rree-tee-voh
dessert	postre	poh-streh
a bottle of white wine	una botella de vino blanco	oo-nah boh-teh-yah deh vee-noh blahn-koh
a glass of red wine	una copa de vino tinto	oo-nah koh-pah deh vee-noh teen-toh
beer	cerveza	sehrr-veh-ssah
mineral water...	agua mineral...	ah-wah mee-neh-rrahl...
with ice	con hielo	kohn yay-loh
without ice	sin hielo	sseen yay-loh
carbonated	con gas	kohn gahss
uncarbonated	sin gas	sseen gahss
soft drink	gaseosa	gahss-say-yoh-sah
fruit juice	jugo de fruta	hoo-goh deh froo-tah

English	*Spanish*	*Pronunciation*
coffee…	café…	kah-f<u>eh</u>…
black	solo	s<u>oh</u>-lo
with milk	con leche/cortado	kohn l<u>eh</u>-cheh/kohrr-<u>tah</u>-doh
tea	té	teh
bread	pan	pahn
salad	ensalada	ehn-sah-<u>lah</u>-dah
fruit	fruta	fr<u>oo</u>-tah
I need…	necesito…	neh-sseh-ss<u>ee</u>-toh…
a knife	un cuchillo	oon koo-ch<u>ee</u>-yoh
a fork	un tenedor	oon teh-neh-d<u>oh</u>rr
a spoon	una cuchara	<u>oo</u>-nah koo-ch<u>ah</u>-rrah
napkin	servilleta	sehrr-vee-y<u>eh</u>-tah
cover charge	cubierto	koo-bee-<u>ehrr</u>-toh
beans	porotos	poh-<u>rroh</u>-tohss
fish	pescado	pess-<u>kah</u>-doh
meat	carne	<u>kah</u>rr-nay
vegetables	verduras	vehrr-d<u>oo</u>-rrahss
vegetarian	vegetariano	veh-heh-tahrr-ee-<u>ah</u>-no
seafood	mariscos	mahrr-<u>eess</u>-kohss
chicken (poultry)	pollo	p<u>oh</u>-yoh
bon appetit	buen provecho	bwehn proh-v<u>eh</u>-choh

Important Addresses

CONTENTS

INTRODUCTION

The following addresses have been gathered from a wide range of sources. We have attempted to verify each address at press time; however, it is likely that some of the information has already changed. Inclusion of an organization, product, or service does not imply a recommendation or endorsement. In many cases we have provided English translations of the names of the organizations. Other translations of the names may be used as well; those included here are given primarily to assist you in deciding which may be the most appropriate for you to contact.

Unless otherwise noted, all addresses are in Argentina; the international country code for calling Argentina is [54] and is not shown in the Argentine listings. City codes are given in parentheses—for example, (1) for Buenos Aires—while non-Argentine country codes are in square brackets—for example, [44] for the UK. For a listing of Argentine city codes, *see* page 316. Refer to "Communications" on page 153 of "Business Travel" for details on making telephone calls in Argentina.

The word "Calle" or "Avenida" is often omitted from street addresses, and the street number follows the name. The four-digit postal code is precedes the city name. Addresses in the city of Buenos Aires may be written with "Capital Federal" on the city line. A few common elements and abbreviations are:

Avenida (Av. or Avda.)	Avenue
Bs. As. (or B.A.)	Buenos Aires
Calle	Street
Casilla de Correo	PO Box
Código Postal (C.P.)	Postal code
Edificio (Edif.)	Building
Esquina (esq.)	At the corner of
Oficina (Of.)	Office
Piso (P.)	Floor, Story
Planta Baja (P.B.)	Ground Floor
Provincia (Pcia.)	Province

TELEPHONE DIALING CODES IN ARGENTINA

The international dialing code for Argentina is [54]. City dialing codes are listed below. Local numbers may be as short as four digits, while those in major cities are usually six or seven digits.

Cities with a * appearing after their names are provincial capitals. There are 23 provinces plus the Federal Capital District. The post office does not require the province name in an address as long as you have the postal code.

Province	Cities	City Code
Capital Federal	Buenos Aires (Ciudad de)	1
Buenos Aires	La Plata*	21
	Mar del Plata	23
	Bahía Blanca	91
Catamarca	Catamarca*	833
Córdoba	Córdoba*	51
Corrientes	Corrientes*	73
Chaco	Resistencia*	722
Chubut	Rawson*	965
Entre Ríos	Paraná*	43
Formosa	Formosa*	718
Jujuy	San Salvador de Jujuy*	882
La Pampa	Santa Rosa*	954
La Rioja	La Rioja*	822
Mendoza	Mendoza*	61
Misiones	Posadas*	752
Neuquén	Neuquén*	99
Río Negro	Viedma*	920
Salta	Salta*	87
San Juan	San Juan*	64
San Luis	San Luis*	652
Santa Cruz	Río Gallegos*	966
Santa Fé	Santa Fé*	42
	Rosario	41
Santiago del Estero	Santiago del Estero*	85
Tucumán	San Miguel de Tucumán*	81
Tierra del Fuego	Ushuaia*	901

GOVERNMENT

ARGENTINE GOVERNMENT AGENCIES AND ENTITIES

Executive Branch

Casa de Gobierno
(Office of the President)
Balcarce 50
1064 Buenos Aires
Tel: (1) 331-5041, 303-608, 331-3183   Tlx: 21464

Legislative Branch

Senado de la Nación
(Senate)
Hipólito Yrigoyen 1849
1089 Buenos Aires
Tel: (1) 953-3081/9

Cámara de Diputados
(Chamber of Deputies)
Rivadavia 1864
1033 Buenos Aires
Tel: (1) 403-441/9

Corte Suprema de Justicia de la Nación
(Supreme Court)
Talcahuano 550
1013 Buenos Aires
Tel: (1) 372-9142

Government Ministries and Secretariats

Ministerio de Economía y Obras y Servicios Públicos
(Ministry of Economy, Public Works and Services)
Hipólito Yrigoyen 250
1310 Buenos Aires
Tel: (1) 342-6411, 342-6421/9, 349-8814, 349-8810/2
Fax: (1) 331-0292, 331-2619, 331-2090   Tlx: 21952
WWW home page: http://www.mecon.ar

Secretaría de Comercio e Inversiones
(Secretariat of Trade and Investment)
Hipólito Yrigoyen 250
1310 Buenos Aires
Tel: (1) 331-2208

Secretaría de Programación Económica
Subsecretaría de Programación Económica
(Subsecretariat of Economic Planning)
Hipólito Yrigoyen 250, Of. 843
1310 Buenos Aires
Tel: (1) 349-5079   Fax: (1) 349-5730

Secretaría de Hacienda
(Secretariat of Finance)
Hipólito Yrigoyen 250
1310 Buenos Aires
Tel: (1) 331-0731, 342-2937, 341-8900
Fax: (1) 331-0292

Secretaría de Industria
(Secretariat of Industry)
Av. Julio A. Roca 651
1322 Buenos Aires
Tel: (1) 334-5068, 342-7822   Fax: (1) 331-3218

Secretaría de Minería
(Secretariat of Mining)
Av. Julio A. Roca 561, Sector 9
1322 Buenos Aires
Tel: (1) 349-3212, 349-3232   Fax: (1) 343-3525

Secretaría de Energía
(Secretariat of Energy)
Av. Paseo Colón 171, Piso 8, Of. 803
1063 Buenos Aires
Tel: (1) 349-8003/5   Fax: (1) 343-6404

Secretaría de Agricultura, Ganadería y Pesca (SAGyP)
(Secretariat of Agriculture, Livestock, and Fisheries)
Av. Paseo Colón 982
1063 Buenos Aires
Tel: (1) 362-2365, 362-5091, 362-5946   Fax: (1) 349-2504

Secretaría de Obras Públicas y Comunicaciones
(Secretariat of Public Works and Communications)
Sarmiento 151
1041 Buenos Aires
Tel: (1) 49-9481, 312-1283

Secretaría de Transportes
(Secretariat of Transportation)
Av. 9 de julio 1925
1332 Buenos Aires
Tel: (1) 381-1435, 381-4007

Instituto Nacional de Estadística y Censos (INDEC)
(National Institute of Statistics and the Census)
Dirección de Difusión Estadística
Centro de Servicios Estadísticos
Av. Julio A. Roca 615
1067 Buenos Aires
Tel: (1) 349-9654
WWW home page: http://www.mecon.ar/indec/indecnet.htm

Dirección General Impositiva
(Customs Authority)
Hipólito Yrigoyen 250, Of. 606
1310 Buenos Aires
Tel: (1) 331-7330   Fax: (1) 331-9839

Subsecretaría de Inversiones
(Undersecretariat of Investments)
Hipólito Yrigoyen 250, Piso 10, Of. 1010
1310 Buenos Aires
Tel: (1) 349-8515/6, 349-5037   Fax: (1) 349-8522
(US mailing address: Miami Business Center, 3896
Biscayne Blvd., Suite 4046, Miami, FL 33137-9012, USA)

Subsecretaría de Comercio Exterior
Dirección de Promoción de las Exportaciones
(Bureau of Export Promotion)
Av. Julio A. Roca 651, Piso 6
1322 Buenos Aires
Tel: (1) 334-2975   Fax: (1) 331-2266

Administración Nacional de Aduanas
(National Administration of Customs)
Azopardo 350
1328 Buenos Aires
Tel: (1) 343-0661/9, 343-0101/9
Fax: (1) 331-9881, 345-1778

Subsecretaría de Puertos y Vías Navegables
(Undersecretariat of Ports)
España 2221
Buenos Aires

Comisión Nacional de Telecomunicaciones (CNT)
(National Commission of Telecommunications)
Sarmiento 151, Piso 4, Of. 435
1041 Buenos Aires
Tel: (1) 331-1203, 49-9481/2

Subsecretaría de Transporte Aéreo, Fluvial y Marítimo
(Undersecretariat of Air, River, and Maritime
Transport)
Hipólito Yrigoyen 250
1310 Buenos Aires
Tel: (1) 349-7205   Fax: (1) 342-6365

Administración General de Puertos
(General Administration of Ports)
Av. Julio A. Roca 734/42
1067 Buenos Aires
Tel: (1) 34-5744, 34-5334   Tlx: 21879

**Ministerio de Relaciones Exteriores, Comercio
Internacional y Culto**
(Ministry of Foreign Affairs, International Trade, and
Cults)
Reconquista 1088
1003 Buenos Aires
Tel: (1) 331-0071/9, 312-1775, 312-3434
Fax: (1) 312-3593, 312-3423   Tlx: 21194
WWW home page: http://www.mrec.ar
WWW home page: http://www.ar/

Secretaría de Relaciones Económicas Internacionales
(Secretariat of International Economic Relations)
Reconquista 1088
1003 Buenos Aires
Tel: (1) 331-7281, 331-4073   Fax: (1) 312-0965

Fundación Exportar
(Trade Information and Opportunities)
Reconquista 1098
1003 Buenos Aires
Tel: (1) 315-4125   Fax: (1) 311-4334

Ministerio de Defensa
(Ministry of Defense)
Av. Paseo Colón 255
1063 Buenos Aires
Tel: (1) 343-1561/9   Tlx: 22200

Ministerio de Salud Pública y Acción Social
(Ministry of Public Health and Social Action)
Av. 9 de Julio 1925
1332 Buenos Aires
Tel: (1) 381-8911, 381-8949

Subsecretaría de Atención Médica y Fiscalización
Sanitaria
(Undersecretariat of Medical and Sanitary Inspection)
9 de Julio 1925, Piso 10, Of. 1003
1332 Buenos Aires
Tel: (1) 383-4814   Fax: (1) 381-8912

Ministerio de Cultura y Educación
(Ministry of Culture and Education)
Pizzurno 935
1020 Buenos Aires
Tel: (1) 424-4551/9, 445-666, 448-410   Tlx: 22646

Ministerio de Justicia
(Ministry of Justice)
Av. Gral. Gelly y Obes 2289, Piso 7
1425 Buenos Aires
Tel: (1) 803-4051/3, 803-5453   Fax: (1) 803-3955

Corte Suprema de Justicia
(Supreme Court)
Talcahauno 550, Piso 4
1013 Buenos Aires
Tel: (1) 401-540   Fax: (1) 402-270

Ministerio del Interior
(Ministry of the Interior)
Balcarce 50
1064 Buenos Aires
Tel: (1) 342-6081, 343-0880

Subsecretaría de Seguridad Interior
Undersecretary of Interior Security
Balcarce 50, P.B.
1064 Buenos Aires
Tel: (1) 342-9440 x579   Fax: (1) 331-7051

Ministerio de Trabajo y Seguridad Social
(Ministry of Labor and Social Security)
Av. L.N. Alem 650
1001 Buenos Aires
Tel: (1) 311-3303, 311-2945

Other Government Agencies and Institutes

Banco Central de la República Argentina (BCRA)
(Central Bank of the Argentine Republic)
Reconquista 266
1003 Buenos Aires
Tel: (1) 394-8411, 394-8119, 393-0021
Fax: (1) 334-6489, 334-6468, 325-4860   Tlx: 1137

Banco de la Nación Argentina (BNA)
(Bank of the Argentine Nation)
Bartolomé Mitre 326
1036 Buenos Aires
Tel: (1) 343-1011, 343-1021   Fax: (1) 331-8745

Consejo Federal de Inversiones
(Federal Board of Investment)
San Martín 871
1004 Buenos Aires
Tel: (1) 313-5557   Fax: (1) 313-4486   Tlx: 21180

Dirección de Desarrollo Minero
(Administration of Mining Development)
Av. Julio A. Roca 561, Piso 8
1322 Buenos Aires
Tel: (1) 349-3133

Dirección de Mercado de Productos no Tradicionales
(Administration of Markets of Non-Traditional
Products)
Paseo Colón 922
Buenos Aires
Tel: (1) 362-1738 y 349-2280/2   Fax: (1) 349-2280

Dirección de Mercados Agricolas y Agroindustriales
(Administration of Agricultural and Agroindustrial
Markets)
Paseo Colón 922, Piso 1, Of. 131
1063 Buenos Aires
Tel: (1) 349-2272/4
Fax: (1) 349-2272

Dirección de Mercados Ganaderos
(Administration of Livestock Markets)
Paseo Colón 922
1063 Buenos Aires
Tel: (1) 349-2287, 349-2294   Fax: (1) 362-5144

Dirección de Producción Forestal
(Administration of Forestry Production)
Av. Paseo Colón 982, Piso 1
1063 Buenos Aires
Tel: (1) 349-2101, 349-2103   Fax: (1) 349-2108

Dirección de Recursos Geológicos y Mineros
(Administration of Geological and Mining Resources)
Julio A. Roca 651, Piso 8
1322 Buenos Aires
Tel: (1) 349-3131

Dirección de Recursos Forestales Nativos
(Administration of Native Forestry Resources)
San Martin 459, Piso 2
1004 Buenos Aires
Tel: (1) 394-1869, 394-5961 x8-489

Dirección de Recursos Ictícolas y Acuícolas
(Administration of Fish and Marine Resources)
San Martin 459, Piso 2
1004 Buenos Aires
Tel: (1) 394-1869, 394-5961 x8557

Dirección Nacional de Combustibles
(National Administration of Fuels)
Av. Paseo Colón 171, Piso 6, Of. 620
1063 Buenos Aires
Tel: (1) 349-8030/1

Dirección Nacional de Pesca y Acuicultura
(National Administration of Fishing and Aquaculture)
Av. Paseo Colón 982, Anexo Jardin, Piso 1
1063 Buenos Aires
Tel: (1) 349-2330/1   Fax: (1) 349-2332

Inspección General de Justicia (IGJ)
(Office of the Inspector General of Justice)
San Martín 665
1004 Buenos Aires
Tel: (1) 312-2427, 373-7609

Instituto Argentino de Sanidad y Calidad Vegetal
(IASCAV)
(Argentine Institute of Plant Sanitation and Quality)
Av. Paseo Colón 982
1063 Buenos Aires
Tel: (1) 343-8311

Instituto Argentino del Petróleo
(Argentine Petroleum Institute)
Maipú 645, Piso 3, Primer Cuerpo
Buenos Aires
Tel: (1) 322-3233, 322-3652, 322-3244   Fax: (1) 322-3233

Instituto Forestal Nacional (IFONA)
(National Forestry Institute)
Julio A. Roca 651, Piso 7
1067 Buenos Aires
Tel: (1) 303-444   Tlx: 21535

Instituto Nacional de Tecnología Industrial (INTI)
(National Institute of Industrial Technology)
Av. L.N. Alem 1067, Piso 7
1001 Buenos Aires
Tel: (1) 313-3013

Instituto Nacional de Tecnología Minería (INTEMIN)
(National Institute of Mining Technology)
Parque Tecnológico Migueletes
Casilla de Correo 327
1650 San Martín
Tel: (1) 754-5151, 754-4141   Fax: (1) 754-4070, 754-8307

Instituto Nacional de Vitivinicultura
(National Viticulture Institute)
A. Julio A. Roca 651, Piso 5, Of. 22
1067 Buenos Aires
Tel/Fax: (1) 343-3846

Junta Nacional de Granos
(National Grain Board)
Av. Paseo Colón 359
1063 Buenos Aires
Tel: (1) 300-641   Tlx: 21793

Instituto Petroquímico Argentino
(Argentine Petrochemical Institute)
Av. Santa Fe 1480, Piso 5
Buenos Aires
Tel: (1) 813-3436, 813-6636   Fax: (1) 813-3436

Secretaría de Turismo
(Secretariat of Tourism)
Presidencia de la Nación
Suipacha 1111, Piso 21
1360 Buenos Aires
Tel: (1) 312-5624, 311-2089   Fax: (1) 313-6834

Servicio Geológico
(Geological Service)
Av. Julio A. Roca 651
1322 Buenos Aires
Tel: (1) 541-3160/2

EMBASSIES AND TRADE OFFICES OF ARGENTINA

Algeria
Embassy in Algeria
7 rue Hamami, 5ème étage
16000 Algiers, Algeria
Tel: [213] (2) 71-8683, 71-8684, 73-1392 (Trade Office)
Fax: [213] (2) 64-3843 (Trade Office)

Australia
Embassy in Australia
MLC Tower, Suite 102
Woden, ACT 2606, Australia
Tel: [61] (62) 82-4555, 82-4855, 82-4855
Fax: [61] (62) 85-3062   Tlx: 67485

Trade Office in Sydney
1 York St., Suite 195
Sydney, NSW 2000, Australia
Tel: [61] (2) 241-1571/2   Fax: [61] (2) 251-4963

Austria
Embassy in Austria
Goldschmiedgasse 2/1
1010 Vienna, Austria
Tel: [43] (1) 533-8463, 533-8577, 533-5171   Tlx: 114512

Belgium
Embassy in Belgium
Avenue Louise 225, B.P. 6
1050 Brussels, Belgium
Tel: [32] (2) 647-7812, 647-9002, 647-9319, 649-0380
(Trade Office)
Fax: [32] (2) 647-9319, 642-9187 (Trade Office)
Tlx: 23079

Bolivia
Embassy in Bolivia
Aspiazu 497, esq. Sánchez
Casilla 64
4677 La Paz, Bolivia
Tel: [591] (2) 32-2172, 37-0335, 32-3511 (Trade Office)
Fax: [591] (2) 647-9319, 39-1046 (Trade Office)
Tlx: 3300

Brazil
Embassy in Brazil
SEPN, Av. W-3 Quadra 513
Bloco D., Edif. Imperador, 4 andar
70442 Brasilia, DF, Brazil
Tel: [55] (61) 273-3737   Tlx: 1013

Trade Office in Brasilia
Shis QL 02 conjunto 01, casa 19
71600 Lago Sul, DF, Brazil
Tel: [55] (61) 328-1198   Fax: [55] (61) 248-1158

Bulgaria
Embassy in Bulgaria
42 Klement Gotvald Blvd.
PO Box 635
1504 Sofia, Bulgaria
Tel: [359] (2) 44-3821/2, 44-1327   Tlx: 23218

Canada
Embassy in Canada
90 Sparks St., Suite 620
Ottawa, ON KIP 5B4, Canada
Tel: [1] (613) 236-2351/4
Fax: [1] (613) 235-2659   Tlx: 053-4293

Trade Office in Ottawa
151 Slater St., Suite 400
Ottawa, ON K1P 5H3, Canada
Tel: [1] (613) 236-9431/2   Fax: [1] (613) 563-7925

Chile
Embassy in Chile
Miraflores 285
Casilla 9867
Santaigo de Chile, Chile
Tel: [56] (2) 639-8617, 638-0890, 633-1076
Fax: [56] (2) 639-3321   Tlx: 24028

Trade Office in Santiago
Ahumada 341, Piso 5
Santiago, Chile
Tel: [56] (2) 639-3653, 639-7464
Fax: [56] (2) 639-3653

China
Embassy in China
11, San Li Tun Dong Lu
Beijing 100060, PRC
Tel: [86] (1) 532-2090, 532-1406, 532-2281
Trade Office Tel: [86] (1) 532-2354, 532-2875
Fax: [86] (1) 532-2319, 532-2875 (Trade Office)

Colombia
Embassy in Colombia
Av. 40A, No. 13-09, Piso 16
Ap. Aéreo 53013
Santa Fe de Bogotá, DC, Colombia
Tel: [57] (1) 288-0900, 285-6342 (Trade Office)
Fax: [57] (1) 285-5794 (Trade Office)   Tlx: 41203

Costa Rica
Embassy in Costa Rica
Calle 27, Av. Central
Apdo. 1963
San José, Costa Rica
Tel: [506] 21-3438, 21-6869, 23-8742
Fax: [506] 23-8742   Tlx: 2117

Trade Office in San José
Av. 3, Calle 3, Piso 4
San José, Costa Rica
Tel: [506] 22-1657, 33-7949   Fax: [506] 55-3204

Cuba
Embassy in Cuba
Calle 36, No. 511
Miramar, Havana, Cuba
Tel: [53] (7) 22-5540, 22-5540/9 (Trade Office)
Fax: [53] (7) 33-2140, 22-7712 (Trade Office)
Tlx: 511138

Czech Republic
Embassy in the Czech Republic
Washingtonova 25
125 22 Prague 1, Czech Rep.
Tel: [42] (2) 223-803/4, 260-320
Fax: [42] (2) 536-501   Tlx: 121847

Trade Office in Prague
Sokolska 29
12000 Prague 2, Czech Rep.
Tel: [42] (2) 293-939, 297-017
Fax: [42] (2) 232-0878

Denmark
Embassy in Denmark
Store Kogensgade 45
1264 Copenhagen K, Denmark
Tel: [45] 33-15-80-82, 33-15-55-74
Fax: [45] 33-15-55-74   Tlx: 27182

Trade Office in Copenhagen
Kastelsvej 15, 1st Fl.
2100 Copenhagen, Denmark
Tel: [45] 31-38-52-11
Fax: [45] 32-56-81-77

Dominican Republic
Embassy in the Dominican Republic
Av. Máximo Gómez 10
Santo Domingo, Dominican Rep.
Tel: [1] (809) 682-0976, 682-2977
Fax: [1] (809) 686-5626   Tlx: 3 460154

Ecuador
Embassy in Ecuador
Amazonas 477, Of. 501 al 509
Apdo. 2937
Quito, Ecuador
Tel: [593] (2) 562-292 566-760 (Trade Office)
Fax: [593] (2) 568-177   Tlx: 22136

Egypt
Embassy in Egypt
8 Sharia as-Saleh Ayoub
Zamalek, Cairo, Egypt
Tel: [20] (2) 341-6862, 341-7765, 340-1501
Fax: [20] (2) 340-8652

Trade Office in Cairo
17 Brasil St., 8th Fl., Apt. 51
PO Box 247
Dokki Zanalek
Cairo, Egypt
Tel: [20] (2) 340-9241   Fax: [20] (2) 340-8652

El Salvador
Embassy in El Salvador
79 Av. Norte 704
Col. Escalón
Apdo. 01-384
San Salvador, El Salvador
Tel: [503] 24-4238, 23-3494, 24-2006
Fax: [503] 79-1333

Finland
Embassy in Finland
Bulevardi 10A-14
00120 Helsinki, Finland
Tel: [358] (0) 60-5249, 60-7630   Tlx: 122794

France
Embassy in France
6 rue Cimarosa
75116 Paris, France
Tel: [33] (1) 45-53-33-00, 43-53-14-69
Fax: [33] (1) 45-53-46-33   Tlx: 645427, 613819, 61158

Trade Office in Paris
2 rue de Sfax
75116 Paris, France
Tel: [33] (1) 45-01-24-55   Fax: [33] (1) 40-67-98-09

Gabon
Embassy in Gabon
BP 4065
Libreville, Gabon
Tel: [241] 73-0216, 73-0105, 74-0549
Fax: [241] 73-1629   Tlx: 5611

Germany
Embassy in Federal Republic of Germany
Adenauerallee 50-52
53113 Bonn, Germany
Tel: [49] (228) 228-010/8, 223-973 (Trade Office)
Fax: [49] (228) 228-0130, 220-277 (Trade Office)

Trade Office in Hamburg
Mittelweg 141
20148 Hamburg, Germany
Tel: [49] (40) 441-807-31

Greece
Embassy in Greece
59 Leof Vassilissis Sophia
Athens 140, Greece
Tel: [30] (1) 72-24-753, 72-24-710, 72-24-158
Fax: [30] (1) 72-27-568

Guatemala
Embassy in Guatemala
2a. Av. 11-04, Apdo. 112
01010 Guatemala City, C.A., Guatemala
Tel: [502] (2) 31-4969, 31-9684, 36-2419
Fax: [502] (2) 32-1654   Tlx: 5285

Haiti
Embassy in Haiti
Impasse Géraud, 20 Bourdon
Port-au-Prince, Haiti
Tel: [509] (1) 45-6180, 45-6881, 22-2063   Tlx: 0176

Honduras
Embassy in Honduras
2 Cuadras al sur del Cenaculo
Apdo. 101-C
Tegucigalpa, Honduras
Tel: [504] 32-3376, 32-3274
Fax: [504] 31-0376   Tlx: 1120

Hong Kong
Consulate General in Hong Kong
2510 Jardine House
Connaught Road
Central, Hong Kong
Tel: [852] 2523-3208, 2523-3251
Fax: [852] 2877-0906   Tlx: 70759

Hungary
Embassy in Hungary
Rippl-Rónai u. 1
1068 Budapest, Hungary
Tel: [36] (1) 115-1094, 115-5213, 122-8467
Fax: [36] (1) 135-959   Tlx: 224128

India
Embassy in India
B-8/9 Vasant Vihar, Paschimi Marg.
New Delhi 110 057, India
Tel: [91] (11) 67-1345, 67-1348, 688-2029
Fax: [91] (11) 317-2373

Indonesia
Embassy in Indonesia
Jalan Duren Ban Ka 22
Jakarta 12730, Indonesia
Tel: [62] (21) 33-8088, 33-3090
Fax: [62] (21) 33-6148   Tlx: 69151

Trade Office in Jakarta
Jalan Lembang Tesuran D 57
Jakarta 10310, Indonesia
Tel: [62] (21) 33-6214   Fax: [62] (21) 33-6148

Iran
Embassy in Iran
7 Argentine Square
Alitalia Building, 4th Floor
PO Box 15875-4335
Tehran, Iran
Tel: [98] (21) 626-244, 628-294
Fax: [98] (21) 622-583

Ireland
Embassy in Ireland
15 Ailesbury Drive
Dublin 4, Ireland
Tel: [353] (1) 269-4603, 269-1546, 269-4713
Tlx: 527-1150

Israel
Embassy in Israel
112 Rehov Hayarkon, 2nd Fl.
63571 Tel Aviv, Israel
Tel: [972] (3) 527-1313/4, 527-1413
Fax: [972] (3) 527-1150   Tlx: 33730

Trade Office in Tel Aviv
Beit Silver, 7th Fl.
Aba Hillel Silver
Ramat Ban
61291 Tel Aviv, Israel
Tel: [972] (3) 661-647/9   Fax: [972] (3) 572-1150

Italy
Embassy in Italy
Piazza dell'Esquilino 2
00185 Rome, Italy
Tel: [39] (6) 474-2551/5, 487-1422
Fax: [39] (6) 481-9787   Tlx: 610386

Trade Office in Rome
Piazza della Rotondo 2, 3 Piano
00186 Rome, Italy
Tel: [39] (6) 687-7022   Fax: [39] (6) 686-1745

Trade Office in Milan
Centro Cooper
Internazionale Largo Africa 1
20145 Milan, Italy
Tel: [39] (2) 481-4927   Fax: [39] (2) 481-3753

Jamaica
Embassy in Jamaica
Dyoll Building, 6th Fl.
40 Knutsford Boulevard
PO Box 119
Kingston 5, Jamaica
Tel: [1] (809) 926-2496, 926-5588, 926-0580
Fax: [1] (809) 926-4296   Tlx: 3812107

Japan
Embassy in Japan
120-1 Moto Azabu 2-chome
Minato-ku
Tokyo, Japan
Tel: [81] (3) 5420-7101/5

Trade Office in Tokyo
Chiyoda House, 6th Fl.
17-8 Nagatcho 2-chome
Chiyoda-ku
Tokyo 100, Japan
Tel: [81] (3) 3593-1280   Fax: [81] (3) 3593-1282

Kenya
Embassy in Kenya
PO Box 30283
Nairobi, Kenya
Tel: [254] (2) 33-5242, 33-9949
Fax: [254] (2) 21-7693   Tlx: 22544

Trade Office in Nairobi
Caxton House, 1st Fl.
Standard St.
PO Box 59716
Nairobi, Kenya
Tel: [254] (2) 24-380, 33-8222   Fax: [254] (2) 72-3564

Korea (South)
Embassy in South Korea
135-53, Itaewon-dong, Yongsan-ku
CPO Box 3889
Seoul 140, Rep. of Korea
Tel: [82] (2) 793-4062, 797-0636
Fax: [82] (2) 792-5820   Tlx: 80124329

Trade Office in Seoul
Namsong Building, Room 202
260-199, Itaewong-dong, Yongsan-ku
PO Box 9276
Seoul, Rep. of Korea
Tel: [82] (2) 795-1145   Fax: [82] (2) 795-5903

Lebanon
Embassy in Lebanon
PO Box 166604
5th Fl., rue de l'Eglise Mar Takla
Hazmieh, Beirut, Lebanon
Tel: [961] (1) 428-960/1, 453-442   Tlx: 43423

Libya
Embassy in Libya
PO Box 932
Tripoli, Libya
Tel: [218] (21) 72160, 70586, 70597   Tlx: 20190

Malaysia
Embassy in Malaysia
3 Jalan Semantan 2
PO Box 11200
50738 Kuala Lumpur, Malaysia
Tel: [60] (3) 255-0176 255-2564
Fax: [60] (3) 255-2706   Tlx: 31854

Morocco
Embassy in Morocco
12 rue Mekki Bitaouri
Souissi, Rabat, Morocco
Tel: [212] (7) 75-5120, 75-4182, 75-5410
Fax: [212] (7) 55410   Tlx: 31017

Trade Office in Morocco
3 Zankat al Yanboua, 2eme etage
Rabat, Morocco
Tel: [212] (7) 75-1293   Fax: [212] (7) 75-1301

Mexico
Embassy in Mexico
Edificio Plaza Comermex, Piso 7
Boulevard M. Avila Camacho 1
Col. Lomas de Chapultepec
11000 México, DF, México
Tel: [52] (5) 520-3412, 520-9430/2, 540-4867
Consulate Tel: [52] (5) 540-0320, 540-7801, 540-5011,
540-4194 (Trade Office)
Fax: [52] (5) 540-5011, 520-4192 (Trade Office)
Tlx: 1774214

Netherlands
Embassy in the Netherlands
Javastraat 20
The Hague, Netherlands
Tel: [31] (70) 365-4836/7   Fax: [31] (70) 392-4900

Trade Office in Amsterdam
Catshuvel 85
2517 The Hague, Netherlands
Tel: [31] (70) 352-2161   Fax: [31] (70) 352-2741

New Zealand
Consulate General in Auckland
Harbour View Building, 11th Fl.
52 Quay Street
PO Box 2320
Auckland, New Zealand
Tel: [64] (9) 309-1757, 309-1434
Fax: [64] (9) 373-5386

Nicaragua
Embassy in Nicaragua
Pasaje Los Cerros No. 111
Reparto Las Colinas
Managua, Nicaragua
Tel: [505] (2) 74-412, 71-822, 78-4824
Fax: [505] (2) 678-406

Norway
Embassy in Norway
Inkognitogaten 10A
0244 Oslo, Norway
Tel: [47] 22-55-24-48/9
Fax: [47] 22-44-16-41   Tlx: 19261

Pakistan
Embassy in Pakistan
PO Box 1015
Islamabad, Pakistan
Tel: [92] (51) 82-0270, 211-117/8

Panama
Embassy in Panama
Edif. Banco de Iberoamerica, Piso 1
Calles 50 y 53
Panamá 1, Panamá
Tel: [507] 64-6561, 64-6989
Fax: [507] 69-5331   Tlx: 2679

Paraguay
Embassy in Paraguay
Av. España entre Boquerón y Saltos del Guaira
Asunción, Paraguay
Tel: [595] (21) 200-034, 212-320/5, 212-617
Fax: [595] (21) 211-029   Tlx: 22067

Trade Office in Asunción
Benjamin Constant 576, Piso 2
PO Box 757
Asunción, Paraguay
Tel: [595] (21) 212-320/4   Fax: [595] (21) 498-582

Peru
Embassy in Peru
Av. Felipe Pardo y Aliaga 640, Piso 12/15
San Isidro
PO Box 270081
Lima, Perú
Tel: [51] (14) 33-1887, 33-9966
Fax: [51] (14) 33-0769

Trade Office in Lima
27 Choqueuanca
1408 San Isidro
Lima, Perú
Tel: [51] (14) 71-1884   Fax: [51] (14) 71-8358

Philippines
Embassy in the Philippines
ACT Tower, 6th Fl.
135 Sen. Gil J. Puyat Ave.
Salcedo Village, Makati
Metro Manila, Philippines
Tel: [63] (2) 87-5655, 88-6091   Tlx: 64666

Poland
Embassy in Poland
Jana Styki 17/19
03-928 Warsaw, Poland
Tel: [48] (22) 17-6028/9
Fax: [48] (22) 17-7162   Tlx: 812412

Trade Office in Warsaw
Zgoda 6, M 19
00-018 Warsaw, Poland
Tel: [48] (22) 17-6028/9   Fax: [48] (22) 17-7162

Portugal
Embassy in Portugal
Av. João Crisóstomo 8 r/c Esq.
1000 Lisbon, Portugal
Tel: [351] (1) 797-7311, 797-7594
Fax: [351] (1) 797-4702   Tlx: 13611

Trade Office in Lisbon
Av. Antonio A. de Aguiar 88.8
Lisbon, Portugal
Tel: [351] (1) 522-094   Fax: [351] (1) 573-388

Romania
Embassy in Romania
Strada Drobeta 11
70258 Bucarest 2, Romania
Tel: [40] (1) 611-7290, 611-7293   Tlx: 11412

Russian Federation
Embassy in the Russian Federation
Sadova Triunfalnaya ul. 4/10
Moscow, Russian Fed.
Tel: [7] (095) 299-1670, 299-0367, 299-2329
Fax: [7] (095) 200-4218   Tlx: 413259

Trade Office in Moscow
Kutuzovsky Pr. 13, Ky. 125
Moscow, Russian Fed.
Tel: [7] (095) 229-3888   Fax: [7] (095) 200-4218

Saudi Arabia
Embassy in Saudi Arabia
PO Box 94369
Riyadh 11693, Saudi Arabia
Tel: [966] (1) 465-3057, 465-2600, 465-6064,
465-1552/3 (Trade Office)
Fax: [966] (1) 465-1632 (Trade Office)   Tlx: 405988

Senegal
Embassy in Senegal
34-36 Boulevard de la République
BP 3343
Dakar, Senegal
Tel: [221] 21-5171, 22-1136
Fax: [221] 22-1136   Tlx: 51457

Singapore
Embassy in Singapore
Tong Building, Office 15-04
302 Orchard Road
Singapore 0923
Tel: [65] 235-4231, 737-4850
Fax: [65] 235-4382   Tlx: 23714

Trade Office in Singapore
268 Orchard Road 06-05
Singapore 0923
Tel: [65] 734-7811/2, 734-4359
Fax: [65] 734-7947

South Africa
Embassy in South Africa
200 Standard Plaza
0002 Pretoria, Rep. of South Africa
Tel: [27] (12) 433-527, 433-516
Fax: [27] (12) 433-521

Spain
Embassy in Spain
Paseo de la Castellana 53
28046 Madrid, Spain
Tel: [34] (1) 442-4500, 442-4089, 442-4532,
442-8446 (Trade Office)
Fax: [34] (1) 442-3559, 441-0088 (Trade Office)
Tlx: 27415

Consulate General in Barcelona
Paseo de la Gracia 11-B, Piso 2
Barcelona 7, Spain
Tel: [34] (3) 317-5882, 317-4149, 302-2216 (Trade Office)
Fax: [34] (3) 301-9472 (Trade Office)

Consulate General in Las Palmas
Av. Franchi No. 5, Piso 2, Of. 10 y 12
Las Palmas, Spain
Tel: [34] (28) 26-1418, 27-6558

Consulate General in Madrid
Ortega y Gasset 62
Madrid 6, Spain
Tel: [34] (1) 402-5115, 402-5248
Fax: [34] (1) 309-1996

Consulate General in Vigo
Marques de Valladares 5, Piso 3
Apdo. Postal 1520
36201 Vigo, Pontevedra, Spain
Tel: [34] (86) 43-5822, 43-9292
Fax: [34] (86) 43-9292

Sweden
Embassy in Sweden
Grevgatan 5
PO Box 14039
10440 Stockholm, Sweden
Tel: [46] (8) 663-19-65, 661-61-97 (Trade Office)
Fax: [46] (8) 782-9035 (Trade Office)   Tlx: 10029

Switzerland
Embassy in Switzerland
Jungfraustrasse 1
3005 Berne, Switzerland
Tel: [41] (31) 352-3565/6, 443-3566/7
Fax: [41] (31) 352-0519   Tlx: 911286

Trade Office in Berne
Spitalgasse 38, 3eme etage
3011 Berne, Switzerland
Tel: [41] (31) 661-6197, 661-7937
Fax: [41] (31) 227-073

Trade Office in Geneva
Route de l'Aeroport 10
3011 Geneva, Switzerland
Tel: [41] (22) 798-8284   Fax: [41] (22) 798-7282

All addresses and telephone numbers are in Argentina unless otherwise noted. The country code for Argentina is [54].

Syria
Embassy in Syria
Rue Ziad ben Abi Soufian
Coin Fauzill-Ghazza
BP 116
Damascus, Syria
Tel: [963] (11) 33-4167, 33-4168, 33-8192
Tlx: 411058

Taiwan
Commercial Office in Taiwan
International Trade Building, Suite 1003
333 Keelung Road, Sec.1
Taipei, Taiwan ROC
Tel: [886] (2) 757-6556

Thailand
Embassy in Thailand
20/85 Prommitr Villa, Soi 49/1
Bangkok 10110, Thailand
Tel: [66] (2) 259-0401/2
Fax: [66] (2) 259-0402   Tlx: 82762

Tunisia
Embassy in Tunisia
10, rue al-Hassen et Housseine
al-Menzah IV
1004 Tunis, Tunisia
Tel: [216] (1) 237-313, 231-222
Fax: [216] (1) 750-058   Tlx: 13053

Turkey
Embassy in Turkey
Iran Cad. 49/2
Çankaya, Ankara, Turkey
Tel: [90] (312) 446-2061

United Arab Emirates
Embassy in the United Arab Emirates
PO Box 3325
Abu Dhabi, UAE
Tel: [971] (2) 216-838   Tlx: 23998

United Kingdom
Embassy in the United Kingdom
53 Hans Place
London, SW1X OLA, UK
Tel: [44] (171) 584-6494, 589-3104 (Consulate General)
Fax: [44] (171) 589-3106   Tlx: 51913348

Trade Office in London
111 Cadogan Gardens
London SW3 2RQ, UK
Tel: [44] (171) 730-9334   Fax: [44] (171) 823-4943

United States of America
Embassy in the United States of America
1600 New Hampshire Avenue NW
Washington, DC 20009, USA
Tel: [1] (202) 939-6400, 939-6431, 939-6416
Fax: [1] (202) 775-4388

Office of the Argentine Counselor for Economic and
Commercial Affairs
1667 K St., NW
Washington, DC 20006, USA
Tel: [1] (202) 387-2527

Office of the Argentine Financial Representative
1901 L St., NW, Suite 606
Washington DC 20036, USA
Tel: [1] (202) 466-3021   Fax: [1] (202) 463-8793

Consulate General and Trade Office in Atlanta
Cain Tower, Suite 401
229 Peachtree St.
Atlanta GA 30303, USA
Tel: [1] (404) 880-0805   Fax: [1] (404) 880-0806

Consulate and Trade Office in Chicago
205 N. Michigan Ave., Suite 4208/9
Chicago, IL 60601
Tel: [1] (312) 819-2620, 819-2610 (Trade Office)
Fax: [1] (312) 819-2626, 819-2612 (Trade Office)

Consulate and Trade Office in Houston
1990 Post Oak Blvd., Suite 770
Houston, TX 77056, USA
Tel: [1] (713) 871-8935   Fax: [1] (713) 871-0639

Consulate and Trade Office in Los Angeles
5055 Wilshire Blvd. Suite 210
Los Angeles, CA 90036, USA
Tel: [1] (213) 954-9155, 954-9233
Fax: [1] (213) 937-3874, 937-3841

Consulate and Trade Office in Miami
800 Brickell Avenue, Penthouse 1
Miami, FL 33131, USA
Tel: [1] (305) 373-7794   Fax: [1] (305) 371-7108

Argentina National Tourist Office
800 Brickell Avenue, Penthouse 1
Miami, FL 33131, USA
Phone: (305) 373-1889, 373-4705, 358-0530
Fax: (305) 371-7108

Consulate General in New Orleans
World Trade Center, Suite 915
2 Canal St.
New Orleans, LA 70130, USA
Tel: [1] (504) 523-2823   Fax: [1] (504) 523-6660

Consulate General in New York
900 Third Ave., 4th Fl.
New York, NY 10022, USA
Tel: [1] (212) 759-6477/8   Fax: [1] (212) 397-3523

Uruguay
Embassy in Uruguay
Agraciada 3397
Montevideo, Uruguay
Tel: [598] (2) 39-5521, 39-1994, 39-3953
Fax: [598] (2) 35-0364   Tlx: 23863

Trade Office in Montevideo
Andes 1365, Piso 10, Of. 1008/11
Montevideo, Uruguay
Tel: [598] (59) 98-7224   Fax: [598] (59) 98-7154

Venezuela
Embassy in Venezuela
Edif. Fedecamaras, Piso 3
Calle El Empalme
Urb. El Bosque
Caracas, Venezuela
Tel: [58] (2) 731-3311, 731-3058, 731-3159
Fax: [58] (2) 731-2659   Tlx: 28053

Trade Office in Caracas
Torre Lincoln, Piso 9, Of. A
Sabana Grande
PO Box 569
Caracas, Venezuela
Tel: [58] (2) 781-1487, 781-1390
Fax: [58] (2) 781-6342

FOREIGN EMBASSIES IN ARGENTINA

Embassy of Algeria
Montevideo 1889
1021 Buenos Aires
Tel: (1) 815-1271   Fax: (1) 815-8837   Tlx: 22467

Embassy of Australia
Villanueva 1400
1426 Buenos Aires
Tel: (1) 771-5620, 777-6580   Fax: (1) 772-3349

Embassy of Austria
French 3671
1425 Buenos Aires
Tel: (1) 802-7195, 802-1400, 802-7096
Fax: (1) 805-4016   Tlx: 18853

Embassy of Belgium
Defensa 113, Piso 8
1065 Buenos Aires
Tel: (1) 331-0066/9   Fax: (1) 331-0814   Tlx: 22070

Embassy of Bolivia
Corrientes 545, Piso 2
1043 Buenos Aires
Tel: (1) 394-6042, 394-6640
Fax: (1) 322-0371   Tlx: 24362

Embassy of Brazil
Cerrito 1350
1010 Buenos Aires
Tel: (1) 812-0035/9   Fax: (1) 814-4687   Tlx: 21158

Embassy of Bulgaria
Mariscal A.J. de Sucre 1568
1428 Buenos Aires
Tel: (1) 781-8644, 786-6273   Tlx: 21314

Embassy of Canada
Tagle 2828
1425 Buenos Aires
Tel: (1) 805-3032   Fax: (1) 806-1209   Tlx: 21383

Embassy of the Central African Republic
Marcelo T. de Alvear 776
Edificio Charcas
1058 Buenos Aires
Tel: (1) 312-2051/5

Embassy of Chile
Tagle 2762
1425 Buenos Aires
Tel: (1) 802-7020/8   Fax: (1) 804-5927   Tlx: 21669

Embassy of China (People's Republic of)
Crisólogo Larralde 5349
1431 Buenos Aires
Tel: (1) 543-8862, 542-0054
Fax: (1) 953-4208   Tlx: 22871

Embassy of Colombia
Carlos Pellegrini 1363, Piso 3
1011 Buenos Aires
Tel: (1) 325-0494, 325-0258   Fax: (1) 332-9370

Embassy of Costa Rica
Av. Callao 1103, Piso 9, Of. I
Buenos Aires
Tel: (1) 815-8159

Embassy of Côte d'Ivoire
Ugarteche 3069
1425 Buenos Aires
Tel: (1) 802-3982

Embassy of Cuba
Virrey del Pino 1810
1426 Buenos Aires
Tel: (1) 782-9049, 782-9089
Fax: (1) 786-7713

Embassy of the Czech Republic
Figueroa Alcorta 3240
1425 Buenos Aires
Tel: (1) 801-3804   Tlx: 22748

Embassy of Denmark
Av. L.N. Alem 1074, Piso 9
1001 Buenos Aires
Tel: (1) 312-6901   Fax: (1) 312-7857   Tlx: 22173

Embassy of the Dominican Republic
Av. Santa Fe 1206, Piso 2
1059 Buenos Aires
Tel: (1) 811-4669

Embassy of Ecuador
Av. Quintana 585, Piso 9 y 10
1129 Buenos Aires
Tel: (1) 804-0073/4 Fax: (1) 804-0074

Embassy of Egypt
Juez Tedín 2795
1425 Buenos Aires
Tel: (1) 805-3913/6   Fax: (1) 801-6145

Embassy of El Salvador
Av. Santa Fe 846, Piso 12, Of. A
1059 Buenos Aires
Tel: (1) 394-7628   Fax: (1) 311-1864

Embassy of Finland
Av. Santa Fé 846, Piso 5
1059 Buenos Aires
Tel: (1) 312-0600   Fax: (1) 312-0670   Tlx: 21702

Embassy of France
Cerrito 1399
1010 Buenos Aires
Tel: (1) 379-2930   Fax: (1) 393-1235

Embassy of Gabon
Av. Figueroa Alcorta 3221
1425 Buenos Aires
Tel: (1) 801-9840   Fax: (1) 801-9832   Tlx: 18577

Embassy of Germany
Villanueva 1055
1426 Buenos Aires
Tel: (1) 771-5054/9   Fax: (1) 775-9612   Tlx: 21668

Embassy of Greece
Av. Roque Sáenz Peña 547, Piso 4
1035 Buenos Aires
Tel: (1) 342-4958   Fax: (1) 342-2838   Tlx: 22426

Embassy of Guatemala
Sante Fe 830, Piso 5
1059 Buenos Aires
Tel: (1) 313-9160   Fax: (1) 313-9181

Embassy of Haiti
Av. Figueroa Alcorta 3297
1425 Buenos Aires
Tel: (1) 802-0211

Embassy of Honduras
Sante Fe 1385, Piso 4
1059 Buenos Aires
Tel: (1) 813-1643, 813-2800   Fax: (1) 813-4734

Embassy of Hungary
Coronel Díaz 1874
1425 Buenos Aires
Tel: (1) 824-5845   Fax: (1) 805-3918   Tlx: 22843

All addresses and telephone numbers are in Argentina unless otherwise noted. The country code for Argentina is [54].

Embassy of India
Córdoba 950, Piso 4
1054 Buenos Aires
Tel: (1) 393-4001   Fax: (1) 393-4063   Tlx: 23413

Embassy of Indonesia
Mariscal Ramón Castilla 2901
1425 Buenos Aires
Tel: (1) 801-6622   Fax: (1) 802-4448   Tlx: 21781

Embassy of Iran
Av. Figueroa Alcorta 3229
1425 Buenos Aires
Tel: (1) 802-1470   Fax: (1) 805-4409   Tlx: 21288

Embassy of Ireland
Suipacha 1380, Piso 2
1095 Buenos Aires
Tel: (1) 325-8588, 325-0849   Fax: (1) 325-7572

Embassy of Israel
Av. Mayo 701, Piso 10
1084 Buenos Aires
Tel: (1) 342-1465   Fax: (1) 342-5307

Embassy of Italy
Billinghurst 2577
1425 Buenos Aires
Tel: (1) 802-0071/4   Fax: (1) 804-4914   Tlx: 21961

Embassy of Japan
Av. Paseo Colón 275, Piso 9
1063 Buenos Aires
Tel: (1) 334-5203

Embassy of Korea (South)
Av. Libertador 2397
1425 Buenos Aires
Tel: (1) 802-8865, 802-1029

Embassy of Lebanon
Av. Libertador 2354
1425 Buenos Aires
Tel: (1) 802-4492, 802-0466
Fax: (1) 802-2909   Tlx: 22866

Embassy of Libya
Cazadores 2166
1428 Buenos Aires
Tel: (1) 788-3745, 788-3760

Embassy of Malaysia
Villanueva 1040-1048
1462 Buenos Aires
Tel: (1) 776-0504   Fax: (1) 776-0604

Embassy of Mexico
Larrea 1230
1117 Buenos Aires
Tel: (1) 821-7136   Fax: (1) 821-7251

Embassy of Morocco
Mariscal Ramón Castilla 2952
1425 Buenos Aires
Tel: (1) 801-8154   Fax: (1) 802-0136   Tlx: 18161

Embassy of the Netherlands
Av. de Mayo 701, Piso 19
1084 Buenos Aires
Tel: (1) 334-3474   Fax: (1) 334-2717   Tlx: 21824

Embassy of Nicaragua
Av. Corriente 2548, Piso 4, Of. I
1426 Buenos Aires
Tel: (1) 951-3463   Fax: (1) 952-7557

Embassy of Nigeria
Rosales 2674
1636 Olivos, Buenos Aires
Tel: (1) 794-4061   Fax: (1) 790-7564

Embassy of Norway
Esmeralda 909, Piso 3, Of. B
1007 Buenos Aires
Tel: (1) 312-2204, 312-1904   Tlx: 22811

Embassy of Pakistan
3 de Febrero 1326
1426 Buenos Aires
Tel: (1) 786-7398

Embassy of Panama
Av. Santa Fe 1461, Piso 5
1060 Buenos Aires
Tel: (1) 811-1254   Fax: (1) 814-0450

Embassy of Paraguay
Las Heras 2545
1425 Buenos Aires
Tel: (1) 802-3826, 802-0437

Embassy of Peru
Av. Libertador 1720
1425 Buenos Aires
Tel: (1) 802-2000   Fax: (1) 802-5887   Tlx: 17807

Embassy of the Philippines
Juramento 1945
1428 Buenos Aires
Tel: (1) 781-4173/5   Fax: (1) 787-1261

Embassy of Poland
Alejandro María de Aguado 2870
1425 Buenos Aires
Tel: (1) 802-9681/2   Fax: (1) 802-9683

Embassy of Portugal
Córdoba 315, Piso 3
1054 Buenos Aires
Tel: (1) 312-3524   Fax: (1) 311-2586   Tlx: 22736

Embassy of Romania
Arroyo 962-970
1007 Buenos Aires
Tel: (1) 322-8656, 326-5888

Embassy of Russian Federation
Rodriguez Peña 1741
1021 Buenos Aires
Tel: (1) 421-552, 428-039   Tlx: 22147

Embassy of Saudi Arabia
Alejandro María de Aguado 2881
1425 Buenos Aires
Tel: (1) 802-4735, 802-3375   Tlx: 23291

Embassy of Slovakia
Figueroa Alcorta 3240
1425 Buenos Aires
Tel: (1) 801-3804, 801-3917
Fax: (1) 801-4654   Tlx: 22748

Embassy of South Africa
Marcelo T. de Alvear 590, Piso 8
1058 Buenos Aires
Tel: (1) 312-3736

Embassy of Spain
Mariscal Ramón Castilla 2720
1425 Buenos Aires
Tel: (1) 802-6031/3   Fax: (1) 802-0719   Tlx: 21660

Embassy of Sweden
Corrientes 330, Piso 3
1378 Buenos Aires
Tel: (1) 328-3080/9

Embassy of Switzerland
Av. Santa Fe 846, Piso 10
1059 Buenos Aires
Tel: (1) 311-6491/5   Fax: (1) 313-2998   Tlx: 22418

Embassy of Syria
Av. Callao 956
1023 Buenos Aires
Tel: (1) 813-2113, 813-5438

Embassy of Thailand
Virrey del Pino 2458, Piso 6
1426 Buenos Aires
Tel: (1) 785-6504   Fax: (1) 785-6548

Embassy of Turkey
11 de Setiembre 1382
1426 Buenos Aires
Tel: (1) 785-7203, 788-3239   Fax: (1) 784-9179

Embassy of the United Kingdom
Dr. Luis Agote 2412/52
Casilla 2050
1425 Buenos Aires
Tel: (1) 803-7070/1   Fax: (1) 803-1731

Embassy of the United States of America
Av. Colombia 4300
1425 Buenos Aires
Tel: (1) 777-0197, 775-4205
Fax: (1) 775-4205, 777-0673

Embassy of Uruguay
Av. Las Heras 1907
1127 Buenos Aires
Tel: (1) 803-6030/9   Fax: (1) 803-6038   Tlx: 25526

Embassy of Venezuela
Virrey Loreto 2035
1428 Buenos Aires
Tel: (1) 544-2618   Fax: (1) 544-6704

Embassy of Yugoslavia
Marcelo T. de Alvear 1705
1060 Buenos Aires
Tel: (1) 811-2860, 812-9133
Fax: (1) 812-1070   Tlx: 21479

Embassy of Zaire
Ituzaingó 915, Piso 5
1272 Buenos Aires
Tel: (1) 303-0751

TRADE ORGANIZATIONS

GENERAL BUSINESS AND TRADE ORGANIZATIONS

Asociación de Dirigentes de Empresas
(Association of Company Leaders)
Paraguay 1338, Piso 2
1057 Buenos Aires
Tel: (1) 811-6735

Asociación de Importadores y Exportadores de la
República Argentina
(Association of Importers and Exporters)
Av. Belgrano 124, Piso 1
1092 Buenos Aires
Tel: (1) 342-0010/9   Fax: (1) 342-1312   Tlx: 25761

Centro de Promoción de Negocios
Bolsa de Comercio de Buenos Aires
(Center for Business Promotion
Buenos Aires Stock Exchange)
Sarmiento 299, Piso 1
1353 Buenos Aires
Tel: (1) 311-5231/4, 313-4812, 313-4544
Fax: (1) 312-9332

Cámara Argentina de Comercio
(Argentine Chamber of Commerce)
Av. L.N. Alem 36, Piso 8
1003 Buenos Aires
Tel: (1) 331-8051/5, 343-9423, 343-7783
Fax: (1) 331-8055   Tlx: 18542

Cámara de Comercio Exterior de Córdoba
(Chamber of Foreign Trade of Córdoba in Buenos
Aires)
Av. Callao 332, P.B.
1022 Buenos Aires
Tel: (1) 374-6912

Cámara de Comercio Exterior de la Federación del
Comercio e Industria
(Chamber of Foreign Trade of the Federation of
Commerce and Industry)
Av. Córdoba 1868
Rosario
Prov. de Santa Fe
Tel: (41) 23896

Cámara de Comercio Exterior del Centro de la
República
(Chamber of Foreign Trade of Central Argentina)
Rosario de Santa Fe 231, Piso 4, Of. 9
5000 Córdoba
Tel: (51) 44-804

Cámara de Comercio Exterior del Centro de la
República
(Chamber of Foreign Trade of Central Argentina)
Av. Callao 332, P.B.
1022 Buenos Aires
Tel: (1) 46-6912

Cámara de Comercio, Industria y Producción de la
República Argentina
(Chamber of Commerce, Industry, and Production)
Florida 1, Piso 4
1005 Buenos Aires
Tel: (1) 342-8252, 331-0813, 343-5638   Fax: (1) 331-9116

Cámara de Consorcios y Cooperativas de Exportación
de la República Argentina
(Chamber of Consortiums and Export Cooperative)
Tte. Gral. Perón 2630, Piso 6
1040 Buenos Aires
Tel: (1) 953-8445, 953-8266, 951-3916
Fax: (1) 953-8445   Tlx: 21420

Cámara de Exportadores de la República Argentina
(Chamber of Exporters)
Av. Roque Sáenz Peña 740, Piso 1
1035 Buenos Aires
Tel: (1) 320-9583, 320-5944, 320-8556
Fax: (1) 328-1003   Tlx: 22910

Cámara de Importadores de la República Argentina
(Chamber of Importers)
Av. Belgrano 427, Piso 7
1092 Buenos Aires
Tel: (1) 342-1101, 342-0523   Fax: (1) 331-9342

Cámara de Sociedades Anónimas
(Corporations)
Florida 1, Piso 3
1005 Buenos Aires
Tel: (1) 342-9013, 342-9225, 342-9272

Consejo Argentino de la Industria
(Argentine Council of Industry)
Piedras 83, Piso 3, Of. E
1070 Buenos Aires
Tel: (1) 343-9977, 208-1032, 208-1398
Fax: (1) 331-2809   Tlx: 17155

Coordinadora de Cámaras de Comercio Exterior del
Interior del Pais (CICATEX)
(Coordinator of Foreign Trade Chambers of the
Provinces)
Callao 332, P.B.
1002 Buenos Aires
Tel/Fax: (1) 46-6912

Foro de Comercio Exterior de la República Argentina
(Forum of Foreign Trade of the Argentine Republic)
Maipú 671, Piso 4
1006 Buenos Aires
Tel: (1) 322-8468   Fax: (1) 322-7813   Tlx: 24247

Fundación Invertir
Bartolomé Mitre 326
Edif. Banco Nación, Piso 1, Of. 109
1036 Buenos Aires
Tel: (1) 342-7723   Fax: (1) 342-7370
*A private organization formed by CEOs of leading
Argentine enterprises and top government officials,
established to promote investments in Argentina of local
and foreign firms; operates in close coordination with the
Undersecretariat for Investment*

Unión Industrial Argentina
(Argentine Industry Association)
Av. L.N. Alem 1067, Piso 10
1001 Buenos Aires
Tel: (1) 313-2012, 313-2512, 313-2561
Fax: (1) 313-2413   Tlx: 21749

World Trade Center Buenos Aires
Moreno 584, Piso 6
1091 Buenos Aires
Tel: (1) 331-3432, 331-2604   Fax: (1) 343-4270

PROVINCIAL FOREIGN TRADE ORGANIZATIONS

Buenos Aires
Subsecretaría de Relaciones Económicas
Internacionales
(Undersecretariat of International Economic Relations)
Calle 12, 53 y 54, Torre II
1900 La Plata
Pcia. de Buenos Aires
Tel: (21) 4-5325, 4-5303   Fax: (21) 25-0141

Córdoba
Secretaría de Comercio Exterior
(Secretariat of Foreign Trade)
Hipólito Yrigoyen 670
5000 Córdoba
Tel: (51) 60-8996, 60-7296, 60-6252   Fax: (51) 69-3483

Mendoza
Dirección de Comercio Exterior
(Directorate of Foreign Trade)
Palacio de Gobierno, Piso 6
5500 Mendoza
Tel: (61) 24-3646, 24-5299, 24-9000   Fax: (61) 24-0385

Salta
Dirección de Comercio Exterior
(Directorate of Foreign Trade)
Alvarado 521, Piso 1
4400 Salta
Tel: (87) 213-3570, 31-1003   Fax: (87) 31-0160

Santa Fe
Subsecretaría de Comercio Exterior
(Undersecretariat of Foreign Trade)
Av. Pellegrini 3100, Piso 1
3000 Santa Fe
Tel: (42) 5-2769, 2-4492   Fax: (42) 5-2769

Tucumán
Dirección de Comercio Exterior
(Directorate of Foreign Trade)
San Martín 469, Piso 4
4000 San Martín de Tucumán
Tel: (81) 21-2369, 22-8373   Fax: (81) 31-0478

FOREIGN BUSINESS ORGANIZATIONS IN ARGENTINA

Asociación Arabe-Argentino-Islámica
(Arab-Argentine-Islamic Association)
Bogotá 3449
1407 Buenos Aires
Tel: (1) 611-2087

Cámara Argentino-Armenia para la Industria y el
Comercio
(Argentine-Armenian Chamber of Commerce)
Av. Santa Fe 969, Piso 2
1059 Buenos Aires
Tel: (1) 393-0101, 393-0151, 393-0334

Cámara de Comercio Arabe-Argentina
(Arab-Argentine Chamber of Commerce)
25 de Mayo 67, Piso 2, Of. 24
1002 Buenos Aires
Tel: (1) 331-6154, 342-1400, 342-5856

Cámara de Comercio Argentino Asiática
(Argentine-Asiatic Chamber of Commerce)
Av. Corrientes 1312, Piso 13
1043 Buenos Aires
Tel: (1) 373-3261, 373-3269

Cámara de Comercio Argentino Centroamericana y
Panameña
(Argentine-Central American and Panamanian
Chamber of Commerce)
Florida 1, Piso 4
1005 Buenos Aires
Tel: (1) 342-8252, 343-5638, 311-0813

Cámara de Comercio Argentino-Austríaca
(Argentine-Austrian Chamber of Commerce)
San Martín 345, Piso 3, Of. 7
1004 Buenos Aires
Tel: (1) 394-2168

Cámara de Comercio Argentino-Boliviana
(Argentine-Bolivian Chamber of Commerce)
25 de Mayo 611, Piso 2
1002 Buenos Aires
Tel: (1) 311-4500, 312-3126

Cámara de Comercio Argentino-Brasileña
(Argentine-Brazilian Chamber of Commerce)
Montevideo 770, Piso 12
1019 Buenos Aires
Tel: (1) 811-4503, 811-4512

Cámara de Comercio Argentino-Británica en la
República Argentina
(Argentine-British Chamber of Commerce)
Av. Corrientes 457, Piso 10
1043 Buenos Aires
Tel: (1) 394-2872, 394-2318, 394-2762

Cámara de Comercio Argentino-Canadiense
(Argentine-Canadian Chamber of Commerce)
Av. L.N. Alem 36, Piso 9
1003 Buenos Aires
Tel: (1) 343-6268, 343-5949, 343-5769

Cámara de Comercio Argentino-Chilena
(Argentine-Chilean Chamber of Commerce)
Viamonte 759, Piso 6, Of. 63
1053 Buenos Aires
Tel: (1) 322-7437

Cámara de Comercio Argentino-Israelita
(Argentine-Israeli Chamber of Commerce)
Av. Corrientes 1312, E.P.
1043 Buenos Aires
Tel: (1) 371-0339, 372-6273

Cámara de Comercio Argentino-Libanesa
(Argentine-Lebanese Chamber of Commerce)
Av. Roque Sáenz Peña 651, Piso 7, Of. 122
1035 Buenos Aires
Tel: (1) 46-6585, 46-7889

Cámara de Comercio Argentino-Mexicana
(Argentine-Mexican Chamber of Commerce)
Marcelo T. de Alvear 976, P.B., Of. D
1058 Buenos Aires
Tel: (1) 312-4408, 343-9748

Cámara de Comercio de los Estados Unidos en
Argentina
(Argentine-US Chamber of Commerce)
Av. L.N. Alem 1110, Piso 13
1001 Buenos Aires
Tel: (1) 311-5420, 311-5126   Fax: (1) 311-9076

Cámara de Comercio Argentino-Arabe
(Argentine-Arab Chamber of Commerce)
Montevideo 513, Piso 6
1019 Buenos Aires
Tel: (1) 372-8167, 371-2561

Cámara de Comercio Argentino-Portuguesa
(Argentine-Portuguese Chamber of Commerce)
San Martín 569, Piso 4
1004 Buenos Aires
Tel: (1) 393-4048, 393-0968

Cámara de Comercio Argentino-Uruguaya
(Argentine-Uruguayan Chamber of Commerce)
Av. Corrientes 545, Piso 3
1043 Buenos Aires
Tel: (1) 394-2709

Cámara de Comercio Argentino-Colombiana
(Argentine-Colombian Chamber of Commerce)
Av. Roque Sáenz Peña 943, Piso 7, Of. 74
1035 Buenos Aires
Tel: (1) 326-0661

Cámara de Comercio Argentino-Ecuatoriana
(Argentine-Ecuadorian Chamber of Commerce)
Lavalle 534, Piso 3
1047 Buenos Aires
Tel: (1) 394-3702, 394-2558

Cámara de Comercio Argentino-Holandesa
(Argentine-Dutch Chamber of Commerce)
Av. de Mayo 701, Piso 19
1084 Buenos Aires
Tel: (1) 334-3247, 342-7329

Cámara de Comercio Belgo-Luxemburguesa en la
República Argentina
(Belgian-Luxembourgian Chamber of Commerce)
San Martín 66, Piso 4
1004 Buenos Aires
Tel: (1) 311-0395

Cámara de Comercio e Industria Franco-Argentina
(French-Argentine Chamber of Commerce)
Bartolomé Mitre 559, Piso 8, Of. 814
1342 Buenos Aires
Tel: (1) 331-6650, 343-2204

Cámara de Comercio e Industria y Turismo Argentino-
Turca
(Argentine-Turkish Chamber of Commerce)
Florida 1, Piso 4
1005 Buenos Aires
Tel: (1) 343-5638

Cámara de Comercio Italiana en la Argentina
(Italian Chamber of Commerce in Argentina)
Marcelo T. de Alvear 1119, Piso 2
1058 Buenos Aires
Tel: (1) 325-0384, 325-5900

Cámara de Comercio Japonesa en la Argentina
(Japanese Chamber of Commerce in Argentina)
Libertad 836, Piso, 2, Of. 38
1012 Buenos Aires
Tel: (1) 325-0288

Cámara de Comercio Suizo-Argentina
(Swiss-Argentine Chamber of Commerce)
Av. L.N. Alem 1074, Piso 10
1001 Buenos Aires
Tel: (1) 311-7187, 311-0253

Cámara de Industria y Comercio Argentino-Alemana
(Argentine-German Chamber of Industry and
Commerce)
Florida 537, Piso 19
1005 Buenos Aires
Tel: (1) 393-5404, 393-9006

All addresses and telephone numbers are in Argentina unless otherwise noted. The country code for Argentina is [54].

Cámara de la Producción, la Industria y el Comercio
Argentino-China
(Argentine-Chinese Chamber of Commerce)
Av. Belgrano 634, Piso 7, Of. A
1092 Buenos Aires
Tel: (1) 342-2639, 343-8677

Cámara Española de Comercio
(Spanish Chamber of Commerce)
Av. Belgrano 836, Piso 8
1092 Buenos Aires
Tel: (1) 342-2509, 342-2335

Cámara Sueca de Comercio
(Swedish Chamber of Commerce)
Tacuarí 147, Piso 4
1071 Buenos Aires
Tel: (1) 334-7103

Cámara de Comercio Argentino-Paraguaya
(Argentine-Paraguayan Chamber of Commerce)
Viamonte 1355, Piso 4, Of. C
1053 Buenos Aires
Tel: (1) 371-9395

Federación Argentina de Cámaras Binacionales
Latinoamericanas
(Federation of Latin-American Binational Chambers)
Av. Roque Sáenz Peña 943, Piso 7
1035 Buenos Aires
Tel: (1) 326-0661

INDUSTRY-SPECIFIC ASSOCIATIONS

Asociación Aeronáutica Argentina
(Aeronautical association)
Bartolomé Mitre 1131, Piso 7, E 2 Cpo.
1036 Buenos Aires
Tel: (1) 381-7154

Asociación Argentina de Acabado de Metales (SADAM)
(Metal finishing)
Medrano 273, Piso 4, Of. C
1178 Buenos Aires
Tel: (1) 983-0525

Asociación Argentina de Cirugía
(Surgery)
Marcelo T. de Alvear 2415
1122 Buenos Aires
Tel: (1) 825-3649, 822-2395

Asociación Argentina de Control Automático
(Automatic control)
Av. Callao 220, Piso 1, Of. B
1022 Buenos Aires
Tel: (1) 372-6746, 46-3780

Asociación Argentina de Criadores de Aves, Conejos,
Abejas
(Poultry, rabbit, and bee breeders)
Av. Rivadavia 2169
1034 Buenos Aires
Tel: (1) 953-6454, 953-3765

Asociación Argentina de Criadores de Cebú
(Zebu breeders)
Av. Córdoba 1525, Piso 6
1055 Buenos Aires
Tel: (1) 42-6071, 42-6224

Asociación Argentina de Criadores de Cerdo
(Swine breeders)
Florida 520, Piso 2, Of. 205
1005 Buenos Aires
Tel: (1) 322-2009

Asociación Argentina de Criadores de Charolais
(Charolais breeders)
Uruguay 469, Piso 10, Of. B
1015 Buenos Aires
Tel: (1) 373-8919

Asociación Argentina de Criadores de Corriedale
(Corriedale breeders)
Av. Roque Sáenz Peña 943, Piso 7, Of. 71
1035 Buenos Aires
Tel: (1) 326-1009, 326-1761

Asociación Argentina de Criadores de Hereford
(Hereford breeders)
M. Obarrio 2948
1425 Buenos Aires
Tel: (1) 802-1019, 802-6864

Asociación Argentina de Criadores de Romney
(Romney breeders)
Montevideo 1745, P.B.
1021 Buenos Aires
Tel: (1) 22-1351

Asociación Argentina de Criadores de Santa Gertrudis
(Saint-Gertrude breeders)
Av. Julio A. Roca 610, Piso 5
1067 Buenos Aires
Tel: (1) 331-6767

Asociación Argentina de Criadores de Shorthorn
(Shorthorn breeders)
Tucumán 994, Piso 5
1049 Buenos Aires
Tel: (1) 326-2212, 326-2225

Asociación Argentina de Empresarios del Transporte
Automotor
(Automotive transportation companies)
Bdo. de Irigoyen 330, Piso 6
1072 Buenos Aires
Tel: (1) 334-3254, 334-3409

Asociación Argentina de Fabricantes de Máquinas,
Herramientas, Accesorios y Afines
(Machinery, tools, and accessories)
Alsina 1609, Piso 6, Of. 33
1088 Buenos Aires
Tel: (1) 476-3833, 322-1050
Fax: (1) 372-5602, 40-6283

Asociación Argentina de Girasol
(Sunflowers)
Av. Corrientes 127, Piso 3
1043 Buenos Aires
Tel: (1) 312-2000, 312-2007

Asociación Argentina de Hormigón Elaborado
(Concrete)
San Martín 1137
1004 Buenos Aires
Tel: (1) 312-3046/8

Asociación Argentina de la Soja
(Soybeans)
Av. Corrientes 127, Piso 3
1043 Buenos Aires
Tel: (1) 312-2000, 312-2007

Asociación Argentina de Preservación del Agua y su
Medio Ambiente
(Water preservation)
Hipólito Yrigoyen 820, Of. 6
1086 Buenos Aires
Tel: (1) 342-6835

Asociación Argentina de Televisión por Cable (ATVC)
(Cable television)
Av. de Mayo 749, Piso 2, Of. 10
1084 Buenos Aires
Tel: (1) 342-3382   Fax: (1) 343-1716

Asociación Civil Argentina de Criadores Fleckvieh
Simmental
(Fleckvieh Simmental breeders)
Esmeralda 582, Piso 5, Of. 15
1007 Buenos Aires
Tel: (1) 393-9161

Asociación Civil Fabricantes de la Industria del
Calzado (ACFIC)
(Shoe industry)
Chilavert 6780, Piso 1
1439 Buenos Aires
Tel: (1) 601-9499

Asociación Cooperativa de Criadores de Caballos de
Pura Sangre
(Purebred horse breeders)
Av. Quintana 191, Piso 2
1014 Buenos Aires
Tel: (1) 815-0034, 815-0136, 815-0435

Asociación Criadores de Caballos Criollos
(Criollo horse breeders)
Larrea 670, Piso 2
1030 Buenos Aires
Tel: (1) 961-2305, 961-3387

Asociación de Clínicas y Sanatorios de la Ciudad de
Buenos Aires
(Clinics and medical centers)
Montevideo 451
1019 Buenos Aires
Tel: (1) 46-1563, 46-2126

Asociación de Cooperativas Hortícolas y
Frutihorticolas Argentinas Cooperativas Limitadas
(Vegetable and fruit cooperatives)
Mercado Central, Piso 3, Of. 332
1761 Villa Celina
Pcia. de Buenos Aires
Tel: (1) 622-1028

Asociación de Distribuidores de Golosinas y Afines
(Candy distributors)
Tte. Gral. J.D. Perón 1610, Piso 2
1037 Buenos Aires
Tel: (1) 382-3350, 382-0780, 382-3218

Asociación de Establecimientos Textiles con Proceso
Industrial
(Textile establishments with industrial processing)
Av. L.N. Alem 1067, Piso 8
1001 Buenos Aires
Tel: (1) 311-0499

Asociación de Fabricantes de Alfombras
(Carpet manufacturers)
Av. L.N. Alem 1067, Piso 8
1001 Buenos Aires
Tel: (1) 311-0499

Asociación de Fabricantes de Cemento Portland
(Portland cement makers)
San Martín 1137
1137 Buenos Aires
Tel: (1) 312-1083, 315-2272   Fax: (1) 312-1700

Asociación de Fabricas Argentinas de Tractores
(Tractor manufacturers)
1015 Buenos Aires
Tel: (1) 49-8573, 49-8590   Fax: (1) 49-8573

Asociación de Fabricas de Automotores (ADEFA)
(Automobile manufacturers)
Marcelo T. de Alvear 636, Piso 5
1058 Buenos Aires
Tel: (1) 312-1306, 312-3483   Fax: (1) 315-2990

Asociación de Fabricantes de Hilos de Coser
(Sewing thread manufacturers)
Av. L.N. Alem 1067, Piso 8
1001 Buenos Aires
Tel: (1) 311-0499

Asociación de Fabricantes de Medias
(Hosiery manufacturers)
Av. L.N. Alem 1067, Piso 8
1001 Buenos Aires
Tel: (1) 311-0499

Asociación de Fabricantes de Tejidos de Algodón
(Cotton fabric manufacturers)
Av. L.N. Alem 1067, Piso 8
1001 Buenos Aires
Tel: (1) 311-0499

Asociación de Fabricantes de Tejidos de Lana
(Wool fabric manufacturers)
Av. L.N. Alem 1067, Piso 8
1001 Buenos Aires
Tel: (1) 311-0499

Asociación de Fabricantes de Tejidos de Lino y
Cáñamo
(Linen and hemp fabrics)
Av. L.N. Alem 1067, Piso 8
1001 Buenos Aires
Tel: (1) 311-0499

Asociación de Fabricantes de Tejidos de Punto
(Knitted fabric manufacturers)
Av. L.N. Alem 1067, Piso 8
1001 Buenos Aires
Tel: (1) 311-0499

Asociación de Ferreterías, Pinturerías y Bazares
(Hardware and paint stores)
1646 Lavalle, Piso 3
Buenos Aires 1048
Tel: (1) 372-6309   Fax: (1) 372-8876

Asociación de Hilanderías de Algodón
(Cotton spinning mills)
Av. L.N. 1067, Piso 8
1001 Buenos Aires
Tel: (1) 311-0499

Asociación de Hoteles de Turismo
(Tourist hotels)
Av. Rivadavia 1157/9, Piso 9, Of. C
1033 Buenos Aires
Tel: (1) 383-2039, 383-1160   Fax: (1) 383-0669

Asociación de Industria Argentina de Carnes
(Meat Industry)
Paraguay 776
1057 Buenos Aires
Tel: (1) 393-8049, 322-0587

Asociación de Industriales Metalúrgicos de la
República Argentina (ADIMRA)
(Metallurgy industries)
Alsina 1609, Pisos 1 y 2
1088 Buenos Aires
Tel: (1) 40-0055, 40-4967, 40-5063, 40-5292, 40-5571
Fax: (1) 814-4407

Asociación de Industriales Textiles Argentinos
(Textile industries)
Uruguay 291, Piso 4
1015 Buenos Aires
Tel: (1) 373-2256, 373-2502, 373-2154

Asociación de la Industria Tintorera, Estampa y Afines
(Dyeing and stamping industry)
Lavalle 1994, Piso 1
1051 Buenos Aires
Tel: (1) 953-2417, 953-1627

Asociación de la Pequeña y Mediana Industria
Electrónica y Eléctrica
(Electronic and electric industry)
Gascón 62
1181 Buenos Aires
Tel: (1) 981-2335

Asociación de Tintorerías de Establecimientos Textiles
(Textile dyeing establishments)
Av. L.N. Alem 1067, Piso 8
1001 Buenos Aires
Tel: (1) 311-0499

Asociación Distribuidores de Dulces y Afines
(Jams and preserves distributors)
Hipólito Yrigoyen 1178
1086 Buenos Aires
Tel: (1) 381-0623, 381-0693, 381-0730

Asociación de Fabricas Argentinas de Terminales
Eléctricas
(Electric terminals)
Av. L.N. Alem 690, Piso 10
1001 Buenos Aires
Tel: (1) 313-2552, 315-3050
Fax: (1) 313-2484

Asociación de Fabricantes de Celulosa y Papel
(Cellulose and paper manufacturers)
Belgrano 2852, Piso 1, Of. 04
1209 Buenos Aires
Tel: (1) 97-0051/4   Fax: (1) 97-0053

Asociación Industrial Artículos de Limpieza, Personal
del Hogar y Afines (ALPHA)
(Personal care products)
Av. L.N. Alem 1067, Piso 12
1001 Buenos Aires
Tel: (1) 312-4605

Asociación Manufacturas de Yute y Fibras Duras
(Jute and hard fibers manufacturers)
Av. L.N. Alem 1067, Piso 8
1001 Buenos Aires
Tel: (1) 311-0499

Asociación Odontológica Argentina
(Dental association)
Junín 959
1113 Buenos Aires
Tel: (1) 961-2377, 961-6062/3   Fax: (1) 961-1110

Asociación Peinadurías e Hilanderías
(Combing and spinning mills)
Av. L.N. Alem 1067, Piso 8
1001 Buenos Aires
Tel: (1) 311-0499

Asociación Productores de Frutas Argentinas
(Fruit producers)
Lavalle 3161 P.B.C.
1190 Buenos Aires
Tel: (1) 862-8333

Asociación Texturizadores de Hilados Sintéticos y
Afines
(Synthetic yarn texturizers)
Av. L.N. Alem 1067, Piso 8
1001 Buenos Aires
Tel: (1) 311-0499

Asociación de la Industria Vitivinícola Argentina
(Wine producers)
Guemes 4464
1425 Buenos Aires
Tel: (1) 774-1887, 774-3370
Fax: (1) 776-2529

Cámara Algodonera Argentina
(Cotton manufacturers)
25 de Mayo 347, Piso 2, Of. 200
1002 Buenos Aires
Tel/Fax: (1) 312-0246

Cámara Argentina de Aserraderos de Madera
(Wood)
Alsina 440
1087 Buenos Aires
Tel: (1) 342-4389

Cámara Argentina de Bebidas sin Alcohol
(Non-alcoholic beverages)
Rivadavia 1823, Piso 3, Of. A
Buenos Aires
Tel: (1) 952-5375 y 953-7982   Fax: (1) 952-5375

Cámara Argentina de Comerciantes e Importadores de
Optica, Fotografía y Afines (CACIOFA)
(Optical and photographic goods)
Pasaje del Carmen 716, Piso 8, Of. A
1019 Buenos Aires
Tel: (1) 383-5399, 812-2751

Cámara Argentina de Consignatarios de Ganado
(Cattle brokers)
Lima 87, Piso 2
1073 Buenos Aires
Tel/Fax: (1) 381-7283, 381-8522, 382-6412, 383-9393

Cámara Argentina de Empresas de Obras de
Saneamiento
(Sanitation work companies)
Piedras 383, Piso 3
1070 Buenos Aires
Tel: (1) 343-1122

Cámara Argentina de Empresas Viales
(Road construction)
Piedras 383, Piso 3
1070 Buenos Aires
Tel/Fax: (1) 343-1122

Cámara Argentina de Especialidades Medicinales
(CAEME)
(Pharmaceutical laboratories)
Av. L.N. Alem 619, Piso 5
Buenos Aires
Tel: (1) 313-0489

Cámara Argentina de Entidades Apícolas
(Apiculture)
Tucumán 1438, Piso 7, Of. 706
1050 Buenos Aires
Tel; (1) 46-7184

Cámara Argentina de Fabricantes de Aberturas
Metálicas y Afines
(Metal door manufacturers)
Luis S. Peña 278
1110 Buenos Aires
Tel: (1) 383-8633, 383-1802

Cámara Argentina de Fabricantes de Acumuladores
(Battery manufacturers)
Av. Pedro Goyena 999
1424 Buenos Aires
Tel: (1) 431-9386

Cámara Argentina de Fabricantes de Envases Metálicos
y Afines
(Metal packaging)
Pedro Goyena 999
1424 Buenos Aires
Tel: (1) 431-9421, 431-9666

Cámara Argentina de Fabricantes de Herramientas e
Instrumentos de Medición
(Measurement tools and instruments)
Alsina 1609, Piso 5, Of. 18
1088 Buenos Aires
Tel: (1) 371-5063, 371-4967, 371-5571

Cámara Argentina de Fabricantes de Lámparas
Eléctricas
(Electric light bulb manufacturers)
Alsina 1607
1088 Buenos Aires
Tel: (1) 371-5063, 371-5571, 371-4967

Cámara Argentina de Fabricantes de Productos
Aromáticos y Afines
(Aromatic products manufactures)
Av. Belgrano 1354
1083 Buenos Aires
Tel: (1) 383-1692, 383-8270

Cámara Argentina de Fabricantes de Rodamientos
(Ball bearing manufacturers)
Alsina 1607
1088 Buenos Aires
Tel: (1) 371-6840

Cámara Argentina de Fabricantes de Vidrios
(Glass manufacturers)
Av. L.N. Alem 1067, Piso 16
1001 Buenos Aires
Tel: (1) 313-0837, 311-7985

Cámara Argentina de Fabricantes Textiles de Artículos
de Limpieza
(Textile cleaning products)
Av. L.N. Alem 1067, Piso 8
1001 Buenos Aires
Tel: (1) 311-0499

Cámara Argentina de Fabricantes, Equipos,
Herramientas e Instrumentos para el Servicio del
Automotor
(Automotive service)
Alsina 1607, Piso 1
1088 Buenos Aires
Tel: (1) 371-5063, 371-5571, 371-4967

Cámara Argentina de Farmacias
(Pharmacies)
Uruguay 60
1015 Buenos Aires
Tel: (1) 381-4141, 381-4945, 381-5213

Cámara Argentina de Ferroaleaciones y Aleaciones
Especiales (CAFAE)
(Iron and special alloys)
Alsina 1607, Piso 1
1088 Buenos Aires
Tel: (1) 371-5063, 371-4967

Cámara Argentina de Gas Natural Comprimido
(Natural compressed gas)
Alsina 1607, Piso 1
1088 Buenos Aires
Tel: (1) 371-5292, 371-0055

Cámara Argentina de Indumentaria para Bebes y Niños
(Baby and children's clothing)
Junín 347, Piso 4, Of. B
1026 Buenos Aires
Tel: (1) 953-9540

Cámara de Industriales de Artefactos para el Hogar
(Housewares)
Paraguay 1855
Buenos Aires
Tel: (1) 813-2673, 812-0232   Fax: (1) 814-2650

Cámara Argentina de Industrias Electrónicas (CADIE)
(Electronic industries)
Bdo. de Irigoyen 330, Piso 5, Of. 121
1072 Buenos Aires
Tel: (1) 334-4159, 334-5752, 334-6672, 334-7763
Fax: (1) 334-6672

Cámara Argentina de Industrias Electromecánicas
(CADIEM)
(Electromechanical industries)
F.D. Roosevelt 2445, Piso 11, Of. C
Buenos Aires
Tel: (1) 788-8502   Fax: (1) 788-8499

Cámara Argentina de la Construcción
(Construction)
Av. Paseo Colón 823
1063 Buenos Aires
Tel/Fax: (1) 361-5036/7, 361-8778

Cámara de la Industria Curtidora Argentina
(Tanning industry)
Av. Belgrano 3978
1210 Buenos Aires
Tel: (1) 981-4393, 983-9623   Fax: (1) 981-5437, 983-8502

Cámara Argentina de la Industria de Autocomponentes
(Car parts industry)
Viamonte 1167, Piso 2
1053 Buenos Aires
Tel: (1) 46-9516, 46-8993

Cámara Argentina de la Industria de Chacinados y
Afines
(Cold meats industry)
Bacacay 2576
1406 Buenos Aires
Tel: (1) 611-3254, 611-7117

Cámara de la Industria de Fibras Manufacturadas
(Manmade fiber industry)
Av. E. Madero 1020, Piso 24
1106 Buenos Aires
Tel: (1) 313-6015   Fax: (1) 319-4258

Cámara Argentina de la Industria de los Oleaginosos
(Oilseeds industry)
Piedras 83
1070 Buenos Aires
Tel: (1) 342-5728

Cámara Argentina de la Industria de Luminarias,
Equipos, Complementos y Afines
(Lighting industry)
Alsina 1607
1088 Buenos Aires
Tel: (1) 371-5063, 371-5571, 371-4967

Cámara Argentina de la Industria de Productos de Higiene y Tocador
(Personal care and toilet products)
Paraguay 1857
1121 Buenos Aires
Tel: (1) 42-5925

Cámara Argentina de la Industria del Aluminio, Metales y Afines
(Aluminum, metals, and related activities)
Paraná 467, Piso 1, Of. 3 y 4
1017 Buenos Aires
Tel: (1) 40-1987, 371-1987, 371-4301

Cámara Argentina de la Industria del Calzado
(Shoe industry)
Av. Rivadavia 4323
1205 Buenos Aires
Tel: (1) 981-0732, 981-2303, 981-5992
Fax: (1) 981-3203

Cámara de la Industria del Petroleo
(Petroleum industry)
Av. Madero 1020, Piso 11
1106 Buenos Aires
Tel: (1) 312-0410, 312-0898, 312-9418   Fax: (1) 312-0898

Cámara Argentina de la Industria Frigorífica
(Meat processing industry)
Lavalle 710
1047 Buenos Aires
Tel: (1) 322-6131, 393-5579

Cámara Argentina de la Industria Plástica
(Plastic industry)
J. Salguero 1939/41
1425 Buenos Aires
Tel: (1) 826-6060, 826-8498   Fax: (1) 826-5480

Cámara Argentina de la Industrial del Juguete
(Toys)
Cochabamba 4067
1262 Buenos Aires
Tel: (1) 922-1537, 922-0169   Fax: (1) 312-3699

Cámara Argentina de la Máquina Herramienta
(Machine tools)
Av. Julio A. Roca 516, Piso 3
1067 Buenos Aires
Tel: (1) 343-1493, 343-3996, 343-9476
Fax: (1) 343-3996

Cámara Argentina de Lubricantes
(Lubricants)
Alsina 943, Piso 6, Of. 603
1088 Buenos Aires
Tel: (1) 334-6328, 334-7832

Cámara Argentina de Papelerías, Librerías y Afines
(Stationery stores and bookstores)
Uruguay 196, Piso 8
1015 Buenos Aires
Tel: (1) 373-2563, 373-1787

Cámara Argentina de Papeles y Afines
(Paper and related products)
Carlos Calvo 1247
1102 Buenos Aires
Tel: (1) 27-5671

Cámara Argentina de Productores Avícolas
(Poultry producers)
Bouchard 454, Piso 6
1106 Buenos Aires
Tel: (1) 312-2000/9, 313-5666 x333, x334
Fax: (1) 312

Cámara Argentina de Productores de Drogas Farmacéuticas (CAPDROFAR)
(Pharmaceutical drug producers)
Carlos Pellegrini 465, Piso 11, Of. 84
Buenos Aires
Tel: (1) 326-6209

Cámara Argentina de Productos de Envases Flexibles
(Flexible packing)
Bacacay 1789
1405 Buenos Aires
Tel: (1) 825-4120   Fax: (1) 205-2276

Cámara Argentina de Productos Químicos (CAPQ)
(Chemical products)
Rodriguez Peña 426, Piso 3
1020 Buenos Aires
Tel: (1) 476-0534

Cámara Argentina de Supermercados
(Supermarkets)
Viamonte 342, Piso 3
1053 Buenos Aires
Tel: (1) 313-1812, 313-1822, 313-1835
Fax: (1) 313-1897

Cámara Argentina de Telefonía y Afines (CATYA)
Av. Paseo Colón 588, Piso 5
1063 Buenos Aires
Tel: (1) 30-8853, 30-7956

Cámara Argentina del Café
(Coffee)
Sgo. del Estero 508
1075 Buenos Aires
Tel: (1) 383-3037, 381-6199

Cámara Argentina del Libro
(Book publishers)
Av. Belgrano 1580, Piso 6
1093 Buenos Aires
Tel: (1) 381-8383, 381-9277, 381-9253

Cámara Argentina de Aviación
(Aviation)
Casilla de Correo 40
1611 Don Torcuato
Pcia. de Buenos Aires
Tel: (1) 748-0471, 748-1685

Cámara de Aceites Vegetables y Subproductos
(Vegetable oils and by-products)
Tucumán 637
1049 Buenos Aires
Tel: (1) 322-7908

Cámara de Armadores, Pescadores, Congeladores de Argentina (CAPECA)
(Outfitting, fishing, and freezing companies)
Tucumán 731, Piso 3, Of. E
1049 Buenos Aires
Tel: (1) 322-1031

Cámara de Ascensores y Afines
(Elevator manufacturers)
Av. L.N. Alem 1067, Piso 13
1001 Buenos Aires
Tel: (1) 313-0837

Cámara de Centros de Servicios Metalúrgicos
(Metallurgy service centers)
Alsina 1607, Piso 1
1088 Buenos Aires
Tel: (1) 371-5063, 371-5571

Cámara de Construcciónes Metálicas Estructurales
(Metallic structures)
Alsina 1607
1008 Buenos Aires
Tel: (1) 371-5063, 371-5571, 371-4967

Cámara de Convertidores de Papel y Fabricantes de
Artículos de Librería
(Paper converters and stationery manufacturers)
Alsina 2178, P.B., Of. A
1090 Buenos Aires
Tel: (1) 951-3001, 951-9021/5

Cámara de Elaboradores de Alambre y sus Derivados
(Wire manufacturers)
Alsina 1607
1088 Buenos Aires
Tel: (1) 371-5063, 371-5571

Cámara de Empresarios Madereros y Afines (CEMA)
(Lumber)
Maza 578, Piso 5
1220 Buenos Aires
Tel: (1) 954-1111, 954-2046
Fax: (1) 97-1556

Cámara de Empresarios Yeseros y Anexos
(Gypsum companies)
Hipólito Yrigoyen 2326
1089 Buenos Aires
Tel: (1) 951-8888

Cámara de Empresas de Obras Ferroviarias y Vias de
Comunicación
(Railway works and communication networks
companies)
Av. Córdoba 890, Piso 3
1054 Buenos Aires
Tel: (1) 322-0555, 322-6453

Cámara de Empresas de Software y Servicios
Informáticos (CESSI)
(Software companies)
Tucumán 1427
1050 Buenos Aires
Tel: (1) 373-0813, 371-1549

Cámara de Empresas Pavimentadoras Argentinas
(Paving companies)
Piedras 383
1070 Buenos Aires
Tel: (1) 342-1122

Cámara de Empresas Petroleras Argentinas
(Oil companies)
Av. L.N. Alem 1067, Piso 2
1001 Buenos Aires
Tel: (1) 313-1544, 313-2589
Fax: (1) 313-1544

Cámara de Entidades de Diagnóstico
(Diagnostic imaging)
R.S. Peña 565, Piso 4
1020 Buenos Aries
Tel: (1) 374-4061   Fax: (1) 374-4096

Cámara de Envases de Cartulina
(Cardboard packaging)
Ramón Falcón 1657
1406 Buenos Aires
Tel: (1) 631-5120, 632-2397, 632-7138

Cámara de Equipamiento Hospitalario de Fabricantes
Argentinos
(Hospital equipment manufacturers)
Alsina 1607
1088 Buenos Aires
Tel: (1) 371-5063, 371-5571, 371-4967

Cámara de Fabricantes de Bulones, Tornillos, Tuercas
y Afines
(Bolts, screws and related products)
Alsina 1607
1088 Buenos Aires
Tel: (1) 371-5063, 371-5571

Cámara de Fabricantes de Caños y Tubos de Acero
(Steel pipe and tube manufacturers)
Alsina 1607
1088 Buenos Aires
Tel: (1) 371-5063, 371-5571

Cámara de Fabricantes de Detergentes
(Detergent manufacturers)
Av. L.N. Alem 1067, Piso 12
1001 Buenos Aires
Tel: (1) 312-4605

Cámara de Fabricantes de Enlozados Sobre Chapa de
Hierro y Afines
(Enameled iron plate and related products)
Alsina 1607
1088 Buenos Aires
Tel: (1) 371-5063, 371-6840

Cámara de Fabricantes de Envases de Acero
(Steel packaging products)
Alsina 1607
1088 Buenos Aires
Tel: (1) 371-5063, 371-5571

Cámara de Fabricantes de Equipos y Máquinas de
Oficina
(Office equipment manufacturers)
Alsina 1607, Piso 1
1088 Buenos Aires
Tel: (1) 371-5063, 371-5055, 371-5071

Cámara de Fabricantes de Grifería Sanitaria de la
República Argentina
(Sanitation faucet manufacturers)
Lavalle 1447, Piso 2, Of. E
1048 Buenos Aires
Tel: (1) 46-2336, 46-0521

Cámara de Fabricantes de Insecticidas y Afines
(Insecticides)
Av. L.N. Alem 1067, Piso 14
1001 Buenos Aires
Tel: (1) 311-7732, 313-1059

Cámara de Fabricantes de Máquinas de Herramientas
Portatiles y Afines
(Power tool manufacturers)
Alsina 1607, Piso 1
1088 Buenos Aires
Tel: (1) 371-5063, 371-5571, 371-6840

Cámara de Fabricantes de Máquinas Para Coser y Tejer
(Sewing and knitting machines)
Alsina 1607
1088 Buenos Aires
Tel: (1) 371-5182, 371-6840

Cámara de Fabricantes de Máquinas Viales
(Road construction machinery)
Alsina 1607
1088 Buenos Aires
Tel: (1) 371-5182, 371-6840

All addresses and telephone numbers are in Argentina unless otherwise noted. The country code for Argentina is [54].

Cámara de Fabricantes de Máquinas y Equipos para la Industria
(Machinery and equipment for industry)
Alsina 1607, Piso 12
1088 Buenos Aires
Tel: (1) 371-5063, 371-6640

Cámara de Fabricantes de Muebles, Tapicerias y Afines (CAFYDMA)
(Furniture and rug manufacturers)
Manuel Ricardo Trelles 1961/87
1416 Buenos Aires
Tel: (1) 583-5606/7   Fax: (1) 583-5608

Cámara de Fabricantes de Papel Tissue
(Tissue paper)
Av. Belgrano 2852
1209 Buenos Aires
Tel: (1) 971-0051/3

Cámara de Fabricantes de Puntillas, Encajes y Afines
(Lace and related products)
Av. L.N. Alem 1067, Piso 8
1001 Buenos Aires
Tel: (1) 311-0499

Cámara de Fabricantes de Refrescos y Afines
(Refreshments manufacturers)
Av. L.N. Alem 734, Piso 7
1001 Buenos Aires
Tel: (1) 311-4271, 311-2882

Cámara de Fabricantes de Tejidos Elásticos
(Elastic fabric manufacturers)
Av. L.N. Alem 1067, Piso 8
1001 Buenos Aires
Tel: (1) 311-0499

Cámara de Fondos Comunes de Inversión
(Investment funds)
Sarmiento 299, Piso 4, Of. 429
1353 Buenos Aires
Tel: (1) 312-4490, 311-5231, 311-5233

Cámara de Industriales Cítricos de la Argentina
(Citrus industries)
Florida 140, Piso 4
1005 Buenos Aires
Tel: (1) 326-9673

Cámara de Industriales Ferroviarios de la República Argentina
(Railway industries)
Alsina 1607, Piso 1
1088 Buenos Aires
Tel: (1) 371-5063, 371-5571, 371-6840

Cámara de Informática y Telecomunicaciones de la República Argentina (CICOMRA)
(Computers and telecommunications)
Av. Córdoba 744, Piso 2, Of. D
1054 Buenos Aires
Tel: (1) 393-7352, 325-8839   Fax: (1) 325-9604

Cámara de Inversores en Valores Mobiliarios
(Securities industry)
25 de Mayo 347, Esc. 627
1005 Buenos Aires
Tel: (1) 311-5231

Cámara de la Industria Aceitera de la República Argentina (CIARA)
(Edible oil industry)
Tucumán 637, Piso 6
1049 Buenos Aires
Tel: (1) 322-3990, 322-7908, 393-8322   Fax: (1) 393-7685

Cámara de la Industria Cervecera Argentina
(Breweries)
Av. Roque Sáenz Peña 637, Piso 5
1393 Buenos Aires
Tel: (1) 362-5767, 326-0125
Fax: (1) 326-5767

Cámara de la Industria Cinematográfica Argentina
(Cinematography)
Av. Callao 157, Piso 8
1022 Buenos Aires
Tel: (1) 40-1378, 476-4148

Cámara de la Industria de la Pintura
(Paint industry)
Av. L.N. Alem 1067, Piso 13
1001 Buenos Aires
Tel: (1) 313-0064, 313-7083

Cámara de la Industria Tabacalera
(Tobacco industry)
Reconquista 656, Piso 3
1003 Buenos Aires
Tel: (1) 313-7705/8, 312-8207
Fax: (1) 312-8205

Cámara de la Industria Química y Petroquímica
(Chemical and petrochemical industries)
Av. L.N. Alem 1067, Piso 14, Of. 58
1001 Buenos Aires
Tel: (1) 311-7732, 313-0944, 313-1059
Fax: (1) 312-4773

Cámara de la Pequeña y Mediana Industria Metalúrgica
(Metallurgy industry)
Av. L.N. Alem 1067, Piso 14
1001 Buenos Aires
Tel: (1) 311-6555, 313-0638

Cámara de Productores de Metales
(Metal producers)
Alsina 1607, Piso 1
1088 Buenos Aires
Tel: (1) 371-5571, 371-4967

Cámara de Sanidad Agropecuaria y Fertilizantes
(Livestock health and fertilizer safety)
Av. Rivadavia 1367, Piso 7, Of. B
1033 Buenos Aires
Tel: (1) 381-2742, 381-6418, 383-0942   Fax: (1) 383-1562

Cámara de Sub-Productos Ganaderos
(Livestock farming by-products)
25 de Mayo 347, Piso 6, Of. 635
1002 Buenos Aires
Tel: (1) 311-4229

Cámara del Forjado (CAFOR)
(Forging)
Alsina 1607, Piso 1
1088 Buenos Aires
Tel: (1) 371-5571, 371-6840, 371-5063

Cámara Empresaria de Piezas de Goma Para Automotores
(Rubber parts for automobiles)
Av. L.N. Alem 1067, Piso 16
1001 Buenos Aires
Tel: (1) 313-2140, 313-2192

Cámara Empresaria de Pinturas y Revestimientos Afines de la República
(Paint and wallpaper manufacturing companies)
Yatay 444
1184 Buenos Aires
Tel: (1) 981-6256, 982-0965

Cámara Industrial de Fabricantes de Autopiezas
(CIFARA)
(Autoparts manufacturers)
Viamonte 1393
1053 Buenos Aires
Tel: (1) 49-5784, 49-6029, 49-6889   Fax: (1) 49-6724

Cámara Industrial Argentina de la Indumentaria
(Apparel industry)
Av. L.N. Alem 1067, Piso 13, Of. 41
1001 Buenos Aires
Tel: (1) 313-6006, 313-6107
Fax: (1) 313-6206

Cámara Industrial de la Seda y de las Fibras Sintéticas
(Silk and synthetic fiber industries)
Av. L.N. Alem 1067, Piso 8
1001 Buenos Aires
Tel: (1) 311-0499

Cámara Industrial de las Manufacturas del Cuero y
Afines de la República Argentina (CIMA)
(Leather manufacturers)
Bernardo de Irigoyen 972, Piso 5
1034 Buenos Aires
Tel: (1) 304-5116, 27-1860   Fax: (1) 304-9448

Cámara Industrial de Productos Alimenticios
(Food products)
Av. L.N. Alem 1067, Piso 12
1001 Buenos Aires
Tel: (1) 312-1929, 312-3508   Fax: (1) 312-1929, 312-3508

Cámara Industrial del Deporte y Afines (CAMIDA)
(Apparel)
Alsina 1433, Piso 7, Of. B
1088 Buenos Aires
Fax: (1) 381-4757

Cámara Industrial Marroquinera Argentina
(Leather goods industry)
Bdo. de Irigoyen 972, Piso 5
1072 Buenos Aires
Tel: (1) 27-1860, 304-9448, 304-5116

Centro Argentino de Ingenieros
(Engineers)
Cerrito 1250
1010 Buenos Aires
Tel: (1) 811-0570

Centro Azucarero Argentino
(Sugar industry)
Reconquista 336, Piso 12
Buenos Aires
Tel: (1) 394-0257, 394-0358, 394-0459   Fax: (1) 322-9358

Centro de Arquitectos y Constructores
(Architects and building contractors)
Tucumán 1539
1050 Buenos Aires
Tel: (1) 46-2664

Centro de Exportadores de Cereales
(Cereal exporters)
Bouchard 454, Piso 7
1106 Buenos Aires
Tel: (1) 311-1697, 311-4627, 312-6924

Centro de Industriales Siderúrgicos
(Iron and steel industries)
Paulea 226, Piso 2
1001 Buenos Aires
Tel: (1) 311-6367, 311-6321/2   Fax: (1) 311-6367

Centro Industrial de Peletería
(Fur industry)
Paraguay 1359, Piso 5, Of. A
1057 Buenos Aires
Tel: (1) 812-1820

Centro Industrial de Laboratorios Farmacéuticos
Argentinos (CILFA)
(Pharmaceutical laboratories)
Esmeralda 130, Piso 5
1035 Buenos Aires
Tel: (1) 394-2963, 394-2978, 394-2981

Centro Marítimo de Armadores Argentinos
(Shipowners)
Av. R.S. Peña 547, Piso 8
1035 Buenos Aires
Tel: (1) 343-4332, 343-2850

Confederación Argentina de Clínicas, Sanatorios y
Hospitales Privados
(Clinics, medical centers, and hospitals)
Tucumán 1668
1055 Buenos Aires
Tel: (1) 372-5762   Fax: (1) 372-5915

Confederación Farmacéutica Argentina
(Pharmaceuticals confederation)
Alsina 655, Piso 2
1087 Buenos Aires
Tel: (1) 343-5632

Confederación Intercooperativa Agropecuaria
(Con.In.Agro)
(Agricultural confederation)
Lavalle 348, Piso 4
1306 Buenos Aires
Tel: (1) 311-4664, 311-1579, 312-6767

Confederación Médica de la República Argentina
(Medical confederation)
Av. Belgrano 1235
1093 Buenos Aires
Tel: (1) 383-5511, 383-9195, 383-8467

Confederaciones Rurales Argentinas
(Rural confederation)
México 628
1100 Buenos Aires
Tel: (1) 361-1501, 361-3343

Consejo Profesional de Ingeniería de
Telecomunicaciones, Electrónica y Computación
(Telecommuications, electronics, and computer
engineers)
Perú 562
1068 Buenos Aires
Tel: (1) 30-8407, 30-8423, 34-6291, 34-7289

Cooperativa de Laboratorios Argentinos de
Especialidades Médicas
(Pharmaceutical laboratories)
Mendez de Andes 24
1405 Buenos Aires
Tel: (1) 982-4637, 982-8963

Federación Argentina de Fabricantes de Abrasivos
(Abrasives manufactures)
Av. L.N. Alem 1067
1001 Buenos Aires
Tel: (1) 313-7544

Federación Argentina de Industriales de la Sanidad
(Health industries)
Av. Belgrano 1354
1093 Buenos Aires
Tel: (1) 383-8270, 383-1692, 381-8381

Federación Argentina de la Construcción
(Construction)
Piedras 383, Piso 3
1070 Buenos Aires
Tel: (1) 343-1122

Federación Argentina de la Industria Molinera
(Milling industry)
Bouchard 454, Piso 6
1106 Buenos Aires
Tel: (1) 311-0898, 312-8717, 313-4185   Fax: (1) 313-4185

Federación de Industriales del Jabón y Afines
(Soap and related products)
Av. L.N. Alem 1067
1001 Buenos Aires
Tel: (1) 312-4605

Federación Industriales Textiles Argentinos (FITA)
(Textile industries)
Av. L.N. Alem 1067, Piso 8
1001 Buenos Aires
Tel: (1) 311-0499, 311-0599, 311-6899, 311-7776, 313-4497
Fax: (1) 311-7602

Federación de la Industria Licorista
(Liquor industry)
Av. L.N. Alem 734, Piso 7
1001 Buenos Aires
Tel: (1) 311-2882, 311-4271

Federación de la Industria del Caucho
(Rubber)
Av. L.N. Alem 1067, Piso 16
1001 Buenos Aires
Tel: (1) 313-2009, 313-2140, 313-2192   Fax: (1) 312-9892

Instituto Argentino del Envase
(Packaging)
Av. Jujuy 425
1083 Buenos Aires
Tel: (1) 957-0968   Fax: (1) 956-1368

Sociedad Argentina de Apicultores
(Apiculturists)
Av. Rivadavia 717, Piso 8
1002 Buenos Aires
Tel: (1) 343-8171

Sociedad de Informática e Investigaciones Operativas
(Data processing and operative research)
Uruguay 252
1015 Buenos Aires
Tel: (1) 476-3950, 371-5755

Sociedad Rural Argentina
(Ranchers)
Florida 460
1005 Buenos Aires
Tel: (1) 322-2030, 322-3431, 322-2070   Fax: (1) 325-8231

Unión Argentina de la Construcción
(Construction)
Av. L.N. Alem 896, Piso 6
1001 Buenos Aires
Tel: (1) 311-2864, 311-2739, 311-2692

Unión Minera Argentina
(Mining)
Av. Roque S. Peña 615, Piso 4
1393 Buenos Aires
Tel: (1) 394-7369

FINANCIAL INSTITUTIONS

BANKS

Central Bank

Banco Central de la República Argentina (BCRA)
Reconquista 266
1003 Buenos Aires
Tel: (1) 394-8411, 394-8119, 393-0021
Fax: (1) 334-6489, 334-6468, 325-4860   Tlx: 1137

Commercial Banks

Banco de Crédito Argentino
Reconquista 40
1003 Buenos Aires
Tel: (1) 334-7261, 334-5673   Fax: (1) 342-4970, 334-8089

Banco de Galicia y Buenos Aires
Juan D. Perón 407
1038 Buenos Aires
Tel: (1) 394-7080, 394-7291
Fax: (1) 393-1602, 325-8886   Tlx: 23906

Banco de la Ciudad de Buenos Aires
Sarmiento 611
1041 Buenos Aires
Tel: (1) 325-5811   Fax: (1) 325-2098   Tlx: 22365

Banco de la Nación Argentina
Bartolomé Mitre 326
1036 Buenos Aires
Tel: (1) 342-4041, 343-1011   Fax: (1) 334-8700, 331-8745

Banco de la Provincia de Buenos Aires
San Martín 137
1004 Buenos Aires
Tel: (1) 331-2561/9, 331-4001   Fax: (1) 331-5154

Banco del Sud
Alsina 153
Bahía Blanca
Pcia. Buenos Aires
Tel: (91) 32047   Tlx: 81763

Banco Francés del Río de la Plata
Reconquista 199
1003 Buenos Aires
Tel: (1) 343-1797, 331-7071   Fax: (1) 334-6269, 953-8009

Banco General de Negocios
Esmeralda 120
Buenos Aires
Tel: (1) 322-1644

Banco Mercantil Argentino
Avda Corrientes 629
1324 Buenos Aires
Tel: (1) 334-9999, 334-1212
Fax: (1) 325-7707   Tlx: 9122

Banco Quilmes
Juan D. Perón 564, Piso 2
1038 Buenos Aires
Tel: (1) 331-8111   Fax: (1) 334-5235   Tlx: 18955

Banco Río
Bartolomé Mitre 480
1036 Buenos Aires
Tel: (1) 331-6627, 331-4978, 331-0555   Fax: (1) 331-6513

Banco Roberts
25 de Mayo 258
1002 Buenos Aires
Tel: (1) 342-0061, 342-6009   Fax: (1) 334-6405

Banco Velox
San Martín 298
1004 Buenos Aires
Tel: (1) 394-0123, 394-0115, 394-0777
Fax: (1) 393-7672, 394-8255

Other National Banks

Banco Hipotecario Nacional
Defensa 192
1065 Buenos Aires
Tel: (1) 331-2778   Fax: (1) 334-9743
Mortgage bank

Banco Nacional de Desarrollo
25 de Mayo 145
1002 Buenos Aires
Tel: (1) 331-2091   Fax: (1) 334-9315   Tlx: 9179
Development bank

Bankers' Associations

Asociación de Bancos de la República Argentina (ABRA)
Reconquista 458, Piso 2
1358 Buenos Aires
Tel: (1) 394-6452   Fax: (1) 322-9642   Tlx: 28165

Asociación de Bancos de Provincia de la República
Argentina (ABAPRA)
Florida 470, Piso 1
1005 Buenos Aires
Tel: (1) 322-6321   Fax: (1) 322-6721   Tlx: 24015

Asociación de Bancos del Interior de la República
Argentina (ABIRA)
Corrientes 538, Piso 4
1043 Buenos Aires
Tel: (1) 394-3439   Fax: (1) 394-5682   Tlx: 28273

Asociación de Bancos Argentinos (ADEBA)
San Martín 229, Piso 10
1004 Buenos Aires
Tel: (1) 394-1430   Fax: (1) 394-6340   Tlx: 23704

Federación de Bancos Cooperativos de la República
Argentina (FEBANCOOP)
Maipú 374, Piso 9, 10
1006 Buenos Aires
Tel: (1) 394-9949   Tlx: 23650

Foreign Banks

American Express Bank Ltd. S.A. (USA)
Arenales 707
1061 Buenos Aires
Tel: (1) 312-0900, 312-1661   Fax: (1) 315-1866

Banca de Roma SPA (Italy)
Maipú 267, Piso 19
1084 Buenos Aires
Tel: (1) 326-2145, 326-4626

Banco Bamerindus do Brasil S.A.(Brazil)
Reconquista 144, Piso 1
1003 Buenos Aires
Tel: (1) 331-1945   Fax: (1) 342-2737

Banco Credit Lyonnais Argentina (France)
Bartolomé Mitre 531
1036 Buenos Aires
Tel: (1) 343-7841, 343-7855   Fax: (1) 331-6435

Banco do Brasil S.A. (Brazil)
Sarmiento 487
1041 Buenos Aires
Tel: (1) 394-9273/4, 394-9480   Fax: (1) 394-9577

Banco Español de Crédito (Banesto) (Spain)
Carlos Pellegrini 1163, Piso 10
1009 Buenos Aires
Tel: (1) 394-5412, 394-5437, 394-4895
Fax (1) 331-6100

Banco Europeo para América Latina S.A. (BEAL)
(Belgium)
Tte. Gral. Juan de Perón 338
1038 Buenos Aires
Tel: (1) 342-7081/9   Fax: (1) 331-8190

Banco Exterior S.A. Argentina (Spain)
Av. Corrientes 441/7
1317 Buenos Aires
Tel: (1) 325-9703, 325-9707, 322-9676   Fax: (1) 325-8309

Banco Holandés Unido (Netherlands)
Florida 361
1005 Buenos Aires
Tel: (1) 394-1022, 394-4192, 394-4282   Fax: (1) 322-0603

Banco Santander S.A. (Spain)
Bartolomé Mitre 575
1036 Buenos Aires
Tel: (1) 334-4871, 331-2525   Fax: (1) 331-3583

Bank of America NT&SA (USA)
Maipú 264, Piso 13
1084 Buenos Aires
Tel: (1) 325-0073   Fax: (1) 325-0067

Bank of Boston (USA)
Florida 99
1005 Buenos Aires
Tel: (1) 342-3051, 342-3061   Fax: (1) 342-8489, 343-7303

Bank of New York S.A. (USA)
25 de Mayo 199
1002 Buenos Aires
Tel: (1) 331-3199, 331-8021/2   Fax: (1) 342-1974

Bankers Trust Río de la Plata S.A.C.F. (USA)
San Martín 140, Piso 15
1004 Buenos Aires
Tel: (1) 331-7724   Fax: (1) 331-7735

Banque Nationale de Paris (France)
25 de Mayo 471
1002 Buenos Aires
Tel: (1) 311-5111, 311-5161   Fax: (1) 311-1368

Chase Manhattan Bank N.A. (USA)
Arenales 707, Piso 5
1061 Buenos Aires
Tel: (1) 319-2487   Fax: (1) 319-2414

Chemical Bank (USA)
Av. L.N. Alem 1110
1001 Buenos Aires
Tel: (1) 312-1767   Fax: (1) 313-4356

Citibank, N.A. (USA)
Bartolomé Mitre 530
1036 Buenos Aires
Tel: (1) 329-1122, 329-1669, 329-1000
Fax: (1) 329-1004, 331-8180

Continental Bank N.A. (USA)
25 de Mayo 537
1002 Buenos Aires
Tel: (1) 313-0334   Fax: (1) 313-0476

Deutsche Bank AG (Germany)
Bartolomé Mitre 401
1036 Buenos Aires
Tel: (1) 343-2510, 343-2519, 343-2541   Fax: (1) 334-2006

Dresdner Bank AG (Germany)
Av. Corrientes 311, Piso 11
1043 Buenos Aires
Tel: (1) 312-8959, 312-9606, 312-4016   Fax: (1) 311-8388

Indosuez Argentina S.A. (France)
Reconquista 1166, Piso 12
1003 Buenos Aires
Tel: (1) 313-5910, 313-4460   Fax: (1) 313-5400

ING Bank (Netherlands)
25 de Mayo 140, Piso 8
1002 Buenos Aires
Tel: (1) 331-5904   Fax: (1) 331-8609

Lloyds Bank Ltd. (UK)
Reconquista 101/151
1003 Buenos Aires
Tel: (1) 343-0361, 343-0309, 343-7281   Fax: (1) 342-7487

Morgan Guaranty Trust Company of New York (USA)
Av. Corrientes 411
1043 Buenos Aires
Tel: (1) 325-8046, 325-8052, 345-8056   Fax: (1) 325-8046

Republic National Bank of New York (USA)
Bartolomé Mitre 343
1036 Buenos Aires
Tel: (1) 343-0161, 343-0179   Fax: (1) 331-6064

Swiss Bank Corporation (Switzerland)
25 de Mayo 555, Piso 15
1002 Buenos Aires
Tel: (1) 313-3361   Fax: (1) 313-3662

The Bank of Tokyo Limited (Japan)
Corrientes 420
1043 Buenos Aires
Tel: (1) 322-7087, 322-7277, 322-5118   Fax: (1) 322-6607

Banco de la Nación
Overseas Offices

Bolivia
Av. 16 de Julio 1486
La Paz, Bolivia
Tel: [591] (2) 35-9211/4   Tlx: 2282, 2501

Brazil
Av. Río Branco 134-A
Río de Janeiro, Brazil
Tel: [55] (21) 252-2026, 252-0201
Tlx: 2123673, 21311101

Av. Paulista 2319
01310 São Paulo, Brazil
Tel: [55] (11) 280-6748, 280-2388, 280-2095
Tlx: 1123615, 1132591

Chile
Morandé 223/239
Santiago, Chile
Tel: [56] (2) 71-2045, 71-2111, 71-2203
Tlx: 340637, 240968

France
3 rue Freycinet
75116 Paris, France
Tel: [33] (1) 40-70-09-38, 40-70-08-16
Tlx: 644297

Germany
Bockenheimer Landstrasse 51/53, 12th Fl.
Frankfurt am Main, Germany
Tel: [49] (69) 726094/5   Tlx: 416301

Italy
Vía di Sant'Andrea Delle Fratte 24
00187 Rome, Italy
Tel: [39] (2) 679-6309

Japan
Yarakucho Denki Building, 14th Fl
Yarakucho 1-Chome, Chiyoda-ku
Tokyo 100, Japan
Tel: [81] (3) 3213-7351/3   Tlx: 222-4018

Panama
Av. Federico Boyd y Av. 3 A
Sur Bella Vista
PO Box 63298
Estafeta el Dorado, Panamá
Tel: [507] 69-4666, 69-1796, 63-8868/9
Tlx: 3440, 02995, 2438

Paraguay
Palma y Chile
Asunción, Paraguay
Tel: [595] (21) 447-433-448-566   Tlx: 157 PY

Spain
José Ortega y Gasset 20
Madrid, Spain
Tel: [34] (1) 576-3703/5, 576-3858,   Tlx: 49242, 23749

United Kingdom
Longbow House
14-20 Criswell St.
London EC1 Y4TD, UK
Tel: [44] (171) 588-2738, 588-3949, 588-3945
Tlx: 883950

United States of America
299 Park Ave.
New York, NY 10017, USA
Tel: [1] (212) 303-0600

777 Brickell Ave, Suite 802
Miami, FL 33131, USA
Tel: [1] (305) 374-3006

Uruguay
Juan C. Gómez 1372
Montevideo, Uruguay
Tel: [598] (2) 960078   Tlx: 22489

STOCKS AND COMMODITIES

Associations and Government Agencies

Banco de Valores S.A.
Sarmiento 310, Piso 9
1041 Buenos Aires
Tel: (1) 343-6836

Cámara de Agentes de Bolsa de la Ciudad
de Buenos Aires
Sarmiento 299, Piso 3, Of. 329
1353 Buenos Aires
Tel: (1) 311-1174

Cámara de Fondos Comunes de Inversión
Sarmiento 299, Piso 4, Of. 429
1353 Buenos Aires
Tel: (1) 312-4490, 311-5231, 311-5233

Cámara de Inversores en Valores Mobiliarios
25 de Mayo 347, Esc. 627
1005 Buenos Aires
Tel: (1) 311-5231

Cámara de Sociedades Anónimas
Florida 1, Piso 3
1005 Buenos Aires
Tel: (1) 342-9013, 342-9225, 342-9272

Comisión Nacional de Valores (CNV)
(National Securities Commission)
25 de Mayo 175
1002 Buenos Aires
Tel: (1) 345-2887 to 2897

Stock and Commodity Exchanges

Bolsa de Cereales de Buenos Aires
Corrientes 127
1043 Buenos Aires
Tel: (1) 312-2000/9, 311-9540

Bolsa de Comercio de Bahía Blanca S.A.
19 de Mayo 271
8000 Bahía Blanca
Tel: (91) 40496, 38285   Fax: (91) 29749   Tlx: 81-664

Bolsa de Comercio de Buenos Aires
(Buenos Aires Stock Exchange)
Sarmiento 299, Piso 1
1353 Buenos Aires
Tel: (1) 311-5231/3, 311-1174, 313-4812
Fax: (1) 312-9332

Bolsa de Comercio de Córdoba
Rosario de Santa Fe 231/43
5000 Córdoba
Tel: (51) 224230, 226550
Tlx: 051774 MODULAR

Bolsa de Comercio de Corrientes
Carlos Pellegrini 1101
3400 Corrientes

Bolsa de Comercio de Entre Ríos S.A.
Urquiza 645
3100 Paraná
Pcia. de Entre Ríos
Tel: (43) 21-3702

Bolsa de Comercio de La Plata
Calle 48 No. 515
1900 La Plata
Tel: (21) 21-4773, 21-8375, 21-7202

Bolsa de Comercio de Mar del Plata
Corrientes 1723, Piso 1
7600 Mar del Plata
Tel: (23) 4-8221, 3-0401
Fax: (23) 2-9579   Tlx: 39821

Bolsa de Comercio de Mendoza S.A.
Sarmiento 199, esq. España
5500 Mendoza
Tel: (61) 23-1937, 23-2489, 23-1650, 23-1203
Tlx: 55231

Bolsa de Comercio de Misiones S.A.
Colón 1628, P.B. y Piso 1
3300 Posadas
Pcia. de Misiones
Tel: (752) 3-2364, 3-2856
Fax: (752) 3-3199   Tlx: 76148

Bolsa de Comercio de Río Negro S.A.
Av. Roca 1281
8332 Gral. Roca
Pcia. de Río Negro
Tel: (941) 2-7558, 2-5667
Fax: (941) 2-7310   Tlx: 85500

Bolsa de Comercio de Rosario
Córdoba 1402, esq. Corrientes
2000 Rosario
Pcia. de Santa Fe
Tel: (41) 21-0043, 21-3470/2, 67544
Fax: (41) 241019   Tlx: 41824, 41894

Bolsa de Comercio de San Juan S.A.
Gral. Acha 278 Sur, esq. I. de la Rosa
San Juan
Tel: (64) 21-4711, 21-4752, 21-4813
Fax: (64) 214813   Tlx: 59139

Bolsa de Comercio de Santa Fé
San Martín 2231
3000 Santa Fe
Tel: (42) 4-0092, 2-5983, 2-4741   Tlx: 048123

Caja de Valores S.A.
Sarmiento 299, Piso 1
1353 Buenos Aires
Tel: (1) 312-6446, 312-6465, 312-8866

Mercado a Término de Buenos Aires S.A.
Bouchard 454, Piso 4
1106 Buenos Aires
Tel: (1) 311-9541

Mercado de Futuros y Opciones S.A.
Sarmiento 299, Piso 4, Of. 458
1353 Buenos Aires
Tel: (1) 312-5141, 312-3679, 311-1541   Fax: (1) 311-1541

Mercado de Valores de Buenos Aires S.A.
25 de Mayo 359, Piso 8, 9 y 10
1002 Buenos Aires
Tel: (1) 311-1174

Mercado de Valores de Córdoba S.A.
Rosario de Santa Fe 235
5000 Córdoba
Tel: (51) 21622, 42827, 37357   Fax: (51) 42827

Mercado de Valores de La Plata S.A.
Calle 48, Piso N 515/17
1900 La Plata
Tel: (21) 25-5033
Fax: (21) 7202, 3-9542, 4-8993   Tlx: 31250

Mercado de Valores de Mendoza S.A.
Paseo Sarmiento 165
5500 Mendoza
Tel: (61) 23-1460, 23-1937
Fax: (61) 31-0074   Tlx: 55-231

Mercado de Valores de Rosario S.A.
Córdoba 1402, esq. Corrientes
2000 Rosario
Pcia. de Santa Fé
Tel: (41) 21-0043, 21-0125, 21-3470   Tlx: 041-824

Nueva Bolsa de Comercio de Tucumán S.A.
Maipú 70 (Suc. Centro Bco. Municipal)
4000 S.M. de Tucumán
Tel/Fax: (81) 31-1942/3   Tlx: 61276

Brokerage Houses

B.A. Brokers Sociedad de Bolsa S.A.
San Martín 439, Piso 11
Buenos Aires
Tel: (1) 326-9866, 326-9863, 394-5645

B.C.P. Bursatil Sociedad de Bolsa S.A.
San Martín 569, Piso 3, Of. F
Buenos Aires
Tel: (1) 393-3122, 394-2314, 326-3135   Fax: (1) 326-3132

All addresses and telephone numbers are in Argentina unless otherwise noted. The country code for Argentina is [54].

Barbenza-Forlano S.A., Sociedad de Bolsa
Corrientes 531, Piso 7
Buenos Aires
Tel: (1) 394-1291, 394-1387, 394-1414

Cantón y Cía. Sociedad de Bolsa S.A.
Reconquista 458, P.B.
Buenos Aires
Tel: (1) 394-7178   Fax: (1) 325-5789

Cia. Privada de Inversiones Sociedad de Bolsa S.A.
Sarmiento 643, Piso 1
Buenos Aires
Tel: (1) 325-4493, 325-2455, 325-1012

Cohen S.A. Sociedad de Bolsa
25 de Mayo 195, Piso 7
Buenos Aires
Tel: (1) 334-0698, 334-0699, 334-5640   Fax: (1) 334-9231

Corsiglia y Cia. Sociedad de Bolsa
Corrientes 456, Piso 8, Of. 86
Buenos Aires
Tel: (1) 394-7703, 394-9890, 326-2589   Fax: (1) 394-9890

Crédito Argentino Sociedad de Bolsa S.A.
Reconquista 40, Piso 4
Buenos Aires
Tel: (1) 334-7263   Fax: (1) 345-1600

De Bary y Cia. Sociedad de Bolsa S.A.
Lavalle 381, Piso 1
Buenos Aires
Tel: (1) 314-9672/3, 314-1182, 314-1482
Fax: (1) 314-9581

De Ganay y Quirno S.A. Sociedad de Bolsa
25 de Mayo 195, Piso 6
Buenos Aires
Tel: (1) 331-0614, 331-7216, 342-9086

Fescina y Cía. Sociedad de Bolsa S.A.
25 de Mayo 347, Piso 3, Of. 359
Buenos Aires
Tel: (1) 311-2246, 311-7224   Fax: (1) 313-9980

Gustavo A. García y Cía. S.A. Sociedad de Bolsa
Reconquista 341, Piso A
Buenos Aires
Tel: (1) 325-4310, 325-0367, 325-0386

Intervalores Sociedad de Bolsa S.A.
Reconquista 144, Piso 6
Buenos Aires
Tel: (1) 343-7079, 343-7187, 343-7406

José E. Brea y Cía. Sociedad de Bolsa S.A.
San Martín 379, Piso 3
Buenos Aires
Tel: (1) 394-6868, 394-6275, 394-6817

Lamarca y Cía. Sociedad de Bolsa S.A.
Reconquista 144, Piso 14
Buenos Aires
Tel: (1) 343-5474, 343-5464, 343-5493

Lascombes, Chlapowski y Cía. Sociedad de Bolsa S.A.
25 de Mayo 168, Piso 9
Buenos Aires
Tel: (1) 343-1847, 343-5472, 343-5602

Luis Domingo Trucco Sociedad de Bolsa S.A.
Tucumán 335, Piso 4, Of. D y E
Buenos Aires
Tel: (1) 311-7680, 313-4092, 313-6721

M.A. Valores S.A. Sociedad de Bolsa
Corrientes 415, Piso 6
Buenos Aires
Tel: (1) 394-0401, 394-9442, 394-9186

M.B.A. Sociedad de Bolsa S.A.
Corrientes 311, Piso 1
Buenos Aires
Tel: (1) 312-4776, 313-3222, 313-1200

Mahosa Bursatil Sociedad de Bolsa S.A.
Roque Sáenz Peña 547, Piso 7
Buenos Aires
Tel: (1) 343-6011/4

Mario S. Fernandez y Cia Sociedad de Bolsa S.A.
25 de Mayo 332, Piso 2
Buenos Aires
Tel: (1) 325-4890, 325-0127, 325-4685

Metrocorp Sociedad de Bolsa S.A.
25 de Mayo 565, P.B.
Buenos Aires
Tel: (1) 312-9440/9   Fax: (1) 313-7844

Norfina Sociedad de Bolsa S.A.
Tte. Gral J.D. Perón 679, Piso 2
Buenos Aires
Tel: (1) 325-8792/4, 349-3560, 349-3482

Orlando y Cía. Sociedad de Bolsa
Florida 780, Piso 5
Buenos Aires
Tel: (1) 394-7773, 394-7762, 394-7786

Oscar V. Quiroga S.A. Sociedad de Bolsa
Tte. Gral J.D. Perón 456, Piso 2, Of. 211 y 219
Buenos Aires
Tel: (1) 342-4130, 342-0987, 343-1193

Patente de Valores S.A. Sociedad de Bolsa
Reconquista 336, Piso 9, Of. "U"
Buenos Aires
Tel: (1) 394-7438, 393-6643, 393-6582

Peralta Ramos Sociedad de Bolsa S.A.
Florida 537/71, Piso 7
Buenos Aires
Tel: (1) 322-1322, 326-4592   Fax: (1) 326-4596

Piano & Parga Sociedad de Bolsa S.A.
San Martín 345, Piso 2
Buenos Aires
Tel: (1) 394-6891, 394-2938, 394-3121   Fax: (1) 325-6776

Provincia Bursatil Sociedad de Bolsa S.A.
San Martín 108, Piso 12
Buenos Aires
Tel: (1) 331-2001, 331-3584, 331-4022   Fax: (1) 342-2563

Quilburs S.A. Sociedad de Bolsa
Tte. Gral J.D. Perón 564
Buenos Aires
Tel: (1) 331-8110/9, 331-8240/9

Rava Sociedad de Bolsa S.A.
25 de Mayo 277, Piso 5
Buenos Aires
Tel: (1) 343-9421, 342-4158, 342-4789

República Valores S.A. Sociedad de Bolsa
25 de Mayo 356/58, Piso 6
Buenos Aires
Tel: (1) 328-4728/9   Fax: (1) 328-4720

Roberto E. Agra y Cía. S.A. Sociedad de Bolsa
San Martín 244, Piso 2
Buenos Aires
Tel: (1) 394-4648, 394-6310, 394-6127
Fax: (1) 394-2745, 394-4487, 394-5698

Títulos Valores S.A. Sociedad de Bolsa
Corrientes 457, Piso 11
Buenos Aires
Tel/Fax: (1) 325-0333, 325-0316, 325-0337

V. Menendez y Asociados S.A. Sociedad de Bolsa
25 de Mayo 555, Piso 11
Buenos Aires
Tel/Fax: (1) 313-2582, 313-2544, 313-2554

Wainbuch y Cía. Sociedad de Bolsa S.A.
San Martín 390, Piso 3
Buenos Aires
Tel: (1) 394-7528, 394-8477, 394-0997

Zarracan Sociedad de Bolsa S.A.
Corrientes 465, Piso 6
Buenos Aires
Tel: (1) 394-2016, 394-2715, 394-2764   Fax: (1) 322-6999

INSURANCE

Associations and Government Agencies

Superintendencia de Seguros de la Nación
(Superintendent of Insurance)
Av. Julio A. Roca 721
1067 Buenos Aires
Tel: (1) 331-8733, 331-9821

Asociación Argentina de Compañías de Seguros
(Argentine Association of Insurance Companies)
25 de Mayo 565
1002 Buenos Aires
Tel: (1) 313-6974   Fax: (1) 312-6300   Tlx: 23837

Asociación de Aseguradores Extranjeros en la
Argentina
(Association of Foreign Insurance Companies)
San Martín 201, Piso 7
1004 Buenos Aires
Tel: (1) 394-3881

Insurance Companies

Aconcagua Compañía de Seguros S.A.
Av. Figueroa Alcorta 3102
1425 Buenos Aires
Tel: (1) 312-0955, 311-9118   Fax: (1) 802-1207

Acuario Compañía de Seguros S.A.
Tucumán 612, Piso 5
1049 Buenos Aires
Tel: (1) 325-5021, 325-5032   Fax: (1) 322-1691

Boston Compañía Argentina de Seguros S.A.
Suipacha 268, Piso 3
1355 Buenos Aires
Tel: (1) 372-6363   Fax: (1) 372-6363

Caledonia Argentina Compañía de Seguros S.A.
San Martín 493, Piso 8
1004 Buenos Aires
Tel: (1) 394-5821   Fax: (1) 394-3451

Cenit Compañía Argentina de Seguros Generales S.A.
Av. de Mayo 637, Piso 2
1084 Buenos Aires
Tel: (1) 342-8491

Compañia Argentina de Seguros de Crédito
a la Exportación S.A.
Av. Corrientes 345, Piso 7
1043 Buenos Aires
Tel: (1) 313-2683, 313-2919   Fax: 313-2919

El Comercio Compañía de Seguros Prima Fija S.A.
Maipú 53
1084 Buenos Aires
Tel: (1) 342-2180/1

El Comercio de Córdoba S.A. Compañía de Seguros
Av. General Paz 323
5000 Córdoba
Tel: (51) 47-070   Fax: (51) 42-074

El Comercio del Norte Compañía de Seguros S.A.
Av. 24 de Setiembre 677
4000 San Miguel de Tucumán
Tel: (81) 31-0447

El Plata Sociedad Anónima Argentina de Seguros
Tte. Gral. J.D. Perón 646, Piso 3
1038 Buenos Aires
Tel: (1) 326-9255

Florencia Compañía Argentina de Seguros Generales
Esmeralda 288, Piso 3
1035 Buenos Aires
Tel: (1) 373-7805

Iguazú Compañía de Seguros S.A.
San Martín 442
1004 Buenos Aires
Tel: (1) 394-6661, 394-3217

Inca Sociedad Anónima Compañía de Seguros
Belgrano 666/72
1092 Buenos Aires
Tel: (1) 331-8795   Fax: (1) 334-5583

Independencia Compañía Argentina de Seguros S.A.
Av. Corrientes 821, Piso 1
1043 Buenos Aires
Tel: (1) 393-8421   Fax: (1) 322-6384

La Buenos Aires
Av. Corrientes 569
Buenos Aires
Tel: (1) 325-0068

La Confianza Compañía Argentina de Seguros S.A.
Av. Paseo Colón 528/36
1063 Buenos Aires
Tel: (1) 331-5840

La Continental Compañía de Seguros Generales
Av. Corrientes 655
1043 Buenos Aires
Tel: (1) 393-8051, 322-2621 Tlx: 121832

La Estrella S.A. Compañía Argentina de Seguros
San Martín 483, Pisos 2 y 3
1348 Buenos Aires
Tel: (1) 393-6556/9

La Fortuna S.A. Argentina de Seguros Generales
Bartolomé Mitre 739, Piso 6
1036 Buenos Aires
Tel: (1) 331-1071, 394-7310

La Franco Argentina S.A. Compañía de Seguros
Hipólito Yrigoyen 476
1036 Buenos Aires
Tel: (1) 342-2151, 343-0912

La Hispano Argentina Compañía de Seguros S.A.
Av. de Mayo 676, Pisos 8 y 9
1002 Buenos Aires
Tel: (1) 331-4889   Fax: (1) 331-6112

La Ibero Plantense Compañía de Seguros S.A.
25 de Mayo 596, Piso 16
1002 Buenos Aires
Tel: (1) 312-4021, 313-7564

La Meridional Compañía Argentina de Seguros S.A.
Tte. Gral. J.D. Perón 646, Piso 3
1038 Buenos Aires
Tel: (1) 331-0941

La Tandilense S.A. Compañía de Seguros
9 de Julio 388, Piso 5
7000 Tandil
Pcia. de Buenos Aires
Tel: (293) 2-6707   Fax: (293) 2-6707

La Union Mercantil Compañía de Seguros
Alsina 756, Piso 3
1087 Buenos Aires
Tel: (1) 342-9216

Providencia Compañía de Seguros de Retiro S.A.
Reconquista 458
1358 Buenos Aires
Tel: (1) 394-0919, 326-2053

Seguros Juncal
Juncol 1319
Buenos Aires
Tel: (1) 394-1018

Victoria Compañía Argentina de Seguros S.A.
Florida 556
1005 Buenos Aires
Tel: (1) 322-2929, 322-1956

SERVICES

ACCOUNTING AND CONSULTING FIRMS

Note: Many of these firms have offices in other Argentine cities, particularly Córdoba, Mendoza, and Rosario, and worldwide.

Abelovich, Polano & Asociados
25 de Mayo 596, Piso 8
1002 Buenos Aires
Tel: (1) 312-1693   Fax: (1) 312-8525

Arrigoni & Asociados
Bartolomé Mitre 688, Piso 7
1036 Buenos Aires
Tel: (1) 343-5338   Fax: (1) 331-2337

Becher Lichenstein y Asociados
Av. Córdoba 1318, Piso 9
1055 Buenos Aires
Tel: (1) 476-3342   Fax: (1) 814-4502

Berge, Giordano, y Asociados
Rivadavia 1367, Piso 11, Of. A
1033 Buenos Aires
Tel/Fax: (1) 381-0416

Bravo & Bravo Losada
Av. Córdoba 1540
1055 Buenos Aires
Tel: (1) 811-2605   Fax: (1) 814-1766

Coopers & Lybrand
25 de Mayo 140, Piso 6
1002 Buenos Aires
Tel: (1) 334-2830   Fax: (1) 331-5325

Counsel
Rivadavia 893, Piso 2
1002 Buenos Aires
Tel: (1) 331-5043   Fax: (1) 331-5044

Deloitte & Touche
Sarmiento 624
1041 Buenos Aires
Tel: (1) 326-0497   Fax: (1) 325-8018

Estudio Dr. Antonio M. Adler y Asociados
San Martín 575, Piso 2
1004 Buenos Aires
Tel: (1) 393-6680   Fax: (1) 325-6989

Estudio Perel
Piedras 519, Piso 9
1070 Buenos Aires
Tel: (1) 331-3137   Fax: (1) 331-3179

Estudio Ratto-Telle-Villares Auditores
Florida 537/71, Piso 22
1005 Buenos Aires
Tel: (1) 393-0954   Fax: (1) 322-3773

Estudio Schenzie, Carballo, Schultz y Asociados
Marcelo T. de Alvear 636, Pisos 3, 8 y 9
1058 Buenos Aires
Tel: (1) 311-4941   Fax: (1) 312-1647

Grant Thornton International
Maipú 1252, Piso 6
1006 Buenos Aires
Tel: (1) 313-0776   Fax: (1) 313-0881

Henry Martin y Asociados
Ernest & Young Consulting
Maipú 942, P.B.
1340 Buenos Aires
Tel: (1) 313-8162   Fax: (1) 313-1528

Horwath Consulting
Cerrito 146, Piso 1
1010 Buenos Aires
Tel: (1) 381-8825   Fax: (1) 953-4517

Jebsen & Co.
Av. L.N. Alem 693
1001 Buenos Aires
Tel: (1) 312-2339   Fax: (1) 312-9116

KPMG Finsterbusch Pickenhayn Sibille
Av. L.N. Alem 1050, Piso 5
1001 Buenos Aires
Tel: (1) 313-9633   Fax: (1) 311-7117

L. Adolfo Penalva y Asociados
Corrientes 311, Piso 7
1043 Buenos Aires
Tel: (1) 311-5643   Fax: (1) 312-6781

Pistrelli, Díaz y Asociados
25 de Mayo 487, Piso 1
1002 Buenos Aires
Tel: (1) 311-6644   Fax: (1) 312-8647

Price Waterhouse
Casilla de Correo Central 896
1000 Buenos Aires
Tel: (1) 381-8181, 382-3005   Fax: (1) 383-6339, 382-2793

ADVERTISING AGENCIES

Ayer Vázquez S.A. de Publicidad
Av. Callao 1046, Piso 3
1023 Buenos Aires
Tel: (1) 815-4850   Fax: (1) 814-0494   Tlx: 23802

Casares, Grey & Asociados S.A.
Suipacha 780
1008 Buenos Aires
Tel: (1) 393-2443, 393-4246/7
Fax: (1) 322-5308, 393-6731

Cicero Dialogo Bates
Paraguay 610, Piso 23
1350 Buenos Aires
Tel: (1) 312-9633, 312-3866, 312-6616
Fax: (1) 311-4086   Tlx: 390-9900

Colonnese Lintas
25 de Mayo 666
1084 Buenos Aires
Tel: (1) 343-0335/9   Fax: (1) 331-4298

Graffiti/DMB&B S.A.
Uruguay 1112, Piso 4
1016 Buenos Aires
Tel: (1) 811-4365, 811-8315   Fax: (1) 811-1629

J. Walter Thompson Argentina S.A.
Alsina 465
1087 Buenos Aires
Tel: (1) 331-4550/9   Fax: (1) 331-3219   Tlx: 18823

Kobs & Draft Worldwide
México 441, Piso 1A
1097 Buenos Aires
Tel: (1) 334-3801   Fax: (1) 331-1381

Lautrec/Nazca S&S
México 472
1097 Buenos Aires
Tel: (1) 345-0961   Fax: (1) 331-1381

Leo Burnett Co., Inc. Sucursal Argentina
Carlos Pellegrini 1363, Piso 12
1011 Buenos Aires
Tel: (1) 394-5062/6, 394-5033
Fax: (1) 112049   Tlx: 24504

McCann-Erickson
Tucumán 512
1049 Buenos Aires
Tel: (1) 322-4361, 322-5922
Fax: (1) 322-4257   Tlx: 24327

Nexo Publicidad S.A.
Florida 1
1005 Buenos Aires
Tel: (1) 342-0946, 342-1263, 342-1300   Fax: (1) 342-9790

Ogilvy & Mather Argentina
Suipacha 568/70, P.B.
1008 Buenos Aires
Tel: (1) 394-3002, 394-3026
Fax: (1) 322-5590   Tlx: 22366

Pragma/FCB Publicidad
Humboldt 1967, Piso 2
1414 Buenos Aires
Tel: (1) 771-7021   Fax: (1) 771-6619   Tlx: 23534

Ratto/BBDO
Quintana 473
1129 Buenos Aires
Tel: (1) 805-4249   Fax: (1) 805-5063   Tlx: 17400

Ricardo de Luca Publicidad S.A.
Carlos Pellegrini 173, P.B.
1009 Buenos Aires
Tel: (1) 326-5133, 394-8915
Fax: (1) 326-5133, 326-5134

Verdino Bates Publicidad
Juncal 4695
1425 Buenos Aires
Tel: (1) 777-3100   Fax: (1) 771-4070

Wundermann Cato Johnson Buenos Aires
Gorostiaga 2021
1426 Buenos Aires
Tel/Fax: (1) 342-4178

Young & Rubicam Argentina
Paseo Colón 275, Piso 13
1063 Buenos Aires
Tel: (1) 331-8491/5
Fax (1) 334-2739

LEGAL SERVICES

Bar Association

Argentine Bar Federation
Av. de Mayo 651
Buenos Aires
Tel: (1) 331-8009

Law Firms

Brons & Salas
Dr. Thomas Boywitt, Partner
Marcelo T. de Alvear 624, Piso 1
1058 Buenos Aires
Tel: (1) 311-9271/9   Fax: (1) 311-7025

Estudio Abeledo Gottheil
Dr. Julio Gottheil, Partner
Maipú 757
1006 Buenos Aires
Tel: (1) 322-4848, 322-4869   Fax: (1) 322-4848

Estudio Allende Brea
Dr. Teodosio C. Brea, Partner
Maipú 1300, Piso 10
1006 Buenos Aires
Tel: (1) 313-9191, 313-9292   Fax: (1) 312-5288, 313-9010

All addresses and telephone numbers are in Argentina unless otherwise noted. The country code for Argentina is [54].

Estudio Beccar Varela
Cerrito 740, Piso 16
1309 Buenos Aires
Tel: (1) 372-5100, 382-0017/9
Fax: (1) 372-6619, 372-6809

Estudio E.P.
Dr. Edgardo Petrakovsky, Partner
Reconquista 671, Piso 1
1003 Buenos Aires
Tel: (1) 311-7392   Fax: (1) 312-1670

Estudio Marval & O'Farrell
Dr. Alfredo O'Farrell, Partner
Carlos Pellegrini 885/887
1338 Buenos Aires
Tel: (1) 322-8336, 322-8266   Fax: (1) 322-4122

Estudio Muñoz del Toro & Quevedo
Dr. Fernando Muñoz del Toro, Partner
25 de Mayo 294
1002 Buenos Aires
Tel: (1) 343-3903, 343-3989   Fax: (1) 334-1718

Estudio O'Farrell
Dr. Uriel O'Farrell, Principal
Av. de Mayo 645/51
1084 Buenos Aires
Tel: (1) 342-5740, 342-4707   Fax: (1) 331-1659

MARKET RESEARCH FIRMS

A&C
Salta 1007
1074 Buenos Aires
Tel: (1) 304-6309, 304-8213   Fax: (1) 27-8800

Commercial Network
Dorrego 2648, Piso 10, Of. A
1246 Buenos Aires
Tel: (1) 777-7121

Guillermo Bravo y Asociados
Av. de Mayo 1480, E.P.
Buenos Aires
Tel/Fax: (1) 381-7892, 381-2540, 381-5625

Jorge Fernandez Bussy y Asociados
Leandro N. Alem 1080, Piso 2, Of. C
1001 Buenos Aires
Tel: (1) 311-7440

Mercados Directos
Lavalle 1515, Piso 1
1048 Buenos Aires
Tel: (1) 375-0772/3   Fax: (1) 375-2012

R.G. Asociados
Defensa 649, Piso 5, Of. A
1265 Buenos Aires
Tel: (1) 342-9355

TRANSPORTATION

AIRLINES AND AIR CARGO CARRIERS

Note: Cargo telephone numbers given are at Ezeiza
International Airport in Buenos Aires.

Aero Expreso Internacional
Bdo. de Irigoyen 308, Piso 4
1379 Buenos Aires
Tel: (1) 334-0154, 334-0659   Fax: (1) 334-3443

Aeroflot
Av. Santa Fe 816, Piso 1
1059 Buenos Aires
Tel: (1) 312-5573, 312-3049   Fax: (1) 313-7589
Cargo: (1) 480-0865

Aerolíneas Argentinas
Av. Paseo Colón 185
1063 Buenos Aires
Tel: (1) 343-2071, 362-5008, 362-6008   Fax: (1) 334-2676
Cargo: (1) 480-0889, 480-0484

Aerolíneas Uruguayas
Paraguay 647
Buenos Aires
Tel: (1) 313-9458, 313-3331

Aeroméxico
Suipacha 512, Piso 1, Of. A
1008 Buenos Aires
Tel: (1) 322-4821, 325-9669   Fax: (1) 325-9669

AeroPerú
Av. Santa Fe 840
1059 Buenos Aires
Tel: (1) 311-6431, 311-6434   Fax: (1) 312-1030
Cargo: (1) 480-0869

Aeroposta
Viamonte 577, Piso 8 y 9
Buenos Aires
Tel: (1) 312-2625, 312-2826, 312-2402

Air Canada
Marcelo T. de Alvear 590, Piso 10
1058 Buenos Aires
Tel: (1) 312-0664, 313-7492

Air France
Paraguay 610, Piso 14
1350 Buenos Aires
Tel: (1) 312-7331, 312-7335   Fax: (1) 814-1487
Cargo: (1) 480-0208, 480-0249

Air New Zealand
Marcelo T. de Alvear 590, Piso 10
1058 Buenos Aires
Tel: (1) 312-0664, 313-7492

Airway Service S.A. (UPS affiliate)
Tacuarí 222, P.B.
1071 Buenos Aires
Tel: (1) 342-1000, 342-4269, 342-8213

Alitalia Líneas Aéreas Iitalianas
Suipacha 1111, Piso 28
1368 Buenos Aires
Tel: (1) 312-4576, 312-4086/9   Fax: (1) 312-3531
Cargo: (1) 480-0876

American Airlines
Av. Santa Fe 887
1059 Buenos Aires
Tel: (1) 342-0031, 315-0031
Cargo: (1) 480-0368

Austral Líneas Aéreas
Av. Corrientes 485/7, Piso 7
1398 Buenos Aires
Tel: (1) 325-0777
Fax: (1) 325-0506

Austrian Airlines
Córdoba 950, Piso 5
Buenos Aires
Tel: (1) 313-3763

Avianca
Santa Fe 865
1059 Buenos Aires
Tel: (1) 312-3621/5
Cargo: (1) 480-0033, 480-0465, 480-0488

British Airways
Av. Córdoba 657, Piso 10, Of. 103
1054 Buenos Aires
Tel: (1) 325-1019

Canadian Airlines International
Córdoba 656
1054 Buenos Aires
Tel: (1) 393-9208, 322-3632, 322-3732
Cargo: (1) 480-0606, 480-0167

CATA
Cerrito 1320, Piso 3
1010 Buenos Aires
Tel: (1) 629-2465   Fax: (1) 627-3721

Cathay Pacific
1006 Maipú 726, P.B.
Buenos Aires
Tel: (1) 322-3179

China Airlines
Marcelo T. de Alvear 590, Piso 10
1058 Buenos Aires
Tel: (1) 312-0664, 313-7492

Circle Freight International Argentina
25 de Mayo 596, Piso 17
1002 Buenos Aires
Tel: (1) 313-6562, 313-6752, 313-6992
Fax: (1) 313-6607   Tlx: 22306

Cubana de Aviación
Av. Corrientes 545, Piso 1
1043 Buenos Aires
Tel: (1) 322-7063, 322-2449   Fax: (1) 394-4875

Delta Airlines
L.N. Alem 884, Piso 2
Buenos Aires
Tel: (1) 312-6633, 311-4913, 311-0207

DHL Internacional
Hipólito Yrigoyen 448, P.B.
1086 Buenos Aires
Tel: (1) 331-3107, 331-3217

Ecuatoriana
Suipacha 1065, P.B.
1008 Buenos Aires
Tel: (1) 311-1117, 311-3010, 311-3019   Fax: (1) 311-4757
Cargo: (1) 480-0423, 480-0089, 480-0367

El-Al Israel Airlines
Maipú 464, Piso 3, Of. 304
1084 Buenos Aires
Tel: (1) 322-8840, 322-6937, 322-7658   Fax: (1) 322-7917

EMS (ENCOTEL)
Av. Antártida Argentina y Comodoro Py
1104 Buenos Aires
Tel: (1) 311-7874, 311-9390, 312-3487

Federal Express Corporation
Maipú 753
1006 Buenos Aires
Tel: (1) 393-6139, 393-6054, 393-6127   Fax: (1) 395-5955
Cargo: 490-9041, 480-9054

Finnair
Florida 826, Piso 4
Buenos Aires
Tel: (1) 313-8144, 313-8107, 312-3323

Iberia Líneas Aéreas de España
Carlos Pellegrini 1165
1011 Buenos Aires
Tel: (1) 393-0621, 393-0639, 393-5680   Fax: (1) 322-5127
Cargo: (1) 480-0323

Internacional Bonded Couriers
(Airborne Express affiliate)
Tacuarí 1050
1071 Buenos Aires
Tel: (1) 27-4872, 27-2949, 26-4546

Japan Airlines
Córdoba 836, Piso 11
Buenos Aires
Tel: (1) 322-2005, 393-0755

KLM Royal Dutch Airlines
Suipacha 1109, Piso 4
1008 Buenos Aires
Tel: (1) 311-9520, 311-9524
Cargo: (1) 480-0938, 442-4668

Korean Air
Córdoba 669, Piso 3
1054 Buenos Aires
Tel: (1) 311-9237, 313-8297

LAB (Lloyd Aero Boliviano)
Carlos Pellegrini 1371
1009 Buenos Aires
Tel: (1) 382-0418, 382-3505, 382-6961   Fax: (1) 382-6961
Cargo: (1) 480-0026, 480-0472

LADE (Líneas Aéreas del Estado)
Perú 714
1068 Buenos Aires
Tel: (1) 361-7071, 361-7174   Fax: (1) 362-4899

Ladeco
Corrientes 617, Piso 9
Buenos Aires
Tel: (1) 394-3554, 394-6141
Cargo: (1) 480-0700

LAN Chile
Córdoba 859, Piso 6, Of. A
Buenos Aires
Tel: (1) 312-1364
Cargo: (1) 480-0439

LAP (Líneas Aéreas Paraguayas)
Cerrito 1026/30
1010 Buenos Aires
Tel: (1) 393-1000, 393-1162, 393-1061   Fax: (1) 393-1469

LAPA
Santa Fe 1970, Piso 2
1123 Buenos Aires
Tel: (1) 812-3322, 812-6773, 812-2105   Fax: (1) 814-2100

Lufthansa
M. T. De Alvear 590, Piso 6
1058 Buenos Aires
Tel: (1) 312-8170/9   Fax: (1) 313-1092
Cargo: (1) 480-0049, 480-9180

All addresses and telephone numbers are in Argentina unless otherwise noted. The country code for Argentina is [54].

Mexicana
Viamonte 1365, P.B.
Buenos Aires
Tel: (1) 372-6531

Million Air
Chacabuco 90, Piso 7
Buenos Aires
Tel: (1) 334-7367/9, 343-1917

Olympic Airways
Viamonte 783, Piso 1
Buenos Aires
Tel: (1) 322-6983, 322-1798

Organización Clearing Argentino
Ramsay 2055
1428 Buenos Aires
Tel: (1) 783-3013/5, 784-7108
Fax: (1) 785-7883   Tlx: 23673

Panalpina Transportes Mundiales
Av. Paseo Colón 728, Piso 9
1063 Buenos Aires
Tel: (1) 345-2633, 345-2643

Philippine Airlines
Marcelo T. de Alvear 590, Piso 10
1058 Buenos Aires
Tel: (1) 312-0664, 313-7492

Pluna (Primera Línea Uruguaya)
Florida 1
1009 Buenos Aires
Tel: (1) 342-9170, 342-4420, 342-8535   Fax: (1) 331-2358

SAA (South Africa Airways)
Av. Santa Fe 794, Piso 3
1059 Buenos Aires
Tel: (1) 311-8184   Fax: (1) 311-5825

SAS (Scandinavian Airline System)
Paraguay 609, Piso 1
1057 Buenos Aires
Tel: (1) 312-8161, 312-8169   Fax: (1) 312-1338

Schenker Argentina
Florida 547/71, Piso 23
1005 Buenos Aires
Tel: (1) 322-3979, 322-4500, 322-4818
Fax: (1) 322-3979   Tlx: 24051

Servicios Choice S.A.
Sarmiento 440, P.B.
1359 Buenos Aires
Tel: (1) 394-7575, 394-9091, 393-7110
Fax: (1) 394-7575   Tlx: 18849, 23967

STAF
L.N. Alem 881, Piso 1
Buenos Aires
Tel: (1) 312-0020, 312-8521
Cargo: (1) 480-0111/9

Swissair
Av. Santa Fe 846
1059 Buenos Aires
Tel: (1) 311-8933, 311-8934, 311-8936
Cargo: (1) 480-0966, 480-0976, 480-0988

TAN
Maipú 42, P.B.
Buenos Aires
Tel: (1) 343-9076, 331-4466

Tap Air Portugal
Cerrito 1146
1010 Buenos Aires
Tel: (1) 811-0984, 811-1625   Fax: (1) 814-4665

Toshin S.A.
Rodriguez Peña 375, Piso 2, Of. B
1020 Buenos Aires
Tel: (1) 382-6086, 382-5022, 382-9638
Fax: (1) 382-6170   Tlx: 17779

TWA (Trans World Airlines)
Av. Córdoba 669, Piso 3
1054 Buenos Aires
Tel: (1) 311-9237   Fax: (1) 313-8297

United Airlines
Carlos Pellegrini 1165, Piso 5
Buenos Aires
Tel: (1) 326-8343
Cargo: (1) 480-0958, 480-0864

USAir
Córdoba 679, Piso 1
1054 Buenos Aires
Tel: (1) 322-7133, 322-8798

Varig
Carabelas 344
1009 Buenos Aires
Tel: (1) 343-5031
Cargo: (1) 480-0027, 480-0028

VASP
Santa Fe 784
Buenos Aires
Tel: (1) 311-6799, 311-2699
Cargo: (1) 480-9022, 480-9056, 480-0715

Viasa (Venezolana Internacional de Aviación)
Carlos Pelligrini 1075
1009 Buenos Aires
Tel: (1) 311-4192, 311-4208   Fax: (1) 311-3774

World Courier
Av. Corrientes 327, Piso 11
1043 Buenos Aires
Tel: (1) 312-8612/5   Fax: (1) 313-5879

FREIGHT FORWARDERS

Amarsac
Piedras 77, Piso 6
1070 Buenos Aires
Tel: (1) 342-1958/9, 342-1985   Fax: (1) 342-5067

Argencargo S.A.
Reconquista 1056, Piso 2
1003 Buenos Aires
Tel: (1) 311-7350, 311-0027, 311-2523   Fax: (1) 311-2511

Centauro S.A.
Lavalle 465, P.B.
1047 Buenos Aires
Tel: (1) 393-8099, 393-8199, 393-8399   Fax: (1) 383-8296

Circle Freight International Argentina S.A.
25 de Mayo 596, Piso 17
1002 Buenos Aires
Tel: (1) 313-6562, 313-6752   Fax: (1) 313-6607

Danzas Argentina S.A.
Reconquista 458, Piso 7
1358 Buenos Aires
Tel: (1) 394-5566, 394-2460, 394-2823   Fax: (1) 325-5075

Eden Air Freight S.R.L.
Perú 345, Piso 10, Of. D
1067 Buenos Aires
Tel: (1) 334-3850, 331-1391   Fax: (1) 343-9829

Eximcargo S.A.
Perú 345, Piso 11
1067 Buenos Aires
Tel: (1) 331-7856, 331-8667, 338-8699   Fax: (1) 331-7833

Express S.R.L.
Florida 716
1005 Buenos Aires
Tel: (1) 322-2393, 322-8308, 322-4341   Fax: (1) 322-5239

Flying Cargo Service S.R.L
Florida 165, Piso 3, Of. 333
1333 Buenos Aires
Tel: (1) 331-3041, 331-3046 x202   Fax: (1) 343-5360

G.R.V.
Alsina 943, Piso 7, Of. 701
1088 Buenos Aires
Tel: (1) 334-1390, 411-2444   Fax: (1) 447-3990

House to House
Belgrano 430, Piso 7
1092 Buenos Aires
Tel: (1) 342-7884, 342-3614   Fax: (1) 343-5149

Interfreight
Perú 367, Piso 6
1067 Buenos Aires
Tel: (1) 342-1696, 342-2068, 342-2628   Fax: (1) 334-1719

Intersea Trade & Services S.R.L.
Reconquista 575, Piso 1
1049 Buenos Aires
Tel: (1) 312-0862, 315-0183/6   Fax: (1) 312-2651

K.N. Newport
L.N. Alem 1002, Piso 5
1001 Buenos Aires
Tel: (1) 313-2868, 313-2873, 313-2807   Fax: (1) 315-4107

Latino S.A.
Talcahuano 750, Piso 10
1013 Buenos Aires
Tel: (1) 476-0125, 476-0664   Fax: (1) 476-0664

Merzario Argentina S.A.
Bartolomé Mitre 797, Piso 6
1036 Buenos Aires
Tel: (1) 393-2548, 393-2620   Fax: (1) 394-1751

Oceal S.R.L.
Perú 689, Piso 5
1068 Buenos Aires
Tel: (1) 362-7196, 361-2262   Fax: (1) 362-6788

Open Cargo S.A.
Defensa 649, Piso 2, Of. C
1065 Buenos Aires
Tel: (1) 345-1295, 331-2456   Fax: (1) 342-9355

Panalpina Transportes Mundiales S.A.
Paseo Colón 728, Piso 9
1063 Buenos Aires
Tel: (1) 345-2633, 345-2643   Fax: (1) 343-6630

Ritasa Argentina
B. de Irigoyen 308, Piso 4
1379 Buenos Aires
Tel: (1) 334-3023/7 Fax: (1) 334-3443

Rohde & Liesenfeld S.R.L.
Lavalle 547, Pisos 5 y 8
1059 Buenos Aires
Tel: (1) 393-7095, 393-8914, 393-3479   Fax: (1) 393-8723

Round Trip Argentina
Santa Fe 1955, Piso 2, Of. F
1059 Buenos Aires
Tel: (1) 815-0138, 815-0441   Fax: (1) 814-0067

Saint Germain
Perú 590, Piso 4
1068 Buenos Aires
Tel: (1) 331-7069, 331-7090

Sea Trans
Viamonte 611, Piso 11
1003 Buenos Aires
Tel: (1) 393-9253, 326-5376   Fax: (1) 326-5376

Servicios Internacionales S.A.
Lafayette 575
1284 Buenos Aires
Tel: (1) 303-2533, 303-2543, 303-2535/6

SIF Transportes Internacionales
Suipacha 576, Piso 5
1008 Buenos Aires
Tel: (1) 322-5726, 322-5826

Solaris S.R.L.
Cerrito 146, Piso 7
1010 Buenos Aires
Tel: (1) 383-3933, 383-4317, 383-4680   Fax: (1) 383-2320

South Export S.A.
Perú 689, Piso 4
1084 Buenos Aires
Tel: (1) 362-8790, 331-1418   Fax: (1) 331-1418

Tiger Cargo S.A.
Belgrano 687, Piso 9
1092 Buenos Aires
Tel: (1) 331-7132, 343-8419   Fax: (1) 331-7132

Tracomsa S.A.
San Martín 448, Piso 5
1004 Buenos Aires
Tel: (1) 394-2149, 394-5241   Fax: (1) 394-4457

Trademar S.R.L.
Moreno 455, Piso 9
1091 Buenos Aires
Tel: (1) 343-7708   Fax: (1) 345-2052

Transportes Universales
Av. Belgrano 615, Piso 9
1092 Buenos Aires
Tel: (1) 343-8904/8   Fax: (1) 331-4293

SHIPPING FIRMS

Agencia Marítima Delfino S.A.
San Martín 439, Piso 2
1359 Buenos Aires
Tel: (1) 394-2913, 394-2713, 394-2264   Fax: (1) 394-5379
General, reefer, and containerized cargo

Agencia Marítima Mundial S.A.
Tucumán 359, Piso 8
1049 Buenos Aires
Tel: (1) 313-2390, 313-8403   Fax: (1) 313-5184
General, liquid bulk, reefer, and containerized cargo

Agencia Marítima Internacional S.A.
25 de Mayo 555, Piso 20
1002 Buenos Aires
Tel: (1) 312-4001/9   Fax: (1) 313-1996
*General, liquid and dry bulk, reefer, and containerized
cargo*

Agencia Marítima Robinson S.A.
25 de Mayo 277, Piso 8
1002 Buenos Aires
Tel: (1) 313-1696, 313-1482, 345-5634   Fax: (1) 334-0109
Containerized cargo

All addresses and telephone numbers are in Argentina unless otherwise noted. The country code for Argentina is [54].

Arpez S.A.
Venezuela 110, Piso 4, Of. "F"
1095 Buenos Aires
Tel: (1) 331-1231, 331-7793   Fax: (1) 331-7793
Liquid bulk cargo

Bowmar S.A.
25 de Mayo 555, Piso 21
1002 Buenos Aires
Tel: (1) 313-4552, 313-4567, 313-4597
Chemical and petrochemical cargo

Ciamar S.A. (CANISA)
Av. Corrientes 327, Piso 3
1043 Buenos Aires
Tel: (1) 313-0707, 313-5150, 313-8149   Fax: (1) 322-7173
General, liquid bulk, and reefer cargo

Cía. de Navegación Atlántico Austral
25 de Mayo 432, Piso 2
1002 Buenos Aires
Tel: (1) 312-4896, 312-4898   Fax: (1) 313-8743
General, dry bulk, and reefer cargo

Cormoran S.A.
Bartolomé Mitre 226, Piso 6
1036 Buenos Aires
Tel: (1) 343-7675, 343-7527   Fax: (1) 331-2862
General, liquid bulk, large bulk and reefer cargo

Del Bene S.A. de Navegación
Piedras 77, Piso 6
1070 Buenos Aires
Tel: (1) 342-1345, 342-1372, 342-4332   Fax: (1) 343-5352
Large bulk cargo

ELMA (Empresas Líneas Marítimas Argentinas) S.E.
Corrientes 389
1327 Buenos Aires
Tel: (1) 312-4861, 312-8111, 312-0987   Fax: (1) 311-7954
General and reefer cargo

Ferry Líneas Argentinas S.A.
Florida 780, Piso 1
1005 Buenos Aires
Tel: (1) 394-5431, 394-1094, 394-8196   Fax: (1) 322-8421
Containerized cargo, not refrigerated

Fletamar S.A.C.
Corrientes 327, Piso 7
1043 Buenos Aires
Tel: (1) 311-6551, 311-8171, 311-8174   Fax: (1) 312-9430
General cargo and reefer services

La Naviera S.A.C
W. Villafañe 19
1160 Buenos Aires
Tel: (1) 362-1278, 362-1876, 312-9055   Fax: (1) 362-1076
Liquid bulk and dry bulk cargo

Lunmar Naviera S.A.
Chile 200
1098 Buenos Aires
Tel: (1) 342-1374, 342-1335, 342-1766   Fax: (1) 334-1261
Liquid bulk cargo

Maruba S.C.A.
Maipú 535, Piso 2
1006 Buenos Aires
Tel: (1) 322-2220, 322-2320, 322-2250   Fax: (1) 322-7173
Conventional cargo, container and reefer services

Navenor S.A.C.I.
Maipú 521, Piso 9
1006 Buenos Aires
Tel: (1) 322-5764, 322-5485, 322-5465   Fax: (1) 322-2866

Oceanmarine S.A.
L.N. Alem 1110, Piso 11
1001 Buenos Aires
Tel: (1) 313-5730, 313-5735, 313-5755   Fax: (1) 311-7941
Dry bulk cargo

Platachart S.A.
25 de Mayo 277, Piso 9
1002 Buenos Aires
Tel: (1) 331-0199, 331-0159, 331-0169   Fax: (1) 342-4808
General, containerized, and reefer cargo

TOBA S.A.
Av. R. Sáenz Peña 720, Piso 1
1035 Buenos Aires
Tel: (1) 342-3532, 342-9098, 342-5162   Fax: (1) 342-2582
Liquid cargo

Transplata S.A.
Reconquista 617, Piso 1
1003 Buenos Aires
Tel: (1) 311-4754/5
General, reefer and containerized cargo

TRUCKING FIRMS

Note: All of these companies provide international trucking services to a number of countries in South America.

Coop. T.A. Cord. Ltda.
Pacheco y Colón
1161 D. Torcuato
Pcia. de Buenos Aires
Tel: (1) 741-0791, 748-0073
Special cargo

Coop. T.A. Cord. Ltda.
Honduras 87
5000 Córdoba
Tel: (51) 94-0511, 94-0729
Special cargo

El Sol Estibajes S.R.L.
Juan B. Palaa 322
1870 Avellaneda
Pcia. de Buenos Aires
Tel: (1) 201-9273, 201-3430, 205-2021   Fax: (1) 201-3430
General cargo, refrigerated cargo

Empresa de Transportes Don Pedro S.R.L.
Gdor. Vergara 4802
1686 Hurlingham
Pcia. de Buenos Aires
Tel: (1) 665-9888, 665-8485   Fax: (1) 665-5807
General cargo

Expreso Suipacha S.A.
Irala 853
1163 Buenos Aires
Tel: (1) 28-2830, 21-5965
General cargo

Expreso Suipacha S.A.
Brown 3048
2000 Rosario
Tel: (41) 3-9050   Fax: (41) 39-3204

Furlong Transportes S.A.
Ruta Panamericana km 35.5
1617 Grl. Pacheco, Buenos Aires
Tel: (1) 327-2165/8   Fax: (1) 327-5227/8
Special cargo

Multiex S.A.
Cerrito 1054, Piso 1
1010 Buenos Aires
Tel: (1) 811-7124/5   Fax: (1) 953-4168
General cargo

Román S.A.C
Río Limay 1853
1278 Buenos Aires
Tel: (1) 21-6131/4, 21-4676/9
Special cargo

Telga S.A.T.
L.N. Alem 538, Piso 21
1001 Buenos Aires
Tel: (1) 311-0484, 311-0868, 313-4619
General and special cargo

Transglobe Trading S.R.L.
Lavalle 652, Piso 8, Of. B
1047 Buenos Aires
Tel/Fax: (1) 322-8916, 322-8773, 322-5969
General cargo

Transportes Lopez Hnos S.A.
Lavalle 465, P.B.
1047 Buenos Aires
Tel: (1) 326-3658, 393-8296
Special cargo

Transportes Lopez Hnos S.A.
Acceso Sur y Bulnes
5507 Lujan de Cujo
Pcia. de Mendoza
Tel: (61) 96-0600   Fax: (61) 96-0621

Transportes Rudaeff S.R.L.
Av. Belgrano 634, Piso 7
1092 Buenos Aires
Tel: (1) 342-6770   Fax: (1) 30-3916
General cargo

MEDIA AND INFORMATION SOURCES

Note: All publications are in Spanish unless otherwise noted.

DIRECTORIES

American Chamber of Commerce in Argentina Directory
(Annual; English)
American Chamber of Commerce in Argentina
Av. L.N. Alem 1110, Piso 13
1001 Buenos Aries
Tel: (1) 311-5420   Fax: (1) 311-9076

Annual Buyers Guide
Top Latin American Processors Directory
(Annual; English)
Stagnito Publishing Company
1935 Shermer Rd., Suite 100
Northbrook, IL 60062, USA
Tel: [1] (708) 205-5660   Fax: [1] (708) 205-5680
Food and food industries

Anuario de la Economía Argentina/Argentine Economy Manual
(Annual; English and Spanish)
Consejo Técnico de Inversiones S.A.
Tucumán 834, Piso 1
1049 Buenos Aires
Fax: (1) 322-4887

Consumer Latin America
(Irregular; English)
Euromonitor
87-88 Turnmill St.
London EC1M 5QU, UK
Tel: [44] (171) 251-8024   Fax: [44] (171) 608-3149
Political and social trends affecting consumer markets in South America

Directory of Argentine Importers
(Annual; English)
Martin D. Garcia
2626 11th Street #2
Santa Monica, CA 90405, USA
Tel: [1] (310) 452-0614

Guía de Exportadores e Importadores Argentinos
Editorial Scott S.A.
Güemes 3440, P.B., Of. A
1425 Buenos Aires
Tel/Fax: (1) 771-7940
Directory of Argentine exporters and importers

Guía Internacional de Tráfico
(Monthly)
Suipacha 207, Piso 3, Ofc. 316
1008 Buenos Aires
Tel: (1) 394-9008   Fax: (1) 394-9034
(US address: c/o Market Links, Dupont Plaza Center 723, 300 Biscayne Blvd. Way, Miami, FL 33131, USA; Tel: [1] (305) 374-1634)
Airline guide providing international travel information and news

Latin America: A Directory and Sourcebook
(Annual; English)
Euromonitor
87-88 Turnmill St.
London EC1M 5QU, UK
Tel: [44] (171) 251-8024   Fax: [44] (171) 608-3149
Statistics and data on the emerging Latin American consumer markets

Latin American International Food Industry Directory
Latin American Textile Industry Directory
(Annual; English, Portuguese, Spanish)
Aquino Productions
Box 15760
Stamford, CT 06901, USA
Tel: [1] (203) 325-3138

Latin Chamber of Commerce—Directorio Comercial
(Annual)
Latin Chamber of Commerce
1417 W. Flagler
Miami, FL 33135, USA
Tel: [1] (305) 642-3870   Fax: [1] (305) 541-2181

Listas Argentinas
Av. Belgrano 673
1092 Buenos Aires
Tel: (1) 342-2421

Nómina de Exportadores Argentinos
(Annual; English and Spanish)
Nóminex S.R.L.
Av. Belgrano 615, Piso 12
1092 Buenos Aires
Tel: (1) 342-2045, 342-2522   Fax: (1) 342-4199
Directory of Argentine exporters

DAILY NEWSPAPERS

Ambito Financiero
(Weekdays)
Pasaje Carabelas 241, Piso 3
1009 Buenos Aires
Tel: (1) 349-1500, 331-5528, 331-5561
Fax: (1) 349-1505, 331-7642
Business daily

Boletín Oficial de la República Argentina
(Weekdays)
Suipacha 767
1008 Buenos Aires
Tel: (1) 322-4164
Official government records publication

Buenos Aires Herald
(English)
Azopardo 455
1107 Buenos Aires
Tel: (1) 342-8476/9   Fax: (1) 334-7917

Clarín
Piedras 1743
1140 Buenos Aires
Tel: (1) 307-0330, 307-0340   Fax: (1) 307-0311/2

Comercio y Justicia
Mariano Moreno 378
5000 Córdoba
Tel: (51) 3-3788
Economic and legal news from Córdoba

Crónica
Av. Juan de Garay 124/30
1063 Buenos Aires
Tel: (1) 361-1001, 361-1051   Fax: (1) 361-6668

El Cronista Comercial
(Weekdays)
Honduras 5673
1414 Buenos Aires
Tel: (1) 777-1234, 775-4476   Fax: (1) 774-1016

La Nación
Bouchard 557
1106 Buenos Aires
Tel: (1) 319-1600, 313-1003   Fax: (1) 319-1611/3

La Prensa
Azopardo 715
1107 Buenos Aires
Tel: (1) 349-1000   Fax: (1) 349-1040

La Voz del Interior
Av. Colón 37/39
5000 Córdoba
Tel: (51) 72-9535   Fax: (51) 72-8550

Página 12
Belgrano 671/7
1067 Buenos Aires
Tel: (1) 334-2334/5   Fax: (1) 334-2330, 313-1299

GENERAL BUSINESS PUBLICATIONS

Americas Trade & Finance: Report on the Emerging Common Markets of the Americas
(Monthly)
Latin American Information Services, Inc.
159 W. 53rd St., 28th Fl.
New York, NY 10019, USA
Tel: [1] (212) 765-5520   Fax: [1] (212) 765-2927
Provides information and analysis one needs to trade, invest and expand financial activities in the Americas

Argentine Economic Development
(Every two years; English and French)
Ministerio de Economía y Obras y Servicios Públicos
Hipólito Yrigoyen 250
1310 Buenos Aires
Tel: (1) 342-6411, 342-6421/9, 349-8814, 349-8810/2
Fax: (1) 331-0292, 331-2619, 331-2090   Tlx: 21952

Argentine Letter
(Monthly)
Ayacucho 1370, P.B., Of. A
1111 Buenos Aires
Fax: (1) 311-4385
(US subscription address: PO Box 855, Bethesda, MD 20817, USA)

Banking: Latin American Industrial Report
Finance: Latin American Industrial Report
(Annual; English)
Aquino Productions
Box 15760
Stamford, CT 06901, USA
Tel: [1] (203) 325-3138

Boletín Estadístico: Banco Central
(Monthly)
Banco Central de la República Argentina
Centro de Estudios Monetarios y Bancarios
Reconquista 266-78
1003 Buenos Aires
Tel: (1) 394-8411, 394-8119, 393-0021
Fax: (1) 334-6489, 334-6468, 325-4860   Tlx: 1137

Bolsa
(Monthly)
Bolsa de Comercio de Buenos Aires
Sarmiento 299, Piso 1
1353 Buenos Aires
Tel: (1) 311-5231/3, 311-1174, 313-4812
Fax: (1) 312-9332

Business Latin America
(Weekly)
Economist Intelligence Unit
111 W. 57th St.
New York, NY 10019, USA
Tel: [1] (212) 554-0600 Fax: [1] (212) 586-1182

Business Trends: Argentine Economic Legislation
(Weekly; English and Spanish)
Consejo Técnico de Inversiones
Tucumán 834, Piso 1
1049 Buenos Aires
Fax: (1) 322-4887

Chronicle of Latin American Economic Affairs
(Weekly; English)
Latin American Institute
801 Yale NE
Albuquerque, NM 87131-1016, USA
Tel: [1] (505) 277-6839 Fax: [1] (505) 277-5989

Comercio Exterior Argentina
(Annual)
Instituto Nacional de Estadística y Censos (INDEC)
Dirección de Difusión Estadística
Centro de Servicios Estadísticos
Av. Julio A. Roca 615
1067 Buenos Aires
Tel: (1) 349-9654

Comments on Argentine Trade (Monthly; English)
AMCHAM Weekly News (Weekly; English)
American Chamber of Commerce in Argentina
Av. Leandro N. Alem 1110, Piso 13
1001 Buenos Aires,
Tel: (1) 311-5420, 311-5126   Fax: (1) 311-9076

Council of the Americas Washington Report: A Summary of Issues of Interest to U.S. Corporations Active in Latin America
(English)
Americas Society Inc.
1625 K Street, NW, Suite 1200
Washington, DC 20006, USA
Tel: [1] (202) 659-1547

Economía
(Quarterly)
Viamonte 1582
Buenos Aires

Economic Report: Summary
(Quarterly)
Ministerio de Economía y Obras y Servicios Públicos
Hipólito Yrigoyen 250
1310 Buenos Aires
Tel: (1) 342-6411, 342-6421/9, 349-8814, 349-8810/2
Fax: (1) 331-0292, 331-2619, 331-2090   Tlx: 21952

El Economista
(Weekly)
Av. Córdoba 632, Piso 2
Buenos Aires
Tel: (1) 322-7360, 322-8157, 322-8187
Economic magazine

Guía Practica del Exportador e Importador
(Monthly)
Lavalle 1125, Piso 3
1048 Buenos Aires
Tel: (1) 35-2829, 35-8533   Fax: (1) 46-1000

Impuestos: Revista Critica Mensual de Jurisprudencia y Legislación
(Monthly)
Ediciones la Ley S.A.
1471 Tucumán
Buenos Aires
Covers Argentine taxation

Latin America Service
(Biweekly)
Buraff Publications
1350 Connecticut Ave. NW
Washington, DC 20036, USA
Tel: (800) 333-1291 (toll-free in the US)
Fax: [1] (202) 862-0999
Regulation of securities markets in Latin America

Latin American Economy and Business
(16 issues/year; English)
Latin American Newsletters
61 Old St.
London EC1V 9HX, UK
Tel: [44] (171) 251-0012   Fax: [44] (171) 253-8193

Latin American Finance & Capital Markets
Latin American Law & Business Report
(Twice a month; English)
WorldTrade Executive, Inc.
PO Box 761
Concord, MA 01742
Tel: [1] (508) 287-0301   Fax: [1] (508) 287-0302

Latin American Markets
(Annual; English)
Washington Researchers Publishing
2612 P St. NW
Washington, DC 20007-3062, USA
Tel: [1] (202) 333-3499   Fax: [1] (202) 625-0656

LatinFinance
(10 issues/year; English)
Latin American Financial Publications, Inc.
2121 Ponce de Leon Blvd., Suite 1020
Coral Gables, FL 33134, USA
Tel: [1] (305) 448-6593   Fax: [1] (305) 448-0718
(In Argentina, call (1) 312-8888 for information)

Legislación Económica/Economic Legislation
(Every 2 weeks; English and Spanish)
Consejo Técnico de Inversiones S.A.
Tucumán 834, Piso 1
1049 Buenos Aires
Fax: (1) 322-4887
Principal laws, decrees, resolutions, central bank circulars, and other official communications

Market: Latin America
(Monthly; English)
W-Two Publications
202 The Commons, Suite 401
Ithaca, NY 14850, USA
Tel: [1] (607) 277-0924   Fax: [1] (607) 277-0925

Mercado
(Monthly)
Editorial Coyuntura S.A.
Perú 263, Piso 2
1067 Buenos Aires
Tel: (1) 342-3322, 343-0639   Fax: (1) 343-3475, 343-7826

All addresses and telephone numbers are in Argentina unless otherwise noted. The country code for Argentina is [54].

Pensamiento Económico
(Quarterly)
Av. L.N. Alem 36
1113 Buenos Aires
Tel: (1) 331-8051   Fax: (1) 331-8055
Review of the Cámara Argentina de Comercio

Prensa Confidencial
(Weekly)
Corrientes 1894
Buenos Aires

Prensa Económica
(Monthly)
Av. Rivadavia 926, Piso 5
1002 Buenos Aires
Tel: (1) 345-4419, 345-0936

Review of the River Plate
(Two per month; English and Spanish)
Casilla de Correo 294 (Suc. 13-B)
1431 Buenos Aires
*Deals with Argentine financial, economic, agricultural,
and shipping affairs*

Superávit
(Monthly; English and Spanish editions)
Edigar S.A.
15 de Noviembre 2547
1261 Buenos Aires
Tel: (1) 941-2344

**US/Latin Trade: The Magazine of Trade &
Investment in the Americas**
(Monthly; English)
Freedom Communications
One Biscayne Tower
2 South Biscayne Boulevard, Suite 2950
Miami, FL 33131, USA
Tel: [1] (305) 358-8373   Fax: [1] (305) 358-9166

San Martín 320, Piso 6
1004 Buenos Aires
Tel: (1) 394-7568   Fax: (1) 394-8607

Progreso (Monthly)
Visión (Every 2 months)
Vision, Inc.
310 Madison Ave., Suite 1412
New York, NY 10017-6000, USA
Tel: [1] (212) 953-1308   Fax: [1] (212) 953-1619

BUSINESS AND TAXATION GUIDES

Argentina, International Series
Ernst & Young, International Operations
153 East 53rd St.
New York, NY 10022, USA
Tel: [1] (212) 888-9100

**Business Corporations in Argentina: An Undated
Handbook of Legislation and Statistics**
Foreign Investment in Argentina
Latin American Linguistic Service
Av. Caseros 796, Piso 5
Casilla de Correo 3699
1000 Buenos Aires
Tel: (1) 26-9831

Doing Business in Argentina
Price Waterhouse & Co.
Distribution Center
PO Box 30004
Tampa, FL 33630, USA
Tel: [1] (813) 876-9000

**Investing, Licensing and Trade Conditions Abroad:
Argentina**
Business International Corp.
One Dag Hammerskjold Plaza
New York, NY 10019, USA
Tel: [1] (212) 750-6326

Investment Laws of the World: Argentina
International Center for Settlement of
Investment Disputes
Oceanus Publications, Inc.
Dobbs Ferry, NY 10522, USA

Laws of Argentina in Matters Affecting Business
Organization of American States (OAS)
Department of Publications
17th St. and Constitution Ave. NW
Washington, DC 20006, USA
Tel: [1] (202) 458-3760   Fax: [1] (202) 458-3967

Reference Book: Argentina
Dun & Bradstreet
Florida 234, Piso 4
1005 Buenos Aires
(US address: One World Trade Center, Suite 9069, New
York, NY 10048, USA; Tel: [1] (212) 938-8400)

Summary of Business Conditions in Argentina
Harteneck, Lopez y Cía.
(Representatives of Coopers & Lybrand)
25 de Mayo 140, Piso 6
1002 Buenos Aires
Tel: (1) 334-2830   Fax: (1) 331-5325

Tax and Trade Guide
Arthur Anderson & Co.
International Tax Department
1345 Avenue of the Americas
New York, NY 10105, USA
Tel: [1] (212) 708-4000

**Tax and Trade Profiles: South and Central America
Taxation in Argentina**
Deloitte & Touche
1114 Ave. of the Americas
New York, NY 10036, USA
(Address in Argentina: Sarmiento 624, 1041 Buenos
Aires; Tel: (1) 326-4046, 326-0497 Fax: (1) 325-8018)

STATISTICAL PUBLICATIONS AND SOURCES

**Anuario de Comercio Exterior: Análisis Estadístico
Boletín de Comercio Exterior Argentino
Comercio Exterior
Indicadores Industriales
Boletín Estadístico Trimestral
Statistical Yearbook Republic of Argentina**
(Frequency varies; English editions of some available)
Instituto Nacional de Estadística y Censos (INDEC)
Dirección de Difusión Estadística
Centro de Servicios Estadísticos
Av. Julio A. Roca 615
1067 Buenos Aires
Tel: (1) 349-9654

**Anuario de la Economía Argentina/Annual Report
of the Argentine Economy**
Consejo Técnico de Inversiones S.A.
Esmeralda 320, Piso 6
1343 Buenos Aires
Tel: (1) 35-0184

Anuario Estadístico Pesquero
(Annual)
Subsecretaría de Agricultura Ganadería y Pesca
Dirección Nacional de Pesca y Acuicultura
Av. Paseo Colón 982, Anexo Jardin, Piso 1
1063 Buenos Aires
Tel: (1) 349-2330/1, 362-2365, 362-5091, 362-5946
Fax: (1) 349-2332, 349-2504
Fishing industry statistics

Economic Report: República Argentina
(Annual with quarterly updates; English and Spanish)
Ministerio de Economía y Obras y Servicios Públicos
Secretaría de Programación Económica
Subsecretaría de Programación Macroeconómica
Hipólito Yrigoyen 250, Of. 843
1310 Buenos Aires
Tel: (1) 349-5079   Fax: (1) 349-5730

Informe Económico: Resena Estadística, Ministerio de Economía
Area de Coyuntura
Hipólito Yrigoyen 250, Piso 8, Of. 829
1086 Buenos Aires
Tel: (1) 30-2916

Memoria Anual
Boletín Estadístico
Banco Central de la República Argentina
Reconquista 266
1003 Buenos Aires
Tel: (1) 394-8411, 394-8119, 393-0021
Fax: (1) 334-6489, 334-6468, 325-4860   Tlx: 1137

INDUSTRY-SPECIFIC PUBLICATIONS

A.G.E.S.
(6 issues/year)
Asociación de Garajes y Estaciones de Servico
Hipólito Yrigoyen 2738
Buenos Aires
Automotive industry

Actividad Minera
(Monthly)
Minera Piedra Libre S.R.L.
Bolívar 187, Piso 4, Of. B
1066 Buenos Aires
Tel: (1) 343-6422   Fax: (1) 343-6138
Mines and mining industry

Aeroespacio/Aerospace
(Bimonthly; English and Spanish)
Casilla de Correo 37, Suc. 12B
1412 Buenos Aires
Tel: (1) 322-2753   Fax: (1) 11-8125/6
Published by the Argentine Air Force

Apparel Industry Internacional
(Bimonthly)
Shore Communications, Inc.
6255 Barfield Rd. NE, Ste. 200
Atlanta, GA 30328-4300
Tel: [1] (404) 252-8831   Fax: [1] (404) 252-4436
Factory management for apparel companies in Latin America

Argentina Automotriz
(6 issues/year)
Av. Belgrano 1580, Piso 6
1093 Buenos Aires
Tel: (1) 381-8383, 381-9277, 381-9253
Automotive industry

Argentina Forestal
(6 issues/year)
Cámara Argentina de Aserradores de Maderas,
Depósitos y Afines
Alsina 440
1087 Buenos Aires
Tel: (1) 342-4389
Forestry

Autoclub; Revista del Automovilismo, Turismo e Informaciones
(Every 2 months)
Automóvil Club Argentino
Av. del Libertador 1850
Buenos Aires
Tel: (1) 824-1837
Automotive transportation

Barcos
(Monthly)
Editorial Barcos S.R.L.
Av. Santa Fe 676
1640 Acassuso
Pcia. de Buenos Aires
Tel: (1) 747-5572
Boats and boating

Bienvenido a Bordo
(Monthly)
Ediciones San Isidro S.R.L.
Obispo Terrero 2981, Of. 2
1642 San Isidro
Pcia. de Buenos Aires
Tel: (1) 742-1328   Fax: (1) 742-0953
Boating

Boletín: Empresa Nacional de Correos y Telégrafos
(Twice a week)
Empresa Nacional de Correos y Telégrafos
Buenos Aires
Fax: (1) 311-3111
Communication and postal affairs

Boletín: Ministerio de Salud y Acción Social
(Irregular)
Ministerio de Salud y Acción Social
Dirección de Estadísticos de Salud
Defensa 120
1345 Buenos Aires
Tel: (1) 340-048, 342-4772, 343-3247
Fax: (1) 953-3223   Tlx: 25064
Public health and safety

C.O.T.A.L.: La Revista del Turismo Total
(Monthly: English and Spanish)
M. Seoane y Cía. S.A.
Lavalle 357, Piso 12, Of.124
1047 Buenos Aires
Tel: (1) 393-5598   Fax: (1) 11-1253
Travel and tourism; a publication of Confederación de Organizaciones Turísticas de la America Latina

Cámara de Industriales de Artefactos para el Hogar
(Monthly)
Paraguay 1855
1061 Buenos Aires
Tel: (1) 813-2673, 812-0232
Fax: (1) 814-2650
Household goods

All addresses and telephone numbers are in Argentina unless otherwise noted. The country code for Argentina is [54].

Campo Moderno y Chacra
(Monthly)
Editorial Atlantida S.A.
Azopardo 579
1307 Buenos Aires
Tel: (1) 333-4591
Agriculture

Cleo en la Moda
(Every 2 months; English and Spanish eds. available)
Ediciones Ariadna
472 Suipacha
Buenos Aires
Leather and fur, shoes and boots, clothing trade, textiles and fabrics

Computerworld Argentina
(Fortnightly)
CW Comunicaciones
Av. Belgrano 406, Piso 9
1092 Buenos Aires
Fax: (1) 331-7672

Comunicaciones: Telecomunicaciones, Comunicaciones de Datos, Computadoras y Satélites
(Quarterly)
Intercom Corp.
9200 S. Dadeland Blvd., Suite 309
Miami, FL 33156-2703, USA, USA
Tel: [1] (305) 670-9444   Fax: [1] (305) 670-9459
Distributed throughout Latin America for the telecommunication and computer technologies.

Confederal
(Quarterly)
Confederación Argentina de Clínicas, Sanatorios y Hospitales Privados
Tucumán 1668
1055 Buenos Aires
Tel: (1) 372-5762   Fax: (1) 372-5915

Corsa
(Weekly)
Editorial Abril S.A.
Leandro N. Alem 896
Buenos Aires
Automotive industry

Cuadernos de Geohistoria Regional
(Irregular)
Consejo Nacional de Investigaciones Científicas y Técnicas
Instituto de Investigaciones Geohistóricas
Av. Castelli 930
Casilla de Correo 438
3500 Resistencia
Fax: (72) 2-39983
Research on: population studies, colonization, agricultural activities, transportation, and communications

Delta
(Every two weeks)
Periódico Delta S.C.A.
General Mitre 320
Tigre
Agriculture and forestry

Diners
(9 issues/year)
Lugones, Lanusse, y Asociados
San Martín 232, Piso 2, Of. 228
1004 Buenos Aires
Travel and tourism

Diners Club
(Monthly)
Editorial Alto Nivel S.A.L.
Carlos Pellegrini 1023, Piso 9
Buenos Aires
Travel and tourism

El Rey; Revista Argentina de Ajedrez
(Monthly)
Hector Ricardo Liso Ed. & Pub.
Casilla de Correo 7
1653 Villa Ballester
Sports and games

Equipamiento Hospitalario
(Quarterly)
Emma Fiorentino Publicaciones Técnicas S.R.L.
Estados Unidos 2796, Piso 1, Of. A
1227 Buenos Aires
Tel: (1) 943-0090   Fax: (1) 942-2970

Exportaciones de Productos Ganaderos
(Monthly)
San Martín 459
1004 Buenos Aires
Tel: (1) 394-6612   Fax: (1) 322-9357
Ranching exports

Fundación Bariloche: Publicaciones
(Irregular)
Fundación Bariloche
Instituto de Economía de la Energía
Casilla de Correo 138
8400 San Carlos de Bariloche
Pcia. de Río Negro

Gaceta Agronómica
(6 issues/year)
Viamonte 494, Piso 2-6
1053 Buenos Aires
Agriculture

Gaceta Textil
(Monthly)
Gaceta Editora Coop Ltda.
25 de Mayo 786, Piso 12
Buenos Aires
Textile industries and fabrics

Galaxia
(Quarterly)
Asociación Argentina de Químicos y Coloristas Textiles
Bulnes 1425
1176 Buenos Aires
Tel: (1) 963-0394
Textile industries and fabrics; textile dyeing

Guía Latinoamericana de Transportes
(Quarterly)
Moreles 691, Piso 5, Of. B
1406 Buenos Aires
Tel/Fax: (1) 631-1108
Travel information and timetables

Ideas en Arte y Tecnología
(3 issues/year)
Universidad de Belgrano
Teodoro García 2090
1426 Buenos Aires
Tel: (1) 774-2133
Covers architecture, engineering and computer science

Industria Alimentaria
(Every 2 months)
Editora Técnica Integral S.R.L.
Av. Corrientes 2763, Piso 2, Of. 9 y 10
1046 Buenos Aires
Tel: (1) 962-6100
*Published by the COPAL, the Argentine Federation of
Food Industries*

Industria Alimenticia
(Monthly)
Stagnito Publishing Company
1935 Shermer Rd., Ste. 100
Northbrook, IL 60062, USA
Tel: [1] (708) 205-5660   Fax: [1] (708) 205-5680
Latin American food processing industry

Industria Avícola
(Monthly, with annual buyers' guide)
Watt Publishing Co.
122 S. Wesley
Mt. Morris, IL 61054, USA
Tel: [1] (815) 734-4171   Fax: [1] (815) 734-4201
Poultry industry in Latin America

Industria Lechera
(Every 2 months)
Centro de la Industria Lechera
Mediano 281
1178 Buenos Aires
Dairy industry

Industria Porcina
(Quarterly, with annual buyers' guide)
Watt Publishing Co.
122 S. Wesley
Mt. Morris, IL 61054, USA
Tel: [1] (815) 734-4171   Fax: [1] (815) 734-4201
Swine industry in Latin America

Industria Textil Sud Americana
(Every 2 months)
Editesa S.A.
Av. Roque Saenz Pena 825
Buenos Aires
Textile industry

**Instituto Nacional de Investigación y Desarrollo
Pesquero. Memoria**
(Annual)
Instituto Nacional de Investigación y Desarrollo
Pesquero
Casilla de Correo 175
7600 Mar del Plata
Fishing industry

La Bobina—Notivest
(Monthly)
Bobbin Blenheim Media Corp.
1110 Shop Rd., Box 1986
Columbia, SC 29202, USA
Tel: [1] (803) 771-7500   Fax: [1] (803) 799-1461
*Serves executives in the Latin American apparel and
sewn products industry*

La Prensa Médica Argentina
(Monthly)
Junín 845
1113 Buenos Aires
Tel: (1) 961-9793   Fax: (1) 961-9494
Medical publication

La Semana Médica
(Monthly)
Arenales 3574
1425 Buenos Aires
Tel: (1) 824-5673
Medial sciences

Latin America Telecom Report
(Monthly; English)
International Technology Consultants
1724 Kalorama Rd. NW, Suite 210
Washington, DC 20009-2624, USA
Tel: [1] (202) 234-2138
Fax: [1] (202) 483-7922
*Latin American telecommunications and information
technology markets*

Latin American Cable & Pay TV
(Monthly; English)
Kagan World Media, Ltd.
126 Clock Tower Place
Carmel, CA 93923, USA
Tel: [1] (408) 624-1536   Fax: [1] (408) 625-3225

Latin American Industrial Reports
(Annual; English)
Aquino Productions
Box 15760
Stamford, CT 06901, USA
*Reports from 22 countries, including Argentina on the
following industries: Agroindustry, Apparel, Appliances,
Automobiles, Beverages, Cement, Ceramics, Chemicals,
Communications, Computers & Office Equipment,
Construction, Cosmetics, Dairy, Electrical Machinery,
Electronics, Energy, Fishing, Food, Forestry, Furniture,
Glass, Hotels & Tourism, Leather, Livestock, Machinery,
Metal Mining, Minerals, Office-Data Processing
Machines, Petroleum, Pharmaceuticals, Rubber, Textiles,
Tobacco, Tools & Hardware, Transportation, Water &
Waste Treatment*

Latin American Mining Letter
(Twice a month)
M.I.I.D.A. Ltd.
PO Box 2137
London NW10 6TN, UK
Tel: [44] (181) 961-7407   Fax: [44] (181) 961-7487
Mines and mining industry

Medicina
(Every 2 months; English and Spanish)
Fundación Revista Medicina
Donato Alvarez 3150
1427 Buenos Aires
Tel: (1) 573-2619   Fax: (1) 573-2619
Medical sciences: original papers in clinical research

Mundo Textil Argentino
(Monthly)
25 de Mayo 267-218
Buenos Aires
Textile industry

Novedades de Industria Alimenticia
(Every 2 months)
Stagnito Publishing Company
1935 Shermer Rd., Suite 100
Northbrook, IL 60062, USA
Tel: [1] (708) 205-5660   Fax: [1] (708) 205-5680
Food processing industry

PC Magazine
Editorial Vanidades
Perú 263, Piso 3
1067 Buenos Aires
Tel: (1) 342-8946, 342-8643   Fax: (1) 334-8053
Computers and software

Prensa Médica Argentina
(10 issues/year; Spanish with English summaries)
Prensa Médica Argentina S.R.L.
Junín 845
1113 Buenos Aires
Tel: (1) 961-9793   Fax: (1) 961-9494
Medical sciences

Quiron
(Quarterly; Spanish with English and French
summaries)
Editorial Quiron
Calle 508 entre 16 y 18
1897 M. B. Gonnet
Pcia. de Buenos Aires
Tel: (21) 71-2616   Fax: (21) 71-2222
Medical sciences

Radio Electrónica Práctica
(Weekly)
Editorial Cul-Tec S.A.
Independencia 1654
Buenos Aires
Radio communications

Revista del Derecho Industrial
(3 issues/year)
Ediciones Depalma S.R.L.
Talcahuano No. 494
Buenos Aires
Fax: (1) 40-6913
*Updated information on economic law, intellectual
property, communications, and computer law, from a
Latin American point of view*

Revista Telegráfica Electrónica
(Monthly)
Arbo S.A.C.E.I.
Av. Martín García 653
Buenos Aires
Telephone and telegraphic communications

Ruralia: Revista Argentina de Estudios Agrarios
(Monthly)
Ediciones Imago Mundi
Sanchez de Loria 1821
1241 Buenos Aires
Fax: (1) 775-6937
Agriculture

Semana Médica
(Monthly)
Arenales 3574
1425 Buenos Aires
Tel: (1) 824-5673
Medical sciences

Sociedad Rural Argentina: Boletín
(9 issues/year)
Florida 460
1005 Buenos Aires
Tel: (1) 322-2030, 322-3431, 322-2070
Agriculture

Southern South America
(Quarterly)
Zagier & Urruty Publicaciones
PO Box 94, Sucursal 19
1419 Buenos Aires
Tel: (1) 572-1050   Fax: (1) 572-5766
(US address: PO Box 526806, Miami, FL 33152-6086,
USA)
Tourism

Técnica e Industria
(Monthly)
Rodríguez Peña 694, Piso 5
1020 Buenos Aires
Tel: (1) 46-3193
Technology and industry review

**Textiles Panamericanos: Revista para la Industria
Textile**
(Quarterly)
Billian Publishing, Inc.
2100 Powers Ferry Rd.
Atlanta, GA 30339, USA
Tel: [1] (404) 955-5656   Fax: [1] (404) 952-0669
Textile and fabric industries

**Universidad Nacional de La Plata. Facultad de
Agronomia. Revista**
(Twice a year; English and Spanish)
C.C. 31, Calle 60 y 119
1900 La Plata
Tel: (21) 3-8168   Fax: (21) 25-2346
Agriculture and forestry

Velocidad
(Every 2 months)
Av. Belgrano 1735
Buenos Aires
Automotive transportation

RADIO AND TELEVISION

Broadcast Organizations
and Government Agencies

Secretaría de Comunicaciones
(Secretaríat of Communications)
Sarmiento 151, Piso 4
1000 Buenos Aires
Tel: (1) 331-1203

Comité Federal de Radiodifusión (COMFER)
Suipacha 765
1008 Buenos Aires
Tel: (1) 394-4274
Controls technical aspects of broadcasting in Argentina

Servicio Oficial de Radiodifusión (SOR)
Maipú 555
1006 Buenos Aires
Tel: (1) 325-9100   Fax: (1) 325-9433

Cadena Argentina de Radiodifusión (CAR)
Av. Entre Ríos 149, Piso 3
1079 Buenos Aries
Tel: (1) 45-2113
*Groups all national state-owned commercial stations
operated by the Subsecretaría Operativa*

Asociación de Radiodifusoras Privadas Argentinas
(ARPA)
Cangallo 1561, Piso 8
1037 Buenos Aires
Tel: (1) 35-4412
Association of privately owned commercial radio
stations

Asociación de Teleradiodifusoras Argentinas (ATA)
Córdoba 323, Piso 6
1054 Buenos Aires
Tel: (1) 312-4219   Fax: (1) 312-4208
Association of private television stations

Radio

LRA Radio Nacional
Ayacucho 1556
1112 Buenos Aires
Tel: (1) 803-5555

Radiodifusión Argentina al Exterior (RAE)
Maipú 555
1006 Buenos Aires
Tel: (1) 325-9100   Fax: (1) 325-9433
Broadcasts in 8 languages worldwide

Radio Nacional
Maipú 555
1006 Buenos Aires
Tel: (1) 325-9433, 325-7390

Radio America
Honduras 5663
1414 Buenos Aires
Tel: (1) 777-1234, 775-1226   Fax: (1) 774-1016, 775-3694

Radio El Mundo Difusora Buenos Aires S.A.
Tte. General Juan De Perón 646, Piso 7
1038 Buenos Aires
Tel: (1) 331-9472, 331-9492   Fax: (1) 325-3108

Radio Argentina
Tacuarí 2035
1139 Buenos Aires
Tel: (1) 362-5432, 362-5533   Fax: (1) 362-0703

Radio Belgrano
Uruguay 1237
Buenos Aires
Tel: (1) 813-9601, 813-9661

Radio Splendid
Arenales 1925
1016 Buenos Aires
Tel: (1) 814-4139, 812-1741   Fax: (1) 814-4162

Radio Mitre
Mansilla 2668
1425 Buenos Aires
Tel: (1) 961-1004, 961-1047   Fax: (1) 963-3060

Radio Municipal de la Ciudad de Buenos Aires
Sarmiento 1551, Piso 8
1042 Buenos Aires
Tel: (1) 476-1085, 374-5535

Radio Continental
Rivadavia 835, Piso 2 y 3
1002 Buenos Aires
Tel: (1) 334-5523, 331-7141   Fax: (1) 334-5220, 331-7311

Radio Rivadavia
Arenales 2467
1124 Buenos Aires
Tel: (1) 824-1080, 824-3808

Radio Buenos Aires
Belgrano 270
Buenos Aires
Tel: (1) 342-1348, 342-1616   Fax: (1) 331-9079

Radio del Plata
Sante Fe 2043
1123 Buenos Aires
Tel: (1) 824-5073, 821-0630   Fax: (1) 821-0629

Television

Asociación Argentina de Televisión por Cable (ATVC)
(Cable television)
Av. de Mayo 749, Piso 2, Of. 10
1084 Buenos Aires
Tel: (1) 342-3382   Fax: (1) 343-1716

Canal 7 S.A. (ATC Canal 7)
Av. Figueroa Alcorta 2977
1426 Buenos Aires
Tel: (1) 802-6001/6, 802-5030
Fax: (1) 802-9878, 801-0566

Canal 9 Libertad (Telearte S.A.)
Pasaje Gelly 3378
1425 Buenos Aires
Tel: (1) 801-5447, 801-4437   Fax: (1) 801-9950, 801-2861

Canal 11 (Telefé)
Pavón 2444
1248 Buenos Aires
Tel: (1) 941-0511, 941-0151, 941-9549   Fax: (1) 942-6773

Canal 13 ArTeAr
San Juan 1170/1132
1147 Buenos Aires
Tel: (1) 27-3661   Fax: (1) 334-3266

Canal 2 America TV
Honduras 5663
1414 Buenos Aires
Tel: (1) 777-1234   Fax: (1) 774-1016, 774-3694

LIBRARIES

Biblioteca del Banco Central de la República Argentina
Reconquista 266
1003 Buenos Aires
Tel: (1) 394-9031

Biblioteca Nacional
México 564
1097 Buenos Aires
Tel: (1) 806-6155   Fax: (1) 812-6038

Sistema de Bibliotecas y de Información (SISBI)
Universidad de Buenos Aires
Azcuénaga 280
1029 Buenos Aires
Tel: (1) 951-1366, 952-6557   Fax: (1) 951-3394

Biblioteca Mayor de la Universidad Nacional de
Córdoba
Calle Obispo Trejo 242
Casilla de Correo 63
5000 Córdoba
Tel: (51) 4-6323   Fax: (51) 3-7841

WORLD WIDE WEB SITES

The number of World Wide Web sites in Argentina has
increased dramatically in 1995. Many sites are still
under development and do not yet provide a great deal
of information. Those listed below are some of the
most important sites, and will also provide links to
other Argentine Web sites as they go online.

All addresses and telephone numbers are in Argentina unless otherwise noted. The country code for Argentina is [54].

Instituto Nacional de Estadística y Censos (INDEC)
(National Institute of Statistics and the Census)
WWW home page: http://www.mecon.ar/indec/
indecnet.htm
Spanish language documents; statistical data and information about INDEC.

Ministerio de Economía, Obras y Servicios Públicos
(Ministry of Economy, Public Works, and Services)
WWW home page: http://www.mecon.ar
English- and Spanish-language documents; information about investment in Argentina and links to other pertinent servers within the Argentine government; gopher sites and ftp servers also available

Ministerio de Relaciones Exteriores, Comercio
Internacional y Culto (MRECIC)
Dirección General de Informática y Comunicaciones
(Ministry of Foreign Affairs, International Trade, and
Cults)
WWW home page: http://www.mrec.ar
WWW home page: http://www.ar/
English- and Spanish-language documents; two of the main Argentine Web sites, with links to many other sites

Secretaría de Ciencia y Tecnología (SECyT)
WWW home page: http://www.recyt.net/secyt/
intro.html
English- and Spanish-language documents pertaining to science and technology

Index